ROSE
THEN AND NOW®
BIBLE MAP ATLAS

with Biblical Background and Culture

PAUL H. WRIGHT, PH.D.

Rose Then and Now® Bible Map Atlas with Biblical Background and Culture

Published by Rose Publishing
An imprint of Tyndale House Ministries
Carol Stream, Illinois
www.hendricksonrose.com

Rose Then and Now® Bible Map Atlas with Biblical Background and Culture has an additional chapter, additional maps and clear plastic overlays, plus some author revisions. Otherwise it is similar to the original version published by Carta, *Greatness Grace & Glory*.

Maps and Graphics: CARTA JERUSALEM unless otherwise indicated
Photographs: Paul H. Wright, Ph.D.
Cover Design: Sergio Urquiza

Library of Congress Cataloging-in-Publication Data

Wright, Paul, 1955-
  Bible map atlas with biblical background and culture / Paul H. Wright ;
editor, Barbara L. Ball.
     p. cm.
  At head of title: Rose Then and Now Bible map atlas with biblical
background and culture
  Includes bibliographical references and index.
  ISBN 978-1-59636-534-6 -- ISBN 1-59636-534-X
  1. Bible--Geography--Maps. 2. Bible--History of Biblical events--Maps. 3.
Bible--Biography. I. Ball, Barbara Laurel. II. Title. III. Title: Rose Then
and Now Bible map atlas with biblical background and culture.
  G2230.W64 2012
  220.95'050223--dc23
                    2012037905

Printed by Regent Publishing Services Ltd.
Printed in Hong Kong
December 2021, 9th printing

INTRODUCTION

Everyone loves a good Bible story. Some stories, like David and Goliath, Jonah and the Whale, and the Birth of Jesus have entered the mainstream of popular culture. Others, such as Sisera's Encounter with Jael, Ahab's Battle at Ramoth-gilead, or Nehemiah's Nighttime Ride, though not as well known, are still a good read. Conflict, intrigue, resolution, local color, character, points of relevance—these and other aspects of storytelling energize the biblical narrative in ways that for centuries have prompted the hearts and minds of Bible readers to hear and respond to the touch of God in their lives.

Great stories are told of great people, and in one sense all of the people of the Bible were great people (some were great in their courage and faith; others in their rascality). The selection of people whose stories are traced here are typical of the whole, and touch on conditions common to all humanity. In this sense their stories transcend time and place. But they're are also *grounded* in time and place, and it is this aspect that gives them a tangible sense of reality. Abraham left his homes in Ur of the Chaldees and Haran, sophisticated places of opportunity and wealth, to go to Canaan, a rocky land with comparatively few natural resources and a marginal economy; understanding the *where* helps us to ponder the *why*. Ahab fought battles and forged alliances on all sides of his expanding kingdom; by mapping his policies on the historical landscape of the mid-ninth century B.C. we are better able to understand not only the realities that he faced but also the response of his contemporaries, people like Jehoshaphat, Elijah and Elisha. Let's listen to what Jesus said, but also to what he did:

> *Again Jesus began to teach by the sea, and a very large crowd gathered around him. So he got into a boat on the sea and sat down, while the whole crowd was on the shore facing the sea. He taught them many things in parables, and in his teaching he said to them: "Listen! Consider the sower who went out to sow...."*
>
> (Mark 4:1–3)

The writers of the Bible knew the land in which God chose to reveal Himself well, for it was their home. They were intimately familiar with the rugged terrain of Judah, with cold winter rain and scorching desert heat, and they had experienced the relief offered by a small spring of water or the shelter of a crevasse in a mighty rock. They knew what it meant for the hills surrounding their city or village to be filled with enemy troops, or to lie down securely at night after a full harvest. Time and again the Bible's historians, prophets and poets infused the divine message they had to tell with geographical information. In fact, such information fills the biblical text—and the biblical authors assumed that their readers knew even more.

This work focuses on aspects of history, geography, culture and personality, exploring ways that tangible *realia* such as these impacted the thoughts, decisions and actions of some of the great people of the Bible. The working assumption is that if we can learn to appreciate details of time and place, we can better see the contours of the characters that grace the pages of the Bible. Such factors of real life, as they can be known through literary, geographical and archaeological data, when reasonably combined with a common-sense approach based on observable patterns of behavior of people, groups and nation states in and around the Middle East today, yields a certain familiarity—even a kind of intimacy—with the people of the Bible that is too often lacking otherwise. By so gazing into their eyes, we can not only begin to grasp the greatness of their stories and the messages that these stories contain, but begin to see ourselves lingering on the corners of the page or even ducking between the lines of the text. Herein lies the immediacy of the eternal truths that the Bible contains. The proof is in the telling—and in the living.

The Book of Genesis ends with Jacob and his family in Egypt, but casts just enough trajectories forward to pull the reader through the rest of the Bible. With an eye toward a future that was very different from both Egypt (the present) and the marginal steppe land that Abraham and his family had called home (the past), Jacob blessed his favorite son with the best that his yet unrealized homeland had to offer: "Joseph is a fruitful bough, a fruitful bough by a spring; its branches run over a wall...."

Old Testament Time Line

Books of the Bible

| 2100 BC | 2000 BC | 1900 BC | 1800 BC |

The period for each book of the Bible shows its historical setting, not the date the book was written. Many dates listed are approximate and may vary according to different scholars.

▶ **Genesis**

Abraham to the Sojourn in Egypt

Bible History

Some scholars place Abraham's birth at 1952 BC. In this case, biblical events through Joseph would slide to the right 214 years.

Abraham c. 2166-1991

Joseph c. 1914-1805

- Joseph becomes and official in Egypt c. 1884

- Abrahamic Covenant

Ishmael c. 2080-1943

- Jacob and his family move to Egypt c. 1876

Isaac c. 2066-1886

Jacob (Israel) c. 2005-1859

KEY	
▨	TIME SPAN MARKER
•	YEAR MARKER
‖	10 YEARS BETWEEN LINES
c.	CIRCA (ABOUT)

| 1200 BC | 1100 BC | 1000 BC | 900 BC | 800 BC |

Books of the Bible

1 Chronicles | 2 Chronicles

1 Samuel | 2 Samuel | 1 Kings | 2 Kings

Psalms, Proverbs, Song of Songs, Ecclesiastes, Job (dates uncertain)

▶ Judges

▶ **Era of Judges** | **United Kingdom Era** | **Divided Kingdom Era**

Bible History

Eli, Priest in Shiloh c. 1100-1060

- Kingdom divides into Northern Kingdom (Israel) and Southern Kingdom (Judah) 931

Judge & Prophet Samuel c. 1060-1020

Prophet Elijah c. 870-845

King Saul c. 1051-1011

Prophet Elisha c. 845-800

King David c. 1011-971

King Solomon c. 971-931

- Solomon's temple (first temple) completed 960

(Kings listed by dates of reign)

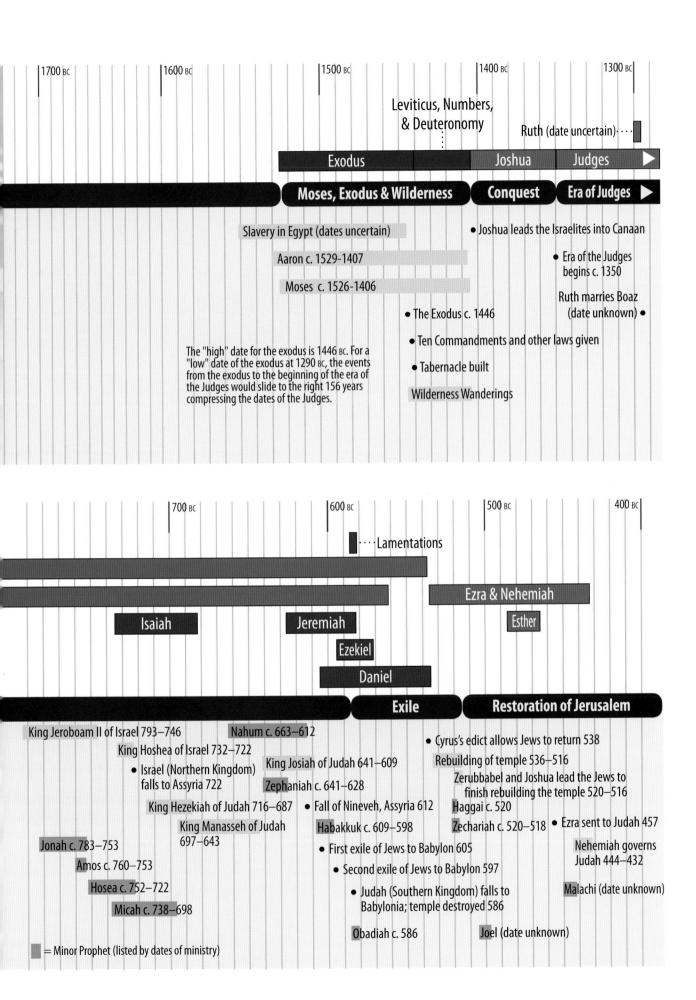

CHAPTER 1
THE LANDED CONTEXT OF THE BIBLICAL STORY

From their spring-fed oasis base at Kadesh-barnea in the northeastern corner of the Sinai Peninsula, Moses gave marching orders to his twelve chosen spies:

> Now see what the land is like, whether the people who live in it are strong or weak, if they are few or many. And what is the condition of the land in which they are living? Is it good or bad? How are the cities in which they live? Are they like open camps or fortified? How is the land itself? Is it fertile or barren? Are there trees in it, or not? (Num 13:18–20)

To find out, Moses instructed Joshua, Caleb and company to go up into Canaan by way of the Negev and hill country. His orders came at a significant time in Israelite history, the year following the Exodus from Egypt. And there was a specific goal in mind: to assess the feasibility of entering Canaan with the intent of settling down. While the context of the spies' task is filled with particulars, Moses' instructions also provide a kind of template for anyone who wants to explore the lands of the Bible today, or to simply understand the biblical narrative better. Indeed, the two endeavors go hand in hand. Each speaks to the other.

Like the modern Middle East, a place chock full of activity and passion, the lands of the ancient Near East (the stage of the Old Testament story) and the eastern Mediterranean basin (the theatre of the New Testament) are all about *location*. The eastern seaboard of the Mediterranean is the zone where these two arenas overlap, and functions as the point of balance (in the phrase of Denis Baly, *The Geography of the Bible*, New York: Harper & Row 1974, 5) of three continents. This observation so dominates discussions of biblical geography that mention of it has almost become cliché. Yet the importance of the reality remains, and though it may seem rather straightforward on the surface it belies a set of relationships, priorities and entanglements between people groups living in the lands of the Bible that provide for a very interesting read.

To start, it is perhaps appropriate to define a few aspects of location that have impacted living conditions in the lands of the Bible over time. The building blocks of biblical geography include the following:

- *Topography*—the shape of the surface of the land, with particular reference to changes in elevation.

- *Climate*—the condition of the weather, with attention focused on widely varying patterns of rainfall.
- *Available resources*—the quality and amount of water sources, arable soil and usable rocks and minerals in any given area.

The particular mix of elements such as these plays a significant role in determining whether any given plot of ground can support permanent settlements and how large and well-established these might have become, or if the land is better suited for herding or desert lifestyles. Specific geographical realities have also helped to shape cultural values and norms that defined individual societies. For instance, protocols of cooperation, hospitality and defense that functioned well in arid, shepherding societies in biblical times developed differently than did those that attained to urban centers located in fertile areas, or to sailors who frequented foreign ports-of-call. And aspects of geography gave rise to specific images that biblical writers used to describe God and the people of ancient Israel. These include terms such as "rock," "water," "shepherd" and "vine" (Ps 18:2; 42:6–7; 78:52; 80:8–11), as well as an overall awareness that God's blessings and judgments affected people and land alike (Isa 33:8–12; 35:1–2).

A helpful way of sizing up the importance of the role that geography played in shaping human priorities and events in the world of the Bible is to identify and describe strategic places, "facts on the ground" in and around the land of ancient Israel that were sought after as points to control. Strategic

A shepherd entertains his flock of goats in a scene typical to the eastern edges of the land of ancient Israel. This landscape, in southern Edom, is a bit too harsh for sheep, though goats manage quite well. "Why did you sit among the sheepfolds, to hear the piping for the flocks?" asks the Song of Deborah, in a verse hoping to rally the disparate tribes of Israel for common defense (Judg 5:16). The great variety of landscapes found along the eastern seaboard of the Mediterranean prompts an equally diverse mix of ways to adapt to living conditions in the region. The biblical record embraces them all.

(right) **Mean Annual Precipitation of the Middle East** (amounts in millimeters); (below) **Mean Annual Temperatures** (temperatures in degrees Celsius).

These maps show a significant correlation between average precipitation amounts and average temperatures across the ancient Near East. The wide swath across the middle of the maps indicates the arid to hyper-arid desert climate that dominates the region. Here rainfall never exceeds eight inches per year, and often barely reaches one or two inches on average. The moderating influence of the Mediterranean Sea and the mountainous lands of Europe and Anatolia to the north allow the middle part of the Fertile Crescent to have a temperate Mediterranean climate, with 20 to 40 inches of rain per year and warm, inviting temperatures.

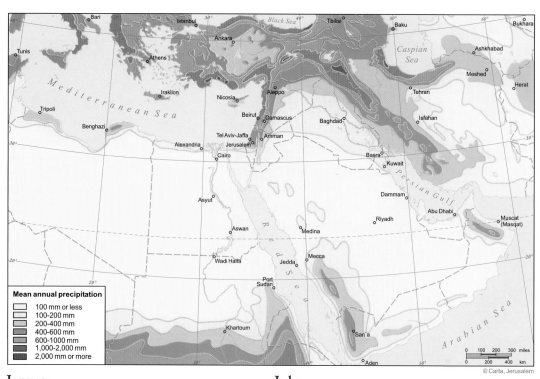

January

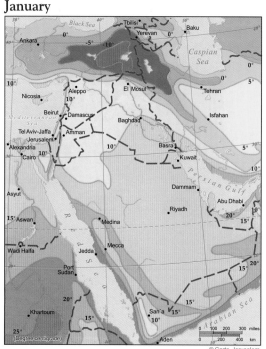

July

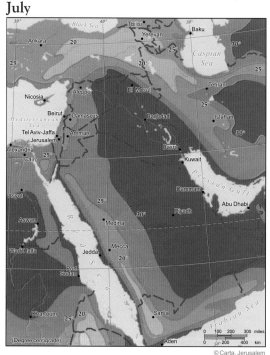

points tend to be "action" points, critical junctures where people groups compete for influence and reward. These are often areas that are rich in natural resources such as fresh water or good soil. They could be as small as an individual spring (Judg 1:15) or as large as the Nile Delta (Gen 42:1–2). A different kind of strategic position is a transportation bottleneck such as a mountain pass (the Cilician Gates) or a tight spot in swampy or sandy terrain (Aphek Pass; 1 Sam 29:1). We should also consider the strategic value of important economic corridors, be they land-based (the Arabian Spice Route) or sea-based (shipping lanes connecting the Aegean with

Phoenicia). Significant crossroads such as Megiddo (2 Kgs 23:29), or natural ports like Acco-Ptolemais (Acts 21:7), were also of vital importance for the biblical story. It is helpful to note that the location of a strategic position is frequently determined by its relationship to nearby areas of difficulty such as high mountain ranges, the open desert or the sea. Folks who came to possess special technologies and skills could manage to cross areas of difficulty, and through such risk reaped great economic or political reward. We can see here the great seafarers of the ancient world (Ezekiel 27), or those who drove camel caravans across the open desert (Isa 60:3–7).

On the other hand, heartlands of people groups, that is, places where folks in the biblical world hoped to settle down and live quiet and productive lives, were often places that were naturally protected. Examples are the hill country of Judah, Ephraim or Upper Galilee, or the highlands of Moab and Edom (Judg 19:1; 1 Kgs 4:25; Obad 3–4). Some heartlands, such as the Philistine coastal plain, lie open to greater opportunities but also to greater threat (2 Chron 2:16; Isa 20:1; Acts 9:43). Tucked between are border or frontier lands which functioned as zones of expansion and, invariably, conflict. Examples are the area of foothills between the Judean hill country and the Philistine coastal plain (the Shephelah), or Bashan, a wide open zone of contention between Galilee and Damascus. Indeed, all nation states located in the lands of the Bible included areas that were relatively protected as well as those of activity and conflict within their territories, and the biblical storyline is wrapped around both.

With these general principles in mind, it is time to overview the geographical shape of the world of the Bible. We will start broadly, with the lands of the ancient Near East and the eastern Mediterranean basin. Once establishing this context, we will turn to the place where these two regions merge, namely, the eastern seaboard of the Mediterranean Sea, with particular reference to the "Dan to Beersheba" homeland of ancient Israel.

The lands of the ancient Near East were dominated by the Fertile Crescent, a great arc of agriculture defined by the river valleys of the Tigris and Euphrates on the east, and the Nile to the west. At least as early as the first century A.D. the river valley located between the Tigris and the Euphrates has been called Mesopotamia ("between the rivers"; Strabo, *Geography*, 2.1.26; 2.5.22). This was the heartland of ancient Babylonia and Assyria. It seems, though, that the term Mesopotamia originally referred to the land lying between the uppermost channel of the Euphrates and the Khabur River, one of the Euphrates' main tributaries in north Syria (*Anabasis Alexandri* 3.8). This original Mesopotamia was the homeland of the Arameans. This is also certainly the sense of the place name Aram-naharaim ("Aram of the two rivers"), the land of Haran to which Abraham sent his servant to find a wife for Isaac (Gen 24:10; cp. Judg 3:8).

The broad river valleys of the Tigris-Euphrates and the Nile share similar natural characteristics. First, each valley is surrounded by harsh landscapes in which, historically, permanent settlement was tenuous or rugged at best. For the Nile these are the Sahara Desert to the west, with a meager scattering of oases, and the Eastern Desert and Sinai Peninsula to the east. In Mesopotamia, the wasteland of the north Arabian Desert pushes to the south bank of the Euphrates, while the soaring Zagros, Ararat

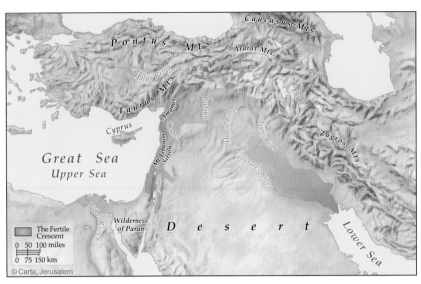

and Taurus mountains, home to a rich village tradition that always seemed at odds with the more urban landscape down below, frame the headwaters of the Tigris and Euphrates. Second, these are all world-class rivers, each with a strong perennial flow bolstered by seasonal rains up in their mountainous headwaters. For the Tigris and Euphrates these rains fall in eastern Anatolia, while for the Nile (the Blue Nile in particular) they inundate central Ethiopia. Throughout history seasonal rains have caused these downstream river valleys to flood at predictable times of the year, bringing new layers of silt to continually renew the already-rich fields along their banks. Third, the river valleys themselves are broad and quite flat. With a constant flow of water (rainfall is minimal in both Mesopotamia and Egypt), fields are relatively easy to irrigate by means of intricate networks of canals (Deut 11:10; Isa 19:5–8). The fertility of the Tigris-Euphrates and Nile river valleys fostered the growth of the world's first urban centers, with the origins of writing happening relatively simultaneously in both Egypt and southern Mesopotamia about the year 3200 B.C. This prompted the development of complex economic and administrative structures and, eventually, the rise of empires. The river valleys on either end of the Fertile Crescent were, in short, centers of highly productive civilizations where opportunities for advancement were attractive and life, for the day, could be good. Indeed, the writer of Genesis compared Egypt to "the garden of the LORD" (Gen 13:10).

The Fertile Crescent. The arc of the Fertile Crescent is defined not only by temperature and rainfall, but elevation. The crescent follows a portion of the southern edge of a large band of mountains that stretches from the Alps in southern Europe to Persia (Iran). The headwaters of the Euphrates and Tigris rivers flow southward out of the towering Taurus, Ararat and Zagros mountains. They combine to form two broad river channels that drain into the Persian Gulf (known in Akkadian texts as the Lower Sea). Smaller rivers flow out of the heights of the Lebanese and Anti-Lebanese ranges. These include the Orontes and an inland river, the Jordan.

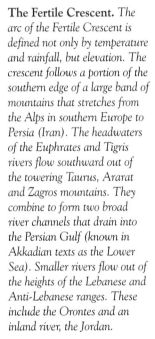

Carts of Sea People drawn by oxen, from relief of Rameses III at Medinet Habu in upper Egypt. This is a battle scene showing the struggle by Egypt to keep groups of Sea Peoples such as the Philistines from settling in Canaan.

This small harbor at Alexandria Troas, in northwestern Anatolia, is typical of hundreds of similar anchorages scattered across the Aegean. It was from near here that the Apostle Paul received his Macedonian Call to cross the archipelago and enter the wellspring of Hellenism on the other side (Acts 16:7–11). Ruins of the city of Troy lie a scant fifteen miles north, foothold of Alexander's invasion which four centuries prior had come the other way. Both crossings forever changed the face of the world.

The Aegean Trade Routes. *Natural sea routes in the eastern Mediterranean hugged a line of ports along the shore, or hopped between Cyprus and the islands of the Aegean. Westward voyages followed the sea currents from Gaza to Rhodes, along the coast. Prevailing westerly winds pushed ships on the return voyage, which could have been across open water if the weather didn't threaten. Open-sea travel was risky, and to be avoided when possible; the floor of the Mediterranean is littered with the wrecks of good sailing intentions. Seaworthy ships represented a large upfront investment, but could haul large quantities of goods relatively inexpensively. Land traffic had a greater human investment and could transport only smaller quantities of goods (the limits were set by the carrying capacity of individual beasts of burden). Land routes in Anatolia and Greece tended to be circuitous, owing to rugged terrain and the availability of suitable mountain passes, and were constantly threatened by bad weather conditions or hostile locals (cf. 2 Cor 11:25–27).*

Ancient Israel's interactions with Mesopotamia and Egypt were usually based on expediency: they were sometimes hostile, sometimes comfortable, and nearly always under the shadow of stronger economic and military structures bent on the ways of Empire. The route between empires passed right through the heartland of the biblical story. The travels of Abraham quickly set the stage for this connection: the Patriarch haled from both Ur of the Chaldees (in southern Mesopotamia) and Haran (in Aram-naharaim), then went immediately to Egypt—as did his descendants—when famine struck the land of Canaan (Gen 11:31–32; 12:10; 42:2; 43:1–2; 47:1). But though each end of the Fertile Crescent was the center of civilization in its own right, Egypt and Mesopotamia were for ancient Israel a necessary frontier—attractive, even a place of origins, but certainly not somewhere to call home.

In contrast to the bounded, elongated river valleys of Egypt and Mesopotamia, the Mediterranean basin can be pictured as a vast amphitheatre of ports and plains facing the sea. A ring of desert on the south (the Sahara) and rugged mountains to the north and east (the Alps, Balkan, Taurus and Lebanese ranges) encloses the basin, separating it and providing protection, at least in theory, from

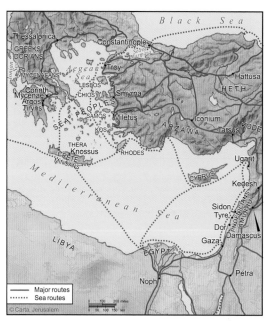

populations beyond which both Greece and Rome considered uncivilized. The main mountain ranges circling the sea are generally concordant to—that is, running the same direction as—the coast. When these ranges run right along the coast, their ragged edges provide inlets suitable for natural harbors and brisk maritime trade. Examples can be found along the Lebanese (Phoenician) and Taurus (Anatolian) coasts. Sometimes the concordant ranges are a bit inland, with broad, level plains separating them from them sea. In these cases the coastline is often straight-lined and generally lacking easy natural harbors, though the plains themselves are typically fertile and densely settled. Examples are the Philistine coastal plain, the plains of Cilicia (Tarsus) in Anatolia and Thessaly (Thessalonica) in Macedonia, and the eastern coast of the Italian Peninsula. Because not more than twenty percent of the land on the mountain slopes surrounding the Mediterranean is arable, the plains edging the coast have always tended to be the larger population centers around the sea. When the mountain ranges are discordant—that is, running perpendicular to the coast—the opportunities are the greatest for deep inlets and large areas of protected water that are favorable for shipping. This is the case for the southern Italian boot, western Anatolia and the Peloponnesus. Indeed, nearly the entire Aegean Sea is bounded by favorable points of anchorage, and when we take into account the thousands of islands and islets scattered between Greece and Anatolia it is clear that this part of the Mediterranean is the sea's heartland of maritime relations and trade.

As for travel and connectedness, the Mediterranean's currents push ships northward from Egypt along the Philistine and Phoenician coasts, then westward toward the Aegean along the coast of Anatolia. Prevailing winds, on the other hand, such as the strong Etesian winds off the Aegean, blow ships the other direction, toward the southeast. The seaborne journeys of the Apostle Paul had to take into account the seasonal affect of these shipping lanes, and shipwrecks were common (Acts 27:4–44). Surprisingly, the Mediterranean lacks a large number of wide river valleys that penetrate deeply inland from the sea and hence could serve as major land-sea corridors. The Nile is one, though its delta coastline has always been too marshy to support a major port (Alexandria lay slightly west). Mention should be made of the Po River in northern Italy and the Meander in western Anatolia. The city of Miletus, the greatest port in western Anatolia and a place visited by the Apostle Paul, was situated just south of the mouth of the Meander (Acts 20:15, 17). For the eastern Mediterranean, the best water route inland started in the estuary of the Orontes, a place dominated in the time of the New Testament by Antioch, the thriving cosmopolitan

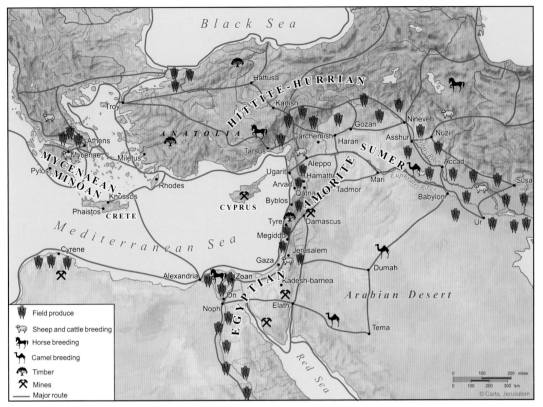

Field produce
Sheep and cattle breeding
Horse breeding
Camel breeding
Timber
Mines
Major route

Culture and Commerce in the Ancient Near East. *This map defines the Fertile Crescent in terms of its fertility for daily produce. Essential commodities as big timber and usable minerals could be found in the more mountainous regions. Routes tended to follow the Fertile Crescent, then branch off toward desert oases or population centers in Persia or the Aegean. The functional complexity of the economy of the ancient world can be seen in two different biblical texts. 1 Kings 10 details the movement of exotic goods from four corners of the ancient world to Solomon's Jerusalem in the tenth century B.C. Ezekiel 27 provides import and export data from which we can locate the origins of commodities that flowed through the port of Tyre in the sixth century B.C. Both show that the lands of the eastern Mediterranean played a crucial role in the development of culture and commerce in the ancient Near East.*

city "where the disciples were first called Christians" (Acts 11:26). Though the course of the Orontes river valley is narrow and quickly turns due south, Antioch provides the anchor point for a relatively short (one hundred mile) portage to the Upper Euphrates and the world of the east. Most other routes leading inward from the Mediterranean Sea had to deal immediately with rugged terrain, and once inland simply sought out the best route which connected paths of least resistance as possible (it wasn't always so simple!).

While economic strength in the world of the Old Testament was defined by camel drivers and charioteers who dominated the long land routes of the ancient Near East, the rulers of the Mediterranean were those who, by means of well-situated ports, could control the sea's shipping lanes. And like the far-flung lands of the ancient Near East, it proved difficult to unite the various corners of the Mediterranean into a single political entity. Throughout history the Mediterranean's coastal mountains tended to separate population centers one from another. This geographic reality fostered the development of diverse cultural contexts around the rim of the sea or on its many islands, though all shared a common knowledge of the sea. The Minoans (in the Aegean), Hittites (in Anatolia), Phoenicians (in Lebanon) and Etruscans (in Italy) all tried, with varying degrees of success, to unify the markets of the Mediterranean. It was not until the late first millennium B.C. that the Mediterranean was finally united, first under the cultural umbrella of Hellenism, then po-

litically by Rome. By the time of the New Testament all roads really did lead to Rome, be they conveying wheat from the Nile Delta and Bashan (Acts 27:6), spices from deep within the Arabian Peninsula, or the message of the Gospel.

With this broad geographical context of the lands of the Bible, it is time to narrow our focus to the place where East meets West. As we have seen, the narrow band of land lying between the eastern seaboard of the Mediterranean and the northern end of the Arabian Desert doubles as the middle section of the Fertile Crescent. This part of the ancient Near East bears greater resemblance to the landscapes of the Mediterranean than it does the broad river valleys that dominate Egypt and Mesopotamia. Here the landscape is defined by two parallel mountain ranges, concordant to the sea and separated from each other by the steep Rift Valley. In the north, where elevations are the highest, the seaward range is called the Lebanese Range (or, simply, Lebanon; Judg 3:3; 1 Kgs 5:9; Song of Songs 4:15), while its twin opposite the Rift is the Anti-Lebanese Range. The southern end of the Anti-Lebanese Range is best known by the name Mount Hermon, though the coastal Phoenicians called it Sirion and to the inland Amorites it was Senir (Deut 3:8–9). The upper elevations of the Lebanese and Anti-Lebanese ranges exceed nine thousand feet, and their well-watered heights are snow-capped for some months every year.

Because the long edge of the Lebanese Range drops directly into the Mediterranean, its coastline contains many natural harbors. This is the historic

This model of a square-rigged Sidonian merchant ship is typical of craft that plied the waters of the eastern Mediterranean in the ancient world.

They have made all your
  planks of fir trees from Senir,
    they have taken a cedar
      from Lebanon to make a
        mast for you…
Your sail was of fine embroidered linen from Egypt
    so that it became your
      distinguishing mark…

(Ezek 27:5, 7)

Geology. *The land of ancient Israel is primarily a land of limestone. Most of the visible surface rock is of three types.* **Turonian-Cenomanian** *limestone dominates the higher hill country. With tight, V-shaped valleys, rugged, terraced slopes and many small springs, hard limestone of this type provides a surface topography that is suitable for small villages. Summer fruit such as grapes, figs, pomegranates and olives thrive in these areas. Such was the heartland of the tribes of Judah, Ephraim and Manasseh, as well as Upper Galilee and the Dome of Gilead east of the Jordan River. Softer Eocene limestone is common in the foothills (Heb. shephelah). There the topographical forms are more relaxed, and the broad valleys are filled with fertile soil. These areas are particularly well suited for grains such as wheat and barley. Areas of soft Senonian chalk can be found in the Judean Wilderness and the Negev, south and east, as well as in troughs that form natural passes between the higher, more durable limestone hills. Areas of Senonian chalk do not hold water well, and unless the rainfall is high they are often best suitable for herding economies.*

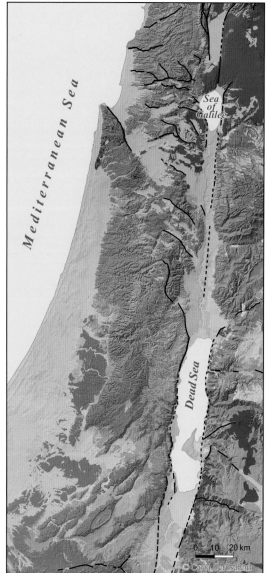

Geological Age			Rock Group					
Cenozoic	Quaternary	Holocene		Dead Sea			Conglomerate Units	Volcanic Units
		Pleistocene	Kurkar					
	Tertiary	Pliocene			Saqiye			
		Miocene						
		Oligocene / Upper Eocene						
		Eocene						
		Paleocene / Senonian						Volcanic Units
Mesozoic	Cretaceous Upper	Turonian / Cenomanian				Kurnub		
	Cretaceous Lower	Albian / Neocomian						
	Jurassic					Arad		
	Triassic					Ramon		
Paleozoic	Ordovician Cambrian					Reed Sea		
	Precambrian							

——— Main fault

- - - - Covered fault

home of the Phoenicians, ancient seafarers *par excellence*. Though lacking an arable coastal plain, Phoenician bellies were fed off the fields of inland powers such as ancient Israel (1 Kgs 5:11; Ezra 3:7; Ezek 27:17; Acts 12:20). We can immediately see the need for ongoing trade partnerships between Israel and Phoenicia, and in them an economic motive for Ahab's marriage to Jezebel (1 Kgs 16:31). The rest of the land within and surrounding the Lebanese and Anti-Lebanese ranges was the homeland of various groups of Arameans. The most important of these was centered at the spring-fed oasis of Damascus (2 Kgs 5:12), facing the open steppe that lines the north Arabian Desert east of the Anti-Lebanese Range. Aram-Damascus used its position astride the great Mesopotamia-to-Egypt trunk route to command inland trade every bit as effectively as the Phoenician ports dominated the seas (e.g. 1 Kgs 22:3; 2 Kgs 8:9; Ezek 27:18).

Both ranges decrease in elevation as they run southward. The Lebanese Range becomes the hills of Upper and Lower Galilee, then drops into the hill country of Manasseh, Ephraim, Judah and finally the Negev. Here elevations rarely exceed three thousand feet, with ample rainfall and only infrequent snow. The Anti-Lebanese Range merges into the hills of Bashan, Gilead, Moab and then Edom. On average the Transjordanian hills are higher than those west of the Rift (up to a mile high in Edom), but their eastward, desert face counteracts much of the benefit that would otherwise come from the rainfall of higher elevations. The Rift Valley, too, drops in elevation south of Lebanon, down to 690 feet below sea level at the surface of the Sea of Galilee (nearly three times as low as California's Death Valley) and to −1,300 feet at the Dead Sea, the lowest place on earth.

We have finally arrived at the heartland of the biblical story, the historic "Dan to Beer-sheba" home of ancient Israel (1 Kgs 4:25). The city of Dan sat up against the southernmost flank of Mount Hermon, adjacent to the most powerful spring feeding the headwaters of the Jordan River. Beer-sheba commanded the middle of the arid Negev basin 110

1	Terra rossa, brown rendzina and pale rendzina
2	Brown rendzina and pale rendzina soils
3	Pale rendzina soils
4	Brown lithosols and loessial arid brown soils
5	Brown lithosols and loessial serozems
6	Rock outcrops and desert lithosols
7	Brown Mediterranean soils and lithosols
8	Protogrumusols, grumusols and pale rendzina
9	Grumusols
10	Dark brown soils
11	Loessial arid brown soils
12	Loessial serozems
13	Reg soils and coarse desert alluvium
14	Hamra soils
15	Sandy regosols and arid brown soils
16	Sand dunes
17	Alluvial arid brown soils
18	Calcareous serozems
19	Hydromorphic and gley soils
20	Solonchak soils

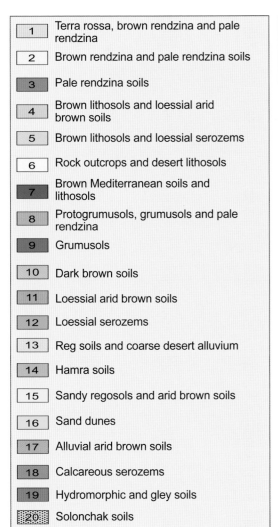

Soils. *The best soils in the land of ancient Israel are the dark brown, hamra soils found on the coastal plain. These are composite soils formed from a mixture of rich loam alluvium that is washed down from the higher limestone hills to the east, and sand that otherwise lines the seashore. The deep clayey grumusol soils of the coastal plain and large inland valleys are also quite fertile, though they do not drain as well. The red-brown terra rossa soils of the higher hill country are also fertile, though best suited for orchard crops. The soils found in the eastern and southern extremities of the land, toward the desert, tend to be immature and not very productive for agriculture.*

(below) This view into the Lebonah Valley, in "the remote interior of the hill country of Ephraim" (Judg 19:1), *offers a template for traditional highland village life in the land of ancient Israel. For protection and community, everyone lives together in town. Village fields, subdivided among family units, stretch as far from home as is practical for a day's work. Crops of winter wheat and barley take good root in the valley's productive soil. The lower levels of the limestone hills surrounding the valley are terraced for summer fruit. Above, open, rocky slopes are suitable for grazing village flocks and herds. The ideal life of an ancient Israelite was lived out in villages such as this one, "each man under his own vine and fig tree"* (1 Kgs 4:25).

miles south, beyond which opens the wasteland of the Sinai Peninsula. Dan provides a picture of the wealth of spring-fed fertility, while Beer-sheba reminds us of the herding resources of the shepherd, the two basic lifestyles of the land of ancient Israel. During the time of the Israelite and Judean monarchies, both cities controlled imperial through-routes that were of interest to the international power-brokers of the day, while the stronger kings of Judah and Israel tried to siphon the revenue flow up to Jerusalem or Samaria.

The homeland core of Judah and Israel was a north-south range of hard limestone hills rising midway between the Mediterranean coast and the Rift Valley. With cool, wet winters and hot, dry summers, this was the ideal setting for small village life supported by a harvest of summer fruit such as grapes, olives, figs, pomegranates and almonds (Gen 49:22–26; Deut 8:8; 33:13–17; 1 Kgs 4:25). To the west, the Philistine and Sharon coastal plains form a wide band of fertile arable soil that have supported a sequence of people groups quite distinct from those living up in the hills. Many of the cities out on the coastal plain sat astride the great trunk route of antiquity where by the advantage of location they were

necessarily tied to—and overrun by—a long succession of peoples from the world beyond. In the biblical period these included the Philistines, who hailed from the Aegean yet made the coast between Joppa and Gaza their home (Amos 9:7), as well as unending waves of conquerors from Egypt, Mesopotamia (Assyria and Babylon) and the Mediterranean (Greece

The Jezreel Valley represents all that's good in the land of ancient Israel. Rainfall and deep, level soil combine to provide some of the best agricultural land in the country. Perhaps more important for the big picture, it was here that the international route connecting Egypt with Mesopotamia crossed the route from Acco-Ptolemais to Transjordan, an intersection for the ages. Of course the benefits came with a down-side: invasion. This view northward from Mount Carmel takes in the western end of the Jezreel Valley and the hills of Galilee beyond. In the time of the Old Testament the tribes of Manasseh, Asher and Zebulun met here; in the first century this was the personal estate of the Herodian royal family (Josephus, Life, 118–119).

and Rome) who were bent on using the coast as a foothold for conquests further afield. Between the hill country of Judah and the Philistine coastal plain are the foothills of the Shephelah (Josh 10:40), a buffer zone which absorbed a constant push and shove by highlanders and plain dwellers on either side. The stories of David and Goliath (1 Sam 17:1–54), Sennacherib (2 Kgs 18:13; 19:8) and the Maccabees (1 Maccabees) are illustrative of the ongoing dynamic for dominance of the Shephelah by one group or another (Isa 9:12; 11:14).

East and south of the hill country of Judah lie areas in which the average rainfall is less than twelve inches per year, which can support neither agriculture nor permanent village life. The Judean Wilderness and much of the Negev fall into this category. Here the economic base is shepherding, with patterns of lifestyle suitable to a mobile, Bedouin-type existence. Shepherds in these regions have typically developed distinct patterns of existence that are different from those of the settled farmer who inhabits the more fertile parts of the land. This has necessarily provoked both conflict and cooperation, as is the case for similar economies worldwide. Even though the more fertile parts of the land were better suited to agricultural lifestyles, ancient Israel's founding memories were nearly all shepherd-based (Abel, Abraham, Moses and David were all shepherds). There is something about the I-will-give-my-life-for-my-sheep persistence of a shepherd that made it one of the most enduring (and endearing) images of faithfulness in the Bible (Ps 23:1; 78:52; Isa 63:11; Ezek 34: 1–31; Jn 10:1–18; 21:15–17).

Further east, opposite the Rift, the lands of Transjordan are dominated by a rise of limestone hills with open desert beyond. While the biblical authors tended to emphasize the ongoing struggles that Israel and Judah had with Ammonites, Moabites and Edomites living east of the Jordan, these eastern lands as a whole can be defined by nearly the same package of traits that characterize the lands lying west of the Rift. They were, after all, the homelands of Israel's tribal cousins (the worst

fights, it's been said, are within the family).

The largest truly international zone in the land of ancient Israel is in the north. The best natural port, Acco-Ptolemais, has a flat-land connection to the resources of Transjordan through the wide-open Jezreel Valley, and this corridor saw brisk activity in international trade and conquest throughout the biblical period. The Jezreel Valley separates the hills of Ephraim and Manasseh from Galilee, and so interest in the region naturally also fell into the orbit of Israel's able kings. Much of the Gospel story focuses on Jesus' activities in Galilee, and his embrace of the role Messiah should be seen within the backdrop of a long litany of royal, priestly and prophetic expectations in the region.

In the Book of Deuteronomy, Moses succinctly described the essential difference between the land of ancient Israel and the flatland Nile Delta which had been his Egyptian home:

For the land into which you are entering to possess is not like the land of Egypt from which you came, where you used to sow your seed and water it with your foot like a vegetable garden. But the land into which you are about to cross to possess is a land of hills and valleys that drink water from the rain of heaven. (Deut 11:10–11)

A land of hills and valleys—this makes all the difference. Canaan was a land of high, rocky hills and limited arability, and lacked a reliable world-class river from which its inhabitants could cultivate large tracts of irrigated land. Indeed, its source of life—rainfall—was both unpredictable and uncontrolled. Because of its many natural blocks to communication and travel, people groups here tended to be separated from each other and as a result tended to develop a matrix of provincial loyalties. More-over, limited natural resources kept overall population levels low. At the same time, because this land was tightly constricted between desert and sea, it also served as the necessary highway connection for empires round about who squeezed the already strapped locals for their own imperialistic ends. The interplay between conquerors and survivors was both constant and active. Responding to the reality of the place, the author of the book of Deuteronomy noted that the only way to a life that was secure and blessed was to recognize the reality of God's choice of this piece of the seam binding the Fertile Crescent to the Mediterranean basin—scrappy as it may be when compared to the better resourced areas of Israel's far-flung neighbors—as the place best suited to raise a people who necessarily had to learn to rely on Him:

It is a land for which the LORD your God cares. The eyes of the LORD your God are always on it, from the beginning even to the end of the year.
(Deut 11:12)

MAP OF THE MIDDLE EAST

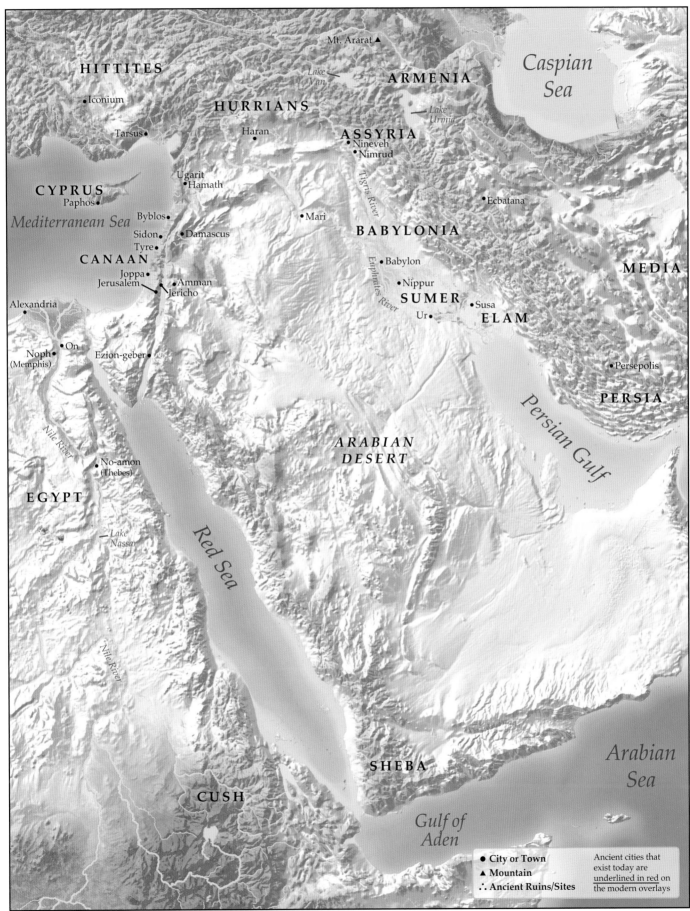

Caspian Sea

Mt. Ararat ▲

HITTITES

ARMENIA

Lake Van

• Iconium

HURRIANS

Haran

ASSYRIA

• Nineveh

• Nimrud

Lake Urmia

Tarsus •

CYPRUS

Ugarit •

• Hamath

Ecbatana •

Paphos •

Mediterranean Sea

Byblos •

• Mari

BABYLONIA

MEDIA

Sidon •

Tyre •

• Damascus

• Babylon

CANAAN

• Nippur

Joppa •

Jerusalem •

• Amman

• Jericho

SUMER

Ur •

• Susa

ELAM

Alexandria •

• On

Noph •

(Memphis)

Ezion-geber •

• Persepolis

PERSIA

Nile River

No-amon •

(Thebes)

ARABIAN DESERT

Persian Gulf

EGYPT

Lake Nassar

Red Sea

Nile River

Arabian Sea

SHEBA

CUSH

Gulf of Aden

● City or Town

▲ Mountain

∴ Ancient Ruins/Sites

Ancient cities that exist today are underlined in red on the modern overlays

CHAPTER 2
THE PATRIARCHS AND MATRIARCHS
Our Fathers and Mothers

As its name suggests, Genesis is a book of beginnings. Here we read of the beginning of family life (Gen 4:1–2, 4:25–26), of music, craftsmen and cities (Gen 4:17, 4:21–22, 10:11–12), of crime and punishment (Gen 4:3–15), of people groups and nations (Gen 10:1–32), of religion and a Divine covenant (Gen 4:26, 9:11–12, 17:1–8), and of hope, promise and redemption (Gen 3:15, 9:12–17, 12:1–3). These stories of life "in the beginning" (from *Bereshit*, the title of the book in Hebrew) coalesce in the lives of the Patriarchs and Matriarchs: Abraham and Sarah, Isaac and Rebekah, Jacob, Leah and Rachel, and Joseph.

As the ancestral head of a family that was to become "as numerous as the stars of the sky and the sand on the seashore" (Gen 22:17), Abraham is held in special regard by Jews, Christians and Muslims alike:

Rabbi Hanan bar Rava said in the name of Rav: On the day our father Abraham departed from this world, all the notables of the world's nations stood in a line and said: "Alas for the world that has lost its leader! Alas for the ship that has lost its pilot." (Baba Bathra 91a–b)

Abraham believed God, and it was reckoned to him as righteousness. Therefore, be certain that the sons of Abraham are those who are people of faith. (Gal 3:6–7)

Recite the account of Abraham according to this Book; he was indeed a righteous person and a Prophet. (Qu'ran 19:42)

From our perspective it is appropriate, then, that the journeys of Abraham and his wife Sarah, as described in Genesis, carried them from one end of the Fertile Crescent to the other, across a great sweep of land that was to become so important in the rise and early history of Judaism, Christianity and Islam. At the same time, Abraham's journey from Mesopotamia (Gen 11:31–12:3), then to and from Egypt (Gen 12:10–13:1), anticipated later journeys that his descendants would make into and out of the same lands: Israel's sojourn in Egypt, the Exodus, the Deportation to Assyria and the Exile to Babylon (Gen 47:27; Ex 13:17–18; 2 Kgs 17:1–23; 2 Chron 36:20–23).

Although ancient Mesopotamia and Egypt were fertile lands, well watered by powerful rivers and offering social and economic opportunities, the envy of the known world, Abraham was not at home in either. Instead, he was called—Divinely compelled—to go to a thin, barren land between, with few of the natural resources that are normally considered necessary for "the good life." Abraham's sojourns in the

(opposite page) Footprints from the past to eternity—Abraham and his family have left their mark on the sands of time, charting the way for generations of their descendants to begin their journey to God.

Israelite captives in Assyria playing the lyre, from the palace of Sennacherib at Kuyunjik (Nineveh). Knowing that their father Abraham had journeyed from Mesopotamia to "the land that I will show you," these captives could only sing songs of sorrow in the land they too wanted to leave behind. One hundred forty years later Judean exiles in Babylon refused to play their lyres as long as they were outside the Land of Promise (Ps 137:1–3).

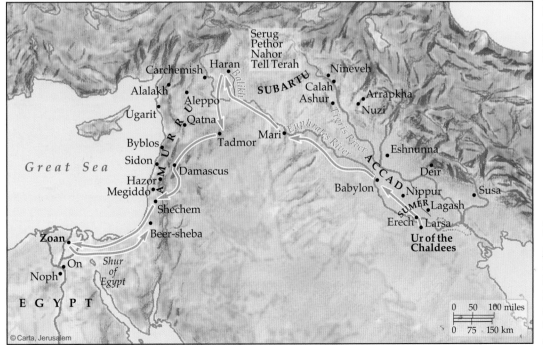

Abraham's Migration.
While Abraham's journeys from Ur of the Chaldees to Haran and then Egypt carried him across the sweep of the Fertile Crescent, he was most at home in Canaan, the land God promised to his many descendants.

19

Rare photograph from the archives of Sultan Abdul Hamid (1876–1909) showing a group of Bedouin in the Negev.

Salt formations along the Dead Sea evoke images of Lot's wife, turned into a pillar of salt for turning her back on the land of God's promise. (photo: Garo Nalbandian)

land of Canaan, where he owned no plot of ground until he bought a cave in which to bury his wife (Gen 23:1–20), set the stage not only for the birth of two great peoples—the Jews through Isaac and the Arabs through Ishmael—but for the human journey taken by each one of his countless descendants through the uncertainties of life (Heb 11:8–19).

Although it is not technically proper to label him as such, Abraham's lifestyle bears certain important resemblances to Bedouin, at least Bedouin who inhabited the Middle East in pre-modern times. For millennia, large extended families of semi-nomadic pastoralists—herders of sheep, goats and cattle grouped along family and clan lines—have inhabited the thin band of arid land that lies between the Fertile Crescent and the inhospitable north Arabian desert. Following the change of seasons in search of adequate pasturage for their animals, these families and clans would move and settle as needed. Most tended to stay within the limits of certain broadly defined territories and developed reciprocal relationships with persons in nearby towns or cities, exchanging goods and services and benefiting from mutually recognized water and grazing rights. There is some evidence for occasional large-scale migrations from one region to another, however, and the movement of Terah with Abram (Abraham), Sarai (Sarah) and Lot from Ur of the Chaldees in Babylonia (southeastern Mesopotamia) to Haran at the upper arc of the Fertile Crescent (Gen 11:31–32), fits this pattern.

Haran was a true urban center in its day (its name derives from a word that means variously "highway," "caravan" or "business finance"), and when Terah entered its social and economic orbit he found a homeland that offered a secure future for his family. Abram, apparently the eldest son (cf. Gen 11:27), stood to inherit the lion's share of the wealth and prestige that accompanied his role

of patriarch in this land of opportunity, but instead he moved on, prompted by the divine call of God, to a place known only as "the land that I will show you" (Gen 12:1). Aging and childless, and lacking both a son and now a home base, the two most essential resources for a semi-nomad, Abram journeyed into the unknown. Following the general line of the great trunk route connecting northern Mesopotamia to Egypt, Abram, his wife Sarai and his nephew Lot entered Canaan from the northeast. They camped on the outskirts of both Shechem and Bethel, two established city-states in the hilly center of the land, and offered due obeisance to the God who had promised *this* rocky landscape, of all places, to his descendants (Gen 12:4–8). We can assume that Abraham's encampment at both places was rather lengthy, for no short-term visitor would be granted the right by the local inhabitants of the land to build an altar to a yet-unknown deity, the reality of his divine call notwithstanding.

From there Abram and his not-yet-a-family journeyed south along the spiny central ridge of southern Canaan, a land fertile enough when the rainfall is good but one that always lies at the doorstep of famine. His movement was slow and deliberate, paced by the speed of grazing sheep and goats, and he certainly interacted with people from every village and city-state along the way including Gibeon, Jerusalem, Bethlehem and Hebron. This portion of Abram's journey ended in the Negeb, a largely barren expanse of fine, powdery soil that lacks sufficient rainfall for agriculture, tucked between the arable hills of Canaan and the dry Sinai desert (Gen 12:9). This biblical Negeb should not be confused with the large V-shaped southern half of the modern state of Israel which, although called the Negev today, is both geographically and historically part of the Sinai. Although the biblical Negeb is suitable for a semi-nomadic lifestyle, a widespread famine soon forced Abram on to the fertile Nile delta in Lower Egypt. Here his initial attempts at establishing a symbiotic relationship with Pharaoh turned sour, and Abram had to be rescued by the hand of God, having nevertheless gained economically for the effort (Gen 12:10–13:1).

Upon returning to Canaan, Abram's growing band faced the consequences of denuding its grazing land and so split into two organic families, with Abram staying in the hills between Bethel and the Negeb and Lot descending into the Rift Valley near the Dead Sea. Lot eventually found grazing rights in the vicinity of Sodom (Gen 13:2–13), a fateful choice that would prove to be his undoing (Gen 19:1–29). The fiery destruction of Sodom and Gomorrah and return of the region to a salty wasteland eventually forced Lot's descendants farther east, into the lands that would one day become Moab and Ammon (Gen 19:30–38). Here the writer of Genesis, like lat-

Megiddo

Great Sea

Jordan Valley

Shechem

Abraham sets up altar at oak of Moreh

Aphek

Lot

Bethel
Ai

LAND OF KEDEM

Salem

Abraham buys cave of Machpelah

Hebron (Kiriath-arba)

Dead Sea

THE LAND OF GERAR

Oaks of Mamre

Capital of Abimelech king of Philistines

Beer-sheba

Sodom
Gomorrah

Zoar

Shur

N e g e b

Abraham goes down to Egypt in year of famine

Way to Shur

Beer-lahai-roi

Kadesh-barnea

Isaac meets Rebekah

Wilderness of Paran

→ Abraham's route
⇉ Isaac's route

0 10 20 miles
0 10 20 30 km

© Carta, Jerusalem

Abraham and Isaac in the Land of Canaan. *Abraham and Isaac traveled throughout southern Canaan, forging important relationships with people from various city-states in the region. Their line of travel along the "Patriarchal Highway" established a tradition of rights to the land for their descendants.*

The Negev—Past and Present. *In the Bible, the Negeb was a tight sideways "8"-shaped basin south of the hill country of Judah. With scant rainfall and powdery loess soil, this was shepherd land. Everything south of that was simply "wilderness," beyond where even shepherds normally would go. Today the entire region is called the Negev.*

er biblical authors, emphasized the geographical movement of persons from the land of promise back to the east, a route opposite that which Abram had originally come, as a way both of setting apart the divine choice of Abram's new land and the people meant to live in it (Gen 3:24, 36:1–43; 2 Kgs 24:14–15).

For his part Abram remained in Canaan, moving alternately between the southern hill country around Hebron and the Negeb (Gen 14:13, 18:1, 20:1, 22:2, 23:2). He set up his main base of operations in the Negeb at a place called Beer-sheba (Gen 22:19), some distance east of Gerar, the closest urban center. Archaeological and literary evidence suggests that in Abram's day Beer-sheba was just an encampment spot near a well (*Beer* means "well"), apparently near the location of the later Israelite (Iron Age) city of Beer-sheba (*Tel Sheva*) or somewhere else in the general vicinity. At one point later in life, probably during another famine, Abram, who by then bore the covenanted name Abraham (which Genesis 17:1–8 takes to mean "father of a multitude"), established his camp near Gerar (Gen 20:1). Gerar controlled a fertile expanse of land at the juncture of the coastal plain and the biblical

Negeb; anachronistically, this was called the "land of the Philistines" in the Genesis account (Gen 21:34; cf. Gen 26:1). Although Abraham won grazing rights from the king of Gerar, water remained a source of friction between the two and prompted a formal alliance that recognized the rights of each within their respective territories (Gen 21:22–34).

Abraham's longest journey after settling in Canaan was not for the benefit of his flocks, but as a man of war. The challenges inherent to daily survival in the harsh conditions of semi-nomadism foster survival skills that are best tested in war, and Abraham had his chance when an alliance of kings from Mesopotamia raided the territory of Sodom and Gomorrah, taking Lot and his possessions as war trophies (Gen 14:1–12). Abraham and 318 trained men of his household, a formidable fighting force, chased the Mesopotamian kings up the Rift Valley to Dan (Laish) and then on to Hobah, a location not yet identified with certainty but somewhere north of Damascus (Gen 14:13–16). Though in the vicinity of his extended family in Haran, Abraham returned to Canaan, pausing on his way to meet Melchizedek king of Salem (likely Jerusalem, a place that Abra-

Encampment at the well of Beer-sheba, 19th century engraving. More than just a watering hole, a well in the desert is a focal point of social life, where acquaintances are made, strengthened or renewed. This is a place where water rights determine social interaction, and the identity and intent of a stranger—like Abraham's servant in search of a wife for Isaac—must be revealed quickly.

Location of Beni Hasan, in Middle Egypt. *Though far from Canaan, evidence of Semitic migrations to Egypt was found here.*

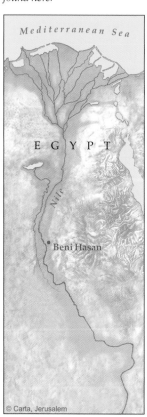

ham would have known from his prior journeys between Bethel and Hebron; (Gen 14:17–24). As a result of this meeting, Abraham's reputation and rights were strengthened in the central hill country.

Abraham's arsenal for survival included skills in the art of diplomacy and with the sword, in hospitality and in living off the land. But these weren't enough, for he lacked what mattered most, a proper heir (Gen 15:1–2). The solution lay in the hands of God alone, and in two dramatic scenes which took place at unnamed locations somewhere in Canaan, Abraham received not only the divine assurance of a son born of he and Sarah (Gen 17:1–27), but of a real homeland for what would be countless descendants (Gen 15:1–21). The borders of this promised land, from the river of Egypt (the *Wadi el-Arish* in the mid-Sinai) to the great river, the Euphrates in northern Syria, were realized in the biblical period only during the United Monarchy, when Solomon maintained some degree of formal control over this vast area (Gen 15:18; 1 Kgs 4:21). In the meantime, Abraham and Sarah had taken matters into their own hands, producing a son through Hagar, Sarah's maid (Gen 16:1–4). Though this was a culturally acceptable solution for a childless couple, it did create jealousies in the home and fell short of the divine promise (Gen 16:5–6; cf. Deut 21:15–17). Hagar and her son Ishmael fled toward Shur in the mid-Sinai, a wasteland barely fit for human habitation (Gen 16:7–15; cf. Gen 20:1, 21:9–21). Exiled from the land of promise, Ishmael became the ancestor of the Arabs; the list of his descendants in Genesis 25:12–18 includes names of tribes and places known in the vast Sinai and Arabian deserts south and east of Canaan.

Finally, but in God's good time, a son was born to Abraham and Sarah (Gen 18:1–15, 21:1–7). It is im-

possible to overestimate the sense of pride, accomplishment and satisfaction that Abraham felt when, during a feast celebrating Isaac's young life, his public honor was restored (Gen 21:8). Then came the bombshell—Abraham was to take Isaac to the land of Moriah and offer him as a burnt offering back to God (Gen 22:1–2). Although the writer of Chronicles understood that the place of this intended sacrifice was just outside the northern wall of Jerusalem on the hill on which Solomon would build the temple (2 Chron 3:1), it is important to distinguish his specific reference to "Mount Moriah" from the more general "land of Moriah" to which Abraham and Isaac journeyed. In fact, the tenor of the account in Genesis suggests that the act was carried out far from human eyes (Gen 22:3–5), probably somewhere in the hill country or wilderness of Judah but certainly not adjacent to an established urban center such as Jerusalem. In the end Isaac was redeemed (Gen 22:9–18); with his life spared, that of Abraham's family was again assured.

Then Sarah died—according to Rabbinic sources (*Tanhuma, Va-yera* 23) it was from fright after hearing what had almost happened to her son—and was buried in the Cave of Machpelah opposite Mamre (Hebron). Abraham purchased the cave from Ephron the Hittite, a local inhabitant of the land (Gen 23:1–20). Abraham refused Ephron's offer to use the cave free of charge; had he accepted Ephron's generosity, Abraham would have been acknowledging that his descendants' rights to the land should remain under the authority of its indigenous inhabitants. Rather, by insisting that he purchase the burial cave outright, Abraham took the first legal step in providing an ancestral land for his descendants, in perpetuity. Abraham's grandson Jacob would continue the process by purchasing land in Shechem (Gen 33:18–20). Eventually Abraham, Isaac and Rebekah, and Jacob and Leah were all to be buried in this family tomb (Gen 25:9–10, 49:29–33).

Abraham's son Ishmael married an Egyptian woman (Gen 21:21), which was probably prudent given his mother's Egyptian bloodline (Gen 16:1) and the fact that he had been exiled from his father's house. But not so for Isaac, the child of promise! To maintain the strength of the family—as well as the integrity of the divine promise—it was essential that the heir marry within and keep the family's human and economic resources intact. For this reason, Isaac's wife had to come from among his closest relatives, the family of Abraham's brother back in Haran. Abraham's servant was entrusted with the sacred task of arranging the marriage. This was perhaps the same Eliezer of Damascus who, before Isaac's birth, had stood in line to inherit everything (Gen 24:1–4; cf. 15:2). Loyalty and honor run deep in semi-nomadic households and so the servant complied, thereby ensuring that his own future would remain subordinate to that of Isaac. Rebekah willingly stepped into the role of matriarch-in-waiting (Gen 24:67) and followed Abraham's footsteps from Haran back to Canaan.

Upon the death of Abraham the responsibility of maintaining the family's welfare fell squarely on the shoulders of Isaac, no small task given the marginal climate of the Negeb and the crucial need to protect the limited resources available there. Another famine drove Isaac west to Gerar, where the prevailing rainfall was predictable enough to support not only herding, but agriculture (Gen 26:1–6, 12–14). Isaac's skills at both, when blessed by the hand of God, tipped the local economy his way. Understandably threatened, Abimelech the king of Gerar rescinded the water rights that he had previously granted to Abraham, forcing Isaac to withdraw toward the desert but to a place still within the valley controlled by Gerar (Gen 26:15, 18; cf. 21:22–34). Taking matters into his own hands, Isaac opened a series of wells that his father had dug, reclaiming his family's rights to the land. In each case, the "Philistines" of Gerar successfully contested these rights, driving Isaac farther away. Finally, back at Beer-sheba, beyond

The sacrifice of Isaac as depicted in a 19th century engraving (Carta, Jerusalem). *This was the great test. Would Abraham be faithful to God? And would God faithfully keep His promises to Abraham?*

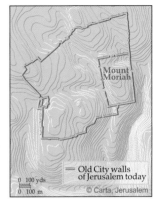

Mount Moriah, the Temple Mount. *The writer of Chronicles connected Mount Moriah with the more general "land of Moriah" where Abraham offered Isaac to God* (2 Chron 3:1).

Gerar's frontier and the limits of Abimelech's immediate economic interests, Isaac was able to camp without outside interference (Gen 26:18–25). With the balance of power restored in the Negeb, Abimelech reestablished with Isaac the covenant that he had previously made with Abraham (cf. Gen 21:22–34).

Meanwhile, Rebekah had given birth to twins. Destined to become two rival nations, Jacob (Israel) and Esau (Edom) already fought for territory in her womb (Gen 25:19–26). Esau, the firstborn, was very much at home in the brutish conditions of the Negeb, while Jacob, part by nature and part by his mother's coddling, preferred a homeland security akin to what Rebekah had left behind in Haran (Gen 25:27–28). The name Jacob is a play on the word "heel," and appropriately throughout his life the more sophisticated Jacob attempted to trip up his churlish older brother. Early on Jacob traded a common pot of lentil stew for Esau's birthright—it was a real steal—and so through the kind of trickery or cleverness that was quietly admired in the art of ancient Near Eastern diplomacy, he moved into the slot of heir-to-the-patriarchy (Gen 25:28–34). Later, toward the end of Isaac's life, Jacob similarly

This 19th century B.C. wall painting from a tomb in Beni Hasan on the east bank of the Nile depicting a caravan of Asiatics journeying to Egypt represents the continual influx of people from the region of Canaan into Egypt during the second millennium B.C. The journeys of Abraham, Joseph and Jacob to Egypt are set against this migratory backdrop.

The remains of the eastern gate of the fortified city of Shechem, dating to Middle Bronze IIB (c. 1750–1650 B.C.), represents the strong, well-established role of the city-state in the central hill country during the time of the Patriarchs. Although they were most at home herding their sheep and goats along the semi-arid seam between the desert and the sown land, Abraham, Isaac and Jacob had to develop and maintain cordial, working relationships with established cities such as Shechem. They were not always successful in doing so.

Although it is too simplistic and overly romantic to equate modern-day Bedouin with biblical characters, various aspects of Bedouin life do preserve ancient patterns of living that can help shed light on the thoughts and deeds of the Patriarchs and Matriarchs.

grabbed the patriarchal blessing from Esau, and with it formal confirmation of his role as head of the family once Isaac had died (Gen 27:1–40). Predictably, Esau plotted to seize back his rights by force (Gen 27:41).

And so Jacob fled, under the convenient suggestion of Rebekah, back to the land where a part of his mother's heart still lay (Gen 27:42–28:10). Tracing the now familiar patriarchal highway from Beer-sheba north along the spiny backbone of the hill country, Jacob stopped one night at Bethel ("the house of God"), where with a glimpse of heavenly geography, Jacob received God's promise that the land would someday belong to his many descendants. With a response true to character, Jacob tried to bargain favorable terms (Gen 28:11–22).

Arriving in "the land of the sons of the east" (Gen 29:1) near Haran, Jacob met Rachel, the daughter of Rebekah's brother Laban, at a well (Gen 29:2–12). This remains a classic "boy meets girl" scene typical of the ageless world of semi-nomadism. By means of the expectations that came with hospitality and negotiation, Jacob attached himself to Laban's household, first as a worker and then as a son, twice over. Typically a man in Jacob's position, already an heir, would take his new bride back to his own home, but the expediency of the moment—his own survival and a chance to marry well—kept him in the neighborhood of Haran. Laban, who, like Jacob, was skilled in the clever art of survival, gained an upper hand on his guest in order to ensure that both of his daughters would receive a proper future, and so Jacob married the older, homely Leah as well as the younger, more beautiful Rachel (Gen 29:13–30).

Jacob stayed in Haran under the patriarchal authority of Laban for twenty years. These were good years, secure and full of opportunity. Jacob honed his skills in animal husbandry so that the flocks under his care multiplied and were strong, but did so at the expense of Laban (Gen 30:25–43). His family eventually numbered eleven sons and one daughter, with another son on the way (Gen 29:31–30:24, 35:16–20). These boys were to become the ancestral heads of the twelve tribes of Israel, and Jacob's deathbed blessing for each carried geographical information that matched the particular part of the land of Canaan where each tribe would settle (Gen 49:1–27).

In the end Laban's extended family had two heads: he by right and Jacob by practice. This was an untenable situation and so the family and its resources were divided, with Jacob and those under his care moving back to the land of his birth (Gen 31:1–55). Like all semi-nomads on the move, Jacob was both strong and vulnerable during his long journey home. He traveled south slowly, along the edge of the open desert, with his wealth strung along, juicy prey for wild animals or desert raiders. In the highlands of Gilead, opposite Canaan, Jacob heard that Esau, with four hundred men, was on the way to meet him. Knowing that memories live long—a characteristic still endemic to the Middle East—Jacob feared the worse. He tried to placate Esau by offering a portion of the hard-earned inheritance from his wives' family, perhaps also hoping that some would count against the debt of the stolen birthright (Gen 32:1–21). Then, in the wild, dark cleft of the Jabbok River, Jacob fought with a man (Heb. *ish*) tooth and nail, all night. "Is it Esau?"— the thought probably raced through his mind. In this melodramatic scene ripe with danger, Jacob finally realized that his lifetime of struggles had really been with God all along (cf. Hos 12:3–4), and that in spite of his own skills of survival and his conniving inner nature, God had chosen to bless him anyway. Jacob "the heel," who had built a career out of his own struggle to supplant others, was now named "Israel," one who strives with God and for *this* reason, prevails (Gen 32:22–32).

By now both Jacob and Esau had become patriarchs and agreed to respect each other's rights and territory (Gen 33:1–17). Esau stayed east of the Rift Valley; his descendants spread throughout southern Transjordan and the northern Arabian Peninsula and can be traced among known tribal and city names in later centuries (Gen 36:1–43). Jacob's family headed west, stopping first at Succoth where the Jabbok River meets the Jordan, a lovely spot in the mid-Jordan Valley (Gen 33:17). From there he followed good grazing land up the Wadi Faria to Shechem, a well-established Canaanite city-state on a hub of hill-country routes blessed with abundant water and fertile fields. Here Jacob settled for some time and gained a degree of permanent status by purchasing land and building an altar to *El-Elohe-Israel* ("God, the God of Israel"; Gen 33:18–19). Eventually, like Abraham before him (cf. Gen 12:6–9), Jacob moved on to Bethel, built another altar and continued south, settling in the vicinity of Hebron (Gen 35:1–27).

Jacob's family matured in the fresh climate of the Hebron hill country. The aging patriarch favored

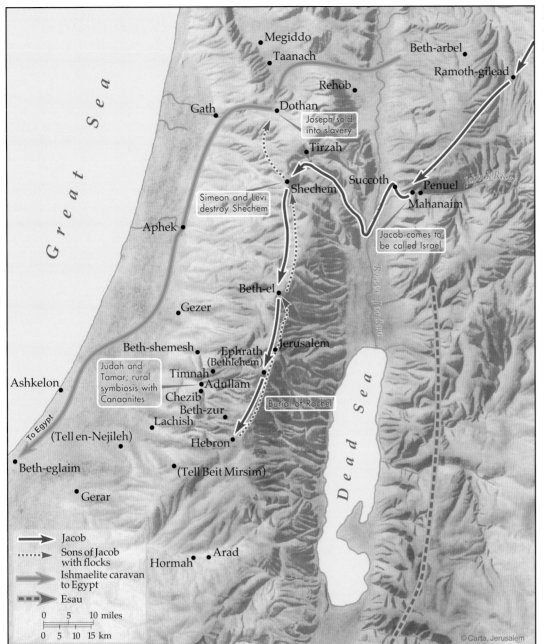

Jacob and His Sons.
Although Jacob spent twenty years of his life in Haran, his return to Canaan with a large family in tow marks the beginning of the history of the "sons of Israel."

Late at night and alone in the cut of the Jabbok River deep in the Dome of Gilead, Jacob had the wrestling match of a lifetime—and one that changed his life. The Supplanter became One who Strove with God.

Joseph, the oldest son of Rachel, his favorite wife, as heir-apparent, a situation that was a continual thorn in the sides of the ten older brothers (Gen 37:3–11). As the years passed and his holdings grew, Jacob routinely split his flocks among his various sons, sending some one way and others another, according to the change of seasons and established patterns of grazing. At one point Jacob's older sons drove their flocks to the fertile land around Shechem, then as far north as the picturesque valley of Dothan (Gen 37:12–17). As recently as the mid-twentieth century some Bedouin families from the Hebron hills still grazed their flocks around Dothan; perhaps each passing generation of shepherds and farmers maintained this ancient grazing pattern by protecting the rights handed down to them from their fathers. Joseph, sent by Jacob to enquire of his brothers' welfare, caught up with his older siblings in Dothan. There Joseph was seized and sold to a passing caravan of easterners—Midianites and Ishmaelites who were tracking the trade routes of the ancient Near East, bound for the lucrative markets of Egypt (Gen 37:18–35).

Joseph ended up attached to the house of Potiphar, a high official in the court of Pharaoh who lived in Goshen (Gen 37:36, 45:10). Goshen lay in the northeastern Nile Delta, a region that had been infiltrated by West Semites—among them shepherds and others looking for a better life—throughout the mid-second millennium B.C. The 15th Egyptian Dynasty (c. 1650–1550 B.C.), composed of foreigners from southwest Asia whom the native Egyptians labeled *hekaw-khasut*, "rulers of foreign lands" (i.e., Hyksos), based its operations here, at Avaris (*Tell ed-*

25

Haram el-Khalil, site of the Cave of Machpelah near Hebron, is holy to both Jews and Muslims. Abraham's right to the place is claimed by all of his descendants. (NEAEHL)

Dab'a). Many scholars find this context to be a comfortable fit for Joseph's migration and rise to power.

The Nile Delta was probably the greatest breadbasket of the ancient Near East, so much so that the writer of Genesis compared it favorably to "the garden of the LORD" (Gen 13:10). Its fertility was due to the annually renewed deposits of fresh silt brought downriver by the late summer floods, and a series of low inundations usually signaled famine. Joseph's career in Pharaoh's court coincided with a particularly severe famine throughout the entire region, so much so that his brothers twice came to Egypt to buy grain (Gen 41:46–45:28).

Realizing the advantages of living under the protection of the Egyptian royal house, Jacob and his family moved to Goshen. His journey took him through Beer-sheba, where God renewed the promise of land and descendants that was first given to Abraham (Gen 46:1–4; cf. Gen 12:1–3, 15:18–21, 17:1–8, 26:2–5, 28:13–15), then across the mid-northern Sinai along the same Way to Shur on which Hagar and Ishmael had fled Beer-sheba years before (cf. Gen 16:7). Jacob and his family rode out the famine in Egypt, then stayed—life was good there, after all, compared to the marginal hills and deserts of Canaan (Gen 47:1–48:22). When Jacob finally died he was buried back home in the Cave of Machpelah outside Hebron. His final resting place was a down payment on the promise that his descendants would someday return to that land of the living (Gen 50:1–21).

And so the story of the patriarchs and matriarchs ended where it began, with a divine promise that a special family would live on a special land under the promise and protection of God. This is the essence of biblical *shalom*, life lived the way it's supposed to be. Although in the end Abraham, Sarah, Isaac, Rebekah, Jacob, Leah, Rachel and Joseph all failed to realize the fullness of their God-given potential (Heb 11:13–15), their lives anticipated the struggles and hopes of future generations that can be traced from the pages of the Bible until today.

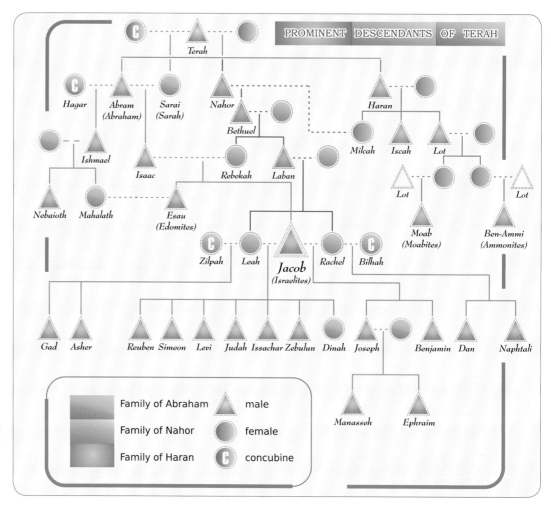

The family line of Terah spread widely over the ancient Near East. This became a family of tribes, fluid, active and jostling for position in a land dependent on God. Their descendants still inhabit the Middle East today in relationships often a little too close for comfort.

CHAPTER 3
MOSES
Showing Us the Way

The name of Moses appears at or near the top of everyone's list of great people of the Bible. Moses was the Great Intermediary, speaking the words of God to His people and carrying their burdens back to God. He was the Great Lawgiver, although if we understand *Torah* in its basic sense of "instruction," perhaps the title Teacher of Right Living might be more appropriate. And he was the Great Example, stepping up to a task far beyond his natural means and being decisive, patient, firm and caring in ways that drove and compelled a new nation into existence.

Moses was born in the region of Goshen in the northeastern Nile Delta, at a time when the protective rights issued by the Pharaoh to Jacob's family had been rescinded (Ex 1:8–22). The descendants of Jacob, by now known as the "sons of Israel," were building for Pharaoh the royal cities of Pithom (perhaps *Tell el-Mashkhuta*) and Rameses (known as Pi-Rameses, "the City of Rameses" in Egyptian documents, probably *Tell ed-Daba'a*, the same site as the earlier Hyksos capital Avaris). Egyptian royal activity was prominent in the northeastern Delta during the New Kingdom's 19th and 20th Dynasties (13th to mid-11th centuries B.C.), when no less than eleven Pharaohs bore the name Rameses.

It should not be assumed that the Egyptians reduced the sons of Israel to the status of slaves akin to the kind of slavery that was prominent in the Greco-Roman world or the pre-Civil War American south. There is no evidence of chattel slavery anywhere in the ancient Near East. Rather, comparative sources from Deir el-Medina, a New Kingdom workman's village adjacent to the Valley of the Kings in Upper (southern) Egypt, suggests that the sons of Israel were government workers who lived in self-contained villages under the control of supervisors (taskmasters) responsible to the Pharaoh. Depending on local conditions life could be good, or hard, and although the basic needs of the workers were supplied (the sons of Israel had their own houses and a large amount of livestock—Ex 9:4, 10:9, 12:22, 12:38), they were at the beck and call of others in a foreign land and certainly didn't feel free (Ex 1:8–14, 5:1–23).

Moses, who was raised in the royal court, never forgot his Israelite identity and so when he had the chance to intervene on behalf of his fellows, even to the extent of killing an offending Egyptian, he did so (Ex 2:11–14). Having fallen out of favor with Pharaoh as a result, this highly educated, sophisticated urbanite became a wandering fugitive in self-imposed exile, far beyond Egypt's harsh eastern frontier. An Egyptian tale from the early second millennium B.C., *The Story of Sinuhe*, carries a similar story line. Moses fled to Midian, the beautiful yet howling wasteland (cf. Deut 32:10) surrounding the Red Sea's Gulf of Aqaba/Elath. There he became attached to the family of Reuel, high priest of Midian, married Reuel's daughter Zipporah and settled into the Abrahamic lifestyle of a semi-nomad. He was as distant from his cultured upbringing as he could be, but somehow more in touch with the land and lifestyle of his ancestors than ever before (Ex 2:15–25).

The divine Pharaoh Rameses II, thought by many to be the Pharaoh of the Exodus, strikes an imposing figure, but his was nothing compared to the power of God that Moses encountered face to face.

Far up the Nile from the land of Goshen, the village of Deir el-Medina housed workmen and their families employed in building royal tombs for the Pharaohs of Egypt's New Kingdom. A wide variety of texts found here describe important details that echo the biblical account of Israel's life under bondage in Egypt. Working for Pharaoh had its advantages if one was an Egyptian, but foreign laborers in the same position felt oppressed and used.

This depiction of Pharaoh Seti I conquering Shasu Bedouin on his march along the Horus Road ("the Way of the Land of the Philistines") is found on the outside of the northern wall of the great hypostyle hall of the Karnak temple in Luxor, Egypt. It is in fact a map showing the location of water sources and fortresses along the route. Travel along this well-supplied but strongly fortified road would have doomed Moses and the children of Israel from the start. (Oriental Institute of the University of Chicago)

It was somewhere in this wilderness, at "Horeb the mountain of God," that Moses had his first encounter with the God of Abraham, Isaac and Jacob. Although outside the land of promise, Moses, standing before the burning bush and the LORD himself, was on holy ground (Ex 3:1–4:17).

Armed with the promise and power of God to redeem his people and bring them home, Moses returned to Egypt, a pilgrim in the unholy land of his birth (Ex 4:18–31). Back in Egypt Moses knew he belonged somewhere else, that who he was now was not who he had once been. Moses' appointment was with Pharaoh, eye to eye, and their tug-of-war tested the iron wills of both men. Through Moses' steady hand God poured nine plagues onto Pharaoh, devastating the Egyptian economy, people and land. Each plague also attacked an important god in the Egyptian pantheon and the natural resource that that god controlled (Ex 7:1–10:29). Finally, with the tenth plague, the death of the firstborn heir to the throne, Pharaoh's will was broken.

After celebrating their newly found freedom with the first Passover, Moses led his people out of Egypt (Ex 11:1–12:37). The most direct route to Canaan followed the north Sinai coast. Called "the Way of the Land of the Philistines" in Exodus 13:17 and the "Horus Road" in Egyptian documents, this was not only the trade route between Egypt and Canaan but an established military road over which the New Kingdom Pharaohs regularly marched in triumph into southwestern Asia. Well-manned, amply supplied Egyptian garrison forts lay at intervals along its length, each a day's journey apart. From the City of Rameses Moses first led the sons of Israel northeast, toward this military route, then veered to the south (Ex 12:37; 13:17–14:2). To Pharaoh this looked like aimless wandering (Ex 14:3); for Moses, it was a brilliant strategic move aimed at avoiding direct combat in the region of Pharaoh's strength in favor of setting a trap that only the God of Israel could spring (Ex 13:17–18, 14:1–12). Moses' path led directly to the Reed (not Red) Sea, which, by its Hebrew name (*yam suph*) must refer to one of the relatively shallow, reedy Bitter Lakes between the Gulf of Suez and the Mediterranean. A strong east wind, blown as it were by the breath of God (cf. Gen 1:9, 2:7), divided the water; Moses and the sons of Israel passed safely through before the wa-

ters swept back over Pharaoh's now-helpless army (Ex 14:13–15:21). With the military threat erased and a renewed faith for the journey ahead, Moses drove Israel into the "great and terrible wilderness" (Deut 1:19) of the Sinai Peninsula.

One of the more perplexing puzzles facing biblical historical geographers is tracing the route of the Exodus through the Sinai. Although dozens of places are mentioned (Ex 12:37, 13:20, 14:2, 15:22–23, 15:27, 16:1, 17:1, 19:2; Num 10:12, 11:3, 11:34–35, 12:16, 13:26, 14:25, 20:1, 20:22, 33:5–49; Deut 1:19), the locations of virtually all of them are unknown. Most were no doubt local names for water sources or natural topographical features, names now lost in the mists of time. Some, like Mt. Sinai, are identified through early church tradition, and although over two dozen suggestions for Mt. Sinai have subsequently been proposed, there is no overly compelling reason to reject *Jebel Musa*, the traditional site high in the crystalline mountains of the southern Sinai Peninsula. The location of the oasis of Kadesh-barnea, where Israel camped "many days" (Deut 1:46; cf. Num 13:26, 20:1), is also known (*Ein el-Qudeirat*, just inside the modern Egyptian Sinai border) and Elath and Ezion-geber (Deut 2:8) were certainly somewhere at the northern end of the Gulf of Aqaba/Elath (one of them was likely *Tell el-Kheleifeh*). However, because the location of most of the rest of the sites in Moses' Sinai itinerary are largely guesswork, it is not surprising that numerous routes of the Exodus have been proposed.

Whatever the exact route, Moses' journey brought him to Mt. Sinai, holy ground where the same word of God that had created the world (Gen 1:3ff.) now created a special people to live in it (Ex 20:1ff.; Deut 32:10–14). Although Israel responded with the same recalcitrance that came to characterize God's people throughout the biblical period, Moses interceded to God on their behalf, showing the way of grace and forgiveness in the midst of the demands of the law (Ex 32:1–33:23). What English Bible readers call the "Ten Commandments" were, after all, Ten Words (Hebrew *devarim*, "words"; Ex 34:28), each of which was an expression of the intimate, deep-down nature of the LORD God himself, spoken in such a way so as to compel guidance and instruction (*Torah*) for life. Moses was radiant at the possibilities and his face shone (lit. "radiated horns"), mostly from his personal encounter with God but partly, no doubt, because he was pleased with Israel's prospects (Ex 34:29–35).

From Mt. Sinai Moses led his people northeastward to Kadesh-barnea, a large perennial oasis within striking distance of Canaan (Num 13:26; Deut 1:19). From there representatives of each of the twelve tribes of Israel, including Joshua (from Ephraim) and Caleb (from Judah), journeyed the length of Canaan, spying out the land of the Patri-

MAP OF THE EXODUS

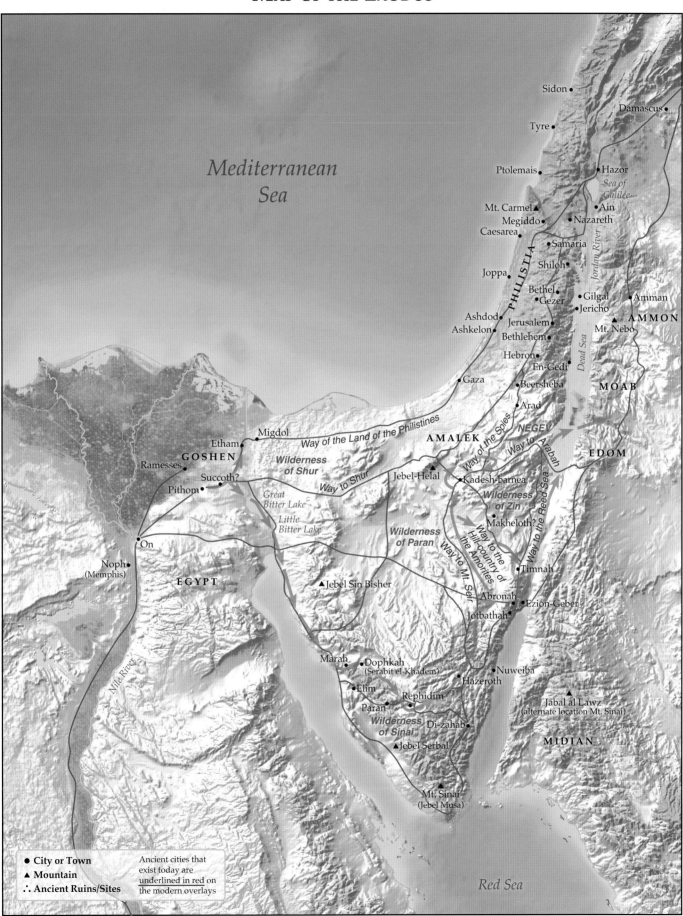

Legend:
- ● City or Town
- ▲ Mountain
- ∴ Ancient Ruins/Sites

Ancient cities that exist today are underlined in red on the modern overlays

AridOcean/shutterstock.com

The Travels of the Spies.
In part retracing the footsteps of the patriarchs, the spies whom Moses sent into Canaan trekked right up the center of the land, the route that offered great vantage points in every direction. Passing by many strongly walled cities, the band of twelve was understandably impressed by the challenges Israel faced in trying to conquer the land.

archs from the Negeb and Hebron to Lebo-hamath north of Damascus (Num 13:1–24). The spies' report of a blessed, fertile land with strong, walled cities met with mixed reviews, and resulted in an initial assault into Canaan from the south that was repulsed by the Amalekites and Canaanites at Hormah, a city in the vicinity of Beer-sheba (Num 13:25–14:45).

According to the biblical chronology, the journey from the City of Rameses to this failed assault on Canaan took two years (cf. Num 14:33; Deut 2:14); by comparison, Pharaoh's army normally marched across the Sinai via the Horus Road in just two weeks. Now thirty-eight years of wilderness wan-

dering lay ahead—not because the distance to Canaan was long or Moses got lost (although one could argue that Israel's heart was), but because all Israel, with their livestock, reverted to a semi-nomadic lifestyle, charged by God to follow the change of seasons and scraps of thorny bushes from *wadi* bottom to *wadi* bottom. Much of this wandering, though within reach of the Kadesh-barnea oasis (cf. Num 20:1, 14), was in the section of the mid-Sinai that today is called *et-Tih* ("the one who is lost"), a vast, rocky, flat and featureless landscape with few springs and no soil. For a people born and bred among the lush, fertile villages and farms

The kingdom of Sihon stretched from the city of Heshbon to its flat horizon as far as the eye could see. Taken by Moses, this provided a wonderful staging ground as he, then Joshua, prepared Israel to enter Canaan. Here the tribe of Reuben found their new home.

of Egypt this was an unbearable change, beyond their human capacity for survival. But like the Exodus itself, it was also part of a Divine strategic plan to teach lessons of dependence and trust (cf. Ex 15:22–16:21, 17:1–7; Num 20:2–13, 21:6–9). If a person's true character becomes apparent only over the long run, then for Moses this was the defining time. Deep in the wilderness, far from the world's limelight and in a position where he had no choice but to rely only on the strength of God and the help of a few close friends (cf. Ex 17:11–13, 18:24–27), Moses met the challenge of a lifetime.

The journey of the sons of Israel to the land of promise finally led them into Transjordan. Here the itinerary is more certain, as many of the place names on the route have been identified (Num 21:10–20, 33:41–49; Deut 1:1, 2:1–5, 2:8, 2:13–14, 2:24, 3:1, 3:8–17, 3:27–29). Three people groups, each related to the sons of Israel, were already settling in the fertile highlands of Transjordan: Moab, Ammon and Edom (cf. Gen 19:37–38, 36:1–43). These emerging nation-states were strung along the King's Highway, the most logical route of travel through the land. Moses approached Transjordan from the south, via Elath, then skirted both Edom and Moab by the more easterly desert route (the "Way of the Wilderness of Edom" and the "Way of the Wilderness of Moab"; Num 21:4–5; Deut 2:8; Judg 11:17–18; cf. 2 Kgs 3:8). By doing so he avoided needless conflicts over grazing and water rights, while finding plenty of pasture and water for Israel's livestock at the upper reaches of the Zered (*Wadi el-Hasa*) and Arnon (*Wadi el-Mujib*) ravines (Num 21:12–13).

Opposite the northern end of the Dead Sea Moses turned westward toward the Plains of Moab. His route had to take him through the Tableland of Moab (the Medeba Plateau), a buffer zone between Moab, Ammon and Canaan that at the moment was controlled by a local king, Sihon of Heshbon. From the point of view of Sihon, the approach of a vast horde of hungry semi-nomads from the eastern desert was a threat that could be repulsed only by war (Num 21:21–32; Deut 2:26–37; Judg 11:19–22; cf. Judg 6:3–5). Upon defeating Sihon, Moses and the sons of Israel gained a valuable foothold at the doorstep of Canaan, established control over a portion of the King's Highway and found land suitable for the tribes of Reuben and Gad in the process (Num 32:1–5, 32:33–36; cf. Josh 13:15–23).

Moses continued north through the highlands of Gilead, skirting west of the Ammonites to Bashan, a northern buffer zone between Ammon, Aram-Damascus (Syria) and Canaan. By defeating Og king of Bashan at Edrei (Num 21:33–35; Deut 3:1–11), Moses assured Israel's influence in northern Transjordan, a reality that would prove valuable during the days of the Israelite Monarchy when David, Ahab and others tried to check the advance of Aram-Damascus into the same region (cf. 2 Sam 10:15–19; 1 Kgs 22:1–40; 2 Kgs 9:1–13). Moses allowed part of the tribe of Manasseh (the Jair clan) to settle in Bashan, and the region took the name Havvoth-jair ("the tent-villages of Jair"; Num 32:33, 32:40–42; cf. Josh 13:29–31). Recognizing the strategic value of the Jordan Valley and the fertile western slopes of the Gilead mountains, Moses placed the tribe of Gad there (Num 32:33–36; cf. Josh 13:24–28).

Returning to the Plains of Moab opposite Jericho, with Egypt and the wilderness far behind and crucial sections of Transjordan secure, Moses now prepared the sons of Israel to move across the Jordan River into their long-awaited homeland. The

The Final Approach to Canaan. *Moses' penetration into Transjordan avoided Edom, Moab and Ammon, distant kinfolk of Israel who were already beginning their own process of developing into nation states. On the other hand, Sihon king of the Amorites, who did not have blood ties to the family of Abraham, faced the brunt of Moses' attack*

The view from Mt. Nebo to the west, across the Dead Sea and into the Land of Promise, remains as majestic as the future that it held for Israel.

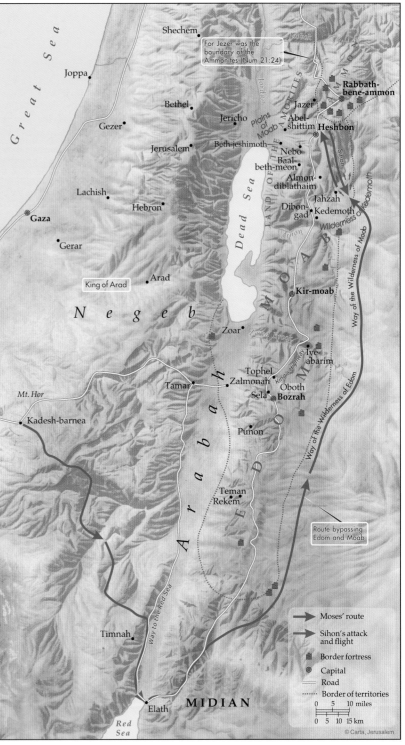

entire book of Deuteronomy finds its setting here, full of imagery of land and climate that fits the landscape of Canaan exactly (e.g., Deut 8:6–10, 11:10–15, 28:1–68, 32:1–33:29). The laws of Deuteronomy (chapters 12–26) were crafted for the needs and conditions of a people settled in a land of agriculture and small villages, rather than the lifestyle of semi-nomads in the wilderness. And so Israel's living conditions would shift again—forty years before it was from Egypt to the wilderness; now it was from the wilderness to a homeland which, although not all that fertile, wasn't a wasteland either. In fact, as Moses reminded his people, this would be a place "in between," where they would have plenty of opportunity but not so much that they would necessarily forget their dependence on God (Deut 11:13–17; cf. Prov 30:7–9). It was, in short, a place especially prepared for them (Deut 32:8).

Moses' job was complete, his lifetime of anticipation almost over. His final view was from Mt. Nebo, where "the LORD showed him all the land" that Israel would possess, "as far as the western sea" (Deut 34:1–4). While it is not physically possible to see all the way to the Mediterranean from the traditional spot of Mt. Nebo—or from any other hill in its vicinity, either—Moses could well have already seen every region of Israel's once and future homeland from afar, from various vantage points on his travels through Transjordan. In the late nineteenth century A.D. travelers to the vicinity of Ajlun high in the mountains of Gilead reported seeing the Mediterranean shore at Gaza through the clear skies following a heavy rain (Bertha Spafford Vester, *Our Jerusalem*, p. 245), and we can expect that Moses saw the same. It was the best view of all—and Moses' eyes, bright to the day of his death (Deut 34:7), saw the best of possibilities for his people.

CHAPTER 4

JOSHUA
Courage to Conquer

Not just anyone can succeed a Moses. Today, conventional wisdom suggests that a towering leader be followed by a caretaker, lest a strong successor be unduly criticized with "that's not the way Moses would have done it!" But as the emerging nation of Israel camped on the Plains of Moab, poised to enter the land of Canaan, the luxury of caretaker leadership was not an option.

Joshua had been the logical choice of succession since the early days of the wilderness wanderings, and it is possible to track the development of his leadership skills as he rose in the ranks to fill the long shadow cast by Moses, the greatest of all mentors. When Israel was just out of Egypt, moving vulnerably into the forbidding wilderness of Sinai, a young Joshua successfully repulsed a persistent attack by the Amalekites, desert raiders bent on easy spoil (Ex 17:9–16). Joshua stayed with Moses everywhere, from the heights of Mt. Sinai (Ex 24:13, 32:15–18) to the daily toil of the tent (Ex 33:11). He was part of a small contingent of men who entered Canaan from the south and traveled

its full length, mapping the land in his mind as a reconnaissance for future conquest (Num 13:1–24). With Caleb, Joshua brought back a favorable report (Num 14:6–9), then withstood a popular uprising against his insistence that the land could be taken in spite of the great risks that conquest entailed (Num 14:10–38). As Moses led Israel on its final approach to Canaan nearly forty years later, Joshua's role as second-in-command was formally ratified (Num 27:18–23). Although one might suppose that by now he was ready to assume the mantle of power, the biblical author underlined the need, at the very moment of Joshua's transition to the greater task at hand, for him to "be strong and courageous" (Deut 3:22, 3:28, 31:7–8, 31:14, 31:23; Josh 1:6–9), a charge that rings refreshingly true for everyone who has stepped into greater areas of responsibility.

Israel entered Canaan from the Plains of Moab, the southeastern, bulbous end of the Jordan River Valley lying just north of the Dead Sea. Opposite was Jericho, the City of Palm Trees (cf. Deut 34:3; Judg 1:16, 3:13), an oasis giving a bit of life to an oth-

The modern city of Jericho preserves much of the character of the ancient site—palm trees, water and an oasis of green. For Joshua it probably looked, on a miniature scale, a bit like Egypt (cf. Gen 13:10).

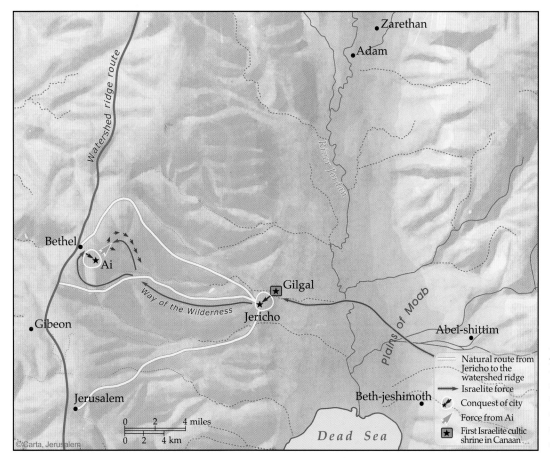

Joshua's Thrust into the Belly of Canaan. *By pushing directly into the heartland of Canaan from the east, Joshua was poised to slice the land in two. It was a textbook example of "divide and conquer."*

33

In the third millennium B.C. Ai (et-Tell) was a well-fortified city surrounded by a strong wall with semi-circular towers. Nothing, however, indicating human habitation at the site remains from the time of Joshua. While the archaeological record poses challenges to the biblical account, the geographical setting of the site fits the story line of Joshua chapter 8 nicely.

erwise stark and salty wasteland (cf. Jer 17:5–8). Beyond rose the sharp, rugged ascent of the Wilderness of Judah, a view that must have reminded Israel of the kind of landscape through which they had just traveled for most of a generation. "For *this* we came?" some no doubt asked themselves, but Joshua's vision was larger, and his experience in spying out the land thirty-eight years before confirmed God's promise that this indeed was "an exceedingly good land…a land flowing with milk and honey" (Num 14:7–8).

A victory at Jericho offered Joshua several strategic advantages as he sought to gain a foothold in Canaan. First, Jericho's destruction would ensure that Israel controlled the routes into the heartland of Canaan from the east, as well as those running between the fertile agricultural land of the northern Jordan Valley and the mineral wealth of the Dead Sea. Moreover, by taking Jericho, Joshua prevented an enemy at his back from hindering his further penetration into Canaan. Perhaps most importantly, although the city of Jericho was to be as thoroughly consumed as a burnt offering to God (Josh 6:21, 6:24), the oasis itself, fed by a powerful spring that still produces one thousand gallons of water per minute, re-

mained fertile and would provide a wonderful base of operations as Israel pressed into the hill country.

The actual attack on Jericho cannot be explained in terms of rational military tactics, nor was it meant to be. Rather, this entire initial episode of conquest, from the time that Israel crossed the Jordan River at spring flood stage in full regalia with the Ark of the Covenant in processional lead (Josh 3:1–17) to the collapse of the city itself, must be seen as a mighty act of God, beyond human capacity to mimic or comprehend. Nor should the lack of archaeological evidence corroborating the biblical description of the battle from *Tell es-Sultan*, the ruins of ancient Jericho, detract from the overall geographical common sense of the narrative account.

With Joshua and Israel firmly encamped at Gilgal, a site not yet firmly identified but probably at the northeastern limits of the urban sprawl of modern Jericho, the midsection of Canaan lay vulnerable before them. Joshua's goal was to sever the road running along the watershed ridge, the north-south lifeline connecting the all-important city-states of Hebron, Jerusalem, Gibeon, Bethel and Shechem. The climb from Gilgal to the watershed ridge, while only 15 miles as the crow flies, was 4,000 feet up through a tangle of dry, rugged *wadis*, a true land of the shepherd devoid of permanent human settlement. Penetrating this mass was difficult, but not militarily dangerous. Near the upper end, however, just below the crest of the watershed ridge and lying squarely in the path of Joshua's ascent to Bethel was Ai, an agricultural village making use of the first bit of arable land above the wilderness. It is likely that Ai was a small satellite (cf. Josh 7:3) of Bethel and could serve, should the need arise, as an advance outpost for the latter; with Joshua on the march the fate of the one hung in the balance of the other.

A lack of appropriate archaeological evidence at *et-Tell*, the commonly accepted site of biblical Ai, has prompted some to suggest other nearby sites, *Khirbet Nisya* or *Khirbet el-Maqatir*, as the site of Joshua's attack, although the physical setting of

Nestled between Mounts Ebal (right) and Gerizim (left) yet adjacent to several broad valleys, the city-state of Shechem was both protected and open to the outside world. Residents enjoyed plentiful water sources, a pleasant climate and fertile soil, and from here kings such as Abimelech (Judg 9) and Jeroboam (1 Kgs 12), as well as Labayu of the Amarna Letters, tried to exert control over other city-states in the region. An early historical geographer, George Adam Smith, called Shechem "the uncrowned queen of the hills," a place that enjoyed every natural advantage for life yet, for the biblical writers, always stood in Jerusalem's shadow.

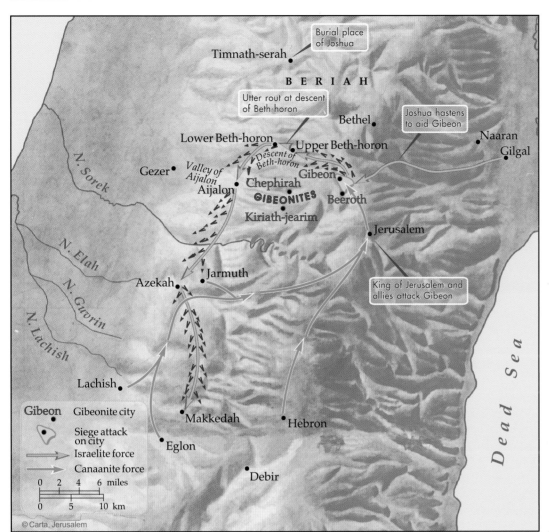

Timnath-serah

Burial place of Joshua

B E R I A H

Utter rout at descent of Beth-horon

Bethel

Joshua hastens to aid Gibeon

Naaran

Gilgal

Lower Beth-horon · Upper Beth-horon

Descent of Beth-horon

Gezer · Valley of Aijalon

Chephirah

Gibeon

Aijalon

GIBEONITES

Beeroth

Kiriath-jearim

Jerusalem

N. Sorek

N. Elah

N. Guvrin

N. Lachish

Azekah · Jarmuth

King of Jerusalem and allies attack Gibeon

Lachish

Gibeon — Gibeonite city

Siege attack on city

Israelite force

Canaanite force

0 2 4 6 miles
0 5 10 km

© Carta, Jerusalem

Makkedah · Hebron

Eglon

Debir

Dead Sea

Cutting the Feet Out from Under Canaan. *In an all-or-nothing gamble, the major city-states of southern Canaan met Joshua at Gibeon where they were summarily routed. Defeated, the kings of Canaan could no longer stand before the Israelite assault.*

et-Tell provides the best fit of the geographical data preserved in the battle account. After an initial military setback blamed on the actions of Achan, an insider from the tribe of Judah who placed personal gain over the common good (Josh 7:1–26), Joshua was able to take Ai. His attack was a brilliant sequence of draw, feint and ambush (Josh 8:1–29), and with it Joshua not only seized productive agricultural land in the hill country but also gained position for an easy strike to the watershed ridge and the road to Shechem.

The biblical narrative of Joshua's campaign through Canaan does not include an account of the conquest of the portion of the hill country that lay between Bethel and the Jezreel Valley, although an episode tucked among various data related to the territorial division of the land notes that the process by which the tribes of Ephraim and Manasseh settled the area included both conquest and natural expansion ("though it is forest, you shall clear it"; Josh 17:14–18). Nevertheless, we read that after taking Ai Joshua moved to Shechem, the main city-state of the region, to renew the covenant of Sinai on Mounts Ebal and Gerizim, twin peaks looming over Shechem from the north and south respectively

(Josh 8:30–35; cf. Deut 27:2–8). Throughout the biblical period Shechem had a reputation as a power base for ambitious men wanting to build a kingdom (cf. Gen 34:1–31; Judg 9:1–57; 1 Kgs 12:1 and the Amarna texts that speak of Labayu). Joshua's ability to penetrate into Shechem in the name of the God of Israel is admirable, yet puzzling, although it is likely that the men of Shechem, with long memories typical to the Middle East, acknowledged the right of the sons of Israel to reestablish roots in the area based on the old landed rights of Abraham and Jacob (Gen 12:6–7, 33:18–20).

Having established a religious and nationalistic presence in the central hill country, Joshua in one sense had already met his goal—and too much so for the other city-states in the region. Most naturally sought to resist the Israelite advance (Josh 9:1–2); the king of Gibeon had other ideas. The city of Gibeon dominated a wide spot on the watershed ridge midway between Jerusalem and Bethel, a plateau that was not only the upper terminus for routes coming out of Jericho but also the most important crossroads within the central hill country. Furthermore, Gibeon was the head of an alliance of cities that controlled the routes from the plateau

The ancient site of Gibeon, on a hill rising from a widened spot of the watershed ridge, commanded not only the only viable north-south route through the hill country but also the best lateral routes between Jerusalem and the coast. Every king of Jerusalem, be it Adoni-zedek or Solomon, had to have a good working relationship with Gibeon or risk isolation and stagnation.

(below) Joshua commanding the sun to stand still (Josh 10:12–13), 19th century engraving (Carta, Jerusalem). Joshua's defeat against the coalition of southern cities led by the king of Jerusalem was so thorough that the day of battle had to be lengthened to finish the fight—at least this is the impression given by the poetic couplet from the Book of Jashar, quoted in Joshua 10:12–13. Several explanations have been given; perhaps a sudden hailstorm (v. 11) or eclipse made the day seem to be extra long. Some simply conclude that earth temporarily slowed its rotation, with negative effects on the force of gravity temporarily suspended!

westward toward the Shephelah (the western foothills) and coastal plain (Josh 9:17). Through a ruse the Gibeonites made peace with Joshua (Josh 9:3–15) and their city, which had been the next logical point of Joshua's attack, was spared. The result, however, was that Israel, without a fight, now controlled the strategic crossroads of the plateau. The importance of realizing this military goal, and Joshua's insistence on keeping the terms of his covenant with Gibeon in light of the divine covenant he had just ratified on Mounts Ebal and Gerizim mandating peace with strangers (Lev 19:33–34; cf. Num 15:15), overrode the demand of some that the land should be conquered only through force (Josh 9:16–27).

The immediate threat was now felt by Adoni-zedek, king of Jerusalem. The city of Jerusalem was—and is—tucked so tightly into the rugged hills that its best access to the world beyond lay through the natural routes that cross the plateau of Gibeon. When the Gibeonites collaborated with Israel—a

betrayal that struck at the root of their indigenous Canaanite loyalty—and choked Jerusalem's access to the coast in the process, Adoni-zedek responded by pulling together an alliance of kings representing the entire southern region of Canaan (Josh 10:1–5). Besides Jerusalem, this alliance included the city-states of Hebron (from the southern hill country), Jarmuth (the northern Shephelah), Lachish (the southern Shephelah) and Eglon (the connection to the Negeb). When the combined forces filled the plateau, Joshua moved to relieve Gibeon. His attack caught the coalition napping. Cresting the eastern ridge of the plateau with the glare of the sunrise at their back, Joshua's army pushed the coalition down the descent of Beth-horon, the natural route to the Aijalon Valley and the coast. Once again, the element of surprise combined with a divine display that defies rational explanation gave Joshua the victory (Josh 10:6–15). A mopping-up campaign through the hill country and Shephelah established an Israel-ite presence throughout southern Canaan (Josh 10:16–43). From Jericho, Joshua had stuck a sword into the belly of Canaan, and with the defeat of the Jerusalem coalition, he undercut its feet. Only the head remained.

Joshua's final campaign was in the north, against the massive city of Hazor. In the Late Bronze Age, Hazor rivaled the great city-states of Mesopotamia in size and influence, as attested by both archaeological and textual (cuneiform) evidence. Its location at the point where the great trunk route from the north enters Canaan, adjacent to the extraordinarily fertile Huleh Basin, ensured Hazor's dominance in the area. Anticipating the Israelite threat, Jabin king of Hazor pulled together a formidable coalition of city-states representing every sub-region in Galilee and controlling every important route and pass in the area; he was "the head of all these kingdoms" (Josh 11:1–4, 11:10). In a surprising move, this combined force rendezvoused not at one of the strategic valleys or passes in Galilee, but at the waters of Merom (Josh 11:5). The location of this meeting place is debated; some suggest the southern, swampy end of the Huleh Basin, others the spring-fed region of Mount Merom high in Upper Galilee. In either case, Jabin chose to leave Hazor open, apparently hoping that the Israelites would be drawn toward the city where they would be easily overrun by his chariot force. But with courage from the hand of God, Joshua turned the tables and

attacked suddenly, in an area—be it either swampy or rugged—where chariots were ineffective and the advantage quickly swung to the Israelite foot soldiers (Josh 11:6–9). Archaeologists have uncovered evidence that Hazor's large Canaanite palace collapsed in a particularly intense conflagration, a circumstance in line with the biblical account of the nature of Joshua's attack (Josh 11:10).

The Bible's point that Hazor was the only Canaanite city "built on its mound" (i.e., on a *tell*) that was burned by Joshua (Josh 11:13) suggests that a search for widespread, archaeologically attestable destruction layers in tells will not provide corroborating evidence of Israel's penetration into Canaan. Rather, it is more helpful to look at changes in material culture (e.g., pottery or housing types), socio-cultural forms (e.g., religion) or aspects of language to track Israel's appearance in the land.

Joshua's campaign through Canaan allowed him to claim the land for the people of Israel and for the LORD their God, but many regions, especially the valleys and plains, were far from subdued (Josh 11:16, 11:23; cf. Josh 13:1; Judg 1:27–36). The focus of operations moved from Gilgal (Josh 14:6) to Shiloh, an isolated spot in the east central hill country where the Ark of the Covenant found a home and from which Joshua apportioned the entire land, subdued or not, among the Israelite tribes (Josh 18:1). Joshua received his inheritance at Timnath-serah in the fresh hills of the south-central hill country. His burial there, the burial of Eleazar the priest at Gibeah, and the reinterment of Joseph's bones on his purchased land in Shechem (Josh 24:29–33; cf. Gen 33:18–20) mark the end of the first phase of Israel's move into Canaan and the beginning of life in their promised homeland.

The biblical narrative of this formative sequence of events is deliberate: Joshua was successful, not because he was a talented and forthright leader but because the hand of God shaped the events of his life. Throughout he needed, and received, courage—to lead the charge of battle, to confront Achan, to walk into Shechem, and to keep covenant with the Gibeonites. In its formative years as a nation, the one-two combination of Moses and Joshua provided Israel with an ideal template for leadership. Sadly, the pattern was too large to fit the next generation.

Now a vast field of grain, the once bustling lower city of Hazor stretched far beyond the shadow of the city's acropolis, which was dominated in the days of Joshua by a strong Canaanite palace. Altogether the site covered 200 acres, placing it in the league of the greatest of the cities of the ancient Near East. Isaiah's comments on the frailty of human kingdoms seems particularly apt: "Scarcely have they been planted, scarcely have they been sown, scarcely has their stock taken root in the earth but He merely blows on them and they wither, and the storm wind carries them away like stubble" (Isa 40:24).

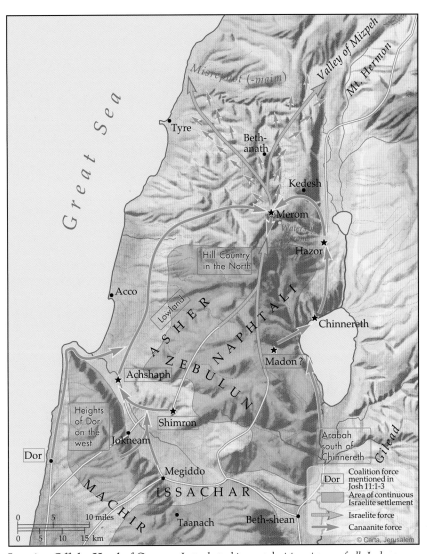

Lopping Off the Head of Canaan. *In perhaps his most decisive victory of all, Joshua defeated a strong coalition led by Jabin king of Hazor, who, until the battle was over, was "the head of all these kingdoms." All of the major routes into and out of Galilee now lay open to Joshua's forces. Unfortunately, Israel was not able to take advantage of their victory and the plains and passes quickly returned to Canaanite hands (cf. Judg 1:27–33).*

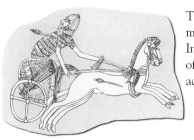

CHAPTER 5
DEBORAH AND JAEL
A Sweet Song of Victory

The history of the Middle East, both ancient and modern, has not been particularly kind to women. In the fifteenth century, a Turkish lady by the name of Mihri Hatun offered the following "so, there!" advice on the relationship between the sexes:

Woman, they say, is deficient in sense, so they ought to pardon her every word.
But one female who knows what to do is better than a thousand males who don't.

While the days of the biblical Judges were troubled enough without dwelling on the underlying social fabric of the times, it must be noted that when Israel, awash in malaise and paralyzed under impotent male leadership, was delivered by the hands of two women, Deborah and Jael, the victory was particularly sweet.

The ebb and flow of the events of the Book of Judges reflects the troubled spirit of the time between the death of Joshua and the birth of Samuel. The writer of Judges organized these events around a repetitive cycle: disobedience, invasion, a cry for help, and military victory. All told, the cycle spiraled downward: each oppression became more difficult to overcome; each judge, or, more properly, deliverer, was less wholesome than the one before.

In fact, Israel faced difficulties on a number of fronts. Although the twelve tribes were loosely united around a common set of ancestor stories, shared a religious site at Shiloh and were bound together by the covenant of Mt. Sinai, each favored local priorities over efforts for the common good. This is, in fact, a characteristic endemic to tribalism. Moreover, whatever success was found on the battlefield was negated by the inability to create a cooperative,

wholesome environment at home, as the stories of corruption and infighting that conclude the book so well attest (Judg 17:1–21:25). On top of this, the Israelite tribes had to settle for the less-productive hill country and steppe land, while the fertile, open and economically productive valleys and plains remained under the control of the established Canaanite city-states (Judg 1:27–36).

The first event in the sequence of invasion and deliverance was in some ways an anomaly: Othniel, nephew of Caleb of the tribe of Judah, delivered Israel from a distant enemy, Aram-naharaim (or, "Mesopotamia"; Judg 3:9–11). It's difficult to reconcile this incident, briefly described, with the stories of the other judges, where each countered a local threat by a near neighbor. Perhaps the writer included Othniel's bout against an enemy from the far north to anticipate Israel's later troubles with Mesopotamian kings in the waning days of the monarchy, and thereby heighten the contrast of what was, to what would be.

Next up was the Benjaminite Ehud, whose tribal gateway city, Jericho, had been overrun by Moabites when their king, Eglon, sought to penetrate the land the same way that Joshua had successfully entered Canaan years before. Eglon got no further; his immense size, at ease in the comforts of the Jericho oasis, was no match for the lean, resourceful and wolf-like fighters of Benjamin (Judg 3:15–30; cf. Gen 49:27).

A brief note mentions Shamgar's heroic defeat of the Philistines, anticipating a similar act by Samson (Judg 3:31, 15:14–17). Linguistic evidence suggests that Shamgar was a non-Israelite associated with the town of Beth-anath in Upper Galilee, a location consistent with his appearance in the Galilee-oriented Song of Deborah (Judg 5:6). Irrespective of Shamgar's ethnicity, Philistine incursions beyond the Jezreel Valley were not to be ignored by those who lived in the area.

The next event is perhaps the single greatest episode in the book. The forces of Jabin (apparently a dynastic name for the kings of Hazor) had overwhelmed the valleys and plains of Galilee, prompting a combined response by all of the tribes that were affected, as well as some on the periphery: Zebulun, Naphtali, Issachar, Machir (Transjordanian Manasseh), Ephraim and Benjamin. Two accounts of the battle have been preserved: a blow-by-blow narrative giving a chronological sequence of events (Judges 4), and a popular victory song of the kind that

For the Israelite tribes scrambling to gain a foothold in their new land, the chariot forces of their Canaanite neighbors must have jarred loose dark memories of the mighty armies of Egypt. It was one thing to flee the chariots of Pharaoh in a foreign land; it was quite another to meet up with the same once back home.

(below) Like a sentinel arising from the floor of the Jezreel Valley, Mount Tabor can be seen from many vantage points both west and east of the Rift Valley, including Kedesh-naphtali, home town of Barak, and Harosheth-ha-goiim, where Sisera's army was stationed. Barak used the protection of the mountain and the folded terrain behind, in the vicinity of Kedesh-naphtali, to muster his troops, then swept around Tabor to encounter Sisera's chariots where the mountain meets the plain. (photo Garo Nalbandian)

38

The Limits of Israelite Settlement during the Time of the Judges. *Although the Book of Joshua portrays a full conquest and division of the land of Canaan by the Israelite tribes, Judges is careful to delineate between areas actually settled by Israel and those in which the Canaanite presence remained strong. In short, Israel clung to the rocky hills largely devoid of natural resources while the Canaanite city-states controlled the fertile valleys and important routes below.*

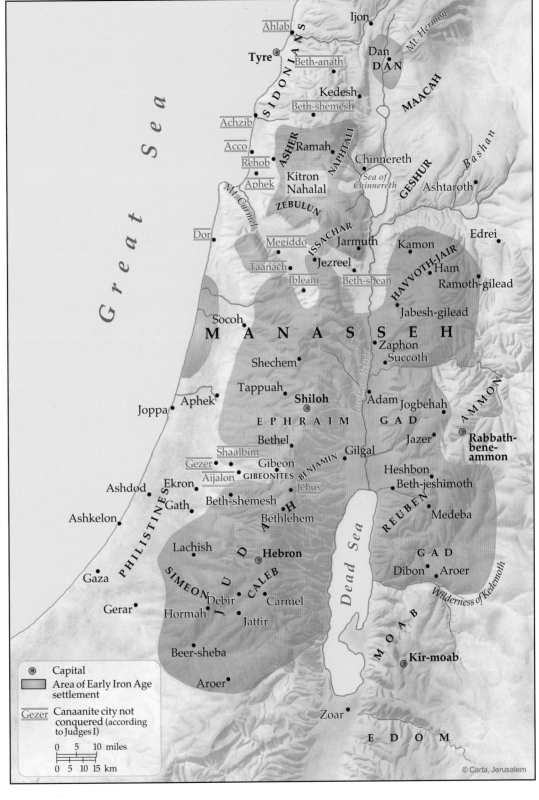

Mesopotamian border marker (kudurru), c. 12th century B.C. *Large nations such as Egypt, Assyria or Babylon formally marked the limits of their control with standing stones, often inscribed by the name and exploits of conquering kings. During the time of the Judges, Israel's tribal borders were too much in flux to be set in stone.*

would have been sung around campfires for generations (Judges 5). Each emphasized different aspects of the whole; together, they offer a telling that is both earthy and delightful, rich in cultural detail while full of geographical common sense.

The story opens with Israel's Galilee tribes squeezed in a pincer between Jabin and his general, Sisera (Judg 4:2–3). Jabin was at Hazor, the old dynastic

Canaanite capital of Galilee (cf. Josh 11:10) where the great international highway connecting Mesopotamia and Egypt entered the land from the north. The army was with Sisera at Harosheth-ha-goiim ("The Cultivated Fields of the Gentiles"), which, from the evidence of the poem (Judg 5:19), must have been between Taanach and Megiddo near the point where the same trunk route approached Galilee from the

39

The Judges According to Their Tribes. *None of the Israelite tribes were immune from the problem of encroachment, as one or another of their neighbors, who were also trying to find living space, pushed into lands recently apportioned by Joshua to Israel. Local problems met with local responses, as Israelite judges (or, deliverers) fought to reestablish the territorial rights of their respective tribes.*

(Josh 11:10–13), some have suggested that the chronological order of the two stories should be switched. It can be argued, however, that the Canaanite army was stationed in the Jezreel Valley precisely because Hazor was no longer a viable Canaanite center, although Jabin still claimed rights to the city.

The solution came from an unlikely source. Deborah, called both a prophetess (Judg 4:4) and "a mother in Israel" (Judg 5:7), perhaps should be understood as standing in the tradition of the wise old village woman, the one who knows everything about everyone, the one to whom everyone comes for advice and who, through intuition, reputation and/or the spirit of God, is able to "see" things others can't (today such women, such as Agatha Christie's Miss Jane Marple, are sometimes thought to be a bit batty by the more "practical" members of society). Deborah's reputation was enhanced by her special spot under a palm—an unusual tree for the highlands of the watershed ridge—between Ramah and Bethel, at the crossroads of the hill country where she could hear news from every quarter of the land (Judg 4:5). It was she, though far from Galilee, who first sensed the initiative from God to do something about Jabin, Sisera and that trouble up north (Judg 4:6, 5:7, 5:12). Deborah marshaled Barak from Kedesh-naphtali, a hill city with a wonderful view of the southern end of the Sea of Galilee, situated above, yet choked by the Canaanite presence in the area. Though Barak surely was a man of some military ability, he sensed that Deborah's special presence on site was important to the outcome of the battle and insisted that she come along (Judg 4:6–9).

The Israelite forces gathered in the gullies and rolling hills behind Mount Tabor, the highest, most recognizable of the peaks surrounding the Jezreel Valley. Sisera's chariots approached Tabor from across the valley and the battle was engaged on the flat plain at the base of the mountain, near the upper reaches of the Kishon, the normally sluggish river that drains the area (Judg 4:12–14). Chariots have a distinct advantage over foot soldiers on a flat, dry battlefield and it should have been a rout for the Canaanites, but a tremendous rainstorm, sent for this moment by God, filled the Kishon, turned the valley into a quagmire and neutralized the bogged-down chariots. The advantage quickly swung to the Israelites, who were skilled at a guerrilla-type of hand-to-hand fighting honed in the difficult conditions of the hill country (Judg 4:15–16, 5:19–21).

Rather than choose to fall nobly on the battlefield, Sisera the mighty general fled, not back to his base by Megiddo but toward Hazor. On the way he came upon the lone tent of Heber the Kenite. The Kenites, a tribe indigenous to the eastern Negeb, were loosely affiliated with the Israelites (cf. 1 Sam 27:10, 30:26, 30:29). At one point Heber had moved his tent, family and flocks north, follow-

south. Harosheth-ha-goiim is a wonderfully descriptive place name, reflecting not only the fertility of the Jezreel Valley but its openness for all who passed through or wanted to control the commercial interests of Canaan. It is suggestive of Isaiah's term *Galil haGoyim* ("Galilee of the Gentiles"—Isa 9:1; 8:23, Heb), which the prophet used to describe the Assyrian advance into the same region just before the fall of the Northern Kingdom and signal a future day when the entire land would find security under the reign of the Prince of Peace (Isa 9:1–7 [8:23–9:6, Heb]; cf. Mt 4:15–16).

The region that lay between Jabin and the forces of Sisera corresponded exactly to that which had been controlled by the kings who sought to resist Joshua's advance into northern Canaan (Josh 11:1–2), namely, a series of valleys and passes through which all of Galilee was easily controlled by Sisera's large chariot force while the Israelites kept to the hills and back roads (Judg 4:3, 5:6). Because the Canaanite city of Hazor had been thoroughly destroyed by Joshua

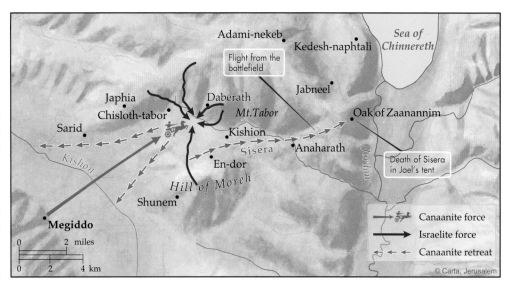

ing the Rift Valley to the oak in Zaanannim above the southwestern end of the Sea of Galilee near Kedesh. He had apparently negotiated grazing rights there from persons loyal to Jabin, and so Sisera, on the run, took advantage of what he assumed was a friendly welcome deep in territory otherwise loyal to Barak (Judg 4:17–20).

But Sisera also had other motives for stopping. In the ancient Near East, a soldier's wage was paid daily—food enough to keep him alive until the next day. What drove every fighter was the chance to grab spoil—to plunder the villages and countryside while on the march and seize whatever could be had from the conquered enemy, including (or, especially) young women (Num 31:17–18; 1 Sam 14:32, 30:2–5, 30:16–20, 31:8; 2 Sam 8:8; 2 Kgs 3:22, 7:15). Being attacked by an enemy was horrifying; simply having an army march through one's land—a frequent enough occurrence for Israel and Judah—was equally frightening (cf. Isa 10:28–32). Both were described graphically by biblical writers who spoke of the horrors of living under siege (2 Kgs 6:24–31; Amos 6:9–11), likening the devastation of war to that caused by a huge swarm of locusts (Judg 6:5; Joel 1:4) and comparing its aftermath to life in a God-forsaken land (Isa 8:21–22).

Sisera's own mother expected that he would fully enjoy the rewards of battle, the best of the goods and at least a couple women (in her words, lit. "a womb, two wombs for every warrior!" Judg 5:28–30). Now that victory and his chance of spoil were gone, Sisera looked for an easy conquest lest he return to Jabin empty-handed. In Bedouin culture, to approach a tent when a woman is alone at home is a horrendous breach of etiquette, even if it is she who initiates the conversation; rather, one can enter only if the patriarch is present and he issues the invitation (cf. Gen 18:1–8). But Jael set the trap and Sisera, sensing his moment, sprung it (Judg 4:18–20, 5:24–25). Jael was proficient with a hammer and tent peg—among her many tasks, she was the one who would set up and take down the tent—and much to the surprise of Sisera, it was *he* who was penetrated (Judg 4:21–22, 5:26–27). Jael's personal victory was a victory for all Israel.

A common, non-heroic peasant woman, Jael was vulnerable and alone, yet she possessed a keen instinct for survival and had an arsenal of skills and resources well honed from a lifetime of living off the land. An unlikely hero is everyone's favorite hero, and Jael's actions in turning the tables on an overpowering enemy precisely in the moment of her weakness became a point of hope for generations of Israelites who relished Deborah's song (Judges 5) and waited for God to use maybe even one of them like he did its two heroines. As for Deborah, although she already had a certain reputation within Israel, her hand in such a great military victory would also have been unexpected. In a sense both women were paradigms of the entire nation, a people who, during their settling-down time after Joshua, needed special protection from God and were capable, at moments when infused by the divine presence, of greatness.

Two Unlikely Victories. *The military victory of Barak's foot soldiers over the chariot force of Sisera was surpassed only by Jael's conquest of the mighty general in the secret folds of her tent. It was a personal triumph that was seized by all Israel, and Jael was remembered as a true folk hero: "Most blessed of women is Jael, the wife of Heber the Kenite; most blessed is she of women in the tent!"* (Judg 5:24)

The table-flat Jezreel Valley is drained by the normally sluggish Kishon, which siphons water from the base of Mt. Tabor all the way to the Mediterranean. Here it flows past the foot of Mt. Carmel in all of today's muddy splendor. Suddenly overflowing its banks by a fierce rainstorm, the Kishon must have seemed to the Israelite foot soldiers like a flash flood—akin to the waters of the Red Sea swallowing Pharaoh's army— pulling Sisera's chariot force under: "The Kishon torrent swept them away, the ancient torrent, the torrent Kishon. March on, my soul, with might!" (Judg 5:21).

41

CHAPTER 6

SAMSON
Greatness Run Amuck

The Migration of the Sea Peoples, 12th Century B.C. *According to Amos 9:7, the Philistines came from Caphtor (Crete). Archaeological and extra-biblical literary evidence spreads the Sea Peoples' homeland into the Aegean. Moving into the eastern Mediterranean by land and sea, the Sea Peoples were repulsed from the Egyptian Delta by Pharaoh Rameses III in c. 1174 B.C. One of these Sea Peoples, the Philistines, settled on the Gaza coast.*

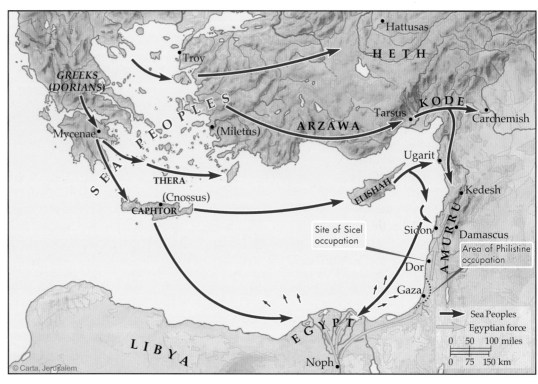

(above) Philistine pottery is most easily recognized by its decoration, with red, brown-red or black designs painted on a light, whitish slip. Most of the designs can be traced to the Aegean world (Mycenae). These include groups of lines divided into triglyphs, and metopes framing stylized motifs, the most characteristic of which is a bird looking over its shoulder. Philistine pottery dates to the 12th and 11th centuries B.C. and is found at many sites on the coastal plain and in the Shephelah.

Samson is the last in a series of deliverers whose deeds and exploits are recorded in the Book of Judges (chapters 13–16). More so than the rest, his is an action-packed adventure story, quickly cutting from one tight-spot episode to the next. Samson's struggle was at the same time against the Philistines and his own weaknesses, and both proved too persistent in the end. In today's terminology we might call Samson conflicted: one part mightily moved by the Spirit of God, one part stumbling oaf, a giant of a man who lived hard and died hard. He was a product of the conflicted times of the Judges and perhaps best represents the frustrated hopes in the days when "there was no king in Israel and everyone did what was right in his own eyes" (Judg 17:6, 21:25).

The Samson story is full of geographical refer-

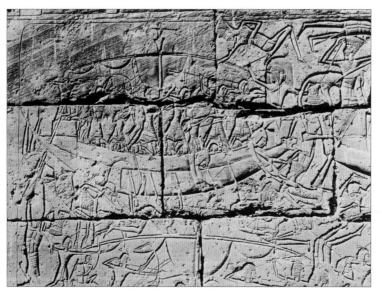

Various groups of Sea Peoples, so called, penetrated the Nile Delta and lands along southeastern coast of the Mediterranean in the late 13th and 12th centuries B.C. The Egyptian Pharaohs were not successful in keeping them out, and several of these groups, including the Philistines, established a beachhead in the region. These newcomers did not belong to the Semitic world but brought with them a material, intellectual and spiritual culture that enriched and challenged the indigenous people of Canaan—and posed a real threat to Israel, themselves just off the desert from the east.

ences and can easily be laid out on the landscape of the Shephelah, a zone of low, rolling foothills separating the high, rugged hill country of Judah from the flat, open coastal plain. The heavy runoff of the western slopes of the hill country flows into a series of six broad, shallow valleys furrowed into the soft limestone of the Shephelah, each of which is a focal point of rich agricultural life. Historically the Shephelah as a whole, and its six valleys in particular, has been a buffer zone between the hill country and the coast. Owing to realities of topography, climate, soil and water resources, the population based in the hills has tended to be rural, closed, conservative and regional, while that of the better-resourced coastal plain can be characterized as urban, open, sophisticated and international. The Shephelah, a true land between, was desired by both.

During the time of the Book of Judges (Iron Age I, 1200–1000 B.C.) the entire land of Canaan was in the process of being transformed from a network of independent city-states into a patchwork of small nation states. Even though the Book of Joshua records the allotment of the entire land to the various Israelite tribes (Josh 13–19), in reality the emerging state of Israel was relegated to the rugged hill country while the plains and valleys remained under indigenous Canaanite control (Josh 13:1–5; Judg 1:27–35). At the same time, the Philistines, whose origins can be traced to a much larger population of "Sea Peoples" hailing from the Aegean (cf. Amos 9:7), were settling the southern coast between Gaza and Joppa. Archaeologists have found distinctive Philistine material culture (pottery, architecture, religious objects and burial techniques) at numerous sites on the coast and in the valleys of the Shephelah. Biblical evidence suggests that the Philistines were organized around a confederation of five cities: Gaza, Ashkelon and Ashdod on or near the coast, and Ekron and Gath at the point where the Sorek and Elah valleys of the Shephelah, respectively, enter the coastal plain (Josh 13:3; 1 Sam 6:4, 6:17). As the Israelite tribes of Judah and Dan attempted to penetrate the rich agricultural valleys of the Shephelah, they met the Philistines coming the other way.

The Samson story is set in the Sorek Valley in the northern Shephelah. The Philistines filled the valley proper, from Ekron to Beth-shemesh, while the tribe of Dan, to which the Sorek had been assigned by Joshua, was compressed into a small wedge of hill country to the east (Josh 19:40–46; Judg 1:34–35). A few Danite families were able to infiltrate the eastern portions of the Shephelah, but could make their homes only on the bare, rocky ridge rising from the northern edge of the fertile Sorek. One of these was the family of Manoah, father of Samson, who was from Zorah.

Samson was born to a woman who had long been barren, a special birth of a special child (Judg 13:1–24;

cf. Gen 18:9–15, 21:1–7; 1 Sam 1:1–20; 2 Kgs 4:8–17; Lk 1:5–25). By the word of an angel of the LORD, Samson was to be a Nazirite, dedicated to God and His service. Samson grew up in Mahaneh-dan ("the camping spot of Dan"), a poor, scratchy hovel of tents and rough houses, if its name is any indication, clinging to the rocky hills between Zorah and Eshtaol. Every day he would look into the rich Sorek Valley below, his by divine right but now under Philistine control (Judg 13:1). The Spirit of the LORD, we read, began to stir in him there, and Samson's life mission took shape (Judg 13:24–25).

Samson's first forays into Philistine territory were to Timnah in the mid-Sorek Valley, a lovely agricultural vale lying a two-hour walk down ridge from Mahaneh-dan. Archaeological excavations suggest that Philistine Timnah was a well-established, fortified, densely populated urban center, an attractive place for a man too big for his own hometown. Here Samson met and married a pretty Philistine maiden, much to the dismay of his parents who, quite naturally, saw no reason for him to break the

According to Judges 1:34, the Amorites pushed the tribe of Dan, which had been given the area of the Sorek and Aijalon valleys in the Shephelah, into the hill country to the east, where they were compressed among the rocky hills and wadis northwest of Jerusalem. The Danite Manoah, with his wife and son Samson, ventured back out into the Shephelah, but were able to settle only on the rocky ridge separating the Sorek from the Aijalon, between the town of Zorah, on the rise shown here, and nearby Eshtaol.

The Sorek Valley below Zorah was the first spot west of the Danite hill country where large-scale agriculture could take place. The Philistines had been able to push into this region, and Samson could only gaze down on what he knew should have been his. Here, adjacent to neighboring Beth-shemesh, a modern Bedouin has won rights to pitch his house and barn—both of them tents—next to a field of tender grain, showing that cooperation and symbiosis in the region is possible even among people whose economic and settlement agendas would otherwise clash.

The Exploits of Samson.
Although the inheritance of the tribe of Dan stretched from the hill country to the Mediterranean Sea, in reality the Danites could scarcely gain a foothold in the valleys of the Shephelah. Samson, hailing from a cluster of towns hanging onto the northeastern corner of the Shephelah, tried to establish a Danite claim in the region—or at least make the Philistines aware that their mountain neighbors to the east were a force to be reckoned with.

The Sorek is a perennial stream as it pushes through the Shephelah to the coast, spreading its blessings across the broad valley at its banks. The city of Timnah, pleasantly situated midway along its course, just above the spot shown here, harvested this river of life. Samson was drawn to Timnah, a city that embraced everything his scraggly home lacked, and here began a series of exploits that swept him across the Philistine stage.

cultural norm and marry outside of his own clan (Judg 14:1–3). Moreover, the wedding festivities, which should have taken place in the home of the father of the groom, were in Timnah (glitz won out over simple homefolk), and even Samson's best man was a Philistine (Judg 14:10–11, 14:20).

We can assume that in the course of daily affairs, Danites and Philistines typically carried on a certain amount of social and personal interaction with each other, as normally happens everywhere between members of ethnic groups that live in close proximity to one another, and Samson and his family no doubt had been to Timnah numerous times over the years. Beneath this everyday interaction on the street, however, was an underlying mistrust and suspicion of each other—also quite normal—which informs the actions swirling around Samson's wedding. The festivities turned raucous, insolent and vengeful (Judg 14:12–18); Samson ended up killing and raiding in Ashkelon, making Philistines pay for Philistine arrogance while excusing his own big talk (Judg 14:19).

Samson, understandably, fell out of favor with his in-laws. His father-in-law arranged for the Iron Age equivalent of a quickie divorce, giving Samson's bride to his best man (Judg 14:20). Samson's devotion to his wife seems to have been nothing more than a matter of convenience anyway (Judg 15:1), and his response to the affront of losing her was aimed at soothing his lost honor. The

price the Philistines paid for wounding Samson's ego lay close at hand (Judg 15:2–3). The agricultural conditions of the Shephelah valleys are best suited for growing grain, and the fields around Timnah typically promise a bumper crop. It was now early summer, the time of the wheat harvest, and Samson set fire to the fields (his method, using foxtail torches, fit his personality to a "T"). The blaze jumped the fields to nearby vineyards and orchards, spreading like wildfire through the grass and stubble that had dried up following the end of the rainy season (Judg 15:4–5; cf. Isa 5:24; Obad 18; Zech 12:6). Dagan, the Philistine god of grain (Judg 16:23; 1 Sam 5:2), would not have been pleased. Suddenly facing the prospect of famine, the Philistines of Timnah struck back at one of their own, Samson's former in-laws, a soft target. His response was sheer vengeance (Judg 15:6–8).

Perhaps realizing that he had finally crossed the line, Samson fled to the hills and hid in Etam, a Judean village just over the crest of the watershed ridge where, he thought, he was out of sight of the Philistines. Intent on blood revenge, the Philistines advanced as far as Lehi in pursuit. The location of Lehi and its spring, En-hakkore (Judg 15:9, 15:19), are unknown, but must have been in the hill country since the Judeans responded as if the Philistine presence there was a real threat (Judg 15:11). Having fled to Etam, Samson had upset the delicate *status quo* of Philistine control over Judah and drawn others into the wake of his cycle of revenge–counter-revenge. Now it was the Judeans' turn to sacrifice one of their own for the common good, and Samson was bound and turned over to the Philistines (Judg 15:10–13). He met them at Lehi ("jawbone") and, using as his weapon the jawbone of a donkey with a toothy, serrated edge, Samson decimated the Philistine squadron (Heb. *eleph*, usually translated "thousand") sent to seize him (Judg 15:14–19).

The final episodes of Samson's life combine his physical prowess with his weakness for women, what for him was a fatal combination. Samson first went to Gaza, at the farthest corner of the coastal plain, passing all of the Philistine cities on his way (did he thumb his nose at each as he went?—Judg 16:1). Apparently occupied for the night with a prostitute (based on his character and in spite of his Nazirite vows, there is no reason to think that Samson was only looking for cover), the Philistines calculated that they could finally seize him easily, in the morning when his strength was spent. But again Samson proved greater than the task at hand. Rising with the city still asleep, he pulled down its gates—rendering the city conquered—and carried them forty miles east to the highest part of the southern hill country, the "mountain which is opposite Hebron" (*Jebel Jalis* or perhaps the mountain of Halhoul to the north) over 3,300 feet in elevation (Judg 16:2–3). Some would argue that Samson's trek from the farthest part of Philistia to the highest part of Judah was too far for him to have been able to carry the entire gate structure, and so he actually seized only its lock and key. In any case, Samson had made his point: the Philistines might have controlled Israel, but at any moment he reserved the right to call the shots.

Samson's success in Gaza set in motion the events of his undoing. He soon developed a relationship ("lover" is not too strong a term) with another maiden in the Sorek Valley, Delilah (Judg 16:4). Delilah's specific home is not mentioned; perhaps she was from a small village like Samson himself and he finally saw in her a soulmate. In fact, their relationship mirrors that of a classic spy novel—he was deceived and seduced from the beginning; she was never anything but Philistine. Samson and Delilah played a game of cat-and-mouse, and Samson, who assumed he was the cat, enjoyed playing the role of the mouse—until his seduction was complete (Judg 16:5–20). Blinded, bound and bald, his honor and strength gone, Samson was taken back to the scene of his last great victory where he was reduced to the lowest level of humanity (Judg 16:21).

Quite naturally, the Philistines celebrated; like Deborah, they composed a song of triumph over their defeated enemy (Judg 16:23–24; cf. Judg 5:1–31). Samson was called to join the fun—as a stumbling giant—and he literally brought the house down (Judg 16:25–30). Archaeological excavations at Tell Qasile in northern Tel Aviv have uncovered extensive Philistine remains, including the foundations of a temple with two interior limestone pillar bases on which two cedar pillars supporting the roof had originally rested. These pillars were spaced just far enough apart that a man of Samson's size could have shifted his weight from one to the next, swaying and then collapsing both. Based on the account of Samson's demise (Judg 16:29–30), it is likely that the temple of Dagan in Gaza was of a similar architectural plan. Samson was buried back home between Zorah and Eshtaol on his rocky ridge above the fertile Sorek Valley, with the Philistine threat temporarily checked but not removed (Judg 16:31).

Even though the Samson story contains some elements bordering on the fantastic (the episode with the fire foxes immediately comes to mind), its overall thrust rings true on a number of accounts. Available historical and archaeological evidence provides the overall context, namely, the prolonged process by which Israel and the Philistines settled the southern Levant at the beginning of the Iron Age and sought to expand their respective spheres of influence in the region, with the Shephelah as a focal point of their efforts. By and large this process was peaceful, although ethnic prejudices and conflict on the personal, village or tribal level were never far from the surface. In addition, the patterns

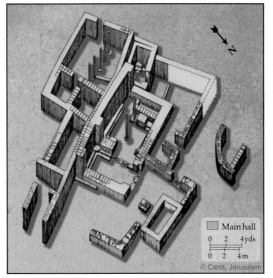

of personal and social behavior in the Samson story reflect what is otherwise known of the cultural and historical context in which the story is set. Underlying the narrative is a geographical reality (topography, soil, water and climate) that fits exactly the landscape of the hill country, Shephelah and coastal plain as it is still known today.

The Samson story also rings true on aspects of human nature. Samson's role as a Nazirite and the reality of his everyday actions were two different things, and seemed to conflict as often as not. But why should the reader necessarily expect otherwise? Samson's rationale to the men of Judah at Lehi is perhaps the best summary of the entire storyline: "As they did to me, so I have done to them" (Judg 15:11). Did Samson's actions help, or provoke? Did his fellow Israelites encourage, or tolerate him? To what extent can heroes be flawed and still be heroes? If one thing is clear in the Samson story it is that God used Samson in spite of himself, and on this account Samson, like Deborah and Jael, became a paradigm for the rest of the biblical story.

The temple found at Tell Qasile remains the most complete Philistine religious complex excavated in Israel. The roof of the main hall was supported by two cedar pillars separated by the distance of the span of a large man's outstretched arms. These archaeological remains evoke memories of a blind yet determined Samson, resting on the pillars of the Philistine temple of Dagan in Gaza before collapsing them and the roof above. (Leen Ritmeyer)

Samson betrayed by Delilah into the hands of the Philistines, 19th century engraving (Carta, Jerusalem). *In the 1st century* A.D. *Josephus praised Samson's heroic deeds while excusing his failings: "And indeed, this man deserves to be admired for his courage and strength...but as for his being ensnared by a woman, that is to be ascribed to human nature..."* (Ant. v.8.12).

CHAPTER 7
NAOMI AND RUTH
The Way It's Supposed to Be

The purple hills of Moab rise from the chasm of the Rift Valley, overpowering the Wilderness of Judah as it drops into the Dead Sea. The modern city of Bethlehem lies in the foreground. The clearer the day, the smaller the land appears, and a journey to the hills "just over there" was a realistic option for someone from famine-stricken Bethlehem.
(photo: Garo Nalbandian)

Naomi's View. *Although it sits on the watershed ridge, Bethlehem is an eastward-oriented city, with its best view to the Judean Wilderness, the Dead Sea and Moab. It was only natural that Elimelech and Naomi followed their gaze to the East. Theologically this was the direction of exile, where strong men die and survival depends on the open hand of God.*

The story of Ruth is a breath of fresh air in the turbulent atmosphere of the time of the Judges. It comes none too soon, for the deeper the reader gets into the Book of Judges, the more outlandish the actions of its characters become until the summary conclusion offers the terse rationale: "In those days there was no king in Israel; everyone did what was right in their own eyes" (Judg 21:25). Out of this maelstrom comes a shining story of courage, faithfulness and life lived the way it's supposed to be. In English Bibles the Book of Ruth follows Judges, an order based on chronology that heightens the contrast between the tenor of the events of the two books and suggests that life can be normal in spite of the chaos of the times. For its part, the Hebrew Bible places Ruth after Proverbs, giving a tangible answer to the question, "A worthy woman (*eshet hayil*)—who can find?" (Prov 31:10; cf. Ruth 3:11). In any case, the story of Ruth is a reminder that behind the craziness of the daily news, people who live under the blessings of God are able to organize their lives in ways that are meaningful and helpful for others.

The story of Ruth is a Bethlehem story, with a sojourn to the fields of Moab. It's a rural, small village story—for such Bethlehem was throughout the biblical period (cf. Mic 5:2). Bethlehem is exactly five miles south of Jerusalem and, like Jerusalem, lies just behind the crest of the watershed ridge. For residents of Jerusalem the view to the east is short, blocked by the Mount of Olives, a ridge that separates the city from the Wilderness of Judah and gives its residents a certain feeling of seclusion (cf. Ps 125:2). Not so for Bethlehem, however. Here the villagers' view is unimpeded and can take in the spectacular plunge of the undulating hills of the wilderness, bare and bright, dropping to the even deeper chasm of the Dead Sea, then the dramatic rise of the gray-purple hills of Moab beyond. Bethlehem lies open, vulnerable and exposed, with the possibility of withering heat and famine—just as real for everyone in the hill country but always with a visible reminder here—ever at hand. The straight-line distance from Bethlehem to the Dead Sea is only 15 miles, but the corresponding drop in rainfall is precipitous, from an average of 24 inches on the watershed ridge to

46

a meager 4 at Jericho. The land of the wilderness is good only for winter grazing of sheep and goats, and so Bethlehem is a base for shepherds (cf. 1 Sam 16:1, 16:11; Lk 2:8). But within the immediate circle of the town lie fertile agricultural lands, with open spaces for barley and wheat, the two grains most suitable for the soil and climate of the region (cf. Deut 8:8).

Historically, for a village on the seam of the desert and the sown land, any slight change in international weather patterns tips the balance of rainfall toward a year of bumper crops, or famine. Three or four consecutive years of marginal or inadequate rainfall would be disastrous for Bethlehem farmers who, in the biblical period, had no recourse to irrigation or government subsidies. At a time such as this Elimelech the husband of Naomi faced three choices: starve (a rather bleak prospect!), change his occupation (not realistic, given the lack of other options for subsistence in a farming village) or move (Ruth 1:1–2). He chose the latter, leaving temporarily (he hoped) the security of his ancestral heritage and homeland for the possibility of surviving another day. Moab was a logical place to go: it was in view; its hills are higher than the eastern slopes of Bethlehem and so potentially wetter and more fertile; and with the Israelite tribe of Reuben commanding the heights immediately east of the northern end of the Dead Sea (Num 32:33–38; Deut 3:16–17; Josh 13:15–23), Elimelech would have had some affinity in the region. Others in Bethlehem may well have migrated south to Hebron, which offered similar advantages.

It is not possible to know exactly where in Moab Elimelech and his family settled, nor in the end does it particularly matter. If Elimelech went around the northern end of the Dead Sea—the easiest track— his journey would have taken him to the tableland (mishor) of Medeba, settled by Reuben but always claimed by Moab. On the other hand, Moab proper lay between the gorges of the Arnon and the Zered opposite the southern half of the Dead Sea. The most direct natural route there from Bethlehem followed a tortuous ridge above the Nahal Arugot, the largest of the wadi systems draining the Judean Wilderness, to the springs of En-gedi on the shore of the Dead Sea, then tracked south to the Lisan Peninsula (near the future site of Herod's Palace at Masada) where the sea is quite shallow and able to be crossed without undue difficulty. Years later, as he began his rise to kingship, David of Bethlehem, the great grandson of Ruth and Boaz, placed his parents under the protection of the Moabite king in Mizpeh of Moab while he stayed in "the stronghold" (metzudah, probably Masada; 1 Sam 22:3–4). David's choice for a place of refuge was probably influenced by family ties through the line of his great grandmother Ruth, and if so, it can reasonably be suggested that his journey paralleled the earlier route of Elimelech.

In any case, Elimelech and his family lived

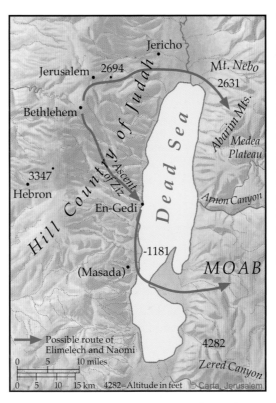

in Moab for ten years, long enough to establish some marriage ties with the people of the land but without putting down formal roots of his own. Elimelech died there, as did his two sons and heirs (Ruth 1:3–5); with names like Mahlon ("sickly") and Chilion ("weakly"), what else could be expected? Landless, childless, out of the land of promise and without legal or economic protection, the widow Naomi faced a bleak future.

Eventually the weather patterns changed and the villagers of Bethlehem again felt the blessing of the open hand of God. For Naomi, it was time to return home (Ruth 1:6–7). Orpah the widow of Chilion and Ruth the widow of Mahlon (cf. Ruth 4:10) faced a difficult choice. According to marriage custom, they belonged under the shelter of Elimelech's household, but his household no longer existed nor was there any real prospect that it would be renewed.

The Sojournings of Naomi and Ruth. *Although separated from Moab by the Rift Valley, the residents of Bethlehem were tied to the region both by line of sight and two rugged, yet passable natural routes. One of these skirted the northern arc of the Dead Sea, the other dropped down the steep Ascent of Ziz (2 Chron 20:16) before crossing the sea at its shallow southern end. The shepherds of Bethlehem would have known these routes well, and either one provides a plausible path for the travels of Naomi and Ruth.*

The powdery soil covering the high, flat tableland of Moab and the Medeba Plateau is poor but plows easily, and with an average of 16 inches of rainfall per year the open fields of the region produce fine (though thin by western standards) crops of wheat and barley, the staple of life. For Elimelech and Naomi Moab was a foreign, but welcoming land.

(above) Naomi on her return to Bethlehem, 19th century engraving (Carta, Jerusalem). *The rabbis commented on Naomi's return: "All the city was astir concerning them, and the women said: 'Is this Naomi, the one whose appearance used to be so comely? At one time she used to be carried out in a palanquin, and now she walks barefoot. At one time she wore garments of fine wool, and now she is covered with rags. At one time her face was ruddy from food and drink, and now her face is a sickly green from hunger.' Naomi replied, 'Call me not Naomi [pleasant], call me Mara [bitter]'"* (Ruth Rabbah 3:6).

It was Naomi's right to allow them to return to their own fathers' households where they could become productive members of a supportive community (Ruth 1:8–13). Orpah, torn, decided to return, while Ruth, for her own part, insisted that she stay with Naomi, sensing that somehow each would be able to help the other (Ruth 1:14). Tired, yet grateful, Naomi accepted Ruth's offer, and together she and her daughter-in-law made the difficult journey back to Bethlehem (Ruth 1:15–18).

They returned in early spring, when barley stood ripe in the fields and the farmers were ready to reap the first fruit of their hard labor (Ruth 1:22). This was during or just after the month of *Aviv* (or, *Abib*), the Canaanite/Old Hebrew month corresponding to the Jewish month *Nisan*. The word *aviv* is an agricultural term designating a young, green ear of barley that is just mature enough to have nutritional value. As such, it signals the potential that the spring season carried every year, that is, the possibility of a good harvest and prosperous life. Moses had commanded Israel to celebrate the Festival of Unleavened Bread/Passover every *Aviv* in order to remember Israel's redemption from Egypt (Ex 23:14–15, 34:18; Deut 16:1), but the celebration also marked the annual freedom and security that comes from God's renewed provision in the land. Naomi, entering Bethlehem during the barley harvest, must have had mixed emotions: even though the possibility of life had returned, her identity had changed. No longer Naomi ("pleasant"), she was now Mara ("bitter"; Ruth 1:19–21). The women of Bethlehem, her new support group, welcomed her home.

So Naomi was not completely bereft. Indeed, Israelite social structure was organized around a tiered series of nested family groups. That is, the basic unit, the household (*ʾbet av*) was a sub-group of an extended family or clan (*mishpaha*); two or three clans lived together in a village or series of neighboring villages. If an entire household was in trouble, it was the responsibility of the clan, and then the village, to help. The women of Bethlehem offered social support, but it was up to the best-positioned member of Elimelech's clan, Boaz, a man of class (*ʾish gibbor hayil*; Ruth 2:1; cf. Josh 6:2; 1 Sam 9:1; 2 Kgs 15:20) and the most eligible bachelor in town, to provide financially. News travels fast in villages, and Boaz heard of Ruth's loyalty and resolve to help a member of his clan who was in distress. Even though both Ruth and Boaz were conscious of her foreignness, they were drawn together—he out of duty and respect; she from need and admiration (Ruth 2:2–22). Common Middle Eastern hospitality extends a welcome to a sojourner or foreigner for a few days; if the stranger proves to be a productive and resourceful member of the community, the possibility is open for he or she to be adopted in some way into their host's family. Ruth gleaned in the fields of Boaz through the barley and wheat harvests until the heat of early summer (Ruth 2:23), proving her character as a woman worthy of Elimelech's clan (she was an *eshet hayil*; Ruth 3:11) in the process.

The days and weeks immediately following the grain harvest were a time of opportunity in the calendar of the ancient Near East. With everyone's bank accounts full, so to speak, it was the season of the year to settle debts and enter into or renew social relationships that had economic ramifications. Naomi knew that the time was ripe for action, and that Boaz was the man with the character, credentials and resources to give Ruth the standing she needed to become a full member of Bethlehem society, and to restore her rightful lot as well. The midnight rendezvous at the threshing floor was the defining moment for everyone (Ruth 3:1–18). The meeting was Naomi's suggestion; older village women are usually wise enough and just meddlesome enough to pull the right strings at the right time, and her resourcefulness here more than made up for her despondency upon first returning to Bethlehem. Ruth placed herself under the protective cover of

Ruth gleaning in the fields of Boaz, 19th century engraving (Carta, Jerusalem). *Though far from her home, the fields of Boaz in Bethlehem were familiar ground for Ruth, whose hands knew well the pull of the sickle through standing grain. Ruth did what she knew how to do, and put her heart and soul into providing for Naomi.*

Every town had a communal threshing floor where for six weeks each spring farmers and their families joined forces to reap the warm bounty that sprang from the cold winter rain. While any exposed area of bedrock would do, the best threshing floors, like this one above the fields of Bethlehem, were on the tops of hills where the brisk wind would separate the tossed chaff from the heavier grain.

Boaz, choosing loyalty to Naomi over the chance for adventure with men nearer her age. And Boaz, full of honor himself, just did the right thing by giving honor to Ruth and restoring lost honor to Naomi. Boaz' primary concern was for Naomi and Ruth; he resolved that if those who *should* have helped chose not to do so, he would step into the role himself (Ruth 3:13).

Many readers of the Book of Ruth see Boaz' actions as a tangible example of levirate marriage, whereby a childless widow marries the brother of her dead husband and their children are counted as those of the deceased (Deut 25:5–10; cf. Gen 38:6–11). Whether or not this instance of Ruth and Boaz is technically levirate marriage, it is clear that the same issues were at stake. These were three, each aimed at maintaining security in a society that placed family and land as the highest of values: that the bereaved widow receive proper care; that the family line continue; and that the property remain within the family. Apparently it was the third that tripped up the nearer relative whom Boaz approached in the city gate to redeem Ruth. If this unnamed relative had simply purchased the land he would increase the capital investment of his own family, but if he also married Ruth he would spend his family's capital for the benefit of the heirs of Ruth's dead husband Mahlon, thereby divesting the rights of his own heirs. But Boaz was willing to do precisely this, partly out of duty to the village, partly out of devotion to Naomi and partly out of what must now be seen as love for Ruth (Ruth 4:10–12).

So Boaz married Ruth, but his actions as redeemer were more far-reaching than simply bringing her into his household. An unresolved issue has to do with the status of Elimelech's land. Clearly the land was out of Naomi's hand or she wouldn't have had

to resort to gleaning, and so it had to be "redeemed" (Ruth 4:4). The land no doubt was productive, and when Elimelech left for Moab someone else apparently had moved in—squatted—and reaped whatever harvests he could for the ten years that Naomi was gone. Naomi's absence had alienated her from her husband's land, and the one who seized possession was unwilling to recognize its rightful owner once she returned. Like the Shunammite widow who faced the same misfortune during the lifetime of Elisha (2 Kgs 8:1–6), Naomi, through Boaz, had to appeal to a higher authority to restore her rights. In a land where possession is nine-tenths of the law, Naomi actually had to buy back from the squatter what was rightfully hers. Financially destitute, she was unable to do so and instead resorted to "selling" the land to her nearest relative so that the money paid would evict the squatter and return the land to her family. The unnamed relative probably would have kept the land for his own use, but Boaz stepped in as Naomi's redeemer, and as her new son through marriage he ensured that she would receive the financial security of Elimelech's ancestral land.

Other than the genealogical comments tying Ruth and Boaz to David (Ruth 4:18–22), the last word in the Book of Ruth is voiced by the women of Bethlehem. Theirs is a word of blessing, sung out at the birth of Naomi's grandson Obed (Ruth 4:14–17). To this day, the older women of Bethlehem still offer special blessings to new brides and new mothers in a chorus of joy shared with the village. Modern Bethlehemites take pride in their biblical ancestors, as they should. Through the actions of Ruth and Boaz, the two greatest values of ancient Israelite society—land and children—were restored to Naomi. Life was the way it's supposed to be.

An Aramaic deed of inheritance on papyrus from Elephantine, Egypt, 460/459 B.C. (Ada Yardeni). *Time-honored custom and law determined rights to inheritance in the ancient Near East. Although specifics varied with time and place, the rights to land were always valued and protected.*

CHAPTER 8
DAVID AND SOLOMON
Our Legacy

(above) Philistine noble as depicted on a faience plaque from the funerary temple of Rameses III, Medinet Habu, Egypt. The Philistines were Israel's greatest nemesis during the time of Saul and David.

(right) Samuel anointing Saul, 19th century engraving (Carta, Jerusa-lem). *Never at a loss for words, the 1st century A.D. historian Josephus* (Ant. vi.4.6) *commented: "[Samuel] the prophet said [to Israel], 'God gives you this man to be your king: see how he is higher than any of the people, and worthy of this dominion.' So as soon as the people had made acclamation,* God save the king, *the prophet wrote down what would come to pass in a book, and read it in the hearing of the king, and laid up the book in the tabernacle of God, to be a witness to future generations of what he had foretold."*

The story of David is a classic example of what can be accomplished by the right person in the right place at the right time. David was one of a rare breed of men who are able to combine personal strength with genuine humility. Devoted to God and receiving the devotion of a loyal band of followers, he forged a network of alliances and built a power base that launched a viable kingdom in Israel. David's son Solomon, born to Bathsheba, reaped the benefit of his efforts and steered Israel through its first—and some would say only—Golden Age. Together, David and Solomon set the standard for political leadership in ancient Israel, so much so that for centuries and even millennia following, a host of Israelite, Jewish and Christian leaders have been gauged by how tall they stood in their shadows.

The story of David is inseparable from that of the rise of kingship in ancient Israel. Whoever aspired to kingship in Israel in the tenth century B.C. faced two nearly insurmountable obstacles. Internally, the problem was a lack of unification among the tribes. The tendency for each of the Israelite tribes to act first and foremost in their own interests was both natural and overwhelming, and attempts at unity for the common good never went very far. If it suited their interests, various northern tribes sometimes rallied around Ephraim and Manasseh, and those from the south would typically find hegemony under

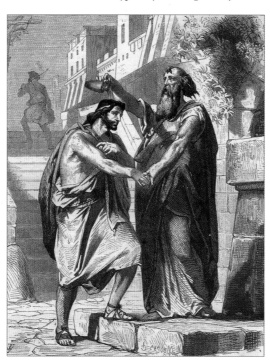

Judah, but not always and not for long. The move from tribalism to monarchy carried enormous social, economic, political, religious and psychological ramifications, and was never complete. Externally, the problem was weak borders, or, perhaps, a lack of realistic borders. The imperialistic Pharaohs of the Egyptian New Kingdom, who pretty much had had their way in Canaan throughout the Late Bronze Age (c. 1550–1200 B.C.), were in decline, and in their wake regional peoples such as Edom, Moab, Ammon, Aram-Damascus, Phoenicia and Philistia, in addition to Israel, found opportunity to express their own political and territorial ambitions. In short, the tribes of Israel faced constant incursions by peoples on every side, most of which were in the process of becoming viable, expanding kingdoms themselves. There was no simple answer to the question of how the Israelite identity, grounded to no small extent in a shared religious experience, would respond to and survive the challenges of tribalism and nationalism.

Over time the Philistines posed the most persistent external threat to several of the Israelite tribes. Philistine pressure in the Sorek Valley pushed the tribe of Dan into the higher hill country to the east, and Samson, a Danite strong man on the front lines, was unable to permanently overcome their incursions (Judg 13–16). The Philistines defeated Israel at Aphek, an important juncture on the international coastal highway controlling access into the hill country of Ephraim (1 Sam 4), and, as is known from archaeological evidence, followed up by destroying Shiloh and its religious sanctuary, Israel's center of tribal unity (cf. Ps 78:60; Jer 7:12). Sometime later, the Philistines pushed deeply into the territory of Benjamin, to Mizpeh on the watershed ridge, in an attempt to drive a wedge between the northern and southern tribes and control the crossroads between them (1 Sam 7:3–12). For the Philistines, Benjamin was a soft target; the tribe was small both in population and land area, though strategically located, and had fairly easy access points from the coast. Samuel, a Benjaminite from the neighboring village of Ramah, rallied the people and drove the Philistines out. Exercising priestly, prophetic and political authority, Samuel had been effective where Samson and the high priesthood of Shiloh failed, and as he aged, the people demanded permanent leadership on a national level, that is, a king (1 Sam 8:5). In fact, it was the need to deal with this jointly-felt external

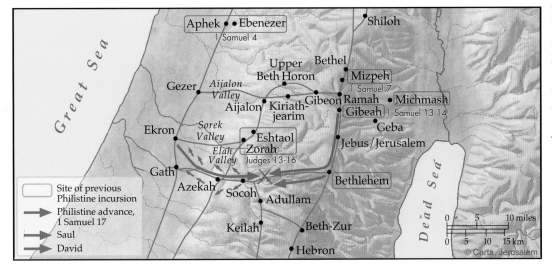

Faceoff in the Elah Valley:
David v. Goliath. *David
cut his teeth on international
politics in his showdown with
Goliath, a battle fit for the
ages. The Philistines of Gath
pushed into the Elah Valley,
their valley they would say,
just as Samson's forays into
the Sorek had been his claim
to his. The Philistine eyes were
on Saul's capital, Gibeah, and
tried this end-around from
the south only after several
more direct assaults farther
north had failed. Bethlehem,
a small village on the way,
should have posed only minimal
resistance—but David had
something else to say about the
matter.*

*Seen from the top of Azekah,
the upper, Judean end of the
Elah Valley offers a wide
highway to the higher hill
country of Judah beyond.
Natural routes climb the hills
to Bethlehem (left) and Hebron
(right), just past the horizon
line. With Goliath's Philistines
seizing this eastern end of the
Elah, Saul's forces likely came
down only to the edge of the hill
country, preferring to remain
in familiar territory rather than
risk entering the Philistine-held
Shephelah. The battle between
David and Goliath must have
taken place at a narrow spot
(Hebrew, gai) of the valley
somewhere along this seam.*

threat that prompted the tribes to come together under a common leader. Because this most recent Philistine thrust was into Benjamin, it was natural that Israel's first king, the man to succeed Samuel, was a Benjaminite, Saul from Gibeah, a village just south of Ramah (1 Sam 9:1–10:27).

All told, Saul's actions as a national leader in the areas where it counted the most were a good start toward statehood, but largely ineffective. His base of operations was his home at Gibeah, and he enjoyed some support from the residents of Jabesh-gilead in northern Transjordan, many of whom had blood ties to the Benjaminites (Judg 21:8–15). While Saul found success on the battlefield by relieving Ammonite pressure on Jabesh-gilead (1 Sam 11:1–11) and checking incursions of the desert-raiding Amalekites on Judah's southern border (1 Sam 15:1–9; cf. 1 Sam 14:47), he was essentially impotent against the Philistines, the problem next door that had prompted his being anointed king in the first place. When the Philistines sliced into Benjamin again, this time east of the watershed ridge to Michmash, it was Jonathan, Saul's son, who took the necessary initiative to drive them out (1 Sam 13:1–14:23). Likewise, Saul's response to the Philistine presence in the Elah Valley was one characterized by decisive inaction (1 Sam 17:1–39). Samuel reserved comment, save to criticize Saul's failures toward God (1 Sam 13:11–14, 15:10–35), but many others no doubt knew the full extent of his shortcomings. It was time for fresh leadership, and this time Samuel sought a young man from Judah.

Judah was by far the dominant Israelite tribe in the southern hill country, with a large land base and growing population. Already the tribe of Simeon was essentially being assimilated into Judah (Josh 19:1–9; cf. Josh 15:21–32), as were other tribes of mixed background that had settled in and around the Negeb (Kenites, Jerahmeelites, Calebites, Cherethites and Kenizzites; cf. Josh 14:6; 1 Sam 27:10, 30:14). For this reason, when Samuel, prompted by

the call of God, anointed David to be the future king (1 Sam 16:1–13), he gave the young shepherd of Bethlehem an early advantage that was never enjoyed by Saul, namely, the possibility of forming a significant base of popular support up front. On the political level, the luxury of time given to David to build a following before he needed one greatly enhanced his chances of reaching, and then hanging on to, the kingship.

David's first appearance in the public eye came as a direct result of Philistine pressure on Judah in the Shephelah. By taking the upper, Judean end of the Elah Valley from Azekah to Socoh, the Philistines laid claim to the two main routes into the mid-section of the hill country from the west, one heading to Hebron, the primary city of Judah, and the other to Bethlehem (1 Sam 17:1). Unchecked, they could walk into both, and Judah's viability as an Israelite tribe would be gone. More pressing for Saul, if Bethlehem fell to the Philistines, Gibeah, his home and Israel's capital, would be next in line and could easily be attacked from the south. In any event, the threat to the land, security and future of Jesse the Bethlehemite was immediate and

Route to
Bethlehem

Route to
Hebron

Dr. Aren Maeir of Bar Ilan University, director of the excavation project at Tell es-Safi (Gath of the Philistines), explains the layout of the site to a group of eager students framed by the remains of the past. Like many ancient sites, the ground on which Gath once stood was inhabited, on and off through the ages, by a variety of peoples, some city or village dwellers, others farmers or shepherds. Evidence of their past—and a window to the city of Goliath—is revealed by the archaeologist's spade.

David's flight took him on one occasion to the wilderness of En-gedi (1 Sam 24:1–2), where an encounter with Saul resulted in an uneasy truce between the two. A relatively recent tourist tradition—understandably attractive due to the natural beauty of the site—holds that David's hideout was among the several waterfalls in a small canyon above the western shore of the Dead Sea that is now called the David Wadi. The region is alive with ibex, providing a convenient link to the "Rock of the Wild Goats" somewhere the vicinity.

real, and so he sent his three oldest sons to help Saul hold the line (1 Sam 17:12–16). Underarmed (cf. 1 Sam 13:19–22), undermanned (1 Sam 17:10–11, 17:16) and lacking the vision of the moment, Saul was paralyzed while David, with survival skills honed in the wilds of the wilderness of Judah, defeated the Philistine hero in hand-to-hand combat (1 Sam 17:20–51). David's victory over Goliath allowed Israel to push the Philistines out of the mid-Shephelah (1 Sam 17:52–53); his greater triumph was to gain a reputation as a warrior mightier than even King Saul (1 Sam 18:6–9).

Saul sensed that David's star was rising, and the two began a game of dodge and feint, move and counter-move, played out on a personal level but with tremendous national ramifications. For Saul, David could be useful (1 Sam 18:17–19; cf. 1 Sam 14:52); he was also a threat that needed to be neutralized. For David, Saul was God's anointed one (lit. "messiah"; 1 Sam 24:6, 26:9; 2 Sam 1:14) and could not be harmed, but at the same time David was not above forging alliances that strengthened his hand at Saul's expense. Throughout, David's actions and statements should be read through the grid of expectations common to Middle Eastern negotiations even today, with a "no, please, after you, I insist" politeness (e.g., 1 Sam 18:18, 18:23) tempering the very practical jockeying for position going on behind the scenes.

So David became the captain of Saul's bodyguard (1 Sam 22:14). He also married Michal, Saul's daughter, for love and out of expediency, and the marriage heightened his standing in both Israel and Philistia. It was expected that the king's son (or son-in-law) would help fight the king's battles, and in Saul's estimation, if David didn't fall to the Philistines (that would be the cleanest way of getting rid of a threat to the throne), at least he would be on a short leash (1 Sam 18:20–30). The situation was endemic to tension and jealousy, prompting David to flee Gibeah (1 Sam 19:1–17). Wisely, he went first to Samuel, the fledgling nation's elder statesman in Ramah, for advice (1 Sam 19:18–24). Apparently Samuel counseled moderation, for David returned to Gibeah, but by now Saul sensed a coup

(1 Sam 20:31). David fled again, this time for good and with the blessings of Jonathan the crown prince in hand (1 Sam 20:1–42).

David stopped briefly at the sanctuary in Nob to secure provisions (with or without the blessing of the priest) and retrieve the sword of Goliath (1 Sam 21:1–9), then sought refuge in the place Saul least expected him to go, Gath of the Philistines (Tell es-Safi). David dared walk into Gath with the sword of their vanquished hometown hero in hand, then feigned to be crazy—Saul would have enjoyed the show—after running afoul of the city's king, Achish (1 Sam 21:10–15). On the run again, David withdrew to the cave at Adullam, a point of refuge above the Elah Valley tucked into the seam between the Shephelah and the Judean hill country. Here, near the scene of his debutante victory over Goliath and away from the centers of power of both Saul and the Philistines, David forged a personal army of valiant men who were not happy with the rule of either (1 Sam 22:1–2). As David's support and reputation grew, others joined him at Ziklag and the Stronghold (perhaps Masada; 1 Chron 12:1–22). Most of these men came from Benjamin—Saul's land—and Judah, but some were from Manasseh (the hill country of Ephraim) and Gad in Transjordan. The Bible records a number of daring exploits of the bravest of the band, men willing to risk life and limb for their leader (2 Sam 23:8–39; 1 Chron 11:10–47). Far from neutralizing David, Saul had given him the opportunity and excuse to pull the southern hill country together—against the Philistines, against Saul, but for David.

The situation was ripe with uncertainties and danger. The first thing David did was find a safe place for his family. He left them with the king of Moab, drawing on the cultural norm by which a sheik (to use a modern term) provides hospitality under the protection of his tent for travelers and long-lost relatives (1 Sam 22:3–5; cf. Job 31:21–32). With David now absent from Adullam, the Philistines raided the nearby threshing floors at Keilah. Some of David's mighty men were probably from the area and took the attacks as a personal threat to their livelihood; they had to react, but with it began to realize the potential consequences of operating as a private militia at odds with both the Philistines and Saul (1 Sam 23:1–13).

It was time to fly below the radar, and David and his band withdrew to the rugged, largely empty Judean Wilderness (he tracked through the Wilderness of Ziph, 1 Sam 23:14–28; En-gedi, 1 Sam 23:29–24:21; the Stronghold = Masada?, 1 Sam 24:22; the Wilderness of Paran and Maon, 1 Sam 25:1–42, and again the Wilderness of Ziph, 1 Sam 26:1–25). This was territory familiar enough for the former shepherd boy, where he could appear and disappear at will, out-maneuvering Saul and his

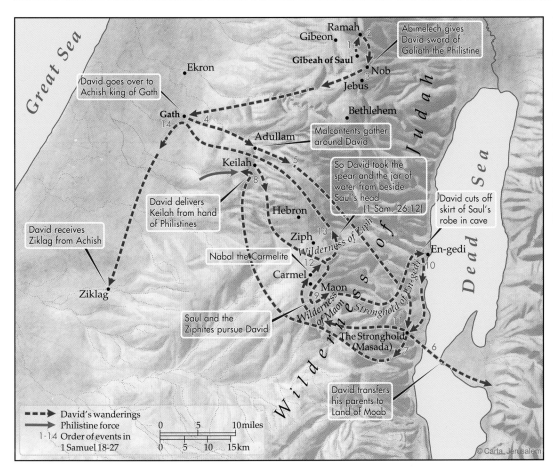

Ramah
Gibeon
Gibeah of Saul
Abimelech gives David sword of Goliath the Philistine
Nob
Jebus
Ekron
David goes over to Achish king of Gath
Bethlehem
Gath
Adullam
Malcontents gather around David
Keilah
So David took the spear and the jar of water from beside Saul's head (1 Sam. 26:12)
David delivers Keilah from hand of Philistines
David cuts off skirt of Saul's robe in cave
David receives Ziklag from Achish
Hebron
Ziph
Wilderness of Ziph
En-gedi
Nabal the Carmelite
Ziklag
Carmel
Maon
Stronghold of En-gedi
Wilderness of Maon
Saul and the Ziphites pursue David
The Stronghold (Masada)
David transfers his parents to Land of Moab
Wilderness of Judah
Great Sea
Dead Sea
Judah

- - - ► David's wanderings
——► Philistine force
1-14 Order of events in 1 Samuel 18-27

0   5   10 miles
0 5 10 15 km

© Carta, Jerusalem

David's Life as a Fugitive.
In a series of dodge and feint moves that must have frustrated Saul to no end, David and his band of fugitives crisscrossed the Shephelah, hill country and wilderness of Judah, staying one step ahead of the Israelite king. At the same time, David worked hard to shift the allegiance of the people of Judah to himself, and built a formidable power base in the process.

loyalists at almost every turn. Saul, a northern villager, lacked the natural affinity that David had in this region. David used his wilderness survival skills to the fullest and practiced a clever kind of diplomacy that won respect among some elements of Judah that previously had found no reason to support him (e.g., 1 Sam 25:2–42). He also continued to marry well—to Abigail, widow of a wealthy Calebite from Maon deep in the southern hill country (1 Sam 25:2, 25:42) and Ahinoam of Jezreel in the north (1 Sam 25:43), a region that would typically be sympathetic to Saul (cf. 1 Sam 28:4). Both marriages cemented alliances with important bases of support for David in Israel.

It is clear that David's experiences in the wilderness, both as a young shepherd and as a leader of men, strengthened his abilities, character and resolve to meet the more difficult challenges that he would face later in life. Many of the Psalms attributed to David speak of rough terrain, mighty rocks, strongholds and deliverers. David drew on a number of very tangible personal experiences to express his dependence on the power and provision of God in times of intense need (Ps 18, 23, 31, 32, 37, 55, 61, 62, 63):

In You, O LORD, I have taken refuge;
    let me never be ashamed;
    in your righteousness deliver me.
Incline Your ear to me, rescue me quickly;
    be to me a rock of strength,

a stronghold to save me.
For You are my rock and my fortress,
    for Your name's sake You will lead me
    and guide me.
You will pull me out of the net which they
        have secretly laid for me;
    for you are my strength.
Into Your hand I commit my spirit;
    You have ransomed me, O LORD, God of truth.
                                        (Ps 31:1–5)

Hear my cry, O God;
    give heed to my prayer.
From the end of the earth I call to You,

Drawing on survival instincts he learned as a shepherd, David and his band fled to the stark landscape of the wilderness of Judah. But they were not alone in this empty land—shepherds attached to cities and villages loyal to Saul silently monitored David's movements, and the hunt and chase was on.

Crags and cliffs abound in the Wadi Suweinit between Gibeah and Jericho, typical of an up-close look at the landscape of the entire wilderness region. For David, the "sweet Psalmist of Israel," the entire region was inspiring: "Lead me to the rock that is higher than I, for You have been a refuge for me, a tower of strength against the enemy…" (Ps 61:2–3).

The Origin of David's Mighty Men. *As Saul's leadership faltered, men who for a variety of reasons were dissatisfied with his rule or otherwise disenfranchised from society hitched themselves to the rising star from Bethlehem. Although most of David's band of mighty men hailed from Judah, some came from regions that should have been loyal to Saul.*

> *when my heart is faint;*
> *lead me to the rock that is higher than I.*
> *For You have been a refuge for me,*
> *a tower of strength against the enemy.*
> *Let me dwell in Your tent forever;*
> *let me take refuge in the shelter of Your wings.*
> (Ps 61:1–4)

The enemies in the Book of Psalms are timeless and usually unnamed, but are certainly no less real than those that David faced on a daily basis. Twice he was betrayed to Saul by the men of Ziph, Judeans he had hoped would be his allies (1 Sam 23:15–29, 26:1–5). The loyalties of these men to Saul can be both understood and excused, for the king had been successful in ridding them of the Amalekite threat (1 Sam 15:1–9). Perhaps unsure of whom he could trust, yet wanting to maintain a base of operations near Judah, David decided to relocate his militia to Gath where he at least knew who his enemies were (1 Sam 27:1–4). His pretext to

Achish was that his band would become mercenaries for the Philistines. David's base of operations was at Ziklag, probably *Tel Sera* in the far southern Philistine Plain. From there he defended the southern border of the Philistines against various desert tribes: Amalekites, Girzites and Geshurites (1 Sam 27:5–9, 30:1–25; the latter is not to be confused with the Aramean kingdom of Geshur in northern Transjordan into which David would later marry; cf. 2 Sam 3:3, 15:8). Ziklag was far enough from Gath for David to operate out of site of Achish, and he reported to Achish that he was raiding tribes associated with Judah (1 Sam 27:10–12). In fact, by securing the southern border of Philistia he was *de facto* ridding Judah of the same enemies. Perhaps more importantly, after David soundly defeated the Amalekites he shared the spoils-of-war with people living in the regions of Judah where he and his band had previously fled from Saul (1 Sam 30:26–31). By doing so, he finally won their support.

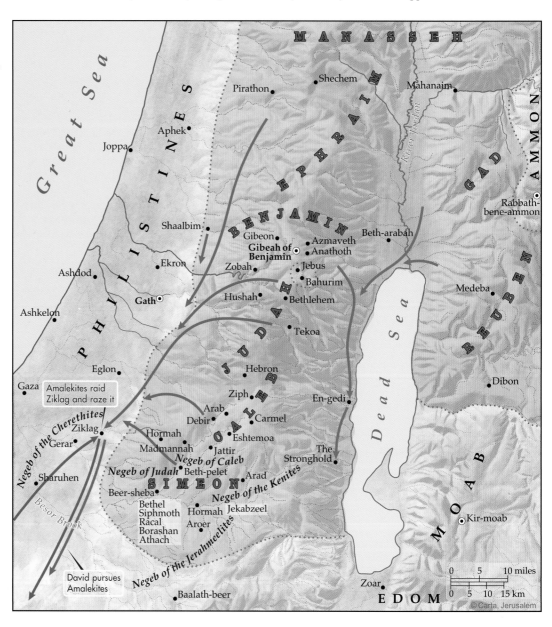

With Saul confined to the northern hill country, the Jordan Valley and Gilead, and with David seemingly now an ally of Achish, the Philistines prepared for their most ambitious strike yet: north along the coastal plain, into and through the Jezreel Valley to Shunem (1 Sam 28:4)—areas apparently already open to Philistine influence (cf. Judg 3:31)—then on to Beth-shean. The strategic importance of Beth-shean is obvious to anyone who stands on the site on a clear day, with Mt. Carmel and the full sweep of Transjordan from the foothills of Mt. Hermon to the rise above the Plains of Moab in view. The Philistine route to Beth-shean followed the international highway through Canaan and mirrored precisely the priorities of Egypt's New Kingdom Pharaohs. But by now Egyptian authority in the region had waned, due in part to Philistine incursions against Rameses III in the early twelfth century B.C., and because the Israelites had not been able to secure the valleys and plains from the Canaanites (cf. Judg 1:27–33), the Philistines seized the opportunity to fill the void. Whoever controlled this international route, with its important junctures and agricultural resources, would be the major player in Canaan.

Achish called on David to support the Philistine thrust from Shunem to Beth-shean. David's answer was diplomatically non-committal, precise yet ambiguous; Achish, giddy over the reports of David's action in the south, took it as a "yes" (1 Sam 28:1–2). The Philistines mustered at Aphek for their march north, but division in the ranks gave David the "out" he needed to avoid the battle against his own people and allowed him—and his patron Achish—to save face (1 Sam 29:1–11). The battle took place at the critical juncture of the Jezreel and Harod valleys, with Israel camped at the village of Jezreel on the lowest flank of Mt. Gilboa and the Philistines at Shunem hugging the base of Mt. Moreh, directly opposite to the north (1 Sam 28:4, 29:1). It was nearly the same battlefield alignment with which Gideon had routed the Midianites (Judg 7:1), but this time the Israelites fled defeated, with both Saul and the crown prince, Jonathan, dead (1 Sam 31:1–6). David's grief-filled response was genuine and overwhelming (2 Sam 1:1–27); he may have been at odds with Saul, but Saul was his anointed king and Jonathan his friend. Worse yet, David's people had been humiliated and his fledgling nation cut in two and gutted.

With Israel on the brink of chaos, David pressed to seize control. He was anointed king over Judah at Hebron by popular acclaim—one might say in triumph—and reigned from there for seven and one-half years (2 Sam 2:1–4, 2:11). Hebron was the most prominent city in the Judean hill country, favored for its commanding geographical position and as such a natural choice for David's capital. Up north, the remnant of Saul's family and army crossed the Jordan River to Mahanaim, a city

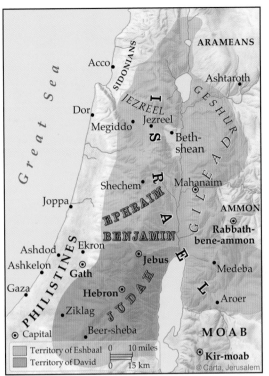

The Kingdoms of David and Eshbaal (Ish-bosheth). *The fledgling kingdom of Israel broke in two at the death of Saul and Jonathan. David seized the smaller, southern block dominated by the tribe of Judah, and one of Saul's remaining sons, Eshbaal (whom the writer of Kings nicknamed Ish-bosheth, "Man of Shame") maintained some control over the north. Though he possessed the lion's share of territory, Eshbaal was generally ineffective as a ruler and his kingdom was quickly swallowed by David.*

tucked into the cleft of the Jabbok River amid the rugged hills of Gilead. Here, in a place of refuge, Saul's general Abner orchestrated the royal line of succession by proclaiming Ish-bosheth (Eshbaal; 1 Chron 8:33), the dead king's son, as king "over Gilead, over the Ashurites, over Jezreel, over Ephraim, and over Benjamin, even over all Israel" (2 Sam 2:8–10). This list of place-names is telling: the house of Saul maintained control over Gilead and Ephraim—the block of hills on either side of the Jordan River—but the northern tribes (Issachar, Zebulun, Naphtali and Asher), if ever under Saul's command, were gone, severed by the Philistine thrust through the Jezreel Valley, as was Judah. It was a truncated, isolated Israel at best. The Philistines must have been ecstatic. Their nemesis to the east had been reduced to two rival petty states, one scrambling to maintain control over bits and pieces, the other trying to jump-start what was left.

David and his supporters fought a long civil war against the remnants of the house of Saul (2 Sam 3:1). A critical first battle, at the pool of Gibeon (2 Sam 2:12–23), was for control over Saul's land of Benjamin, a strategic region for Judah as it provided not only a buffer to the north but the best access point from the watershed ridge to the coast (via Gezer) and to the Jordan Valley (through Jericho). A mammoth, circular stone-cut pit that has been found at Gibeon, with a stepped tunnel providing access to the city's spring, is a good candidate for this pool. The battle was personal and fierce—the mighty men

This stone-cut staircase, spiraling down a 37-foot wide, 35-foot deep cylindrical pit at Gibeon, is connected to a sloped tunnel dropping another 45 vertical feet to a freshwater chamber below. The ones who hewed out this water system at Gibeon during the Iron Age removed approximately 3,000 tons of limestone in their effort. Although the pit itself didn't hold water, it is usually identified with the "pool at Gibeon" where David's mighty men defeated the mighty men of Saul in hand-to-hand combat. (photo: Garo Nalbandian)

David's Move to Jebus (Jerusalem). *David's choice of Jebus (Jerusalem) as the new capital of Israel was intended to establish common ground between south and north, and to found a city that belonged not just to one tribe but to everyone—and to the royal house. The Philistines twice tried to snip David's kingdom in the bud by attacking Jerusalem through the rugged hills southwest of the city; twice David drove them back to the coast (2 Sam 5:17–25).*

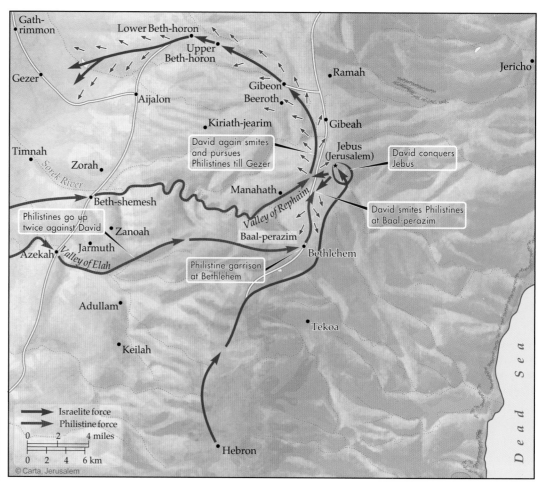

This engraving of the so-called Upper Pool of Siloam appearing in Charles Wilson's Picturesque Palestine, Sinai and Egypt *(1880) shows a water collection pool near Jerusalem's Gihon Spring as it looked in the 19th century. Many early European explorers described the spring and the rubble remains in its vicinity. Wilson commented: "[The water's] taste is slightly salt and decidedly unpleasant, owing chiefly to the fact that the water has filtered through the mass of rubbish and filth on which the city stands…the people make matters worse by bathing and washing their clothes in the same place from which they draw water for drinking purposes"* (Wilson, Jerusalem, 103)

of David, led by his general Joab, against the mighty men of Abner, general of Saul—and David's men prevailed (2 Sam 2:24–32).

David's efforts at bringing all Israel under his control were focused not only on the battlefield. His diplomatic skills, already proven effective during his rise to power in Judah, gained him inroads among the supporters of the house of Saul. David's first entreaty was to the residents of Jabesh-gilead, Saul's family stronghold in northern Transjordan (2 Sam 2:4–7). David also renewed his marriage to Saul's daughter Michal, thereby hoping to unite the royal houses under his single control. Earlier Saul had given Michal to Paltiel to undercut David's growing popularity (1 Sam 25:44) and now her current husband had to take a back seat to political expediency (2 Sam 3:12–16). Most importantly, David attempted to strike a peace deal with Abner. For David, the goal of the coalition was to build strength through alliance; for Abner, who was at odds with Ish-bosheth, it was a means of survival (2 Sam 3:17–25). When Joab assassinated Abner in an act of single-minded zeal, David's overtures to the house of Saul were nearly torpedoed, but by offering his open hand, David saved his reputation among Saul's supporters (2 Sam 3:26–39). Ish-bosheth, too, was assassinated, a tragic victim of his own weak-

ness and the rash act of subordinates who had decided to do David a favor (2 Sam 4:1–8). Again, in avenging the murder of his rival, David showed the kind of honor that compelled the majority of Israel to accept his rule (2 Sam 4:9–5:5).

One of David's first acts as king of all Israel was to move his capital from Hebron to Jerusalem (2 Sam 5:6–9). This was a wise political move on a number of counts. David realized that Hebron was too far south geographically and too Judean culturally to give him credibility with the tribes in the north. He had to find a city more centrally located, preferably one that would not give priority to one tribe over another. Jerusalem (Jebus) had been allotted to the tribe of Benjamin (Josh 15:8, 18:16, 18:28), yet remained a Jebusite (Canaanite) enclave deep in the central hill country. Although Saul's Gibeah lay only five miles north, Israel's first king was unable to, or uninterested in, bringing Jerusalem into the Benjaminite orbit. David redeemed the city and its holdings—thereby gaining favor among the people of Benjamin—but rather than turn Jerusalem over to them he maintained the city's independence, transforming it into a capital for all Israel. The Jebusite fortress had been called the Stronghold of Zion; with its capture, Zion became the City of David, the royal seat of an Israelite national dynasty.

Although the significance of the archaeological and pre-biblical documentary evidence for Jebusite Jerusalem is debated, it appears that the city was an important, well-fortified center in the centuries prior to David's conquest. Jerusalem boasted a sophisticated water system that improved public access to the water of the Gihon Spring at the base of its eastern wall, and a palace complex at the city's higher, northern end. Although Jerusalem was nearly two thousand years old when David got there, this was the beginning of a very special relationship between the city and its new inhabitants. Jerusalem's rise to international prominence under the Davidic dynasty cannot be explained on geopolitical factors alone; in terms of sheer strategic presence and defensibility the capital cities of Israel's eastern rivals, Ammon (Rabbah), Moab (Kir) and Edom (Bozrah), are all better situated, and Aram-Damascus is located at a point to control international traffic in the entire southern Levant. Rather, Jerusalem would become one of the world's greatest cities, a city of emotion, song, hope and praise, on the strength of its unique tie to God and the dynasty that He chose to represent His Name on earth (Ps 48, 121, 122, 125):

> [He] chose the tribe of Judah,
>   Mount Zion which He loved.
> And He built His sanctuary like the heights, like the
>   earth which He has founded forever.
> He also chose David His servant,
>   and took him from the sheepfolds.
> From the care of the ewes with suckling lambs He
>   brought him,
> to shepherd Jacob His people, and Israel his
>   inheritance.
> So he strengthened them according to the integrity
>   of his heart,
>   and guided them with his skillful hands.
>   (Ps 78:68–72)

David's move to unite the tribes of Israel at Jerusalem drew a response from Israel's neighbors. Now that David was a *bona fide* player in the international arena of the southern Levant, Hiram king of Tyre initiated commercial contacts with him (2 Sam 5:11–12). The seafaring Phoenicians were the recognized economic middlemen of the region, especially with Egypt in decline, always ready to develop new markets and reestablish old ones. Because Phoenicia lacked adequate agricultural land to support itself, it relied on good relations with its neighbors to the south, formerly Egypt but now also Israel, for foodstuffs (1 Kgs 5:10–11; Ezek 27:17; Acts 12:20), and Israel admired and coveted Phoenician timber (1 Kgs 5:10; 2 Kgs 19:23; Isa 60:13). Established trading practices in the ancient Near East prompted kings to send "greeting gifts" to other kings in an attempt to win favorable trade relations (cf. Amarna texts 5, 9–10, 15–17, 37, 40); David benefited to the tune of a new palace built with the finest Phoenician materials and workmanship. Economic cooperation overrode the need for military conquest, and the Phoenicians remained allies of Israel throughout the biblical period.

The Philistines responded to David's conquest of Jerusalem too, but with a show of military force. Clearly David was no longer a Philistine vassal; his move to unite Israel through Jerusalem was a gauntlet that could not be ignored. Twice the Philistines penetrated the rugged hills west of Jerusalem and besieged the new Israelite capital from the Valley of Rephaim (2 Sam 5:17–25; cf. Josh 15:8); twice David flushed them out of the hills. With these victories and a follow-up campaign at Gath (1 Chron 18:1; called the Philistine's "chief city" in 2 Sam 8:1), David—at least for the time being—had removed the Philistine threat from Israel. It can be assumed that Philistine control of the northern coastal plain and Jezreel Valley also fell to David, and that Israel was able to subdue old Canaanite urban centers of the region such as Beth-shean, Taanach, Ibleam, Megiddo and Dor (cf. Judg 1:27–28). It would be a mistake, however, to assume that the Philistines stayed put, for they were never really conquered by David, only temporarily contained. Notices toward the end of David's reign speak of ongoing Philistine incursions in the Shephelah, perhaps sparked by the notion that if David was growing old, the nation of Israel must be weakening as well (2 Sam 21:15–22).

In the meantime, with the city-states and kingdoms to the west and northwest under Israelite control David could turn his attention to some domestic matters. Problems of tribal unification still loomed large and David took two steps internally to bring the nation together. One was essentially symbolic, yet with clear practical ends. David allowed Mephibosheth, Saul's lame son and the last hope of his truncated dynasty, to "eat at the king's table." By doing so, David bestowed status, honor and provision on Mephibosheth (2 Sam 9:1–13; cf. 2 Sam 4:4), gaining his loyalty and hopefully that of others who had supported Saul in the process (but cf. 2 Sam 16:1–4). The second was distinctly practical, yet had important symbolic aspects. With great pomp and circumstance David brought the Ark of the Covenant from Kiriath-jearim—it had lacked a proper home since the Philistines had destroyed Shiloh—to Jerusalem (2 Sam 6:1–23; cf. 1 Sam 6:1–21).

Every city and kingdom in the ancient Near East melded religion and politics into a single powerful force. For instance, David's inner cabinet included men in charge of affairs-of-state (e.g., the judiciary, revenue and the army) and religion (2 Sam 8:15–18, 20:23–26). It was necessary and proper, therefore,

The hulking mass of stones over the traditional tomb of Hiram, king of Tyre, preserves for all time the memory of one of the greatest of the Phoenician kings. Hiram rode a surging wave of sea-borne trade to reinforce Phoenician commercial dominance in the eastern Mediterranean. By the end of the 10th century B.C. the Phoenicians had established colonies in Cyprus, Sicily and Sardinia. Hiram's land partners, David and Solomon, only benefited from their economic ties to Phoenicia.

The Ark of the Covenant was meant to give tangible form to the presence of God dwelling among His people. Its proper resting place was in the Temple in Jerusalem. (Leen Ritmeyer)

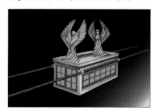

that David provide opportunity for himself and all Israel to give full expression to their national covenant with the LORD God in Jerusalem, now the political *and* religious capital of Israel. David knew that a formal temple for the LORD must be built. Through his prophet Nathan, God told David that his "house and kingdom shall endure forever," but that his son—yet unnamed—would build the temple (2 Sam 7:1–29).

David's efforts at fostering tribal unification through national and religious means are admirable. In the end, however, the centrifugal forces pulling the kingdom apart were never overcome and continued to hound both David and Solomon throughout their reigns.

Equally troubling were threats on Israel's eastern frontier. It is difficult to construct an exact chronology of David's wars of conquest in Transjordan, and it can be assumed that his battles there consumed a significant portion of his reign. A probable sequence of events becomes apparent based on the overall geographical and political realities that faced David and the kings of Moab, Ammon, Edom and the Aramean states. David aimed not only to secure his eastern frontier but to make his nation the most powerful single state in the Levant. His enemies were largely reduced to defensive strategies to check Israel's influence in Transjordan and the north.

David's first move was against Moab, a decisive thrust in the face of his blood-ties with the people of the land and his history of peaceful relations with its king (2 Sam 8:2; cf. Ruth 4:13–22; 1 Sam 22:3–4). Moab always had eyes for the Medeba Plateau, the former kingdom of Sihon that Moses had given to Reuben (Num 21:21–32; Deut 2:26–37). This was a strategic gateway between peoples living on either side of the Dead Sea, and David's main concern was to restore unimpeded access to the region for Israel. David's move posed a threat to Hanun king of the Ammonites, who also needed the plateau as his own front line of expansion. Hanun marshaled support from Beth-rehob, Zobah, Maacah and Tob, emerging Aramean states in northern Transjordan and the northern Rift Valley, and engaged David's army east of Medeba, but the Ammonite-Aramean coalition was routed by Joab (2 Sam 10:1–14).

With the Medeba Plateau under David's control, Hadad-ezer king of Zobah pulled together an even larger coalition of Aramean states from as far north as the Euphrates to try to stop David from advancing to Damascus. The battle lines were drawn at Helam in eastern Bashan, across the same pivotal land between Israel, Ammon and Aram-Damascus that Moses had taken from Og (Num 21:33–35; Deut 3:1–11). David had already established some influence in the area by marrying Maacah, the daughter of the king of Geshur, an autonomous kingdom in western Bashan

(2 Sam 3:3), but for Hadad-ezer, David's current series of campaigns forced a military response. Again, David's forces routed the Arameans, and many members of the coalition became David's vassals (2 Sam 10:15–19). When Hadad-ezer tried to restore his control over the north Aramean states who were now Israel's allies, David took the battle directly to Damascus, routing the Aramean army, decimating its chariot force and occupying the city with garrisons (2 Sam 8:3–8). Under the Middle Eastern adage "the enemy of my enemy is my friend," Toi king of Hamath, the major Aramean kingdom just north of Damascus and a state always at odds with its southern neighbor, established a treaty of joint-recognition with David (2 Sam 8:9–10).

At some point during David's wars of conquest in Transjordan the battle was taken directly to the Ammonite capital, Rabbah (2 Sam 11:1). The site of ancient Rabbah—the modern Citadel of Amman—is well situated to withstand attack, and Israel fell into a prolonged siege against the city. It was during the course of the siege that David committed his greatest sequence of sins—adultery, cover-up and murder (2 Sam 11:1–12:23). One of his prized generals, Uriah, was dead, as was David's illicit infant son. Bathsheba, the woman of the affair, ended up as David's favorite wife and the mother of the crown prince, Solomon (2 Sam 12:24–25). Rabbah finally fell to David, and Ammon became Israel's vassal (2 Sam 12:26–31).

David certainly didn't need the "Bathsheba Affair," which came just as his efforts at kingdom building were reaching a climax. Every other monarch in the ancient Near East would have responded, "So what's the big deal? The land, everything and every*one* in it belong to me and I can do whatever I want with them." Some later kings of Israel had the same idea (e.g., 1 Kgs 21:1–29). But for David, God's anointed one, the expectation that a king should care for the fatherless and widows—and everyone else under his charge—was more than just the image-enhancing rhetoric typical of others. The righteousness and justice that extended from Israel's covenant with the LORD on Mt. Sinai demanded that the rights of everyone be protected, privilege notwithstanding. And certainly David, a commoner by birth, would have known better. Perhaps he initially tried to justify his cover-up by reasoning that he *was* performing his kingly duty by taking care of this new widow. In the end, David's heart-felt remorse (Ps 51:1–19) is not only a timeless example of true repentance, but shows that *this* king was different than the others and worthy of launching a very special kingdom.

With Rabbah in the Israelite fold, only southern Transjordan was left. David's army defeated Edom in the Valley of Salt, the wasteland of the Rift Valley abutting the southern end of the Dead

David's Campaign Against Moab. *In order to secure his eastern frontier, David had to subdue Moab. The victory was necessary yet difficult on a personal level, as this was the homeland of David's great-grandmother, Ruth.*

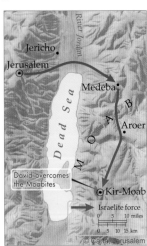

DAVID'S KINGDOM

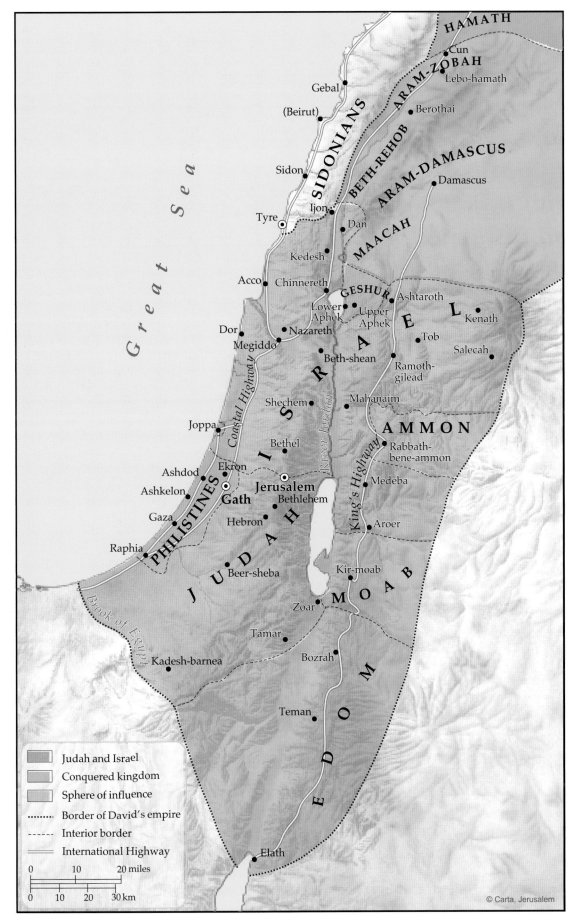

HAMATH

Cun

ARAM-ZOBAH

Lebo-hamath

Gebal

Berothai

(Beirut)

SIDONIANS

BETH-REHOB

ARAM-DAMASCUS

Sidon

Damascus

Ijon

Tyre

Dan

MAACAH

Kedesh

Acco   Chinnereth

GESHUR   Ashtaroth

Lower   Upper

Aphek   Aphek

Kenath

Dor

Nazareth

Tob

Megiddo

Beth-shean

Salecah

Ramoth-

gilead

Shechem

Mahanaim

AMMON

Joppa

Bethel

Rabbath-

bene-ammon

Ashdod

Ekron

Medeba

Ashkelon

Jerusalem

Gath   Bethlehem

Gaza

Hebron

Aroer

Raphia

PHILISTINES

Beer-sheba

Kir-moab

JUDAH

MOAB

Zoar

Tamar

Bozrah

Kadesh-barnea

EDOM

Teman

Great Sea

ISRAEL

River Jordan

Coastal Highway

King's Highway

Brook of Egypt

Elath

	Judah and Israel
	Conquered kingdom
	Sphere of influence
⋯⋯⋯	Border of David's empire
---	Interior border
═══	International Highway

0   10   20 miles

0   10   20   30 km

© Carta, Jerusalem

59

Sea, and established garrisons throughout the land of Edom. Edomite hopes rested with their crown prince, Hadad, who fled to exile in Egypt where he was wined and dined as an Egyptian tool to someday help restore Egypt's hegemony in the Levant (1 Kgs 11:14–22).

David's nominal control of the entire Levant, from the Sinai to the Euphrates River, was now complete; with it, the covenant that God had made with Abraham, "to your descendants I have given this land, from the river of Egypt as far as the great river, the River Euphrates," had been realized (cf. 1 Kgs 4:21; cf. Gen 15:18). This is the kingdom that God had bequeathed to David, and David passed on to Solomon. The borders of Israel and Judah were at their maximum and included the lands that Moses had conquered in Transjordan; Israel's Transjordanian neighbors, Edom, Moab, Ammon and Aram-Damascus, were also conquered and occupied, and the Philistines and north Aramean states were reduced to vassal status. David's census, implemented by Joab, was aimed at gauging the relative military strength of the Israel-Judah core of the empire (2 Sam 24:1–9). The task of actually governing this complex behemoth eventually fell to Solomon, and taxed that king's abilities to the fullest.

Unfortunately, David's success on the battlefield was not replicated at home. His own family was plagued by the bitter fruit of raw ambition, jealousy and strife, and mirrored the internal weaknesses that would always threaten the moral fiber of Israel. In particular, David had trouble with several of his sons, born to different mothers and motivated more by rivalry than filial affection. Kings typically had multiple wives in the ancient world, partly to cement diplomatic relations and partly as a sign of wealth and prestige. Often a lesser queen would try to advance her influence within the royal household—and the nation at large—by positioning one of her sons as heir-apparent at the expense of the oldest son of the favorite wife. David's house was not exempt from such palace intrigue.

David's son Amnon, whose mother was Ahinoam from the northern city Jezreel, raped his half-sister Tamar. Her full-brother, Absalom, one of David's favorites, arranged Amnon's murder, then fled to Geshur, the homeland of his mother, Maacah, where he remained for three years (2 Sam 13:1–39; cf. 2 Sam 3:2–3). Ironically, although the name Absalom means "father of peace," his actions brought just the opposite to a beleaguered David, who, in spite of fatherly yearnings for his son, had trouble forgiving Absalom's deed (2 Sam 14:1–33).

Eventually restored to favor, Absalom promptly began to position himself as the crown prince. Apparently David was too preoccupied with larger affairs of state to notice, and his attention to all the tribes of Israel rather than just Judah caused the old guard of Hebron to feel neglected. Absalom, handsome and ambitious, played on the sympathies of the people of Judah and ignited a revolt against David in Hebron that quickly spread to all Israel, including key people in David's court (2 Sam 15:1–13). Years before, God had spoken through the prophet Nathan and promised that upon David's death, the kingdom would pass to one of his sons (2 Sam 7:12–16); Absalom advanced the notion that the prophet had spoken of *him*, and, like the Prodigal (Lk 15:11–12), was unwilling to wait for his father to die.

With all previous loyalties—sincere and otherwise—in question, David had to act wisely, and quickly. Realizing that Absalom's full power had yet to be tapped, David fled from Jerusalem up and over the Mount of Olives, weeping in the face of uncertainties to come (2 Sam 15:14–37); centuries later, a descendant of David would descend the same mount, weeping over the future of the same city (Lk 19:37–44). Taking advantage of their king's plight, remnants of the house of Saul found opportunity to vent their long-suppressed hostility to David's rule (2 Sam 16:1–14). David planted a trusted friend, Hushai, as undercover agent in Jerusalem (2 Sam 15:32–37), and Hushai's counsel to Absalom allowed David to escape across the Jordan River to Mahanaim, the same place, ironically, to which Ish-bosheth had fled at the death of Saul to try to reestablish his own kingdom (2 Sam 16:15–17:24; cf. 2 Sam 2:8). The battle was joined in the Forest of Ephraim, the densely overgrown western slopes of Gilead above the Jordan Valley. David's loyalists defeated Absalom's army of Israel, and, much to the dismay of David, Absalom himself was killed (2 Sam 18:1–33). As at the death of Saul, David's anguish over his fallen foe was genuine. By sharing the grief of Absalom's followers rather than gloating in triumph over their downfall, and by dealing kindly with those who had encouraged Absalom's revolt, including Absalom's general Amasa, David compelled the loyalty of all Israel (2 Sam 19:1–43).

But not of everyone. In a now familiar storyline, Sheba, who belonged to Saul's tribe of Benjamin, attempted to rally the northern tribes against Judah, playing on their local pride, regional nationalism and age-old suspicion of anything southern (2 Sam 20:1–2). David directed Amasa to crush the revolt; Amasa's delay in carrying out David's orders betrayed his true loyalties and gave occasion for Joab, Amasa's personal rival, to assassinate him (2 Sam 20:4–12). It was now a matter for David's mighty men and personal bodyguards (the Cherethites and Pelethites, Philistine mercenaries from David's early days [2 Sam 15:18–22]), those who were above personal squabbles and whose loyalty to their king was unquestioned. Sheba was tracked down in Abel-beth-maacah, a city guarding the northern frontier of

Israel, where the townsfolk did him in rather than confront the horrors of siege (2 Sam 20:13–22).

David faced revolt for the last time on his death-bed. Adonijah, born of the lesser queen Haggith and possessing the charisma and charm of his half-brother Absalom, rallied key support from David's inner cabinet, including Joab, and proceeded to have himself anointed king (1 Kgs 1:1–10). While the festivities were in progress at En-rogel, a spring at the juncture of the Kidron and Hinnom valleys just south of Jerusalem, the prophet Nathan advised Bathsheba, David's favorite wife, to prompt the king to have his chosen successor, Solomon, anointed immediately (1 Kgs 1:11–37). This was done at the Gihon Spring, within the protection of the fortified tower above the spring (lest the people prefer Adonijah's rule to that of Solomon), yet within shouting range of the crowds down at En-rogel to let them know the tide had just changed (1 Kgs 1:38–40). This tower, though not mentioned in the biblical text, has been uncovered by archaeological excavations and offers a reasonable setting for the anointing ceremony. David's decision to anoint a successor while he was still alive was both expedient and brilliant. The precedent of co-regency was followed by many of David's successors and gave internal strength to the Davidic dynasty by establishing a known chain of succession. The kings of the northern kingdom of Israel, who did not adopt this practice, suffered one *coup d'état* after another.

David died in peace, his kingdom established and borders secure (1 Kgs 2:1–12). In some ways the tasks that Solomon faced were as difficult as his father's, for loyalties could not be assumed and Solomon's own hands had not been hardened in battle. Moreover, a rich son in the public eye too often succumbs to the playboy syndrome, and Solomon had certain tendencies that had to be refined. Because a new nation is most at risk during its first transfer of power, Solomon had to show decisive leadership or David's legacy would be in vain.

His first order of business was to remove any hint of insurrection among those close to the throne. Abiathar the priest, who had been loyal to David from the early days, was removed from office and banished to his home in Nob because he had chosen to side with Adonijah (1 Kgs 2:26–27). Solomon had the chief of David's personal bodyguard, Benaiah, kill David's general, Joab, whose loyalties had also turned to Adonijah (1 Kgs 2:5–6, 2:28–35; cf. 2 Sam 20:23). As for himself Adonijah created the excuse to be executed by insulting David's honor when he asked to marry Abishag. The noble Abishag (a Shunammite northerner!) had shown David the respect due his position and age during his frail last days while Adonijah had been plotting to take the throne (1 Kgs 2:19–25; cf. 1 Kgs 1:1–4). Finally, Shimei, one of the most dangerous members of Saul's family, one

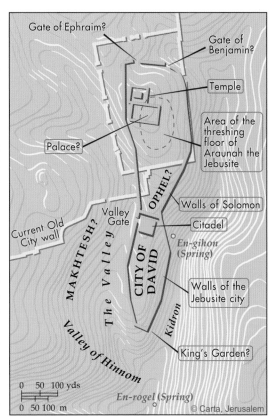

The Jerusalem of David and Solomon. *The ancient city of Jebus became the City of David with the Israelite king's conquest of its citadel, the Jebusite "stronghold of Zion." The city grew to the north to encompass Araunah's threshing floor, a mount which became the site of the great Temple to the LORD and eventually took the name Zion for itself.*

who showed his true colors when given the opportunity and hid them when it was expedient to save his own neck, was also put to death (1 Kgs 2:36–46; cf. 2 Sam 16:5–14, 19:16–23; 1 Kgs 2:8–9). In a region of the world where strength and honor are among the highest values, and where insurgents—and there are always plenty to be found—exploit any show of weakness in their rivals, Solomon had to have an iron hand, even against members of David's trusted old guard. At the same time, faithfulness was rewarded; Zadok was named high priest, and Benaiah, general (1 Kgs 2:35). With these few quick strokes, the kingdom was established and Solomon could look forward to a long reign of prosperity and peace.

The focal point of Solomon's kingdom was the city of Jerusalem, where two magnificent new buildings were constructed. These were the royal palace and the temple, and each represented one of the two primary institutions of the state. Although no archaeological remains of either have been found, it is certain that the palace would have been at the northern, higher and more secure end of the city where Solomon could have full view of his subjects (and they of him), and the temple above that. (On the other hand, the King's Garden was located on the opposite end of the city in the fertile confluence of the Kidron and Hinnom valleys. This was the setting of the "nature rendezvous" in the Song of Songs, where the prince could meet his young lady friend far from daddy's eyes.) David had purchased a threshing floor from Araunah (Ornan) the Jebusite, and it was over this exposed expanse

Simple lives lived securely, each with sufficient provision for the day—this was the idea behind the biblical phrase that characterized the reign of Solomon: "every man under his own vine and fig tree" (1 Kgs 4:25). We could add the olive to this list, the most beautiful and productive tree in the hill country of Judah and a fitting reminder of the quiet endurance of Israel in the land.

Solomon fortified three cities on the international highway: Hazor, Megiddo and Gezer (1 Kgs 9:15). He walled all three with casemate (double) walls and six-chambered gates. The approach to the gate at Gezer, shown here, was from the direction of Jerusalem. Perched above the outer end of the Aijalon Valley, Gezer was Jerusalem's eyes to the coast, and control of the region was critical if Solomon hoped to maintain his edge on the economy of the Levant.

of bedrock north of the city that the temple was built (2 Sam 24:18–25; 2 Chron 3:1–2). Appropriately the temple was the highest building in Solomon's Jerusalem, commanding a hill to which worshippers would ascend toward God. This became *Mount Zion*, co-opting the name of David's conquered Jebusite fortress (Ps 74:2; 125:1; cf. 2 Sam 5:7). Ironically, the hills surrounding Jerusalem were all higher than the temple mount, and it was perhaps this geographical reality that prompted the Psalmist, in a holy burst of local pride, to compare Mount Zion favorably to Mount Sion (Hermon), the lofty, blessed, divine mountain of the far north (Ps 48:1–2, 68:15–16; cf. Deut 4:48).

Solomon's royal palace and temple were built with the help of Hiram, king of Tyre, who provided the necessary construction materials, workmen and expertise to do the job (1 Kgs 5:1–12). By doing so, Hiram renewed the economic treaty that he had established with David (2 Sam 5:11–12). Israel is a land overgrown with stone and scrub brush, wholly lacking fine timber, so now that Solomon had access to cedar and cypress from Phoenicia, he used the strength, size and beauty of their logs to build structures the like of which had never been seen in Israel. Solomon's palace and the temple were adorned with wooden floors set on large, cut stone foundations, walls paneled in cedar and ceilings spanned by great wooden beams (1 Kgs 6:1–7:51). Both buildings incorporated north Syrian and Egyptian designs and motifs, and reflected nicely Solomon's growing status in the ancient Near East. Of course, the temple was first and foremost a place worthy of the presence of the LORD God, and its architectural and artistic elements portrayed God's interaction with His people at creation and on Mt. Sinai, while allowing the Israelites to publicly express their ongoing covenantal relationship with Him. The temple was dedicated in a fantastic ceremony in which Solomon bound himself and his people to God, and then blessed and thanked God for fulfilling the promises He had made to Abraham, Moses and David (1 Kgs 8:1–66).

Solomon was not above acknowledging that God's promises had *him*, specifically, in mind (1 Kgs 8:15–21, 8:25–26), and it would take all the wisdom that he could muster (and God could give) for him to govern his kingdom in ways that benefited his people (1 Kgs 3:3–15, 9:1–9). Problems facing families and individuals, such as that of the two women with one live baby (1 Kgs 3:16–28), were always at hand. More intractable were those that had the potential to tear at the entire social fabric of the kingdom, such as the ongoing need to foster tribal unity and the dilemma of how to bring indigenous Canaanite elements still found in the land under the Israelite umbrella. The list of Solomon's twelve district governors (1 Kgs 4:7–19) indicates that the new national administration respected the old tribal boundaries, while incorporating the Canaanite lowlands conquered by David into new districts. In this way Solomon struck a balance between the expediency of allowing established tribes to maintain their individual identities, and the necessity of binding everyone to the good of the kingdom. Each of the districts was responsible for sending the equivalent of one month's supply of foodstuffs and provisions to the "king's table" (taxes to support the royal bureaucracy; 1 Kgs 4:21–28) and providing corvée workers for royal projects (1 Kgs 5:13–18, 9:15, 9:17–23). While the lifestyle of the rich and famous (Solomon and his inner circle) was extravagant (1 Kgs 4:21–24, 4:26–28), the people of the land were generally satisfied, each living "under his own vine and his fig tree" (1 Kgs 4:20, 4:25). It's a picture of "the good life" such as a typical tenth-century B.C. Israelite could hope to gain, with everyone rejoicing in God and king and secure in their station in life.

David had forged political alliances throughout the Levant, alliances that Solomon reaffirmed with a series of royal marriages and sealed by building shrines in Jerusalem dedicated to his wives' homeland deities (1 Kgs 11:1–8). But now he cast a wider net. The closest major player in the international arena was Egypt. Egypt's ability to control affairs in the Levant had declined steadily over the previous two centuries, and with the rise of the United Kingdom of David and Solomon, the Egyptian Pharaoh (probably Siamun) had to play the game of international relations with all the skill he could muster. Egypt's goal was to try to foster good relations with its former vassal states in order to maintain commercial interests along the coast, all the while with an eye to destabilizing Israel and reestablishing Egyptian imperial interests there. Complicating matters, it is likely that with the death of David, the Philistines tried to re-exert their influence along the coast (cf. 2 Sam 21:15–22). In response, Egypt would have first needed to check the Philistine advance—their major threat in the region since the days of Rameses III—in order to maintain open land and sea routes to Phoenicia.

To do so, Siamun turned to Israel. Forging an economic alliance, he allowed his daughter to marry Solomon, and then, in an unprecedented move signaling the superior position of the Israelite king vis-à-vis Pharaoh, allowed her to live in Jerusalem rather than forcing Solomon to move to Egypt as had been the case with previous arrangements of a similar nature according to Egyptian texts (1 Kgs 3:1, 9:16). More importantly, Siamun tied the marriage to the status of Gezer, an unconquered Canaanite city that controlled Jerusalem's access to the coast. If Solomon would have conquered Gezer, he could have dictated Egyptian interests up and down the coast, but by taking Gezer first, Siamun reestablished an Egyptian presence in Philistia. When he turned Gezer over to Solomon, Siamun guaranteed Solomon's rights in the region via the gateway of Gezer and Lower Beth-horon, and in return Solomon ensured Egypt's security throughout the Negeb and eastern Sinai (at Tamar; 1 Kgs 9:17).

In order to solidify his position as an international player, Solomon rebuilt three cities on the international highway: Gezer at its juncture to Jerusalem; Megiddo astride the great crossroads of the Jezreel Valley; and Hazor, the gateway to the Aramean kingdoms of the north (1 Kgs 9:15). All three were rebuilt on the same general city plan, with casemate walls and straight-access, six-chambered gates. Solomon also built a series of store cities and chariot cities throughout Israel in order to reinforce his economic and military control of the land (1 Kgs 9:19, 10:26).

Solomon was now in position to become the major economic force in the Levant. He controlled both the International Coastal Highway and the King's Highway, including the upper terminus of the Arabian Spice Route. Solomon's agents in Egypt and Kue (Cilicia, the gateway between the Levant and Anatolia) facilitated a network of trade in horses and chariots—and certainly also other expensive commodities—in which Israel was the all-important middleman (1 Kgs 10:28–29). But his most dramatic move was south, to the Red Sea. With Egypt and Edom pushed from the Arabah and eastern Sinai, Solomon was able to open a route through the awful wasteland of the wilderness to Ezion-geber/Eloth. From here, with the help of the seafaring Phoenicians, he launched a fleet of ships that sailed the length of the Red Sea (1 Kgs 9:26–28). This was a completely different world than the Mediterranean, and Solomon siphoned off gold and exotic commodities to Jerusalem that used to be channeled through Egypt (1 Kgs 10:11–12, 10:22). Solomon built a series of fortresses in the Negeb, including at Tamar and the strong fort at Arad, to protect this route. The revenue from Solomon's trade network paid for his vast building programs and supported his lavish lifestyle. In a visit reminiscent

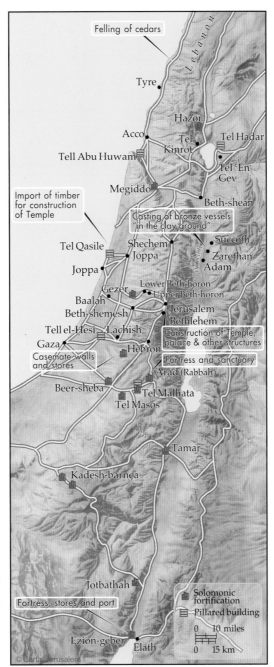

Solomon's Building Projects. *Wealth from abroad fueled building projects back home, and Solomon, like Herod the Great a thousand years later, had visions of architectural greatness. The Solomonic footprint included pillared buildings, casemate walls and six-chambered gates—although not all appeared at all sites that he built. The crown jewel, of course, was the palace and temple complex in Jerusalem, the holy royal City of David.*

of that of the Queen of Punt to Hatshepsut in the early fifteenth century B.C. (recorded in pictures on Hatshepsut's funerary temple at Deir el-Bahri in Upper Egypt), the Queen of Sheba (from a land found either in today's Yemen or Somalia) made a call on Solomon and was duly impressed with what he had accomplished (1 Kgs 10:1–13).

Solomon stands in the tradition of great men of state who had the time and opportunity to turn their talents to more refined pursuits, men like Ashurbanipal, Ptolemy II Philadelphus and Thomas Jefferson, renaissance men who engaged in science (as it was known), literature and the arts. Solomon is best known for his wisdom, which he was more successful expressing in the form of proverbs, poetry and song (1 Kgs 4:29–34; Prov 1–29; Song of Songs; Ps 72) than

Solomon's Kingdom. *With the network of trade routes blanketing the eastern seaboard of the Mediterranean safely within the Israelite fold, Solomon became one of the greatest middlemen of the ancient world. Here wealth from the desert and the sea met that from Egypt and Mesopotamia. The Israelite king filled well God's promise to Abraham that "to your descendants I have given this land, from the river of Egypt as far as the great river, the river Euphrates" (Gen 15:18).*

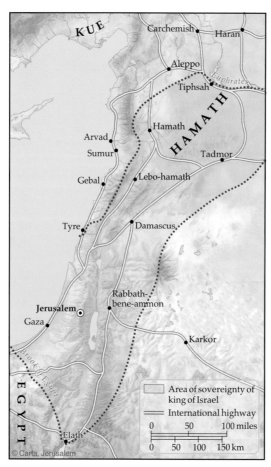

(below) After the death of Solomon the royal line of David remained a bright spot throughout the history of the Judean monarchy. Even though the line was cut when the Babylonians destroyed Judah in 586 B.C., the idea survived that someday the Davidic dynasty would be restored. Choosing a brilliantly simple image, the prophet Isaiah likened the coming Messiah to a tree stump: "Then a shoot will spring from the stump of Jesse, and a branch from his roots will bear fruit, and the Spirit of the Lord will rest on him…" (Isa 11:1).

by his own actions. When read through the grid of his own experiences, the wisdom literature of Solomon reveals a conflicted soul, a man torn between the simple pleasures of life and the fatal attraction of life in the fast lane. Or, perhaps Solomon's counsel can be believed precisely *because* it was hammered out on the hard anvil of experience.

In the end, Solomon's lifestyle—and other factors—caught up with him. The writer of Kings roundly condemned Solomon for making concessions to the gods of his foreign wives, thereby tainting the unique call of God on Israel (1 Kgs 11:1–13). But this was just one aspect of the deep-seated social and economic unrest that had never stopped tearing at the underbelly of his kingdom. Eventually the extraordinary effort that it took to keep the country together from the top was overwhelmed by any number of factors down the line, some within the government, some among the masses, some at the borders. The economy was propelled partly by revenue from vassals and trade, and partly by taxation. It was the latter that seemed particularly unjust to the still independent-minded northern tribes and prompted their revolt soon after Solomon died, when the kingdom passed to his son, Rehoboam (1 Kgs 12:1–20). The economy as a whole was tripped by a negative balance of trade with Hiram king of Tyre (and probably others), and aggravated by rebellion all along the frontier.

In order to pay for his expensive imports, Solomon ended up ceding a large portion of the tribal inheritance of Asher to Hiram. Apparently exasperated with his junior partner's financial excesses, Hiram named this payment Cabul, "good for nothing" (1 Kgs 9:10–14).

For all its grandeur, the kingdom that Solomon left to Rehoboam was weaker than the one he had inherited from David, and Egypt was waiting in the wings. Egypt, the Land that Time Forgot, was patient, with all the time in the world to act. Expecting that one day the façade of Solomon's kingdom would crack, Pharaoh Shishak patronized Jeroboam, head of the Ephraim district's royal corvée, in Egypt (1 Kgs 11:26–40) the same way that Siamun had supported Hadad of Edom during the reign of David (1 Kgs 11:14–22). As soon as Solomon died, and with the blessings of Shishak, Jeroboam returned home with the confidence and encouragement he needed to restore independent rule to the northern tribes. Then, in the fifth year of Rehoboam and with a sly smile, Shishak attacked, slicing and dicing the weakened Levant—thanks to the unsuspecting advance work of Jeroboam—and reducing Israel and Judah to two hollow shells (1 Kgs 14:25–26; 2 Chron 12:1–12; cf. 2 Chron 11:5–12). Shishak's route, known from his city list engraved on the outside of the southern wall of the great hypostyle hall at Karnak, shows that he was particularly interested in seizing the trade routes in the south and confining Israel and Judah to the high hill country. The Edomites and the Arameans of Damascus broke away at the same time, if not before (1 Kgs 11:23–25). The United Kingdom of David and Solomon collapsed to two rump states as truncated as the kingdom had been at the death of Saul.

The story of David and Solomon says something about courage in the face of danger, single-minded devotion to tasks larger than life, the power of forgiveness and the grace to honor others, the need to temper strength and privilege with humility and decency, and the transience of human success. Perhaps most of all, this is a story that reflects the human potential for greatness when lived in tune with the needs of others and supported and shielded by the power and grace of God. But it also suggests that the very best that people can do is, in the end, never quite enough. For the biblical writers, David became a type, a symbol, an image of what yet could someday be, and real hope for the future rested on the belief that a son of David, one who was truly anointed (*messiah*), would someday arise to instill Davidic greatness in all God's people (Isa 55:3; Jer 30:9; Ezek 37:24–28; Zech 12:8, 12:10; Mt 1:1; Lk 2:11).

CHAPTER 9
RIZPAH
When Not-So-Little-Things Really Matter

What an odd story. A woman no one's heard of suffers one horrible tragedy after another, then reacts in a way that is simply bizarre. To sit and silently watch the bodies of her two dead sons decompose in the hot sun, day after agonizing day, defies all rational explanation. It is nothing short of shocking—and was meant to be for those who saw the horrible events unfold that led to this gruesome climax. But these were not the actions of a crazy woman, someone with a mind of mush who had become excusably deranged in the face of abuse and brutality beyond her control. No, this was a powerful protest, carefully calculated to move the heart of the king, with a great deal at stake. Indeed, for Rizpah, a tragic victim if there ever was one, it was life, loyalty and honor that mattered most.

The story, told in 2 Samuel 21:1–14, ties up some loose ends in the longer narrative of the rise of David to the kingship of Israel. David's march to the throne was a complicated affair, full of twists and turns, with many dangers and threats along the way. David was a man after God's own heart (1 Sam 16:7), yet not exempt from the pitfalls inherent to anyone who attempts to do great things. A man with a pure heart but a weak backbone would have failed to establish the kingdom, while someone driven by conniving and ruthless strength might have gained the throne, but who among his subjects would have wanted to call him king? David's work in establishing the kingdom of Israel was remarkable but not perfect, and as year gave way to year certain issues that had been overlooked in the process—intentionally or otherwise—reared their heads and demanded attention. All were relatively minor items, considering the larger task at hand, and could easily have been dismissed as irritants to progress, perhaps—except that for the little people involved, they were often a matter of life and death.

For David, the prompt that all wasn't right in his kingdom was a famine (2 Sam 21:1). Israel's rocky landscape, with scant soil and capricious weather patterns, lay at the edge of the semi-arid wilderness and was all too frequently overrun by the ghost riders of drought, famine and death (cf. Rev 6:7–8). The result was predictable. The prophet Jeremiah, for instance, described the gaping reality of famine this way, sometime toward the end of the lifetime of the kingdom of Judah:

Judah mourns and her gates languish;
everyone sits on the ground in mourning, and the

cry of Jerusalem has ascended [to heaven].
The nobles sent the servants for water;
they came to the cisterns and found no water,
so returned with their vessels empty;
shamed and humiliated, with heads covered.
For the ground is cracked,
there has been no rain on the land;
the farmers have been put to shame,
with heads covered.
Even the doe in the field has given birth
only to abandon her young because there is no grass.
The wild donkeys stand on the bare heights panting for air like jackals;
their eyes fail, for there is no vegetation. (Jer 14:2–6)

The worst part was not knowing when a famine would end—like staring down a long, dark tunnel and seeing no opening—and not being able to know how far to plan ahead, how much to skimp today to have something to eat next year. David and everyone in his kingdom endured this particular famine for three agonizing years. In the sweep of history three years may be only a blink, but for those facing yet another sunrise without a realistic hope of finding even the most basic necessities of life for the coming day, it felt like an eternity. Of course to make matters worse—was it supposed to make it easier in situations like these?—was a world view that understood that people and land, under God, were inextricably bound together as a kind of organic and theological unity, and that if one cried out in pain, it was because there was something wrong with the other. Clearly God, giver of life to both, was angry about *something* in the realm of hu-

Mourning scene from the Bible, 19th century engraving (Carta, Jerusalem).

Consider and call for the
mourning women,
that they may come;
and send for the wailing
women, that they may come!
(Jer 9:17)

The festival of Passover, celebrated every spring, is timed to coincide with the annual barley harvest. Fields of ripened grain and the Passover meal, the seder, *speak of the same reality: God's good provision in a promised land. Spring is a time of hope, though for Rizpah, this particular season's famine mocked hers, tearing it out by the roots.*

Straddling the watershed ridge above a plateau forming the heartland of the tribe of Benjamin, the hill of Gibeah became the first capital of Israel by virtue of the choice of Saul, its favorite son, to be king. Fertile soil and a pleasant climate helped foster the good life here, a place where Rizpah, widow of the slain king, probably chose to live out her days. Gibeah sat at a crossroad frequently used by residents of Jerusalem five miles south. Here Rizpah's silent protest could not help but be noticed.

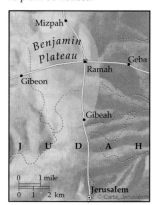

Saul's Forced Heritage.
The Benjamin Plateau north of Jerusalem was a critical crossroads for the Israelite capital and provided important agricultural land for its residents. The most important city in the region often controlled the others. For Saul of Gibeah, this meant that Gibeon should be subject to him.

man activity, *somewhere* within David's kingdom (cf. 2 Sam 24:1–14). But what? And where?

Once it was clear to David that the famine must have been caused by something other than a simple blip in weather patterns, he sought the presence of the LORD. David was blindsided by God's answer: the famine that was wasting his kingdom away wasn't due to *his* actions (cf. 2 Sam 24:1–25), but those of his predecessor, Saul, whose "bloody house" had put the Gibeonites to death (2 Sam 21:1). To help the reader understand, the writer of the Book of Samuel added the detail that even though Israel had made a covenant with the Gibeonites, "Saul had sought to kill them in his zeal for the sons of Israel and Judah" (1 Sam 21:2; cf. Josh 9:1–27). The Gibeonites, in fact, claimed that Saul had "planned to exterminate [them] from remaining within any border of Israel" (2 Sam 21:5), a kind of ethnic cleansing that went beyond even the intent of Joshua's conquest of Canaan. For Saul it was particularly ironic, because his own ancestors, the men of neighboring Gibeah, had been nearly exterminated in a fit of misguided zeal by the other tribes of Israel a few generations earlier (Judg 20:1–48). Gibeah was eventually shown grace in that episode (Judg 21:1–24); Saul refused to return grace in this.

Perhaps Saul's actions can be understood on the economic and political levels. It is reasonable to suppose that Saul saw the indigenous (Hivite) Gibeonites as a threat to his attempt to build a power base in the central hill country. Saul's home, now the capital of Israel, was the village of Gibeah, which lay a scant five miles from the much larger city of Gibeon. Both shared important resources (water, agriculture and routes) on a wide spot of the watershed ridge between Jerusalem and Bethel, the political and economic heartland of the tribal inheritance of Benjamin. Based on archaeological evidence from the seventh century B.C. (names in-

scribed on pot handles found at Gibeon), we can surmise that members of Saul's clan, the clan of Ner (1 Sam 14:50–51), tried to wrestle these resources away from the indigenous inhabitants of Gibeon. If Saul had any hope of strengthening his own family and then expanding his control over all of Israel, he couldn't afford to have a strong Canaanite enclave looking over his shoulder back home, Joshua's covenant with the Gibeonites (Josh 9:1–27) notwithstanding.

Early in his reign David had taken out the Jebusite stronghold of Jerusalem, the Canaanite city nearest his own home village of Bethlehem (2 Sam 5:6–10), and so in the game of *realpolitik* he must have sympathized with or at least understood Saul's actions. But a greater issue was at hand. Israel had made a covenant of peace with the Gibeonites and even though the circumstances that led to this covenant were motivated by insincerity on the part of the Gibeonite king, Joshua insisted (in the face of intense public opposition back home) that its terms be upheld. After all, Israel was no more worthy of being included in *God's* covenant than Gibeon was in theirs. The result was that the Gibeonites were absorbed into the greater people of Israel, as other indigenous people groups in Canaan had been during the early days of Israel's settlement in the land (e.g., the Kenites, Jerahmeelites, Calebites, Cherethites and Kenizzites; Josh 14:6, 14:13; Judg 4:11; 2 Sam 15:18). The Gibeonites' particular fate was to become temple servants, a role that, by design or otherwise, should have fostered their integration into the religious and social fabric of ancient Israel, and once in, the principle of covenantal loyalty (*hesed*, "lovingkindness") should have ensured that their rights be protected. But for Saul, the political realities of the moment overrode this foundational value.

Launching an investigation, David asked the Gibeonites what in their mind would constitute justice in the matter. The Gibeonites wanted blood for blood: they demanded that seven of Saul's remaining sons be publicly executed in Gibeah. But why should the sons (and their families) have to pay for the sins of the father? For that matter, with Saul dead and his dynasty deposed, why should David and all Israel have to suffer through a debilitating famine for something that the reigning king didn't do? Here the operative factor was the cultural norm of corporate solidarity: like a human body composed of many parts, the people of Israel were an organic unity. If one part was honored, all were honored, but if one part suffered, all suffered (cf. 1 Cor 12:12–26). In a tribal society in which the honor of the family was paramount, sins were indeed visited upon the third and fourth generations (Ex 34:7; Josh 7:1–26; 2 Sam 14:7). David hand-picked the victims who would restore the honor of both Gibeon and all Israel: two of Saul's sons born to Rizpah and five of

Saul's grandchildren, sons of Saul's daughter Merab (2 Sam 21:7–9).

So Rizpah, by virtue of a tragic enforcement of rights, was dragged into the affair. Rizpah had been Saul's concubine, a lesser queen in his harem who had enjoyed all of the status and responsibilities that being so attached to the royal court implied: certain prerogatives, yes, but also knowing that she was number two, chosen by Saul probably either for political reasons (to seal an alliance) or, more likely, for sexual expediency (2 Sam 3:7). Rizpah's future indeed lay with the royal house, but when her husband was killed on the battlefield (1 Sam 31:1–6) and what was left of the house of Saul was ground to rubble under the inexorable rise of David (2 Sam 3:1), Rizpah's status and fortunes took a serious hit. Now outside looking in, Rizpah knew that her future was tied to the mercy of the new king.

With the crown prince Jonathan also dead, Rizpah's older son Armoni may have stood a chance to inherit Israel's throne, or at least lead the charge against David to retain northern political control over all Israel. But Abner, Saul's general, had other ideas. Abner seized Rizpah as his own concubine in an attempt to re-establish the line of Saul by force, with himself as king. For Ish-bosheth, Saul's only surviving full son, and those loyal to the full bloodline of Saul, this was an act of treason (2 Sam 3:7–11; cf. 1 Kgs 2:13–25). We can surmise that Rizpah, the mother of two of Saul's sons, simply felt used.

But there was more. Neither Rizpah nor any of the other surviving members of the house of Saul could be at ease with the world as long as the bones of their dead king did not rest in peace in the family tomb of Kish, Saul's father, located in Zela, their ancestral village neighboring Gibeah (cf. 2 Sam 21:14; Josh 18:28). Instead, the bodies of Saul and Jonathan had been burned and their bones buried secretly and in haste, without the security of a tomb, under the branches of a wizened tamarisk tree in Jabesh-gilead east of the Jordan River (1 Sam 31:11–13). Saul apparently had family ties to Jabesh-gilead through an unnamed female ancestor (Judg 21:8–15), but in a patrilocal society such as ancient Israel where a bride became part of her new husband's family, the homeland for the living—and only proper resting place for the dead—was with the male line. Dead and buried abroad, Saul was in exile, his dust scattered far from the land of his birth. Rizpah was left with a gaping hole deep in her heart, her life restless and incomplete.

So Rizpah was already tragically wounded on a number of accounts when David earmarked her only two sons to publicly bear the humiliation of the Gibeonites—and pay the highest price in the process. The execution took place in the springtime at the beginning of the barley harvest, during the Passover season when Israel should have been re-

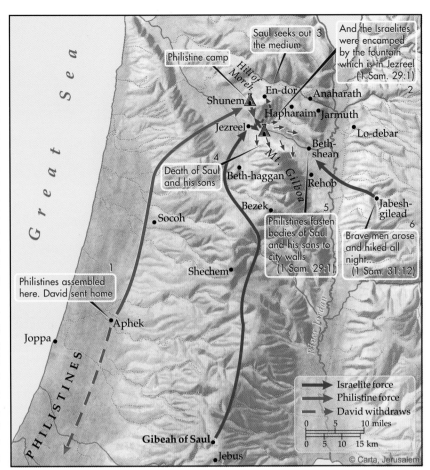

joicing in freedom and new life. With it, Rizpah the widow was made childless, her legacy, security and future forever gone. In terms of redeeming the honor of the Gibeonites, reaffirming the need to keep covenant and restoring his land from the ravages of famine, David was on the right track. As to the effect on Rizpah personally—that for David, in the larger scope of national affairs, was small potatoes. For Rizpah, of course, it was a not-so-little-thing that really mattered.

Rizpah could have sought a private audience with David to plead justice for herself, but decided on another tactic. Silent throughout the entire narrative, she found power in a course of action much louder than words. Rizpah fashioned a rough lean-to of coarse sackcloth (the verb "to spread out" often refers to the act of pitching a tent; e.g., Gen 12:8) on a large expanse of exposed bedrock to make a place of mourning. There she sat in a silent vigil before the corpses of her only two sons "from the beginning of harvest until it poured rain on them from the sky" (2 Sam 21:10). Day turned into night then back to day, week followed week, month stretched into month. Of course it wasn't going to rain until David responded to Rizpah's plea (cf. 2 Sam 21:11–14), but the rains always stopped after the spring harvest anyway, leaving the land parched and dry until the early rains of the fall renewed the yearly agricultural cycle six months later (cf. Deut 11:14).

Saul's Last Battle. *When Saul and Jonathan lost their lives battling the Philistines on the slopes of Mt. Gilboa, the kingdom of Israel was sent into a tailspin. The Philistines hung the bodies of the dead king and crown prince on the wall of Beth-shean to rot in the sun. The men of Jabesh-gilead, whom Saul had delivered from the hand of the Ammonites, risked life and limb to rescue the bodies—although a decent burial awaited the actions of Rizpah.*

Clinging to the edge of the mound of Beth-shean, the skeleton of a once-proud tree stands in silent witness that the bodies of Saul and Jonathan once hung from the city's walls. Much later, the same stigma of death exposed was attached to the act of crucifixion. Rizpah, Mary—it was women, bent but unbroken, who remained to carry the grief of their son's executions.

Saul's Final Burial. *It was a long journey home, but when Saul's bones finally reached his ancestral estate at Zela near Gibeah, the land could rest in God's blessing and peace.*

The text doesn't have to be any more specific in describing the scene—everyone who heard or read the story knew from first-hand experience what would happen. The sight and smell was common enough, for dead animals weren't buried in ancient Israel (they often still aren't) but were left exposed where they fell, slowly bloating and rotting away, the hard remains (bones and hair) becoming as parched and dry as the stony ground on which they lay. The first give-away is always the smell—pungent, penetrating and sharp. Even today it's a frequent enough encounter off-road anywhere in the Middle East, on hillsides, in wadi bottoms, or along the edges of paths between village and field. Birds and wild animals scavenging for carrion hasten the decomposition process. Eventually nothing is left. This was a natural fate for animals in the ancient world, even large ones such as camels, donkeys or cattle. But for a human body to be left exposed to the elements was an indignity worse than death, for it not only profaned the sacredness of the person, it left nothing to bury on one's ancestral estate (cf. Ps 79:1–5; Jer 16:4). In a sense, to lie unburied and be eaten by animals condemned the person to the sentence of having never been born. Such was the fate of Jezebel (2 Kgs 9:33–37) and the intent of Goliath's curse on David (1 Sam 17:43–44) and David's on Goliath (1 Sam 17:46). And in the first century, this was often the last phase of crucifixion: bodies would hang on the cross until the dry and dismembered bones fell into a heap at its base (cf. Mt 27:33: Golgotha, "Place of the Skull"). The cultural norm in ancient Israel to care for the bodies of dead people was so strong that the Mosaic law made provision for the proper burial even of executed criminals (Deut 21:22–23).

And so Rizpah sat, driving away birds by day and wild animals by night to preserve what little dignity for the dead that she could, personally witnessing the slow decomposition of the bodies of her only two sons. With each passing day her own future rotted away, slowly but inexorably swallowed by the ground out of which it had come (cf. Gen 2:7, 3:19; Job 7:5, 10:9, 20:11). It was a public display, exposed to all, accompanied by heart-rending, ear-splitting silence. Rizpah was left with but a memory and the determination not to let it die.

But if memory was all that motivated Rizpah, she could have preserved that better by safely enclosing it in a rock-cut tomb. No, something much larger was at stake. Rizpah chose to discomfort herself and to dishonor her own sons in order to restore honor to the house of Saul. Her loyalty was to his family, not herself, and she saw in David's complicity to annihilate her king's line an opportunity to redeem his legacy. Even though nothing was left of Saul but his charred bones and a rival now sat on his throne, he still had the right to a decent burial and to be remembered for the good that he had done: *zichrono l'vracha*, "may his memory be for a blessing." It was an issue of dignity and honor, the greatest source of security or wealth that an individual in the ancient Near East could possess.

There was one final, ironic twist. It wasn't only the two sons of Rizpah that David had executed, but the five sons of Saul's oldest daughter Merab as well (2 Sam 21:8; cf. 1 Sam 14:49). This was this same Merab whom Saul had twice promised in marriage to David, and both times the marriage did not take place (1 Sam 17:25, 18:17–19). "Who am I to marry the king's daughter?" David had said with all the proper Middle Eastern self-deprecation he could muster—and Saul, certainly to David's chagrin, took him seriously. Merab did raise five fine sons, but by another man, and we should not think that David did not have a personal score to settle in his choice of those who had to die for their father's sins. But it still must have been a tortuous decision for David, who instead had married Michal, Merab's sister (1 Sam 18:20–29), making these five whom he condemned to death his own nephews. What a tangled mess it had all become.

David finally heard, and his heart was moved by Rizpah's silent protest. He arranged that the remains of Saul and Jonathan be interred in the family tomb of Kish, on Saul's ancestral estate (2 Sam 21:11–14; cf. 2 Sam 2:4–7). God himself approved, and only now released the blessing of his open hand, rain in its season (cf. Deut 11:14), upon the land. Of what happened to Rizpah no further details are given, but perhaps none need be. From this event alone we see a woman who was resourceful, forthright and loyal, a survivor who was able to turn the worst tragedy that life could throw at her into good and maintain not only her dignity but that of others in the process. Was it only David who strove after God's own heart?

CHAPTER 10
AHAB AND JEHOSHAPHAT
The Fine Line Between Failure and Success

People, it seems, love to watch others at conflict—"competition," it's called in its milder form—especially if the opposing sides are represented by two great personalities, drawn together by forces larger than themselves or sometimes, as ambition melds with the greater task at hand, by the sheer force of their own wills. Are great rivalries—those such as breed a certain kind of camaraderie among the two protagonists—driven more by grand vision, or personality? Octavian and Antony. Hamilton and Burr. Churchill and Stalin. Mozart and Salieri. Men striving with, and against, each other. And so it was with Ahab and Jehoshaphat, the kings of Israel and Judah during the mid-ninth century B.C., as one stepped into, then out of, the shadow of the other. Who was the protagonist? The antagonist? Either? Both? In the troubled ninth century B.C., what made for success? Or failure?

Ahab took the throne of the Northern Kingdom of Israel in 874 B.C., fifty-seven years after the death of Solomon, and Jehoshaphat began his sole reign over Judah after a two-year co-regency with his father Asa four years later. Jehoshaphat was 37 years old when he became king; Ahab's age, though unknown, must have been roughly the same (1 Kgs 15:24, 16:29, 22:51; 2 Chron 20:31). Ahab and Jehoshaphat, contemporaries, were also comrades and rivals. In the decades following the death of Solomon, the circumstances that for better or worse locked their nations into a common struggle spun out differently north and south of their shared border, and produced two kings who were quite different in outlook and temperament yet who both tried to reestablish a bit of the glory days of Solomon.

The decades following the split of Solomon's kingdom had indeed been a traumatic time for Judah and Israel. The kingdoms of Rehoboam and Jeroboam were humiliated by Shishak's run through the southern Levant, and even though the Egyptian Pharaoh was unable to follow up his conquest with occupation, Israel and Judah were left staggering (1 Kgs 14:25–26; 2 Chron 12:1–12). Rehoboam built fortresses in the hill country of Judah and the upper, eastern Shephelah "for the defense of Judah" (2 Chron 11:5–12)—no pushing the borders outward here—which allowed the king to hold Judah and Benjamin but nothing else. With their backs turned toward their neighbors, the kings of Israel and Judah faced off against each other, the strategic land of Benjamin the prize.

The narrow land of Benjamin had already seen its share of invasion during the biblical period: Joshua and Eglon penetrated from the east, and the Philistines and Shishak pushed in from the west (Josh 6–10; Judg 3:12–30; 1 Sam 7:7, 13:3–12; 1 Kgs 14:25–26). Jerusalem was particularly vulnerable, for the best routes into and out of the Judean capital ran through the plateau of Benjamin, a wide area of the watershed ridge outlined by the cities of Gibeah, Ramah, Mizpah and Gibeon. For the kings of Judah to have any chance at reestablishing their economic ties to the larger world, they had to maintain control of this corridor. Israel's best access to the coast and the Jordan Valley lay elsewhere and so its kings were less dependent on the Benjamin plateau, but still found

Barely containing his excitement when Solomon died, the Pharaoh of Egypt, Shishak, tore into the kingdom of Israel, ripping it in pieces and reducing its holding to two rump states, Israel and Judah. In the manner of his triumphant predecessors, Shishak left memorial stelae in his wake; this fragment from Megiddo bears Shishak's identifying name in a cartouche.

The Division of the Kingdom. *By the time Ahab and Jehoshaphat took their respective thrones, the international priorities of Israel and Judah were coming into focus. Judah remained landlocked, hemmed in by the Dead Sea to the east and the resurgent Philistines on the coast. Israel, on the other hand, aided by a more open geographical setting and a king bent on expansion, tapped into the lucrative international routes of the Mediterranean and Transjordan.*

69

The land of Judah was blessed; Israel, the inheritance of Joseph, doubly so. Moses said it well: "Blessed of the LORD be [Joseph's] land, with the choice things of heaven, with the dew and from the deep lying beneath; with the choice yield of the sun and that of the months" (Deut 33:13–14). It was a land that could be twice cropped, with winter wheat sharing the same soil as summer olives. Ahab reaped the benefit of this double blessing, with ample resources to fuel his rising kingdom.

The Battle for Benjamin. *The early decades of the divided monarchy were consumed with a fraternal fight: Israel and Judah jockeying for strategic position on the central Benjamin plateau. Purchasing Aramean intervention, Asa of Judah was able to repulse Baasha's thrust to Ramah, and the border was fixed somewhere between Mizpah and Bethel (1 Kgs 15:17–22). In subsequent years Judah used the crossroads of Ramah to push to the coast, while Israel claimed Jericho by developing the route running southeast out of Bethel.*

it necessary to hold the area if only to resist Judah's advance north.

During his short reign (913–911 B.C.), Rehoboam's son Abijah penetrated Benjamin and pushed into the hill country of Ephraim, seizing Bethel, Jeshanah and Ephron from Jeroboam (2 Chron 13:1–19). In response, within a year or two Nadab, Jeroboam's

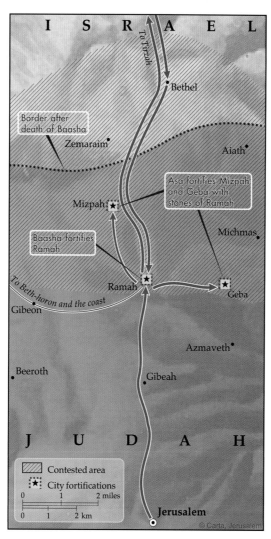

son, attacked the Philistines at Gibbethon west of Gezer, with a side-glance toward the Jerusalem-Gezer route. Before Nadab could seize Gibbethon and do an end-around on Judah, however, he was assassinated by Baasha, a usurper from Issachar who seized the throne (1 Kgs 15:27–33).

Baasha ended up reigning for twenty-three years and his contemporary, Asa the son of Abijah, forty-one. After an initial period of respite, the battle for Benjamin was rejoined and waged throughout their reigns (1 Kgs 15:16, 15:32; cf. 2 Chron 14:1). The writer of Kings mentions only the defining episode in this struggle (1 Kgs 15:17–22). In an attempt to put a chokehold on Asa, Baasha fortified Ramah in the heart of the Benjamin plateau. Prompted by a well-placed bribe, Ben-hadad I of Aram-Damascus (a place name often rendered in English Bibles as "Syria") invaded Israel from the north, allowing Asa to push Baasha back to Bethel. The Israel-Judah border, drawn between Mizpah and Bethel (the rebuilt city gate of Mizpah faced north) and between Geba and Michmash, remained essentially stable throughout the divided monarchy, with the land of Benjamin dissected but more Judean than Israelite. Jerusalem enjoyed access to the coast through Gibeon and Beth-horon, while Israel was able to develop the Bethel-Jericho connection to Moab (cf. 1 Kgs 16:34).

Baasha's son Elah reigned less than two years (886–885 B.C.) before he was assassinated by Zimri, commander of the Israelite chariot force, during a drinking binge in his capital at Tirzah (1 Kgs 16:8–14). Within a week, Elah's general Omri, who had renewed the assault on Gibbethon, was proclaimed king by his troops and Zimri committed suicide (1 Kgs 16:15–20). Omri's rule was not accepted by everyone, and it took nearly six years of civil war for his army to suppress the followers of one Tibni son of Ginath, apparently a man of some competence but otherwise unknown to history. With the full accession of Omri to Israel's throne, the kingdom's fortunes took a noticeable step forward. His dynasty (Israel's third, not counting the aborted reign of Zimri) gained so much international attention that Jehu, who overthrew Omri's royal house in 841 B.C., was nevertheless called "Jehu son of Omri" by the Assyrians (Black Obelisk of Shalmaneser, ANET 280).

In his six years as sole king of Israel (880–874 B.C.), Omri laid a strong foundation for the kingdom to return, at least in part, to the glory days of David and Solomon. Omri was probably around sixty years old when he became king. He would have personally remembered both the closing days of the United Kingdom and the ignominy of Shishak's invasion, a national wound that festered for decades as a new generation arose, and he no doubt impressed the need to restore the lost honor of Israel upon his impressionable young son, Ahab. Now that he had seized the throne, Omri could position himself

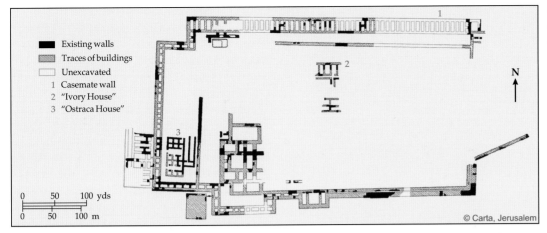

Nearly 250 meters in length, Ahab's palace at Samaria dominated the acropolis of the ancient city. The strong casemate wall was constructed of finely cut ashlar masonry in the "header and stretcher" style, which was copied in the summer palace of Hezekiah at Ramat Rachel south of Jerusalem and in the contemporary royal palace in the Ammonite capital of Rabbah in Transjordan.

Existing walls
Traces of buildings
Unexcavated
1 Casemate wall
2 "Ivory House"
3 "Ostraca House"

0   50   100 yds
0   50   100 m

N

© Carta, Jerusalem

and his son to receive the glory for erasing Israel's shame.

One of Omri's most important acts was to move the location of his capital. The first capital of the Northern Kingdom had been Shechem, an established city-state in the heartland of the tribal territory of Manasseh and a hub of routes in the hill country (1 Kgs 12:25). With a history of strong leadership as a Canaanite city-state and ancestral ties to the patriarch Jacob, Shechem was the natural choice for Israel's capital. But perhaps the city was *too* accessible, for in the wake of Shishak's attack and by the time the battle for Benjamin kicked into high gear, Jeroboam had moved his capital to Tirzah at the upper end of the Wadi Faria (1 Kgs 14:17, 15:21, 16:8–9, 16:23). Tirzah was tucked in the eastern hills of Manasseh, with good access only to the Jordan Valley and Transjordan, and its choice signaled Jeroboam's political priorities: give Israel time to lick its wounds and regroup. But for Omri, a capital that served only the regional needs of an inland kingdom was clearly insufficient. With vision for a revived empire, Omri purchased the settlement of Shemer on a hill facing west, in view of the coastal plain, to both symbolize and facilitate his goal of reestablishing economic ties with Phoenicia. Now he could run with the big boys. Like the Jebusite city of Jerusalem that had been conquered by David, Shemer was an established settlement when Omri made the site his royal, dynastic home. He renamed the place Samaria and built Israel's third, last, and most magnificent capital there (1 Kgs 16:24). Although Ahab gets the credit (or blame), it was certainly Omri who arranged the marriage of his son to Jezebel, daughter of the Phoenician king (1 Kgs 16:31). What the writer of Kings condemns as evil, Omri meant for good, for the marriage sealed a renewed relationship between Israel and the commercial outlets of Phoenicia that pumped money in both directions.

With these gains in the west, Omri took back the tableland of Medeba from the king of Moab, who himself had seized it from Israel sometime after the death of Solomon. Omri also rebuilt Ataroth farther south on the Medeba Plateau, thereby pulling the tribe of Gad back to Israel and reinforcing his hold in Transjordan. These events, not directly mentioned in the Bible, are clear from the Mesha Stele (Moabite Stone) and consistent with the notice of the rebellion of Mesha, a later king of Moab, against Israel recorded in 2 Kings 3:4. Omri and then Ahab acted as middlemen in the delivery of sheep and ram's wool from Moab to the Phoenicians who, in addition to controlling the sea lanes, had a monopoly on red-purple dye and trade in fine garments (cf. Ezek 27:7). In order to make sure that the route between Moab and the coast would pass through Israel, Hiel from Bethel rebuilt Jericho, Israel's southeastern gateway, probably early in the reign of Ahab (1 Kgs 16:34). As a result, Judah's access to the east around the northern end of the Dead Sea was hindered, forcing Jehoshaphat to concentrate on the difficult but potentially more lucrative southeastern routes into Edom instead.

Ahab, then, inherited both a kingdom on the rise and the hardscrabble genes of his father. Like father like son, both were tough, opportunistic fellows who loved a show of strength, and although Omri reigned only six years in Samaria, he set the tone for his son to claw his way up and over the top.

While Omri and Ahab had to fight for their rights, Jehoshaphat was given his on a platter. The early kings of the Davidic dynasty—Rehoboam, Abijah and Asa—maintained a certain aura of propriety that continued to envelop Judah in spite of Shishak's raid. Asa's long reign (911–870 B.C.) brought stability to the throne in the south just when the northern kingdom was churning out one *coup d'état* after another, and with it came success on the battlefield in Benjamin (1 Kgs 15:16–22) and against Zerah the Cushite, who met Asa at Mareshah in the southern Shephelah (2 Chron 14:8–15). Moreover, Asa fostered a religious conservatism that gave priority to the LORD as the proper God of Judah, over against certain tolerant, internationalizing elements of Judah's population that paid homage to the gods of the nations (2 Chron 15:8–19). The

A large concentration of ivories carved with geometric designs and motifs common to Egyptian and Assyrian art were found in Ahab's palace in Samaria. Other ivories, recovered in the Assyrian capital of Nimrud, were apparently taken there as booty when Samaria was destroyed in 722 B.C. Some of these ivories were probably inlays in wooden furniture. The writer of Kings mentions that Ahab built an "ivory house" (1 Kgs 22:39), and the prophet Amos condemned residents of Samaria "who recline on beds of ivory and sprawl on their couches" (Amos 6:4). (NEAEHL)

The Campaign of Zerah the Cushite. *One of Asa's foreign policy success stories came at the expense of Zerah, who attempted to push into the southern Shephelah at Mareshah (2 Chron 14:8–15). It is a debated point whether Zerah's Cushites were an Egyptian dynasty from Ethiopia or a local Arab tribe. In any case, Asa was able to hold the line at the outer end of the Shephelah, but not establish a Judean presence on the coast.*

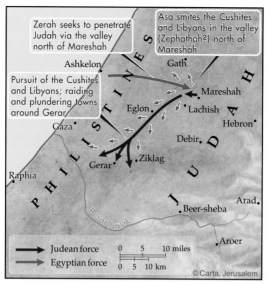

The view from Ahab's winter capital at Jezreel took in the sweep of the Jezreel and Harod valley system. This was not only rich agricultural land (the name "Jezreel" means "God sows"), but the line of the major east-west corridor through Israel. Running along the base of Tel Jezreel today lies the modern equivalent of this great ancient highway; farther north rises Mt. Moreh, with Israel's breadbasket in between.

northern kings never seemed to be too bothered by such issues. According to the writers of Kings and Chronicles, the kings of the south who were most successful in religion (devotion to the LORD and His temple in Jerusalem) were also the most successful in politics (fostering a secure, stable society and promoting a favorable international policy). Asa, on the balance, was one of these, and his son Jehoshaphat learned the role well. Grounded in a solid dynasty, Jehoshaphat was born to a sense of duty and understood the need to foster the welfare of the people of his kingdom. He was a conventional man, taking the throne of Judah in the fourth year of the pretentious Ahab.

Ahab inherited rights to the coast through Omri's alliance with Phoenicia, and continued his father's policy of control over Moab. With this intact, he turned his attention to the Arameans, a perennial threat to Israel's goal of dominating the King's Highway in Transjordan. The only way that Ahab could concentrate on things north, however, was by formalizing a truce in the south, with Judah. Is-

rael's aspirations for control over all of the land of Benjamin would have to be put on the back burner; more important matters lay at hand. This easing of relations was sealed with the marriage of Ahab's daughter Athaliah to Jehoshaphat's son Jehoram, the crown prince of Judah (2 Kgs 8:16–18, 8:25–27). Like all royal marriages in the ancient world (and a good many today), this one was born of political expediency. The alliance bound the nations together and allowed Israel and Judah the respite needed to expand their borders in other directions. The northern tribes had always felt themselves superior to the upstart Judah, and since Rehoboam had been unable to hold the United Kingdom together, Ahab hoped to position himself as the proper heir to that legacy. Surely Samaria could succeed where descendants of David had failed! As it turned out, Israel and Judah did in fact together approach the level of influence, at least in the southern Levant, that the United Kingdom had enjoyed under David and Solomon.

Athaliah, like Jezebel, was a strong personality and seems to have been a dominant player in affairs of state in Judah, constantly reminding Jehoshaphat that he lived under the shadow of his stronger and more politically ambitious northern neighbor. Like Jezebel, Athaliah outlived her husband, even becoming for a time sole ruler in the land (queen by proxy, so to say; 2 Kgs 11:1–16; 2 Chron 22:1–23:15). For the writers of Kings and Chronicles, however, Athaliah's similarity to Jezebel lay in her role as a queen of Baal and Asherah. Both women, they insisted, undermined the true strength of Israel and Judah, nations which had been founded on the Kingship of the LORD God, and for this they were condemned.

To establish a base of operations against Damascus, Ahab built a large rectangular fortress at Jezreel on a broad mound hugging the western slope of Mount Gilboa at the point where the Jezreel Valley spills into the Harod Valley. Archaeological remains show that Ahab surrounded the entire top of the mound with strong walls marked at the corners and the mid-point of each by square towers (cf. 2 Kgs 9:17, 9:31–32, 10:8). From here Ahab not only had direct access to his capital city, Samaria, and the cities of Galilee, but could control the best route between the King's Highway and the Mediterranean Sea. Moreover, the climate during the rainy season was more favorable here than in Samaria, and so Jezreel became Ahab's winter capital (Amos mentioned several royal palaces of the Northern Kingdom, including a "winter house" which was apparently in Jezreel, and a "summer house," probably in Samaria; Amos 3:15). As a point-counterpoint to Ahab's military ambitions, the only events that the Bible mentions as having taken place in Jezreel during the reign of Ahab focus on his nemesis, the prophet Elijah (1 Kgs 18:45–46), and Naboth, whom Ahab murdered and despoiled (1 Kgs 21:1–29). Fittingly, it was at

Jezreel that the house of Omri was eventually overthrown and the aging queen mother, Jezebel, assassinated (2 Kgs 9:14–37).

In spite of Ahab's preparations, or maybe because of them, the Arameans struck first. In 857 B.C., Ben-hadad II (Hadad was the Aramean equivalent of the storm-god Baal, the male god of fertility; Ben-hadad, "the son of Hadad," was a common name of kings from the Aramean state of Damascus; 1 Kgs 15:18, 20:1; 2 Kgs 13:25) formed a coalition of thirty-two Aramean kings and penetrated as far as Samaria, laying siege to the Israelite capital. Ben-hadad not only sought to curtail Israel's expansion toward Aram-Damascus, but to open a clear corridor for himself to the outlets of the Mediterranean Sea. The description of pre-battle boasting (1 Kgs 20:1–12) is timeless, as real on the ancient battlefield as it is on gang turf or in the sports arena today. Ben-hadad settled back to enjoy a long siege; Ahab led Israel in a quick counterattack, catching the Arameans off-guard and routing their army (1 Kgs 20:13–21).

By the next spring Ben-hadad had centralized the command of his army under captains directly responsible to himself. He attacked Israel at the Aphek located on the eastern shore of the Kinneret/Sea of Galilee (either at the plains of today's Kibbutz En Gev or on the flats of the Golan Heights immediately above). Already stung once, this time Ben-hadad chose to attack a site not quite as deeply exposed in Israelite territory and on terrain that was better suited to his chariot forces (1 Kgs 20:22–26). Again the Aramean army was defeated by Israel; this time Ahab used his advantage to force territorial and economic concessions from Ben-hadad (1 Kgs 20:27–34). Ahab was content to restore Israelite political control throughout northern Galilee (cf. 1 Kgs 15:20) and gain favorable trading rights in Damascus; the prophets of the LORD God, who had now twice assured victory (cf. 1 Kgs 20:13–15, 28), were not, and condemned Ahab for not getting rid of Ben-hadad when he had a chance.

This truce lasted three years (1 Kgs 22:1). The short period between 856 and 853 B.C. saw a measure of cooperation (forced or otherwise) between the kingdoms of the southern Levant, resulting in a degree of prosperity for Israel and Judah that had not been seen since the days of Solomon. Ahab was the primary recipient, with Jehoshaphat not far behind. Economically, it was a brief taste of a golden age. Ahab's kingdom had survived a severe, three-and-a-half-year drought that gripped Israel in the early part of his reign (1 Kgs 17–19; cf. Jas 5:17–18). Because Israel was the breadbasket for Phoenicia, the drought must have been particularly hard for Jezebel's homeland (cf. 1 Kgs 17:8–16), yet neither she nor Ahab were particularly moved by Elijah's insistence that their devotion to Baal and Asherah, the Canaanite god

Established political and commercial ties with Tyre; royal marriage of Jezebel and Ahab

Transfer of royal capital

Omri besieges Gibbethon at time of Zimri's revolt

Renewed ties with Judah; Athaliah marries Joram son of Jehoshaphat

Renewed control over tableland of Moab

and goddess of fertility, was the source of the problem (1 Kgs 18:17–18). Ahab and Jezebel survived this initial battle with Elijah, and having by now also infiltrated the dynasty of Judah, twice defeated Aram-Damascus on the battlefield and raped Moab in the meantime, the self-confidence of Israel's royal house must have been pretty high. Israel's old landed aristocracy—tribal, clan and city elders—largely fell in line behind their powerful and charismatic leader (1 Kgs 20:13–14, 21:8–13). To cover his bases, Ahab surrounded himself with a loyal band of prophets who were quick to soothe his conscience and ensure that the will of the gods would bend his way (a common practice in the ancient world). Of what consequence could a few nagging prophets who took their orders from the LORD God be in the meantime (1 Kgs 22:6–8)? When challenged, Ahab pouted, then went right back to business (1 Kgs 20:41–43, 21:4, 21:27, 22:8). Could his conscience still be touched, or was he like a recalcitrant child that too quickly forgets its spanking? The economy was good and the borders of his nation were expanding; why, Ahab no doubt thought, should a few individuals stand in his way? So the king acted with all the headiness that was appropriate to his position in life and his view of the circumstances around him, and men like

The Capitals of Israel. The Davidic monarchy was stable throughout the time of the kingdom of Judah and reigned from a single capital city, Jerusalem. Not so the Northern Kingdom of Israel, where uncertainty and opportunism prompted a series of five capitals: Shechem, Penuel, Tirzah, Samaria and Jezreel. It was from Samaria and Jezreel that Ahab overshadowed his neighbors.

As the priests of Baal are slaughtered on Mt. Carmel, the prophet Elijah warns Israel's defiant King Ahab that life-giving rain—a commodity of the LORD God alone—was about to inundate the land; 19th century engraving (Carta, Jerusalem).

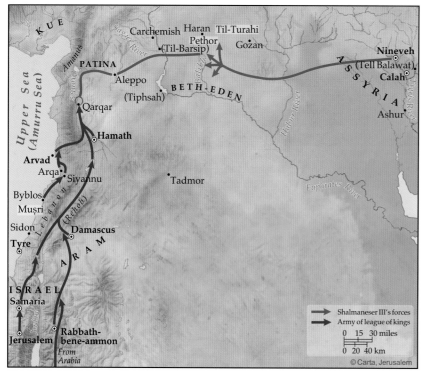

The Battle of Qarqar. *The first real Assyrian threat to the lands of the eastern Mediterranean came in 853 B.C. when Shalmaneser III advanced to Qarqar on the Orontes. Met by a coalition of kings in which Ahab played a major role, the Assyrian advance was safely checked. The coalition forces showed classic signs of tribalism: unity against a common enemy, then back to scrappy infighting once the crisis from the outside had passed.*

had too much Aramean fodder to chew through before Egypt would be threatened. Judah, more at risk, is not mentioned in the list of coalition forces, and it is likely that Jehoshaphat simply placed his resources at the disposal of Ahab. In any event, although Shalmaneser claimed a resounding victory (to believe him, he dammed up the Orontes with the dead bodies of his enemies), it is apparent that the coalition held the line. Shalmaneser returned to his capital at Nineveh and didn't campaign to the west again for four years.

Assyria was not yet a concern of the biblical authors and so the great battle at Qarqar was not mentioned in either Kings or Chronicles, although it is clear from the chronological accounts that it should be placed at the end of the three-year respite mentioned in 1 Kings 22:1. With the Assyrian threat temporarily checked (Assyrian kings would continue to hassle the north Aramean states throughout the ninth century B.C. and return in full force by the end of the eighth), the coalition that had successfully opposed Shalmaneser III quickly resumed their infighting.

Buoyed by his role at Qarqar, Ahab finally took the offense against Aram-Damascus: "Don't you know that Ramoth-gilead belongs to us, and we still aren't doing anything to take it out of the hand of the king of Aram?" he asked his royal officials (1 Kgs 22:3). Ramoth-gilead, the bone of contention, commands both the King's Highway and the region of Bashan. The latter, once an important part of the kingdom of David and Solomon, was a buffer zone and battleground between Israel, Aram-Damascus and Ammon (Num 21:33–35; Deut 3:1–11; 2 Sam 10:15–19).

Maintaining their coalition relationship, Ahab sought the support of Judah for this fight, and Jehoshaphat, the junior partner, willingly agreed (1 Kgs 22:1–4). Jehoshaphat had the presence of mind to ask the outcome of battle from a true prophet of the LORD rather than be snowballed by Ahab's prophetic yes-men, and the prophet Micaiah foresaw Israel's defeat. Ahab and Jehoshaphat marched to battle anyway, the former because his character demanded it and the latter, still largely Ahab's lapdog, for essentially the same reason (1 Kgs 22:5–29).

The battle was joined at Ramoth-gilead (*Tell Ramith* near er-Ramtha in northern Jordan), a site open and exposed on the eastern flats of Bashan,

The basalt Mesha Stele (Moabite Stone) preserves the official Moabite account of Mesha's conquests in Transjordan following the death of Ahab. The text augments the biblical story as it is preserved in 2 Kings 1–3 (or, vice versa) and, although Ahab doesn't come off too well in the Moabite version, Mesha's rendition of events makes perfect historical and geographical sense. (NEAEHL)

Naboth—as well as many nameless others, we can assume—paid the highest price (1 Kgs 21:1–29).

Ahab's ease was not to last. Assyrian storm clouds loomed on the northern horizon, the beginning stages of two hundred years of "calculated frightfulness" (in the words of A. T. Olmstead, an early Assyriologist) aimed at Egypt and the west. This period of imperialistic expansion was initiated by Ashurnasirpal II (883–859 B.C.) who, according to Assyrian sources, plowed through the north Aramean states and Phoenicia, exacting tribute from Arvad, Byblos, Tyre and Sidon. His son and successor, Shalmaneser III (859–824 B.C.), enjoyed a long and prosperous reign, fueled largely by tribute from Assyria's neighbors. In his sixth year (853 B.C.), Shalmaneser III crossed the Euphrates near the old patriarchal city of Haran, smashed through Aleppo and drew his battle line against the Arameans at Qarqar on the Orontes River. Realizing that everyone in the Assyrian path stood to lose alike, the kingdoms of the Levant, plus Egypt and Arabia, put aside their differences and formed a coalition to stop Shalmaneser. Shalmaneser's "Kurkh Stele" lists the members of this coalition and the relative strength of each. Although the number of men and chariots itemized in the list are probably exaggerated, it is clear from the order of participants that the coalition was led by the new king of Aram-Damascus, Hadad-ezer (Hadad-'idri), by the king of Hamath and by Ahab. The king of Israel is listed as commanding 2,000 chariots, the largest of the chariot forces mentioned. Egypt, Assyria's ultimate goal, played a minor role in the coalition; Pharaoh Osorkon II apparently hoped that Shalmaneser

just south of a low range of hills that separates it from a level expanse leading straight to Damascus. Ahab knew he was a long way from home; the Rift Valley dropped away far to the west, and he was safe only beyond that. Hoping for security in a ruse, Ahab had Jehoshaphat enter the battle as king and commander while he played a common foot soldier. Apparently anxious for his moment of glory, Jehoshaphat agreed, either too trusting of Ahab or too duped to know the difference. Jehoshaphat survived but Ahab was killed and the Israelite army fled, defeated (1 Kgs 22:29–40).

Only a few months had passed since the battlefield success at Qarqar yet now, with the death of Ahab, everything had changed. Ahab was succeeded by two of his sons, Ahaziah (853–852 B.C.) and then Jehoram (852–841 B.C.), neither of whom inherited a full measure of their father's skills (1 Kgs 22:51–53; 2 Kgs 1:1–18, 3:1). Aram-Damascus was certainly strengthened, and although Israel would continue to fight for control of Ramoth-gilead for another twelve years (2 Kgs 8:28, 9:14–15), the remainder of the ninth century B.C. saw the Aramean kings pretty much have their way with Israel (cf. 2 Kgs 13:7; Amos 1:3). Mesha king of Moab, too, seized the moment, throwing off the hated Israelite yoke and reclaiming the Medeba Plateau. Mesha's battles across the plateau, his repulsion of a counterattack by Ahaziah at Jahaz and fortification of strategic sites throughout the region, are described in some detail in the Mesha Stele (Moabite Stone), quite naturally from the perspective of the victor and his god, Chemosh (cf. 2 Kgs 1:1, 3:4–5).

And as for the king of Judah—he could finally be his own man. Jehoshaphat's skills and abilities, until now somewhat latent and subservient to Ahab, suddenly had the freedom to develop and mature. Judah no doubt had enjoyed a measure of prosperity that came hand-in-hand with the success of Ahab (2 Chron 18:1), but according to the sequence of events recorded in 2 Chronicles—and there is a certain cause-and-effect logic to its flow—it was only after Jehoshaphat witnessed the violent death of Ahab that the Judean king realized the priority of fostering a religious-nationalistic revival in his land, centered on the will of the LORD God (2 Chron 19:1–4).

It is unclear how many of Jehoshaphat's initiatives and reforms were begun while Ahab was still alive; certainly those related to matters of state must have been taken either in response to Ahab or with his encouragement. "There is some good in you," the prophet Jehu told Jehoshaphat upon the death of Ahab (2 Chron 19:3), not hiding the mixed message and uncertain future his words contained. The king, at a crossroad (cf Jer 6:16), responded wisely, and the flowering of Jehoshaphat's kingdom seems to have reached its fullness only after Ahab had passed from the scene.

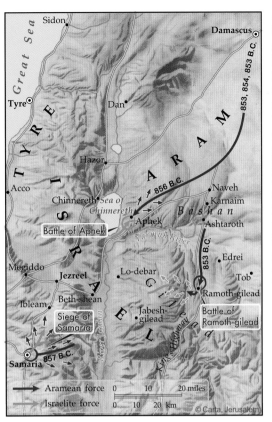

Ahab's Wars with Aram, 857–853 B.C. *Facing each other on opposite sides of the Rift Valley, Israel's Ahab and the Aramean Ben-hadad had the same goals: control of the region's routes and resources. The crossroads of Galilee were particularly important, for by seizing them Ben-hadad could open ports on the Mediterranean. After repulsing thrusts to the Israelite capital Samaria, then at Aphek above the Sea of Galilee, Ahab lost his life in the battle for Ramoth-gilead. Israel retained control over Galilee, but its influence in Transjordan was checked.*

Jehoshaphat appointed a line of judges to serve in the fortified cities of Judah, and priests, Levites and high-level officials (a sort of court of last resort) in Jerusalem in order to centralize and enforce a single standard of justice throughout the land (2 Chron 19:5–11). It is possible that the division of the cities of Judah into districts recorded in Joshua 15:20–63 reflects Jehoshaphat's efforts. Perhaps the king was motivated to save Judah the excesses of social and economic injustice that had taken root in Israel under the patronage of Ahab, or maybe he simply wanted to strengthen his kingdom from the top down. In any case, Jehoshaphat's success in the face of the honored line of village elders—dispensers of justice from time immemorial—and in spite of the influence of Athaliah toward things of Ahab,

The view from Ramoth-gilead toward the north takes in a low rise of hills separating the site from land beyond that was easily controlled by Aram-Damascus. Ramoth-gilead was the Transjordanian terminus of the road heading east from Jezreel, as well as the jumping-off point for conquests to Ammon and places south. Here Ahab chose to make his stand: the Aramean king could not be allowed to press any further. Ahab staked his life on the outcome of the battle, and lost both.

The Campaigns of Mesha, King of Moab. *Ahab's persistent thorn in the side to the southeast was Mesha, the Moabite king who reigned from his family home at Dibon. Held in check during the lifetime of Ahab, Mesha's military prowess matched his pride when Ahab died. Most ominously for Israel Mesha was able to seize the tableland of Medeba, which had first been the land of the kingdom of Sihon, then became the territory of the tribe of Reuben, and was one of the best natural staging grounds for thrusts into or out of Israel.*

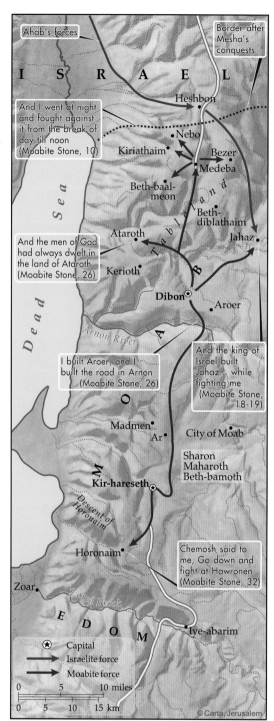

Ahab's forces

Border after Mesha's conquests

ISRAEL

Heshbon

And I went at night and fought against it from the break of day till noon (Moabite Stone, 10)

Nebo

Kiriathaim • Bezer

Medeba

Beth-baal-meon

Beth-diblathaim

Ataroth

Jahaz

And the men of Gad had always dwelt in the land of Ataroth (Moabite Stone, 26)

Kerioth

Dibon ⊛

Aroer

Arnon River

And the king of Israel built Jahaz... while fighting me (Moabite Stone, 18-19)

I built Aroer, and I built the road in Arnon (Moabite Stone, 26)

Madmen

Ar •

City of Moab

Sharon Maharoth Beth-bamoth

Kir-hareseth ⊛

Descent of Horonaim

Chemosh said to me, Go down and fight at Hawronen (Moabite Stone, 32)

Horonaim •

Zoar •

Zered Brook

E D O M

Iye-abarim

⊛ Capital
→ Israelite force
→ Moabite force

0   5   10 miles
0 5 10   15 km

© Carta, Jerusalem

(below) "Now Mesha king of Moab was a sheep breeder," the writer of Kings tells us, "and used to pay the king of Israel 100,000 lambs and the wool of 100,000 rams every year." Although head of a kingdom, Mesha also had a "day job" in a land best suited for shepherding. Flocks of sheep and goats still graze at Dibon amidst the ruins of the once-proud capital of Mesha's realm.

is admirable, and can be credited to both the stable relationship of the people of Judah to their ruling dynasty and the personality of Jehoshaphat himself. Although Jehoshaphat's actions win both the praise and condemnation of the biblical writers, it is clear that his devotion to the LORD God did play an important role in his personal life and in the way that he led his kingdom.

Much of Judah's prosperity came from Jehoshaphat's control of the southern trade routes, especially the movement of exotic goods from Arabia to Philistia and ports on the Mediterranean (2 Chron 17:10–13). To strengthen his hold on these lucrative markets, Jehoshaphat replaced the king of Edom with a governor loyal to Judah (1 Kgs 22:47). This was understandably intolerable for Edom, but also threatened Moab and Ammon, each of whom sought to reestablish their own rights as middlemen on the Spice Route. Prompted by his success against Israel on the Medeba Plateau and in league with the Ammonites and Meunites (a tribe from Mount Seir, i.e., Edom), Mesha crossed the Dead Sea and camped at the springs of En-gedi (Hazazon-tamar). He intended to invade Judah and capture its share of these markets (2 Chron 20:1–4; cf. Gen 14:7). Armed with a Levitical blessing, Jehoshaphat's army marched south and east, stopping just beyond Tekoa where the limestone hill country suddenly gives way to the rugged, chalky and waterless wilderness below. The fight was over before it began: Mesha's coalition couldn't survive its ascent through the wasteland above En-gedi to meet Jehoshaphat. The harsh conditions of the Judean Wilderness apparently sparked tribal infighting that fractured the unity of Mesha's forces (2 Chron 20:5–25). Understandably, Mesha fails to mention this defeat in his victory stela.

With control over the southern routes ensured, Jehoshaphat attempted to reestablish Solomon's profitable commercial ventures on the Red Sea (1 Kgs 22:48–49; 2 Chron 20:35–37; cf. 1 Kgs 9:26–28). Given the many risks of this enterprise (harsh climate, lack of water, long supply lines and difficult sailing conditions), Jehoshaphat needed all the assistance he could get. Israel's king Ahaziah helped Jehoshaphat build his fleet (in an unholy alliance that incurred the wrath of the Chronicler), but Jehoshaphat shut Ahaziah out of a share of the profits by refusing his request to man the voyage. Ahaziah's sailors must have been fairly competent given Israel's longstanding alliance with Phoenicia, but the general lack of sailing expertise by the landlocked Judeans spelled disaster for their effort. Jehoshaphat was bitten by a leader's ultimate frustration: he was condemned for asking for help, yet fell on his face when trying to make a go of it on his own.

Ahaziah, still green behind the ears and wallowing in the legacy of his father Ahab, died after reigning less than two years, a victim of his own clumsiness (2 Kgs 1:2–4, 1:17). After taking the throne, his brother Jehoram set about righting the wrongs inflicted on Israel by Mesha, now that the Moabite king was reeling from his thwarted invasion of Judah. Avoiding a frontal assault through Jericho, Jehoram curried the favor of Jehoshaphat for an end-around from the south. A follow-up attack against Moab east of the Dead Sea would also serve Jehoshaphat's interests and so he willingly offered to attach the armies of Judah and those of his vassal, Edom, to Israel (2 Kgs 3:6–8). The seven-day march down to the eastern Negeb, through the Rift Valley and up to the edge of the incredibly rugged heights of Edom was exhausting, and the armies ran out of water. As before the battle at Ramoth-gilead, Jehoshaphat again had the sensitivity to ask counsel on the feasibility of the upcoming battle from a prophet of the LORD (2 Kgs 3:11; cf. 1 Kgs 22:7). Were it not for the prophet Elisha's intervention on his behalf (Jehoram could run to Baal for help as far as Elisha was concerned; cf. 2 Kgs 3:13), bringing water as dramatically as had his prophetic predecessor on Mt. Carmel, no one would have had the strength to fight (2 Kgs 3:9–20; cf. 1 Kgs 18:41–46). Although the region just south of the Dead Sea receives less than one inch of rain per year, the heights of Edom above frequently catch heavy thunderstorms. In this instance the rainwater from a timely nighttime storm above simply followed the *wadis* back into the Rift Valley where the armies drank their fill. Revived, Jehoshaphat and Jehoram drove the Moabites back to their capital, Kir-hareseth (Kerak), where the battle was broken off after Mesha sacrificed "his oldest son who was to reign in his place" on the city wall (2 Kgs 3:21–27). A plain reading of the text would indicate that Mesha sacrificed the Moabite crown prince in order to prove his desperation and force the hand of his god, Chemosh, thereby confounding the allied attackers in the process. On the other hand, Anson Rainey (The Sacred Bridge, p. 205) suggests that "his oldest son" was the crown prince of Edom who had been captured in battle (cf. 2 Kgs 3:27 in which "his" could refer to the king of Edom; Amos 2:1). If so, this assassination forced Edom to break ranks with Israel and Judah, and sway the tide of battle to Moab.

Jehoshaphat died four years later in 848 B.C. His legacy did not survive him. In a story that smacks of the behavior of the northern kings, Jehoshaphat's own son and successor, the husband of Ahab's daughter Athaliah, a man who was also named Jehoram, purged the Judean royal household in fear of internal threats (2 Chron 21:4), then faced open rebellion on every frontier (2 Kgs 8:20–23; 2 Chron 21:8–17). By the time this Jehoram died in 841 B.C., Judah's holdings in land and capital had been gutted. Within months his son Ahaziah was assassinated, along with Jehoram of Israel, at Jezreel by the Israelite

general Jehu (2 Kgs 9:27–29). The old queen mother Jezebel met her fate, too. Hearing that Jehu had seized the throne, she "painted her eyes, adorned her head and looked out the window" of her upper chambers—from which she was promptly thrown to her death (2 Kgs 9:30–37). At least the old gal went out in style. For better or worse, a new age had dawned in Israel and Judah.

The writer of Kings emphasized the deeds of Ahab, while the post-exilic Chronicler, concerned with the reestablishment of the nation of Judah, naturally focused on Jehoshaphat. Both writers judged human events by how closely their participants—especially the kings of Israel and Judah—adhered to the commands and expectations of the LORD God. While this is a common theme throughout the Bible, it is perhaps most pronounced for the events of the ninth century B.C., as Israel and Judah, left largely alone by the world powers, sought to establish patterns of national behavior that were favorable for their own interests. What made for failure, or success? For Ahab always, and Jehoshaphat sometimes, success was defined in terms of secure borders, a strong national economy and a role on the regional stage. Those who served as the mouthpiece of the LORD God—prophets and the writers of the Bible itself—agreed, but only to a point; after all, these *had* been important ingredients in the Golden Age of David and Solomon. But the lesson was learned on Jehoshaphat: it is better to be faithful to God *even if* life's circumstances side more with what is seen as failure by those who are pushing the boundaries of success. If Ahab wanted to strut, let him strut. Life is good enough when it is lived with the human concerns of the LORD God in mind: justice, righteousness, fairness and common decency, something that was all too uncommon in the court of Ahab.

Jehoshaphat joined Jehoram, the new king of Israel, to attack Moab from the south. This meant first a rugged march through the Wilderness of Judah, then climbing the wall of eastern mountains that rise from the Rift Valley. Nearly dead of thirst before the battle even began, it took water flowing out of the Edomite mountains such as these between the Rift Valley and Edomite capital of Bozrah to revive the coalition forces for the fight.

It was one thing for a king of Judah to try to gain access to a port on the Mediterranean. It was quite another for Jehoshaphat to try to reestablish Judean control over the Red Sea. Here even the water looks exotic—warm, green-blue and rich. Jehoshaphat tried to mimic Solomon's efforts to launch a fleet of ships from Ezion-geber, but failed miserably. The Golden Age was not to be revived.

CHAPTER 11
ELIJAH AND ELISHA
Going About Doing Good

Elijah the Prophet depicted as a Christian saint on a Russian icon from the second half of the 13th century A.D. Here in face, dress and gesture he resembles Jesus. Other Christian iconographers chose to make Elijah a rough ascetic, like John the Baptist. New Testament writers saw him as a forerunner of both.

Achieving greatness is remarkable; doing so in two completely different arenas is something quite special. This is not to say that Elijah, the great prophet of the mid-ninth century B.C., and Elisha, his even greater successor, were the kind to aspire to greatness. Quite the opposite—they just did as they were bidden by the call of God, whether it was in the corridors of power or in cottages scattered across the countryside. By living lives that rang straight and true, fueled by righteousness and compassion, Elijah and Elisha reached greatness not only in the presence of kings, but face-to-face with Everyman. And in the end, it became apparent that the most pronounced differences between kings and peasants were not that significant after all.

In his unsurpassed volume *The Prophets*, Avraham Heschel, one of the greatest philosophers of religion of the twentieth century, described with unrivaled eloquence the essential character of the biblical prophets. "The prophet is a man who feels fiercely" (p. 5). "Prophecy is the voice that God has lent to the silent agony" of people when "no human voice can convey its full terror" (p. 5). "It is a form of living, a crossing point of God and man" (p. 5). "The prophet's theme is, first of all, the very life of a whole people, and his identification lasts more than a moment…it is an involvement that echoes on" (p. 6). Indeed, the prophet's response to the human condition is relentless—it has to be, for "those who are hurt, and He who inhabits eternity, neither slumber nor sleep" (p. 9). Whether one is a prince or a pauper, "the purpose of prophecy is to conquer callousness, to change the inner man as well as to revolutionize history" (p. 17). Everyone stands equal in the eyes of God.

Elijah the prophet hailed from Tishbe, an otherwise unknown town in northern or northwestern Gilead (1 Kgs 17:1). (Perhaps the word "tishbe" simply indicates that Elijah was "among the sojourners of" [Heb. *tishbe*] Gilead.) In any case, most of Elijah's ministry took place in haunts and hollows far from urban areas, fitting locations for one known for his rough look and coarse dress (2 Kgs 1:8). Nothing is known of Elijah's life prior to his sudden and dramatic entrance onto the national stage in 1 Kings 17:1; we can only assume that like most who were raised on the frontier, he possessed a certain toughness and resiliency that proved handy in many situations throughout life.

Although the specific location is not mentioned in the biblical story, it is likely that Elijah first met Ahab on the king's own turf, probably in or near the sumptuous royal palace of Samaria, a building of finely cut stone with paneling and furniture of inlaid ivory (cf. 1 Kgs 22:39; Amos 3:15). Ahab's kingdom was on a heady rise, with its borders pushing outward and the economy expanding. But this Age was Golden only on the surface—an unfortunate circumstance typical to much of Middle Eastern history—riddled with corruption from the top down and hollowed by a huge gap between the thin, wealthy upper crust and the mass of peasants far below.

Springtime growth on Mt. Carmel promises another year of life in the fields and villages of Israel. In the world-view of the indigenous Canaanites, for whom the mountain expressed tangible qualities of the divine, it was in springtime that Baal and Asherah smiled on the land.

For Elijah and the writers of Kings and Chronicles, the problem was rooted in matters of the heart. Jeroboam, the first king of the northern kingdom of Israel, had merged the indigenous Canaanite fertility religion of Baal and Asherah with that of the LORD God. In doing so he declared that it was the calves sanctified at the shrines of Bethel and Dan who were really the gods of Israel's founding epic and who had brought Israel out of Egypt (1 Kgs 12:26–29). Eighty years later Ahab called a spade a spade. When he married Jezebel, the daughter of the king of the Phoenicians (Sidonians), Ahab found it politically expedient to go beyond Jeroboam's syncretism and elevate the Canaanite gods of fertility—the storm cloud treading, rain-giving Baal and his life-giving consort, Asherah—as the official, state-sponsored gods of Israel (1 Kgs 16:31–33). This was far more than a change of Divine Name in the halls of power; it entailed a complete denial of the world-view of the prophets of the LORD God.

The motor that drove Baalism was an understanding that gods shared a common character and set of behaviors with people, and the latter had to strive to placate the former to gain an edge on the good life. In stark contrast, the LORD God revealed himself to Moses as a single Divine Being whose essence was entirely different than humans and who is both unable and unwilling to be put on a chain. Among other things it was a matter of control, an issue that was particularly ripe in a land such as Israel, where the normal change of seasons saw six months of not-a-drop-of-rain every year and where the fertility of the land and flocks and herds always lay just beyond the human grasp. For the dirt-farming masses, the beck and call of Baal and Asherah, the divine-earthy givers of life, was always close at hand, and Ahab's choice to legitimize the Canaanite deities from the palace down was natural, expedient…and fateful. For Ahab and his kingdom the words of the prophet Moses, that "[this is] a land for which the LORD your God cares; the eyes of the LORD your God are always on it, from the beginning even to the end of the year" (Deut 11:12), were no longer relevant.

And so Elijah, whose name means "The LORD is God," attacked Ahab at precisely the point on which his kingdom's greatness rested: the fertility of the land (1 Kgs 17:1). Israel was Phoenicia's breadbasket (1 Kgs 5:10–11; Ezek 27:17; Acts 12:20), and its leadership now chose to depend on Phoenicia's gods to ensure this fertility. Elijah cut to the source (no rain or dew!), devastating everyone in hope of saving some: "When all hopes are dashed and all conceit is shattered, man begins to miss what he has long spurned" (Heschel, *The Prophets*, p. 193). The immediate response of Ahab, who might have expected prophetic comfort from someone named Eli-baal instead, is not recorded. However, as the years passed and famine strengthened its grip on the land, Ahab

came to blame Elijah for his troubles (1 Kgs 18:16–17), clearly aware that the power of Baal and Asherah was being confounded by someone, or something, beyond his control.

A time-worn verse from the *Tale of Aqhat*, a fourteenth-century B.C. Ugaritic (north Syrian) legend of this earthy world of the divine, expresses exactly the Canaanite's fear of the capriciousness of Baal:

> Seven years shall Baal fail,
> eight, the Rider of the Clouds.
> No dew, no rain, no welling-up of the deep,
> No sweetness of Baal's voice.

(Aqhat C 42–46; ANET 153)

To the Canaanites the "voice" of Baal of course was thunder, rolling over the waters of the Mediterranean in front of the darkened rain cloud, lit by flashes of lightning to signal the onrush of rain (cf. Ps 29:3–11).

Having delivered his sentence Elijah fled east, where rainfall was relatively scarce even in good years. He stayed within the crevice of the brook Cherith east of the Jordan River (today identified in Church tradition as the *Wadi Qilt*, a majestic canyon flowing into the Jordan from the west), where the power of Baal was weak, so to speak, and Elijah had to depend on provision supplied by a God not limited by local conditions (1 Kgs 17:2–6). Eventually the flow of water in the Cherith dried up and Elijah, directed as always by the word of God, traversed the width of both Israel and Phoenicia to Zarephath (modern Sarafand), a large city-state with an active harbor midway between Tyre

Elijah's first point of retreat was to the brook Cherith, remembered in church tradition as the Wadi Qilt above Jericho. Before Herod the Great channeled the spring flow of the Qilt into an aqueduct to supply his nearby winter palace, the wadi carried some water year around. Now, the water flow is limited to a few days in the winter when rainfall from the hills above washes—sometimes suddenly and always majestically—into the Rift Valley below. In years of poor rain, the spring water of the Qilt would quickly be absorbed into the wadi floor: "And after a while, the brook dried up because there was no rain in the land" (1 Kgs 17:7).

Ahab's royal palace in Samaria set the standard for other palaces in Israel (at Megiddo and Hazor), Judah (Jerusalem and Ramat Rachel) and Transjordan (Rabbath-bene-ammon). All had pillars of ashlar masonry topped by "proto-Aeolic" stone capitals, which were likely meant to be stylized representations of palm trees.

(above, left) The most common artistic representation of Baal from the ancient world shows the god in full stride, with his upraised right hand holding a club or lightning bolt about to be hurled to earth. This is the onrushing thundercloud, taking the dry land of Canaan by storm and impregnating the earth with rain, the fluid of life.

(above, right) In a pose reflecting images of Baal, this statue of Elijah slaying the god's prophets freeze-frames the prophet's righteous indignation. Towering over the courtyard of the Carmelite Monastery of Muhraqa on Mt. Carmel, the image depicts Elijah as a man driven by the wrath of God, fed up with the direction that the religious and political leadership of his nation has been taking the people he loves.

and Sidon on the Phoenician coast. This place represented everything that was foreign to Elijah. Yet in spite of its obvious prosperity (attested by both textual and archaeological sources), the city was also home to people who were impoverished. In Zarephath Elijah met the personal and very real needs of a widow and her son, an insignificant family destitute to the point of death (1 Kgs 17:7–24). Basic human needs were familiar ground even deep in enemy territory, and Elijah, who was motivated neither by the opportunity for riches or for power, simply went about doing good.

By the third year the famine was particularly severe. For all its resources, Ahab's capital of Samaria lay prone and nearly strangled (1 Kgs 18:1–2). Although Ahab didn't know it yet, rain was about to inundate the land (cf. vs. 1). To set the stage for the LORD's dramatic entrance, Elijah, again prompted by the divine call, arranged a public showdown with the king and his prophets on Mount Carmel.

The promontory of Carmel rises abruptly out of the Mediterranean, soaring to a height of nearly 1,800 feet. Its bold, westward face is the first bit of land in Israel to catch the brunt of the winter storms rolling off the sea (cf. Ps 29:3–11) and so this well-watered, always green mountain was held in divine reverence by the Canaanites. Here Baal, a god represented in ancient art and literature by the thunder cloud and lightning bolt, was most at home and here his fertile consort Asherah, the sacred tree, was most visibly impregnated by Baal's life-giving rain. Elijah, in total command of the situation, chose this of all places to uproot the Canaanite gods. Ahab, sensing that his own prophets had home-court advantage, was convinced Baal couldn't lose.

Ahab and his gang were up first. Their orgiastic actions around the sacrificial altar were consistent with what is known from Ugaritic texts describing the means by which north Syrians—and by implication, Canaanites—placated their gods (1 Kgs 18:20–29). Everyone expected that Baal would appear as the sudden fire of lightning, signaling the onrush of rain. As the scene unfolded and the gods remained silent, Elijah's amusement grew. The climax came when the prophet took center stage. The presence of an ox on Elijah's altar was particularly expressive, for in the popular iconography of the day Baal was also represented by the bull, the strongest, most fertile of the domesticated animals, now butchered and emasculated before the LORD and doused, in mocking tribute to his impotence, with a fluid he could no longer control (1 Kgs 18:30–35). The fire of the LORD was quick, dramatic and complete, and followed by heavy rain (1 Kgs 18:36–45).

> ...the one who rides on the clouds—
> his name is the LORD! (Ps 68:4; cf. Deut 33:26)

Ahab took off in his chariot, trying to outrace the storm to his winter capital in Jezreel, which lay directly across the Jezreel Valley to the east. When he began his ride, the normally swampy floor of the valley was still rock-hard from three years of drought, but by the time Elijah had picked his way to Ahab's capital by foot along the edge of the hills to the south, the Jezreel Valley had filled with runoff water, bogging Ahab's chariot to the axles as surely as Baal had mired his kingdom (1 Kgs 18:45–46).

Jezebel, comfortably at home in Jezreel, was incensed and swore to execute the troublesome prophet of the LORD. Based on oath-taking formulae found in earlier texts from Mari on the upper Euphrates, it is possible that Jezebel followed the old practice of touching her own throat (in a slitting motion?) when she swore "may the gods do to me and even more so..." (1 Kgs 19:2). This visible drama aside, Elijah fled south, bisecting the length of Israel and Judah to Beer-sheba, the gateway to the great and terrible wilderness (cf. Deut 1:19) of Moses' wanderings. Then, under the strength of the LORD, Elijah made his way to Horeb (Mt. Sinai), called here by the writer of Kings "the mountain of God" (1 Kgs 19:3–8).

The reason Elijah fled from Israel's Phoenician queen is unclear; that he caved in her presence after standing before Ahab and his horde of prophets is possible, but unconvincing. Inferences in the story line suggest that Elijah, a great prophet but someone certainly not immune to the limits of being human, might have been seized by a sudden fit of ontological doubt. After all, when the fire of the LORD fell from heaven on Mount Carmel, the physical image that everyone saw was probably lightning, what *Baal* was supposed to look like. In the downtime of post-battle reflection the question arises, *who was it that* appeared, anyway? And is the LORD God in the end of the same *essence* as Baal, lightning for lightning, stronger today but perhaps not so tomorrow? So Elijah retraced the steps of both the patriarchs (cf. Gen 12:1–9) and Moses, a journey from the mountain of Baal to the mountain of God, where he stood alone and in need of a very different kind of divine encounter (1 Kgs 19:8).

There, lost in solitude deep in the awesome majesty of the Sinai Peninsula, high on the great Mount of Revelation and standing at the opening of what the writer of Kings intended to be the very cave of Moses, Elijah finally saw the LORD God for what He is—not bound to natural phenomena and patterns of human behavior like Baal (although he could choose to appear that way if he wanted to) but, in the translation of Chanan Brichto, as "the sound of thinnest silence" (1 Kgs 19:9–12; *Toward a Grammar of Biblical Poetics*, 141). The sound—the voice—of the LORD: incredibly powerful (cf. Ps 29:3–11), but wholly other; total peace rather than noise and chaos. It was only when Elijah saw personally that in his essence the LORD God is a different kind of reality altogether than the earthy, crowded Canaanite-now-Israelite pantheon, that Elijah was empowered to talk with God face-to-face and became equipped to anoint kings and prophets. On Horeb, greatness became greater.

Elijah returned north, crossing into Transjordan where, in a steppe land called "the wilderness of Damascus" he anointed Hazael as the next king of Aram-Damascus (i.e., Syria) and Jehu the future king of Israel (1 Kgs 19:15–16). According to Assyrian annals Hazael was "son of a nobody" (ANET 280), that is, not of royal blood, although he must already have been a man of some standing in the administration of Ben-hadad II, the reigning king of Aram-Damascus. Jehu was as an officer in Ahab's bodyguard (2 Kgs 9:25) and later became a general in the Israelite army. As was the case when Saul anointed the young shepherd boy David king over Israel,

neither of these men were to assume the throne for some time (2 Kgs 8:7–15, 9:1–13; cf. 1 Sam 16:1–23), although with the prophetic news in hand it is likely that they, like David, spent the intervening years in silent yet sure preparation for their appointed role. The "wilderness of Damascus" was an appropriate setting for Elijah's pronouncement, as this frontier was part of the large buffer zone between Israel and Aram-Damascus over which both nations would expend a great deal of military and economic energy trying to put a stranglehold on each other.

Elijah also anointed Elisha son of Shaphat, a farmer from Abel-meholah (probably *Tell Abu Sus*) in the north-central Jordan Valley, as his heir-apparent (1 Kgs 19:19–21). Elijah found his disciple hard at work, twelfth in a line of plowers all turning furrows in the same field by single-share plows, each pulled by a pair of oxen (vs. 21). Plucked from a prosperous and secure future (cf. Lk 9:62), Elisha would wear the mantle of prophetic authority well.

Elijah's prophetic ministry probably began relatively early in Ahab's reign (c. 870–865 B.C.) and ended shortly after the death of Jehoshaphat (848–847 B.C.). Yet we know of only a few specific events in which Elijah was involved during these two decades other than those connected with his confrontations with Ahab on Mount Carmel and the LORD on Mount Sinai. It is significant that men such as Jehu the soldier, Elisha the farmer and especially Hazael, a foreigner, recognized Elijah and his authority immediately: apparently Elijah's face and reputation were widely known. Wise, forthright and somewhat eccentric personalities tend to draw followers, and we can assume that Elijah had his share. He seems to have had a close association with a school or company of prophets (lit. "sons of the prophets") at Bethel and one at Jericho (2 Kgs 2:3, 2:5), with probably another from Gilgal (2 Kgs 2:1) and certainly others at locations throughout the northern kingdom of Israel. Elijah was the master example, they the disciples. While it is reasonable to suppose

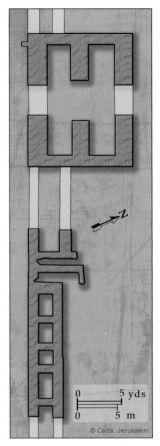

This solid four-chambered gate attached to a casemate wall uncovered in archaeological excavations at Tel Jezreel in 1992 and 1993 is typical of Ahab's building projects.

Backtracking Israel's journey into the land of promise, Elijah's flight from Jezebel took him to Mt. Horeb (Mt. Sinai), reliving a 40-year wandering in a 40-day "sprint." The silent view from Mt. Sinai whispers the awesome majesty of God. Here, Elijah finally understood that God's essence was—and is—wholly Other.

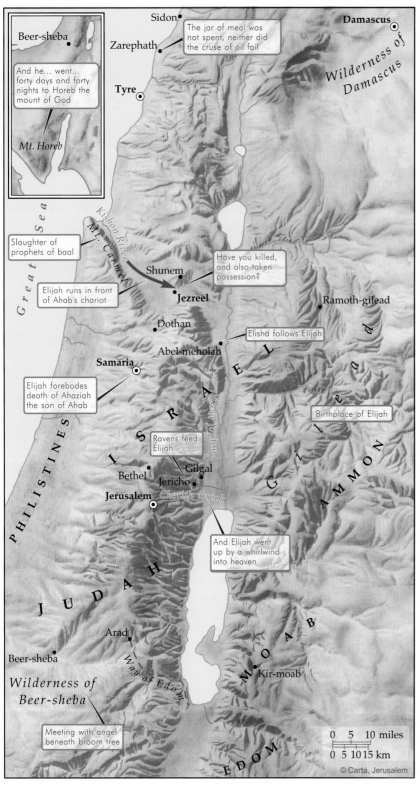

On the map:

Beer-sheba

Sidon

Damascus

Zarephath

The jar of meal was not spent, neither did the cruse of oil fail

Wilderness of Damascus

Tyre

And he... went... forty days and forty nights to Horeb the mount of God

Mt. Horeb

Kishon River

Mt. Carmel

Slaughter of prophets of baal

Shunem

Have you killed, and also taken possession?

Elijah runs in front of Ahab's chariot

Jezreel

Ramoth-gilead

Dothan

Elisha follows Elijah

Abel-meholah

Samaria

Elijah forebodes death of Ahaziah the son of Ahab

Birthplace of Elijah

Ravens feed Elijah

Bethel

Gilgal

Jericho

Jerusalem

Cherith Brook

And Elijah went up by a whirlwind into heaven

Great Sea

I S R A E L

G i l e a d

A M M O N

P H I L I S T I N E S

J U D A H

M O A B

Arad

Beer-sheba

Way of Edom

Kir-moab

Wilderness of Beer-sheba

Meeting with angel beneath broom tree

E D O M

0   5   10 miles

0   5   10 15 km

© Carta, Jerusalem

Elijah's Prophetic Ministry. *With the exceptions of a journey into Phoenicia and another to Mt. Horeb—both with clear pedagogical goals—Elijah's prophetic ministry as recorded in the Book of Kings took place in the heartland of the northern kingdom of Israel. Here, where rainfall was more predictable than in Judah, the clash between the devotees of the Canaanite fertility deities Baal and Asherah and the followers of the LORD God was most pronounced.*

and saw in the great prophet a hope for direction and purpose that was somehow missing in their lives back home. It is also reasonable to conclude that for Elijah to develop this kind of reputation and position in Israel, he must have had significant contact with people in towns and villages throughout the land. To fill in the blanks is impossible.

Three key episodes in his life yet remain, and it is from these that a framework for the rest can be supposed. In the first, Elijah met Ahab in the vineyard of Naboth after Naboth was murdered and his patronage seized (1 Kgs 21:17–20). Elijah had a penchant for confronting Ahab at locations precisely where the king thought he had dealt himself a winning hand; in each case, Ahab's strong suit was trumped by the prophet. As opposed as Elijah was to Ahab's devotion to Baal and Asherah, it was because the king had deliberately violated the rights of his own people that the prophet announced the LORD God would overthrow his dynasty (1 Kgs 21:21–24). Many texts from the ancient Near East mention the culturally expected norm that the primary responsibility of the one in power was to help those who could not help themselves, although kings who crowed the loudest that they had done so were almost certainly covering up the fact that they didn't. In any case, virtually all failed on this account, and some, like Ahab, miserably so. Meanwhile, Elijah's greatness was honed on the quest for justice among the vineyards and villages of Israel.

The second and third episodes focus on Elijah's confrontations with the next generation of kings: Ahaziah son of Ahab and Jehoram, who was not only the son of Jehoshaphat but also the husband of Ahab's daughter, Athaliah (2 Kgs 1:1–18; 2 Chron 21:8–15). Both fell under God's judgment for matters of the heart, seeking after gods other than the LORD. Ahaziah was critically injured in a fall from an upper room in his palace in Samaria. Even though his sickness to death fell within Elijah's area of expertise (cf. 1 Kgs 17:17–24), Ahaziah sought help from a Philistine god, Baal-zebub of Ekron. Because Ekron guarded Jerusalem's access to the coast, we are left to wonder if Ahaziah was working on forging a political alliance with Philistia at Judah's expense at the time. In any case, when Elijah announced that Ahaziah would die of his injuries, the king responded with a show of military strength—if his father's prophets of Baal couldn't best Elijah, surely Israel's army could! But like on Mount Carmel the LORD again appeared as fire from heaven, and again Elijah was victorious.

For his part, Jehoram of Judah received a written message from Elijah containing a scathing pronouncement against the king for walking in the footsteps of his father-in-law Ahab (2 Chron 21:12–15). Elijah recognized that the same issues his own people were facing also plagued Israel's neighbor to the

that Elijah's followers represented a cross section of Israelite society, it is also likely that not a few hailed from the dissatisfied or disenfranchised underclass

south. Old and approaching the end of his ministry, he sent a letter to Jehoram rather than make the trek to Jerusalem personally. The prophet was not to be long on this earth and so Jehoram, sensing that the old man would soon leave him alone, preferred business as usual, Ahab-style. The Chronicler's litany of Jehoram's reign focuses on the ways that Jehoshaphat's legacy crumbled under the incompetence of his son, and ends with the matter-of-fact notation that the king died in great pain, to no one's regret and mourned by no one (2 Chron 21:18–20). We can only suppose that this utter lack of public sympathy for Jehoram was a result of the king's abject failure in every aspect of his reign, and that the people of Judah longed for their own Elijah, someone who could not only eyeball those in power but bend to their own untold pleas. Again, Heschel: "The prophet's ear perceives the silent sigh" (p. 9).

Elijah's end—if it's even proper to speak of his presence in Israel as ending—was as dramatic as his beginning. Accompanied by Elisha, Elijah had walked the highways and byways of Israel for years, prophetic father with protégé son. Now their last journey together took them from Gilgal to Bethel to Jericho and across the Jordan River, locations with strong historical and spiritual ties to the mighty acts of God. The itinerary is a bit odd: from Gilgal they went "down" to Bethel (2 Kgs 2:1–2). Perhaps their point of departure was not the Gilgal in the lower Jordan Valley near Jericho that had served both as Joshua's base camp during the conquest of Canaan and Israel's spiritual center throughout the time of the Judges (*Khirbet el-Mafjar?*; Josh 4:19; 1 Sam 7:16, 10:8, 11:14, 15:10–31), but a place in the hill country of Ephraim north of Bethel whose memory is preserved in Jiljiliya, the name of the modern Arab village in the vicinity (cf. Deut 11:30). In any case, the name Gilgal evoked great emotions for ancient Israel. As for Bethel, the company of prophets loyal to Elijah there kept their city's connections to the God of the patriarchs alive in spite of the shrine that Jeroboam had erected for the golden calf (2 Kgs 2:3; Gen 12:8, 13:3, 28:18–19, 35:1–3; 1 Kgs 12:26–29). And Jericho, the site of Joshua's first victory after crossing the Jordan River, marked the down payment for the realization that the Land of Promise held lifelong blessings for its new inhabitants.

From Jericho, Elijah and Elisha crossed the Jordan on dry ground, a dramatic reversal of Joshua's march into Canaan and one that echoes both the crossing of the Red Sea and parting of the primeval waters of

Like Moses, the other great prophetic voice who channeled the words of the LORD to a recalcitrant people, Elijah took his last breath east of the Jordan River. Somewhere here, on the Plains of Moab beneath Mt. Nebo, Elijah was caught up in a chariot of fire taking him on a journey far above anywhere that Baal, the Rider of the Clouds, could go.

creation (2 Kgs 2:7–8; cf. Josh 3:7–17; Ex 14:21–31; Gen 1:9). Then, in front of the rise of hills of the Medeba Plateau and somewhere near the unknown place where God had buried Moses the greatest of all prophets (Deut 34:5–6), Elijah once more saw the LORD appear as fire, this time lifting him into a final, triumphant encounter with the Divine (2 Kgs 2:10–12).

Elisha crossed back over the Jordan, again on dry ground and now with Elijah's mantle of power in hand, possessing a double portion of his mentor's spirit (2 Kgs 2:9–14). Elisha knew that he needed something more than normal human strength for the task ahead, what with Ahaziah's undistinguished younger brother Jehoram on the throne of Israel (2 Kgs 1:17) and his country facing serious incursions from both Aram-Damascus and Moab. But while Elisha did end up playing an important role in Israelite and Judean politics, the writer of Kings tended to emphasize Elisha's affinity for individuals instead, be they actors in a larger royal play such as Naaman or the silent, common people of the land.

Elisha's first miracle back in Israel was to purify the water of the spring of Jericho (2 Kgs 2:19–22; cf. 1 Kgs 16:34). This powerful spring, issuing 1,000

It is possible to locate Naboth's vineyard with reasonable certainty on the eastern slope of Jezreel, between Ahab's citadel up top and the city's spring at its base. Surely royal land connected the two, but Ahab, already sitting pretty in his winter capital, was bent on getting more. Ignoring his first impulse that patriarchal land was not to be disinherited, Ahab killed, seized and enjoyed—until he felt the wrath of Elijah in Naboth's vineyard, the scene of the crime, as shown in this 19th century engraving. (Carta, Jerusalem)

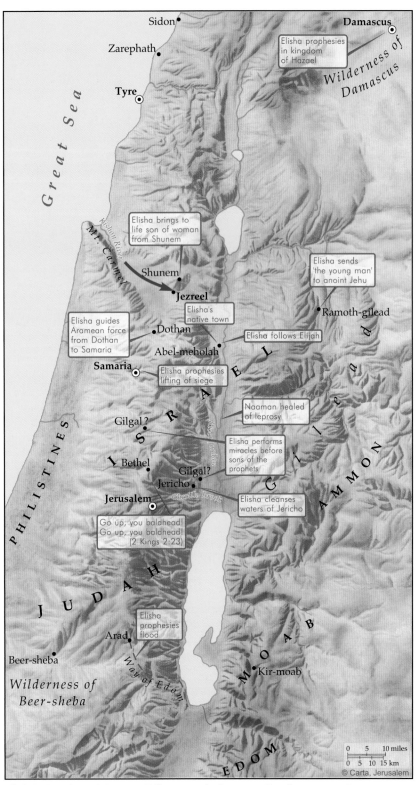

Elisha's Prophetic Ministry. *Following in the footsteps of his illustrious predecessor Elijah, Elisha focused his ministry on things northern. Unlike the prophets of the 8th to 6th centuries B.C., most of whom were southern and left written accounts of their messages and ministries, Elijah and Elisha verified their prophetic words by performing miracles. Centuries later Jesus of Nazareth, also a northern prophet (among other things), fostered a ministry that began in a similar way.*

ants to be "unfruitful" and "miscarry," a most unfortunate circumstance for those in the area still depending on the work of Baal (vss. 19, 21). Elisha purified the spring with salt in a ritual that has been variously explained both symbolically and rationalistically. The event itself placed Elisha in a special kind of prophetic pattern: Moses' first miracle after passing through the Red Sea was to make bad water good (Ex 15:22–26); Elisha's first miracle after similarly crossing the Jordan was to do the same; and in a statement intentionally declaring the revival of prophetic authority in Israel, the gospel writer John recorded that Jesus' first miracle after passing through the waters of the Jordan in baptism was to make already good water better (Jn 2:1–11).

Elisha's initial journey as prophet took him to places in Israel that were particularly significant in the clash between Baal and the LORD: Bethel, Mount Carmel and Samaria (2 Kgs 2:23–25). He surely stopped at Bethel to confirm his role as Elijah's successor with the city's company of sons of the prophets, although on the way Elisha had a run-in with a very different kind of gang who taunted his authority. Mount Carmel by now seems to have become a mountain of the LORD, and during his ministry Elisha stopped there on more than one occasion (cf. 2 Kgs 4:25). That Elisha ended his journey by "returning" to Samaria is indication enough that a large part of his ministry was focused in the Israelite capital (2 Kgs 2:25).

Elisha's first foray into affairs of state had already come a year or two earlier when he accompanied Jehoram king of Israel, Jehoshaphat and the combined armies of Israel and Judah on a strenuous march through the eastern Negeb to attack Moab from the south (2 Kgs 3:11–12). Chronological clues in 2 Chronicles 21:12–15 indicate that Elijah was still alive although elderly at the time, and we can assume that Elisha was already acting on his mentor's behalf when the situation so warranted. Before any risky venture kings in the ancient world habitually invoked the blessing of their gods through a royal cadre of prophets, and although a robust Elisha was probably obliged to join the battle entourage along with Jehoram's yes-men, his heart and mouth answered only to the LORD. Israel's army succeeded in the fight only because of Elisha's timely intervention bringing water out of the rock-face of Edom, Moses-style, in spite of the grumbly and disbelieving Jehoram (2 Kgs 3:10, 3:13–20).

Next up was a most remarkable event when seen within the context of the ongoing Israelite-Aramean struggle for military and economic supremacy in the region. Naaman, a high-ranking commander in the army of the Aramean king, Ben-hadad, came to Elisha to be healed of leprosy (2 Kgs 5:1–14). His debilitation from this wasting disease could only mean good news for Jehoram and the regional pri-

gallons of water per minute, should have been the primary source of life for the Jericho oasis but for reasons unknown caused the land and its inhabit-

orities of Israel, but Elisha saw the bigger picture. Naaman can be excused if he had trouble focusing on the means of his cure, for the water of the rivers that flow through the plain of Damascus, the Abana (modern *Nahr Barada*) and Pharpar (*Nahr el-ʿAwaj*), are cold, clear and refreshing, while the Jordan below the Sea of Galilee, where he surely washed, is often sluggish and muddy. Elisha healed Naaman willingly, opening a window that reveals the extent to which God's grace overrode national and religious priorities back home (2 Kgs 5:1, 5:18–19; cf. Jonah 4:11; Lk 4:24–27).

During the reign of Ahab, the Arameans had twice penetrated into Israel, and twice were repulsed by the Israelite king (1 Kgs 20:1–30). Now Ahab's death on the battlefield at Ramoth-gilead gave the Arameans the chance to take their campaign back to Israel's heartland. Ben-hadad's first strike in this new campaign was to order his army to lay siege to Dothan, ostensibly to kidnap Elisha who, in the Aramean king's reasoned opinion, was a spy who knew too much (2 Kgs 6:8–14). The route to Dothan must have taken the Aramean army past the Israelite winter capital at Jezreel (was Elisha a more important target than Jehoram?), then through the Jezreel Valley to Dothan, the northern doorway to the hill country of Israel and the fast track to Samaria itself. Israel's victory arose from a combination of Elisha's boldness and God's active hand on behalf of his people (2 Kgs 6:15–23).

Ben-hadad's effort to throttle Israel was only temporarily checked. The next year the king took command of the army himself, pushed all the way to Samaria and besieged the city. Naaman, now revived, probably played a role in this campaign, although the Bible is silent on details. It was a long, drawn-out affair, and soon Israel's capital was gripped by famine, its starving, desperate inhabitants reduced to acts of barbarism (2 Kgs 6:24–31). Jehoram blamed Elisha for the situation, but so did Ben-hadad. Inside the city gate, where real life counted, however, Elisha maintained rapport with the city's elders, offering hope that the siege would be broken—and it was, when the Arameans, in a panic, thought they were being attacked by Hittite and Egyptian mercenaries in the hire of the king of Israel and fled back across the Jordan River (2 Kgs 7:1–20).

Affairs of state make for grand designs, but in the end the things that matter the most happen on the streets where we live. Throughout the larger flow of events was dominated by kings and battles, the writer of Kings interspersed stories of Elisha's interaction with people who were tangled up in the normal circumstances of life. Most cited misfortunes that fell on the sons of the prophets or their families. One could argue that Elisha simply took care of his own; or, more favorably, it is likely that these stories are among the many once known that illustrate the

prophet's dedication to the task of going about doing good. In any case, these stories focus on the interplay of trouble and hope that was part of normal life for everyone in ancient Israel.

Of these stories, only one does not mention a specific geographical location, perhaps out of recognition that it relates an unfortunate circumstance too common in ancient Israel to be localized. A village woman, a widow of one of the sons of the prophets, fell into debt and was about to lose her two dependent children to a creditor who intended to seize them as slaves until they could pay off the amount owed, likely with interest (2 Kgs 4:1; cf. 1 Kgs 17:8–16). Widows held an inferior status in Israelite society, and those with young children to support were often reduced to poverty, falling prone to the whims and charity of others (cf. Deut 26:12–13; Job 29:11–12). Prophetic invectives against unjust creditors indicate that laws to prevent this kind of injustice were either not fully in place, not well enforced, or enforced capriciously (Isa 1:17, 1:23; Jer 7:4–7, 22:3; cf. Deut 24:17–18, 27:19). Recognizing that God alone was the ultimate provider for his destitute followers (Deut 10:17–18; Ps 146:9), Elisha opened the way for God to provide enough olive oil for the poor woman to pay off her debt and live besides (2 Kgs 4:2–7).

Two of Elisha's "every-day" episodes had to do with food, one taking place at Gilgal (2 Kgs 4:38–41) and the other, probably also at Gilgal, involving a visitor from Baal-shalishah (2 Kgs 4:42–44). A usually reliable record of early Church tradition (Eusebius and Jerome, *Onomasticon*) places Baal-shalishah above the southeastern edge of the Sharon Plain (*Khirbet Sirisiya*) in a fairly well-watered area a bit east of the powerful Yarkon springs. If Eusebius's location is to be accepted, the Gilgal mentioned here was probably the site in the rocky hills of Ephraim north of Bethel that had been visited by Elijah and

The spring at the eastern foot of Jericho, Tell es-Sultan, is one of the strongest in the Rift Valley. Here the oldest city on earth first found life, and here death came creeping into the oasis in the days of Elisha, its spring fouled and land unproductive. Local tradition has renamed the spring "Elisha's Spring" in gratitude of the prophet's miracle of healing the water. Now enclosed in a large building covering two reservoirs, the spring is depicted here in a 19th century engraving. (Carta, Jerusalem)

Jericho Today. *Remains of the Old Testament city of Jericho, Elisha's Spring at its base, and New Testament Jericho are all easily accessible within the city limits of Jericho today.*

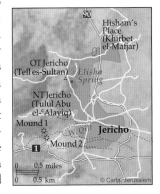

This bronze bull, c. 7 inches long, was found within the remains of a circular enclosure wall on a low rocky ridge 5 miles east of Dothan. With no evidence of contemporary settlement in the immediate vicinity, the site appears to have been a local "high place" for Baal worship, either by Canaanites or Israelites, at the beginning of the Iron Age. This was the time when Israel began to shift from desert to village life and the pull of Baal was strong. (NEAEHL)

Uncovered during the 1993 and 1994 excavations at Dan, the Tel Dan inscription preserves a victory shout of Hazael over Israel and Judah. This was the same Hazael Elijah had anointed king of Aram-Damascus. When Elisha healed Naaman, the Aramean general, the people of Israel and Judah must have wondered on whose side their prophets stood—or, perhaps, how inclusive God's kingdom actually could be.

Elisha on their last journey together (cf. 2 Kgs 2:1–2). The winter rains in the region were poor that year and the sons of the prophets were forced to scavenge plants from the hillside for food. Wild plants probably always made up a portion of the ancient diet, and skilled foragers could easily differentiate between good plants and bad. Mistakes were sometimes made, however, and in this case Elisha fortunately knew a home-brewed remedy to restore flavor and nutrition to the stew. The famine was broken for the sons of the prophets when a man from Baal-shalishah brought Elisha a supply of barley bread and grain, his springtime offering of first fruits for God's prophet (cf. Deut 26:12–13). The gift was generous but not sufficient as a meal for everyone, yet at Elisha's insistence it fed a multitude of one hundred men with a surplus left for later. This miracle is a mini-parallel of the multiplication of the loaves and fishes by Jesus, who fed 5,000, then 4,000, both times with leftovers (Mt 14:13–21, 15:32–39).

A fourth miraculous story took place on the bank of the Jordan River near the Gilgal just outside of Jericho. One of the sons of the prophets lost an iron ax-head in the water while chopping trees for building materials (2 Kgs 6:1–7). The possibility of work accidents was frequent enough in ancient Israel, and sometimes led to disastrous results (Deut 19:4–5). In this case the loss was only financial, but the owner of the ax was a third-party whose rights for restitution had to be recognized. Elisha showed requisite concern—he righted wrongs whether they were accidental or intentional, done to his prophets or by them—and the ax-head floated to the surface.

But the best-known of Elisha's miracle stories took place at Shunem, a sizeable farming village at the edge of the Jezreel Valley hugging the southern slope of Mount Moreh, opposite the Israelite winter palace at Jezreel. Shunem was half-way between Elisha's family home at Abel-meholah and Mount Carmel, and as such was a convenient rest stop on the two-day journey between the two. As he traveled, Elisha received gracious hospitality from a prosperous Shunammite farmer and his wife, and he eventually became an informal member of their household (2 Kgs 4:8–17). When their only son died of heatstroke in the heat of the wheat harvest early one summer, Elisha, driven with compassion, raised the boy to life, a dramatic confirmation of his own prophetic authority (2 Kgs 4:18–37; cf. 1 Kgs 17:17–24). Eight centuries later the village of Shunem was long gone but the population of the region still lived on the slopes of Mount Moreh, now in a town called Nain. Here Jesus raised another boy to life, the only child of his mother, prompting the villagers to gasp in amazement, "A

great prophet has risen among us [—again!]. God has visited his people [—again!]" (Lk 7:11–17).

Back in the royal courts of Jehoram and Ben-hadad, Elisha's reception was mixed—on the one hand, his powers were feared; on the other, both kings were fascinated with the man and knew he had access to something they needed. Elisha's reputation prompted Jehoram to restore the Shunammite woman's land to her after a seven-year absence due to famine (2 Kgs 8:1–6). This act of justice should have been the norm in Israel, but seems all the more remarkable in light of Ahab's seizure of Naboth's vineyard (cf. 1 Kgs 21:1–29) and Jehoram's own track record of running in the ways of his notorious father. As for the king of Aram-Damascus, Ben-hadad knew that only a man as connected to God as Elisha was could foresee the result of his final illness. Elisha knew, all right, and with his prophetic word Hazael, whom Elijah had anointed king years before, murdered Ben-hadad and seized the Aramean throne (2 Kgs 8:7–15; cf. 1 Kgs 19:15). Two years later, in 841 B.C., Jehu, who had also been anointed as king by Elijah, assassinated Jehoram and seized the throne of Israel (2 Kgs 9:14–26; cf. 1 Kgs 19:16).

An era had passed; new dynasties arose in Israel and Aram-Damascus, but the new blood was like the old. Elisha foresaw that Hazael would be just as aggressive against Israel as Ben-hadad had been, an eventuality attested by both the biblical record (2 Kgs 9:14, 10:32–33, 13:3, 13:22) and archaeology (the Tel Dan inscription). For his part, Jehu destroyed the entire royal house of Omri, purging the land of Ahab's ties to Baal but coming no closer to the ethical demands of the LORD God than did his predecessor (2 Kgs 10:1–31). The years passed and Israel's struggles with Aram-Damascus—and their own soul—became more and more intractable, sliding from one desperate strait to another. Elisha finally faded from the scene, an old, sick man who had fought the good fight but had to leave the battle and its results to others (2 Kgs 13:14–21).

Elijah and Elisha set the standard for prophetic leadership in Israel, a nation ripe with the potential for both greatness and despair. Elijah's style—his dress, boldness and uncanny ability to slice to the core—became the mark of the great prophet that God would one day send to announce the climax of His work on earth (Mal 4:5; Sirach 48:10–11; Mt 3:1–12). Elisha followed, touching people where they were and challenging and compelling them to follow the LORD God in both the big things and little things of life. Much of what Elisha did was mirrored in the ministry of Jesus, who also "went about doing good and healing all who were oppressed...for God was with him" (Acts 10:38). Through this trajectory, linking the Testaments, Elisha's work was certainly not in vain.

CHAPTER 12

JONAH
Not on My Watch

For all its familiarity, the story of Jonah is an enigma. The narrative is cast in simple language, presenting a point-A-to-point-B sequence of events in four short episodes, only forty-eight verses in all, told in a way that even a child can understand—except that scholars, theologians and students of the *belle-lettres* can never quite seem to get their hearts and minds around the book. The plot is simple but the stakes are immense, for at every moment in the flow of action questions arise about the nature of God and people (especially *His* people), and a host of other issues that are part of all of our attempts to figure out our place in the world: responsibility and resolve, justice and fate, action, reaction, repentance, mercy, grace and second chances. Given this complexity, perhaps a base-line understanding of the book should start with the basics: the historical and geographical context in which the storyline itself is set.

Jonah was a man of the mid-eighth century B.C., a product of the times that for Israel was an age of both heady nationalism and social complacency. It was a great time to be one of the "haves," this in spite of the fact that Israel was overshadowed by the ominous presence of the Assyrian empire just off-stage to the right. For over two hundred years Assyria had filled the northeastern horizon, gathering energy like a giant thunderstorm and occasionally hurling lightning bolts of destruction to the west. Assyria was after the wealth of Egypt, and to realize this goal a succession of the stronger of the Assyrian kings pushed across Western Asia, slowly but relentlessly grabbing the imperial trade routes that bisected the lands lining the eastern Mediterranean seaboard. Every kingdom and people group that stood in the way capitulated to the Might that was Assyria (in the phrase of H. W. F. Saggs), be it through conquest or surrender, and were forced to bury their own nationalistic aspirations under the weight of vassal or provincial status. By the late ninth and early eighth centuries B.C. Shalmaneser III (858–824 B.C.) and Adad-nirari III (810–783 B.C.) had struck as deeply as Mount Carmel (841 B.C.) and Damascus (in 841 and 796 B.C.), forcing tribute from Israel and Phoenicia in the process.

Israel was bent but not broken. When under a succession of three weak kings (Shalmaneser IV, 782–773 B.C.; Ashur-dan III, 772–755 B.C.; and Ashur-nirari V, 754–745 B.C.) the Assyrians became preoccupied with internal matters and had to ward

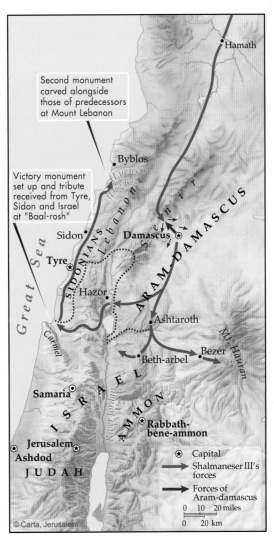

off attacks by Urartu on their northern border, the power vacuum in the west gave Israel its chance. Absent Assyria, Jehoash (798–781 B.C.) and his son Jeroboam II (781–753 B.C.) steered Israel through its last great hurrah, restoring Israelite control over the trade routes of the Jezreel Valley and Transjordan and subduing the Aramean states that had been unable to fully recover from the blow to the head they had taken from Assyria in the late ninth and early eighth centuries B.C. (2 Kgs 13:14–19, 14:28; cf. 1 Chron 5:1–17).

All evidence suggests that Israel enjoyed a booming economy under Jeroboam II, fueled largely by good harvests, full storehouses and well-oiled administrative machinery—precisely the conditions that also bred complacency and, eventually, exploitation of the poorest strata of society. The cries of

The Campaign of Shalmaneser III, 841 B.C.
As the national fortunes of Israel and Judah began to wane after the deaths of Ahab and Jehoshaphat, Assyrian pressure on the kingdoms of the southern Levant increased. Shalmaneser III, who had been repulsed by a coalition of kings at Qarqar in 853 B.C., bided his time for twelve years, then pushed all the way to Damascus, Bashan and Mt. Carmel. This was the year that Jehu purged the royal houses of both Israel and Judah, in theory setting the stage for a resurgence in Judah and Israel but in fact adding to the instability of the region. For the next five decades Israel and Judah wallowed under foreign domination.

This golden seal impression (an Israel Museum reproduction—the original is lost) depicting an aggressive male lion, roaring and in full stride, is inscribed "[Belonging] to Shema servant of Jeroboam." Found at Megiddo, this impression belonged to a high government official within the royal administration of Jeroboam. The lion, a common symbol of royalty and strength throughout the ancient Near East, reflects the tenor of the age of Jeroboam II: Israel was on the attack mode. Lions were also favorites of the Assyrian kings, posing a certain amount of irony as to who the true lion in the region actually was.

The Campaign of Adad-nirari III, 796 B.C.

Throughout the late 9th and early 8th centuries B.C., *the Assyrian juggernaut rolled across western Asia and into the southern Levant. One of the Assyrian goals was to control the ports of the Mediterranean. Adad-nirari III put it this way: "[I conquered] Amurru in its full extent, Tyre, Sidon, Israel [lit. 'the land of Omri'], Edom, Palestine, as far as the shore of the Great Sea of the Setting Sun. I made them all submit to my feet, imposing on them tribute"* (ANET 281). *A more elusive goal was to reach Egypt, but when Adad-nirari stalled at Damascus and was then succeeded by a series of three weak kings, this greatest of prizes would have to wait for another hundred years.*

U R A R Ṭ U

805 B.C. - Adad-nirari campaigns against Arpad

Samal
Carchemish
Hadattah · Haran · Gozan
Til-Barsip
Arpad
Aleppo

Name of Hazael appears on ivory found at Hadattah, evidently brought from Damascus by Adad-nirari

Nineveh
Calah

A S S Y R I A
Ashur

Adad-nirari III visits the Phoenician coast and sets up a stele

Arvad
Hamath
Sumur
Tadmor

Byblos

Sidon
Tyre

Damascus

Forced submission to Adad-nirari III 796 B.C.

Samaria
Rabbath-bene-ammon
Jerusalem

EDOM → Subject kingdoms paying tribute to Adad-nirari
⊙ Capital

0 20 40 60 miles
0 40 80 km

© Carta, Jerusalem

The large granary of Megiddo, thought by many archaeologists to date to the mid-8th century B.C., *can be taken as an indication of the accumulation of wealth in the top echelons of Israelite society during the reign of Jeroboam II. Measuring over 20 feet across and just as deep, this granary would have fed 300 horses for 150 days—or kept a large bureaucracy fat and sassy and at odds with the little people on whose backs the kingdom was sustained.* (NEAEHL)

injustice that echoed in the streets and marketplaces of Israel were ignored by the elitist upper crust, which was otherwise preoccupied with maintaining its own interests. These conditions coincided exactly with the first of the so-called "writing prophets," Amos and Hosea, whose prophetic invectives were hurled at everyone on the Israelite landscape who used his or her own position for personal gain at the expense of others:

Thus says the LORD:
"For three transgressions of Israel and for four
I will not revoke the punishment,
because they sell the righteous for money
and the needy for a pair of sandals…"
[those who say] "When will the New Moon be over
so that we may sell grain,
and the Sabbath
that we may open the wheat market,
to make the bushel smaller and the shekel bigger,
and to cheat with dishonest scales…?"
(Amos 2:6, 8:5)

Listen to the word of the LORD, O sons of Israel,
for the LORD has a case against the
inhabitants of the land.
There is no faithfulness or kindness,
or knowledge of God in the land.
[Instead], there is swearing, deception,

murder, stealing and adultery.
They employ violence, so that bloodshed follows
bloodshed.
(Hos 4:1–2)

Within three decades, as these prophets so clearly saw, both the land and people of Israel would be "snatched away with meat hooks" (Amos 4:2) and swallowed by the ravenous Assyrian Empire, bite by ripping bite.

But not all of Israel's prophets shared this vision. Jonah son of Amitai of Gath-hepher, apparently a prophet of Jeroboam's royal court, was less concerned about individual human rights than the glory of his monarch's kingdom. While Amos and Hosea decried the social rot that stemmed from Jeroboam's policies, Jonah spoke of territorial expansion, encouraging Jeroboam's conquests "from Lebo-hamath to the Sea of the Arabah" (i.e., from the "entrance to Hamath" lying near the headwaters of the Orontes and Litani rivers in north Syria to the Dead Sea; 2 Kgs 14:25, 14:28). For the writer of the Book of Kings, the fact that Jeroboam was able to recoup territory that had last fallen under Israel's control only in the days of Solomon was good (2 Kgs 14:26–27; cf. 1 Kgs 4:21) for by it God had restored hope to his people, but one wonders to what extent Jonah's support of these nationalistic overtones blinded his eyes to larger issues at hand which Amos and Hosea so clearly saw (Amos 6:14). Jonah had a personal stake in the matter, for his own home town, Gath-hepher (*Kh. ez-Zurra'*, modern Mashhad), on the northeastern shoulder of the high limestone ridge that separates Galilee from the Jezreel Valley, lay directly in Assyria's line of attack. If Israel could hang on to its Aramean vassals in the north, one or another of these states could act as a buffer the next time Assyria burst on the scene.

Better yet, what if Assyria just didn't come back at all?

Then came the divine message: Jonah was to travel to Nineveh, Assyria's capital, to the core of the evil empire, and cry against it, for the LORD had declared that "their wickedness has come up before Me" (Jonah 1:1–2). To walk into Nineveh was dangerous enough, but should Jonah go, both his people and his own conscience would label him a traitor for warning their enemy of God's displeasure. On the other hand, should he refuse the call and Nineveh fall under divine judgment, Israel would finally be rid of the Assyrian threat, and, with a clear eastern horizon, the nation could bask in the political and economic revival of Jeroboam II. After all, one hundred years before Elisha had healed the Aramean general Naaman only to have the Aramean army turn around and invade Israel (2 Kgs 5:1–14, 6:8–24). For the prophet there was only one choice: God may have called, but Jonah fled in the opposite direction. Save Assyria? "Not on my watch," we can hear the prophet saying.

Jonah headed for Judah's Mediterranean port at Joppa, 180 degrees from Nineveh (Jonah 1:3). His intent was to "flee from the presence of the LORD"— as if that were geographically or even ontologically possible—but by his actions Jonah betrayed that his provincial understanding of God was no larger than that of prophets from other nations who operated under the assumption that every land or city-state was protected by a god who was effective only within its own borders (cf. 1 Kgs 20:23, 20:28). Maybe Jonah wanted to buy time (if God would forget the call, Jonah could strut his stuff as the one responsible for ridding Israel of the Assyrian threat); maybe he wanted to start a new life; maybe he panicked—or maybe, realizing that the LORD was right, Jonah just couldn't come to terms with the ramifications. A rabbinic midrash offers the following:

> There are three types of prophets. One insisted on the honor due the Father [God] as well as the honor due the son [the prophet]; one insisted on the honor due the Father without insisting on the honor due the son, and one insisted on the honor due the son without insisting on the honor due the Father.
>
> (Mekilta de-Rabbi Ishmael, *Pisha*, 1:111.6)

The example the midrash gives for the first was Jeremiah, for the second, Elijah; the third, of course, was Jonah. Indeed, Jonah's run the other way had

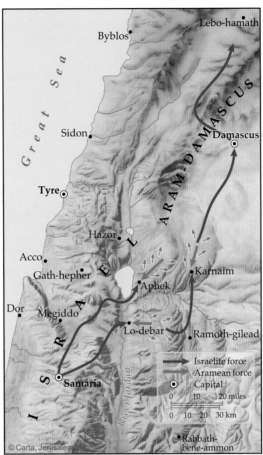

more than geographical reference. As a prophet, his job was "to arise!" (Jonah 1:2); instead Jonah "went down"—to Joppa, onto a ship, into the hold of the ship and eventually into the angry sea (Jonah 1:3, 1:5, 1:15), a four-fold punctuation of his renunciation of God's prophetic call.

Jonah headed for Tarshish, a point somewhere on the far shipping lanes of the Mediterranean (places in Cilicia, North Africa, Italy and Spain have been suggested; cf. Gen 10:4; 1 Kgs 22:48; 1 Chron 1:7; Isa 66:19; Ezek 27:12). These sea routes were controlled by the Phoenicians, full-bore cultural heirs of the world view of the Canaanites whose god *Yam* was the deified Sea, a god that personified the uncontrollable cosmic chaos that could overwhelm creation at any

The Glory Days of Jehoash and Jeroboam II. *A window of opportunity opened for Israel when Assyrian pressure in the region relaxed at the death of Adad-nirari III. Jehoash and his son Jeroboam II recouped Israel's former territorial losses to Aram-Damascus, which had been left weakened from Adad-nirari's incursions, then pushed as far north as Lebo-hamath (c. 790–782 B.C.; 2 Kgs 13:15–19, 13:25, 14:25, 14:28). For Israel at least it was a time to harken back to the greatest days of the kingdom, the reign of Solomon, when the economic and political arm of Jerusalem reached the Euphrates.*

Jonah's home, Gath-hepher, was a village perched on a hill in Galilee that is now dominated by the Israeli Arab town of Mashhad. In the 8th century B.C. Gath-hepher would have been a pleasant place to call home, near a fertile valley and strong spring with fresh Mediterranean breezes stirring the air. As long as Israel was at peace, Galilee was quiet and life could be good, but with the Arameans constantly knocking at Israel's northern door and the Assyrians gathering forces to smash it down, the threat of what might be always lay at hand.

Jonah's Journeys. *Living squarely in the path of the next Assyrian attack, the recalcitrant prophet from Gath-hepher left his Galilean home for a point as far away from Nineveh as he could get—not because he was afraid of battle but because if he could reverse God's call to go to Nineveh, Israel's most feared enemy would fall under divine judgment and Galilee would be spared. In the end Jonah went anyway, where his encounter with the LORD was more real than it had ever been back home.*

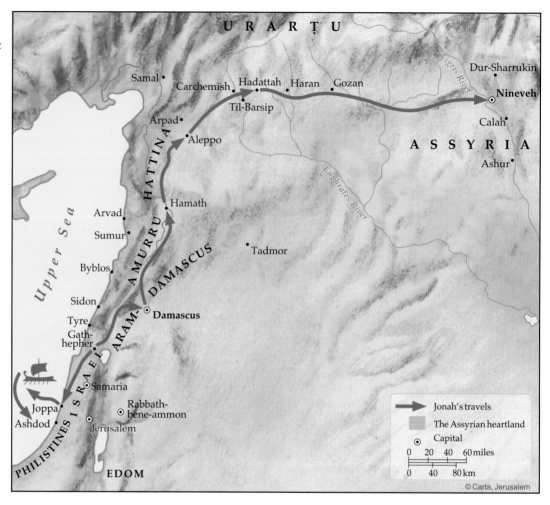

This model of a square-rigged merchant ship, with bow and stern raised to replicate a mythical creature of the high seas, fairly represents the "ships of Tarshish" that plied the waters of the Mediterranean during the mid-1st millennium B.C. From planks to oars to mast to sail, these were the finest ships that had yet sailed (cf. Ezek 27:5–9). Such ships carried specialized commodities from across the ancient Near East and Mediterranean worlds (cf. Ezek 27:12–25), including, once, a below-deck cargo labeled "Jonah." (Haifa, Maritime Museum)

given moment. For Israel, a people at home among the dry hills of the southern Levant, a journey onto the face of the primordial deep was asking to be swallowed alive (cf. Ps 107:23–32). Even the Phoenician mariners, who made a living on the waters, knew their limitations when they ventured into the domain of the relentlessly churning *Yam* (cf. Ezek 27:25–36).

When the storm hit, the sailors threw themselves at the mercy of their normally unforgiving gods while Jonah, a spokesman for the one true God, hunkered down in his recalcitrance (Jonah 1:4–6). He spoke only when ordered to, and that with only the briefest of testimonies, yet this was enough: by the time the storm ended his seafaring hosts had become "good Israelites," looking out for the welfare of the stranger in their midst and sacrificing and making vows to the LORD, the God whom they now feared (Jonah 1:13, 1:17). Jonah's fears had been proven right: if God could save the pagan mariners, of course Nineveh would also be spared. For his part, he would rather have died (Jonah 1:12).

Sinking into the waters,

Jonah scraped bottom, his body nearly lifeless and flopping against the gates of Sheol (cf. Jonah 2:5–6). Rabbinic sources state that the great fish that swallowed Jonah was appointed to his special task all the way back at the time of creation (Genesis Rabbah 5:5); other than calling on the sovereignty of God, how else can the events in the story be explained?

Jonah's prayer in the belly of the fish is often called a cry of repentance, but the tenor of his words fall far short of the emotion that galvanized David, for instance, when he admitted personal responsibility in the Bathsheba/Uriah affair (Ps 51). Jonah was glad that his life had been saved (did he know that the mariners had already sacrificed and vowed to the LORD when he promised that, once out of his foxhole, he would do so?—Jonah 2:9), but blamed God for his troubles (Jonah 2:3–4a) rather than look at himself. His words all sounded good—most were quotations from or allusions to various Psalms—but the intent behind them can be questioned. Maybe the fish knew, for although it was the instrument of Jonah's salvation, it gagged when the prophet finally finished speaking (Jonah 2:10). A local tradition—surely spurious—holds that Jonah was spit up on the beach at Ashdod.

Back on dry land and no doubt looking rather worse for the wear, Jonah picked his way back home. If he had truly repented, we can expect that he would have gone directly to Nineveh. But God, as relentless as the surging sea, called Jonah again, and this time Jonah went—after all, whatever fate awaited him in the Assyrian capital couldn't be any worse than being swallowed alive (Jonah 3:1–3).

The Nineveh of Jonah's day was growing into a world-class city, with hints of the nature it would attain in its heyday in the mid-seventh century B.C. It was a place that was cosmopolitan, sophisticated, learned and in-your-face powerful—at least in terms of the ancient Near East. The city Jonah visited was probably three miles (five kilometers) in circumference, spanning the Khosr River (a tributary of the Tigris) and centered on a raised plateau (today called Kuyunjik) dominated by spacious palaces and large temples dedicated to the city's chief deities, Nabu and Ishtar. This was indeed "an exceedingly great city" (Jonah 3:3), not necessarily in terms of brute size (the reference "three day's journey in breadth" may refer to the environs lying between Nineveh, Calah/Nimrud and Dur Sharrukin/Khorsabad) but certainly so in aura, reputation, sheer presence and potential. A visitor from a small village in Galilee should have been spellbound.

Jonah was not. He simply went through the city shouting out its impending destruction, without mentioning either the reason for, or the name of the deity behind its doom (Jonah 3:4). This was a minimalized message that did not allow the people of the city a chance to repent, one that for Jonah was short, sweet, and would hopefully force God to bend to the will of Jeroboam II. After all, God wouldn't want his own reputation to be tarnished out here among the nations by failing to fulfill the prophecy of one of his own. But repent the people of Nineveh did, from the king on down, as quickly as had the mariners at sea (Jonah 3:5–9). The reaction of the LORD God, One who is "gracious and compassionate, slow to anger and abundant in loving-kindness" (Jonah 4:2; cf. Ex 34:6–7; Num 14:18–19), was true to his divine character, even on behalf of Israel's most detested enemy (Jonah 3:10). But did Jonah also suspect the inevitable, that within a few short decades the Assyrians would overrun Galilee and that his own children and grandchildren might well pay the ultimate price?

Jonah, displeased, angry and thoroughly confounded, believed that his reputation as a prophet and political confidant was shattered. With his honor and dignity gone and not wanting to face the shame of returning to Israel, Jonah again preferred to die (Jonah 4:1–3). And, once again, he ignored the greater events of the day and blamed God for his troubles. Understandable? Certainly. Unforgivable? Not at all.

The prophet withdrew to a rise east of the city with a view to await its fate, unaware that it was his own fate that was under divine scrutiny. Over-

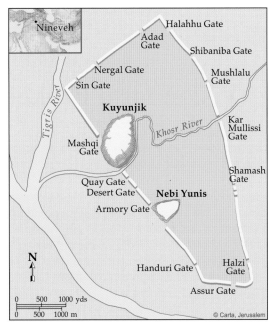

come by the heat of the day, Jonah found relief in the shade of a leafy gourd-plant specially appointed, like the great fish, for such a time as this. Again he sulked in his own comfort then was thrown headlong as the worm-eaten plant died and a sultry desert wind, a full-forced *hamsin* such as is common throughout the Middle East in the spring and fall of the year, sucked his remaining energy and life away.

Jonah nearly died because of too much water and now, because of not enough ("You prefer dry land? Take it!"). Throughout, in the style of good rabbinic pedagogy, God simply asked questions, slowly plodding after his recalcitrant prophet and nudging him—and the readers of his story—to face reality (Jonah 4:4, 4:9–11). One wonders what the biggest miracle of the story really was: That the fish was able to save Jonah? That the people of Nineveh would repent and be spared? Or that God can save *anybody*, even someone as privileged as his prophet?

Back at home, Jonah had been a big fish in a little pond. Perhaps he can be excused for not realizing that he was really just a small fish in a pond that was quite a bit bigger. Jonah's hometown, Gath-hepher, lay just three miles (five kilometers) from a point on its limestone ridge where the village of Nazareth would one day arise. Nearly eight centuries later, when the land of Israel wallowed in the grip of another foreign oppressor, the Prophet of Nazareth (Mt 21:11) carried the message of God's grace and compassion to all peoples, filling out the prophetic role in a way that Jonah refused or was unable to do (cf. Mt 12:38–41). In the end, God's great work is always done, be it either *with* a Jonah—or in spite of him.

Surrounded by rich farmland and commanding major trade routes radiating from an important ford of the Tigris River, Nineveh became one of the greatest cities of the ancient world when Sennacherib made it the Assyrian capital in the late 8th century B.C. By the mid-7th century B.C. Nineveh was a sprawling urban center, rich in commerce and deep in tradition. One hundred years earlier, when Jonah made his renowned visit, the city sat at the cusp of greatness. The prophet must have known what a rising Assyria would mean for Israel.

(below) When Jonah turned his back on Nineveh he also went into voluntary exile from the land of Israel, preferring instead like this modern-day sailor to become a bobbing speck in the middle of an unending sea. When calm, the Mediterranean's sea lanes are clear and someone with backbone and common sense could reap the harvests of far-off shores. Jonah had neither, and gave up every bit of security that solid ground offered. The greatest of His mighty acts—from Creation to the Flood to the crossing of the Red Sea—God pushed aside water so dry land, a place suitable for human life, could appear. Now Jonah tried to reverse the flow.

CHAPTER 13
ISAIAH
Vision for a Broken World

With storm clouds gathering on the horizon, the prophet Isaiah had the ear of Hezekiah the king. But though his land was under attack and people were distraught, Isaiah's counsel often went unheeded. (Carta, Jerusalem)

An iron sentinel, rusted with time, tirelessly stands guard on a reconstructed 8th-century B.C. watchtower at Hazor. Prepare as they might, the efforts of the kings of Israel and Judah to withstand Assyria went largely for naught. The Psalmist's refrain was short and sweet: "Unless the LORD guards the city, the watchman keeps awake in vain" (Ps 127:1). Isaiah certainly agreed.

Looking back, the news reporter said that it was otherwise a beautiful day. His words were carefully measured and reflective. The sky, he said, was cloudless and brilliantly blue, the grass warm and green and the temperature quite pleasant for a September day, as summer began to turn to fall in Manhattan. It was a wonderful day to be alive—except that on the horizon two huge pillars of fire and smoke rose to the heavens, choking the air and blackening mind and soul with shock, fear, anger, uncertainty and panic. For everyone who was an eyewitness to the event, and the millions who followed each moment on live television, it was a day of untold horror, a personal attack with unimaginable consequences. As the shock began to give way to a host of other emotions, many felt at the same time utterly helpless—yet fiercely resolved to do something. Anything. But what? And how?

Without detracting in any way from the horror of the events of 9/11, they were, within the context of a host of personal and national struggles that have been waged across the face of the globe for millennia, certainly not unprecedented. While the specifics were unique—specifics always are—the crisis of attack was not. The entire career of the great prophet Isaiah for instance was defined by a huge cloud of horror and uncertainty that billowed and blew and enveloped the lands of the eastern sea-board of the Mediterranean, including Israel and Judah. This was the Assyrian threat, ripping apart nations and people alike, and destroying everything in its path. One generation before, the prophet Amos had foreseen the inevitable consequences of the Assyrian attack and described it as nothing but rubble and body parts:

> *Just as a shepherd snatches from the lion's mouth a*
> *couple of legs or a piece of an ear,*
> *So will the sons of Israel dwelling in Samaria be*
> *snatched away—*
> *with the corner of a bed and the cover of a couch!*
> (Amos 3:12)

The things that everyone in Israel had grabbed on to for security were swept away, and the future was bleak. The only thing that was certain was that life would never be the same again. Everyone was in for a nasty time. The prophet Isaiah put it this way, the brightness of the Mediterranean climate notwithstanding:

> *And they will pass through the land hard-pressed and famished, and it will turn out that when they are hungry, they will be enraged and curse their king and their God as they face upward. Then they will look to the earth, and behold, distress and darkness, the gloom of anguish; and they will be driven away into darkness.*
> (Isa 8:21–22)

Called to the greatest of tasks at the time of his people's greatest need, Isaiah had to do something—and not just anything. But what? And how?

Isaiah's mission as a prophet coincided with the arrival of the Assyrians in the southern Levant. He witnessed Tiglath-pileser III's quick thrusts to the coastal plain, Galilee and Transjordan (734–732 B.C.), looked in horror as the northern kingdom of Israel fell to Shalmaneser V (722 B.C.) and Sargon II chewed through Philistia (720, 713 and 712 B.C.), and barely survived Sennacherib's assault on Judah and Jerusalem (701 B.C.). It was nothing but trouble for king and people alike as the Assyrian flood came "up to the neck" of Judah (Isa 8:8).

If this were all that the people of Judah had to face, their spiritual and moral backbone as God's Chosen People could have seen them through. But the real tragedy lay not so much in the devastation of the Assyrian attack as in the fact that Judah was already so shot through with moral failings that the social fabric of society was fatally wounded before Tiglath-pileser even arrived. With a mind that penetrated to the real problem Judah was facing, Isaiah spent most of his time blasting his own people—then picking up the pieces. This was an unpopular task and certainly one that was not "politically correct." It took a special kind of person to stand in this kind of gap, and with God's help, Isaiah proved equal to the challenge at hand.

The first part of the Book of Isaiah (chaps. 1–39) is framed by accounts of Isaiah's interaction with two of Judah's kings, Ahaz and Hezekiah. Each encounter is set in the context of a military attack on Judah, the first by Aram-Damascus and Israel in 735 B.C. in anticipation of Tiglath-pileser's dramatic entrance into the land (Isa 7:1–9:7), and the second by Sennacherib in 701 B.C. (Isa 36:1–39:8). The latter part of the book (chaps. 40–66), a glorious, sweeping view of Israel's future, is as much a reflection of the need for vision in a broken world as it is a picture of what would some day be. There is a long-standing discussion in scholarly circles as to the suitability of using these latter chapters to understand Isaiah as a late eighth-century B.C. prophet, although the present, canonical shape of the book does encourage a holistic reading. In any case, when read together, the disparate parts of the Book of Isaiah provide a vibrant picture of the man for whom the book is named and the greatness of one whose vision was grounded in the reality of a God who controlled past, present and future. The greatness of Isaiah the prophet, in fact, lay in his ability to pierce the blackness of the moment and see that not only was a great light shining somewhere behind the dark cloud that enveloped his land (Isa 9:2), but that that light, the glory of the LORD God, would allow his people to "arise and shine" themselves (Isa 60:1). The people of Israel would become attractive forces for redemption

and good throughout the world (Isa 60:2–3), not just Israelites, but "Israel-lights."

Isaiah's prophetic ministry began sometime late in the reign of Uzziah (767–740 B.C.), spanned the reigns of Jotham (740–732 B.C.), Ahaz (732–716 B.C.) and Hezekiah (716–687 B.C.), and most probably extended into the early part of the reign of Manasseh (Isa 1:1; Isaiah reported the death of Sennacherib, which occurred in 681 B.C., although this note may be a later editorial insertion; Isa 37:38). Most of these Judean kings apparently held co-regency with both their fathers and sons, a policy that ensured a strong and smooth transition of power. As prophets go Isaiah's career was lengthy, and provided a sense of spiritual continuity to a royal dynasty that was otherwise prone to follow only the geopolitical exigencies of the day, shifting policies and alliances as the needs of the moment dictated.

Isaiah was apparently a native of Jerusalem, certainly closely connected to the Judean royal court as an advisor and confidant and perhaps even related to it by marriage (a tradition mentioned in the Babylonian Talmud notes that Isaiah's father Amoz was a brother of King Uzziah; Megillah 10b). He was married, with children (Isa 7:3, 8:3), and certainly literate, probably trained as a scribe (Isa 8:1). One can assume that Isaiah was a man of privilege and standing and could hobnob with the best of them. At the same time, his message ran counterculture to Jerusalem's aristocracy. Tightly woven throughout the prophet's political commentary was the theme of justice and righteousness—Isaiah focused on the injustice and unrighteousness, to be exact, that was rampant throughout Judah—a whole-cloth condemnation of a way of life that flowed through society from the top down. If privilege begets responsibility, Isaiah certainly had his share.

Though an urbanite, Isaiah was also at home in the countryside, out and about in the hills and valleys of Judah and Israel. This we can assume, for his

Even though Isaiah lived in the largest city of Judah, he was a man of nature. His was an agrarian society, with water, wind and soil an important part of everyone's life. The natural world offered a limitless supply of images evoking conditions of heart and mind of individuals and nation alike. "[When] the Spirit is poured out upon us from on high, the wilderness will become a fertile field and the fertile field will be like a forest.... Then my people will live in a peaceful place, in secure houses and undisturbed resting places" (Isa 32:15–18).

In traditional Palestinian viti-culture, vines trail along the ground until the moment that grapes first appear. The farmer then lifts the vine by means of a flat stone to allow the fruit to develop hanging free, as if on a trellis. Isaiah's song of the vineyard (5:1–7) speaks of the care by which a vinedresser coaxes fruit from his vineyard, and of the tragedy of spoilage on the vine: "but it produced rotted grapes."

For an outsider, it is one more nondescript rise in the Shephelah. For Micah, the site of Moresheth-gath (Tel Goded) was home. Because Moresheth-gath lay far enough out into the Shephelah to be rustled by every threat on the coast, Micah's call for a return to the LORD God in the face of Assyria's march down the International Highway carried a genuine and believable sense of urgency.

vividly descriptive prophetic imagery was energized by an intimate knowledge of land and nature, of trees, grass and flowers, and of animals, birds and insects. Isaiah enjoyed the outdoors and likely owned a patronage of fields and orchards somewhere in the environs of Jerusalem. He probably also had marketable skills in addition to those of a scribe—like Amos, for instance, who was called from the flocks, herds and sycamore trees to the royal court of Samaria (Amos 1:1, 7:14), or like the farmer Elisha (1 Kgs 19:19), or maybe even Jesus, a skilled craftsman in local building materials who was certainly more than just a "carpenter" (cf. Mt 13:55). Like Amos, Isaiah would have had personal experience in business matters and been keenly aware of issues of interpersonal propriety and what makes for justice and righteousness on the street—and between nation-states.

All this can be assumed from the kind of information that filled Isaiah's oracles and teachings. His overall message was one of judgment and hope, but the detail of the verbal pictures painted on the prophetic canvas was brilliant, full of the minutiae of everyday life in Judah and lands beyond. His descriptions were vibrant, colorful and full of real life. For instance, how did a farmer prepare a vineyard? Isaiah tells us: He started with a fertile hill (such as the terraced slopes on the hills drained by the Sorek wadi west of Jerusalem—the Hebrew word *sorek* refers to the rich, red grapes grown there). Then,

He dug it all around and removed its stones,

> *and planted it with the choicest vine (sorek).*
> *He built a tower in the middle of it and hewed out a*
>   *wine vat in it*
> *and expected it to produce good grapes....* (Isa 5:2)

Or, what did a rich lady keep in her trousseau? Isaiah took a peek:

> *In that day the Lord will take away the beauty of their anklets, headbands, crescent ornaments, dangling earrings, bracelets, veils, headdresses, ankle chains, sashes, perfume boxes, amulets, finger rings, nose rings, festal robes, outer tunics, cloaks, money purses, hand mirrors, undergarments, turbans and veils.*
> *Instead of sweet perfume—there will be*
>   *putrefaction;*
>   *instead of a belt—a rope;*
>   *instead of well-set hair, a plucked-out scalp;*
>   *instead of fine clothing—a donning of sackcloth;*
> *and instead of beauty—a branding.* (Isa 3:18–24)

Although he had likely never been to Egypt, Isaiah knew the landscape of the Nile—what grew along its banks, how fishermen caught its fish and what kind of plants were good for making clothing:

> *...the river will be parched and dry*
>   *and the canals will emit a stench;*
> *the streams of Egypt will thin out and dry up,*
>   *and the reeds and rushes will rot away.*
> *The bulrushes by the Nile, by the edge of the Nile,*
>   *will become dry,*
>   *be driven away and be no more.*
> *The fishermen will lament and all those who cast a*
>   *line into the Nile will mourn,*
>   *and those who spread nets on the waters*
>   *will pine away.*
> *Moreover, the manufacturers of linen*
>   *made from combed flax*
>   *and the weavers of white cloth*
>   *will be utterly dejected.* (Isa 19:5–9)

Isaiah knew how to prepare a field for planting (Isa 28:24–25), what a proper crop yield should be (Isa 5:10) and the different techniques for harvesting dill, cumin or grain (Isa 28:27–28; cf. 41:15–16). He could set a table for a lavish banquet (Isa 25:6)—or one for drunkards (Isa 28:7–8). He knew how to manufacture an idol (as if he ever *would*; Isa 40:19–20), how to prescribe medicine (Isa 38:21), what kind of flora and fauna to find in the open desert (Isa 13:20–22, 30:6, 34:13–15) and the road-map of Moab (Isa 15:1–9). Isaiah could describe the sudden collapse of a wall as surely as he did the collapse of Judah—and why not? Both surely happened before his very eyes (Isa 30:13–14).

Isaiah can also be compared to Micah, his contemporary from Moresheth(-gath) (*Tel Goded*), a town on a prominent rise in the southern Shephelah (Mic 1:1, 1:14). Isaiah and Micah were of one prophetic mind, even sharing some words nearly verbatim (Isa 2:2–4; Mic 4:1–3). Unlike Isaiah, however, Micah's home lay directly on the front line of the Assyrian attack, and was not far from Lachish, the city that would feel the brunt of Sennacherib's assault on Judah in 701 B.C.. While Isaiah eventually felt the hot breath of Sennacherib bearing down on Jerusalem, Micah's own position was much more vulnerable. It is almost certain that Moresheth (-gath) was one of the "46 strong cities" of Judah that Sennacherib claimed to have destroyed during his campaign against Judah, and that Micah's home and land and perhaps even his person fell in the onslaught (cf. Mic 1:14). The strength of Micah's message arises from the fact that he was both a prophet and a victim. His words were personal, experienced and driven from within. They can be believed—and *felt*. Isaiah's message was no less real, but focused on the experience of the people of Jerusalem.

Isaiah's prophetic ministry, which had begun sometime during the latter part of the reign of King Uzziah (Azariah), took on a fresh intensity "in the year that King Uzziah died" (Isa 6:1). The news that the king was dead, when first announced, would have sent shockwaves throughout Judah and Jerusalem. Uzziah and his mid-eighth-century B.C. contemporary in Israel, Jeroboam II, had steered their respective kingdoms through periods of growth, prosperity and strength. This was during a period of Assyrian decline, when there was a power vacuum in the Levant. Uzziah revived the Judean economy through a series of agricultural initiatives that opened up development in the Negeb, Judean Wilderness and Shephelah (2 Chron 26:10). This, combined with his control over Ammon, the "Arabians" and the Meunites in southern Transjordan, allowed Uzziah to push to Elath and restore to Judah its Red Sea trade connections that had lagged since the days of Jehoshaphat and Solomon (2 Chron 26:7; 2 Kgs 14:22; cf. 1 Kgs 9:26–28, 22:47–48).

He also extended Judean control over the northern Philistine coastal plain, subduing Gath, Jabneh and Ashdod in the process and reaping the harvest of their fields and trade routes (2 Chron 26:6–8). Assyrian records suggest that Uzziah (there called Azriyau) led a coalition of south Levantine states against Tiglath-pileser III (named Pul by the writer of Kings) in the region of Hamath in 743 B.C., temporarily checking this first of the renewed Assyrian attacks in the region (cf. 2 Kgs 15:19–20). To accomplish these goals Uzziah reorganized and bolstered his army. He also refortified Jerusalem, installing on its walls and towers newly-invented war machines that could shoot arrows and heave large stones onto the enemy below (2 Chron 26:9, 11–15). Uzziah hoped to prepare his kingdom to be able to fight on its own terms. All of this was accompanied by a general, although not always exclusive, sense of devotion by the king to the LORD God (2 Kgs 15:3–4; 2 Chron 26:4–5).

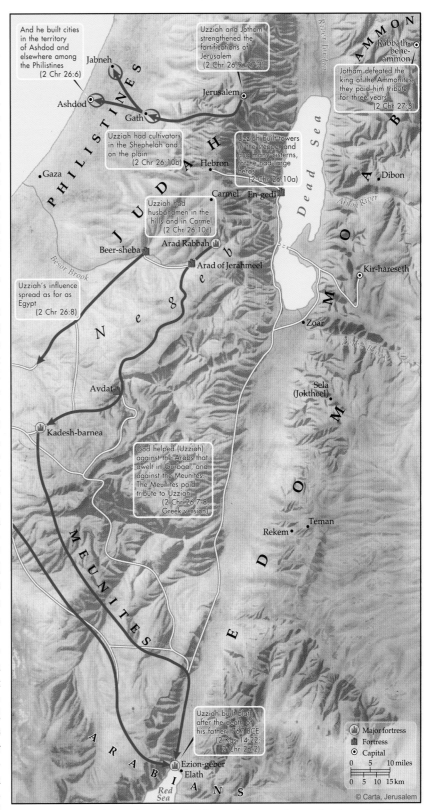

The Campaigns of Uzziah. *Landlocked during the reigns of its weaker kings, Judah's fortunes revived when Uzziah, like his predecessors Jehoshaphat and Solomon, was able to establish control over land and sea routes from the Mediterranean to the Red Sea. These days just prior to Isaiah's ministry were heady times, but happened only once every century or so.*

Uzziah was stricken with leprosy in his latter years, then died just as Assyria again reared its head above the northeastern horizon (2 Chron 26:16–23).

95

The modern seaport of Ashdod, Israel's busiest, lies below the rise of Tel Mor. Ancient Ashdod, tucked behind a sheet of sand dunes three miles inland, maintained its port in the same location. Although today's tonnage far exceeds the volume of goods that moved through the port in the days of Uzziah or Sargon, the raison d'être *for their move to control the region's land and sea commerce through Ashdod remains unchanged.*

The timing could not have been more ominous, and sometime during that year Isaiah, still a young man, had a vivid and dramatic encounter with the LORD (Isa 6:1–7). The setting, God's throne room in the Temple, was one of intense majesty. Overcome with the realization of his own inadequacy and failings, Isaiah received Divine assurance that his sins were forgiven. Then came the nearly impossible commission: the prophet was to tell his people that in spite of the obvious economic, political and military strength of their nation, their spiritual and moral condition was hopeless and everyone stood in line for judgment; only a remnant would survive (Isa 6:8–13). While Isaiah was willing (Isa 6:8), his spirit was overwhelmed. Not only was his beloved nation about to be invaded by the most feared and efficient war machine the world had ever known, his people lacked the moral and spiritual fiber necessary to find a way to survive.

Fortunately for Judah, Uzziah's son Jotham followed in his father's footsteps. The two had acted as co-regents for ten years, including the period of Uzziah's leprosy (750–740 B.C.; 2 Chron 26:21). After his father died, Jotham not only continued Uzziah's policy of fortifying Judah but also moved to curtail the interests of Israel and Aram-Damascus in Gilead and Bashan (2 Chron 27:1–9; cf. 1 Chron 5:16–17). All of this can be interpreted as an anti-Assyrian stance, preparing Judah for an eventual conflict with Assyria while not wanting to make concessions to anyone else in the meantime.

But the tide was turning. Israel's old nemesis to the northeast, Aram-Damascus, saw in Uzziah's death a chance to restore its control over the trade routes of Transjordan, while the Northern Kingdom of Israel also tried to revive their own interests there. At the same time, Tiglath-pileser III advanced into north Syria, annexing to the Assyrian Empire nineteen political districts around Hamath up to the very doorstep of Aram-Damascus. The Assyrian long-term goal was to conquer Egypt, and everything that lay in the way, including Israel and Judah, either had to capitulate or be eaten up.

For the nation-states of the southern Levant it was time for action. In league together, Pekah king of Israel and Rezin king of Damascus turned against Judah, the first overture of the so-called "Syro-Ephraimite War." Both opposed Jotham's moves into Transjordan, but also wanted the Judean king to join their coalition against the Assyrians. Sensing trouble, a party of pro-Assyrian supporters in Jerusalem deposed Jotham in 735 B.C. and placed his son Ahaz on the throne instead. But Ahaz's own feelings were that it was better to cooperate with the Assyrians. After all, it was clear that Assyria would soon be calling the shots in the southern Levant anyway; if Judah could get on Assyria's good side, the kingdom would stand to inherit the lion's share of Assyria's influence in the region. Or, perhaps Judah could even restore its prosperity to the level of the days of Uzziah, albeit controlled by a distant landlord. The deposed king Jotham, marginalized in his own home, died three years later.

For the kings of Israel and Aram-Damascus, Judah's shift in foreign policy was tantamount to international treachery. Pekah of Israel and Rezin of Damascus immediately attacked Jerusalem, intent on subduing the city and replacing Ahaz and the dynasty of David with an unnamed "son of Tabeel" who had the guts (or foolishness) to stand up to the Assyrian king (2 Kgs 16:5; Isa 7:1–2, 7:6). The Tabeel family apparently resided in Gilead; the family name has been connected with the Tobiads of the same region who were Gilead power brokers in the Intertestamental Period. They offered Israel and Aram-Damascus not only the chance to restore Judah to the anti-Assyrian fold but to remove Judean control over Transjordan in the process. Smelling blood, the Philistines took advantage of the situation and recaptured Uzziah's gains in Philistia and the Negeb, while the Edomites attacked Judah from the southeast and Aram-Damascus grabbed Elath (2 Kgs 16:6; 2 Chron 28:16–19). Ahaz, lost in a flow of events far beyond his control, was understandably shaken (Isa 7:2).

In stepped Isaiah, a man who loved both God and country. Isaiah was no fan of Ahaz's pro-Assyrian policy, yet respected both the office of king as well as the individual—*whoever* he was—who filled the throne at any given moment. After all, Ahaz was of the Davidic dynasty, the royal line of God's promise and protection, and had to be acknowledged as such. And so, under the instruction of the LORD, Isaiah met Ahaz as the latter was on his rounds inspecting the infrastructure of the city and counseled a cautious, stay-put approach: this local threat, Isaiah said, was just that, and would soon be swept away by the floodtide of Assyria (Isa 7:3–9, 8:1–7). Then came the scary part: Isaiah warned Ahaz that Assyria would nearly swallow up Judah as well—the king's pro-Assyrian leanings would do nothing to prevent that—but offered hope that his kingdom would survive in spite of Ahaz's reckless policies (Isa 7:17–25, 8:8).

Ahaz, blinded by his love of all things Assyrian, took this as permission to speed up the inevitable—"surely Assyria will be reasonable when it comes to me, their eager ally," he apparently thought—and so ran to Tiglath-pileser for help (2 Kgs 16:7–9; 2 Chron 28:16). And help Assyria did, but on its own terms. Over the next three years, from 734 to 732 B.C., Tiglath-pileser III attacked, conquered and annexed the northern coastal plain, all of Galilee, Damascus and northern Transjordan, killing Rezin and reducing the northern kingdom of Israel to a rump state isolated in the hills of Ephraim and Manasseh (2 Kgs 15:29). Through it all Ahaz had hoped to buy Assyria's favor by paying a sizable tribute to Tiglath-pileser and trying to act like a good Assyrian in the process (cf. 2 Kgs 16:10–16). Tiglath-pileser, glad that the tribute he would have taken anyway came so easily, didn't need Judah's help, thank you, and reduced Ahaz's shrinking kingdom to vassal status (2 Chron 28:19–21).

So much for the historical context of the biblical record of Isaiah's first run-in with a king of Judah. What is often tragically overlooked when offering any account of the sweep of battles and kings is the personal devastation that is foisted on the mass of little people underneath, the folk forgotten in the face of "more important things." Ahaz was lost by the flow of swiftly moving events, but everyone else was lost *in* it. While the king and his capital city were the target of attack, the people of the land were so much battle fodder. There was no escape: just try to hide in a steep ravine, Isaiah said, or high on a cliff ledge, among a patch of thorn bushes or at scattered watering holes, places characteristic of haunts in the nearby Judean Wilderness—the Assyrians would find you anyway (Isa 7:19). Lives would be broken, shattered, "hard-pressed and famished" (Isa 8:21; cf. Isa 7:21–25, 8:9). If this weren't bad enough, Isaiah declared in no uncertain terms that the people of Judah weren't going to see their lives destroyed because of the Assyrians *per se*, but because they themselves deserved it:

How the faithful city has become a harlot, she who
 used to be so full of justice!
Righteousness once lodged in her,
 but now—murderers.
Your silver has become dross,
 your drink diluted with water.
Your rulers are rebels,
 and companions of thieves;
everyone loves graft and chases after bribes.
They do not defend the orphan nor does the
 widow's plea come before them.

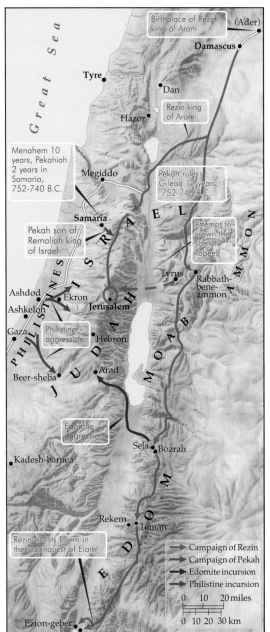

The Campaign of Rezin and Pekah Against Judah, 735 B.C. *In advance of the Assyrian tsunami that was about to crash into the southern Levant, the kings of the region started scrambling for position. Two, Rezin of Aram-Damascus and Pekah of Israel, thought it best to form a combined front against Assyria. When Ahaz of Judah didn't agree, Rezin and Pekah tried to overthrow the Judean dynasty in favor of a more pliable "son of Tabeel" who would tow the new company line. Ahaz resisted, but in the process the borders of Judah, hard won by Uzziah, collapsed.*

(below) "…and they will all come and settle on the steep ravines, on the ledges of the cliffs, on all the thorn bushes, and on all the watering places" (Isa 7:19). *If even the rough places were filled with Assyrians, what can be said for the fertile land and cities?*

The Campaigns of Tiglath-pileser III, 734–732 B.C.
In the first direct Assyrian assault on Israel, the armies of Tiglath-pileser III poured into the land from the north, seizing the international routes along the Mediterranean coast and those in Transjordan, as well as the great crossroads of Galilee. These regions taken by Tiglath-pileser correspond to Isaiah's litany "by the way of the sea, on the other side of the Jordan, Galilee of the Gentiles," a land that, though now in anguish, would one day again see light (Isa 9:1).

Therefore the LORD God of hosts,
the Mighty One of Israel declares,
"Aha! I will gain satisfaction against My foes!
I will take revenge against My enemies!
I will turn my hand against—you!"

(Isa 1:21–25a)

Living in a society that was corrupted from within and caught between the threat of an imminent attack from Aram-Damascus and Israel on the one hand and the reality of an invasion by Assyria on the other, coupled with the fear that the only thing that was sure was that lives would be destroyed, Isaiah offered a path of security and hope: *Immanuel*, "God is with us" (Isa 7:14, 8:8, 8:10). Isaiah's own son Shear-jashub, whose name means "a remnant will return" (Isa 7:3), should have been witness enough to God's ultimate hand of grace. But through the gloom, the prophet saw a great future for his people. He made his point on the back of five specific geographical regions: while at the moment, it was true, the lands of (1) Zebulun and (2) Naphtali writhed in anguish, some day the (3) Way of the Sea, (4) the

Other Side of the Jordan and (5) Galilee of the Gentiles would again be made glorious (Isa 9:1). Isaiah was commenting on the attack of Tiglath-pileser, who conquered areas that corresponded precisely to these five regions, leaving the northern kingdom truncated and helpless with only ten short years to survive. The tribes of Zebulun and Naphtali formed the heartland of Galilee (cf. Josh 19:10–16, 19:32–39), and it is certainly because there was a village in Zebulun called Nazareth and an important town in Naphtali called Capernaum in the first century that Matthew drew on these words of Isaiah to announce the coming of Jesus to a similarly insecure and precarious land (Mt 4:12–17; cf. Mt. 2:23, 9:1). It was, after all, because the entire region was geographically open and hence so susceptible to the military, political and cultural challenges of foreigners that Isaiah insightfully called the area Galilee of the *Gentiles*, this in spite of the fact that all or parts of five Israelite tribes lived there in his day. Alluding to the battle of Gideon in which gentiles conquered, occupied and then were driven out of the great international crossroads of the Jezreel Valley in southern Galilee (Isa 9:4), Isaiah foresaw a great day when a child born in the line of David would establish and uphold justice and righteousness throughout the kingdom forever. This child was aptly given the throne name "Prince of Peace" (Isa 9:6), a title announcing the very reality the land so badly needed.

In the devastation following Tiglath-pileser's invasion, Israel's king Pekah was assassinated by Hoshea son of Elah, the ninth change of dynasty in Israel's troubled two-hundred-year history (2 Kgs 15:30). In his annals Tiglath-pileser claimed that it was the people of Israel who had assassinated their own king; that it was he, Tiglath-pileser, who appointed Hoshea king of Israel; and that Hoshea traveled all the way to Babylonia to receive his commission as a loyal Assyrian vassal (ANET 284).

When Tiglath-pileser died in 727 B.C. his successor Shalmaneser V renewed the Assyrian push to Egypt, and with Galilee and the northern coastal plain already annexed as Assyrian provinces (called Megiddo and Dor, respectively), the truncated kingdom of Israel was next in line to be gobbled up. Hoshea chose to play a dangerous cloak-and-dagger game, paying tribute to Assyria while at the same time looking to Egypt to help overthrow his Assyrian master (2 Kgs 17:3–4). Shalmaneser correctly interpreted this Israel-Egypt alliance as an act of open rebellion and the Assyrian king, supreme commander of a war machine that ruthlessly crushed disloyal vassals, attacked Israel with a vengeance. Hoshea was captured and taken to Assyria and his capital city, Samaria, besieged (2 Kgs 17:4). The siege lasted three grueling years, time enough for many Israelites to flee south into Judah, placing themselves as refugees under the protection of Ahaz and, later,

his son Hezekiah. Archaeological evidence suggests that many of these refugees settled immediately west of the walled city of Jerusalem, on the higher, broad hill that today is part of the Old City's Jewish and Armenian quarters.

When the city of Samaria finally fell in 722 B.C., many of its people were exiled to areas scattered across Assyria's northern and eastern frontier (2 Kgs 17:6). Israel was annexed into the Assyrian Empire under the name Samaria (this name would continue to designate the region throughout the time of the New Testament) and people from Babylonia were brought in to resettle the land (2 Kgs 17:24). By permanently uprooting people from their ancestral homelands, the Assyrians hoped to break the spirit of rebellion across their empire.

The writer of Kings, peering out from deep within the Babylonian exile nearly two hundred years later, had a great deal to say about the root cause of Israel's demise: it was because "the sons of Israel had sinned against the LORD their God" and turned aside after foreign gods (2 Kgs 17:7–41). While Isaiah certainly would have agreed with this overall assessment, his own understanding of the problem was not that Israel chased after foreign gods *per se*, but that such apostasy inevitably led to a deplorable lack of justice and righteousness throughout the land, weakening the moral fiber of the nation and hence its resolve to withstand foreign threats (e.g., Isa 5:7, 9:8–21). Because Isaiah's point of view was from within, it was current, practical and anything but simplistic, wholly taken instead by the swirling mass of personal and social problems that plagued his people as a result of their broken covenant with the LORD God. His was a voice of immediacy that carried a great sense of urgency:

> Behold, brave men cry in the streets,
>   the ambassadors of peace weep bitterly.
> The highways are deserted, travel has ceased.
> [Everyone] has broken the covenant,
>   despised the cities, shown regard for no one.
> The land mourns and pines away,
>   Lebanon is shamed and withers;
> Sharon is like a desert plain,
>   and Bashan and Carmel lose all their leaves.

The majestic vistas, abundant rainfall, green hills and stately cedars of Lebanon—from Upper Galilee northward—gave rise to the notion that this portion of the land was especially favored by God. Biblical writers such as Isaiah spoke of "the glory of Lebanon" that would overtake the barren wilderness when God's open hand of blessing touched his land (Isa 35:2). When the divine hand withdrew, it was as if Lebanon, evergreen even in a year of drought, "was shamed and withered" (Isa 33:9).

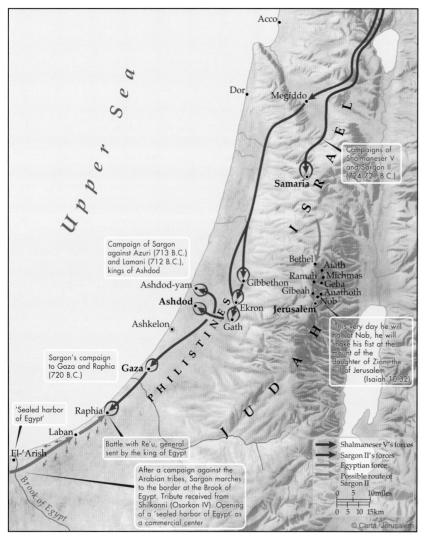

The Campaigns of Shalmaneser V and Sargon II (724–721 B.C.)

Campaign of Sargon against Azuri (713 B.C.) and Lamani (712 B.C.), kings of Ashdod

Sargon's campaign to Gaza and Raphia (720 B.C.)

'Sealed harbor of Egypt'

Battle with Re'u, general sent by the king of Egypt

After a campaign against the Arabian tribes, Sargon marches to the border at the Brook of Egypt. Tribute received from Shilkanni (Osorkon IV). Opening of a 'sealed harbor of Egypt' as a commercial center

'This very day he will halt at Nob; he will shake his fist at the mount of the daughter of Zion, the hill of Jerusalem' (Isaiah 10:32)

→ Shalmaneser V's forces
→ Sargon II's forces
→ Egyptian force
→ Possible route of Sargon II

0   5   10 miles
0 5 10 15 km

©Carta, Jerusalem

Upper Sea · Acco · Dor · Megiddo · ISRAEL · Samaria · Bethel · Aiath · Ramah · Michmas · Gibeah · Geba · Anathoth · Nob · Gibbethon · Ashdod-yam · Ashdod · Ekron · Jerusalem · Ashkelon · Gath · PHILISTINES · Gaza · JUDAH · Raphia · Laban · El-'Arish · Brook of Egypt

The Campaigns of Shalmaneser V and Sargon II, 724–712 B.C. *In their resolute push to Egypt, each successive Assyrian king took up the fight where the previous one had left off. The main line of attack was along the international coastal highway, but nations that lined the route like Israel and Judah were caught in the wake. Assyrian military policy was ruthless and precise, and demanded that anyone left in the vicinity who might disrupt the Assyrian supply lines, here stretched to their limit, be crushed.*

"Now I will arise," says the LORD,
"Now I will be exalted, now I will be lifted up
[to act!]
You have conceived chaff,
you will give birth to stubble;
My breath will consume you like a fire,
and the peoples will be burned to lime,
like cut thorns that are burned in the fire…"

(Isa 33:7–12)

Israel had been given their ancestral home, their land of promise, by Moses. But Moses was clear that the land was a gift—to be enjoyed, yes, but also a place where life was to be lived, with family, friend and the stranger-in-your-midst, the way life was meant to be, with the good of each other in mind. If not, people and land would suffer together, and the land would eventually lie desolate, its people torn out and scattered across the face of the earth (Deut 28:1–68). With Israel gone and Assyria still on the march, Isaiah understood all too well that this threat was as real for Judah as it had been for their northern neighbor.

Sargon II succeeded his father Shalmaneser in 722 B.C., just as Samaria was being annexed to the

Assyrian Empire. Sargon was a true military man, with unbridled ambition to raise the empire to new heights across all its frontiers. Not long after the beginning of his reign (in 720 B.C.), however, Sargon faced an initial setback on the battlefield east of the Tigris River, prompting what was left of the native populations of the Levant to revolt against Assyrian rule. Sargon's own annals indicate that Judah also joined the fray. All came to naught for these Levantine states as the Assyrian king quickly put down the revolt in a battle at Raphia, a city of the southern coastal plain between Gaza and the "River of Egypt" (*Wadi el-Arish* in the Sinai). Realizing that his entire western flank (and access points to Egypt) was no longer in friendly hands, Ahaz wisely capitulated to Assyria before the fight reached Jerusalem. It has been suggested by M. A. Sweeny (*Biblica* 75/1994: 457–470) and others that the final line of march of this, the first direct Assyrian threat to Judah, may be recorded in Isaiah 10:28–32. This itinerary passed point by point from Aiath (somewhere in the vicinity of Bethel) to Nob. Even though the location of some of these named towns and villages is unknown, the force of the onrush, scattering people like animals before a forest fire, is clear:

He has come against Aiath,
he has passed through Migron.
At Michmash he stored his baggage, [Then] advanced through the pass, saying "Geba will be our overnight place."
Ramah is terrified,
and Gibeah of Saul has fled away.
Cry aloud with your voice, O daughter of Gallim!
Pay attention, Laishah and wretched Anathoth!
Madmenah has fled;
the inhabitants of Gebim have sought refuge.
Even today he will halt at Nob;
he will shake his fist at the mountain of the daughter of Zion, the hill of Jerusalem.

(Isa 10:28–32)

Nob, perhaps on the southern end of the Mount of Olives, was clearly within fist-shaking distance of Jerusalem, and so if the battle-weary Ahaz wasn't already convinced that *his* kingdom was about to be swallowed, just as Israel had been, he was now:

The fading flower of [your] glorious beauty,
which is at the head of the fertile valley,
will be like the first-ripe fig prior to summer.
Whoever sees it, as soon as it is in his hand,
will swallow it.   (Isa 28:4)

With the campaign of 720 B.C. Assyria had made its move to the border of Egypt, and over the next decade worked to mop up the entire Philistine coastal plain. By 716 B.C. Sargon had seized the upper, Philistine end of the Gaza-to-Edom trade route and settled Arabians in Samaria in order to consolidate his commercial gains. Pharaoh Osorkon

IV recognized Sargon's growing monopoly in the area by paying tribute, thereby keeping Assyria out of Egypt for the time being. In Judah, meanwhile, Ahaz died and was succeeded by his son Hezekiah (715 B.C.), who inherited a kingdom nearly bereft of hope (2 Chron 28:27–29:2).

But Hezekiah was just the king Judah needed. Not only full of energy and ambition but also loyal to the LORD God and the temple priesthood in Jerusalem, Hezekiah sought to revive the national strength of Judah, albeit tempered somewhat by the pragmatic counsel of Isaiah. Quite early in his reign, Hezekiah re-instituted the Passover festival, a celebration that had not been properly observed in Jerusalem since the days of David and Solomon (2 Chron 29:3–30:27). Hezekiah hoped to restore Judean influence "from Dan to Beer-sheba" (2 Chron 30:5), but realistically was only able to bring the remnants of Samaria (Ephraim and Manasseh) into the Judean fold (2 Chron 31:1–2). His efforts were wisely focused on religious festivals and cult centers, matters that Sargon let slide so long as Judah's payments of tribute were not affected.

Sargon, in any case, was busy elsewhere, campaigning across Assyria's vast frontier. He reached the Philistine coast again in both 713 and 712 B.C., squelching revolts by the kings of Ashdod that had been egged on by Egypt's pharaoh, Shabako. Edom, Moab and Judah all had a hand in Ashdod's insurrection, and Isaiah strongly and publicly urged Hezekiah to leave well enough alone. This time Isaiah's actions spoke louder than his words. For three years the prophet walked the streets of Jerusalem without shoes or sackcloth, "naked and barefoot"—although probably with loincloth in place—as a graphic sign that Assyria would so lead Egypt into exile, clothed only in the shame of nakedness (Isa 20:1–6; cf. Isa 30:1–5, 31:1–3). Apparently Hezekiah needed both a strong sign and continual reminding to not disturb the status quo, and so Isaiah, prominent resident of Jerusalem that he was, placed the future of his people above his own reputation and comfort.

In the meantime Sargon had his own way on the Philistine coastal plain, turning the region into the Assyrian province of Ashdod. However, rather than formally annexing the province as his predecessors had done with Israel and Damascus, Sargon allowed the kings of the local city-states on the Philistine coast to remain in power. This might have been in deference to their role as maritime trading centers (especially in the case of Ashdod and Ashkelon), a status quo that Sargon needed to protect in order to ensure that the lucrative Arabian-Mediterranean commerce continued unabated, but with Assyria now skimming the top off the profits. The result was that Judah was now surrounded, its revenue from sources outside of its own shrinking borders greatly

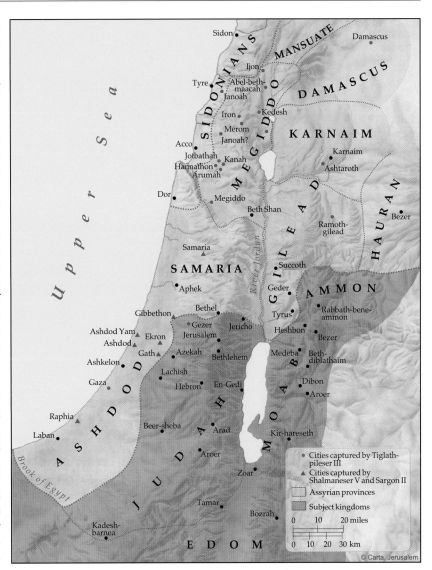

curtailed. It all appeared to mirror the fate of the northern kingdom of Israel, déjà vu.

Sargon died on the battlefield repulsing a surprise attack by the Cimmerians in the mountains of eastern Anatolia in 705 B.C.; his body was not recovered. The rest of the world celebrated: it was just desserts for a man who had crushed so many during his iron-fisted march for world supremacy. Sargon's violent, ignoble end was interpreted by even his son and successor, Sennacherib, to be an omen of disfavor of the gods. Sensing (or maybe just hoping) that Assyria was headed into a period of instability, Hezekiah saw his chance. For the last seven years he had prudently and dutifully paid tribute to Sargon, but not any more (2 Kgs 18:7). Revolt spread like wildfire from Babylon to the Levant. Hezekiah, too, immediately moved to strengthen his kingdom: if Assyria stayed away, perhaps Judah could assume the role as the major player in the southern Levant, but even if Sennacherib returned (and Hezekiah must have known that he would), he would be ready for the fight.

Assyrian Provinces, 710 B.C. *The Assyrians reorganized land that they conquered in the southern Levant into provinces, most renamed after their major administrative centers. After the conquests of Tiglath-pileser III the kingdom of Israel was reduced to its hilly interior, cut off from the outside by three Assyrian provinces. Upon the death of Sargon II, Judah was bereft of all but its heartland, confined to the high hill country, Shephelah lowlands and wilderness and with only nominal control over lands to the east.*

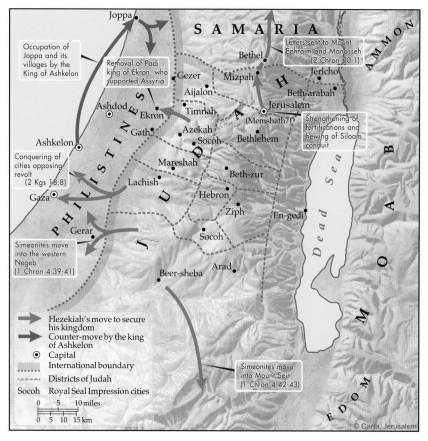

Map legend:
- Hezekiah's move to secure his kingdom
- Counter-move by the king of Ashkelon
- ⊙ Capital
- International boundary
- Districts of Judah
- Socoh Royal Seal Impression cities

0   5   10 miles
0 5 10 15 km

Map labels:
- Joppa
- SAMARIA
- AMMON
- Bethel
- Letters sent to Mount Ephraim and Manasseh (2 Chron 30:1)
- Jericho
- Mizpah
- Gezer
- Beth-arabah
- Occupation of Joppa and its villages by the King of Ashkelon
- Removal of Padi king of Ekron, who supported Assyria
- Aijalon
- Jerusalem
- (Memshath?)
- Strengthening of fortifications and hewing of Siloam conduit
- Ashdod
- Ekron
- Timnah
- Gath
- Azekah
- Socoh
- Bethlehem
- Ashkelon
- Conquering of cities opposing revolt (2 Kgs 18:8)
- Mareshah
- Beth-zur
- Gaza
- Lachish
- Hebron
- Ziph
- En-gedi
- Dead Sea
- MOAB
- Gerar
- Socoh
- Simeonites move into the western Negeb (1 Chron 4:39-41)
- Beer-sheba
- Arad
- Simeonites move into Mount Seir (1 Chron 4:42-43)
- EDOM
- JUDAH
- PHILISTINES
- © Carta, Jerusalem

Hezekiah's Preparations for Sennacherib's Invasion, 705–701 B.C.

The window of opportunity didn't open far, but Hezekiah took full advantage of the extent that it did. In the four years between Sennacherib's accession to the throne and the massive Assyrian assault on Judah, Hezekiah bolstered Judah's economy for the war effort, strengthened his army and threw up bulwarks around his kingdom. Particular attention was paid to the capital city of Jerusalem and to the Shephelah, which would surely face the brunt of the Assyrian attack.

And so the Judean king built and fortified. It is a testament to Hezekiah's vision and skill as a leader that throughout the years that he paid tribute to Sargon, he was still able to reap a good deal of wealth from the southern caravan routes that passed by Judah and from his own agricultural lands (2 Chron 32:27–29). It was these sources of revenue that allowed Hezekiah to expand so quickly once he had the chance. Although some of these preparations undoubtedly began while Sargon was still alive, Hezekiah's work took on a sense of urgency after the Assyrian king died. The Judean king fortified a number of cities that commanded strategic junctures or observation points throughout the hill country of Judah and in the Shephelah and outfitted them with provisions and armaments for war, pushing Judah's influence "as far as Gaza and its ter-

ritory" (2 Kgs 18:8). Sennacherib himself witnessed the extent of Hezekiah's efforts when he later boasted to have "laid siege to forty-six of [Hezekiah's] strong cities, walled forts and countless small villages in their vicinity" (ANET 288). Archaeological excavations at Lachish, Judah's second capital and a royal chariot city (cf. Mic 1:13a) overlooking the coastal plain to the southwest, have uncovered evidence of impressive fortifications. Hezekiah surrounded Lachish with two parallel walls and built a strong gate complex and an impressive palace there. Archaeology also provides ceramic evidence that at least part of the Judean economy was centralized for the war effort. Archaeologists have found over one thousand handles of large storage jars affixed with seal impressions reading "[belonging] to the king," (in Hebrew, *lmlk*). These seal impressions, dating to the late eighth century B.C. and found at sites throughout Judah and its outlying areas, indicate that the contents of the jars (perhaps wine or oil) were registered as royal property, apparently collected either as revenue for the war effort or as direct rations for the troops.

But it was Jerusalem that received the most attention. Hezekiah expanded the size of the walled-in area of the section of Jerusalem that had been David's city and encircled the broad hill lying immediately to its west with a massive wall. It was here that refugees from Israel and others looking for protection and better economic opportunities had settled over the course of the last several decades. Hezekiah also improved the city's water supply by having gangs of workmen hew a 1,750-foot-long conduit through bedrock under David's city (the so-called "Hezekiah's Tunnel") to channel the water of the Gihon Spring to a large pool within the city walls (2 Kgs 20:20; 2 Chron 32:30). South of Jerusalem, on a prominent rise exactly half-way to Bethlehem (modern Ramat Rachel), Hezekiah built for himself a magnificent royal palace in the style of the now-destroyed palaces of the northern kingdom of Israel.

After the fighting was over, Isaiah looked back and described Hezekiah's war preparations this way (with explanatory comments added):

After Sennacherib subdued Judah and returned home to Nineveh, he commissioned a large relief showing the siege of Lachish for one of the most prominent walls of his palace. Now in the British Museum, this relief preserves significant details of the fortifications of Lachish, of warfare techniques (both offensive and defensive), of dress and personal grooming, and of personal items such as Sennacherib's royal throne. Of particular note is the scene showing Sennacherib, now defaced, receiving prisoners and booty after the fall of the city (left). Isaiah and all Jerusalem heard well the Assyrian demand for surrender: "Who among the gods of the nations has delivered their land from my hand, that the LORD should deliver Jerusalem from my hand?" (Isa 36:20).

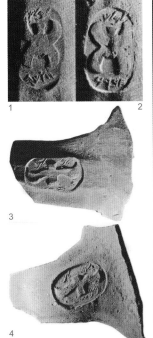

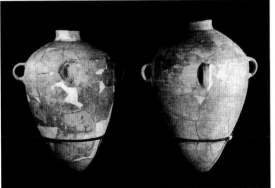

Numerous storage jars bearing stamped seal impressions showing two- or four-winged scarabs on their handles have been found in cities throughout Judah in archaeological contexts dating to the end of the eighth century B.C. Each seal bears the inscription in Hebrew lmlk, "[belonging] to the king," and the name of one of four cities, (1) Socoh, (2) Hebron, (3) Ziph and the enigmatic (4) mmšt. Apparently part of Hezekiah's war effort, these jars carried commodities either originating on royal lands or destined for government (probably troop) use. (NEAEHL)

In that day you depended
   on the weapons of the Forest House [the
   armory];
You saw that there were many breaches in [the wall
   of] the city of David [so you repaired them];
You collected the waters of the lower pool
   [to withstand a prolonged siege];
You counted the houses of Jerusalem
   [to declare eminent domain]
   and tore them down to fortify the wall;
And you made a reservoir between the two walls
   for the waters of the old pool.
But—you didn't depend on the One who made it,
   nor did you take into consideration the One who
   planned all this long ago.   (Isa 22:8b–11)

Isaiah was all in favor of a strong kingdom and a healthy national economy, and was probably impressed with Hezekiah's skills in administration and governance, as far as they went. But having a paid-up insurance policy, Isaiah cautioned his king, was a poor use of resources if it lulled its owner (and beneficiaries!) into the complacency of self-sufficiency. Isaiah preferred a life well lived to an attitude that squawked "let's eat and drink, for tomorrow we may

Dr. Gabriel Barkay, who excavated at Ramat Rachel in 1984, explains the form and function of the site's fortifications, preserved only in bits and pieces today. Here Hezekiah built a palace in the style of royal palaces of the Northern Kingdom of Israel. It was surrounded by a casemate (double) wall of well-dressed ashlar masonry laid in the header-stretcher technique (shown here). While Isaiah spoke only of Hezekiah's building projects in Jerusalem, it is likely that this palace, midway between the capital and Bethlehem, reflected the grandeur of the king's main palace there.

die" (Isa 22:13). In spite of the careful preparations and expensive trappings of his too-sophisticated king, it was clear to Isaiah that without the help of the LORD God, the emperor (and his kingdom) had no clothes (cf. Isa 20:4–6). Since the Assyrians were bent on destroying Judah anyway, Isaiah reasoned, it would have been better to die honorably with mind and soul intact than fall into a self-complacent national stupor that gave way to confusion and panic when things went sour (cf. Isa 22:5).

But it was even worse. For all his greatness (or maybe because of it), Hezekiah carried within him a fatal character flaw. At one point during his preparation for war Hezekiah fell mortally ill, cut down by an internal infection of some kind. Isaiah's initial word to the king was to set his house in order, for he would surely die. Devastated, Hezekiah threw himself on the mercy of God, but with a twinge of self-righteousness ("Heal me—I deserve it"; 2 Kgs 20:1–3).

(above) When Hezekiah instructed his workmen to hew a tunnel through bedrock beneath the City of David in order to channel water to a pool within the protection of the city's walls, he didn't intend that it would become a tourist attraction. Still, the tunnel was well-known in his day. According to the writer of Kings, it was the singular work most fitting Hezekiah's reign: "And the rest of the acts of Hezekiah and all his might, and how he made the pool and the conduit and brought water into the city, are they not written in the Book of the Chronicles of the Kings of Judah?" (2 Kgs 20:20).

Jerusalem, 701 B.C.

Hezekiah's efforts to prepare Jerusalem for Sennacherib's invasion have left important marks in the archaeological record of the city. It is possible to reconstruct the line of the "broad wall" around the western hill (Mishneh, or Second Quarter) of Jerusalem, to identify expansion of the oldest section of the city (the City of David) and to trace at least a portion of Hezekiah's renovated water system.

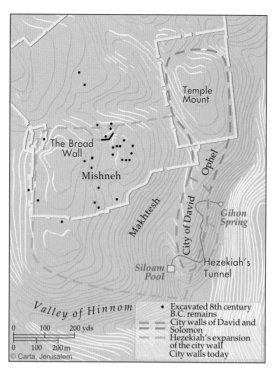

In anticipation of the Assyrian siege on Jerusalem, Hezekiah surrounded the hill lying west of the City of David and the Temple Mount with a wall, laid bare by excavations in the Jewish Quarter in the late 1960s. By doing so Hezekiah brought the extramural settlements scattered across the hill into Jerusalem's urban framework, and in the process enlarged the city fourfold. The massive wall, in places 22 feet thick, was called, appropriately, the "Broad Wall" (cf. Neh 3:8). (NEAEHL)

God relented and granted Hezekiah an additional fifteen years of life, enough to see the nation through the worst of the Assyrian threat (2 Kgs 20:4–11).

It was Isaiah who took charge of the situation and directed the healing process: "Let them take a cake of figs and apply it to the boil that he may recover" (2 Kgs 20:7; Isa 38:21). This notation is probably not so much a clue that Isaiah was an expert in medicine as an indication that the prophet maintained a certain degree of authority even over the king's personal life.

The two men were colleagues, their missions in life intertwined, but they didn't always see eye-to-eye. After Hezekiah had recovered, Merodach-baladan, the king of Babylon, sent emissaries and good-will gifts to the Judean king. Merodach-baladan had been plotting to throw off the Assyrian yoke which also strangled him, and he apparently saw in Hezekiah a willing accomplice. Hezekiah was completely taken by the overture, no doubt enjoying his "big-boy" status in the eyes of Babylonian king (2 Kgs 20:12–15; Isa 39:1–4). Isaiah, however, was not impressed, and warned that one day Judah certainly *would* be going into exile—but to *Babylon*, not Assyria. Hezekiah's response was tragic to the core: "The word of the LORD is good," he told the prophet, feigning acceptance of Isaiah's words, while all the while thinking, "So what? At least there will be peace in *my* days" (2 Kgs 20:16–19; Isa 39:5–8). Isaiah, whose eyesight was crystal-clear

(cf. Isa 6:8–10), saw right through his transparent king, and his heart must have broken. It was bad enough that the moral failings of the people Judah were taking its toll on the spirit of the nation, but now the king, too? A man with so much talent and promise who had made a loud public profession of following the ways of the LORD God (cf. 2 Chron 29:5–31:21), instead harbored within the privacy of his own mind such a short-sighted, me-only view of things? The very best that the house of David had to offer was falling short at the exact moment of its biggest crisis. Isaiah now knew that his most important message to Judah must be not that God would intervene on Israel's behalf in times of intense national stress only, but that one day He would step into history in a personal and redemptive way far greater than could be done through a normal Judean king (Isa 41:8–20, 42:1–9, 49:1–7, 50:4–11, 52:13–53:12, 61:1–9).

But first there was a battle to fight. Sennacherib's goal was to force Judah back into the Assyrian fold. According to Assyrian annals his army drove to the Philistine Coastal Plain, then plunged into Judah from the west. The line of attack was through the broad valleys of the Shephelah, each of which was a gateway into the hill country—or, taken together, a line of defense if Hezekiah fortified them properly (as had Rehoboam; cf. 2 Chron 11:5–12). Sennacherib's plan was to take the fortified city at the midpoint of a given valley in order to isolate and then conquer the more prominent city at that valley's western end: first Timnah (*Tel Batash*) and then Ekron (*Tel Miqne*) in the Sorek Valley, followed by Azekah and then Gath (*Tell es-Safi*) in the Elah Valley. In the process, Sennacherib also repulsed an Egyptian attack at Eltekeh that was apparently launched in support of the Judean effort. Isaiah described the result this way:

> Then your [i.e., Judah's] choicest valleys were full
> of chariots,
> and the horsemen took up fixed positions at the gate.
> He removed the defense of Judah.   (Isa 22:7–8a)

With the strategic Sorek and Elah valleys in Assyrian hands, the Judean defense was sufficiently weakened for Sennacherib to attack the most formidable of Hezekiah's fortified cities, Lachish. This was the decisive battle, and when Sennacherib eventually returned to Nineveh he commissioned his artisans to portray the full assault and violent end to Lachish in all its brilliant and gory detail in high relief on one of the most prominent walls of his royal palace.

During the heat of battle but when the fate of Lachish was still certain, Sennacherib sent his emissary, the Rabshakeh ("Rabshakeh" was not a personal name but an Assyrian title for a high official) to Jerusalem to demand Hezekiah's surrender (2 Kgs 18:17–37; Isa 36:1–22). In Sennacherib's own words, Hezekiah was now trapped "like a caged bird" (ANET 288). Realizing that his enormous efforts to prepare Judah were no match for the Assyrian onslaught, Hezekiah finally turned to the LORD for help—something Isaiah had been counseling he do all along (2 Kgs 19:1–34; Isa 37:1–35). According to the biblical account Sennacherib broke off the siege of Jerusalem and returned home—although not before repulsing another Egyptian attack and laying waste to Libnah (perhaps *Tel Bornat*) and the rest of the southern Shephelah in the process (2 Kgs 19:8–9, 19:35–37; Isa 37:8, 37:36–38; cf. Mic 1:10–16). The kingdom of Judah was devastated; only Jerusalem survived—and that, barely. But it was enough so that the remainder of people who were left to scratch out a living in their wasted land developed the notion over the coming years that Jerusalem was inviolable; God would never let His holy city fall.

Sennacherib's attack on Jerusalem in 701 B.C. is the only event that is described in historical detail in the Old Testament three times (2 Kgs 18–19, 2 Chron 32 and Isa 36–37). Clearly this greatest moment of crisis was a pivotal point in the ebb and flow of the nation of Judah. It was not the Judeans' finest hour—but it was one of God's. Isaiah fully recognized Assyria's strength as the horrifying events of the attack unfolded, describing it as if the prophet had personally witnessed Sennacherib's "scorched-earth" policy on the march from Lebanon to Judah:

> I [Sennacherib] cut down its tall cedars and its
> choice cypresses…
> and with the sole of my feet I dried up all the rivers
> of Egypt
> …turning fortified cities into ruinous heaps
> so that their inhabitants became…as grass on the
> housetops, scorched before it could grow.
>
> (Isa 37:24–27)

While not denying the utter shock of the events of his day, Isaiah had the vision to lift his eyes to the larger picture. He was a realist, one who had to come to terms with the fickle human potential for good and stare full-face into a life that had become "solitary, poor, nasty, brutish and short" (borrowing words from an even more horrifying scenario described by Thomas Hobbes in *Leviathan*, 1651). But Isaiah was also a visionary. Sennacherib left Judah devastated, but the reason for the tragedy was not because the Assyrians were inherently stronger

Young olive trees grace the terraced hillsides of the Judean hill country. Supple and full of life, they promise harvests for many generations. Faced with the possibility that his people might be cut off in his own generation, Isaiah insisted on hope for the future. "Don't let even the eunuch say 'Look, I'm nothing but a dry tree.' For thus says the LORD, 'To those who…choose what pleases me…I will give them, in my house and within my walls, a memorial and a name (yad vashem) better than sons and daughters" (Isa 56:3–5).

than the Judeans, nor were the events that chewed up Isaiah's land simply part of the natural ebb and flow of nation-states. For Isaiah, the normal rules of political science didn't apply. Rather, the prophet declared that the entire event had been orchestrated by God in order to show his divine power over the affairs of men (Isa 37:26–35). If Jerusalem survived—and both it and a remnant of its people surely would—it was because God had ordained such from the beginning of time. The One who herds the starry host as if it were a flock of sheep (Isa 40:26) would surely be able to care for his own people. For the prophet, living in deeply troubled times, this was comfort enough (Isa 40:1–2, 40:21–31).

And so Isaiah looked to the future.

* * * * *

It was the Edomites, also bewildered by the events that shook the southern Levant during the lifetime of the prophet Isaiah, who asked the most relevant question:

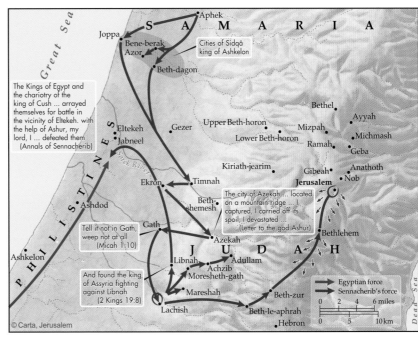

The Kings of Egypt and the chariotry of the king of Cush … arrayed themselves for battle in the vicinity of Eltekeh. with the help of Ashur, my lord, I … defeated them (Annals of Sennacherib)

Cities of Sidqâ king of Ashkelon

The city of Azekah … located on a mountain ridge … I captured, I carried off its spoil, I devastated … (Letter to the god Ashur)

Tell it not in Gath, weep not at all (Micah 1:10)

And found the king of Assyria fighting against Libnah (2 Kings 19:8)

Egyptian force
Sennacherib's force

© Carta, Jerusalem

Sennacherib's Assault on Judah, 701 B.C. *Hezekiah prepared well, but not well enough for the Assyrian onslaught. After taking the port of Joppa, Sennacherib turned his attention to Hezekiah's front line of defense. The attack was methodical and quite effective as first one, then another of the valleys of the Shephelah, each carrying an important highway from the coast to the hill country of Judah, was brought into the Assyrian fold. With the fall of Lachish the kingdom of Judah was reduced to its bare minimum. Only when Jerusalem stood alone did Hezekiah finally heed Isaiah's call to look to the Lord rather than himself for survival.*

With warm spring days following full winter rains, wildflowers burst into bloom across the hills of Judah. But the scorching heat of early summer follows close behind, and beauty lasts just for a moment. "All flesh is grass, and all its loveliness is like the flower of the field," said Isaiah, who if anyone should know. "The grass withers, the flower fades when the breath of the LORD blows upon it. Surely the people are grass…" (Isa 40:6–7).

A fertile terrace west of Jerusalem brings to mind the promise of Isaiah, spoken in a land of stubble that was about to be licked by flame: "The LORD will continually guide you and satisfy your desire in scorched places, giving strength to your bones. And you will be like a watered garden, like a spring whose waters never fail" (Isa 58:11).

> *Watchman, how far gone is the night?*
> *Watchman, how far gone is the night?*
> (Isa 21:11)

By the first century, the rabbis had turned Edom's query into Israel's question: When would *our* night give way to the light of dawn? According to a midrash in the Palestinian Talmud, Isaiah gave an answer:

> *"When you wish it, God will wish it; when you desire it, God will desire it." So the people asked, "Then what prevents it from coming?" Isaiah replied, "Your lack of repentance. So return, come."*
> (Palestinian Talmud 1:1, 64a)

Isaiah recognized that there was a direct connection between the woes of his nation and the behavior of his people, and that a corrupt heart corrupted everything else (Isa 1:16–17, 33:15–16). But there was also a solution. Israel could be redeemed. Drawing on the age-old notion that the identity of the people of Israel was so intertwined with their ancestral homeland that the health of one invariably affected that of the other, Isaiah described his vision of a renewed future for his people in terms of what would happen to the land itself:

> *The wilderness and the desert will be glad,*
> *and the Aravah will rejoice and blossom;*
> *like the crocus it will blossom profusely and rejoice*
> *with rejoicing and shouts of joy.*
> *The glory of Lebanon will be given to it,*
> *the majesty of Carmel and Sharon.*
> *They will see the glory of the LORD,*
> *the majesty of our God.*
> (Isa 35:1–2)

Lebanon, Mount Carmel and the Sharon Plain—three regions on Israel's periphery, always green, fertile and blessed, were verdant reminders of the open hand of God. But if even the parched wilderness could bloom, why not also the shriveled lives of the remnant of people that had survived the Assyrian attack?

Isaiah didn't intend for a simple restoration of the fortunes of days gone by, however. No, the prophet spoke in terms of righteousness and justice, of salvation and redemption, qualities that would finally define not just the nation of Israel but also its people, individuals who would live together in a special community with God (Isa 42:1, 42:4, 49:6–7). And the vehicle to bring it all about, Isaiah saw, was a divinely-appointed Servant, someone who was inherently part of Israel yet also able to redeem Israel (Isa 42:1–9, 49:5–7, 50:4–11, 52:13–53:12). This Servant would succeed where Ahaz and Hezekiah—and everyone else—had failed. It was a wonderful, redemptive vision, a lofty trajectory launched by Isaiah that landed squarely in the fertile ground of the first century where it took deep root among the earliest followers of Jesus (Mt 12:18–21; Lk 4:18–19; Acts 8:26–37, 13:47). The darkest night required the brightest dawn.

CHAPTER 14
JOSIAH
The Last Hope

One of the things that makes greatness great is that it doesn't happen all the time. In the normal ebb and flow of events people are usually adequate to the task at hand—on the ball enough to keep everything moving in the right direction, but rather comfortable with a routine that becomes mundane. Life grinds along from one year to the next, lacking moments of distinction or merit. Many forces—a prolonged economic downturn, the loss of freedom, dignity or rights, or a breakdown of the values and traditions of the past—can drag on a person's spirit. In extreme cases an entire society can slip into the abyss of malaise. It's not an attractive picture, and one that, once in place, is very hard to overcome. Solutions usually begin in fits and starts until the moment arrives—never quite quickly or often enough—when a gifted individual is able to seize the advantage offered by a number of favorable circumstances and pull his people back toward greatness. Quite rightly, the biblical writers saw periods of personal and national renewal in Israel as a divine work, stirring events in a way that restored favor to a chosen people until, in a moment of greatness, someone reached up to seize the hand of God.

Such was Judah in the seventh century B.C. during the long aftermath of Sennacherib's invasion. The Assyrian attack of 701 B.C. left the people of Judah staggering, their land devastated and local economy in ruins. Hezekiah their king survived, but only as an Assyrian vassal holding a rump state with reduced territory and limited autonomy. The land's most productive areas—parts of the outer Shephelah and the coastal plain—were given to the kings of Ekron and Ashdod, who had showed a greater will to collaborate with the Assyrians than had Judah. The challenge facing Hezekiah and his successor, Manasseh, was how to restore the hope and fortunes of Judah without arousing the ire of Assyria, which needed a pacified Levant for its imperialistic drive into Egypt. Eventually Jerusalem's religious hierarchy would interpret the survival of Judah as proof that God would never let Jerusalem, His chosen city, fall (cf. Jer 7:4). In the meantime everyone was just glad to be alive, the reality of their shattered dignity and clipped rights notwithstanding.

Scholars have labeled the first half of the seventh century B.C. a time of *Pax Assyriaca*, when the "peace of Assyria" governed the political, social and economic priorities of the lands that bordered the eastern Mediterranean seaboard. Archaeological and written evidence suggests that the economic infrastructure of the entire region was reconfigured to funnel its profits to the Assyrian capital, Nineveh, much as in the nineteenth century European colonial powers manhandled the resources of their empires for the good of God, King and Country. Although he continued to enjoy the support of Judah's prophetic circles and the powerful Jerusalem priesthood, Hezekiah was left to chafe under heavy economic and political bondage. We can easily assume that the competent and freedom-loving king spent his last years greatly frustrated by what could have been.

Conquest of Lachish by the Assyrian army, on a relief from the palace of Sennacherib at Nineveh. The Assyrian war machine was ruthless, efficient and complete. Short of a miracle, nothing could stand in its way.

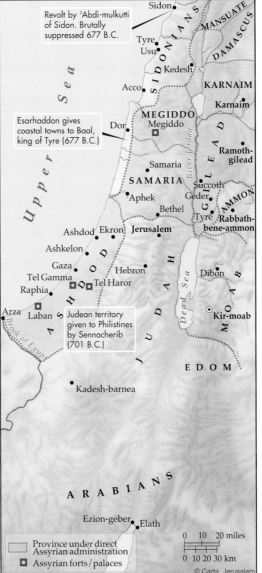

Revolt by ʿAbdi-mulkutti of Sidon. Brutally suppressed 677 B.C.

Esarhaddon gives coastal towns to Baal, king of Tyre (677 B.C.)

Judean territory given to Philistines by Sennacherib (701 B.C.)

Province under direct Assyrian administration

Assyrian forts / palaces

0   10   20 miles
0 10 20 30 km

© Carta, Jerusalem

The Southern Levant During the Reign of Manasseh. *Written records left by Sennacherib, Esarhaddon and Ashurbanipal portray a consistent picture of Assyrian subjugation over the southern Levant throughout the first half of the 7th century B.C. The Assyrians created an access corridor to Egypt by converting land lying along the international coastal highway into imperial provinces. Judah and other kingdoms maintained a semblance of independence, though submissive to Assyria's beck and call. Assyria's clenched fist hovered over the province of Ashdod, aimed at Egypt but also keeping Judah's aspirations safely in check.*

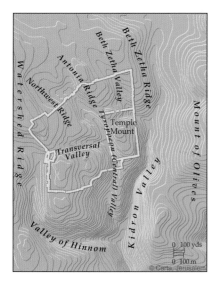

Jerusalem, a city of hills and valleys, is framed by two ridges, the Mount of Olives to the east and the Watershed Ridge to the west. Both are higher than Jerusalem and provide a nice frame for the city and its residents.

Hezekiah died in 686 B.C.; his evil nemesis Sennacherib outlived him by five years. Unfortunately he didn't live long enough to enjoy hearing the news of the Assyrian king's murder (cf. 2 Kgs 19:36–37). Hezekiah was succeeded by his son Manasseh, who had begun his reign as a co-regent in 697 B.C. at the age of twelve. After the death of Hezekiah Manasseh reigned as sole monarch for another forty-four years, until 642 B.C. In spite of the overall negative assessment of his deeds by the writers of the books of Kings and Chronicles (2 Kgs 21:10–16, 23:26–27; 2 Chron 33:1–9), Manasseh's long reign (the longest of any king of ancient Israel or Judah) must have provided a measure of stability and relief to the people of Judah.

Taking a page from the policy handbook of his grandfather Ahaz—one that was categorically rejected by Hezekiah—Manasseh recognized that the world was changing and that Judah's best chance for revival lay in its ability to willingly accommodate to the priorities of its neighbors, be they near (Phoenicia, Ammon and Moab; cf. 2 Kgs 23:13) or far (such as Assyria itself). The biblical writers focused their commentary on Manasseh's adoption of foreign religious practices, and between the lines we can see wholesale efforts by the king to meld Judah's identity with that of "the nations whom the LORD dispossessed before the sons of Israel" (2 Kgs 21:2; cf. vs. 11). While there is no evidence that the Assyrians imposed their cultic practices on conquered peoples, it is reasonable to suppose that Manasseh, the new-world-order head of an Assyrian vassal state, would have thought it expedient to adopt visible elements of his overlord's identity (cf. 2 Kgs 21:5, 23:11–12; Jer 7:17–18, 19:13; Zeph 1:8). The priesthood and prophetic circles of Jerusalem were understandably angered, and in a fit of divine rage likened Manasseh's Jerusalem to a dish that needed to be wiped clean:

> Behold, I am bringing such a calamity on Jerusalem and Judah that whoever hears of it, both his ears will tingle! I will stretch over Jerusalem the measuring line of Samaria and the plummet of the house of

In the sixth century B.C. all roads led to Nineveh, where Ashurbanipal and his queen, shown here on a relief from the royal palace, enjoyed the hard-won fruit of their empire.
(original in The British Museum)

> Ahab, and I will wipe Jerusalem as one wipes a dish, wiping it and turning it upside down.
>
> (2 Kgs 21:12–13)

The image was graphic and powerful: when viewed from the hill south of Jerusalem it is easy to imagine the shape and dimensions of the topography around the city as a large dish, with the royal quarter, the old City of David, lying on the bottom like a lump of spoiled food needing to be scraped away—then great cosmic hands reaching down from the sky to seize the scene from horizon line to horizon line (the Mount of Olives to the watershed ridge) and flip the entire landscape over, "turning it upside down" like a wiped dish. In spite of this prophetic condemnation, however, it seems as though Manasseh's policies, combined with the stability of his long reign, allowed Judah to begin to regain its economic footing.

Hezekiah's vision for a renewed Judah was hampered by the grip of the Assyrian vice, while Manasseh's ran afoul of powerful circles in Jerusalem. For most of the seventh century B.C. the pieces just didn't come together right. Then, in the last years of his life, something happened that allowed Manasseh to begin to lay the groundwork for a realistic attempt at restoring the national fortunes of Judah. In his account of the reign of Manasseh, the writer of Chronicles noted that the Judean king was hauled before the king of Assyria in Babylon—it must have been before Ashurbanipal, who was besieging Babylon in 648 B.C.—where he realized the error of his ways and returned to the LORD (2 Chron 33:10–13). The detail of what actually happened at this fateful meeting can be fleshed out from the verses that follow, in which the Chronicler reported that upon returning home, Manasseh refortified Jerusalem and the cities of Judah and removed the images of foreign gods from Jerusalem and the Temple (2 Chron 33:14–15). These acts won guarded praise from the Chronicler (2 Chron 33:17–19), but hint at a larger reality behind the event. Although the Assyrian Empire was on its last legs, Manasseh could not have strengthened Judah militarily without Ashurbanipal's permission and blessing. We can assume, then, that by the waters of Babylon (cf. Ps 137:1) the Judean king cast his nation's future squarely in the Assyrian lap. At the same time, Manasseh's eradication of foreign elements of worship in Jerusalem suggests that he severed certain diplomatic ties or initiatives with his near neighbors. Perhaps Ashurbanipal and Manasseh had cut a deal: Judah pledged loyalty to Assyria in return for Assyrian guarantees that Judah would now be Assyria's point guard in the southern Levant. Assyria was teetering on the edge of a quick downward spiral (within a generation the feared empire would be nothing but rubble), and Ashurbanipal needed to shore up his support in the west. Apparently Judah became the vassal chosen to hold Assyrian interests in the region, and Manasseh stood to reap whatever political and economic benefits this cozy relationship might bring his way. As a result, Judah's economy received a much-needed boost, and as long as Temple worship was directed toward the LORD God, the high priesthood was happy. After all, they, too, probably recognized the expediency of the times.

Manasseh's son and successor, Amon, reigned for only two years (642–640 B.C.) before being assassinated by his own "servants," persons who held official positions within the government (2 Kgs 21:19–23; cf. 2 Kgs 14:19). Clearly the royal bureaucracy was not happy with the direction that Amon was taking Judah, although not enough information is available to determine the source of their discontent. It is tempting to look for a cause in Amon's foreign policy, but was he too pro- or too anti-Assyrian for their sentiments? Had he strayed from Manasseh's policies, or towed the line too closely for those wanting change? Or should the reason be found in something more mundane? In any case, the "people of the land," a group of influential landed aristocrats who, though not of the royal blood line, had a history of exercising their will in affairs of state, killed the assassins and placed Amon's son Josiah on the throne (2 Kgs 21:24–26; cf. 2 Kgs 11:19–20, 14:21). We should understand that Josiah, only eight years old, thus began his reign with the support of a very significant element of Judean society (cf. 2 Chron 35:24–25), and that he probably was chosen as king because he was young enough to be shaped by their will.

And what was that will? This can only be implied from the kind of king that Josiah turned out to be. Briefly put, the forces of conservative, religious nationalism had again risen to the top of Judean society and were able to shape the policy of state. But it should be noted that those who advocated a return to the glories of a strong, independent Judah found opportunity to express their will not because of dissatisfaction with Amon *per se*, but for a much larger reason, namely, the imminent collapse of Assyria's evil empire.

Assyria's centuries-long goal of world domination had been realized only in 663 B.C., when Ashurbanipal sacked Thebes (the city of No-amon; cf. Nahum 3:8), Egypt's ancient religious and political capital far up the Nile. But Ashurbanipal's Assyria was not able to bask in the glow of his grand accomplishment for long. Like a firework rocket, Assyria had slowly risen to great heights, then burst into brilliance for a brief, glorious moment before quickly fizzling to nothingness. By the time that Josiah was thrust onto the throne of Judah in 640 B.C., the grandeur of Assyria was already fading, and within another generation the mighty empire would forever cease to exist. Apparently Judah's old aristocracy

sensed that with Assyria on the edge of collapse everything could change, and for provinces on the periphery such as Judah that meant sooner rather than later. So all of the circumstances for a return to glory had come together: Assyria was on the way out, Manasseh's policies had begun to revive the economic and nationalistic aspirations of Judah, Josiah enjoyed prophetic, priestly and popular support at home, and the new king was young and energetic enough to do something about it all. God smiled again on his people; the possibility of greatness had returned.

The writers of the books of Kings and Chronicles were wholly taken by the religious aspects of Josiah's reign, and by all indications his was the most thorough-going of the revivals in ancient Judah. The Chronicler gives the chronology: in Josiah's eighth year "while he was still a youth, he began to seek the God of his father David"; in his twelfth year "he began to purge Judah and Jerusalem of the high places" and other aspects of foreign and indigenous cults; and in his eighteenth year he gave instruction "to repair the house of the LORD his God" and "celebrate the Passover to the LORD in Jerusalem" (2 Chron 34:3, 34:8, 35:1). These dates should not necessarily be taken as exact intervals of events but well-positioned summary statements of a lifetime of royal effort to return Judah to the glory days of David and Solomon. The Chronicler's outline gives logical coherence to the

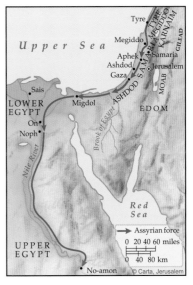

The Kingdom of Judah in the Days of Josiah. *As Assyrian power collapsed in the southern Levant, Josiah was able to pull areas that had belonged to the Northern Kingdom of Israel back into the orbit of Jerusalem. The result was a kingdom with borders that were essentially the same as those of Israel during the United Kingdom of David and Solomon, excluding the vassal states of Transjordan and Syria. Short-lived, Josiah's kingdom was like a piece of summer fruit, ripening just before falling (cf. Isa 28:4).*

The Conquest of Egypt by Assyria, 671–663 B.C. *Assyria's goal of reaching Egypt was realized when Esarhaddon conquered the Delta in 671 B.C. and Ashurbanipal sacked Thebes (No-amon) seven years later. The victory was short-lived, as Assyria itself fell within a generation.*

Students of biblical geography are briefed on archaeological remains at Tel Zayit (Zeitah) in the southwestern Shephelah. The site, more closely connected to the coast than the hill country of Judah, is one of the candidates for biblical Libnah, the home of Josiah's favored wife, Hamutal. If this identification is correct, it provides personal motivation for Josiah's political expansion into the region.

The prophet Jeremiah, 19th century engraving (Carta, Jerusalem). *Commented Heschel* (The Prophet, vol. 1, p. 106), *"Jeremiah has often been called a prophet of wrath. It would be more significant to say that Jeremiah lived in an age of wrath."*

events, but also makes historical-geographical (and common) sense. Each of these dates (years eight, twelve and eighteen of Josiah's reign) correspond to other actions or events that impacted the life of the young king and offered him both the opportunity and encouragement to pursue a path of greatness.

Josiah's first formative years, before his eighth on the throne (age sixteen), were spent under the guidance of "the people of the land," those widespread voices of conservatism that had brought him to power. He responded well to their tutelage. The writer of Kings offers a clue, in his account of the reign of Josiah's son Jehoahaz (also called Shallum; 1 Chron 3:15; Jer 22:11), that helps us understand Josiah's coming of age in his eighth year, when he began "to seek the God of his father David." Like Josiah, Jehoahaz was anointed king by "the people of the land" (2 Kgs 23:30), doubtless to ensure that the popular conservative agenda would continue. Two things are significant in this regard, as Anson Rainey has pointed out (The Sacred Bridge, p. 256). First, we are told that Jehoahaz took the throne at the age of twenty-three (2 Kgs 23:31), which means that he was born in Josiah's fateful eighth year, when the king was sixteen (cf. 2 Kgs 22:1; by this time Josiah had already fathered three other sons! cf. 1 Chron 3:15). Second, Hamutal, the mother of Jehoahaz, Josiah's favorite wife, was from Libnah, a Levitical priestly city in the southwestern Shephelah (2 Kgs 23:31; cf. Josh 21:13; 1 Chron 6:57). The Levitical cities were centers of religious and political conservatism in Judah and probably served as regional focal points for the work of the "people of the land." The reasoned conclusion? Josiah, who probably married Hamutal not too long before, must have been shaped by the political and religious priorities of his father-in-law's family from Libnah. As he came of age and faced the reality of not only governing a kingdom but raising a family, Josiah chose to embrace what he had been taught to hold dear from childhood and "began [personally] to seek the God of his father David" (2 Chron 34:3). It was a fortuitous choice.

The real meat of Josiah's reign was in the years that followed, and is summarized in a long list of reforms that took place between (or in connection with?) the king's twelfth and eighteenth years (2 Kgs 23:4–20; 2 Chron 34:3–7). The Chronicler put it succinctly:

> Now Josiah removed all the abominations from all the lands belonging to the sons of Israel, and made all who were present in Israel to serve the LORD their God. (2 Chron 34:33)

These words presuppose the resurgent nationalism that aimed to restore the political and religious fervor of the kingdom of David. But from the point of view of the ancient Judeans, it would have been impossible or at least nonsensical to separate the political aspects from the religious; both were integral for a successful state.

The twelfth year of Josiah, 628 B.C., coincided with the demise of Ashurbanipal. Shortly before his death the Assyrian king turned the reigns of power over to his successor, the young Ashur-etil-ilani, who faced unrest at home and abroad. The Assyrian Empire was fading fast, and everyone knew it. As a result, Josiah had a chance to reclaim land that not only had been seized as Assyrian provinces one hundred years before, but also the former territory of the Northern Kingdom that had stood in rebellion against the House of David for two centuries before that. As a political leader, Josiah's destiny was clear.

Within six years, by 622 B.C. (Josiah's eighteenth as king), Nabopolassar of Babylon (the father of Nebuchadnezzar) had consolidated his power and stood as likely heir to the Assyrian Empire. But it would be awhile before the Babylonians would be able to reach the lands of the eastern Mediterranean, and in the meantime Josiah had all the freedom for kingdom building he needed. His reforms reached their climax in 622 B.C., when the Temple was refurbished, the covenant with the LORD God of Israel was renewed, and Passover, Israel's great freedom festival, was celebrated.

But other factors also came into play during these critical years. Jeremiah began his ministry in 627 B.C., in the thirteenth year of Josiah's reign (Jer 1:2, 25:3). The prophetic ministry of Zephaniah, a man perhaps of the royal house (cf. Zeph 1:1), also coincided with Josiah's rule. Both spoke forcefully of the dire straits into which the people of Judah and Jerusalem had fallen, and although their loudest message was one of impending judgment (Jer 3:1–5; Zeph 1:7–18, 3:6), it was a tirade consistent with Josiah's call for reform (cf. Jer 3:20–4:1; Zeph 3:8–11). The great irony is that Judah saw its greatest potential for social, moral and religious revival only on the eve of its final destruction. Like Assyria, Judah's flame burned brightest just before it was extinguished. Josiah stood in as the last great hope.

The political and nationalistic aspects of Josiah's revival can best be charted by combining archaeological evidence with the clues provided by the writers of Kings and Chronicles. Of course we can suppose that the lion's share of Josiah's effort fell in Jerusalem and the towns and villages of Judah "from Geba to Beer-sheba" (2 Kgs 23:8). Taking care of home was the first priority of the Judean kings. But to protect his land and expand its limited economy, Josiah pushed outward.

The southwestern frontier, toward Egypt, always called for attention. Judah had a love-hate relationship with Egypt, the sleeping giant that lay across the Sinai. Throughout the time of the monarchy Judah had benefited from Egyptian commercial interests in the region (as long as Egypt didn't seize too dominant a role on the Levantine coast); of late the Egyptian army could be relied upon to help drive Assyria back to the Euphrates. Now Josiah drew a line in the sand: he rebuilt the fortress at Kadesh-barnea (*Ain el-Qudeirat*), a large oasis on the border between the Negeb and Sinai, to control the inland road to Egypt. At the same time, this fort kept the southern desert tribes in the area in check.

A late sign of Judean-Egyptian cooperation was the presence of a Jewish colony on the island of Elephantine (adjacent to modern Aswan), far up the Nile where the first cataract separates Egypt from Nubia. The Elephantine Papyri, a rich trove of documents dating to the fifth century B.C., speak of a temple at Elephantine at which animal sacrifices were offered to YHW, the LORD God of Israel. It has been suggested, and reasonably so, that this colony (and maybe others of which no evidence remains) was founded by Josiah, who offered Judean mercenaries to Pharaoh Psammetichus (Psamtik) to assist the Egyptian fight against the Babylonians. In theory it would be a smart move—should the Babylonians try to push their empire into the Levant, the Egyptians would bear the brunt of the fight and Babylon hopefully would leave Judah alone. The temple, then, would have been a mechanism for this community to maintain its Judean/Jewish identity so far from home. Deep in Egypt, it would not have affected Josiah's reforms back in Jerusalem.

To guard his southeastern frontier, Josiah rebuilt the fortress at Arad where a Judean temple had stood since the days of Solomon. Archaeological evidence suggests that as Josiah rebuilt Arad's fortress, he destroyed its temple in the drive to centralize worship in Jerusalem.

The Edomites were also rebounding nicely in the vacuum left by the Assyrian demise and had their eyes on both the Negeb and the southern wilderness all the way to Ezion-geber/Elath on the Red Sea. The Edomites eventually joined the Babylonians in destroying Judah and Jerusalem in the early sixth century B.C. (cf. Obad 10–14), overrunning Arad and its

satellite fortresses in the process, but in the meantime Josiah was able to hold the line.

Josiah also built three small fortresses in the Buqei'ah, a small valley in the Judean Wilderness above the northwestern corner of the Dead Sea (at *Kh. Abu Tabaq*, *Kh. es-Samrah* and *Kh. el-Maqari*, possibly the Middin, Secacah and Nibsham of Joshua 15:61–62, respectively). In addition to their military value guarding the approaches to Jerusalem from the east, these fortresses, with nearby dams and catchment basins for runoff rainfall, seem to have been an attempt to wrest agricultural productivity from an otherwise stark and arid landscape. The real success of this bold and creative endeavor remains uncertain. Also uncertain is the extent of Josiah's efforts, if any, to reclaim Israelite interests in Gilead lying farther to the east.

Judah's main points of access lay to the west, and it is here that Josiah stood the most to gain (economically) and lose (militarily). The king had both the incentive and the opportunity to make a firm stand here. Josiah's mother, Jedidah, was from Bozkath (2 Kgs 22:1), a village that appears elsewhere only in the list of towns of the administrative district of the southern Shephelah (Josh 15:37–41). The order of the cities listed suggests that Bozkath was

The Elephantine Papyri, dating to the 6th and 5th centuries B.C., mention a temple to YHW located somewhere on the southern end of the Nile island of Elephantine, a site now dominated by palm trees and ruins of a temple to the Egyptian god of the inundation, Khnum. The Israelite/Jewish temple here could have been founded as early as the mid-7th century, and seems to have been active throughout the reign of Josiah.

The temple found within the confines of the fortress of Arad was built on the same general plan as was the Temple in Jerusalem—and existed for about the same time period. The most significant difference between the two buildings was the holy of holies, where in Arad archaeologists found two incense altars and two standing stones, shown here. This evidence strongly suggests that two deities were worshiped in the Arad temple.

Three fortresses were strung the length of the Buqei'ah Valley in the Judean Wilderness during the late 7th century B.C. The one with the most prominent remains, Khirbet es-Samrah (perhaps biblical Secacah) on a low rise in the middle of the valley, was walled with large, roughly-hewn stones forming a square enclosure shown here. The three sites apparently served a double purpose: they provided a Judean military presence east of Jerusalem and attempted to establish an agricultural base in the region. Today, the Israeli army uses the entire Buqei'ah Valley for military training and security purposes.

(above) Thousands of female figurines from the time of the monarchy have been found at sites throughout Israel and Judah. The physical features of these figurines strongly suggest a connection to the feminine (rather than warlike) aspects of the Canaanite female goddess(es) of fertility: Asherah, Ashtoreth and Anat. It is likely that these images were "household gods" intended to protect and provide for women during the period from procreation to childbirth. Hundreds of such images, including this one, were found in Jerusalem. From the evidence of 2 Kings 23, it appears that homage to Asherah was given even within the confines of the Temple enclosure itself.

located between Lachish and Eglon, in the extreme southwestern Shephelah. In addition, Josiah's wife Hamutal, the mother of Jehoahaz, came from Libnah, a prominent city at the outer edge of the mid-Shephelah (likely in the Guvrin Valley at either *Tel Bornat* or *Tel Zayit*; 2 Kgs 23:31; cf. Josh 15:42). These family ties drew Josiah's interests to the far side of the Shephelah, within striking distance of the coast. To get there his efforts in the Shephelah probably mirrored those of Hezekiah: archaeological and textual evidence points to strong fortifications being rebuilt at Lachish and Azekah in the late seventh century B.C.

The practical extent of Josiah's interests on the coast, however, is unclear. Certainly his eyes turned toward Ashkelon and Ashdod, both a fairly straight shot from Libnah, but all available evidence suggests these cities fell outside of his orbit. A chance archaeological find farther north, however, at Mezad Hashavyahu, indicates that Josiah did maintain control over at least part of the coastal plain. Archaeological excavations there reveal a large L-shaped fortress on a rise of sand near the shore of

(right) This strong fortress at Mezad Hashavyahu protected Josiah's interests on the Mediterranean coast. The local governor resident in this fortress managed Judean commercial and agricultural affairs in the region.

The ostracon (below) contains a plea of a farm worker whose garment had been confiscated. Written in Hebrew and addressed "my lord, the governor," the letter suggests that during the reign of Josiah the Judean cultural orbit had reached at least a portion of the coast.

the Mediterranean, about one-third of the way from Ashdod to Joppa, Judah's natural seaport. (Today the site is on the site of a nuclear research center and inaccessible to the public.) Much of the pottery found at Mezad Hashavyahu is categorized as "East Greek," indicating either important trade connections with the Aegean or the presence of persons, perhaps mercenaries, from that area. What ties the site to Judah is the discovery of an ostracon, written in good biblical Hebrew and containing a Yahwistic personal name, Hashavyahu. The text of the ostracon contains the complaint by a farm laborer, employed in the harvest, that his garment had been taken from him, with a plea to the governor that it be returned (cf. Ex 22:26–27). While the presence of the fort indicates that Josiah was able to push to the Mediterranean and hold at least a narrow corridor between Joppa and Ashdod, information contained in the text of the ostracon shows that Judeans were also able to settle and farm the region and that the standards of justice advocated in the ancient Mosaic law formed the basis for complaint and redress.

Of course Josiah also looked north. His destruction of the high place of Jeroboam in Bethel and local cultic shrines throughout "the cities of Samaria" (2 Kgs 23:15, 23:19) presupposes political control over the now defunct Assyrian province of Samaria, the mountainous heartland of the former Northern Kingdom of Israel. The archaeological record of Megiddo indicates that although that city was unfortified in the late seventh century B.C., a large rectangular fortress was constructed on the northern edge of the site, apparently reflecting Josiah's move to control the Jezreel Valley together with its important resources and international routes. The

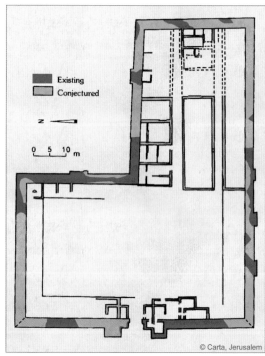

Chronicler notes that Josiah's efforts reached "even as far as Naphtali" (2 Chron 34:6), bringing the Sea of Galilee (the Kinneret) and Upper Galilee into the Judean fold and pushing the northern limits of his control toward Dan.

This region, in the far north, was certainly known to the residents of Jerusalem in Josiah's day, and Jeremiah used a precise description of its water resources to drive home a point to the people of Jerusalem:

> Does the snow of Lebanon ever melt from the
> highland crags?
> Or does cold water flowing from a foreign
> [land] ever fail? (Jer 18:14)

These are rhetorical questions: the answer is "No! The waters of Mount Hermon never fail." Jeremiah's point? That all of nature does exactly what it was created to do—except for people, who

> ...have forgotten Me,
> they burn incense to worthless gods
> and they have stumbled from their ways, from the
> ancient paths,
> to walk in bypaths, not on a highway. (Jer 18:15)

Jeremiah's assessment of the human condition was well taken, and Josiah would have agreed. But how would Jeremiah have known that on the highest parts of the Mount Hermon range, in basins out of eyesight from the land of Israel, the snow in fact does remain throughout the summer—unless Josiah had reestablished communication, influence and control in the area?

Enough clues exist, then, for us to assume that Josiah's kingdom reached to most, if not all, of the regions embraced by the old Solomonic phrase "from Dan to Beer-sheba" (cf. 1 Kgs 4:25). Politically it was Judah's last great hurrah, in which Josiah was able to find enough jockey-room among the remnants of the local kingdoms of the southern Levant to fill the vacuum left by the collapse of Assyria.

Politics aside, for Bible readers the more visible aspects of the revival of Josiah's kingdom were those that impacted its religion. Foremost among these were his efforts to purge Jerusalem and Judah of the high places and ritual objects associated with deities other than the LORD. Certainly among the first to go were the solar and astral cults most closely related to the high pantheon of Assyria, together with the centers of worship on the mountains around

Active during the reign of Josiah, the prophet Jeremiah never tired of likening the LORD God to life-giving water, while equating Baal and Asherah, the local deities of rainfall and fertility, with dryness and death. This was a powerful image for Israel, whose historic identity was grounded in a desert experience. "My people have forsaken Me, the fountain of living waters" (Jer 2:13), Jeremiah declared as God's spokesman, setting the record straight that even the powerful spring at Dan, in Baal's home territory, fell under the sovereignty of the LORD.

Jerusalem that Solomon had built for Ashtoreth of the Sidonians, Chemosh of Moab and Milcom of Ammon (2 Kgs 23:4–5, 23:11–13; cf. 1 Kgs 11:7–8). Josiah also tried to root out the cults of Baal and Asherah, the persistent, indigenous deities of the land who had taken up residence in Jerusalem and even in the Temple (2 Kgs 23:4–10, 23:14; 2 Chron 34:3–4). This part of the purge was bloody, and many of the priests attached to cultic sites in Samaria were killed, "slaughtered on the altars" according to the writer of Kings in a fate most fitting their deeds (2 Kgs 23:20). One of the ironies of his account is that by giving so much information about what Josiah did in his purge, the writer of Kings has unwittingly preserved for historians many details concerning the worship of foreign gods in Jerusalem that would have otherwise been lost (e.g., 2 Kgs 23:7, 23:10–14).

But perhaps the force of Josiah's purge was directed most strongly at those who were spiritually closest to home, the priests of the LORD God who served local shrines throughout the towns and villages of Judah and who "burned incense from Geba

"On every high hill and under every green tree you have lain down as a harlot" (Jer 2:20). The prophet Jeremiah issued a blanket condemnation of the loyalties of the men and women of Israel and Judah who preferred a world-view that posited the reality of Baal and Asherah rather than the LORD God. Open-air religious sites dotted the landscape, from small, local shrines to large regional temples such as this one at Dan. Josiah was indiscriminate, destroying them all and curtailing their activities in favor of the priesthood in Jerusalem.

As if it wasn't bad enough that Israel and Judah turned from the LORD, "the fountain of living waters," they compounded their plight by committing a second evil: "hewing for themselves cisterns, broken cisterns that don't hold any water" (Jer 2:13). Many of the residents of Jerusalem—and most of those living outside of the city—depended on cistern water for their daily needs. Here a small watering trough rests near a cistern opening. Clearly an inferior method of getting water when compared to a spring or flowing stream, cisterns would sometimes crack and leak, rendering the supply of already stale water within to become nothing but dampness and muck.

Shaphan reading the book of the law before King Josiah (2 Kgs 22:8–10), 19th century engraving (Carta, Jerusalem). Shaphan's son Gemariah had a chamber in the Temple (Jer 36:10), and it was from there that Baruch later read the words of Jeremiah to the people of Jerusalem.

(below) A clay seal impression bearing the name "Gemariah son of Shaphan" was found in archaeological excavations in Jerusalem (NEAEHL).

to Beer-sheba" (2 Kgs 23:8). Josiah destroyed their worship centers and bade them come to Jerusalem, the only remaining legitimate center of worship for the LORD. Jerusalem's Temple priests, with their own established interests to protect, weren't keen on the idea (once attained, privilege is difficult to share), but most of the local priests preferred to stay at home anyway (2 Kgs 23:8–9). Each of these men was probably the most influential person back in his respective home town; now all were alienated from the larger flow of events that were redefining the kingdom. If the temple found within the confines of the fortress at Arad is any indication of the whole, we can assume that up to this moment, these local priests had been able to function outside of Jerusalem under royal sponsorship and support. Now the rug was pulled out from under them, and the dissatisfied elements of society that all of this produced must have played a role in the social, political and religious chaos that buffeted Judah after Josiah's death. This was the downside of his reform.

It may be helpful to think of Josiah's acts as analogous in some ways to those of Akhenaten (Amenhotep IV), who tried to redirect Egyptian religion and society to the exclusive worship of the divine sun disk Aten in the mid-fourteenth century B.C., or perhaps to the Babylonian king Nabonidus who neglected other Mesopotamian deities in favor of the moon-god Sin in the mid-sixth century B.C. In both cases the backlash of disenfranchised priests, whose political and economic roles had been undercut by the zeal of reform, returned society to its pre-reform status quo with a vengeance after the death of the king. But Josiah's reform was exceptional: its lasting strength was found not in centralizing the nation around a newly-elevated deity but in reaching back to the origin of Israel and reestablishing the prominence of the Deity who founded both people and state in the first place. Josiah rode the forces of conservatism rather than run counter to them. By doing so, he ensured that even though the people of Judah might slide back into Baalism after his death, those who guarded the religious and cultural heritage of society (the prophets, priests and scribes) would guarantee that the ways of the LORD God would not be forgotten.

A fortuitous find provided the mechanism for this trusteeship. An important part of Josiah's reform was to refurbish the Temple in Jerusalem. During the repair work, the high priest Hilkiah reported that he had found "the book of the law" somewhere within the confines of the building (2 Kgs 22:8). A scholarly consensus, suggested by no less a man of learning than Jerome, holds that the document that was found by Josiah's workmen was some form of the Book of Deuteronomy. Reasons for this consensus abound: Deuteronomy speaks of a single (though unnamed) place of worship (Deut 12:1–14); the book emphasizes a covenant between the LORD and His people in which blessings and curses related to staying on the land or being exiled from it figure prominently (Deut 11:13–32, 27:1–28:68); the terminology and imagery in Deuteronomy perfectly describes the actual physical features of the land of promise (e.g., Deut 8:7–8, 11:11–14, 32:14); and the overall theological themes of Deuteronomy mirror the words of Jeremiah (Jer 5:24, 7:5–11, 11:1–5, 30:1–3, 30:22, 31:27–37, etc.). That is, the Book of Deuteronomy speaks precisely to the spiritual, political and lifestyle concerns of Judah in the closing days of its kingdom.

It is inconceivable that this kind of a book, a document as close to a national constitution as ancient Israel ever had, would have been lost for so many years; it is equally beyond the bounds of normal reason to conclude that it was written whole cloth by Josiah's conservative tutors in order to justify their takeover of the kingdom. The overall thrust of the stipulations would have come as no surprise to Josiah, his priests or the people of Judah. The "deuteronomists," as these conservative forces in society have been called, who counted Josiah among their supporters (and vice versa), were finally able to legitimize the ancient traditions of the divine Yahwistic covenant that had remained alive in Israel and Judah throughout the ebb and flow of the monarchy. Now that a formal, written document acknowledging their understanding of this covenant was in hand, the reform could formally express this legitimization as coming from the hand of God. Moreover, this book of the law ensured that the ideals of Josiah's reform would remain alive, at least among their guardians, even if the nation slid into apostasy and exile. Textless, the followers of Baal, Asherah, Chemosh, Milcom and the rest would fade from history, while the disciples of the LORD God, armed with the certainty that was provided by documents that would one day make up the Bible, had a vehicle to bridge whatever national tragedy the world might throw at them, and hold on for the future. If for nothing else, Josiah reached greatness for fostering an environment in which his people, reaching out to the open hand of God, could build a bridge that would allow them to survive the catastrophe of the coming exile.

The climax of Josiah's revival came when the

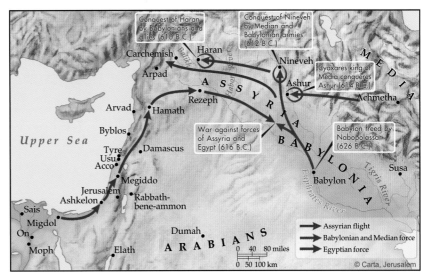

king, standing within the confines of the Temple, read the book (now called "the book of the covenant"; 2 Kgs 23:2) "to the priests, the prophets and all men small and great" from Jerusalem and Judah. On behalf of his people, Josiah established a formal covenant with the LORD God "to walk after the LORD, and to keep His commandments and His testimonies and His statues with all his heart and soul, to carry out the words of this covenant that were written in this book" (2 Kgs 23:2–3). To prove their determination by their deeds, Josiah commanded that the people celebrate the festival of Passover (*Pesach*) in Jerusalem (2 Kgs 23:21–23; 2 Chron 35:1–19). It was a glorious celebration, one that Judah had not seen to this extent since the days of Samuel (2 Kgs 23:22; 2 Chron 35:18; cf. 2 Chron 30:1–27). In some ways, Josiah's kingdom surpassed even the glory days of David and Solomon.

But everything came to a screeching halt in 609 B.C., Josiah's thirty-first year on the throne. Once again the context involved the Assyrians who, even in their death-throes, seemed to wreak havoc in Judah. Five years before, in 614 B.C., a coalition of Babylonians and Medes (the two rising stars in the ancient Near East) had destroyed Ashur, the old religious capital of Assyria, then overran Nineveh, its political capital, in 612 B.C., killing the Assyrian king Sin-sharra-ishkun in the process. An Assyrian government-in-exile headed by Ashur-uballit II, the last Assyrian king, took off for the sunset with the Babylonians and Medes in hot pursuit. Next comes one of the greatest ironies of ancient Near Eastern history. The Egyptians, long-sworn enemies of the Assyrians, realized that if Assyria fell the Babylonians would pour into the Levant, and so Pharaoh Psammetichus sent an Egyptian force to help Ashur-uballit hold the line. All was for naught, as the Assyrians were overrun at Haran in 610 B.C. and continued their flight westward, toward Carchemish.

Necho II succeeded his father Psammetichus as Pharaoh in 609 B.C. and immediately set out to assist the Assyrians for one last stand at Carchemish. His armies crossed the coastal plain that Josiah by now counted as part of Judah, then pushed to the great crossroads of the Jezreel Valley, which was

The decisive moment for Josiah's Judah was on the Plain of Megiddo, one of the ancient world's greatest battle theaters. Caught up in the flow of the times, Judah proved to be no match for an Egyptian army that was used to having its way in the international arena. The tel of Megiddo shown here was sliced deeply by an excavation team from the Oriental Institute of the University of Chicago in the 1920s and 1930s, revealing twenty-five destruction layers from the Neolithic to Persian periods; Josiah's city, perched high on a storied past, was second from the top. The Plain of Megiddo, or Jezreel Valley, with Mount Gilboa in the distance, lies beyond.

guarded by the Judean fortress at Megiddo. It was there that Josiah came out to meet Necho, and where the Judean king met his death (2 Kgs 23:29–30; 2 Chron 35:20–24). The episode is tragic beyond all measure, and leaves many questions unanswered. Why did Josiah pick a fight with the Egyptians? Was he an ally of Babylon as Hezekiah had been? Or with Necho new on the throne, did Josiah hope to catch the Pharaoh unprepared and conquer Egypt outright? And why make the challenge at Megiddo rather than at Lachish, Gezer or Aphek, all points the Egyptian army would have had to pass on the way and all closer to Judah and hence more easily defended by Josiah? Did Josiah actually think that his small kingdom could succeed against the great empires of the day, or was he so overcome with his own zeal that his judgment was clouded? Or, perhaps Necho called Josiah to Megiddo, the site of many Egyptian military triumphs of the past, to secure an oath of Judean loyalty, but then Josiah seized the opportunity to push his kingdom's expansion to its logical conclusion. Josiah's Judah was already large

The Collapse of the Assyrian Empire, 626–610 B.C. *Long to rise and quick to fall, the might that was Assyria collapsed in rubble during the reign of Josiah. A combined assault by the Babylonians and the Medes—an uneasy coalition born of opportunism and veiled second-intentions—drove the remnants of the Assyrian Empire west along the rim of the Fertile Crescent. The Babylonians under Nebuchadnezzar would be the first to fill the vacuum left by Assyria's demise.*

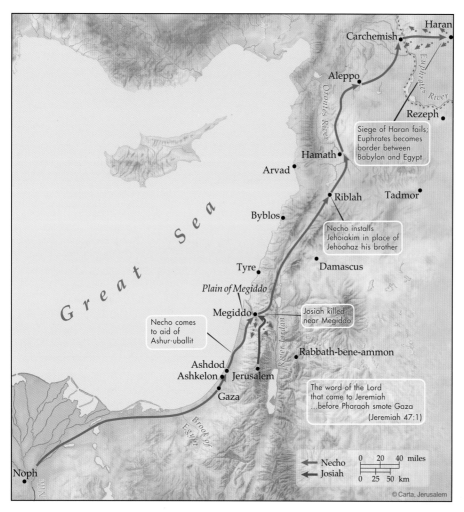

Map labels: Haran, Carchemish, Euphrates River, Aleppo, Orontes River, Rezeph, Siege of Haran fails; Euphrates becomes border between Babylon and Egypt, Hamath, Arvad, Riblah, Tadmor, Byblos, Necho installs Jehoiakim in place of Jehoahaz his brother, Tyre, Damascus, Plain of Megiddo, Megiddo, Josiah killed near Megiddo, Necho comes to aid of Ashur-uballit, Rabbath-bene-ammon, River Jordan, Ashdod, Ashkelon, Jerusalem, Gaza, The word of the Lord that came to Jeremiah ...before Pharaoh smote Gaza (Jeremiah 47:1), Great Sea, Noph, Nile, Brook of Egypt

→ Necho
→ Josiah

0   20   40 miles
0   25 50 km

© Carta, Jerusalem

The Campaigns of Necho and the Death of Josiah, 605–601 B.C. *Sensing that the coming new world order wouldn't be any more favorable to Egypt than the old one dominated by Assyria had been, Pharaoh Necho sent his armies to Carchemish to help Assyria make a final drive to push the Babylonians out of Haran. Josiah's intervention on the Plain of Megiddo defies rational explanation, but spelled doom for the Judean kingdom. Squeezed between Egypt and Babylon, Judah's days as an independent nation were nearly over.*

enough without trying to take on the big boys, but after a series of wins at home just one more role of the dice....

Josiah was badly wounded in battle, shot through by an Egyptian arrow. The rip through his body must have been excruciating, and all the more so on the long, torturous journey back to Jerusalem, the stricken king wrapped in what would become his death-shroud and huddled on the floor of his chariot, bouncing along from rut to rock, in and out of wadis, with each jolt searing his nerves and shocking his brain. It was a long time to think, and Josiah must have replayed the events of his entire life over and over in his mind: "Why this? Why now?" Like Abel, righteous, just and so full of unrealized promise, Josiah was cut down in his prime (cf. Gen 4:1–8). Eventually blood poisoning would have set in and, like countless soldiers before and since who survived an initial battle wound (cf. 1 Sam 31:3–4; 1 Kgs 22:34–35), Josiah succumbed in delirium and pain.

The nation's agony was no less acute:

All Judah and Jerusalem mourned for Josiah. Then Jeremiah chanted a lament for the king. All the male and female singers speak about Josiah in their lamentations to this day. (2 Chron 35:24b–25)

Life had to go on, but how? The swell tide of reform dropped overnight, leaving residue from the bottom to define the future of the kingdom. Josiah's youngest son, Jehoahaz, was made king by "the people of the land," but he cared little for their conservative ways or the religious aspects of the reforms of his father ("he did evil in the sight of the LORD according to all that his fathers had done"; 2 Kgs 23:32). Within three months the Egyptians deposed Jehoahaz and placed his brother Eliakim (Jehoiakim) on the throne, effectively reducing Judah to a vassal state once again (2 Kgs 23:34–37). This began a chain of events that led to the destruction of Jerusalem and the exile of Judah to Babylon twenty-three years later (2 Kgs 24:1–25:21). Caught between Assyria, Egypt and Babylon, Judean independence under Josiah had lasted scarcely two decades.

With the exile bearing down full force on Judah, Josiah was the nation's last hope—not that the exile could be avoided, but that it could be survived. The prophets Jeremiah and Ezekiel rebuked, urged, condemned and encouraged the people of Judah during the days of their greatest catastrophe, but it was Josiah the king who established public policy that gave official voice to the forces of religious and social conservatism that so needed to be heard during Judah's last days. On the one hand, the prophetic tradition in ancient Israel didn't need state support to be a restorative influence on society. In fact, the prophets are known for running counter to the culture of the throne. But Josiah fostered an environment whereby these prophets could gain a hearing among the people that even his successors and their royal court couldn't silence (e.g. Jer 26:7–24). We can only suppose what could have happened if their effort, like the life of the king, hadn't been cut short.

Other than David whom he sought to emulate, Josiah most closely filled the expectations of an ideal monarch for God's people. He may have lacked foresight in meeting Necho at Megiddo, but, at least according to a story preserved in the Babylonian Talmud, he had it when it counted most. In the tractate *Yoma* (52b), we read that in anticipation of the Babylonian invasion, Josiah hid the Ark of the Covenant lest it, too, be taken into exile. The story is certainly fanciful, but it preserves an understanding about Josiah that is an appropriate memory of a king who was forthright and acted decisively on behalf of his people. One wonders what the history of Israel and Judah might have been like if a king like Josiah had lived a few decades or a century or two earlier. Perhaps there wouldn't have been a need for a "last hope" after all.

NEO-ASSYRIAN AND BABYLONIAN EMPIRES

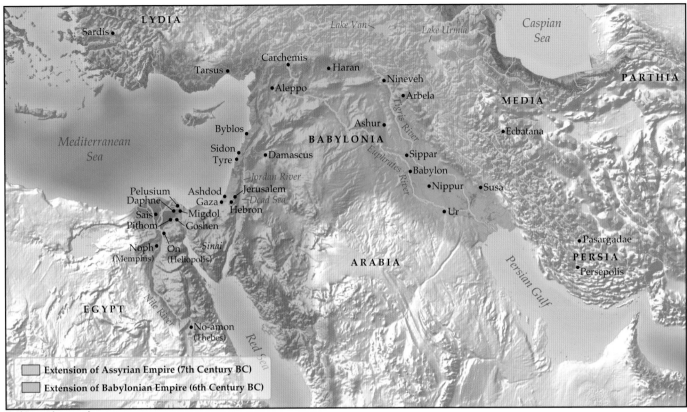

AridOcean/shutterstock.com

* Territory controlled by both Empires overlaps in extension (orange color), though they were in power at different times

PERSIAN EMPIRE IN THE FIFTH CENTURY

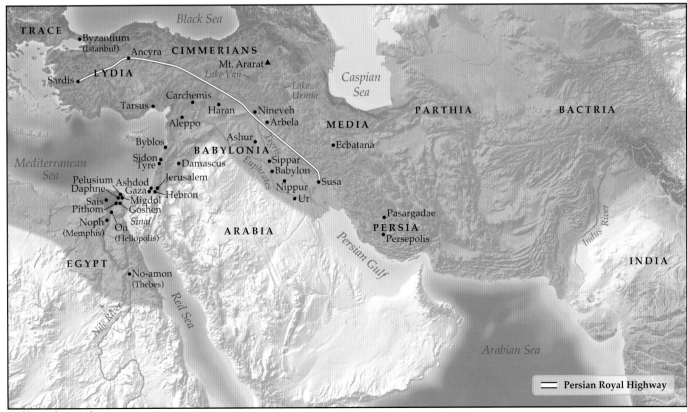

AridOcean/shutterstock.com

CHAPTER 15
EZRA AND NEHEMIAH
Courage to Start Over

The god Marduk on a piece of lapis lazuli, from Babylon. "You, Marduk, are the most honored of the great gods, your decree is unrivaled, [even over] the sky-god. From this day onward your pronouncements shall be unchangeable, to raise up or bring low—those shall be in your hand" (Enuma Elish [the Babylonian Genesis] IV, 5–8).

(right) He was a great warrior, statesman and visionary, one who forged the largest empire the world had yet known. He was also a man of clemency and toleration, whose iron fist reached to lift back up those whom he had conquered. To the world, Cyrus was "the Great." For Isaiah he was "the anointed one," God's messiah "taken by the right hand to subdue nations before him" (Isa 45:1) *and prepare the way for the Jews to return to Jerusalem. His reputation assured, Cyrus was killed on the battlefield fighting the nomadic Massagetae tribe on Persia's northeastern frontier. He was buried in this limestone block tomb outside his capital city, Pasargadae (modern Murghab in southern Iran). Like the rest, it was robbed long ago.*

It is impossible, so the proverb says, to step into the same stream twice, and this to the regret of those who want to relive good events and remake bad ones. "Do-overs," unfortunately, work only in kids' games. Sometimes, however, people or groups of people are offered second chances, and in the face of tragedy these opportunities are the most welcome, for by them wrongs can be righted and people redeemed.

For the men and women of Judah, the destruction of Jerusalem and its temple by Nebuchadnezzar in 586 B.C. and the subsequent exile of many of the people of Judah to Babylon was a tragedy of the highest proportion. While not discounting the impact of the lives and livelihoods lost in the process, or of the collectively shattered national aspirations of the people of Judah, this was first and foremost a violation of sacred space, a desecration of that "charged and highly significant locus" on Mount Zion (in the words of Adolfo Roitman, *Envisioning the Temple*, p. 12) in which people could touch the world of the divine and learn how to live lives pleasing to God and each other in the process. In the religiously-charged atmosphere of the ancient Near East, the Babylonians knew good and well that they were not just destroying a building when they burned Jerusalem's temple, but proving once and for all that the way that their own gods organized the universe—with Babylon of course on top of the earthly heap—was superior to the ways of the others across their far-flung empire, the LORD God included. The ancient-yet-ever-young Babylonian national god Marduk and his royal representative, Nebuchadnezzar, crowed that together they finally reigned supreme.

Once the initial shock subsided (for some it must

have taken merely years; for others, a lifetime), those who had been dragged off to the waters of Babylon (cf. Ps 137:1; Hab 1:15), as well as the multitude left behind in Judah, had to come to terms with the loss not just of their homeland and temple, but also potentially their world view. The tragedy was of cosmic proportions. Was the gateway to heaven closed? Or had it moved to *Esagila*, the magnificent temple of Marduk in Babylon (in the Akkadian languages, Babylon, *Bāb-ili*, was popularly understood to mean "gate of the gods")? The biblical record gives voice to the determined faithful whose vision refused to let the reality of the LORD's choice of Jerusalem die. But for many—those whose cries aren't preserved in poetry or song—the feeling might just as well have been, "Why should I sing *the LORD's* song in a foreign land?" (cf. Ps 137:1). Didn't He prove himself unable or unwilling to help when I needed him most?

Not so, said Jeremiah, who had announced before Jerusalem fell that God would *allow* the city to be destroyed because of the sins of its people (Jer 5:1–17), but the extent to which Jeremiah's message actually penetrated the consciousness of the men and women of Judah in the years following the Exile is unknown. Eventually this became the understanding of the majority and shaped the response of men such as Ezra and Nehemiah as they returned to Jerusalem. But in the meantime there must have been a clash of voices trying to come to terms with the reality of the day. For many, as one decade gave way to the next, the pull of the present was strong: life *could* be good by the waters and among the fertile fields of Babylon. And as for Judah—those rocky hills were never all that productive anyway.

Forty-seven years later, in 539 B.C., the Babylonian Empire was swallowed by the tidal wave of Persia and all indicators pointed to these newcomers sticking around for quite awhile. Unlike the Assyrians who had tried to force subservience by moving whole people groups from one land to the next and cutting local landed ties in the process, or the Babylonians who thought that by bringing the best and brightest from their conquered territories to their glorious capital (cf. 2 Kgs 24:14) those left back home would toe the line, the Persians adopted a more benevolent policy. After entering Babylon, the victorious Cyrus the Great (539–530 B.C.) issued a series of edicts allowing cult statues taken by Nabonidus, the last Babylonian king, to be returned their home temples. A similar edict permitted the exiled Judeans (by now properly called Jews) to return to Jerusalem with the temple vessels that had been taken by Nebuchadnezzar, and to rebuild their temple (2 Chron 36:22–23; Ezra 1:1–11; cf. Dan 1:1–2). By tolerating the local religious and national feelings of peoples throughout his empire ("fostering their aspirations" would be too liberal a phrase), Cyrus hoped to instill compliance to Persian will. It should be noted that most of the Jews in Babylon, however, preferred to remain put. Only the oldest retained a first-hand memory of Judah anyway; those of the newer generation were becoming well-established culturally and economically in the only home they had ever known and, according to Josephus, were "not willing to leave their possessions" (Ant. xi.1.3).

A relatively few number of Jews elected to return to Judah in 538 B.C. with Sheshbazzar, a member of the defunct royal line of David who had been newly appointed "prince" and "governor" of Judah (Ezra 1:8, 5:14; cf. 1 Chron 3:10, 3:18, where Shenazzar = Sheshbazzar). These Jews were certainly grateful for this second chance at life back home, but faced a fateful choice. Should they try to recreate the state that had existed before the Exile (monarchy and all), hoping to withstand a sure Persian reprisal as they did against Assyria back in the days of Hezekiah (cf. 2 Kgs 18–19)? Or should they learn to live under the political hegemony of someone else, currying imperial favor so that whatever rights they could salvage would be protected? Face to face with the reality of a new world order, Sheshbazzar and his fellow Jews wisely chose the latter, recognizing that political independence was a thing of the past and that the right to live in Jerusalem and rebuild the temple would offer life enough. In the end it actually wasn't much of a choice: Isaiah had called Cyrus God's messiah, the "anointed one" (Isa 45:1). Many (but certainly not all) of the Jews who had remained in Judah must have agreed that this expediency was the better part of valor. By themselves they had been unable to rebuild the ruins of Jerusalem in the years following the destruction of the city; with Cyrus's decree and the return of Sheshbazzar, they could at least gain rights that would give them an edge on others who also still lived in the region.

With mixed doses of resignation and courage, this was the first step in the right direction. The four-month overland journey (cf. Ezra 7:9) was long and arduous, and Sheshbazzar's small band of followers received a mixed reception once back in

The returning exiles lay the foundation of the Second Temple, 19th century engraving (Carta, Jerusalem). *Josephus described the progress of the work this way: "The building of the temple went on apace…and so the temple, by the great diligence of those that had the care of it, was finished sooner than anyone would have expected"* (Ant. xi.4.2).

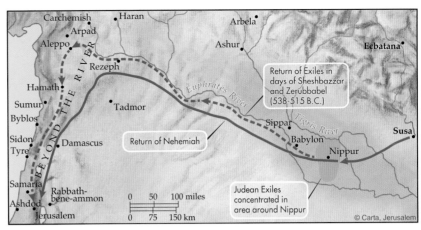

their ancestral home. Now *they* were the newcomers, and the land was far from empty when they arrived. Sheshbazzar's first public act was to raise the flag of a restored Jewish homeland by rebuilding the altar in Jerusalem and celebrating the autumn Festival of Booths (*Succot*; Ezra 3:1–5). Here are faint echoes of Abraham, who had erected altars upon entering the same land—then inhabited by Canaanites—over a millennium before (Gen 12:6–8). Then, like David and Solomon, Sheshbazzar arranged for cedar wood from Sidon and Tyre to be brought to Jerusalem as building material for the temple (Ezra 3:7; cf. 1 Kgs 5:1–12). The foundations of the temple were laid a year later, then consecrated to the once-frequent sound of the Levitical choir (Ezra 3:8–11; cf. 2 Chron 5:11–14). Sheshbazzar had done his best to begin to restore elements of active Jewish religious life to Jerusalem under the permissive eye of Persia. His fellow Jews were grateful although some, remembering the glory of the temple that once was, recognized that the new building—and the possibilities for a fully restored religious/national life that it offered—would fall short of life as it once had been. But at least they had an address again.

Outright opposition soon followed from unspecified "enemies of Judah and Benjamin" who had been living in the region for over one hun-

The Return from Exile.
Clues from the Bible, when combined with information from Babylonian cuneiform records of the fifth century B.C., indicate that the Judean exiles lived in the vicinity of Nippur, one of the great cities of Mesopotamia's venerable past. Numerous canals (including the Chebar; Ezek 1:1) crisscrossed the flats of southern Mesopotamia, bringing hope to an otherwise hot and arid land. Life could be good here—but for the Jews it wasn't home. When they finally returned to their promised land the Jews followed the route that Abraham had taken to Canaan over a millennium before. Nehemiah, once at home in the cultured Persian capital of Susa, also found his legacy after trekking the same route to Jerusalem.

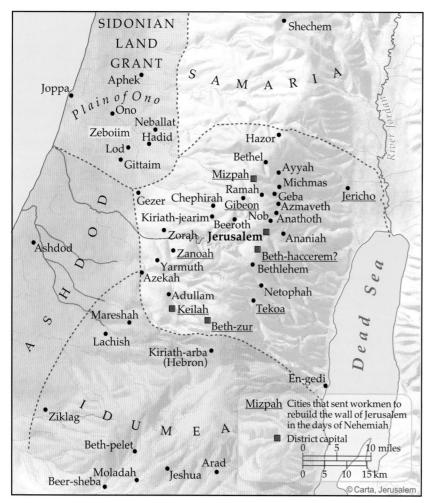

Map labels:
SIDONIAN LAND GRANT
SAMARIA
Shechem
Joppa
Aphek
Plain of Ono
Ono
Neballat
Zeboiim
Hadid
Lod
Gittaim
Hazor
Bethel
Ayyah
Mizpah
Michmas
Ramah
Geba
Gezer Chephirah
Jericho
Gibeon Azmaveth
Kiriath-jearim Nob
Beeroth Anathoth
Zorah Jerusalem
Ananiah
Ashdod
Zanoah
Beth-haccerem?
Yarmuth Bethlehem
Azekah
Netophah
Adullam
Keilah Tekoa
Mareshah Beth-zur
Lachish
Kiriath-arba (Hebron)
En-gedi
ASHDOD
IDUMEA
Ziklag
Beth-pelet
Arad
Moladah Jeshua
Beer-sheba
Dead Sea
River Jordan

Mizpah Cities that sent workmen to rebuild the wall of Jerusalem in the days of Nehemiah
■ District capital
0   5   10 miles
0 5 10 15 km
© Carta, Jerusalem

The Province of Yehud. *The extent of the province of Yehud, the old-new homeland of the Jewish people of the post-exilic period, can be determined by the place names included in the list of persons who returned from exile that are recorded in Ezra 2:1–67 and Nehemiah 7:6–69. The towns of Lod, Hadid and Ono, mentioned in these lists, lay exposed on the plain near Joppa and likely were transferred to the coastal district of Sidon by the time Ezra and Nehemiah gave Yehud a distinctly Jewish identity in the mid-fifth century* B.C. *(cf. Neh 6:1–2).*

dred years, since the days of Esarhaddon (Ezra 4:1–2). These were apparently remnants of populations that had been moved into the area in the wake of the Assyrian conquests in the eighth century B.C., and they cannot be faulted for wanting to protect their interests in what in the meantime had become their home. The feeling of mistrust was mutual (Ezra 4:3) and although the Jews, now led by Sheshbazzar's nephew Zerubbabel, recognized the strength of the right of return decreed to them by Cyrus (interestingly, they neglected to appeal to their divine right which reached back to the call of Abraham), work on the temple stopped for nearly twenty years (Ezra 4:4–5, 4:24). These were "days of small things" (Zech 4:10) compounded by poor harvests (Hag 1:9–11, 2:15–19), a stagnant economy (Zech 8:10), and envy and hostility between the returnees—who considered themselves to be the true Israel—on the one hand, and everyone else on the other, be they long-term residents of the land (among them Samaritans) or other Jews who were deemed less orthodox than the returnees (Hag 2:10–14).

Prompted by the prophets Haggai and Zechariah, Zerubbabel and the high priest Jeshua son of Jozadak finally restarted work on the temple around the year 522 B.C. (Ezra 5:1–2). They were immediately challenged by Tattenai, the governor of Beyond the

River (*eber nari*), the sprawling Persian satrapy lying west of the Euphrates that encompassed the entire Levant, including Jerusalem. This time Zerubbabel had the wherewithal to continue working, Middle Eastern style, until a direct appeal was made to Darius I (522–486 B.C.), now on the Persian throne. Darius reissued Cyrus's decree in 520 B.C. and work on the temple continued apace until the building was completed and dedicated with great fanfare on the 3rd of Adar (March 13), 515 B.C. (Ezra 5:3–6:22).

How shall we magnify Zerubbabel?
He was like a signet ring on the right hand,
*   and so was Jeshua the son of Jozadak.*
In their days they built the house and raised a
*   temple holy to the LORD,*
prepared for everlasting glory.

(ben Sirach 49:11–12)

The persistence of the Jews proved effective. Rather than chafe under the rule of Persia, they considered Cyrus and Darius to be God's instruments, raised to protect their rights. This was a critical and courageous shift in world view: foreign control could have its benefits if one could learn to work within the system.

While the Jews who remained in Babylon continued to assimilate Babylonian cultural forms (they picked up the Aramaic language and script, the Babylonian calendar and took Babylonian personal names such as, even, Zerubbabel, "the seed of Babylon"), those living in and around Jerusalem also adopted aspects of the lifestyles of the locals. Many lived in Yehud, the hilly province that the Persians had circumscribed around Jerusalem. This was a smaller area than had been controlled by the pre-exilic kingdom of Judah and excluded Hebron and regions south as well as the outer Shephelah. Jews also lived in parts of several surrounding provinces (Idumea, Ashdod, Sidon and possibly even Samaria), places that sometimes had been under Judean control before the exile (cf. Neh 11:25–36), and we can assume that the tendency toward assimilation with non-Jews was stronger here than in Yehud. Because the Jews in and around Yehud lacked the cohesion of their own state, boundaries marking their distinctiveness as a people had to be redefined. The institution of the temple, already an important element in pre-exilic Judah, became the primary focus for defining "who is a Jew" after the return.

But matters of religious and personal propriety, already hard to define, are even more difficult to control. Enter Ezra, a priest and "scribe skilled in the law of Moses" who, in 458 B.C., made the journey from Babylon to Jerusalem "to study the law (*Torah*) of the LORD and to practice it and to teach His statutes and ordinances in Israel" (Ezra 7:1–10). Because the biblical account traces Ezra's ancestry through Zadok to Aaron (Ezra 7:1–5; cf. 2 Sam 8:17; 1 Kgs 1:32), some have suggested that Ezra himself was (or should have been) high priest, although if this were so, given his zealousness for *Torah* we should expect that he (and his father and grandfather) would have already been attached to the rebuilt temple in Jerusalem. Ezra's genealogy indicates that he had some standing in the Jewish exilic community prior to his return to Jerusalem, and that he saw himself as a legitimate leader in religious matters and a bridge binding the Jews of his own day to the institution of the pre-exilic temple.

Ezra was also a scribe. This term could either indicate that he, like Nehemiah (cf. Neh 1:11), held an official administrative position within Persian society or, more likely, that he was a scholar learned in Jewish affairs who functioned in tasks so related. Certainly literate in Hebrew and Aramaic, the question arises to what extent Ezra might also have been familiar with the rich and ancient cuneiform scribal tradition of his home city, Babylon, or even that of Persia, just as Moses "was educated in the learning of the Egyptians" (Acts 7:22; Josephus, *Ant.* ii.9.7–10.2). Clearly Ezra's appointment had both Jewish and Persian interests in mind (cf. Ezra 7:25–26) and it is unlikely that the Persian king would have designated an individual for this demanding task who was not already familiar with the greater ways of the empire. This being so, Ezra apparently saw a distinction of essence between the ways that he had already adapted to (collaborated with?) greater Babylonian and Persian society, and the syncretistic practices of the Jews that he so vehemently opposed once he arrived in Yehud.

Ezra left Babylon for Jerusalem under the patronage of Artaxerxes I (464–424 B.C.), who provided funding and tax concessions for the effort (Ezra 7:6, 7:11–24). Perhaps as many as two thousand persons, many connected to priestly and levitical families, accompanied Ezra in this *aliyah* (to use the modern term of immigration to Israel; Ezra 8:1–20; cf. 2 Chron 36:23), and they surely supported his determination to define Jewish distinctiveness in terms of religious behavior consistent with the law of Moses. Many already living in Yehud disagreed, and Ezra faced a stiff test of wills. He took the matter of mixed marriages in particular very seriously, using it as the criterion that could most easily be measured to determine the proper ethnic and religious boundaries of his people (Ezra 9:1–10:44; Neh 13:23–31). Ezra's wintertime sermon perhaps best indicates his resolve: by keeping the offenders out in a cold driving rain, seated in puddles of water on a wet stone pavement listening to a preacher-shaking-his-forefinger-at-the-audience sermon, Ezra forced his fellows to see that in the sight of God, their actions left their souls chilled to the bone (Ezra 10:9–13). Eventually many (but not all) Jews in the province seem to have fallen in behind Ezra's leadership in the matter (Ezra 10:14–17). It was to be an ongoing struggle, one

that received a much-needed boost when Nehemiah arrived in Jerusalem sometime later, in 445 B.C.

Ezra's efforts were not limited to matters of internal Jewish affairs, however. Artaxerxes' decree included the stipulation that Ezra "appoint magistrates and judges" to teach and enforce not only "the law of your God" but also "the law of the king" under strict penalty of death, banishment, confiscation of goods or imprisonment (Ezra 7:25–26). The word used for "law" in both instances is the Aramaic term *dat*, a term borrowed from Persian meaning "decree" or "royal command." Clearly Ezra's official backing had ramifications that extended beyond a mere promulgation of Mosaic *Torah*. It appears as though Ezra's journey to lay down the law was also part of an official mission in keeping with the benevolent Persian policy of affirming local legal traditions throughout the empire—under the larger umbrella of Persian legal statutes—in order to foster gratitude and loyalty to the king. Ezra, then, found opportunity to instill a sense of cohesiveness among the Jews of Yehud and the surrounding provinces by piggybacking on the larger legal and judicial agenda of the Persian king.

The revival of a viable Jewish community in the southern Levant after the return from Exile took some time. Even after the Temple had been rebuilt and Ezra's reforms started to take hold, the people of Jerusalem continued to live in a depressed environment. The province of Yehud lacked an adequate administrative infrastructure, its major city, Jerusalem, was severely underpopulated and the local economy was anemic. A daily reminder of this distress lay close at hand: portions of the wall of Jerusalem were broken down and many houses and other buildings still lay in ruins from the Babylonian attack nearly a century and a half before. The magnificent Holy City, once embraced by strong ramparts and towers and adorned with fine palaces (cf. Ps 48:12–13), held but a shell of its former glory. Prophets and psalmists had once spoken of Jerusalem fondly, as if its stones lived, as if it were a member of their own family:

> Pray for the peace of Jerusalem:
>   "May they prosper who love you;
>   may peace be within your walls,
>   and prosperity within your palaces."
> For the sake of my brothers and my friends
>   I will now say, "May peace be within you."
> For the sake of the house of the LORD our God
>   I will seek your good.   (Ps 122:6–9)

But now the city was destroyed, its gaping holes and piles of rubble (cf. Neh 4:2) overgrown with thistles and weeds, a wound hard to heal, and the Jews continued to ache for the glory of Jerusalem that once was:

Coinage began in Phrygia (western Anatolia) in the 7th century B.C., then spread across the known world under the commercial initiatives of the Persian Empire. Sometime in the 4th century B.C., a century after Nehemiah's work in Jerusalem, the Persians allowed Yehud and other provinces in the southern Levant to mint their own coins. With this came a degree of local autonomy not enjoyed by Nehemiah and his fellow Jews. Yehud coins were tiny, about half the size of an American dime, and bear the inscription YHD written either in the old (pre-exilic) Hebrew script or the contemporary block-letter Aramaic script. Numerous designs appear on these coins; some were copies of images found on coins from Greece, while others bore strictly Jewish symbols.

The elders and the virgins of Jerusalem lament the desolation of the city, 19th century engraving (Carta, Jerusalem).

The elders of the daughter of
    Zion sit on the ground in
    silence;
they have cast dust on their
    head and put on sackcloth;
the maidens of Jerusalem
    have bowed their heads to
    the ground.   *(Lam 2:10)*

Artaxerxes I died of natural causes during the winter of 425–424 B.C., after a reign of forty years. He was buried in this tomb at Naqsh-i-Rustam, near Persepolis, in modern Iran. The Jews benefited from Artaxerxes' long and relatively stable reign.

*The LORD determined to destroy the wall of the
    daughter of Zion.
He has stretched out a line,
    He has not held back His hand from destroying.
He has caused rampart and wall to lament;
    They have languished together.
Her gates have sunk into the ground,
    He has destroyed and broken her bars....*

                    (Lam 2:8–9)

The rebuilt temple and its revived order of service deserved a city worthy of God's presence.

The opportunity to clean up the city of Jerusalem and rebuild its walls coincided with an uneasy political situation on the western frontier of the Persian Empire. As the Persian kings pushed westward into the Mediterranean they met a growing Greek presence coming the other direction, but also had to contend with an aging but still active Egypt to the southwest. Military defeats on the Greek mainland at Marathon (490 B.C.) and in the bay of Salamis off-shore of Athens (479 B.C.) checked the Persian advance in the Aegean, and a revolt in Egypt against Persian rule in 488 B.C., though successfully suppressed, kept the Persian kings on their toes. The Egyptians revolted again in 460 B.C., this time with Greek help, and Artaxerxes I was not able to bring Egypt back in line until 454 B.C. Ezra in the meantime had arrived in Jerusalem to strengthen the moral fiber of the residents of the city. Shortly afterward, according to the Greek writer Ctesias *(Persica*, Epit. 68–70), the governor of Beyond the River led an unsuccessful revolt against Persian rule. Locally, archaeological evidence shows that several cities in the hill country north of Jerusalem were destroyed in the early fifth century B.C. (Shechem, Mizpah, Bethel, Gibeah and Gibeon), and while there is no specific historical event to which this can be attributed, their destruction does reflect the general instability of the time. Clearly the Persians had to strengthen their hold on the Levant if they

hoped to continue dominating the eastern Mediterranean and they could tolerate no rebellious province there that might disrupt their long supply lines, already stretched to the limit.

It was about this time, apparently bolstered by the overall conditions of unrest and uncertainty in the region, that the residents of Jerusalem decided to refortify their city. It is unclear whether they were pushing the initiatives of Ezra to their logical conclusion, acting to protect their own interests against possible local attack or wanting to signal their independence from Persia. It was the latter that was reported to Artaxerxes in a pointed letter of complaint sent by local adversaries, reminding the Persian king that Jerusalem had a reputation for rebelling against foreign domination (Ezra 4:7–16; the writer of the Book of Ezra inserted this letter into the account of the opposition that Zerubbabel had faced in rebuilding the temple). Artaxerxes, naturally, stopped the work (Ezra 4:18–23); one wonders if he also regretted his decision to send Ezra to Jerusalem.

The letter prompted the leaders of the Jewish community in Jerusalem to send an official delegation to Nehemiah, the cupbearer of Artaxerxes who lived in Susa, an important Persian administrative center on the eastern edge of the flatter than flat Babylonian plain. This was in December, 446 B.C. (Neh 1:1, 1:11; cf. 1 Kgs 10:5; Esth 1:2; Dan 8:2). Nehemiah was a respected and capable Jew who had risen to a position of influence in the royal Persian court. His responsibilities as cupbearer included supplying the court with drink, but were certainly not limited to that. Nehemiah perhaps might be compared to a social director for palace affairs or even a kind of chief-of-staff, as cupbearers sometimes controlled access to the king (cf. Xenophon, *Cyropaedia* 1.3.8); it was a position, noted Herodotus, "of no small honor" (*Histories* 3.34). The delegation, which included Nehemiah's own brother Hanani, played to Nehemiah's longing for his ancestral homeland and asked that he intercede on their behalf and petition Artaxerxes to allow the wall of Jerusalem to be rebuilt (Neh 1:1–3).

Wanting to help his fellow Jews in Jerusalem yet realizing the sensitivity of the matter, Nehemiah waited for three months before approaching Artaxerxes (Neh 2:1). A royal order had already been given to stop the work and it was no small task to reverse "the law of the Medes and Persians" (cf. Esth 1:19, 8:8). Although specifics are not given, the timing of Nehemiah's request was clearly of God, as was his spiritual sensitivity and courage in the matter (Neh 1:4–11). Artaxerxes not only granted the request that the walls be rebuilt but commissioned Nehemiah as governor of the province of Yehud (cf. Neh 5:14), sending him off to see that the work was carried out (Neh 2:2–8).

But what did Artaxerxes have to gain by all of this? It would be naïve to think that he was acting out of altruism. Knowing Jerusalem's reputation for chafing against foreign domination and obviously aware of Ezra's success in galvanizing the religious and social energy of its inhabitants, Artaxerxes may have calculated that the Jews of Yehud were on the verge of revolt. If he appointed a friendly governor and issued a decree to rebuild Jerusalem's walls, he stood a better chance that they, grateful to be *given* the chance to fortify their city, would remain loyal to the throne. Alternatively, some of the provinces surrounding Yehud (e.g., Samaria and Ammon) were ruled by powerful men with dynastic intentions (e.g., Tobiah), and Artaxerxes may have wanted to support the initiative of the men of Yehud as a countercheck to them.

Either of these scenarios can be subsumed under a third. Nehemiah was commissioned to build a fortress and city wall for Jerusalem (Neh 2:8). In language typical of the Persian Empire, "fortresses" and "walls" were built to house military garrisons (including cavalry, a chariot corps, foot soldiers, officers and staff, some of whom accompanied Nehemiah to Jerusalem; Neh 2:9). Such fortresses—and apparently Artaxerxes decreed that Jerusalem would be one—served not only wartime needs but were centers to control and tax the local population. The move to fortify Jerusalem made perfect sense for Artaxerxes. For the residents of Yehud, the honor gained in the chance to rebuild the wall of Jerusalem was worth the increase in Persian control that it entailed.

It was impossible for someone sent on an official mission by the Persian king to travel incognito, and Nehemiah's presence in Jerusalem aroused immediate suspicion (Neh 2:9–10). Soon after his arrival he surveyed the broken-down walls of the city. Late at night, by donkey, on foot and in the company of only a few trusted confidants, Nehemiah picked his way around piles of debris, gazing on the burned-out remains of the past (Neh 2:11–16). With a clear view of the need to strengthen the city of his ancestors and armed with the favor of God and king, Nehemiah convinced the leadership of Jerusalem that the time was right to rebuild their city's walls (Neh 2:17–18).

Even with royal backing Nehemiah quickly discovered that actually carrying out his commission would take courage, persistence and wisdom. Those most upset with his plans to rebuild the walls of Jerusalem were the ones with the most to lose: Sanballat the governor of Samaria (the Persian province lying just north of Yehud), Tobiah the governor of Ammon (the province to the east), Geshem governor of Arabia to the south and, to the west, the province of Ashdod (Neh 2:10, 2:19). Their opposition would continue throughout the project (Neh 4:1, 4:7–8, 6:1–14). Each represented a people that historically had fought Judah for territorial and economic control of the region, and when Judah was weakened by the Babylonian Exile each gladly tried

to establish their rights to the leftovers. The last thing Sanballat, Tobiah and Geshem wanted was for a strong Jerusalem to reclaim its historic place in the mix, or for Persia's control in the region to be channeled through Jerusalem. Challenged from the outset that the Jews had lost the right to their homeland, the newcomer Nehemiah retorted: "It is *you* who have no portion, right or memorial in Jerusalem" (Neh 2:20).

In order to mobilize its residents to build their own stake in the city, Nehemiah divided the entire line of Jerusalem's wall into sections and assigned individuals or groups of persons to each. When possible, an individual or group rebuilt the portion of the wall that was adjacent to their own houses (e.g., Neh 3:10, 3:21–23, 3:29–30), or a section that lay near a place connected to their profession. For instance, goldsmiths and perfumers, whose specialized crafts were connected with temple activity, repaired portions of the wall that ran just west and east of the temple complex (Neh 3:8, 3:31–32). Some of the workers haled from cities other than Jerusalem (Jericho, Tekoa, Gibeon, Mizpah, Zanoah, Beth-haccerem, Beth-zur and Keilah;

Nehemiah's Jerusalem.
Nehemiah's nighttime journey around the broken-down walls of Jerusalem began at the Valley Gate on the western side of the city not far from the ruined governor's residence (cf. Neh 3:7; Nehemiah was probably staying nearby). He proceeded down the valley, around the southern tip of the city and back up the scarp above the Kidron Valley to a place opposite the Valley Gate where the wall was broken enough that he could reenter the city from the east. The city he restored was small and narrow—about the size that it had been under David and Solomon, but like the Jerusalem of the old United Kingdom, it was a city with great potential.

Tower of Hananel
Tower of the hundred
Sheep gate?
Fish gate?
Muster gate?
Temple
East gate?
"Broad Wall"
Horse gate?
House of Jedaiah son of Harumaph
OPHEL
Great projecting tower
Older wall
En-gihon
Valley gate
Water gate?
Nehemiah continues on foot
Nehemiah's nighttime ride
Fountain gate?
Stairs descending from City of David
0 50 100 150 yds
0 50 100 m
© Carta, Jerusalem

Rebuilding the walls of Jerusalem, 19th century engraving (Carta, Jerusalem). *In a classic scene of "heave-ho" that anticipated a Hollywood cast of thousands, the walls of Jerusalem were repaired and rebuilt in just fifty-two days.*

The only part of the wall of Jerusalem mentioned in the Book of Nehemiah that is visible today is the "broad wall" (Neh 3:8), the foundations of which were discovered by Nahman Avigad in the Jewish Quarter in the late 1960s. This wall encircled the large hill lying immediately west of the oldest part of Jerusalem during the last century and a half of the kingdom of Judah. Nehemiah apparently left it unrepaired, choosing instead to refortify only the portion of the wall that had defined David and Solomon's city on Jerusalem's narrow eastern hill. For the renewed population of Jerusalem, this was enough.

Dedication of the walls of Jerusalem (Neh 12:27–43), 19th century engraving (Carta, Jerusalem). "Then I had the leaders of Judah come up on top of the wall and I appointed two great choirs...some of the sons of the priests had trumpets..." (Neh 12:31,35).

Neh 3:2, 3:5, 3:7, 3:13–14, 3:16–18), and we can be sure that by the time the work was finished they, too, had gained a special interest in the part of the city that they helped to fortify.

The list of persons and repair stations recorded in Nehemiah 3 includes a wealth of information about the infrastructure of Nehemiah's city. Unfortunately, of all of the sections of the wall or adjacent structures that are mentioned in the list, only the Broad Wall (Neh 3:8) has been positively identified by archaeology. Various suggestions have been made to connect a few others with structures uncovered by excavation (e.g., the Valley Gate—Neh 3:13; Fountain Gate—Neh 3:15; and "the steps that descend from the City of David"—Neh 3:15), but these identifications are less sure and none, except for the Broad Wall, are able to be seen today. The location of a very few others can be inferred by written sources (e.g., the Sheep Gate, which must have been on the northern wall of the city near what was to become the Sheep Pool—cf. Jn 5:2). Nevertheless, it seems reasonably clear that the list follows a counterclockwise sequence around the eastern hill of Jerusalem—the oldest part of the city—beginning with the Sheep Gate in the north. In spite of the uncertainties, the list offers a tantalizing map of the circumference of the walled city of Jerusalem in Nehemiah's day.

The eastern stretch of the wall along the scarp above the Kidron Valley appears to have been more heavily damaged by the Babylonian attack than other portions since Nehemiah assigned the greater number of persons to work there (this is confirmed by the archaeological record which reveals graphic evidence of the fierceness of the Babylonian attack along the midpoint of the eastern wall). The city's fortress and the governor's official residence, both located in the northern part of the city near the temple complex, were also repaired (Neh 2:8, 3:7). Left unrepaired was the Broad Wall itself, the massive

wall that Hezekiah had built around the expansive western hill of Jerusalem in the late eighth century B.C.; Jerusalem's small population no longer warranted such a large walled-in area (Neh 7:4).

Everyone worked hard; some zealously (Neh 3:20, 4:6). Sanballat, Tobiah and Geshem worked equally hard trying to stop Nehemiah's progress. When word reached Nehemiah that they were gathering forces to mount an attack, he responded by posting a 24-hour guard in the city and arming those who were working on the wall (Neh 4:9–23). Failing to stop the work by threat of violence, Sanballat and company next devised a plan to lure Nehemiah out onto the plain of Ono for a peace conference where, out of the safety of the hill country, they would do him bodily harm. Wisely Nehemiah refused the meeting (Neh 6:1–4). Nehemiah's enemies then switched tactics again and started a rumor that he was attempting to restore the Judean monarchy and have himself declared king, thereby forcing a reprisal from Artaxerxes. This, too, Nehemiah thwarted, calling it an invention of their minds (Neh 6:5–9). Finally, Sanballat and Tobiah planted an agent in Jerusalem to claim that reliable sources had confirmed that Nehemiah would be assassinated some dark night, in an attempt to push the wall-builder toward paranoia. Here Nehemiah drew the line: "Should a man like me flee? Never!" (Neh 6:10–14). In the end it proved to be mostly hot air and mind games. This was pressure enough, but with courage, resolve and the strength of God (Neh 6:9) Nehemiah prevailed. The job was completed in fifty-two days (Neh 6:15). It had been a massive undertaking, and even though parts of the wall were a bit shabby (cf. Neh 4:3; few of the workers were skilled masons), a complete wall once again surrounded Jerusalem.

Now was the time to celebrate, and celebrate Nehemiah and the people did. The wall was dedicated amid great fanfare, "with gladness, with hymns of thanksgiving and with songs to the accompaniment of cymbals, harps and lyres" (Neh 12:27). Nehemiah called in the Levites from the surrounding towns and villages and the Levitical choir, accompanied by dignitaries (including Ezra) and crowds of people, formed a great, joyous processional. Together they moved from the Dung Gate at the southern tip of the city to the temple complex in the north. Half of the people (including Nehemiah) followed the line of the wall along the western side of the city, while half proceeded along the eastern wall following the scarp above the Kidron Valley (Neh 12:28–43). The two choirs met in the courtyard of the temple where

the singers sang, with Jezrahiah their leader, and on that day they offered great sacrifices and rejoiced because God had given them great joy, even the women and children rejoiced, so that the joy of Jerusalem was heard from afar. (Neh 12:42–43)

Thanks to the efforts of Nehemiah, Jerusalem's standing among its neighbors—and with the Persian king—was restored.

> The memory of Nehemiah also is lasting:
> He raised for us the walls that had fallen, and set
>   up the gates and bars
>   and rebuilt our ruined houses.
>
> (ben Sirach 49:13)

People could feel good about their city, their society and *themselves* again, and embrace their religious and ethnic identity without cause for shame.

Building on his previous attempts to reform the religious and social consciousness of the Jews living in Yehud, Ezra organized a public reading of the *Torah* in the open square in front of the Water Gate, southeast of the temple complex in Jerusalem (Neh 8:1–6). Because many of the people who attended were Aramaic speakers and no longer understood Hebrew well enough to follow what was being read, the Levites translated for Ezra (who of course knew Aramaic himself) and added explanatory comments so that everyone could make sense out of it all (Neh 8:7–8). Times had changed; the relevance of *Torah* had not. The people again celebrated the autumn Festival of Booths (*Succot*), confessed their sins before the LORD and pledged themselves in writing to follow the stipulations of *Torah* and support the work of the temple community (Neh 8:9–10:39).

Throughout, Nehemiah had also been busy exercising the social and economic aspects of his role of governor. Walled cities in the ancient Near East tended to become "exclusive" cities that attracted and cultivated an urban elite at the expense of the rural poor. To counteract this tendency in Jerusalem, Nehemiah revised the tax structure in a way that gave relief to the common people while providing adequately for those attached to the temple (Neh 5:1–13, 12:44–47, 13:10–14). He also encouraged people who lived elsewhere in Yehud to move into Jerusalem. Those who did so maintained their estates in the outlying parts of the province, but by spending a significant portion of their time in the "holy city" (so Jerusalem is called in Neh 11:1), they fostered the process by which Jerusalem, a place with unique needs and a *raison d'être* not shared by any other, could become fully integrated into the social and economic life of the rest of the province. The city was underpopulated anyway, and could use an influx of new residents (Neh 11:1–19; cf. Neh 7:4). Nehemiah also enforced public observance of the Sabbath day (*Shabbat*) within the walls of Jerusalem; the special city deserved a special day, even if it meant cutting the growth of the economy by one-seventh in the process (Neh 13:15–22).

Nehemiah returned to Susa after spending twelve years in Jerusalem (Neh 13:6). In his absence, his old nemesis Tobiah had gained access to a large room within the confines of the temple courtyard through the influence of Eliashib the high priest, to whom he was related (Neh 13:4–8; cf. Neh 3:1, 3:20). There Tobiah lived a life of pomp and luxury. Having lost the war Tobiah tried to profit from the peace: since he hadn't been successful in stopping the rebuilding of Jerusalem, he figured that he might at least enjoy its physical comforts. But when Nehemiah returned to Jerusalem sometime later he smelled a snake—and threw Tobiah out, household goods and all (Neh 13:8–9).

And so the story continued. The city of Jerusalem was restored and its residents committed themselves before the LORD to live their lives with the best interests of each other in mind, though daily problems kept pressing for attention. It was, after all, real life.

It had taken about a century and a half for the Jews to go from hopes dashed to hopes restored. The temple had been rebuilt—although many thought the building wasn't as large or magnificent as the one before. The Jews lived in their ancestral homeland—but now under the thumb of Persia rather than as free people with their own king. The walls of Jerusalem were repaired—though the city was smaller and less elaborate than it had once been. The riverbank hadn't moved, but the stream flowed on. Ezra's goal was to rebuild a religious community by which the Jews might survive as a distinct, yet vibrant part of the Persian Empire. Nehemiah's was to strengthen the infrastructure of Jerusalem and give its people a sense of presence and propriety within the region. With courage tempered by experience and a faith rooted in the protection and promises of God, both were successful. The crisis passed; the people had survived and one day they would thrive again.

Rock solid, the words of God spoken through the prophet Ezekiel are permanently engraved above the entrance gate to Israel's holocaust memorial, Yad vaShem: "I will put my spirit in you and you will live, and I will place you in your own land" (Ezek 37:14). Ezekiel's hope became that of Ezra and Nehemiah, and continues to root the Jews of Israel in their ancestral homeland today.

Ezra reads the law "before the congregation, both men and women and all who could hear with understanding… and the ears of all the people were attentive to the book of the law" (Neh 8:2–3), 19th century engraving (Carta, Jerusalem).

The wanna-be kingdom of Tobiah the Ammonite was nestled in the majestic hills of Gilead, east of the Jordan River. The family name, written in Aramaic, has been found inscribed adjacent to two rock-cut openings in a prominent limestone cliff in Wadi es-Sir near the ruins of a Hellenistic palace (Iraq el-Emir). These were apparently living quarters for family members during the 2nd century B.C., testimony to the resilience of the Tobiad family in Transjordan during the latter half of the first millennium B.C.

" וְנָתַתִּי רוּחִי בָכֶם וִחְיִיתֶם וְהִנַּחְתִּי אֶתְכֶם עַל אַדְמַתְכֶם... "

125

Chapter 16
ESTHER
For Such a Time as This

Designed by internationally renowned architect Moshe Safdi, the rail-car exhibit at Yad vaShem speaks of the journey into oblivion for countless Jews of the Holocaust. Twenty-five hundred years earlier Haman's order to round up the Jews of the Persian Empire for a journey to annihilation came to naught by the timely (and early) intervention of Esther, who came to power "for such a time as this" (Esth 4:14).

Yad vaShem, Israel's memorial to the Holocaust, is a living testimony to the cruel horror of the most seductive of all evils: sacrificing others on the altar of one's own ambition. The many exhibits, artifacts and monuments displayed throughout the site, both indoors and out, portray aspects of the deliberate and systematic attempt by Nazi Germany to wipe the Jewish people from the face of the earth. Among them is a small cattle car, once jammed with over one hundred men, women and children—sealed in, dehumanized and suffering in horror, standing in their own filth, pushing their noses to cracks in the wooden sides like so much livestock on the way to slaughter. The car now stands at the end of a broken bridge jutting over a yawning chasm, perched on the brink of oblivion. From the belly of a similar car there once came a gasp, originally scribbled in pencil, now indelibly inscribed on a stone wall nearby the railcar exhibit, forever yet never silenced, vaporous and enduring:

> Here in this carload I am Eve,
> with Abel my son.
> If you see my other son Cain Son of Man,
> tell him I….

Tell him….

Man's inhumanity to man is endemic to the human race. Cain and Abel were both created in the image of God, but something happened to skew the picture horribly. Abel was dead and Cain, turning his back, denied responsibility for his brother's welfare. It's a familiar story, all the more real because of the magnitude with which it unfolded during the years of the Third Reich. The Holocaust was unparalleled among acts of human savagery. Still, it contains echoes of other attempts to destroy Abel, black spots on the course of human history.

The Book of Esther, for instance, recounts a much earlier attempt to annihilate the Jewish people. That one was perpetrated by the coldly calculating Haman and his unwitting (and somewhat dim-witted) sovereign Ahasuerus, king of a Persian Empire that was otherwise relatively tolerant of its subjected peoples. (Then again, the Germany of the Weimar Republic and Third Reich was otherwise among the most highly educated and culturally advanced nations on earth.) The story focuses on four individuals: Ahasuerus and his trusted but twisted vizier Haman, Mordecai the Jew who "sat in the king's gate" (Esth 2:19), and Mordecai's younger cousin Esther. Woven into the primary plot line are multiple sub-plots and motifs, including the rags-to-riches rise of the orphaned Esther; Haman's vain attempts to glorify himself; and the recurring—and comically redundant—sequence in which the highest affairs of state are decided at drunken banquets. Most of the scenes take place in and around Ahasuerus's royal palace in Susa with Haman, the evil genius upon whom the tables deliciously turn in the end, lurking in its corridors of power. But it is Mordecai, solid and reliable, and especially Esther, the charming and beautiful heroine, first naïve then rising to the occasion, who carry the day. It was she, after all, who was born "for such a time as this" (Esth 4:14).

Aspects of the story of Esther fit nicely with what is known about the Persian Empire, the largest the world had yet known. Persian control stretched "from India to Ethiopia" (Esth 1:1), that is, from the Indus River to Upper (southern) Egypt and the Aegean Sea. Herodotus (*Histories* 3.89–95) reports that

It was all pomp and circumstance in the Persian royal court, with everyone in their proper order and place. Here, on a relief from Persepolis Darius I, stern of face, sits on his throne with scepter in hand to receive a visitor who approaches with a rather cowed demeanor. Darius's son and successor, Xerxes, the Ahasuerus of the Book of Esther, stands behind the throne, learning well the rights and privileges of authority.

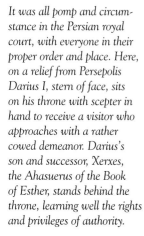

The Persian Empire. *During the course of the sixth century* B.C., *energetic kings of Persia left their home on the southwestern Iranian Plateau to gobble up huge tracks of land in every direction. Cyrus the Great conquered Sardis in western Anatolia in 547* B.C. *and seized Babylon with its empire eight years later. He had already pushed to what is now Afghanistan and the border of India. Cyrus's successor, Cambyses II, became the first Persian Pharaoh of Egypt. Then, sitting on a large and unwieldy empire, the Persian monarchs fostered a policy of good-will among their many subjected peoples and built a network of highways, including the Susa-to-Sardis Royal Road, to bind everything together.*

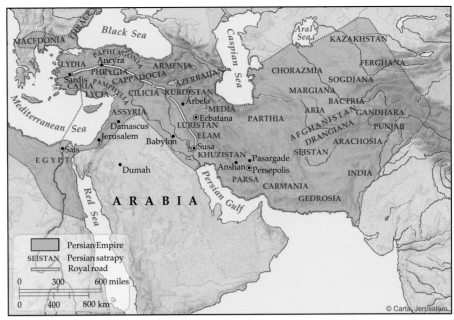

Darius I (521–486 B.C.) organized the empire into twenty satrapies; these were subdivided into the 127 provinces mentioned in Esther 1:1. Jews were scattered at various places throughout, though certainly not in each of the 127. Besides in the southern Levant, Jews (or persons of Israelite descent) lived along the northern and northeastern bend of the Fertile Crescent (thanks largely to the Assyrian deportation of Israel; 2 Kgs 17:6), in Egypt (2 Kgs 25:26) and in the vicinity of Babylon (2 Chron 36:20). Some became well off in their new surroundings, such as those connected to the Murashu family, financiers from Nippur, an ancient city-state on the Babylonian plain midway between Babylon and Susa; this is attested in cuneiform records dating to the reigns of Artaxerxes I (464–424 B.C.) and Darius II (423–404 B.C.). The story of Esther is set slightly earlier during the reign of Ahasuerus (= Xerxes; 485–465 B.C.), a context comfortable with a situation in which a Jewish man such as Mordecai could "sit at the king's gate" (Esth 2:19). This was a position of honor and influence among those who hobnobbed among royal circles, and the phrase "to sit at the king's gate" could even indicate that Mordecai was a Persian official of some rank (Xenophon, *Cyropaedia* 7.1.6 and Herodotus, *Histories* 3.120). Nor should this be surprising, as he counted among his ancestors some of the best and brightest that Judah had to offer (Esth 2:5–6; cf. 2 Kgs 24:14).

The Persian royal city of Susa, where the action of the Esther story takes place, lay on the eastern edge of the Babylonian plain. Susa had been the ancient capital of Elam; now it was in the heart of the sprawling Persian Empire, a great crossroads on the network of imperial highways that ran hither and yon to the farthest reaches of the empire. The winter weather was much more pleasant in Susa than in Persepolis and Ecbatana, other Persian capitals high on the Iranian plateau, and so the Persian kings preferred to spend up to half the year here, carrying on all manner of diplomatic and administrative duties that affected everyone who lived under the long arm of the Persian law. If a Jew wanted to gain influence in the Persian court, Susa would have been a good place to do it (cf. Neh 1:1). Darius I and Xerxes rebuilt the extravagant royal district of Susa on top of the remains of the older Elamite palaces, and archaeological and textual evidence confirms the overdone splendor of the Persian court that is so garishly described in the Book of Esther (Esth 1:6–7 and 6:8, where even the royal horses wore crowns!).

All of this, and other details of names, genealogies, terms and the like, provide a context for the story of Esther that fits nicely with the workings and trappings of the Persian court. But with King Ahasuerus things become strange. Simply put, Ahasuerus doesn't act the role of Xerxes, the great visionary and military leader who put down rebellions in Babylon and Egypt and amassed a vast navy for battles against the Greeks in the Aegean. Classical writers do point out certain excesses back home: Xerxes had a soft spot for lavish banquets and extravagant gifts and, typical to many in his position, could be easily driven to anger and quick decisions. But the Xerxes of the story of Esther, Ahasuerus, plays a bit of a stooge, a fool too dependent on his hormones and wholly given over to suggestion and subterfuge (this is nicely portrayed by Maurice Samuel in *Certain People of the Book*). If Ahasuerus had acted as responsibly in his dealings with Haman and Mordecai as he did with Egypt, Babylon and Greece, the sequence of events described in the Book of Esther could have never taken place. No matter; any one of the conquered peoples of the Persian Empire would have enjoyed portraying Xerxes as the Book of Esther does—"we would like to hope to think that he really *is* a fool who doesn't stand a spitting chance of holding his own, one-on-one, to one of *us*, if we would only be given the chance."

Mordecai and Esther, on behalf of their people the Jews, got that chance. It started with a great

Two Persian nobles stand at rapt attention on a relief adorning a wall in the royal palace in Persepolis. The position of the hands, one clenched to a staff, the other at rest, suggests the ease that accompanies many years of experience on the job, while the expressionless face reflects the cold and calculating power of the king whose will they wait to enforce. The tightly rolled hair and beard, a style held over from the Assyrians, speaks of people who have time to take care of the finer things of life. As for dress, the long, voluminous sleeves, plaited robe and crown—prominent though not nearly as elegant as that of the king—give visible weight to the important office these nobles held.

The royal palace in Susa was built by Darius and used by subsequent kings including Xerxes. The entire complex was constructed on a terrace raised 50 feet above the surrounding plain. A Propylaeum (ceremonial pavilion) lay outside the gate to the east. Adjoining the royal quarters to the north was an Apadana (hypostyle hall of massive columns), which was probably surrounded on three sides by lavish gardens. The buildings were made of mud brick with walls of important rooms covered by slabs of stone or baked clay, or by colorful glazed tiles.

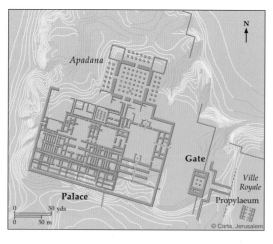

display of kingly splendor—only three years on the throne and Ahasuerus held a six-month show-and-tell with all the pomp and circumstance that only he could muster, topped off with a seven-day banquet, open to the public, in his decked-to-the-hilt royal garden (Esth 1:1–10). By the end of the revelry the king was "merry with wine"—let's call him drunk to silliness—and he commanded that his own dear Queen Vashti present herself before all his merry subjects so that the entire city could admire her physical beauty (and she *was* beautiful) in some detail. Understandably unwilling to submit herself, let alone her office, to the whims of a rousing house of revelry—that is what slave girls are for—Vashti point blank refused (Esth 1:10–12). But public humiliation is never becoming a man of high standing,

especially when everyone should be enjoying themselves watching him enjoying himself, and so Ahasuerus, in cahoots with his pompous advisors, did the only sensible thing his foggy mind *could* do—banish her and create an empire-wide cover-up: she *had* to go or women everywhere would start to treat their husbands with the same kind of disrespect she dared show him. Men, after all, must be men, even if it takes a royal edict to make them so (Esth 1:13–22).

With morning comes the morning after and the "oops" of the night before was pretty apparent. Of course the simple thing would have been for the king to admit his wayward ways and beg Vashti back, but this Ahasuerus could never do. Absolute monarchs never err. (Fortunately he was covered by the conveniently irreversible "laws of the Medes and Persians" that prevented such an embarrassment; Esth 1:19.) So a new queen had to be chosen, and what better way than an empire-wide beauty contest (Esth 2:1–4)? Ahasuerus liked his queens to be beautiful. Chauvinistic, yes, but at least this time he was sober—and without excuse. Among the beautiful young virgins gathered to Susa was Esther (there is no hint what any of *them* might have thought about the idea; presumably the honor of a night with the high and mighty king should have been motive enough). She was "beautiful in form and face," the orphaned cousin of Mordecai (Esth 2:7). Both were already residents of Susa (Esth 2:5–7; cf. Esth 2:19) and one wonders if either had witnessed the public humiliation of Vashti. Esther went through the proscribed twelve-month beauty treatment for would-be queens while faithful Mordecai nervously paced outside the harem, then had her night with Ahasuerus. Lucky her!—the king called Esther back for full-time duty and a new queen was crowned (Esth 2:9–18).

Under the advice of Mordecai, Esther had not revealed her birth name—Hadassah, "myrtle"—or the identity that it would have given away: that she was Jewish (Esth 2:19–20). Being queen was, of course, the highest honor to which a woman of the Persian Empire could attain, and Esther came to the position with no qualifications except those that were God-given. Better to be quiet about everything else unless or until circumstances

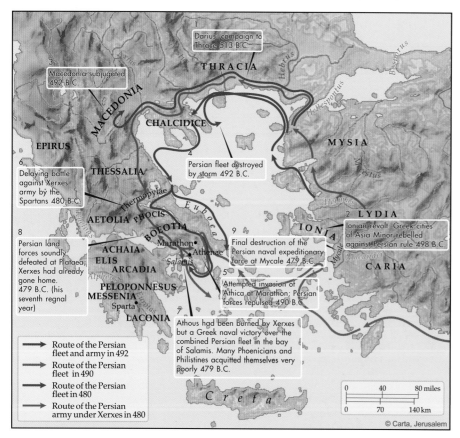

Persian Wars in the Aegean. *Darius I, father of Xerxes, twice tried to invade the Greek mainland from Persian bases in western Anatolia and twice was turned back; first by a storm (492 B.C.) and then at the battle of Marathon, only 20 miles from Athens (490 B.C.). Xerxes' combined land and sea invasion ten years later was routed at Salamis, Plataea and Mycale. The Greek writers had a field day with the Persian defeat; they would have enjoyed the way that Xerxes was portrayed as Ahasuerus in the Book of Esther.*

might demand otherwise. So Esther began her new career as a dutiful wife in the high and mighty royal palace in Susa.

Mordecai, too, had his time in the limelight, but it was for a much briefer moment. Recorded then forgotten—the fate of many a good deed done by many an unassuming person—Mordecai uncovered a plot on the king's life. His only reward was that his name was buried in the official Book of the Chronicles of the kings of Persia (Esth 2:21–23). Ahh, such is life lived in the shadow of the only one who counts.

But at least the king was busy recognizing *somebody*. Ahasuerus appointed one Haman "over all the princes who were with him" (Esth 3:1). The title of Grand Vizier might do nicely. Haman was an Agagite, which probably meant nothing to the king but to the queen and her people an "Agagite" must somehow have been a descendant of Agag the Amalekite, Israel's nemesis in the days of King Saul (cf. 1 Sam 15:1–35). At least this is how Josephus and the rabbis understood the story (Ant. xi.6.5; Esth. R. 7:13, 9:4; Targ. Sheni on Esth. 9:7). Haman took his job as second-in-command to heart and demanded that all the princes beneath him do just obeisance to his lordly presence. This Mordecai resolutely refused to do; his identity as a Jew demanded that he bow to no human being. For high-horse Haman, the act of one implicated all and so the only punishment suitable for the crime was the eradication of every Jew in the empire (Esth 3:2–6).

Haman's plan was cut and dried: just tell Ahasuerus that a people (he was careful not to give them a name) scattered throughout the empire followed laws other than those decreed by the king. First a little suggestion whispered in the ear—"it is not in the king's best interest to let them remain"—then the final solution: they must be destroyed and their property in the amount of 10,000 talents of silver confiscated by the royal treasury (Esth 3:7–9). Even though in Ahasuerus's eyes three-quarters of a million pounds of silver at the going rate was a pretty fair exchange for a troublesome people, we have to wonder why he didn't ask any questions about the affair. Wasn't he the least bit curious about who these people were? About where they lived? Or how Haman knew? Whether any had infiltrated the palace? Or if they were such a big threat, why hadn't he heard of their lawless deeds before? Maurice Samuel:

> Not that Ahasuerus was a Jew-hater; he was merely the kind of person who votes a Haman into office and then says: "Buchenwald? I never heard of the place." Also, in the more familiar phrase: "Why, one of my dearest friends is a Jew"—or "a Jewess."
>
> (Certain People of the Book, p. 18)

No, Ahasuerus simply gave the order (he would probably say he was just following orders) that every

single one be rounded up and "destroyed, killed and annihilated" (as if any one of these fates alone wasn't enough!). The act was to take place exactly eleven months hence, on the thirteenth day of Adar in the twelfth year of Ahasuerus (March 9, 473 B.C.; Esth 3:7–15). Eleven long months to stare death in the face and know that Death would not be the first to blink.

The order went out by royal courier across the empire, from pillar to post. Herodotus commented on the efficiency of the Persian mail service:

> Now there is nothing mortal that accomplishes a course more swiftly than do these messengers [sent] by the Persian's skillful contrivance. It is said that as many days as there are in the whole journey, there are that many men and horses standing along the road, each horse and man at the interval of a day's journey. Neither snow nor rain nor heat nor gloom of night stays these couriers from the swift completion of their appointed rounds. (Herodotus, Histories 8.98)

No chance this order wasn't going to be carried out! Satisfied with a day's work well done, Ahasuerus and Haman congratulated each other with a long drink, confident that soon *Kristallnacht* would be in full swing with rail cars grinding their way to the ovens.

And everyone else said, "What??!!" (Esth 3:15).

Jews throughout the empire immediately went into loud, public mourning. Their grief was of true biblical proportions (Esth 4:1–3). Esther, meanwhile, was apparently locked up somewhere in the palace, totally unaware of the goings-on in the kingdom and ignored by even her husband (cf. Esth 4:11). She had to be told by her maidens and eunuchs (servants always seem to know the latest scuttlebutt), then sent one of them to Mordecai (her heart must have longed for the good old days, just she and Mordecai taking care of each other back home) to find

Of the many decorated scenes depicting mythic and real images lining the walls of the royal palace in Susa, those made of richly glazed tiles are the most striking. The most complete is the frieze of archers, the "Guard of the Ten Thousand Immortals" standing ready for the king's every command. Craftsmen added colors to the outlines of the figures by mixing metal oxides to the liquid glazes before the third firing of the bricks. The patterns depicted on the archer's long and elegant robes indicate a highly developed textile industry in the region—a fact confirmed by earlier Elamite inscriptions from the site. How could Esther hope to influence such a court as this?

The most important Persian capital was Persepolis. This was the location of coronations, royal burials, the magnificent New Year's celebration and other ceremonies of the imperial pomp and circumstance. Every New Year's Day dignitaries from across the empire—such as these Median nobles in bold relief—converged on Persepolis, then marched in solemn procession up a wide, low set of stairs to a raised terrace on which were built the residential and ceremonial palaces of the king. Here was the great audience hall; nearby, rooms for banquets. With most of the empire living in huts and hovels, the reality of the royal court was nothing but opulent—as the story of Esther suggests.

Esther was known among her people as Hadassah (the Hebrew word for "myrtle"; Esth 2:7), a name fit for a queen. The evergreen myrtle, more a bush than a tree, has dense, upright branches with rich, green leaves that secrete a fragrant oil held to have healing qualities. Even when cut, the branches remain upright, fresh and fragrant, and so became a symbol of immortality in Jewish tradition. Esther's grace, strength and charm, qualities critical to her success as queen, mirrored the plant after which she was named. "…instead of the thorn the myrtle will come up, and it will be a memorial to the LORD, for an everlasting sign which will not be cut off" (Isa 55:13).

Esther, in the presence of Ahasuerus, touching the royal scepter (Esth 5:1–2), 19th century engraving (Carta, Jerusalem). Josephus provides a number of imaginative details of the meeting: "He looked at her somewhat severely, his countenance on fire with anger, and her joints failed her immediately out of dread so that she fell down sideways in a swoon. Concerned for his wife, he leapt from his throne, took her in his arms and recovered her by embracing and speaking comfortably to her…then put the scepter in her hand" (Ant. xi.6.9). Why not? Josephus would have made a great Hollywood screenwriter.

out what was happening. How Mordecai knew even the exact amount of money to be stolen from the Jews is not said; apparently he was the kind of fellow who just *knew*, and in that Esther found some familiar comfort (Esth 4:4–8). And now Mordecai, dear, dear always-knows-what-to-do-to-get-us-out-of-a-jam Mordecai, asked Esther, wide-eyed, silent and wondering, to help. Esther of course saw only the obstacle—Ahasuerus banishes those who refuse his summons and kills those who come in without his call. "How could I *possibly?*" (Esth 4:9–12). Mordecai laid all the cards on the table:

> *Don't imagine that just because you are in the king's palace that you can escape any more than all of the other Jews. If you remain silent at this time, relief and deliverance will arise for the Jews from another place, while you and your father's house will perish. Who knows? Perhaps you have attained royalty for such a time as this.* (Esth 4:13–14)

Of course Mordecai was right. And now that the problem was clear, now that a situation made by men and wholly unable to be solved by men was *Kristall*-clear, the woman Esther rose to the occasion. "Fast and pray," she said, "for I am going to the king. If I perish, I perish!" (Esth 4:15–17). This was no Masada suicide-wish, but the quiet yet firm realization that sometimes one has to sacrifice one's own ambitions on the altar for others.

Sensing that her husband the king was one who liked to know a secret ("shhh! Did you know that there's a rabble out to get you?") and that he simply *loved* a good banquet, Esther concocted a plan to twist him, bit by bit, around her little finger. First she approached the throne room, wholly unannounced, coyly distant yet near. Ahasuerus perhaps felt a little guilty ("has it really been *thirty days* since we were last together?") and allowed her to remain (Esth 5:1–2; cf. Esth 4:11). In fact, he offered her half the kingdom, quite an overture to someone who was already his wife. Esther's only request was that Ahasuerus and his beloved Haman be guests of honor at a special banquet that night. (Was half the Persian Empire really worth this little? Then again, Esau had given up his chance at chosen-peoplehood for a bowl of len-

til stew…; cf. Gen 25:27–34.) Evening came and Ahasuerus, never one to keep honor waiting, fully enjoyed himself, no doubt wondering what his queen had on her mind. Just another invitation to another banquet tomorrow night (Esth 5:3–8). Twist, twist. "Why didn't I notice how much fun she was before?"

Haman, also invited, shared the king's pleasure. He left the banquet stuffed with himself. On the way out he passed Mordecai, who again refused to bow. Barely controlling his anger, Haman couldn't wait for Slaughtering Day. He ordered a "gallows" (lit. "tree") seventy-five feet high be erected and vowed that in the morning he would ask the king to hang that impudent Mordecai on it (Esth 5:9–14). Most commentators note the impossible height of the gallows, although Rabbinic tradition solves the problem by adding that Haman cut a cedar (the tallest of trees in the Near East, from which ship's masts were made; Ezek 27:5) out of the palace garden and, with chants and shouts, had it set up at the entrance to his house. This was not "hang by the neck until dead." According to Herodotus (*Histories* 3.125, 159), the going form of capital punishment in Persia was to be impaled on a stake. Hang Mordecai above the city like a flag, Haman thought. Stick him up on a high pole. *That* ought to show the Jews! Then, off to the banquet.

For a king who didn't seem too concerned about higher affairs of state, sleep came surprisingly hard for Ahasuerus that night. Perhaps it was something he drank. Rather than toss and turn, he asked to hear a chapter or two from the Chronicles of the Kings of Persia; that way he could reminisce on other good days and fall asleep content, shuttering the cries outside his window that he didn't hear anyway. The page was opened exactly—for such a time as this!—to the record of Mordecai's good deed and how the king's life had been saved. No day is done without a good deed repaid and so Ahasuerus, full of the need to be gracious, summoned his faithful Haman to right the wrong (Esth 6:1–5).

And now one of the greatest sets of dialogue lines in the Bible (Esth 6:6–10). Both men spoke exactly according to character.

> Ahasuerus to Haman: "What should be done to the one the king desires to honor?"
> Haman to himself: "Surely the king means me!"
> Haman to Ahasuerus: "Let him be decked in royal splendor and led through Susa on a royal horse with criers shouting that he is the one most honored by the king."
> Ahasuerus to Haman: "Perfect! See that it's done—to Mordecai!"

The next morning Haman did as he was bidden, looking like death warmed over. And Mordecai, dutifully receiving the honor, surely couldn't have enjoyed being paraded around the city square knowing that his people, even those looking on, were still as doomed as ever. Later in the day, while Haman was pouting about the house, his wife Zeresh saw the omen coming: "If Mordecai is Jewish, you will surely fall before him" (Esth 6:12–13).

That night, with banquet #2 in full swing, Ahasuerus again asked the question, and again promised half the kingdom to his suddenly enchanting wife. This time Esther surprised him. Certainly he expected a favor, but likely had in mind something, shall we say, a bit feminine—a personal request perhaps, or some concession for the harem. But what Ahasuerus heard was something much different.

> We have been sold, I and my people, to be destroyed, killed and annihilated. Now if we had only been sold as slaves I would have remained silent, for that trouble alone would not be worth annoying the king.
>
> (Esth 7:4)

(Haman jerked to attention, but tried to look disinterested.) Esther was decisive and forthright, yet careful to first arouse the king's interest, then his anger, then his will to act. Lingering on every syllable, she deliberately dragged out the accusation: "A foe, an enemy…is…this…wicked…*Haman*!" Suddenly neither the queen nor the king were the center of attention in the room. Things were unraveling fast for the evil vizier. As Ahasuerus stormed out to the garden to try to figure out what was happening and why *he* was the last to know, Haman, reduced to a sniveling shell, plead for mercy from the queen (Esth 7:5–6).

Ahasuerus was in a real quandary. His wife, isolated in the harem, had been the perfect detective: identifying the crime, finding the perpetrator, making the accusation and, he was sure, getting a confession. And he, the king…"Someone must have *tricked* me into being a part of the conspiracy! That traitor Haman is to blame. He didn't tell me they were the queen's people…but why didn't I ask?" The king had been a fool, a drunken fool. He knew it, and now everyone would know. As frustrated and angry as his sauced male ego could be, Ahasuerus reentered the banquet hall to find Haman sprawled out on Esther's couch, begging for his life. The timing was most unfortunate for Haman and Ahasuerus, looking for a place to focus his rage, locked on to his suddenly *former* vizier: "Will he even assault the queen when I'm still in the house?!" Then one final nail for Haman's coffin: an attendant eagerly offered a welcome piece of news. Haman had just erected a huge hanging tree, intending to impale Mordecai, the newly honored friend of the king. The solution was easy; justice swift: "Hang *him* on it!" (Esth 7:7–10). And it is easy to imagine all of Susa, already confused by the edict to kill, destroy and annihilate the Jews (cf. Esth 3:15), looking up in the sky the next morning and remarking, "Why, that poor fellow up there bears an uncanny resemblance to Haman."

Haman's property was given to Esther and his position to Mordecai (Esth 8:1–2, 10:1–3). In the palace everything was resolved, but the real problem still remained. Esther, in an emotional plea for her people, reminded the king that the order to kill all the Jews of the empire was still in effect. The law of the Medes and Persians, once evoked, could not be rescinded (Esth 8:3–7). The solution was ingenious, and quite effective. Mordecai, in the name and power of the king, issued a follow-up edict to all 127 provinces of the empire giving the Jews the right "to assemble and to defend their lives, to destroy, kill and annihilate their enemies" on the thirteenth day of Adar, what had been decreed as Slaughtering Day. And defend themselves they did, with the help of the governors of the provinces, against everyone throughout the empire who had conspired to do them harm (Esth 8:8–9:17).

This was a great victory over the forces of evil, certainly one worth celebrating. Mordecai, in fact, mandated that Jews everywhere celebrate their triumph the next two days "with feasting and rejoicing and sending portions of food to one another and gifts to the poor" (Esth 9:17–32). This is the festival of Purim, now a wonderful holiday for children (when every boy dresses like Mordecai and every girl like Esther), and the one day of the year when "it is the duty of a man to mellow himself [with wine]…until he cannot tell the difference between [someone who says] 'cursed be Haman' and [someone who says] 'blessed by Mordecai'" (Babylonian Talmud, *Megillah* 7b).

Time and distance have turned the events surrounding Purim into a good story, a time to poke fun at Haman and Ahasuerus and to cheer Mordecai and Esther. The fun of the story, however, shouldn't mask the dead seriousness of the edict that prompted Esther's bold acts. A terrible massacre had been averted. Mordecai and Esther were fortunate: their monarch was only a fool. Not so with the Holocaust, the most horrible atrocity of the living past. The Holocaust has no parallels, yet there are some points of connection between it and the events of the Book of Esther. Mordecai, the proud partisan, refused to bend the knee. He survived, but even if he had not, his life would be remembered for the strength that God gives to his people and the honor that cannot be taken away even in death. And Esther, the lovely heroine, stands for help that comes from unexpected places, often at the last possible moment. In spite of—and in the midst of—widespread horror or unbearable challenges, individual acts of greatness, through the grace and strength of God, still exist and become most pronounced when a person leaves behind "what can *I* possibly do?" to grasp "I am here for such a time as this."

In the ancient Near East the stately cedar was to plants what the lion was to animals (Ps 104:16; Ezek 31:1–18). Cedar beams were used to span the roofs of palaces and temples and planks of cedar paneled walls of the houses of the wealthy (1 Kgs 5:6, 5:10, 6:14–18; Song of Songs 1:17). Soaring to heights of over 100 feet, the cedar remains the tallest tree in the Middle East today, still a tree fit for kings. Rabbinic tradition holds that Haman constructed his 75-foot "gallows" from a cedar tree, perhaps as a sign of mock-royalty for Mordecai.

This brick and stone mausoleum in Hamadan, Iran (ancient Ecbatana) dating to the 13th century A.D. is believed by the faithful to house the graves of Esther and Mordecai. Inside the modest Islamic structure, capped with a simple dome, are two exquisite wooden tomb-boxes, one of which bears a Hebrew inscription. The site was restored by Iran's Jewish community and is cared for by Islamic authorities.

New Testament Time Line

300 BC	200 BC	100 BC	AD 1	AD 20

Books of the Bible

Matthew

Luke

Mark

John

The period for the Gospels and Acts shows its historical setting, not the date the books were written. Many dates listed are approximate and may vary according to different scholars.

Intertestamental Period

Life of Christ

Bible History

• Dead Sea Scrolls (copies of Scriptures) written c. 200 BC–AD 100

Maccabean Revolt 167–160

• Alexander the Great conquers Palestine; Spreads Greek culture (Hellenization) 332

• Jerusalem temple rededicated; First Hanukkah 164

Hasmonean Dynasty 164–63

• Septuagint (Scriptures translated into Greek) 255

Roman General Pompey invades Jerusalem 63 •

Herod the Great, king of Judea 37–4 BC

King Herod begins refurbishing the temple 20 •

• John the Baptist born 7–5 BC

• Jesus born in Bethlehem 6–4 BC

Herod Antipas rules Galilee 4 BC–AD 39

• Jesus (age 12) goes to Jerusalem for Passover c. AD 7

Jesus baptized; ministry begins c. 26 •

Crucifixion, death, and resurrection, of Jesus c. 30 •

Ascension of Jesus and commission to the disciples c. 30 •

KEY

▬	TIME SPAN MARKER
•	YEAR MARKER
c.	CIRCA (ABOUT)

AD 40	AD 60	AD 80	AD 100

Books of the Bible

Acts

General epistles written

Paul's epistles written

Revelation written

Early Church Era

Bible History

Felix, governor of Judea 52–57

Herod Antipas 4 BC–AD 39

Emperor Nero 54–68

Emperor Domitian 81–96

• Pentecost; disciples receive Holy Spirit c. 30

• Stephen martyred c. 32

• Paul's conversion 37

• Gospel preached to Gentiles 40

Herod Agrippa I, King of Judea 41–44

• James the apostle martyred c. 44

Paul's first missionary journey c. 48

• Jews expelled from Rome 49

• Jerusalem Council c. 49

Paul's second missionary journey c. 50–52

Paul's third missionary journey c. 53–57

• Paul arrested in Jerusalem 57

Paul's Journey to Rome and house arrest 57–62

• Paul shipwrecked 59

• James, brother of Jesus, martyred 62

• Paul released from house arrest in Rome 62 or 63

Fire in Rome; Nero blames and persecutes Christians 64–68

• Paul imprisoned in Rome c. 64–68

• Peter and Paul martyred in Rome c. 64–68

First Jewish Revolt; Jerusalem Christians flee rather than join the revolt 66–73

• Fall of Jerusalem; temple destroyed by Romans 70

Apostle John exiled to Island of Patmos c. 85–96

Some scholars believe John's exile was under Domitian's rule (c. 85-96) and others believe it was under Nero's rule (c. 68).

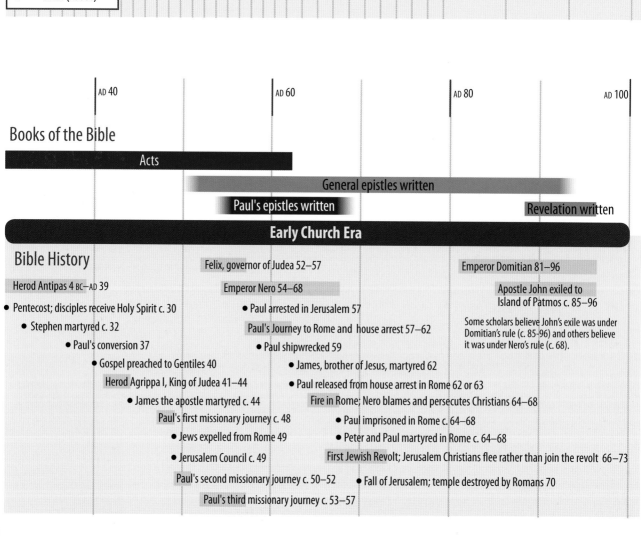

CHAPTER 17

THE HERODS
Magnificent to a Fault

For a century and a half the Herod family dominated the political landscape of Roman Palestine. Herod the Great; his father and grandfather, both named Antipater; his three sons, Archelaus, Philip and Antipas; and his grandson and great-grandson, both Agrippa—these were the home-grown powers-that-be for the region, and even during the years when Rome ruled the land directly through procurators or other high officials the kings produced by the Herod family could carry enough influence to sway Rome's hand. Herodian power was strongest between the years 37 B.C., when Herod the Great took the throne, and A.D. 44, when Agrippa I, his grandson, died. This was a time of great political, social and economic energy, of unrest, accommodation and confrontation, of suppression, innocence and intrigue. Throughout, to be a Jew was to have options, and Judaism sparkled under the opportunities and pressures of the times. And it was here, in a swirl of Jewish religious nationalism buffeted by strong Hellenistic winds and caught in the surge tide of Rome, that the *am ha-aretz*, the common people of Judea and Galilee, looked for someone to provide real answers for life and deliver on their hope for peace, prosperity and security.

Much had changed for the Jews in the centuries following their return from exile in Babylon. By the time Herod the Great gained the throne, the geopolitical center of the world had swung westward to the Aegean and then Rome, and the old Jewish homeland in the rocky hills beyond the Mediterranean's southeastern shore was reduced to a far-flung corner of the Roman Empire. The ramifications of this for the story of the Bible are immense, and prompt an overview of the political, cultural and religious forces that gave shape to this change. By all accounts the individual who was most responsible for the new world order of the late Intertestamental Period was Alexander of Macedon, the Great.

Alexander launched his campaign to conquer an aging Persian Empire in 334 B.C. Fearless and dynamic, the 20-year-old warrior rode the rising tide of Hellenism, a vibrant way of life that would forever change the world. After sweeping through Asia Minor in just one year, Alexander fought his first major battle at Issus on the Cilician Plain where the daring general routed the Persian king Darius III. While Darius fled east, Alexander turned south, conquering Tyre in 332 B.C. after a seven-month siege and then easily subduing the remaining petty city-states that hugged the eastern Mediterranean seaboard. After being crowned Pharaoh in Egypt, Alexander retraced his steps before catching up with Darius at Gaugamela in northern Mesopotamia. Here was the decisive battle, and after his ringing victory Alexander faced little real resistance as he marched all the way to the Indus Valley and the steppes of central Asia. When he died at the age of 32, his energy spent in a vengeance, the seeds of a new world order had been sown across the ancient

Reliving the conquests of the heroes of his own past, Alexander of Macedon crossed the Hellespont at the southern tip of the Gallipoli Peninsula, thrust his spear into Asian soil, advanced across the Plain of Troy to Achilles' tomb and laid a wreath before mortal remains of the demi-god he sought to emulate—or so Alexander's chroniclers liked their own hero to be remembered. The Hellespont—the modern Dardanelles—separates Europe (Greece) from Asia (Turkey), and the Black Sea from the Mediterranean. Then, as now, it's hard to pinpoint a more strategic juncture of routes on earth.

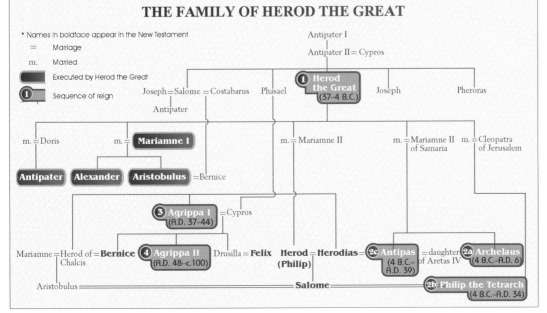

THE FAMILY OF HEROD THE GREAT

* Names in boldface appear in the New Testament
= Marriage
m. Married
▬ Executed by Herod the Great
① Sequence of reign

Antipater I
Antipater II = Cypros

Joseph = Salome = Costabarus   Phasael   ① **Herod the Great** (37–4 B.C.)   Joseph   Pheroras
Antipater

m. = Doris   m. = **Mariamne I**   m. = Mariamne II   m. = Mariamne II m. = Cleopatra
                                                                              of Samaria   of Jerusalem

Antipater **Alexander** **Aristobulus** = Bernice

③ **Agrippa I** (A.D. 37–44) = Cypros

Mariamne = Herod of **Bernice** ④ **Agrippa II** (A.D. 48–c.100)   Drusilla = **Felix**   **Herod (Philip)** = **Herodias** ②c **Antipas** (4 B.C.–A.D. 39) = daughter of Aretas IV ②a **Archelaus** (4 B.C.–A.D. 6)
Chalcis

Aristobulus ══════════════════════════ **Salome** ══════════════════════ ②b **Philip the Tetrarch** (4 B.C.–A.D. 34)

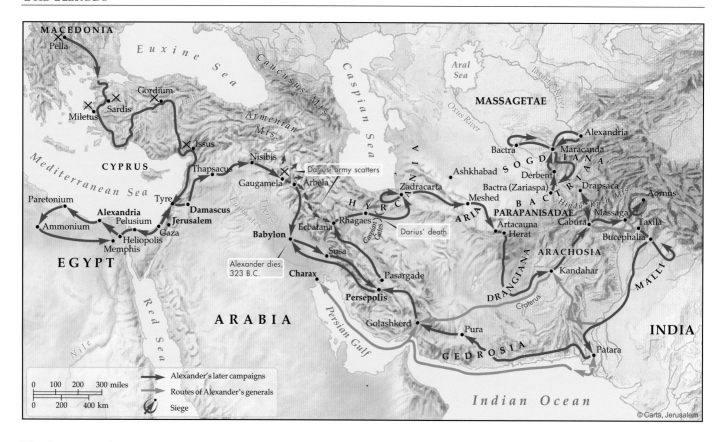

The Conquests of Alexander the Great, 334–323 B.C. *Alexander marched his armies on a circuitous but efficient route from his Macedonian home all the way to the doorway of India. He died en route in Babylon, leaving the world's largest empire in his wake. Europe, Asia and Africa were cemented together by the glue of Hellenism, spread in liberal doses over the seam binding West to East in the Middle East. The lands of the Bible would never be the same.*

Near East. Alexander's soldiers settled down in his wake, establishing Macedonian colonies and cities throughout the former Persian Empire, including one in Samaria, once the capital of the Northern Kingdom of Israel.

Upon his death the fruit of Alexander's conquests passed to his generals. After two decades of war during which each sought to gain advantage over the others, the world from Greece to Persia fell into an uneasy peace. The southern Levant came under the control of the Ptolemies, a long line of successors of Alexander's general Ptolemy who ruled from Egypt. Lands from Damascus to the Indus River were ruled by the successors of Seleucus, another of Alexander's generals, most of whom were named Seleucus or Antiochus. The Seleucid kings established a series of military colonies and Greek cities—many named Seleucia or Antioch—throughout the territory under their control. These served several purposes: to bind together an otherwise diverse and divisive land, to foster loyalty to the king, and to disseminate Hellenism among the indigenous populations of the empire. In reality, because locals had no citizenship rights in these cities a sharp division arose between those who stood to benefit from Hellenism and the rest who just had to put up with it.

Like Judaism, Hellenism was an all-encompassing way of life, a package of thought and behavior that defined one's view of oneself, others and the world of the divine. Hellenism had political, social, economic, cultural and religious aspects, and to be a good citizen of the world and participate in the

socioeconomic opportunities of the time, one had to be a good Hellenist. This of course was cultural imperialism, with a strong economic incentive for the relatively few who could take advantage of the system. The mass of Judean and Galilean peasants in Palestine were used to being protected, at least in theory, by built-in provisions for the poor found in the *Torah*, but in time Hellenistic thinking wrapped itself around the Jewish aristocracy that ran their country and most of the people underneath simply felt exploited. Jews who were able to participate in the opportunities of Hellenism generally separated themselves from its religious aspects. It was relatively straightforward, for instance, to denounce Hellenistic idolatry and refuse to participate in the activities and celebrations of the pagan cult. Defining the proper boundaries of other aspects of Hellenism remained problematic. For most Gentiles, this slice-and-dice response to the Greek way of life was bewildering, maddening and ultimately unacceptable. A classic statement is that of Hecataeus of Abdera, a contemporary of Alexander the Great who, though generally sympathetic to the Jews, noted that they "were somewhat anti-social and hostile to strangers" (quoted by Diodorus Siculus, *Bibliotheca Historica* 40.3.4). Perhaps more than any other single issue of the times, it was the Jewish response to Hellenism—and vice versa—that came to define life in the land of the Bible during the Intertestamental Period.

This process began in the late fourth and early third centuries B.C. as Greek language and customs began to take deep root in Seleucid and Ptolemaic

Hellenistic Cities in Palestine, 312–167 B.C. *The face of the map of the southern Levant changed in the aftermath of Alexander's conquest. Certain regional names—Judea, Samaria, Galilea, Phoenicia—persisted, with new spellings, from Old Testament times, while others, such as Perea and Gaulanitis, took root. Greek city names were sown over the top: Jerusalem became Antiochia, Gaza was now Seleucid Demos, Acco was renamed Ptolemais, and so on. The Hellenistic ideal fostered a vibrant city life favoring aristocrats and world citizens. But most of the local folk just kept using the indigenous names for the places around them, and in the end it was the original Semitic identity of the land that survived.*

During the thousand years between Alexander and the Islamic conquest, West flowed East through ports lining the Mediterranean shore. Today it's everything from coal and oil to fashion and Hollywood, the promise of everything golden the rest of the world has to offer. Then it was the attraction of things Hellenistic—ways of building and dressing and thinking and living that brought light for some, nothing but clouds for others.

soil, finding life among many peoples—including Jews—who were attracted to the new economic and cultural opportunities now available to them. At the same time the eastern Mediterranean was also buffeted by war, as Seleucids fought Ptolemies for dominance over the region. With the Battle of Panias in 198 B.C. in the vicinity of what in the first century A.D. would become Caesarea Philippi, the border of Seleucid control was pushed south to Gaza. The Jews of Jerusalem welcomed the Seleucid king Antiochus III (223–187 B.C.), who granted them rights and privileges that allowed relatively free expression of Jewish religious practices. But within a decade Antiochus III lost his holdings in Asia Minor to Rome, an ominous sign that an emerging world power was already poised to sweep into the lands of the eastern Mediterranean.

Antiochus IV Epiphanes ("Illustrious") took the Seleucid throne in 174 B.C. as Roman war clouds gathered on the western horizon. Perhaps in part to meet this rising threat, Antiochus sought to strengthen his own far-flung empire by uniting its diverse lands and peoples under the cultural and religious flag of Hellenism, integrating all gods under the supremacy of Zeus. Certain elements among the population of Jerusalem accepted these decrees while most, of course, resisted. At the highest levels, the office of the high priesthood was "purchased" by Jason, an ardent hellenizer, and then by Menelaus (2 Maccabees 4), two powerful men who tried to use their position to bend the cultural and religious loyalty of the Jews toward Hellenism. It was Jason who established a gymnasium in Jerusalem, a formal school of Hellenism that taught the finer (and necessary) points of Greek civilization: proper civic and military life, physical culture, philosophy, literature and piety toward the gods. When Antiochus IV invaded Egypt to try to forge a single political alliance of all of the eastern lands, Rome stepped in. Humiliated and frustrated on the world stage, Antiochus turned his wrath against the Jewish population of Jerusalem who had largely rebuffed his earlier attempts to bring their city into his cultural and political fold. Antiochus forbade the exercise of religious

135

The Campaigns of Antiochus IV Epiphanes in Egypt and Judea, 170–167 B.C. *Bent on creating a Syrian empire that could withstand the tidal wave of Rome, Antiochus IV Epiphanes decided to conquer Egypt. After winning an initial battle against Ptolemy VI near Pelusium, Antiochus had himself crowned Pharaoh in the ancient Egyptian capital Memphis, then besieged Alexandria. He broke the siege for a quick trip to Jerusalem where the deposed high priest Jason was trying to retake the city with the help of the Tobiads of Transjordan. After depleting the Temple treasury Antiochus returned to Egypt but was stopped outside of Alexandria by a very determined Rome. Turning tail, Antiochus retraced his steps to Jerusalem where in 167 B.C. he forced Hellenism down the throats of its Jewish inhabitants.*

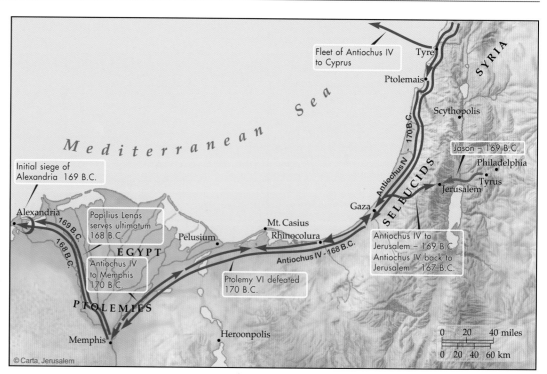

Archaeologist Gabriel Barkay explains the architectural significance of the courtyard of Jason's Tomb to attentive students of biblical archaeology. Located in the fashionable Rehavia neighborhood of Jerusalem, the tomb contains a charcoal drawing of Mediterranean-style ships and an Aramaic inscription identifying the inhabitants as the priestly family of Jason, likely the same Jason who was high priest in the Jerusalem Temple in the early 2nd century B.C. Jason is best known for bribing his way to the high priesthood and then using the office to actively foster Hellenism among a generally unwilling populace. It was this tendency toward things Greek that led to the Hasmonean Revolt a few years later.

practices essential to Judaism (such as keeping the Sabbath, yearly feasts, sacrifices and circumcision) and in December 167 B.C. turned the Temple into a sanctuary of Zeus (1 Macc 1:41–64).

With this the Jews mounted an armed revolt, prompted by Mattathias, a priest of the Hasmonean family who hailed from the village of Modiin (*el-Midye*) northwest of Jerusalem on the edge of the hellenized coastal plain. Jews had tried to gain a foothold in this, Jerusalem's most necessary frontier, back in the days of Nehemiah (Ezra 2:33; Neh 7:37, 11:35). Now it was here that things most essential to Judaism first came to a head. Mattathias' son Judas Maccabeus ("the hammerer") waged what amounted to a guerrilla war against the Seleucid army which was trying to link up with the Hellenistic forces in Jerusalem and crush the Jewish revolt. Judas was a brilliant battle tactician who routed the Seleucid forces at each attempt, finally

taking his own army into Jerusalem. In December 164 B.C. he cleansed and rededicated the Temple (1 Maccabees 2–4); the festival of Hanukkah ("Dedication"; cf. Jn 10:22–23) commemorates this event.

Not content with rescuing the Temple from Seleucid hands, Judas launched a series of defensive campaigns aimed at strengthening the Jewish position in their historic homeland. Judas himself fell in battle in 161 B.C., but over the next two decades his brothers Jonathan and Simon gained decisive victories over the Seleucids in Samaria, Galilee, Transjordan (Gilead and Syria) and even on the coastal plain, long a stronghold of Greek culture and power (1 Maccabees 10–15). The Seleucid king formally recognized Judea's independence under Simon in 142 B.C. (1 Macc 13:33–42), signaling the rise of the first independent Jewish state since the fall of Judah to the Babylonians in 586 B.C. In response, the ecstatic Jews made Simon "their leader and high priest forever, until a trustworthy prophet should rise" (1 Macc 14:25–49). For all practical purposes he was their king.

With political and religious independence in hand, the new Jewish state (the Hasmonean kingdom) began to consolidate and expand power in its ancestral homeland. In 135 B.C. Simon was succeeded by his son John Hyrcanus who, with the tacit approval of Rome, conquered Medeba in Transjordan, Samaria (where he destroyed the Samaritan temple on Mt. Gerizim; cf. Jn 4:20) and Idumea, thereby securing for Judea the lands which were best placed strategically for later territorial expansion. The region of Idumea, encompassing the southern areas of the Shephelah, hill country and Judean Wilderness, had become home to a gentile population, mostly

The Hasmonean State, 142–63 B.C. *At the beginning of the Maccabean Revolt the Jews controlled nothing politically, and the province of Judea—their homeland—was limited to the high hill country around Jerusalem and the arid wilderness to the east. Over the course of the next eight decades the Jews not only gained their independence from the Seleucids but were able to expand their kingdom, systematically and deliberately, bit by bit, until it included nearly everything that lay within the old biblical boundaries "from Dan to Beer-sheba" (cf. 1 Kgs 4:25) plus Transjordan. It didn't last long. Thirteen years after the death of Alexander Jannaeus the Hasmonean kingdom was gobbled up by Pompey and the Romans.*

Edomite, after the Judean Exile to Babylon. The Jewish historian Josephus relates that after subduing the Idumeans, Hyrcanus

> *permitted them to stay in that country if they would circumcise their genitals and make use of the laws of the Jews. They were so desirous of living in the country of their forefathers that they submitted to the use of circumcision and the rest of the Jewish ways of living . . . so that from this point on they were nothing but Jewish.* (Ant. xiii.9.1; cf. Ant. xiii.15.4)

It was from Idumea, an all-too-fitting setting where culture was conquered by force of arms, that the family of Herod the Great would arise.

Toward the end of his reign Hyrcanus sided with the Sadducees over against the Pharisees in inter-Jewish religious affairs, signaling a gradual shift toward hellenization within the ruling administration of Judea. (As the party of the wealthy Jewish aristocracy, the Sadducees were more in touch with the social and economic opportunities that arose with Hellenism than were the Pharisees, who represented the conservative masses of the population.) That Hyrcanus gave his sons (and successors) Greek names (Aristobulus and Alexander Jannaeus) is a further indication of the inter-Jewish religious and cultural strife that lay ahead. The Jewish Hasmonean kingdom was fast becoming a semi-Hellenistic kingdom, with all the trappings of just one more despotic oriental state. But at least it was *their* semi-Hellenistic despotic oriental state. Independence was, after all, independence—the rest could work itself out later.

In 104 B.C. Hyrcanus was succeeded by his oldest son Aristobulus, whom Josephus called "a lover of the Greeks" (Ant. xiii.11.3). During his one-year reign Aristobulus was able to conquer the Itureans, an Arab tribe living in the vicinity of the Huleh Basin between Mount Hermon and Galilee. Taking a page from his father's policy handbook, he forced the Itureans to convert to Judaism (Ant. xiii.11.3). Aristobulus' successor, his brother Alexander Jannaeus, pushed the borders of the Hasmonean kingdom to their greatest extent, encompassing essentially the same territory that had been under the direct control of David and Solomon back in the glory days of ancient Israel. Of particular importance was the conquest of all of the Greek cities on the coastal plain except for Ascalon.

An expanding state needs a proper show of pomp and force, and the Hasmonean kings wasted no time in the effort of both. Among their many palaces and fortresses, four lining the Rift

Not much is left of Modiin, the hometown of Judas Maccabeus and his family, and even the location of the site is debated. Tradition identifies several tombs at Sheik el-Gharbawi near el-Midye as the tombs of the Maccabees, even though they likely date to the Byzantine period seven hundred years later. These tombs have rectangular body-sized openings covered by heavy stone lids—impressive enough today, but rather simple compared to the elaborate tomb adorned by columns, pyramids and carved ships constructed by Simon for his family (1 Maccabees 13:25–30).

Map labels: Tyre, Panias, Cadasa, Dan (Antiochia), PHOENICIA, Seleucia, Hazor, Bascama, Ptolemais, Bethsaida, Gamala, Gennesaret, Taricheae, Dathema, Arbela, Sea of Galilee, Hipppus, GALILEE, Sepphoris, Philoteria, Dora, Jezreel Valley, GALAADITIS, Strato's Tower, Scythopolis, Pella, SAMARIA, Geresa, Samaria, Shechem, Amathus, Apollonia, Mt. Gerizim, Alexandrium, Joppa, Acrabeta, PEREA, Adida, Aramathea, Apharema, Gadora, Lydda, Docus, Philadelphia, Jammia, Gazara, JUDEA, Jericho, Esbus, Azotus, Emmaus, Jerusalem, Samaga, Accaron, Hyrcania, Ascalon, Herodium, Medeba, Machaerus, Anthedon, Marisa, Beth-zur, Dead Sea, Gaza, Adora, Hebron, MOABITIS, Gerar, En-gedi, Orda, IDUMEA, Masada, Raphia, Beer-sheba, Malatha, Rhinocorura, Wadi el-Arish, NABATEANS, Mediterranean Sea, Mt. Carmel

Legend:
- Judea at the beginning of the revolt
- Additions of Jonathan, 160–142 B.C.
- Additions of Simon, 142–134 B.C.
- Additions of Hyrcanus I, 134–104 B.C.
- Additions of Aristobulus I, 104–103 B.C.
- Additions of Alexander Jannaeus 103–76 B.C.
- Kingdom of Alexander Jannaeus
- Fortresses

0   10 miles
0   15 km

© Carta, Jerusalem

Having established a beachhead along the eastern Mediterranean shore, Rome drove inland through the thin band of arable land along the mid-point of the Fertile Crescent, then spilled out onto vast seas of sand as formidable as the oceans themselves. Here Nabateans threaded their ships of the desert from oasis port to oasis port, hugging rugged islands of rock with cargoes of spices from Yemen and beyond. Rome coveted Nabatean wealth and their expertise at controlling the sand lanes to get it.

Valley bear special mention because of their later connection to Herod the Great. These were apparently first built by Alexander Jannaeus: Alexandrium (*Sartaba*), north of Jericho, named after himself; Hyrcania, in the Buqei'ah Valley above the northwestern corner of the Dead Sea, named after his father; Machaerus east of the Dead Sea (*Ant.* xiii.16.3), and the palace in Jericho at the point that the Wadi Qilt exits the limestone cliff fronting the Judean Wilderness. Josephus also mentions a Hasmonean palace at Masada, along the western shore of the Dead Sea (*War* vii.8.3). All had architectural elements common to Hellenistic buildings elsewhere as, we can assume, did the Hasmonean palace in Jerusalem. Political sentiment aside, by now Judea was also beginning to *look* Greek.

Jannaeus appointed Antipater, a local man of some standing, to be the chief magistrate (*strategos*) of Idumea. Seizing the opportunity to expand his own power base, Antipater made friends "by means of many and large presents" with the leading men of Ascalon, Gaza and Arabia (*Ant.* xiv.1.3). This has been a time-honored way of launching a political career in the Middle East for millennia. Antipater's opportunism allowed Jannaeus to push Judea's influence south and west—which surely endeared the gover-

nor to the king—but also gave Antipater enough momentum to position his own son, Antipater II, as a future power-broker in Judea. Antipater's political deftness also set the tone for the actions of his more famous grandson, Herod the Great. Ambitious genes ran deep in the family.

In internal affairs, however, Jannaeus was less successful. His favor for things Greek, combined with gross personal moral failings, brought him into open conflict with the socially conservative Pharisees. Jannaeus suppressed the Pharisees cruelly, at one time crucifying 800 of them. Then, at the very end of his life when seized by the death throes of alcoholism, Jannaeus made peace with the Pharisees, apparently seeing in them a stronger political base by which the Hasmonean kingdom might survive the coming onslaught of Rome

Jannaeus' queen, Salome Alexandra, succeeded him in 76 B.C. Her largely peaceful reign was marred by conflict between her two sons and heirs-apparent, Hyrcanus II (the elder) to whom she granted the high priesthood (although weaker than his brother, he was favored by the queen and the Pharisees), and Aristobulus II (favored by the Sadducees) who controlled the army. Upon her death in 67 B.C. the brothers waged civil war. Antipater II, now coming into his own and, in the undisguised musings of Josephus, "a man who was very rich and in his nature active and seditious" (*Ant.* xiv.1.3), placed himself at the disposal of Hyrcanus over against Aristobulus. After four years of fraternal squabbles that were played out on the international stage, Rome intervened at the behest of each ("Help *me*! No, take *my* side!") and Pompey entered Jerusalem. Aristobulus, the greater threat, was taken prisoner to Rome while Pompey confirmed Hyrcanus II in his role as high priest—the highest remaining office over internal Jewish affairs—apparently calculating that he could buy the Jews' political loyalty if he threw them this at-least-one-of-our-own-is-in-charge-of-matters-that-most-define-our-identity bone. Hyrcanus remained the official ruler of Judea but was soon sidelined by his ambitions yet cautious power-broker, Antipater II who, as the most savvy local military strategist left standing, wormed his way up the channels of influence under the tacit approval of Rome. Antipater preferred to veil his power behind the scenes. In reality, were it not for his support, Hyrcanus probably wouldn't have lasted as long as he did. ("But with friends like him," the overwhelmed high priest probably thought on more than one occasion, "who needs enemies?")

Ever eager to prove his worth to Rome, Antipater II helped secure Roman control over the Nabateans and Egypt and, most tellingly, in Jerusalem itself. In 47 B.C., a year after he defeated Pompey in Egypt, Julius Caesar granted Roman citizenship to Antipater and appointed him procurator (chief financial

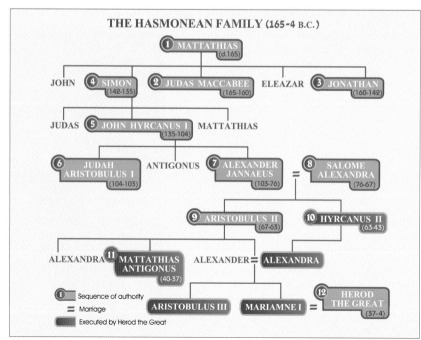

THE HASMONEAN FAMILY (165-4 B.C.)

- ① MATTATHIAS (d.165)
- JOHN
- ④ SIMON (142-135)
- ② JUDAS MACCABEE (165-160)
- ELEAZAR
- ③ JONATHAN (160-142)
- JUDAS
- ⑤ JOHN HYRCANUS I (135-104)
- MATTATHIAS
- ⑥ JUDAH ARISTOBULUS I (104-103)
- ANTIGONUS
- ⑦ ALEXANDER JANNAEUS (103-76) = SALOME ALEXANDRA (76-67)
- ⑨ ARISTOBULUS II (67-63)
- ⑩ HYRCANUS II (63-43)
- ALEXANDRA
- ⑪ MATTATHIAS ANTIGONUS (40-37)
- ALEXANDER = ALEXANDRA
- ① Sequence of authority
- = Marriage
- ▬ Executed by Herod the Great
- ARISTOBULUS III
- MARIAMNE I = ⑫ HEROD THE GREAT (37-4)

officer) of Judea; this pact of mutual friendship was useful for the ambitions of both (*Ant.* xiv.1–8). Caesar allowed Antipater to appoint his two oldest sons, Phasael and Herod, as military prefects over Jerusalem and Galilee, respectively. Herod was only 25 years old at the time, Josephus reports, "but youth was no impediment to him, as he was a youth of great mind." This was a welcome relief to Antipater, who reckoned Hyrcanus "slow and slothful" and generally unfit to rule (*Ant.* xiv.9.2). A puppet dynasty was arising out of the ashes of the Hasmonean kingdom, one that preferred to pull its own strings. Antipater the opportunistic Idumean had reached the top of the local heap by schmoozing with power-hungry Romans and climbing over the backs of his Jewish subjects. His son Herod, unwilling to wait in the wings, was cut from the same cloth, though a piece with bolder colors.

There was an immediate and very practical outcome of all of this political intrigue for the Jews, however. Out of gratitude for Antipater's help in establishing Roman control in the region (and in particular, help that favored Julius Caesar, who was fighting his own political battles at the time), Caesar granted them a special series of privileges. Among those which proved to be the most important in the decades that followed were a reduction of the Jewish tax burden, an exemption from the usual obligation of providing auxiliary troops for Roman campaigns, a return to Jewish control of the commercially strategic cities of Joppa, Lydda and the agricultural villages of the Jezreel Valley, and the guarantee of assembly and *Torah* observance in the synagogue (*Ant.* xiv.10). These privileges were reconfirmed by Caesar's successors and provided not only a context for Judaism to thrive in Judea and the Diaspora but helped prepare the ground for the spread of the Gospel throughout the Roman world.

Power politics, always a dangerous game, was especially so in the years that Rome was trying to establish control in the eastern Mediterranean. Antipater the procurator and Hyrcanus, whom Caesar had appointed "ethnarch of the Jews" the same year Antipater received his commission, were uneasy dance partners, often stepping on each other's toes, each insisting on taking the lead himself. The music stopped in 43 B.C. when, in the general disorder following the assassination of Julius Caesar, Antipater was poisoned by Malichus, a man of like temperament and ambitions as Antipater but who preferred the rule of Hyrcanus instead. Herod avenged the murder (*Ant.* xiv.11).

In his historical narrative of the Jewish people, Josephus introduced Antipater as someone who by nature was "seditious." He looked with kinder eyes at the notice of Antipater's death: "The man," Josephus said, "had distinguished himself for piety and justice and love to his country" (*Ant.* xiv.11.4; cf. xiv.1.3).

Herod was to meet with similar ambivalent feelings by his fellow Jews. The family founded by Antipater was magnificent in presentation and accomplishment, but obsessive to a fault.

As for his part, Herod came charging out of the gate the first chance he got. Shortly after receiving military control over Galilee, when his father was still alive, Herod "met with an opportunity to show his courage" (*Ant.* xiv.9.2) and set out on a campaign to rid Galilee and parts of Syria (the Golan) from a band of robbers that had been ravaging the countryside. The bandits' victims were likely not just anyone but those who had something to lose, namely, the aristocratic Jewish landowners for whom the mass of Galilean peasants toiled. Herod promptly squashed the gang and arrested and executed its popular leader, Ezekias (Hezekiah), without a trial. It was a quick, firm and decisive act. In principle this angered members of the Sanhedrin, the highest Jewish ruling body, who held that under Jewish law only they could enact capital punishment (*Ant.* xiv.9.3; cf. Babylonian Talmud, *Sanhedrin* 7.1). Summoned before the Sanhedrin in Jerusalem, Herod dared to appear in full royal regalia with armed bodyguards. The confrontation went something like this (*Ant.* xiv.9.4):

> Herod: "I have a powerful daddy. You can't touch me."
> The Sanhedrin: "You impudent whelp!"

The Sanhedrin caved, but for Herod this wasn't enough. Years later, after he had become king, he executed the members of the Sanhedrin before whom he had stood, as well as Hyrcanus II who put them up to it (cf. *Ant.* xv.1.2; 6.1–4). By that time Herod had married Hyrcanus' granddaughter but that was irrelevant; power was power, after all.

Herod's actions against Ezekias and his band of brigands also alienated him from a large number of his Jewish subjects. Most Galileans were peasants and many considered outlaws such as Ezekias to be

Aristocracy is aristocracy, and in the late 2nd and early 1st centuries B.C. the Hasmonean kingdom brought enough wealth and wherewithal to Jerusalem that the city's leaders had ample opportunity to publicly flaunt their positions. Among the most enduring "monuments of the righteous" (cf. Mt 23:29) are several tombs lining the Kidron Valley, including the columned tomb of the priestly Hazir family and a pyramid-topped monument that tradition wrongly connects with the prophet Zechariah. Architecturally, these tombs combine Greek, Egyptian, Nabatean and local forms, a witness in stone of the land bridge that is Palestine.

The Battle for Herod's Kingdom, 39–37 B.C.

Landing at Ptolemais in 39 B.C. with the strength of Rome in hand, Herod quickly secured the lowlands and plains of Galilee, the coast and the Negeb, then drove his army to Jerusalem along the spiny central ridge of the hill country from the south. Breaking off the siege, his army wintered on the coast, then cleaned out Galilee from Sepphoris to Arbela the next spring. With the help of his brothers Joseph and Pheroras, Herod's army again approached Jerusalem, this time from the north and east, finally overcoming Pappus, Antigonus' general, and entering Jerusalem in 37 B.C.

folk heroes, partisans who stood up for their rights against the daily oppression of a landed gentry who, for personal gain, had become too friendly with things Roman. Of course this gentry formed an attractive power base for Herod as he sought to gain his footing in higher Galilean society; later on, persons of a similar ilk were called Herodians (perhaps a bit pejoratively) by the Gospel writers (Mt 22:16; Mk 3:6, 12:13).

This was Herod's opening salvo, and with it he cleared the deck. As far as Herod was concerned, he was subject only to the will of Caesar, certainly not to the scruples and local laws of all those little people (including the Sanhedrin) who stood in his way. Yet in spite of Herod's excesses in this and much larger incidents throughout the rest of his life, there was an overall acquiescence to his rule. There's something assuring in having strong leadership, all in all, even if it is of the Herodian type. Rome recognized that Herod was the kind of person that

the empire needed to maintain law and order in the region (though not necessarily in that sequence of priority) and so in 42 B.C., after the assassination of Antipater and with the consent of the thoroughly-cowed Hyrcanus, Mark Antony appointed him and his brother Phasael tetrarchs of Judea (*Ant.* xiv.13.1).

It didn't take long, though, for Herod to (temporarily) meet his match. Two years later, sensing weakness in Rome's eastern frontier, the Parthians invaded Syria and Palestine. Heirs of the Persian Plateau, the Parthians were Rome's great enemy to the east. They found an eager local ally in Matthias Antigonus, the son of the deposed Aristobulus II, who believed that he, not his old uncle Hyrcanus II and certainly not anyone from the family of the dead Antipater, was the rightful heir to the Hasmonean throne. Perhaps, Antigonus thought, he could squeeze a true Jewish kingdom out of the Roman-Parthian fight in the process. Hyrcanus and Phasael went to Galilee to meet the invading Parthian king

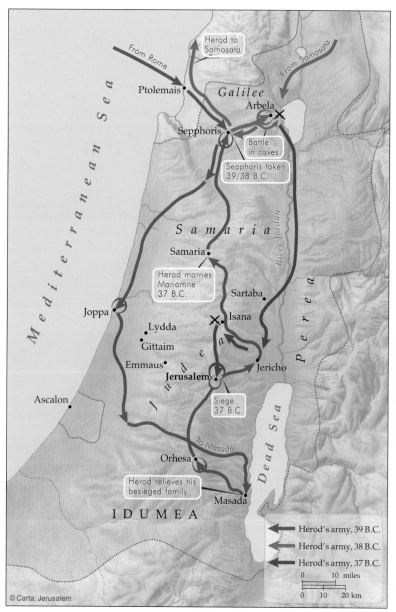

The cliffs of Arbel are one of the most distinctive landforms—and popular hiking spots—in Galilee. An international route ran at the base of the cliff, linking the coast and Galilee's interior with the Sea of Galilee in the distance. The cliff face is honeycombed with caves, and it is to them that Herod chased some of his "political opponents" (so remnants of the Hasmonean kingdom were labeled by Josephus) en route to a massacre by sword and suicide as Herod seized his kingdom. Intrepid hikers can easily visit many of the caves in the cliff today.

and negotiate terms of peace; they were immediately arrested, Antigonus was crowned king of Judea, and Herod, mighty Herod of the purple and gold, turned tail and fled for his life to Rome (Ant. xiv.13.3–14.3).

There Herod was welcomed with empathy and honor ("such things sometimes happen to those who arise to great position and fortune," thought Antony, according to Josephus; Ant. xiv.14.4. "Just a bump in the road," we could paraphrase). In the summer of 40 B.C. the Roman Senate, at the behest of Antony and Octavian, named Herod king of Judea with authority over all lands formerly held by Hyrcanus (Galilee, Idumea, Perea, Joppa and the Jezreel Valley, with Samaria thrown in for good measure), granted him the right to raise an army and sent him off to conquer his kingdom (Ant. xiv.14.4–5). He wasn't absolute monarch, but a client king of Rome. It is important to note that Herod was King of Judea, not King of the Jews (cf. Mt 2:2, 27:37); that title would have given him authority over a people scattered throughout the Roman Empire, a situation clearly untenable for proper lines of governance and control.

Herod landed at the Galilean port of Ptolemais ("He's baaack!") and for two and a half years slashed and burned his way through his promised land. Battles at Joppa and Orhesa secured the coast and Idumea. Sepphoris was taken during a snowstorm (quite rare for the elevation), and with it Galilee came back into Herod's fold. As before, Josephus called Herod's Galilean enemies "robbers"; freedom-loving Jewish partisans might be more accurate. At one point Herod chased his opponents to the caves of Arbel where, after an impassioned struggle, some chose suicide rather than imprisonment or death at the hand of their new king (the Masada-motif struck early). The final battle was of course over Jerusalem, which fell to Herod in the summer of 37 B.C. Antigonus was beheaded at Herod's insistence (it was the first time Rome executed a conquered king); with this slash of the sword the Hasmonean line formally (and finally) came to an end. The new king, Herod, received his kingdom when he was about 33 years old (Ant. xiv.15–xv.1; cf. Lk 3:23).

Herod started to don his regalia but soon found that the blessing of Rome only went so far on the international stage. By 32 B.C. Antony and Octavian were embroiled in civil war. Herod preferred to back his old ally Antony, but Cleopatra, Egypt's last pharaoh and a monarch with a lot more pull than Herod back in Rome, had other ideas. Placing territorial ambition over love (for all its hyped romance, Cleopatra's feelings for Antony were first a matter of political expediency), Cleopatra insisted that Herod instead bide his time by keeping the pesky Nabateans in check. She apparently hoped that by doing so, Herod would be weakened enough that she could overrun his kingdom and Egypt

could once again realize its millennia-old dream of imperial domination over the Levant. But the tide came in differently: Herod handily crushed the Nabateans (it was to be his only military victory apart from the initial fight to gain his kingdom), Octavian defeated Antony in the Battle of Actium (31 B.C.) and Cleopatra, finding an honorable solution, took the suicide sting of an asp (Ant. xv.4.1–5.5). By mixed doses of groveling and pomp, Herod threw his loyalty to Octavian (now Caesar Augustus), who responded by enlarging his kingdom with Hellenistic cities along the coast (Gaza, Anthedon, Joppa and Strato's Tower) and in the northern Jordan Valley (Gadara and Hippus). By the end of the next decade Caesar had also given Herod the unruly frontier lands of Transjordan east of Galilee (Gaulanitis; Panias; Batanea, Trachonitis and Auranitis; Ant. xv.6.5–7, xv.7.3, xv.10.1,3). With equal doses of skill, charm and luck, Herod's kingdom had reached its greatest extent, the turbulent political world of Rome notwithstanding. He likely rather enjoyed the process.

Herod also found out that the blessing of Rome only went so far back home, but overcoming this one was much more difficult and here he was ultimately unsuccessful. The problem was one of perception and identity. Herod had been born into an aristocratic Idumean family that had been forcefully converted to Judaism by Hyrcanus I only a few decades before (perhaps Herod's grandfather Antipater I, or maybe his father, was the first of the line to become a Jew; cf. Ant. xiii.9.1). What made mat-

Caesar Augustus gave the springs of Panias at the foot of Mt. Hermon to Herod in 20 B.C. Herod was most grateful— it was a region of wet and wild beauty that had never been conquered by the Hasmoneans. Out of gratitude Herod built a temple to the divine Augustus in the vicinity. While popular tradition places this temple at the mouth of a large cave at Panias out of which a power stream of water flowed in Herod's day, a better candidate for this Augusteum has recently been found a couple of miles south, at Omrit. The ruins at Omrit are clearly those of a Roman Temple, and closely resemble Herod's Augustus Temples at the port of Caesarea and at Sebaste.

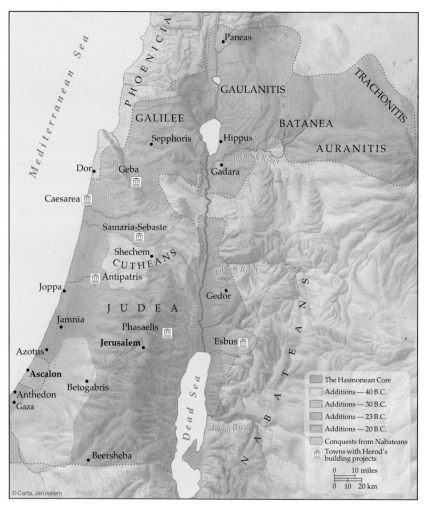

The Growth of Herod's Kingdom, 40–4 B.C.
Springing out of territory left over from the old Hasmonean kingdom, Herod's sovereignty grew primarily by additional land grants from Caesar. In addition to lands "from Dan to Beer-sheba," Herod controlled a much larger portion of northern Transjordan than did the Hasmoneans. And, unlike Alexander Jannaeus, he made no attempt to shape his kingdom around a primarily Jewish identity. Quite the contrary: Herod preferred things Roman.

ters worse was that the Idumeans were descendants of the Edomites, the Jews' historic enemies (cf. Obad 1–21). Nor was there any help on Herod's mother's side: Cypros, the wife of Antipater II, was an Arab (probably Nabatean), without a drop of Jewish blood in her veins (Ant. xiv.7.3). For the Jews of Judea and Galilee, then, Herod was *barely* Jewish, certainly not of the house and lineage of David but an outsider, a hopeless pretender to the Hasmonean throne. During the war for control of Judea, Antigonus derisively called Herod "nothing but a commoner, an Idumean, a *half*-Jew" (Ant. xiv.15.2). But to the gentiles in the Hellenistic city-states under Herod's control he was too Jewish. They didn't take kindly to being ruled by someone who represented a people they considered "somewhat anti-social and hostile" to outsiders who lived next door (Diodorus Siculus, *Bibliotheca Historica* 40.3.4). And so Herod, mistrusted by Jew and gentile alike, enforced his will with an army of other "half-Jews" like himself (be they Idumeans, Galileans, Pereans and Samaritans), with the always-ready help of mercenaries on the side.

Herod's heart was in Rome, but reality kept pulling him back toward the Jews of Jerusalem who held the key to *shalom habayit* (peace at home) in his domain. The king and the remnants of the Hasmonean aristocracy made strange bedfellows, but for bet-

ter or worse they were stuck with each other. Herod decided to solidify his position as king of Judea the old-fashioned way: by marriage and by murder.

Herod married ten times; the one that mattered most was his second, to Mariamne, granddaughter of both Hyrcanus II and Aristobulus II. The ceremony was in Samaria in 37 B.C. during the siege for Jerusalem, just in time for Herod to enter into his kingdom with proper (though manufactured) Hasmonean credentials (Ant. xiv.12.1, xiv.15.14). Although it was a marriage of convenience, Mariamne appears to have been the only wife that Herod truly loved; their betrothal, after all, had lasted five years (Ant. xv.7.1–2, 6). She was "a woman of an excellent character, both for chastity and greatness of soul," commented Josephus in his usual musings giving honor to those to whom honor was due, "but lacked moderation and was too contentious in her nature" (Ant. xv.7.6). While she was alive Mariamne was the undisputed queen of Herod's court and spared no effort in pushing the Hasmonean agenda. It would do her in.

Thirteen years later—five years after Mariamne's death—Herod married another Mariamne (II), this one the beautiful daughter of a priest named Simon. Wholly smitten by her beauty, Herod fired the current high priest, elevated Simon into the position and married the daughter (Ant. xv.9.4). Except for propriety, everyone gained.

There is no direct evidence that any of the rest of Herod's marriages were taken to elevate his standing in higher Jewish social circles, although most if not all likely had political overtones. We can be sure that at least one, to Malthace the Samaritan (his fourth), strengthened his ties to non-Jewish elements under his rule (Ant. xvii.1.3). Lost in the flow was Doris, wife #1, a plain Idumean, the love of Herod's youth who was shoved aside for things more expedient (Ant. xiv.12.1).

Marrying into the Hasmonean line to win the heart of his kingdom brought with it a certain measure of intrigue. A parallel track to secure the throne was simply to remove everyone else who could claim rights to it, and this Herod did with a vengeance. Those he murdered reads like a Who's Who of Jewish Higher Society in the latter first century B.C. Of course the first to go was Antigonus, son of Aristobulus II, the natural heir to the Hasmonean throne and puppet king during the time of the Parthian invasion (Ant. xiv.16.4, xv.1.2). Next up was Aristobulus III, Mariamne's younger brother whom Alexandra, Mariamne's mother (Herod's meddlesome mother-in-law) was grooming for the high priesthood. Herod had no intention of placing a member of the Hasmonean family in that office, preferring his own candidate from the older, more authentic (and loyal) Zadokite line instead (Ant. xv.2.5–3.1; cf. 2 Sam 8:17; 1 Kgs 4:2; Ezek 40:46). Both Antony and Cleopatra intervened on Alexandra's behalf (Cleopatra was an old friend), forcing a humiliated Herod to make the appointment. Herod never wore humiliation well, yet had to find the right circumstances for pay-back since the 17-year-old Aristobulus was widely popular and had personally done nothing to undermine the king's rule. The chance came about a year later in the winter of 35 B.C., when Alexandra, Aristobulus and Herod were all enjoying themselves at the Hasmonean pleasure palace in Jericho. As evening turned to night and Aristobulus was swimming in the large palace pool, Herod's servants and friends playfully (and obligingly) held him underwater just a bit too long. (Herod, the perfect guest, smiled all the while.) Alexandra didn't buy the official version of this most unfortunate drowning "accident"—of course she was right—and had Antony charge Herod with murder. Facing his own execution, Herod-of-the-silver-tongue bribed Antony to find him innocent of the affair (*Ant.* xv.3.2–4).

The war between Antony and Octavian in 31 B.C. provided the opportunity for further house cleaning. The old high priest Hyrcanus II was still kicking, ten years after being hauled off to Parthia during Herod's war for Judea. Hyrcanus had returned to Jerusalem after the war and remained the most viable hope for restoring the Hasmonean line. Herod, thinking that he himself might not survive his meeting with Octavian after the Battle of Actium—and thereby giving Hyrcanus the opportunity to fulfill his lifelong goal of becoming king of Judea—decided that it was best just to execute Hyrcanus straight away. This he did on the pretext that Hyrcanus had supported the Nabateans in their fight against Herod (*Ant.* xv.6.1–4). Herod had similar feelings about Alexandra and Mariamne; they, too, would surely steer the kingdom back to the Hasmoneans if he failed to return. The solution? Lock them up in the desert fortress at Alexandrium while he was gone with instructions that if he was killed, they, too, should be executed. Mariamne, at first thinking that she had been sent to Alexandrium for her own safety, was astute enough to figure out otherwise and made life miserable for her husband once she had put all the pieces together ("You think you have trouble at work? Just wait until you get home!") Taking advantage of the confusion, Herod's mother Cypros and sister Salome, neither of whom liked Mariamne anyway, reminded the king of certain earlier and continuing allegations of infidelity on her part. After a few long months of anything but *shalom habayit*, a fed-up (and blinded by passion) Herod had Mariamne executed. The wife Herod loved the most faced the sword "with an unshaken firmness of mind" (*Ant.* xv.7.1–5).

Herod never got over the deed. The immediate realization of what he had done made him physically ill and so he went to Samaria (Sebaste), the place of his wedding, for some peace and quiet among his

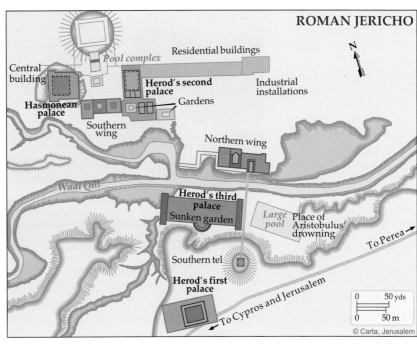

ROMAN JERICHO

Roman friends. Mariamne's mother Alexandra, true to form, kicked him when he was down. Smelling blood, she seized two fortresses in Jerusalem in his absence in an attempt to take back the throne for her beloved Hasmoneans by force. Herod mustered enough presence of mind to realize what was going on and had her executed: like daughter, like mother (*Ant.* xv.7.6–8). Many others, friend and foe alike, were caught in the backlash (*Ant.* xv.7.9–10). Politically, the kingdom was now secure. Magnificent. At least the royal executioners had job security.

In everything, Herod was a Colossus. He married big, killed big and built big. His megalomania is probably best preserved in the footprints of stone that marked his realm, many of which can still be seen by modern visitors to his domain. Everywhere Herod went, he left permanent images on the landscape: theaters, temples, palaces, baths, aqueducts, fortresses, hippodromes, gymnasia, and these only of the most magnificent kind. The Talmud cautions against constructing monuments to draw attention to oneself:

> It has been taught: Rabban Simeon b. Gamaliel says, "Do not make monuments for the righteous. Their teachings [or, deeds] are their memorial."
> (Jerusalem Talmud, *Sheqalim* 2:5)

For Herod, who only tolerated Jewish sensibilities, such advice was far too sentimental. His best deeds were those that glorified himself, his most enduring legacy magnificent works of stone. By them Herod sought to appease his insatiable ego, to secure his rule, to impress his boss in Rome, to provide his people with work and to entice their loyalty and devotion. But most of all, Herod built because he could. A man of his talents and ambitions would normally expend energy on the battlefield, but since

The highest peak on the edge of the limestone cliff above Herod's palace at Jericho commands a view of the entire southern Jordan Valley. Line of sight from the top takes in a large portion of the Judean Wilderness, the northern end of the Dead Sea and the rise into Transjordan. The real value of the fortress that both the Hasmoneans and Herod built on top, however, was to control the palaces of Jericho and the road ascending to Jerusalem at its base (this was the line of the route between the two cities until the early 20th century A.D.). Herod named the place, "notable for its security and a place most pleasant to stay," Cypros, after his mother (Ant. xvi.5.2), perhaps the only woman in his life with whom he felt secure.

(*opposite page*) **Herodian Jerusalem.** *While Jerusalem received special attention by every member of the Herodian family who ruled over the city, the architectural footprint of Herod the Great on its urban landscape was the most enduring. Our knowledge of the shape and character of Herodian Jerusalem comes partly from first-century* A.D. *written sources such as Josephus and the New Testament, partly from archaeology (Jerusalem is the most intensively excavated living city on earth) and partly from geographical and logical common sense. Still, many gaps in our understanding remain. What is known about first-century Jerusalem reveals a city with a complex and expensive infrastructure, a place that was attractive to see and pleasant to call home.*

The so-called "Straight Joint" in the eastern wall of the Temple Mount separates masonry that is clearly Herodian to its left (south) from rougher stones on the right (north). Although scholars debate the date of the stones on the right, they most likely formed a portion of the retaining wall of a Hasmonean Temple Mount. Herod enlarged the Hasmonean platform by constructing extensions to the south, west and north, provided a series of stairways, gates and tunnels as access points, and completely rebuilt the Temple on top.

Herod's architectural pièce de résistance *was the Temple in Jerusalem, a thorough remodeling of Zerubbabel's Temple into a structure that not only matched Herod's own sense of grandiose size, but his taste for Roman building forms. The Temple is best represented in stone today by the scale model built for Jerusalem's Holyland Hotel, recently moved to the grounds of the Israel Museum. Behind its expansive colonnaded courtyard rises the Antonia Fortress, garrison spot for imperial troops who kept an eye on temple proceedings and who could easily respond to any attempt of anti-Roman sedition anywhere in the city—especially in the courtyard below.*

he was confined to a rather small plot of land by Caesar, Herod turned his efforts inward and made Judea a showplace for the best and brightest architects he could find to do their finest work. And it wasn't enough just to build—Herod had to build in ways never even considered before in his part of the world. Part was engineering; part was location. Herod moved mountains; he defied gravity; he made oases in the desert and conquered the currents of the sea. Of course, he reasoned, everyone in his kingdom would fall in love with him—or at least hold him in reverential awe—as they participated vicariously in the splendor due his name (cf. *Ant.* xv.9.5). As usual, Josephus said it best:

> [Herod desired most to] publicly demonstrate the generosity of his soul, for in all his undertakings he was ambitious to do only things that exceeded things of the same kind that had been done before. It is related that Caesar and [Marcus] Agrippa often said that the dominions of Herod were too little for the greatness of his soul, and that he deserved to have all the kingdoms of Syria and Egypt as well.
>
> (*Ant.* xvi.5.1)

Given the chance, what would Herod have built in the shadow of the pyramids?

Herod became a master at transferring the symbols of his reign into stone, with the idea that by the time eyewitness descriptions of what he had accomplished filtered back to the villages and fields of Judea and Galilee and then all the way to Rome, the mental pictures they created would be even greater than the reality itself. And what better image was there to portray than that Herod had one-upped the Creator?

The list of Herod's building projects is long. Although he built actively throughout his reign, his most impressive projects were undertaken between 25 and 14 B.C., after his kingdom was secure and while he still had ample energy to expend in the effort. While the extant remains of Herod's works are impressive enough yet today, equally so was the vision to build in the first place (the blueprint sessions

must have been fascinating) and the administrative skill that it took to coordinate the planning, supply and implementation of not just one, but several projects at the same time. The sheer magnitude of it all, so much in such a short time, was unparalleled for Judea and, pound for pound, probably hasn't been matched to this day.

It is difficult to say which of Herod's building projects was the greatest, although his makeover of Jerusalem could rightly claim the honor. Here Herod constructed what was likely his largest palace (on the western side of today's Armenian Quarter in the Old City) and encircled it with ramparts and towers. He also built a theater and amphitheater in Jerusalem (archaeological remains have yet to be found) and the massive Antonia Fortress to guard the city's vulnerable northern approaches and overlook the Temple esplanade (*Ant.* xv.8.1,5). But Herod's most ambitious project in Jerusalem was the Temple Mount complex. Herod rebuilt the Temple—enlarged and glorified it—in a way that was faithful to its ancient plan but now with a decidedly Roman look (it had been a rather pedestrian structure since being rebuilt by Zerubbabel in the late sixth century B.C.; cf. Hag 2:3). When finished the Temple, with its Royal Stoa, vast columned courtyard and huge retaining wall, must have been one of the wonders of the ancient Roman world (*Ant.* xv.11.3–7).

Equally impressive was the method by which Herod was able to convince the Jewish temple authorities to allow him to alter their sacred space. (When it comes to moving holy stones in the Middle East, everyone assumes pretext and subterfuge.) The Jews knew that Herod was building temples to the divine Caesar Augustus elsewhere—what was to keep him from profaning their Temple under the guise of repairs? Josephus tells us that Herod first swayed them over with an eloquent speech about the honor due the Jewish nation and a return to the glory days of Solomon when the Temple had first stood in splendor, then arranged for priests to be trained in the necessary skills of construction so that the Holy Place would not be desecrated by those forbidden to

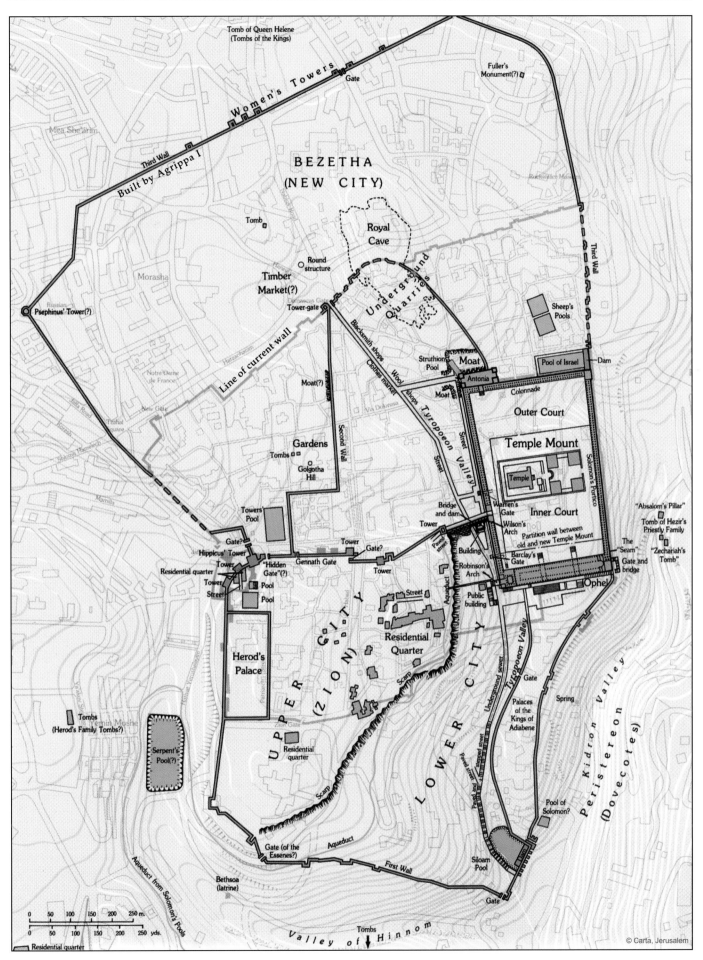

Tomb of Queen Helene
(Tombs of the Kings)

Women's Towers

Gate

Fuller's
Monument(?)

Third Wall
Built by Agrippa I

Mea Sheʿarim

Third Wall

B E Z E T H A
(NEW CITY)

Tomb

Royal
Cave

Morasha

Round
structure

Underground
Quarries

Psephinus' Tower(?)

Timber
Market(?)

Damascus Gate
Tower-gate

Sheep's
Pools

Notre Dame
de France

Line of current wall

Moat(?)

Blacksmith shops

Clothes market

Wool shops

Struthion
Pool

Moat

Antonia

Moat

Pool of Israel

Dam

New Gate

Via Dolorosa

Tyropoeon Valley

Street

Colonnade

Outer Court

Gardens

Second Wall

Tombs

Golgotha
Hill

Temple Mount

Temple

Solomon's Portico

"Absalom's Pillar"

Tomb of Hezir's
Priestly Family

Towers'
Pool

Bridge
and dam

Tower

Warren's
Gate

Wilson's
Arch

Inner Court

Partition wall between
old and new Temple Mount

"Zechariah's
Tomb"

Gate?

Hippicus' Tower

Tower

Residential quarter

Tower
Street

"Hidden
Gate"(?)

Gennath Gate

Gate?

Tower

Pool

Pool

Paved street

Building

Barclay's
Gate

Robinson's
Arch

Public
building

The
"Seam"

Gate and
bridge

Ophel

U P P E R   C I T Y

Street

Residential
Quarter

Aqueduct

Herod's
Palace

(
Z
I
O
N
)

Scarp

Underground sewer

Gate

Palaces
of the
Kings of
Adiabene

Spring

Tombs
(Herod's Family Tombs?)

Yemin Moshe

Residential
quarter

Scarp

L O W E R   C I T Y

Tyropoeon Valley

Paved and stepped street

Kidron Valley

Peristereon
(Dovecotes)

Serpent's
Pool(?)

Pool of
Solomon?

Gate (of the
Essenes?)

Aqueduct

First Wall

Siloam
Pool

Aqueduct from Solomon's Pools

Bethsoa
(latrine)

Gate

0   50   100   150   200   250 m.

0   50   100   150   200   250 yds.

Tombs

V a l l e y   o f   H i n n o m

© Carta, Jerusalem

Residential quarter

Herod's roots were in the Idumean desert, but his heart tug faced the sea. Of his many palaces, the one that perhaps best represented his world view was in Caesarea. Here Herod built a palace on a promontory point of calcified sandstone that jutted into the Mediterranean. The palace boasted dining halls, living quarters, an audience hall and ritual baths (for guests who wanted to keep kosher) *surrounding a freshwater pool. A semicircular colonnaded terrace faced the sea at the palace's Rome-ward end. Here were Herod's private, and probably favorite, quarters. Facing the sea and with his back toward Jerusalem, it was in this palace that Herod was all he could be.*

enter by Jewish law. Herod's plan worked: the Jews' desire for a beautiful building overrode their initial fears of what could happen if their king got his dirty little hands on it (*Ant. xv.11.1–2*), and in the end it was a cooperative effort.

In non-Jewish areas of his realm Herod founded two thoroughly Hellenistic cities, Caesarea Maritima and Sebaste, naming them after his patron in Rome (Sebaste is Greek for Augustus). Herod wanted a single, new port to serve the seaward needs of his kingdom, and a location on the northern end of the Sharon Plain provided fairly direct land access to both Galilee, Samaria and Judea. Well planned and developed, Caesarea boasted a theater, amphitheater and hippodrome, a magnificent royal palace on the sea, a temple dedicated to Augustus, an aqueduct and, most importantly, a harbor projecting far into the Mediterranean held together by underwater concrete, a building material that Herod introduced to the region. Caesarea became the administrative seat of the province and, oriented as it was to the call of the sea, Herod's favorite place to be (*Ant. xviii.3.1*).

Herod built Sebaste on the remains of the ancient Israelite capital Samaria. Here veteran soldiers loyal to Herod's cause lived out their lives in manorial ease. The grandest edifice in Sebaste was a great white temple for Augustus built on the acropolis of the city. Boats sailing into the harbor of Caesarea could see the temple of Sebaste nestled amidst the inland hills of Samaria, gleaming in the bright Levantine sun over the skyline of Herod's port city.

(above) Rome's footprint implanted itself deeply in the sand of Caesarea Maritima on the coastline of the Sharon Plain, midway between Judea and Galilee. Among the treadmarks left in the sand of Caesarea are remains of a hippodrome (or, circus) that Herod laid out parallel to the shore. Chariot races followed a long U-shaped track with 1,000-foot runs to encourage speed and a tight bend for quick crack-ups. Up to 5,000 spectators sat in 12 tiers of seats, waiting for accidents to happen. As far as conservative Jews in Jerusalem were concerned, the entire city was an accident waiting to happen. The Great Revolt began in Caesarea in A.D. 66.

The economic advantages of these two cities aside, nothing was lost on image: a visitor from Rome arriving in Herod's domains was made to feel from the start right at home. The Roman eagle had landed (*Ant. xv.8.5, xv.9.6; War i.21.5*).

Herod's Idumean blood gave him a special affinity for the desert and it was there, in and along the sides of the Rift Valley, that Herod erected a string of luxurious palace fortresses. Each was an oasis of water and green in a most inhospitable landscape. Most (with the exception of Herodium and possibly Masada) were elaborate modifications of earlier Hasmonean palaces. Masada was the most dramatic, in part for location, in part for the sheer impossibility of its construction. The palace fortresses at Machaerus, Hyrcania, Alexandrium, Herodium and Cypros (the last named in memory of Herod's dear mama—who said he wasn't sentimental?) were all variations on a theme. Each was perched high on a prominent rounded mountaintop, each controlled

Lying on the geological seam that separates the limestone hill country of Judea from the chalky wilderness to the east, the volcano-shaped mountain of Herodium dominates the skyline southeast of Jerusalem. To create Herodium, Herod's workers artificially raised the hill to its present height, partly to protect and partly to camouflage the luxurious palace fortress within. A colonnaded garden, banqueting hall, full bath complex and guest suites are hidden in the mountain's core. Herod ran a spur line from the aqueduct serving the Temple Mount to Herodium where it filled a large pool at its base, shown here. There Herod could float to an island gazebo and lounge in the shade while the rest of the kingdom baked under his political sun. Here Herod lived in splendor, and here he was buried. His tomb has only recently been located.

Herod's most celebrated desert fortress was built on the top of the sheer-faced table rock mountain, Masada. Even without taking into account the difficulty of the climb to the top (the drop on the right reaches 1,200 feet), reaching Masada from Jerusalem was an exercise in persistence and determination. With less than one inch of rainfall in the region per year—and that sporadic at best—Herod's workmen created a walled compound that boasted baths (of both the ritual and recreational kind), a swimming pool, and a million-gallon cistern in addition to the requisite suites, storehouses, towers and workrooms. Herod likely built and furnished Masada as his refuge of last resort. It served this purpose for Jewish zealots during the Great Revolt as well.

an important juncture or highway on the eastern approaches to Jerusalem, each had columns, courtyards and baths, and each was a place for Herod to enjoy the pleasures of Rome without ever leaving home. On a more practical level, these fortresses allowed Herod to keep a lid on the unrest that he was never quite able to suppress, and provide places for a quick get-away should things again turn sour (*Ant.* xv.9.4–5, xvi.2.1, xvi.5.1–2; *War* i.21.9, vii.6.2, vii.8.3–4).

The palace complex at Jericho, straddling the Wadi Qilt as it exits the limestone cliffs just north of the Dead Sea, perhaps marked the epitome of Herod's royal ease. Here the king could escape the winter chill of Jerusalem and banquet in decadent splendor amid pools, fountains, baths, gardens and columned courtyards, oblivious to the drowned ghost of Aristobulus nearby (*War* i.21.4, ii.4.2). The opulence of Herod's Jericho, which controlled the world's supply of balsam (a soft tree grown at Engedi used for medicine and spice) attracted both rich opportunists (cf. Lk 19:1–8) and the desperately poor (cf. Lk 18:35–43).

Although these are the best known of Herod's building projects, Josephus mentions a number of others both at home and abroad. These include the harbor of Anthedon south of Gaza; the garden city of Antipatris at the headwaters of the Yarkon springs (near modern Tel Aviv); the royal estate at Phasaelis north of Jericho; palaces and fortresses east of the Dead Sea at Heshbon and Haramtha, and possibly at Sepphoris in Galilee; and two cities for retired soldiers (one on Mt. Carmel at modern Geva Haparashim, the other, Biethura, on the Golan; *Ant.* xvi.5.2, xvii.2.1). Remains of a temple at Panias have been uncovered in a setting that bears strong resemblance to Josephus' description of the temple Herod built to the divine Caesar in the area (*Ant.* xv.10.3), although some archaeologists have identified Herod's "Augusteum" with temple remains at nearby Omrit. Ironically, the Herodian structure that is best preserved today, the edifice above the Tomb of the Pa-

triarchs at Hebron, is not mentioned by Josephus at all. Herod was also active funding temples, theaters, gymnasia and other centers of Roman cultural life throughout the eastern Mediterranean world, including in Ptolemais, Tyre, Sidon, Berytus (Beirut), Damascus, Antioch, Rhodes, and Nicopolis in western Greece (*Ant.* xvi.5.3; *War* i.21.11). And even though he knew that it broke Jewish custom and law, Herod introduced the Quinquennial Games to his kingdom, celebrated in honor of Caesar every five years with full Greco-Roman sport (*Ant.* xv.8.1, xvi.5.1).

When enough of Herod's building projects were completed to show them off properly, General Marcus Agrippa, Octavian's son-in-law and hero of the Battle of Actium, paid a visit to Judea. Giddy with excitement, Herod held nothing back that might please his honored guest, providing him with "all sorts of the best and most costly dainties." (A Latin inscription found at Masada dated to 19 B.C. tells of a special shipment of fine wine from southern Italy—the empire's best vineyards—consigned to the storehouses of Masada for Herod, *Regi Herodi Iudaic.*) It wouldn't do for Marcus Agrippa to come all this way just to eat *felafel*. Agrippa visited Caesarea, Sebaste and Jerusalem (where he offered sacrifices in the Temple; cf. Acts 21:28), as well as the desert fortress at Alexandrium, Hyrcania and Herodium (*Ant.* xvi.2.1). He left fully satisfied with Herod's good work. But when Marcus Agrippa was gone and Herod entertained Jews, the king was careful to make at least an outward showing of keeping *kosher*. No need to offend needlessly.

Herod banked his legacy on his building. The Jews certainly appreciated their new Temple and even had a say in the planning stages:

> It has been taught: He who has not seen the temple of Herod has never seen a beautiful building. Of what did he build it? Rabbah said: of yellow and white marble [i.e., hard limestone]. Some say, of blue, yellow and white marble. Alternate rows [of the stones]

Two aqueducts supplied the freshwater needs of the population of Caesarea. A high-level aqueduct, raised and leveled by a long row of arches, brought drinking water from springs on the southern slopes of Mt. Carmel more than 6 miles away. The low-level aqueduct shown here, running on ground level, drew water for irrigation from the Crocodile River (Nahal Tanninim) 3 miles to the north. While there is a debate about who was the first to construct these aqueducts, it is likely that both served Herod's Caesarea.

The Temple precincts needed lots of water, more than the annual rainfall of Jerusalem could provide. At least by the time of Herod and probably as early as the Hasmonean kingdom a series of aqueducts were hewn in bedrock to carry water from the hills of Hebron to the Temple Mount. Meandering around the curve of hills, the water channel, its covering stones now gone, followed the natural gradient along its 45-mile course. Three large storage pools near Artas south of Bethlehem, anachronistically labeled "Solomon's Pools," stored water for the journey north.

projected so as to leave a place for mortar. He originally intended to cover it with gold, but the Rabbis advised him not to, since it was more beautiful as it was, looking like the waves of the sea.

(Babylonian Talmud, *Baba Bathra* 4a)

They certainly took a measure of pride in Herod's other building projects as well, especially those in Jerusalem, and enjoyed the new ambiance of the city. The elevated portion of Jerusalem adjacent to Herod's palace, for instance, contained many spacious mansions, finely decorated and furnished, some of which no doubt belonged to Herod's special friends (e.g., the Herodians), while others were the homes of high-ranking priests. Herod enjoyed a certain measure of support among the Sadducees, the sophisticated urban priests who were more likely to benefit from ties to the Roman world than were the more conservative village-based Pharisees, and many must have enjoyed living between the shadows of Herod's palace and the Temple. Yet Josephus was probably not far from the mark when he explained why, in spite of Herod's magnificence, the Jews never quite accepted him as their king. Herod built a Temple to the LORD and cities in honor of Caesar; why, Herod wondered, wouldn't the Jews give similar honor to *him*?

After giving the most excellent present he could make to another, Herod discovered the inclination to have the like presented to himself. But the Jewish nation is by their law a stranger to all such things, and accustomed to prefer righteousness to glory. It is for this reason that that nation was not agreeable to him, because it was beyond their ability to flatter the king's ambition with statues or temples or any other such performances.

(Ant. xvi.5.4)

Herod and the Jews (with the exception of the Herodian-type minority) were simply moving along non-intersecting lines. They would never meet.

Nor did they really want to. Herod was one of Rome's client kings and his job description was short: keep a lid on things and send money. All empires, ancient as well as modern, are driven by

revenue: conquer the most fertile lands; control the most lucrative routes; funnel the revenue, in this case, to Rome. The tax burden on the outlying client kingdoms was excessive. Caesar needed his cut; local kings wanted theirs; so did those who patrolled the lower levels of society to enforce the will of every greedy pocket above. Over ninety percent of the people of Herod's realm were peasants—grunts—near-commodities themselves—the multitude who toiled for the benefit of the elite few in whose hands the resources rested. Farming Herod's fields or building Herod's buildings may have kept food on the table, but the prospects for an easy life remained dim. By the time Herod died the economy of Judea was exhausted and the backs of the people on which it rested were nearly broken. Again Josephus, describing the situation as it was reported to him early on around 20 B.C., before the cumulative weight of the system had taken effect:

It was at this time that Herod [temporarily] remitted to the people of his kingdom a third part of their taxes, under the pretext of letting them recover from a period of lack of crops, but really for the more important purpose of getting back the goodwill of those who were disaffected. For they resented his carrying out of such arrangements as seemed to them to mean the dissolution of their religion and the disappearance of their customs. And these matters were discussed by all of them, for they were always being provoked and disturbed. Herod, however, gave the most careful attention to this situation, taking away any opportunities they might have [for agitation] and instructing them to apply themselves at all times to their work. No meeting of citizens was permitted, nor were walking together or being together permitted, and all their movements were observed. Those who were caught were punished severely, and many were taken, either openly or secretly, to the fortress of Hyrcania and there put to death. Both in the city and on the open roads there were men who spied upon those who met together. And they say that even Herod himself did not neglect to play

(left) Jerusalem's citadel, a walled castle just inside Jaffa Gate on the highest, western part of the Old City, is largely a medieval structure today. An imposing square tower sits astride its northeastern corner, clearly visible from both inside and outside the citadel. Since medieval times this tower has been popularly called "David's Tower," although the stonework in the lower section is clearly Herodian. Herod built his lavish Jerusalem palace in the area, guarded on the northern side, according to Josephus, by three towers: one named after his favorite wife Mariamne, a second in honor of his friend Hippicus and the third for his brother Phasael (War v.4.3). Scholars identify "David's Tower," shown in the back corner of the Citadel courtyard here, as that of either Hippicus or Phasael. Remains of earlier Hasmonean and Hellenistic monumental structures were also found in the area.

a part in this, but would often put on the dress of a private citizen and mingle with the crowds by night so as to get an idea of how they felt about his rule. Those who obstinately refused to go along with his practices he persecuted in all kinds of ways. As for the rest of the populace, he demanded that they submit to taking an oath of loyalty, and he compelled them to make a sworn declaration that they would maintain a friendly attitude to his rule. Now most of the people yielded to his demand out of complaisance or fear, but those who showed some spirit and objected to compulsion he got rid of by every possible means. (Ant. xv.10.4)

To make matters worse the masses didn't get a lot of sympathy from the Jewish aristocracy either. Once a peasant, always a peasant, and the educated, high-society upper court labeled the ninety percent on whose back the country ran *am ha-aretz*, "people of the land," uneducated, poor, ignorant commoners, with nothing to say or contribute to the real workings of life (cf. Jn 7:40). Ostracized politically, culturally and economically by Roman and Jewish aristocrats alike, the multitude groaned for a real king, one of their own who, like David, would come from common stock to rule with justice and righteousness.

As Herod aged the intrigue between rival factions for his throne heated up. Herod's favorite sons, Alexander and Aristobulus (IV), born to his favorite wife Mariamne I, were his apparent heirs. While still young Herod sent them to Rome for proper schooling in the ways of the empire. The boys returned to Judea in 17 B.C., when Herod's kingdom was at the height of its glory (Ant. xvi.1.2). But it was not to be a smooth transition. Alexander and Aristobulus developed an obnoxious habit of flaunting their Hasmonean bloodline and Herod's sister, Salome, a rival to all things Mariamne, wanted her own son to succeed Herod instead. Salome began the rumor (perhaps true) that Alexander and Aristobulus were intent on avenging their mother's death (Ant. xvi.3.1). In 14 B.C. Herod made Antipater (III), son of his first wife Doris, sole heir to the throne but two years later, having been reconciled to the sons that he loved, appointed all three joint-heirs. It wasn't going to work. The older that Herod grew, the more paranoid he became (and justifiably so). The crazed passion he felt for Alexander and Aristobulus mirrored that which had killed their mother, and the result was the same. In 7 B.C. Herod had his golden boys strangled in Sebaste, where he had married Mariamne three decades before, then buried them in the Hasmonean tomb at Alexandrium (Ant. xvi.3.3–4.6, xvi.10:6–11:7). Judging from Josephus' lengthy ramblings trying to rationalize how Herod could possibly have done such a thing to his own sons, "who were handsome, greatly admired by others and no way deficient in their conduct," the world must have stopped in dis-

Herod was the first to bring the art of mosaics to the Holy Land. This mosaic, found in the hallway leading to the bathroom of Masada's large Western Palace, and another, with an even more intricate design found just inside the rear entrance of the palace nearby, are as beautiful as the mosaics of palaces of Herodian Jerusalem. Mosaics were already widespread in other parts of the Roman world by this time and typically featured human and animal figures. Herod was careful to depict only Jewish motifs and geometric designs on his so as not to needlessly offend those who tried to keep the Second Commandment. He didn't care so much about the Sixth.

belief, then recoiled in horror (Ant. xvi.11.8). Again Antipater was named sole heir, but by now he was too impatient to wait for the throne. Twice Herod uncovered plots against his life and after the second, in 4 B.C., had Antipater executed (Ant. xvii.2.4–7.1). Deathly ill, the king himself had only five days to live. Henry VIII was an amateur.

Likely only a few months before, magi from the east came to Jerusalem and announced that they were looking for the one "born king of the Jews" (Mt 2:1–2). While the event is not mentioned in any first-century documents outside of the Gospel of Matthew, it rings entirely true to the way Herod was portrayed by Josephus. Here was Herod at the end of his life—certainly he knew he was dying—and rather than enjoying the adulations of a faithful populace for a job well done he was hated, maligned, feared and attacked, even by his own sons. Thirty-six years before, Herod had fled for his life before an invading army of Parthians who set up Antigonus the Hasmonean as the rightful king of Judea; now, after years of struggle to marry, kill and build his way to legitimacy, easterners were back looking for someone born to the kingdom. Still silver-tongued and sly, Herod tried to trick the magi into turning the babe over to him; but when he was tricked instead, Herod did the only thing the prior four decades of life had taught him to do—kill everyone in sight who could possibly fit the description of king (Mt 2:3–18).

In the early fifth century A.D., the Roman philosopher Macrobius commented on the purported reaction of Caesar Augustus to Herod's paranoia:

When [Augustus] heard that the king's own son was among the boys under the two years of age in Syria [i.e., Judea] whom Herod the king of the Jews had ordered to be put to death, he exclaimed: "I'd rather be Herod's pig (hus) than Herod's son (huios)."
(Macrobius, Saturnalia ii.4.11)

Herod, cautious of Jewish sensibilities, at least would never kill a pig. But Macrobius' testimony also includes a clear allusion to the Slaughter of the Innocents in Matthew 2, the only time Herod the Great is mentioned in the Bible. Whether Macrobius confused Herod's Antipater with one of the

Herod the Great had a thing for kids—and it wasn't good. Between his own sons, the children of Bethlehem and who knows how many others caught in the routine battles and purges of his reign, the lives of many innocent children were lost. These two kids (the author's) are content not to belong to the Herodian bloodline as they rest after a long hike to the top of Hyrcania, Herod's desert fortress deep in the Judean Wilderness. Enjoy the view, not the man who made it possible.

© Carta, Jerusalem

The Division of Herod's Kingdom, 4 B.C.–A.D. 6.
When Herod died his kingdom was divided between his three surviving sons. Each portion contained good agricultural land and access to important trade routes. Archelaus received the historic core, which included cities stridently conservative (Jerusalem) and unabashedly liberal (such as Caesarea). It proved to be too difficult for a young man who was neither wise nor judiciously strong to govern, and Archelaus could hold on for only ten years. Life was simpler, perhaps, in the territories inherited by Antipas and Philip, and these sons of Herod enjoyed long reigns.

children of Bethlehem or posited another son of Herod otherwise unknown to history is immaterial. Herod's reputation as a butcher was sealed and has provided easy typecasting ever since for writers from Chaucer to Shakespeare to Browning and Shaw who sought to reference Herod as the epitome of human evil while portraying villains in their own works. But to be fair, even though Herod gets the bad rap, his actions were typical of many of his contemporaries and of a bloody sequence of despots who have stained the course of history ever since.

In his prime, Herod was a man of great prowess and physical strength, one who could out-ride, out-hunt and out-fight everyone else, whose javelins and arrows always found their mark—or so Josephus would like his readers to believe (*War* i.21.13). This was also the reputation of Pharaoh Amenhotep II and Assyria's Ashurbanipal—and King Arthur. But by the end, Herod was a miserable shell of his former self, whose physical ailments matched the torment of his mind and soul. Herod's guts rotted away within his body, producing an unbearable stench and worms, and Josephus, never missing a beat, explained this final illness as God's punishment on the king's rotted soul (*Ant.* xvii.6.5). In a final attempt for relief Herod's attendants bathed him in the hot springs of Callirrhoe on the eastern shore of the Dead Sea. Slightly revived, Herod lived just long enough to be hauled up to Jericho where he gave orders to execute Antipater, then follow his son into

the grave. It was 4 B.C.; Herod was not quite seventy years old. He was buried at Herodium with a great show of pomp arranged by his newest heir-apparent, Archelaus, to the feigned sadness of a few and the relief of many (*Ant.* xvii.7.1–8.3). Josephus had some final words on the matter:

> [Herod was] a man who showed great barbarity equally toward all, who was a slave to his passions and too high up to consider what was the right thing to do. Yet he was favored by fortune as much as any one ever was, for though he was a commoner, he became king....But through it all, in my opinion, he was very unfortunate. (*Ant.* xvii.8.1)

When he had only months to live, Herod named sixteen-year-old Antipas, his youngest son born to Malthace the Samaritan, as sole heir instead of Antipater. Then, the day he executed Antipater, Herod designated Antipas' eighteen-year-old brother Archelaus as heir instead, bumping Antipas down to the lesser position of tetrarch of Galilee and Perea. At the same time Herod appointed his son Philip, born to Cleopatra of Jerusalem, tetrarch of Gaulanitis (*Ant.* xvii.6.1, xvii.8.1). All three were young and inexperienced, though raised by a private tutor in Rome (*Ant.* xvii.1.3) and none carried Hasmonean blood.

Archelaus promised to be more tolerant than his father but didn't get off to a very good start. During his first Passover—the Jewish freedom festival when expectations for political independence typically ran high—Archelaus sent troops and cavalry onto the Temple Mount to quell an anti-government riot, massacring about three thousand Jewish pilgrims in the process (even Herod hadn't done *that*). He then took off for Rome to receive Caesar's formal approval of kingship (*Ant.* xvii.8.4–9.3). Antipas followed his brother to Rome to argue that their father was not of sound mind and body when he made his last will and testament and that he, not Archelaus, was the rightful king. Augustus, likely shaking his head in exasperation ("What am I going to *do* with these boys?!"), compromised. Philip and Antipas remained tetrarchs of their respective territories but Archelaus would only be ethnarch of Judea, Idumea and Samaria, with the promise that if he behaved himself, he would be promoted to king (*Ant.* xvii.9.5–6, xvii.11.1–4). He didn't—and wasn't.

As soon as Archelaus had left for Rome widespread revolt broke out across the province, from Jerusalem and Judea to Perea and Galilee. Many soldiers and slaves who had served Herod joined the rebellion. Some rioted in Jerusalem during the Festival of Shavuot (Pentecost), others burned the royal palace at Jericho and villages here and there. The revolt spread without coordination or unified leadership, giving eschatological and messianic expression to an undercurrent of dissatisfaction that had long afflicted the peasantry, especially in Galilee. Philip, who hadn't gone to Rome with his brothers, was largely ineffective in taking care of the mess and so Varus, the Roman governor of Syria, had to intervene. Varus put out what fires he could and started a few of his own, burning Sepphoris, the capital of Galilee, where the armory had been seized by the rebels, and Emmaus on the road to Jerusalem. Thousands were enslaved in a general roundup of perpetrators, and two thousand of the most troublesome were crucified. Archelaus finished the job when he returned, then continued his reign of terror and oppression for the next ten years, treating both Jews and Samaritans "barbarously and tyrannically" (Ant. xvii.10.1–10; cf. Ant. xvii.13.2). It is no wonder that Mary and Joseph, upon hearing that Archelaus reigned in Judea in the place of his father, preferred to settle in Galilee where Antipas was beginning his rule with a more even hand (Mt 2:22–23).

Things came to a head in A.D. 6 when the Jews and Samaritans, who usually didn't agree on much, brought a common complaint to Augustus against the excesses of Archelaus. Antipas and Philip joined the charge. Much to everyone's relief Augustus fired Archelaus and banished him to Gaul (the Roman equivalent of Siberia), then confiscated his assets. Heeding a Jewish delegation that begged Augustus not to replace Archelaus with another member of the Herodian line, the emperor reduced Judea to an imperial province and placed it under the direct Roman rule of military prefects and procurators (Ant. xvii.13.1–5; War ii.7.3–8.1).

Twenty-five years later, after Archelaus was long gone but not yet forgotten, Jesus told a parable about a certain nobleman who went to a distant country to receive a kingdom for himself, then returned to reward those who were loyal to him and punish those who weren't. "I was afraid of you because you are an exacting man," said one who had failed his responsibility. "You take up what you did not lay down and reap what you did not sow." The nobleman was incensed—not that his servant recognized him to be a hard overlord but because he wasn't willing to participate in the system: the poor work hard so that the rich can get richer. Then came the nobleman-now-king's pronouncement, full of royal prerogative and inequity (Lk 19:12–25):

> I tell you, everyone who already has will be given more, but to the one who has only a little, even that will be taken away from him. And as for these enemies of mine who did not want me to reign over them—bring them here and slay them in my presence! (Lk 19:26–27)

Jesus told this parable as he was ascending to Jerusalem for the last time, passing within the shadow of the royal palace in Jericho that Archelaus, a nobleman who had left to receive a kingdom, rebuilt more extravagantly than the burned palace of his

father (Ant. xvii.13.1). Another Passover was coming; the remnants of Archelaus' kingdom still adorned the road. On track to receive a very different kind of kingdom, Jesus climbed on, resolutely, to the cross.

Philip, in the meantime, had had a relatively peaceful reign as tetrarch over the northeastern portion of his father's kingdom: Gaulanitis, Auranitis, Trachonitis, Batanea, Panias and Iturea (Lk 3:1). Here were some of the best wheat fields in the Roman Empire as well as the most powerful springs in the Middle East, those forming the headwaters of the Jordan River. Demographically, Philip's territory was primarily gentile (Syrians and colonized Hellenists), although important Jewish communities thrived in Iturea and on the slopes of Gaulanitis above the northeastern shore of the Sea of Galilee (cf. War iii.3.5; Jn 1:44). Philip was a person "of moderation and quietness in the conduct of his life and government" (Ant. xviii.4.6), much to the relief of his subjects who had had enough of the Herodian excesses of his father and brothers, and they responded well to his rule. Philip was content with what Augustus had given him and governed efficiently and fairly with the help of a few trusted friends. He married his half-niece Salome, the same Salome whose dance was responsible for the death of John the Baptist (the Philip of that story was Salome's father; cf. Mt 14:1–12).

Philip built two magnificent cities around the remains of smaller sites, Bethsaida at the edge of the marshy alluvial plain just above the point where the

Herod's son Archelaus didn't reign long enough to leave a large footprint of stone in his land, but he did rebuild the palace at Jericho and constructed a new site—Josephus calls it a village—about seven miles north of Jericho named, of course, after himself (Ant. xvii.13.1, xviii.2.2). The region was known for its fine stands of date palms. Today the site of Archelais lies largely neglected, just east of the highway between Jericho and Beth-shean, with a few columns and bits of tumbledown walls overgrown with brush and weeds. Still, it's a fine stop for anyone wanting to poke around a bit....

Gaulanitis, part of the tetrarchy of Herod's son Philip, was a fertile land blessed by a thick layer of black basaltic soil. Its flatlands stretched eastward above the climb of what is today called the Golan Heights. A line of extinct volcanic cones, including this double cone, produced a strong lava flow far in the geologic past, and over the eons ample rainfall has eroded the pumice to a rich soil well suited for growing grain. This, and Egypt, were Rome's eastern breadbaskets, and Philip reaped a wealthy harvest every spring.

Nothing suited a Roman soul like running water, but Herod's land had precious little of this most essential commodity. In the north, though, in Philip's territory, water flowed in abundance. The most refreshing may have been the Banias stream, flowing from Mt. Hermon springs dedicated to Pan, the woodland god venerated throughout the Greco-Roman world. This was the vicinity of Caesarea Philippi, a Mediterranean-looking locale if there was one in these dry eastern lands. Philip inherited a special place, and reigned contentedly.

Jordan River dumps into the Sea of Galilee, and Caesarea Philippi at the foothills of Mount Hermon. Once likely the capital of the tenth-century B.C. kingdom of Geshur (cf. 2 Sam 3:3), Bethsaida's fortunes had fluctuated during the centuries since until Philip raised it to the status of a *polis*. Philip renamed the city Julias in honor of Livia-Julia, wife of Augustus and mother of Tiberius, a worthy namesake of an important city on the sea. (Tiberius had become emperor in A.D. 14 and three years later Antipas built a new city for him on the western side of the Sea of Galilee, within site of Bethsaida. It is likely that Philip and Antipas enjoyed a camaraderie of urban one-upmanship for their bosses back in Rome.) The status of a *polis* presupposes a certain level of building activity consistent with the new role that Bethsaida would play in the region (a theater, gymnasium, hippodrome, etc.), but few significant remains dating to the first century A.D. have been found at *et-Tell*, the generally accepted location of the city. In any case, Bethsaida maintained its character as a fishing center throughout the centuries and was home to several of Jesus' disciples, including Peter, Andrew, Philip (Jn 1:44) and, according to an early tradition, the sons of Zebedee James and John.

Philip also rebuilt Panias (modern Banias), a cultic site dedicated to the worship of the Greco-Roman nature god Pan. Here a powerful spring exited a large cave at the base of Mount Hermon, a delightful setting for those given to devotion of Pan and the divine Caesar, Augustus, whose temple Herod had built at the mouth of the cave. For Greeks and Romans familiar with the lavish scenery of the Mediterranean, this was a wonderful Rome-away-from-home on the dry eastern edge of the empire, where one could enjoy life to the fullest. Philip built extensively here and made Panias the capital of his tetrarchy, renaming it Caesarea (after Augustus) Philippi (after himself). It was a setting aptly suited for Jesus to first mention the church (Mt 16:13–19).

Josephus relates an anecdote involving Panias that hints that Philip was more of a "renaissance man" than a fighter. Curious about the source of the Jordan, Philip had chaff thrown into the Pool of Phiale (the volcanic cone of *Birkat Ram*) high on the southern slopes of Mount Hermon and supposedly saw it emerge in the Panias spring below. Because there is no underground channel connecting the two, his willing assistants must have planted the evidence so as not to disappoint their tetrarch (*War* iii.10.7).

Philip died in A.D. 34 after ruling for thirty-seven years and was buried at Bethsaida-Julias. He had no sons—perhaps this contributed to his peaceful reign!—and so Tiberius annexed his tetrarchy to the province of Syria. Tiberius allowed taxes that were collected after Philip's death to remain in the tetrarchy rather be pooled under the governor of Syria (*Ant.* xviii.4.6). In a time and place where heads of state routinely exercised the right to place excessive tax burdens on their subjects, Tiberius' concession to the people who lived under authority of Philip is perhaps the greatest testimony to the only Herodian who can be called benevolent.

Antipas, whose wings were clipped by Augustus, ruled over a largely Jewish population in Galilee and Perea. These were free-spirited lands with a history of open anti-Roman sentiment. But there was no armed rebellion during Antipas' reign, a tribute to his skills as a fair (relatively speaking) and able tetrarch. In order to encourage loyalty to Rome, Antipas rebuilt two cities as centers to disseminate Greco-Roman culture and life: Sepphoris in Galilee (the main work was done between A.D. 8 and 10) and Livias-Julias (Beth-ramatha) in Perea (completed in A.D. 13; *Ant.* xviii.2.1). After Augustus died Antipas also built a brand-new city on the western shore of the Sea of Galilee, laid out from the beginning as a *polis* and named it after the new emperor, Tiberius. By the time the initial construction of Tiberias was finished in A.D. 25, the city had replaced Sepphoris as the capital of Galilee. Tiberias was built in part on a cemetery, and Antipas had to offer economic incentives (free houses and land, and tax concessions) to Jews of the area in order to entice them to move there (*Ant.* xviii.2.3). It is clear that many of the Jews of Galilee were careful, in the face of the corridors of Hellenism that pushed into their land, to maintain a lifestyle of strict *Torah* observance that prohibited, for instance, living on land that was ritually unclean. The Gospels don't record any instances of Jesus visiting Tiberias in spite of his willingness to interact with people of a variety of backgrounds (cf. Jn 6:23) in the towns and villages of Galilee; perhaps he, too, was careful about not treading on ground profaned by the Romans—or perhaps the Gospel writers just preferred to emphasize Jesus' rural ministry. In the end, rather than sway the opinions of the people of Galilee to things Roman, these cities remained bulwarks of imperial domination, vehicles of exploitation and symbols of oppression that kept the embers of revolt alive.

Antipas was married to the daughter of the Nabatean king Aretas IV (perhaps the same Nabatean king responsible for the well-known tomb façade dubbed "the Treasury" at Petra). The Nabatean kingdom, which controlled the lucrative spice routes out of the Arabian Peninsula, was still politically independent of Rome, and it was in the best interests of Caesar to keep the Nabateans pacified to act as a buffer between Rome and the Parthians. Rome's direct control in the region ended at Perea, and so it is possible that Antipas was encouraged by Augustus to marry into the Nabatean royal family for matters of political expediency. In about the year A.D. 29, when Antipas was nearly fifty years old, he fell in love with his own niece Herodias, who was younger (and likely prettier) than his Nabatean queen. Marrying one's niece was not considered a problem, unless she was already married to one's half-brother at the time, which happened to be the case here. Herodias left her husband, Herod Philip, for Antipas (trading in a minor member of the royal family for a tetrarch had its advantages), and Antipas divorced his Nabatean queen for her. Royal marriages to family members are always sticky, especially so when powerful and jealous outsiders are insulted in the process. Daddy Aretas had been slapped in the face and vowed revenge (Ant. xviii.5.1). In the meantime John the Baptist, who like the prophet Elijah made a career of publicly denouncing perpetrators of unrighteousness in high places, called Herodias and Antipas on their actions. Antipas did what anyone in his position would do—he put John (considered to be one more source of insurrection) in prison at the desert fortress of Machaerus east of the Dead Sea. Antipas didn't dare execute him because of his popularity with the crowds. Herodias, however, didn't need to heed the same caution and, catching her new husband in an awkwardly weak moment during the fun of a raucous birthday banquet, pressed for John's execution. Antipas complied to save face (Ant. xviii.5.2; Mt 14:3–12; Mk 6:14–29; Lk 9:7–9).

As news of Jesus' miraculous powers began to spread throughout Galilee, Antipas (called Herod in the Gospel accounts) thought, likely sarcastically and mimicking the crowds, "This must be John the Baptist risen from the dead!" (Mt 14:2; cf. Mk 6:14–16; Lk 9:7–9). He scarcely had gotten rid of one popular agitator when another popped up in his place. Antipas wanted to personally meet Jesus (and put the squeeze on him), but Jesus left Galilee for Bethsaida in Philip's territory, out of reach (Lk 9:9–10). Later, as his Galilean ministry was nearing its end, Jesus called Antipas a "fox" (the common people, skeptical of trusting anything Herodian, would have enjoyed the image), and sent a message to the tetrarch that his, Jesus', ministry would continue in the direction and according to the timetable that he himself, not the power of Rome or anyone else, would set (Lk 13:31–35).

For nearly three years Jesus and Antipas moved in their respective spheres of influence, aware of each other by reputation and word of mouth but leaving each other alone (much like the relationship of Elijah and Ahab during Israel's great three-year drought; cf. 1 Kgs 18:1). They finally met after Jesus had been arrested, in the spring of perhaps A.D. 30 or 31. Antipas was in Jerusalem for the Passover, as was Pilate, prefect of Judea. The two maintained an uneasy relationship (Judea used to be the land of Antipas' brother Archelaus, and even though they had been rivals at least Archelaus was family). At one point Pilate, a rank foreigner, dared to kill

some Galilean pilgrims in Jerusalem, slaughtering them like the sacrifices they were presenting to God (Lk 13:1). Antipas was soured that Pilate would touch some of his subjects without first consulting him on the matter, but came when Pilate called him to interrogate Jesus. The two finally met; Antipas hoped to see some sign of Jesus' power, perhaps to be entertained, likely to finally have just cause to accuse him of insurrection. Antipas grilled Jesus mercilessly, with mixed doses of contempt and sarcasm; Jesus remained maddeningly silent. Although Antipas got nowhere with Jesus at least he was reconciled to Pilate, since by bringing Antipas into the affair Pilate had acknowledged the tetrarch's authority over Galilean matters (Lk 23:6–12).

Pilate was removed from office in A.D. 36 for gross negligence of duty, the same charges that had done in Archelaus. Aretas the Nabatean attacked and soundly defeated Antipas on the battlefield the same year. The next year Antipas' patron, Tiberius, died and was succeeded by Caligula. Caligula had an old friend in the Herodian dynasty, Agrippa I, brother of Herodias and both nephew and brother-in-law of Antipas. This was not good news for Antipas, though, because Agrippa was of the Hasmonean bloodline, a grandson of Mariamne I. Fed up with the ineffectiveness of direct Roman rule in Judea, Caligula decided to reinstall the Herodian dynasty with Agrippa I as king. Antipas of course went to Rome to object; if anyone deserved the title king it was him; he deserved to receive the unfulfilled promise of Augustus to Archelaus that kingship awaited years of faithful service. Agrippa meanwhile accused Antipas of collaborating with the Parthians (an accusation that was not without merit) and in A.D. 39 Caligula, anxious to place his own stamp on Judean affairs, banished Antipas to Gaul and installed Agrippa I as king. Herodias, who began her career as queen under scandal, loyally chose to follow her husband where, like Archelaus,

The façade of the "Treasury" at Petra is one of the most recognizable monuments from the ancient world, thanks in part to recent movie exposure. This magnificent structure, combining Greek, Roman, Egyptian and local Nabatean architectural and artistic motifs, is likely the front-piece of a royal tomb. Unfortunately, it comes without an identifying inscription. The most frequent suggestion is that this is the final resting place of the Nabatean king Aretas IV, based at least in part on logic—Nabatea's most prolific king deserved its most elaborate tomb. In any case, Aretas IV was the original father-in-law of Herod Antipas, whose tetrarch bordered Nabatea. Antipas disposed his Nabatean queen for Herodias, wife of his brother Philip, a move that failed on both geopolitical and moral grounds.

The Kingdom of Agrippa I,
A.D. 37–44. Agrippa's kingdom grew from the top down, north to south, as he quickly gathered up lands that had belonged to Philip, Antipas and Archelaus. Agrippa was not a military man—his conquests were in the political arena, and the territory that he controlled came as land grants from Caesar for friendships won and loyalties kept. Agrippa was a Herodian born of Hasmonean blood, and his reign was a short Golden Age for the Jews of his realm.

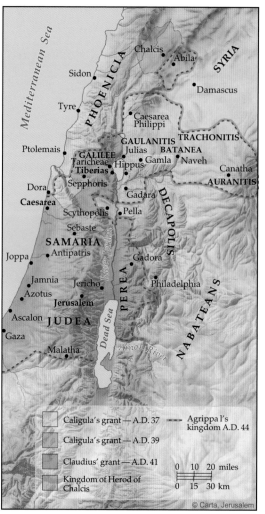

Caligula's grant — A.D. 37

Caligula's grant — A.D. 39

Claudius' grant — A.D. 41

Kingdom of Herod of Chalcis

Agrippa I's kingdom A.D. 44

0   10   20 miles
0   15   30 km

© Carta, Jerusalem

This coin of Agrippa I, minted in Caesarea Maritima toward the end of his reign, shows the king in full rounded profile, well-fed and healthy, with the prominent Herodian nose and head crowned with a diadem. The reverse, badly rubbed, depicts the goddess Tyche holding a rudder and a palm branch. Maritime themes were common on Hasmonean and Herodian coins—a far cry from symbols of Jewish Jerusalem.

they lived out their years in exile. Antipas was a tough sixty years old, having ruled for forty-three, the longest of any ruler of the Herodian period so far (*Ant.* xviii.5.1–7.2).

Agrippa I became king through the time-honored route of having friends in high places. As a grandson of Herod the Great, he was close enough to the throne to be a "royal" but far enough away to think that he would never inherit the crown. This was the perfect formula for producing an irresponsible playboy (a common pitfall of many a royal in the centuries since), and Agrippa wrote the dictionary definition of the term.

Agrippa was three years old in 7 B.C. when his grandfather killed his father Aristobulus, who was a bit of a pretty boy himself. Agrippa and his mother were sent to Rome under the protection of Caesar's household (cf. Phil 4:22). There Agrippa befriended the future emperor Claudius (they were the same age) and Drusus, son of Tiberius. The future king of Judea learned the life of leisure (i.e., debauchery) well, and ran up many debts with careless and extravagant living. It was a habit that was to plague him the rest of his life—spend too much on a good time; borrow to cover the debt; run from one creditor to the next. When his protector Drusus was poi-

soned in A.D. 23, Agrippa fled Rome for his Idumean home, leaving a tangled mess behind. Agrippa was about 33 years old at the time, the age of his grandfather when he had inherited his kingdom. Instead, the grandson was out of favor, nearly broke and bundled off to Malatha, a weather-beaten fortress on an unobtrusive rise in the stark landscape of the eastern biblical Negeb—a fate as far from the comforts and high life of Rome (or the glories of Herod's kingdom) as one could possibly imagine (*Ant.* xviii.6.1–4).

There Agrippa considered suicide—a Roman's stock solution for bad fortunes—but Antipas intervened, playing the part of the patronizing older uncle, and gave his nephew (and brother-in-law) an allowance and a bit part in the tetrarchy. Sometime before A.D. 30 Agrippa became inspector of markets (*agoranomos*) in Tiberias, a position that allowed him to regain a measure of honor while rubbing shoulders with the common folk of the land (*Ant.* xviii.6.2). He held this position during the time of Jesus' later Galilean ministry. The Tiberias market was the eastern terminus on the "sea to sea" international route linking the Sea of Galilee to the Mediterranean, and as such felt the heartbeat of Galilee's expanding economy. Tiberias' markets would have dealt in fish, among other commodities, and it is reasonable to suppose that fishermen from Capernaum to Bethsaida would have been familiar with its personnel (and inspector) and inner workings as they sought to sell the product of their daily toil around the lake.

Agrippa's position was inadequate to his lifestyle expectations and Antipas publicly mocked his inability to be anything but a leach on society. Sometime around A.D. 33 Agrippa left Antipas for the protection of the governor of Syria, then returned to Rome via Alexandria on borrowed money and borrowed time. There he befriended Caligula on the strength of flattery that Caligula would make a better emperor than Tiberius. When Caligula became Caesar in A.D. 37, he gave Agrippa the former tetrarchy of Philip (who had died in A.D. 34) and Chalcis (the tetrarchy of Lysanias) in the Beq'a Valley farther north, and bestowed on him the coveted title of king (*Ant.* xviii.6.4–10).

Like his grandfather Herod eight decades before, Agrippa returned to Palestine to receive his kingdom, but unlike the rest of the Herodians, this one had real Hasmonean blood flowing in his veins. Antipas refused to accept Agrippa's appointment—the title that had eluded him his entire life was given to that uncouth nephew of his in an instant!—and hurried to Rome to complain. Agrippa immediately showed his mettle by accusing Antipas of conspiracy against Rome and so Caligula not only stripped Antipas of his power but gave his lands to Agrippa, that wily snake (*Ant.* xviii.7.1–2). *Ouch.*

When Caligula was assassinated in A.D. 41 Agrippa, who happened to be in Rome at the time, helped his boyhood friend Claudius to the throne. Claudius rewarded Agrippa with control of Judea, Samaria and Caesarea (*Ant.* xix.4.1–5.3). King Agrippa I now ruled a territory as large as that of Herod the Great. Although he carried the official titles "Great King, Friend of Caesar, Pious and Friend of the Romans" (cf. Jn 19:12), Agrippa showed a genuine concern for the welfare of his Jewish subjects. He was careful to observe Jewish laws and traditions, was "generous without bound" (here Josephus used a kind phrase for Agrippa's unchanged spending habits) and generally liked by many:

> He was not at all like that Herod who reigned before him…but Agrippa's temper was mild and equally generous to all. He was humane to foreigners and made them aware of his liberality.…He loved to live continually in Jerusalem and was exactly careful to keep the laws of his country. (*Ant.* xix.7.3)

Even the Pharisees felt a camaraderie with their king. The Rabbis told a story of Agrippa's attendance in the synagogue. Upon accepting the honor of being asked to read from the *Torah*,

> King Agrippa received [the scroll] standing up and kept standing while he read, and the Sages praised him for it. And when he reached the portion that says "You may not put a foreigner over you who is not your brother" [Deut 17:15], [Agrippa's] eyes flowed with tears [because of his Idumean blood], but they called out to him, "You are our brother! You are our brother! You are our brother!" (*Sotah* 7.8)

Many Jews were getting used to Rome's rule by now (*Ant.* xix.6.3, xix.7.3, xix.8.3) and saw Agrippa's ties to the imperial family as a good thing. Friends in high places had the potential to win Caesar's goodwill, with all due rights and privileges in tow (cf. *Ant.* xix.5.3). The possibilities of having a Hasmonean on the throne with such ties posed some nice options (other than insurrection, for instance) for Jewish-Roman relations. In this respect Agrippa rose to the occasion presented to him, and Judea entered a kind of mini-Golden Age—the last the Jews experienced in ancient Judea.

Agrippa began a project to encircle the extramural suburbs north of Jerusalem with a strong wall (called by Josephus "the Third Wall"), thereby strengthening the vulnerable northern defenses of the city, but was stopped by Claudius who feared he was getting ready to revolt. Claudius' fears were probably not without warrant, as sentiments for the restoration of an independent Hasmonean kingdom ran high among some elements in the land (*Ant.* xix.7.2; *War* 2.11.6, 5.4.2).

In his zeal Agrippa also persecuted prominent leaders of the early Church, killing James the brother of John (he was the first apostolic martyr) and imprisoning Peter during the Passover festival (Acts 12:1–19).

In spite of the goodwill Agrippa enjoyed with his

Jewish subjects, he quickly became intoxicated with power and couldn't contain his flair for extravagant living now that he finally had the reason and resources to strut. Both Josephus and the writer of Acts note with relish that Agrippa's sudden and untimely demise coincided with a public show of pomp. As he made an appearance during a festival in Caesarea in A.D. 44, fully decked in a gleaming silver robe, gentiles in the city declared Agrippa to be a god. It was, in its context, perhaps the greatest show of devotion subjects could give to a king who aspired to something even greater than magnificence. For a brief moment Agrippa must have enjoyed the "promotion"; only Caesar, he knew, was the divine man-god, "but surely it won't hurt if my people want to bestow that honor on me, Caesar's friend, too," he apparently thought. But blasphemy is blasphemy, and the angel of the Lord struck Agrippa with a sudden case of the same kind of putrescence (worms and such) that had killed his grandfather. (Edgar Allan Poe would have taken keen interest in the case.) Agrippa died five days later and was genuinely mourned by Jews. Many gentiles, not used to a king who favored the Jews, rejoiced that Agrippa was gone (Acts 12:20–23; *Ant.* xix.8.1–9.2).

The 17-year-old heir-apparent, Agrippa II, was in the middle of his obligatory in-Rome schooling when his father died. Under the advice of counselors who held that this Agrippa was too young and inexperienced to keep such an important province in line, Claudius returned the land to direct-Roman rule (*Ant.* xix.9.2). But in A.D. 50 when Agrippa's uncle, Herod the king of Chalcis, died, Claudius appointed him successor. Three years later Agrippa II received

The upper (western) city of Jerusalem during the Hasmonean and Herodian periods was the place-of-choice for the upwardly mobile to live. Archaeological excavations have uncovered the remains of several palatial mansions nestled between Herod's palace and the Temple Mount—a high-rent district if there ever was one. Evidence of mosaic floors, frescoed walls, decorative ceilings and fine furniture and wares attest to the good life of Jerusalem's aristocrats, among them Sadducees, high priests and Herodians. Among the finds in these mansions are thin-walled plates and bowls, locally produced and painted with intricate floral designs to look like the more exquisite Nabatean-ware used farther east. Perhaps Herod himself, fan of the eastern desert as he was, helped popularize the style.

Although over half a mile of the length of the "Third Wall" of Jerusalem has been excavated, only bits and pieces are visible here and there among the infrastructure of modern Jerusalem a quarter-mile north of the Old City wall today. This piece of the wall, a large squared stone block enclosed within a small courtyard along a sidewalk near the American Consulate in East Jerusalem, is typical of the whole. Josephus reports that the wall, which nearly doubled the size of the city, was lined by ninety towers (War v.4.3). A project this size wasn't completed overnight; begun by Agrippa I sometime between A.D. 41 and 44, it was finished only on the eve of the Great Revolt two decades later.

The Kingdom of Agrippa II, A.D. 50–c. 100. *Agrippa II, the last of the Herodian kings, was able to exercise sovereignty over a portion of northern Transjordan only. Judea, Samaria and most of Galilee were governed by a series of Roman procurators, and there the authority of Agrippa II was limited to internal Jewish religious affairs. The procurators consulted Agrippa on matters of religious law and allowed him to control Temple finances. It was an arrangement that would not have suited any of his predecessors, but did allow Herodian lands to pass naturally to direct Roman rule when he died.*

Herod the Great brought special workmen from Italy to construct a portion of his palace in Jericho. Rather than build in mud brick (the normal local building material in the region), he imported a technique that was common in Italy but very rare in the East: constructing walls of poured concrete held in place by "forms" of stone called opus quadratum *(rectangular in shape) and* opus reticulatum *(diamond-shaped). The latter not only gave strength to the walls but allowed them to be constructed on curved lines. The completed walls were covered with lime plaster and frescoes so that the casual observer wouldn't know what was inside, though Herod did and probably bragged on the fine way his house was built to any guest who might care to listen.*

Although the territory governed by Agrippa II never included areas of large Jewish settlement, Claudius granted him the right—also given to his father—to control Temple finances and appoint high priests (*Ant.* xx.1.1–3). This was consistent with Rome's overall policy of allowing Jews a degree of sovereignty over internal religious affairs, whether or not a Jewish client king held political control over Jerusalem at the time. Later Rabbinic tradition remembered (or invented) discussions on matters of Jewish law between Agrippa and Eliezer ben Hyrcanus, an influential rabbi of the time (*Babylonian Talmud, Pesachim* 107b and *Sukkah* 27a). Agrippa occasionally stood in as Rome's advisor for religious affairs and was asked to get involved in a case brought against the Apostle Paul in Caesarea by some Jewish elders from Jerusalem. The new procurator, Festus, asked Agrippa to determine whether or not Paul had committed a capital offense according to Jewish law, as he appeared to be innocent of wrongdoing against Rome (Acts 25:1–27). Paul's defense was before both men, but his words—an account of his personal encounter with the resurrected Jesus—were clearly directed at Agrippa, who had an insider's understanding of Jewish messianic expectations (Acts 26:1–27). The king's response was tinged with sarcasm:

> *In such a short time you will persuade me to become a Christian?!* (Acts 26:28)

Agrippa's sister Bernice was present at the hearing. She appeared with the king "amid great pomp" (Acts 25:23), much as only a queen accompany her husband could do. Bernice had been married to Agrippa I's brother Herod, king of Chalcis, but after Herod died and Agrippa II inherited his kingdom strong and persistent rumors arose that he and Bernice had begun an incestuous relationship. Agrippa II and Bernice reportedly continued their affair, on and off, for years, perhaps even after she became Titus' mistress in Rome following the destruction of Jerusalem.

Agrippa II used Temple finances to make important improvements to the infrastructure of Jerusalem in the years leading up to the Great Revolt of A.D. 66–70. Partly to curb mass unemployment and partly because the work needed doing, Agrippa approved a project to repave the streets of Jerusalem with new white limestone (*Ant.* xx.9.7). Evidence of this has been found in archaeological excavations under Robinson's Arch at the southwestern corner of the Temple Mount. Agrippa also made preparations at great expense to raise the level of the Temple Mount platform 30 feet in one location to offset its sinking foundations, but with the outbreak of the Revolt the great wooden beams he had imported for the

the old territory of Philip as well, and in A.D. 54 the new emperor, Nero, gave Agrippa certain cities in Galilee and Perea including Tiberias and Julias. Agrippa was so grateful that he enlarged Caesarea Philippi and renamed it Neronias in his honor (*Ant.* 5.2, 7.1). Archaeological remains at the site reveal a very large fortified palace built with finely cut limestone lined with marble. Apparently Agrippa II was the first Herodian king to use marble as a building material; for all his magnificence, Herod the Great had only painted plaster in Masada, Herodium and Jericho to make it *look* like marble.

Map legend:
Area help by Agrippa II — A.D. 50–53
Area transferred to Agrippa II — A.D. 53
Area transferred to Agrippa II — A.D. 54
Area of Roman procuratorial rule in Judea
Agrippa II's kingdom—A.D. 61

0 10 20 miles
0 15 30 km

© Carta, Jerusalem

work were used to manufacture engines of war instead (War v.1.5). With the onset of the Revolt in A.D. 66, war preparations took priority over everything else.

Caught between loyalties Agrippa first tried to play peacemaker, but when the crowds, egged on by the *Sicarii*—a fanatic faction that advocated violence against Jews who accommodated to Rome—burned his Jerusalem palace, he threw his support to the cause of Rome (War ii.17.6). Agrippa played a relatively minor role in the Revolt, preferring to watch much of its course from Berytus (Beirut) and Rome while leaving important decisions and actions to others. The Jews, who badly needed unified leadership, were left to their own devices and the Roman general Vespasian pretty much had his way in Galilee and Judea. After he became emperor in A.D. 69, Vespasian appointed his son Titus to finish the task of subduing the Jews. Agrippa, eager to support the new Caesar, returned to Judea to assist him in his work. When Jerusalem fell, Titus went to Caesarea Philippi where

> he stayed for a considerable time and put on a great number of shows. Here many of those captured [in Jerusalem] were destroyed, some being thrown to wild beasts while others were forced to kill one another in combat, as if they were enemies.

(War vii.2.1)

Because Agrippa's great palace was in Caesarea Philippi it is reasonable to suppose that he attended these "games" and watched—perhaps half-willingly, half-forced by Titus-the-conquering-hero who wanted to reward his puppet king with a good show—while Agrippa's people were systematically slaughtered before his eyes. "Come on! Enjoy! Be a good Roman! You deserve it!"

Vespasian enlarged Agrippa's kingdom, probably with lands to the north. The last of the Herodian monarchs lived out his days in literary obscurity. Josephus mentions little else about Agrippa except that the king collaborated with him as he wrote *The Jewish Wars* and that he praised the book's reliability and even purchased a personal copy (Life 65; Against Apion i.9). Agrippa probably died in either A.D. 93 or 100, in any case having reigned longer than any other member of the Herodian family. As he left no children, his kingdom was likely incorporated into the province of Syria and with its demise the Herodian line finally came to an end.

It had been quite a ride. Each of the members of Herod's family had made their careers on balancing the power of Rome with the needs and aspirations of the people they ruled. It was an uneven bar—and they never forgot whom they were working for. By the end of the first century A.D. Rome reigned supreme. But what of its legacy? Certainly many positive aspects of Roman life and culture have been inherited by the West, including forms of government, law, language, and art and architecture to name a few. But it is worth noting that today people name their dogs Caesar or Herod, and their kids after first-century rabbis or Jesus' disciples. Now *that's* magnificent.

The Great Revolt began in Caesarea in A.D. 66 and quickly spread to Galilee. Just as quickly, Vespasian brought the full weight of the Roman army against the Jewish forces of Galilee and within a year had retaken the region. The critical battle was at Jotapata (Yodfat) north of Sepphoris. The Jewish army was under the control of Josephus, a much better writer than soldier. Josephus' account of the battle is lengthy, no doubt a literary tribute to his own importance (War iii.7.1–8.9). (Note as well that this is one of the few events related in his books that Josephus actually witnessed firsthand.) In the end Josephus hid in the network of cisterns and caves that honeycomb the city—some, as this one, are easily identified yet today—before giving himself up as a prisoner to Rome. Josephus wrote of honorable suicide in other battles—perhaps he had to live vicariously in the deaths of others to soothe his own choice to surrender.

It doesn't take too many years for heavy foot and cart traffic to wear down rough paving stones to a surface as smooth as glass—the slick streets and alleys of Jerusalem's Old City are ample testimony to that. So when the white limestone blocks that paved Jerusalem's main street on the eve of its destruction in A.D. 70 were uncovered recently in archaeological excavations, it was a surprise that they all bore a new, rough look. Then Josephus came to the rescue: Agrippa II, we read, repaved the streets of Jerusalem in the years just before the Great Revolt. Keep on building and hope for the best. Given the alternative of falling into despair, what else could Agrippa do?

Early Caesars of the Roman Empire

Caesar	Years of Reign	New Testament References	Selected Notes of New Testament Significance
Julius Caesar	49–44 B.C.	—	—
Second Triumvirate (Mark Antony, Octavian, Lepidus)	44–31 B.C.	—	—
Augustus (Octavian)	31 (27) B.C.–A.D. 14	Luke 2:1	Patron of Herod the Great; Caesar at Jesus' birth
Tiberius	A.D. 14–37	Matthew 22:17, 22:21; Luke 3:1, 23:2; John 19:12, 19:15	Caesar during Jesus' ministry; namesake of Herod Antipas' capital on the Sea of Galilee
Caligula (Gaius)	A.D. 37–41	—	—
Claudius	A.D. 41–54	Acts 11:28, 17:7, 18:2	Caesar during Paul's first two missionary journeys
Nero	A.D. 54–68	Acts 25:11–12, 26:32, 27:24, 28:19; Phil 4:22	Caesar during Paul's third missionary journey and Roman imprisonment; executed Paul and Peter
Galba, Otho and Vitellius ("the year of the three emperors")	A.D. 68–69	—	—
Vespasian	A.D. 69–79	—	As general, led Roman forces against the Jewish Revolt in A.D. 66–69
Titus	A.D. 79–81	—	As general, defeated Judea and destroyed Jerusalem in A.D. 70
Domitian	A.D. 81–96	—	Caesar during John's exile in Patmos; great persecution of the church
Nerva	A.D. 96–98	—	—
Trajan	A.D. 98–117	—	Annexed the Nabatean realms in A.D. 106
Hadrian	A.D. 117–130	—	Suppressed the Second Jewish (Bar Kochba) Revolt

The Herods

Name	Relationship to Herod the Great	Greatest Extent of Territory Ruled	Title and Dates of Reign	New Testament References
Antipater I	Grandfather of Herod the Great	Idumea	Governor during the reign of Alexander Jannaeus	—
Antipater II	Father of Herod the Great	Greater Judea (including Idumea, Samaria, Galilee and Perea)	*De facto* administrator from 63–55 B.C.; procurator from 55–43 B.C.	—
Herod I (the Great)	—	Greater Judea (including Idumea, Samaria, Galilee, Perea, Gaulanitis and surrounding regions)	King from 37–4 B.C.	Mt 2:1–22; Lk 1:5
Archelaus	Oldest son of Herod the Great	Judea, Samaria and Idumea	Ethnarch from 4 B.C.–A.D. 6	Mt 2:22
Herod Philip	Son of Herod the Great	Gaulanitis and surrounding regions	Tetrarch from 4 B.C.–A.D. 34	Lk 3:1
Herod Antipas	Son of Herod the Great	Galilee and Perea	Tetrarch from 4 B.C.–A.D. 39	Mt 14:1–11; Mk 6:14–29; Lk 3:1, 3:19, 13:31–33, 23:7–12
Herod Agrippa I	Grandson of Herod the Great	Greater Judea (same land as ruled by Herod the Great)	King from A.D. 37–44	Acts 12:1, 12:18–23
Herod Agrippa II	Great grandson of Herod the Great	Chalcis (southeastern Lebanon); Gaulanitis and surrounding regions; parts of Galilee and Perea	King of Chalcis from A.D. 48–53; Tetrarch of Gaulanitis and surrounding regions and parts of Galilee and Perea from A.D. 53–c. 100	Acts 25:13–26:32

CHAPTER 18

JOHN THE BAPTIST
A Voice Crying in the Wilderness

The usual fate of people from the past, if they're remembered at all, is to be hung from a hook on the wall ("Ah, great Uncle Harold. What a fine man he was!") or placed safely in a glassed-in cabinet and brought out occasionally for curiosity's sake ("That belonged to old cousin Dora. Now *there* was an odd one. She ironed her socks"). Truth be told, it's the same with Bible people. We look at Elijah and Jeremiah and the like from a safe distance, where through the antiseptic of time they fade into old pictures or storybook characters—and, often enough, eccentric ones at that (certainly real people wouldn't dress in Elijah's garb or be as constantly obsessed with his nation's self-inflicted national doom as was Jeremiah). If someone like that actually showed up today, he or she would receive plenty of not-so-guarded smirks, then likely be dismissed as a curio, either an obsessed attention-seeker or an out-of-touch fanatic—harmless in the end, or crazy, or both, but not really part of modern-day life. Prophets are good to have around to check certain personal or social excesses, but only if they criticize the same things that the senses of the majority already say need criticizing.

That's not, of course, just in our generation. The early part of the first century A.D. was a fairly prosperous time for residents of Judea and Galilee, all things considered, and folks were generally learning to work within the Romanized political and economic systems that had enveloped their land. "Just keep things level," was a common sentiment, one well attuned to self-interest and expediency. Many were still looking for "the Elijah that was to come" (cf. Mal 4:5–6), but preferred that he make an appearance on their terms rather than someone else's (including, perhaps, even his). And so, when "in those days John the Baptist came preaching in the wilderness of Judea, crying out 'Repent! The Kingdom of Heaven is at hand!'" (Mt 3:1), dressed like the Elijah of old (nine hundred years had passed since the first Elijah's coming) and playing the already ancient prophetic role to the hilt, he drew decidedly mixed reactions. His wasn't exactly a bolt out of the prophetic blue—John wasn't the only prophet (or prophet wannabe) of the day (cf. Acts 5:33–39)—but he did cast a jarring counter-culture pose and in the end even gained the attention of the governing tetrarch, Herod Antipas. A one-off kook? A there-you-go-again holy man? A potentially dangerous subversive? Just another one of many varieties of

Jewish self-expression in the desperately fertile years of the first century A.D.? But for the writers of the Gospels, John the Baptist was the real thing, the bridge from then to now, the long-awaited flesh and blood arc spanning the chasm of time and binding the God-spoken Testament of Moses with the New Testament of the long-awaited Anointed One, Jesus the Messiah (Lk 16:16). The divine clock, ticking in silence for hundreds of years, was about to strike twelve. And who could have guessed that it would sound like that?

A role as special as this required a special kind of birth. Both of John's parents, Zechariah and Elizabeth, were of priestly descent (Lk 1:5). Luke describes them as "righteous in the sight of God and walking blamelessly in all the commandments and requirements of the LORD" (Lk 1:6); that is, devout folk living responsible lives with all proper public and private expressions of first-century Jewishness in place. Zechariah was an active priest, one for whom the priesthood was a sincere calling, unencumbered by the aristocratic tendencies or obsessions that seemed to seize too many of his colleagues up in Jerusalem during the last days of the reign of Herod the Great. He and Elizabeth were well along in years but childless, and carried the public stigma that God had withheld his blessing in spite of their lifetime of faithful service (cf. Lk 1:25). In such a time and place as this the fault for barrenness always adhered to the woman, but Zechariah, in the solid values of his rural upbringing, refused to push Elizabeth aside for a more promising womb. And so the two lived

John the Baptist was born and raised in an unnamed village in the hill country of Judea and continued to live in the open countryside (or, "empty places") of the region until the day of his public appearance to Israel (Lk 1:80). The ruggedness of the Sorek wadi west of Jerusalem, with steep, rocky hillsides and narrow canyons, precluded dense settlement and left plenty of open places for a person such as John to roam. John was close to God when he went up to the Temple in Jerusalem to fulfill his Nazirite vows, but also here in a place inhabited only by traces of the nameless and faceless multitudes of Judea.

159

Mary's Visit to Elizabeth.
Of the cycles of life in a Judean village, none was as momentous as the birth of a firstborn son. Always the midwife, never the mom, Elizabeth finally became the center of attention after Gabriel's announcement that she would bear a child in her old age. Family and acquaintances no doubt flocked to her home in her hill country village (tradition identifies the place as modern En Kerem, west of Jerusalem) to dote on the mother-to-be. Even Mary, Elizabeth's cousin from far-off Galilee, paid a visit, no small trip for young peasant woman. Mary ended up staying about three months, enough time to offset the hardships of the trip.

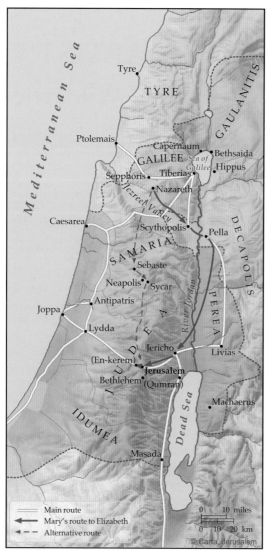

Mosaic on façade of the Church of the Visitation in En Kerem, traditional birthplace of John the Baptist. The church preserves the memory (and supposed location) of the house of Zechariah and Elizabeth. The mosaic depicts the arrival of Mary, the Holy Mother, dressed in the garb of tradition, to the home. (photo: Garo Nalbandian)

together as the years slipped by, resigned to the fact that although their family line would end, life could be dignified and full in the meantime. Zechariah knew that Sarah, Rachel, Hannah and the mother of Samson were all barren at one point in their lives, yet their families, blessed by God, ended up taking on biblical proportions (Gen 18:9–15, 30:2; Judg 13:1–2; 1 Sam 1:1–2). But that was then; simple fortitude would have to suffice for now.

Zechariah belonged to the priestly division of Abijah, one of twenty-four groupings of priests who served in the Temple in Jerusalem (Lk 1:5; cf. 1 Chron 24:1–19). Each individual from each division had the opportunity to personally offer the daily incense offering in the Temple. Because they all took turns doing so, this honor came only a very few times during each priest's lifetime. After the incense was burned, the day's officiating priest customarily lingered alone before the altar—just outside the door of the Holy of Holies—to bring his private petitions to God. In what was likely Zechariah's last time to stand in

this holy place, he was thoroughly taken aback by the very thing he never dared hope could ever happen. Suddenly, in that ripe moment, an angel of the LORD appeared to Zechariah—Gabriel, who usually stood in the presence of God, now stood before the awestruck priest and even called him by name. This chief of all of God's messengers promised that not only would Elizabeth become pregnant, but that their much-awaited child would be a most special son, born in the ascetic, separatist tradition of the biblical Nazirites and filled with the Holy Spirit from the womb (Lk 1:8–15, 19; cf. Num 6:1–21; Judg 13:4–5, 13:14). Moreover, he would enter the world in the spirit and power of Elijah "to turn the hearts of the fathers back to the children and the disobedient to the attitude of the righteous, so as to make ready a people prepared for the LORD" (Lk 1:17; cf. Mal 4:6). And if that wasn't enough, he was going to be the forerunner of someone even greater who was also on the way.

It was, perhaps, too much all at once. Zechariah was left speechless—literally (Lk 1:18–22). Returning home, everything happened—quite *supernaturally*—exactly as Gabriel had said that it would. Six months into her pregnancy and quite unable to hold either her shape or her joy, Elizabeth had a special visitor. Mary, a near relative (probably a cousin) made the five-to-six-day journey down to Judea from Nazareth of Galilee. By now Mary had also received a visit from Gabriel (this angel got all the fun jobs) and was likely in the beginning stages of her own divine pregnancy. The expectant mothers knew that something quite extraordinary was happening, and the two formed a special bond between themselves (Lk 1:26–56). So would their sons.

When Elizabeth's baby was circumcised on the eighth day of his new life, he was given the name Yohanan (John), "the LORD is gracious." This was an angel-given-God-given name, one that stood outside the family line, an identity that announced that John's intended ministry—for all its voiced fire and brimstone—marked the birth of a new era in God's gracious dealings with people (Lk 1:13, 1:57–66). Zechariah knew that John, like Jeremiah and Ezekiel, would be a prophet-priest of the Most High,

*[to] go before the LORD to prepare His ways,
to give to His people the knowledge of salvation by
    the forgiveness of their sins . . .
to shine upon those who sit in darkness and the
    shadow of death,
[and] to guide our feet into the way of peace.*
(Lk 1:76–77, 79; cf. Isa 9:2)

In a day rich with political and social opportunities and thick with intrigue, what did all this mean? That people could be restored. Families could become reconciled. Society could be made whole. And life could be the way it was supposed

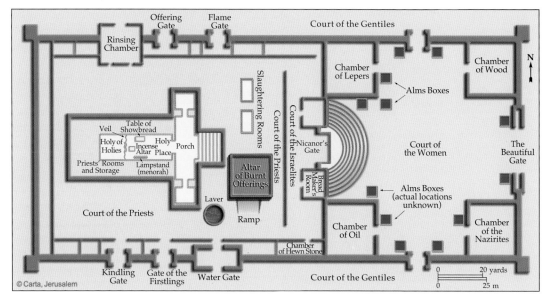

Offering Gate / Flame Gate / Court of the Gentiles

Rinsing Chamber

Chamber of Lepers / Chamber of Wood / Alms Boxes / N

Slaughtering Rooms

Court of the Priests

Veil / Table of Showbread / Holy of Holies / Incense Altar / Holy Place / Porch / Priests' Rooms and Storage / Lampstand (menorah)

Nicanor's Gate / Bread Maker's Room / Court of the Women / The Beautiful Gate

Court of the Israelites

Altar of Burnt Offerings

Laver / Ramp / Alms Boxes (actual locations unknown)

Chamber of Oil / Chamber of the Nazirites

Kindling Gate / Gate of the Firstlings / Water Gate / Chamber of Hewn Stone / Court of the Gentiles

0 — 20 yards / 0 — 25 m

© Carta, Jerusalem

to be (cf. Lk 1:68–79). But would the proud papa and mama have also wanted to know that their son's role would entail other necessary consequences of old-time prophecy: wrath, alienation, hardship and death? It's likely that neither Zechariah nor Elizabeth lived long enough to find out.

Nothing is known of John's formative years except that he grew in body and mind like Samson and Samuel before him and Jesus to follow, and became strong in the Spirit (Lk 1:80; cf. Judg 13:24–25; 1 Sam 3:19; Lk 2:40). Luke identified John's hometown as only a village in the hill country of Judea (Lk 1:39, 1:65), and it wasn't until the eighth century A.D. that *The Gregorian Lectionary*, recording a very late early-Church tradition, first gave a name to the place, Encharim (modern En Kerem in the far western suburbs of Jerusalem). This village of tradition is nestled in a wonderfully picturesque valley (a branch of the Sorek), now as well as then, and was far enough from Jerusalem to be surrounded by expanses of "open countryside" (so "deserts" or "empty places" should be rendered in Luke 1:80) in which a young John must have often hiked and explored. But whether his Judean hill country home was in Encharim or elsewhere, John was raised in a fresh and joyful land of strong hills, quiet valleys and springs of living water. This was an optimistic landscape, mirroring the unbounded expectations that Zechariah had set for his one and only son (Lk 1:67–79).

Were it not for the unusual circumstances of his birth, John would have followed in his father's footsteps as the local village priest, serving dutifully in the Temple of the LORD, turn by turn, with the next generation of priests of the division of Abijah. It is likely that he did so at first, before what Luke termed "the day of his public appearance to Israel" (Lk 1:80). If he had not—if he had chosen to stay only in the quiet countryside in silent meditative preparation until well into adulthood—John would have

brought shame to his parents as only an of-sound-mind-and-body-yet-economically-inactive-first-born-son of first-century Judea could do. Norms of righteousness, in fact, demanded that he support his elderly parents, or honor their memory with responsible, gainful employment if they had already died. (Pharisees, too, often held down "night jobs" in order to make a living.) Turn-by-turn service in Jerusalem would also have given John ample opportunity to see first-hand the excesses, insincerity and corruption that had come to infect too much of the Herodian-style Temple leadership in his day. (Perhaps he even stood once, or maybe even twice, in the holy spot of his father and Gabriel.) Certainly a righteous anger as pointed as John's must have been honed on the anvil of personal experience; one thing his opponents *didn't* say was "John, you don't know what you're talking about."

Sometime in A.D. 28 or 29 (cf. Lk 3:1–3), when John was a little over 30 years old, he climbed over the Mount of Olives and withdrew deep into the wil-

Although no archaeological remains of Herod's Temple have been found, it is possible to reconstruct the likely shape and position of its various rooms, elements and furnishings from written sources, primarily the Mishnah Middot and Josephus, Jewish Antiquities. Zechariah the priest was standing in the Holy Place next to the Altar of Incense, just before the veil that hid the Holy of Holies, when the angel Gabriel appeared before him in heavenly glory. Because he belonged to a priestly family, Zechariah's son John must also have had access to the Court of the Priests and to the Holy Place. But because John was also a lifetime Nazirite, he was required as well to visit the Chamber of the Nazirites in the Court of the Women where he would bring sacrifices upon completing special vows.

A rainbow lightens the northern end of the Dead Sea, piercing the clouds somewhere between Qumran and Bethany beyond the Jordan. The Torah light of Judaism diffused into several bright colors in the first century, offering fresh opportunities for religious expression that brought hope to a people who for too long had been "sitting in darkness and in the shadow of death" (cf. Mt 4:16; Isa 9:2).

The Ministry of John the Baptist. *John's public ministry took place in the great chasm of the Jordan Valley, mostly in the south above the Dead Sea but also farther north, toward Galilee. Stark yet full of life—the valley was a haunt of prophetic voices of the past, voices crying in the wilderness to whatever or whomever would listen. And plenty did. The Baptist wasn't that far away from civilization—a lot of traffic moved on the road from Jerusalem to Jericho to Livias, as well as up and down the course of the river connecting Judea with Galilee. Here John could play the role of the ascetic prophet, yet interact with people as sophisticated as the world had to offer—and it was they who came to him.*

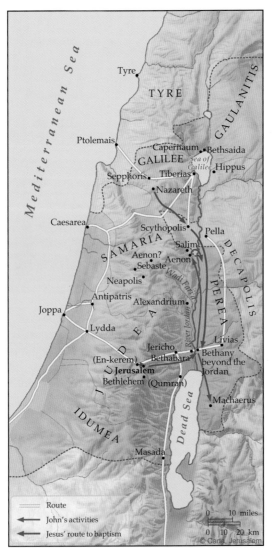

Trading one set of open places for another, John moved east to the wilderness along the Jordan River. Physical survival was exponentially more difficult here, "in stony wastes in the wilderness, a land of salt without inhabitant" (Jer 17:6). Yet this, too, was part of the land of promise, seen from afar by Moses and given by God to Joshua as part of the down payment on a place most suited for his people to live. A bit of water, a scrap of green—not much, but enough for prophets to speak of the need for stony hearts to become flesh "so that they may walk in my statutes and keep my ordinances, and do them. Then they will be my people, and I will be their God" (Ezek 11:19–20). John the Baptist certainly agreed.

derness of Judea, to the arid wasteland above the northern end of the Dead Sea. Traditionally, such wilderness areas were places of death, purification and rebirth (cf. Deut 32:10–12; Jer 2:6–7; Ezek 47:1–12; Hos 2:3–4, 2:14–20, etc.) and so formed an appropriate backdrop for the ascetic prophet. What prompted his move must remain a matter of speculation. Was it simply a divine nudge (perhaps another angelic

voice) saying "It's time?" John was certainly motivated by religious sensibilities, but to what extent did social or economic or even political issues also come into play? Did a specific event set him so strongly against Jerusalem's religious aristocracy that he felt he had to flee to the wilderness? Was it an accumulation of frustrations with the *status quo*? His journey to the eastern wastelands was not the extreme response of an anonymous, low-level rural priest at the disappointment of being shut out of the inner circles of power in Jerusalem. No, something altruistic was involved, and the overall impression given by the writers of the Gospels depicts a man who was genuinely moved by the power-sanctioned injustices of his day and so sacrificed his own reputation and career as a young priest to call the entire system into account. Priests tended to be members of The Establishment, while Old Testament-style prophets usually stood counter-culture (beneath their wrathful front was a broken heart). John's divine call as the latter drove him from the comforts of home to a life of alienation in a place wild and alone. It was a willful move throughout, and this as much as anything likely prompted John's former colleagues from Jerusalem to make the trek into the harsh wilderness to see what the fuss was all about.

It was a long and tiring walk from Jerusalem to "the district around the Jordan" where John established his new position preaching "a baptism of repentance for the forgiveness of sins" (Lk 3:3). When members of the priestly aristocracy (Pharisees and Sadducees are specifically mentioned in Matthew 3:7) made it down to be baptized, they got an earful:

You brood of vipers! Who warned you to flee from the wrath to come? Bear fruit that's consistent with repentance! Don't even begin to say to yourselves, "Abraham is our father," for I say to you that God is able to raise up children of Abraham from these very stones. The axe is ready to hack up even the roots of the trees. Every one that doesn't bear good fruit will be cut down and thrown into the fire.

(Lk 3:7–9; cf. Mt 3:7–10)

With mixed doses of venom and sarcasm, John didn't leave a lot of room for self-justification or philosophical discussions. Reversing the imagery of Jeremiah (who himself, like all prophets, turned images on their heads), "the stony wasteland of the wilderness" would spring to life while "the tree planted by the water, extending its roots by the stream" would be chopped into firewood (Jer 17:5–8). What is surprising is not that Pharisees and Sadducees came to John in order to submit to his baptism (Mt 3:7), but that he dismissed them out of hand. The most plausible scenario would suggest either that John was simply fed up enough to make a blanket condemnation of the entire religious aristocracy (the personal sincerity of specific individuals aside), or that these particular Pharisees and Sadducees were somehow playing the role of interested hearers in order to bring a report of the renegade's actions back to Jerusalem (cf. Jn 1:19–24). If John hadn't burned his bridges with the Temple authorities yet, he surely did so now. The initial likely response back in Jerusalem? "He wants to hang out down in the wilderness? Good. He can holler and kick around down there all he wants. At least now he's out of our hair."

But some—perhaps many—did respond. Luke calls them "the multitude"; Matthew and Mark simply say "everyone" from Jerusalem, Judea and the district around the Jordan (Mt 3:5; Mk 1:5; Lk 3:7, 3:10), areas with a predominately Jewish population. The multitudes are present throughout the Gospel story, from the birth of John (Lk 1:58) to the crucifixion of Jesus (Lk 23:48). These people of the land (am ha-aretz) are not exactly background fill (they serve throughout as an indication that John's ministry, and Jesus', had strong popular followings), but neither are they typically fronted in the storyline (the Feeding of the Five Thousand is an exception; Mt 14:13–21). Surely their response to John was as individualized as that of any mass gathering: some responded and were baptized; some scorned (he was even called a demon! Mt 11:18), while others probably wanted to hear more (Lk 3:15; cf. Acts 17:32–34). Of those who were particularly moved (or who had little to go back to), some remained and became disciples; Elijah had had a school of prophets in the same area (2 Kgs 2:15). Most, however, certainly returned home to their families and jobs, changed for the better for the effort of seizing the grip that God had placed on their lives.

John's intended audience, however, was perhaps a level above, persons a bit higher on the power ladder who had immediate influence over the socio-economic matrix in which the multitude lived. These included tax collectors and soldiers—collaborators and Gentiles who represented and enforced the everyday face of Rome in the land (Lk 3:12, 3:14). In the ancient world an occupying force was primarily bent on securing an unlimited pool of healthy young bodies to enlarge its army and an unbroken supply of tax revenue to fuel their march. Rome needed money for its soldiers; the soldiers made sure that the tax collectors could get it, and both had relatively free rein to skim off as much as they wanted in the process. But some of each also came to John for baptism, asking, "Teacher, what shall we do?" John's response was not that they should quit their jobs, but that in the normal course of their duties they should treat others fairly, righteously and honorably (Lk 3:12–14). He demanded no more or no less of everyone else (Lk 3:10–11). John didn't advocate political change; he only demanded that the political system—be it Rome or Jerusalem-based—govern

benevolently (this was bound to anger both zealots and friends of Caesar). It was the Kingdom of Heaven that was coming (Mt 3:1), and for John, personally-changed lives that could influence society for good was the key to getting ready for it. This call for social and economic justice echoed across the corridors of time; John's integrity as a priest of the LORD Most High received the mandate from the prophets of old and awoke the charge for a new generation (cf. Ps 51:14–17; Isa 1:10–17; Jer 7:1–7; Amos 2:6–8; Mic 6:6–8).

Those who responded by confessing their sins were baptized (Mt 3:5–6; Mk 1:4–5; Lk 3:3). While ritual acts of washing were common in Judaism in the first century A.D., there must have been something particularly striking about John's immersion that gave him the nickname "the Baptist" (or, "the Baptizer"; Mt 3:1; Mk 1:4, etc.). In John's day observant Jews repeatedly took miqveh baths to cleanse their bodies from ritual impurities. This practice was heightened at Qumran, in the vicinity of the Baptist's activities in the wilderness, where members of that community (the Essenes) saw themselves as priests in a kind of substitute, purified temple (they believed the Jerusalem Temple to be corrupt and that God had chosen them as a select, separatist group for final redemption). But unlike the Temple Jews, the Essenes—and John—reserved immersion for people who first repented for their sins:

John baptized on both sides of the Jordan River above the northern shore of the Dead Sea. In his day the river's flow was unimpeded by human intervention, spilling its banks into a wide and irregular pattern during the heavy winter rains and falling back into a relatively narrow channel during the hot, dry months of summer and early autumn. The growing need for fresh water to quench the thirst of modern states of Israel and Jordan has reduced the Jordan River's flow in the south today to a sluggish trickle, making its channel in Galilee, shown here, a more attractive place to imagine John's locale in the first century.

One of the largest water reservoirs at Qumran bears marks of the classic miqveh—stepped access to the water below, with low ridges of stone (here, two) running the length of the steps and symbolically dividing persons entering from those exiting the purifying waters. According to rabbinic law, a miqveh also had to contain a minimum of 40 seah (c. 125 gallons) of water that entered under its own flow (such as by rain or a spring via a channel). The reservoir had to be deep enough so that the person could fully immerse his body (while standing, sitting or reclining) up to his extended fingertips. This miqveh was cracked by a severe earthquake that destroyed Qumran in 31 B.C., and was not repaired when the site was rebuilt a few years later.

Qumran (Khirbet Qumran) is unique among archaeological sites of the land of Israel. Situated on a soft marl terrace a short distance from the base of the high limestone cliff just off the northeastern corner of the Dead Sea, and surrounded on three sides by canyons of the Nahal Qumran, the site commands the region, including the road from Jericho that runs south along the western side of the Dead Sea. Various rooms in Qumran are connected by an aqueduct that spilled water into cisterns and stepped reservoirs, many of which were surely miqva'ot, Jewish ritual immersion baths of the first century. Caves in the cliffs above and in the marl terrace at the base of the site contained the Dead Sea Scrolls. In spite of a plethora of explanations of the site in recent scholarly (and other) literature, the dominant understanding of Qumran remains that of its excavator, Fr. Roland de Vaux, who connected the site with the Essenes and identified them with the Yahad ("community") of the Scrolls.

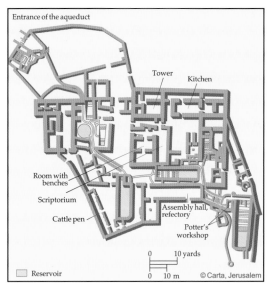

It is impossible to be purified [by the waters of immersion] without first repenting of evil, since impurity adheres to all who transgress His word.

(The Community Rule 1QS 5:13–14)

A second type of immersion was required of Gentile proselytes converting to Judaism. These underwent a single initiatory rite of baptism to remove the defilement which had adhered to them, as non-Jews, from birth. Similarly, the Essenes also conducted an initiatory one-time immersion for each prelate marking the beginning of his (men only were allowed) new life as a member of the exclusive, purified Qumran community.

Those who witnessed John's baptism would have heard and seen things that reminded them of aspects of any or all of this, but also would have noticed that something about how the Baptist did things was fundamentally different.

The historian Josephus described John's baptism with language comfortable to normative Judaism, speaking of the soul becoming purified through acts of righteousness and the body by water:

John, who was called the Baptist, was a good man

and commanded the Jews to exercise virtue, both as to righteousness toward one another and piety toward God, and so to come to baptism. This washing [with water] was acceptable to him, not in order to put away sins but to purify the body, assuming that the soul had been thoroughly purified beforehand through acts of righteousness. (Ant. xviii.5.2)

The Gospel writers, for whom John the Baptist was first and foremost a forerunner of Jesus the Messiah, portrayed John's baptism somewhat differently. Mark's account is the most succinct:

John the Baptist appeared in the wilderness preaching a baptism of repentance for the forgiveness of sins. And all the country of Judea was going out to him, and all the people of Jerusalem; and they were being baptized by him in the Jordan River as they confessed their sins. (Mk 1:4–5)

John the Baptist made no mention of any of the priestly ceremonial rites that characterized either normative Judaism or the teachings of the Qumran community, including the need to repeatedly purify one's body through ritual washings. Instead, he made a direct connection between right living and a one-time immersion that signaled that the individual had adopted (or was in the process of adopting) a lifestyle characterized by acts of justice and righteousness, and had (or was) sincerely repenting of his sins. Or, *her* sins—while women are absent in the Gospel story of John the Baptist, they did participate in traditional *miqveh* immersions and some likely became followers of John, as they would of Jesus. John's one-time "baptism of repentance for the forgiveness of sins" was an initiatory rite aimed at emphasizing the need for living righteously (defined in terms of social, not liturgical, acts) in a Kingdom of Heaven that was inclusive of anyone who submitted to its waters, regardless of gender, ethnicity, status or former life. It was a bold, visible and decisive way of signaling the need for both Jews and Gentiles (everyone from Sadducees to soldiers) to start over, as it were, from scratch ("don't call yourselves

Modern-day explorers catch the first hour of dawn in the entrance of Cave 11 high in the limestone cliffs above Qumran. This was the last of the caves containing the Dead Sea Scrolls to be discovered. In addition to scrolls, the cave contained fragments of white linen garments of the type worn by priests, and the corroded head of a pick-axe which the excavator, Roland de Vaux, suggested was used by new members of the Qumran community to dig latrines—a handy reminder for initiates of the community's commitment to ritual and practical purity. Primary among the scrolls and scroll fragments found in Cave 11 is the Temple Scroll, at 27-feet long the largest of all of the Dead Sea Scrolls. For the Essenes this was the book of Law par excellence, containing detailed instructions and regulations for a revived Zadokite priesthood that would one day serve in a purified, renewed Temple in Jerusalem.

children of Abraham…"; Mt 3:8). In essence, John's baptism undercut an important cornerstone of Jerusalem's Temple apparatus (and of Qumran) in favor of direct access to God. It was, in the words of Mark, "the beginning of the gospel (lit., 'good news') of Jesus Christ" (Mt 1:1; cf. Acts 1:22, 10:37).

The first century was an ideological hey-day, with vast tracts of fertile ground ready to receive seeds of revelation and thought. Judaism was erupting into a kaleidoscope of colors, and John reflected a vibrant hue. He didn't exactly fit any of his contemporary modes—not the Pharisees or Sadducees, not Qumran, not the social or political critics of his day, not even the messianic hopefuls who, with the exception of Jesus, all looked for the overthrow of Rome. His message was religious, but with clear social and political implications. These implications were welcomed by the masses, although they seem to have been aimed particularly at people who held enough institutionalized power to effect real change. Yet by following John's call, it was precisely this group of professionals who had the most to lose—or to gain (cf. Mt 16:25–26). In spite of his clear ties to the mainstream Judaism of his day, perhaps the best way to characterize John is by the words of all four Evangelists (who quoted the Greek Septuagint text of Isaiah 40:3): he was "a Voice Crying in the Wilderness" (cf. Mt 3:3; Mk 1:3; Lk 3:4 and Jn 1:23).

John's prophetic ministry took him up and down the Jordan Valley where he encountered many kinds of people. Matthew speaks of John baptizing "in the wilderness of Judea," which must have been somewhere along the west bank of the Jordan River north of the Dead Sea (Mt 3:1). This was part of the province of Judea and, during John's ministry, was under the direct Roman rule of procurators. On the other hand, John the Evangelist mentions that John the Baptist's first (and perhaps most frequented) baptismal spot was "beyond the Jordan" (Jn 1:28, 3:26, 10:40), on the Jordan's eastern bank. This was in the district of Perea, governed by Herod Antipas who, as tetrarch, also ruled Galilee by proxy for Rome. Perhaps the Baptist crossed to Perea in search of a greater degree of tolerance for his religious and social commentary. Luke's simple synopsis, that John preached and baptized in "all the district around the Jordan" (Lk 3:3), quite reasonably implies that John could be found in both places.

This was a region that had been frequented by Elijah, a prophet who had fled beyond the Jordan after bursting onto the Israelite scene in his initial confrontation with a religiously corrupt, Baal-driven Ahab (1 Kgs 17:1–7). Elijah also ascended to heaven across the Jordan in the fire of the LORD (Elisha received a double portion of his prophetic spirit there; 2 Kgs 2:1–14), and maintained a school of followers in Jericho (2 Kgs 2:15). Enough geographical clues are present to suggest that John, who ate off

the land like Elijah and dressed in the fashion of the prophet (Mt 3:4, 11:18; Mk 1:6; cf. 1 Kgs 17:6; Zech 13:4; Mal 4:5–6), chose this region to emphasize these prophetic associations. (Whether John saw himself as the Elijah to come or as the one preparing for Elijah's return remains a matter of, primarily, theological debate; cf. Mt 11:9–14 in which Jesus suggested that John could be Elijah, and Jn 1:19–23 where John insists that he isn't.)

Of the Gospel writers, only John the Evangelist mentions specific places by name where John baptized. The most prominent was "Bethany beyond the Jordan" (Jn 1:28), a place otherwise unknown in literary sources. An early tradition favored by the church fathers Origen and Eusebius (Onomasticon 58:18) emends the name Bethany to Bethabara, a known site (Qasr el-Yehud) on the west side of the Jordan. Bethabara means "the place of crossing over" and clearly indicates a natural ford that could be reached from both sides of the river. This particular ford, at the juncture of the Jordan River with the Wadi el-Kharrar just five miles north of the place where the Jordan empties into the Dead Sea, carried the main route between Jerusalem and Livias (Beth-ramatha; Tell er-Rame), the capital of Perea. The presence of this route made it a convenient place for the tradition to develop that John's ford was here; Christian pilgrims, after all, could arrive at the site easily to be baptized in the same waters used by John. Byzantine-era churches were built on both sides of the river (until modern times, the

(right) There is no need to suggest that "locust," the mainstay of John's diet in the wilderness, was a strange euphemism for the carob pod, a suggestion often made to soothe modern dietary sensibilities. On this Assyrian relief one servant carries racks of pomegranates while another leads with skewers of locusts, both delicacies fit for a royal banquet. One Old Babylonian letter implores: "send me one hundred locusts and [other] food!" But locusts were also a ready source of nutrition for the common people who were left to forage off the land (each contains 75% protein and 20% fat, with plenty of riboflavin and Vitamin B²). And, locusts were declared "clean" by Jewish law (Lev 11:21–22), an important detail for someone such as John who might have found it otherwise hard to keep kosher out in the wilderness. As for the taste—that was acquired like anything else.

The eastward-oriented Medeba Map, a mosaic now badly broken but once covering the entire floor of a 6th-century A.D. church in Medeba, Jordan, is an invaluable first-hand source revealing how Byzantine Christians understood the relationship between the biblical story and the land on which its events took place. The map places "Bethabara the Baptism of St. John" on the west side of the Jordan in the vicinity of Jericho, city of palm trees, and locates an Aenon-Sapsaphas, next to a hardy desert shrub of balsam, just across the river to the east. Between the two a fish swims against the current, away from sure death in the salt-saturated Dead Sea. This location of Aenon as the site of John's baptism mentioned in the Gospel of John 3:23 has otherwise little merit in the sources.

Sixteen springs saturate a three-square-mile landscape of flat farmland in the vicinity of Umm el-'Umdan in the northern Jordan Valley, just west of the cut of the Jordan River. Even though today all are fully tied into Israel's national water system, enough groundwater remains to keep the surrounding area green even in the searing heat of late summer. This was likely the region of Aenon near Salim (Tel Shalem is the mound rising just beyond), where John baptized "because there was much water there" (Jn 3:23). Mount Gilboa frames the valley to the west. Elisha's hometown, Abel-meholah, lay nearby, with fields so vast and fertile that a farmer could "plow with twelve pair of oxen before him" (1 Kgs 19:19). The water also attracted the main route running the length of the Jordan Valley between Galilee and Judea.

(below) Herod Antipas was fond of putting images of a palm tree or a reed on coins minted in his name, ΗΡΩΔΟΥ ΤΕΤΡΑΡΧΟΥ ("Herod, Tetrarch"). Reeds were common throughout Antipas' kingdom, in the wetter areas of Galilee and along the banks of the Jordan River. In Jewish lore and literature of the time the reed symbolized fresh water, fertility and wisdom, and so it became a suitable founding image for the city of Tiberias, Antipas' new capital on the shore of the Sea of Galilee. Perhaps this connection prompted Jesus' specific reply to John's disciples, who came to him after Antipas had locked their master in prison. "What did you go out into the wilderness to see? A reed shaken by the wind? People dressed in soft clothing live in king's palaces!" (Mt 11:7–8).

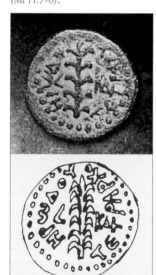

course of the Jordan changed relatively frequently due to heavy flooding and landslides, so that any given shrine may have changed sides of the river from time to time!) and today pilgrimage spots face each other, within spitting distance, across a much-reduced water flow. Nevertheless, if this tradition of place is correct, then John intentionally chose a spot to baptize that was frequented by many travelers, including influential folk of all kinds passing from one capital city to the next. The great prophets of the Old Testament found a ready audience on the crowded streets and public squares of Jerusalem; perhaps John found a way to reach similar crowds even while playing the role of the prophetic loner.

On at least one occasion John also baptized at Aenon near Salim (Jn 3:23). Because Aenon (derived from the word Ein, "spring") was a fairly common place name in the region, this particular Aenon is further identified as being near Salim, but with the odd qualifier "because there was much water there." Of course John couldn't baptize at a place unless there was water, and of course there would be water at a place called Aenon, so why mention the obvious? It is possible that the Evangelist made the point of saying Aenon had much water to offer an explanation as to what the Baptist was doing there, as if his presence in the place was otherwise unexpected. Why the issue? Because this there was either at springs (Aenon) near the remains of the Old Testament city of Tirzah at the head of the Wadi Faria in Samaria or, more likely, at the springs of Umm el-'Umdan just south of the modern village of Tirat Tzvi in the upper Jordan Valley, eight miles due south of Beth-shean/Scythopolis (so Eusebius, Onomasticon 40:1). The Aenon near Scythopolis has the advantage of being on a more important north-south route and in the vicinity of places connected to the Elijah-Elisha stories (it was quite near Elisha's hometown of Abel-meholah and close to the route Elijah traveled between his home in Gilead and Mt. Carmel; cf. 1 Kgs 17:1, 19:16). The significant point, though, was that because the one Aenon was in Samaria and the other was in the Gentile

region of the Decapolis, John's audience for as long as he remained at either must have been primarily persons who were not Jewish. This should not be surprising—a move up the Jordan Valley to the Decapolis would put John in an area where he would meet a wider circle of tax gatherers, soldiers and the like (cf. Lk 3:12–13), but also plenty of Jews traveling between Judea and Galilee (Jn 3:23–25).

But it was back at Bethany beyond the Jordan that John met up with Jesus, his most significant candidate for baptism (Mt 3:13–17; Mk 1:9–11; Lk 3:21–22; Jn 1:19–34). It was to be the beginning of Jesus' public ministry, and the climax of John's. Jesus, who apparently had been watching John's activities with keen interest from afar, came to the prophet from his home in Nazareth of Galilee. John already knew who Jesus was as well—they were cousins, after all (Lk 1:36), although the realization that this was the one for whom he had been preparing the way now struck John with full force (Jn 1:29–34)—and he was put off by Jesus' request to be baptized. "I need to be baptized by you—and you come to me?" (Mt 3:14; cf. Jn 1:26–27, 1:30). For all the hype attached to himself, John knew that his role was to prepare the way for the Kingdom of Heaven—and now here came the king. Jesus tacitly acknowledged that John was right, but replied,

Permit it now anyway, for by doing it in this way it is fitting for us to fulfill all righteousness.   (Mt 3:15)

That is, in the context of lives lived according to the Torah, it was the right thing to do. Jesus neither could nor would become a leader of those he hoped would follow if he refused to identify with them fully from the start. It's the one who comes up through the ranks (working in the mailroom or peeling potatoes like the little guy) who wins the right to be heard ("he's one of us…but so much more!"), and so Jesus joined with his future followers in their confession and dedication to God (cf. 2 Cor 5:21). Emerging from the water, the Spirit of God descended on Jesus like a dove from on high—more so even than the mantle of Elijah falling back from the sky to Elisha (cf. 2 Kgs 2:7–14), and a voice from heaven declared,

This is my beloved Son in whom I am well pleased.

(Mt 3:17)

Even John hadn't heard *that* before.

From this point on the Gospel writers fade John from the scene. John himself would have approved: "He must increase," the Baptist later told his disciples, "and I must decrease" (Jn 3:30). Understandably, some of them had trouble with the idea and were a little jealous of Jesus' success which appeared to detract from the work of their own master (Jn 3:26). John could have solved the problem by simply disbanding his own ministry in favor of that of Jesus, since his specific calling had been to prepare the way for Jesus' appearance in the first place. But he continued to preach and baptize to all who still would come, and Jesus even endorsed his ministry by heading back into Galilee so as not to visibly override John's work (Jn 4:1–3).

John's prophetic ministry, in any case, could not have lasted much longer; altogether it covered no more than a year (or two at the most) from start to finish. His work was cut short when he was arrested and put in prison—familiar ground for prophets, to be sure—ostensibly because of personal criticism of the conduct of the tetrarch, Herod Antipas (Mt 14:3–12; Mk 6:14–29; Lk 9:7–9). John publicly called Antipas to account for divorcing his wife to marry Herodias, the wife of his (half-)brother, Philip. John's point could have been that Antipas' divorce was foolish politically, since the tetrarch's divorced wife was a powerful Nabatean queen, but ramifications on the nation-state level didn't concern the prophet. What irked Antipas was that John had held him to the same moral standards of everyone else ("I'm the *tetrarch*, after all"). While the proverbial straw that broke the camel's back was personal, John had already been in Antipas' bull's eye anyway for advocating "subversive" economic changes in the tetrarch's corner of the empire. If enough soldiers and tax collectors heeded John's mandate to collect only what was technically due the empire (i.e., the minimum amount that righteousness allowed), the revenues that flowed upward through the Roman imperial system would be slowed and Antipas' own neck would be on the line. Clearly this fell in the category of political insurrection. So, Josephus:

> Now when [many] people came to crowd about [John]—for they were greatly moved by hearing his words—Herod [Antipas] feared lest the great influence John had over the people might put it into his power and inclination to raise a rebellion (the people seemed ready to do anything he should advise). He then thought it best, by putting John to death, to prevent any mischief he might cause and thereby not bring himself into difficulty [with Rome] if he waited until it was too late. (Ant. xviii.5.2)

The gruesome act came during Herod's birthday

party as he celebrated in bawdy splendor before a multitude of leading officials of his realm. (The scene was strangely reminiscent of the drunken banquets of the Persian king Ahasuerus, who, like Antipas, made promises while under the influence of pomp and drink that he later regretted; Esth 1:1–22; cf. Mt 14:9). "What a great feast!" we can hear him crowing. "Bring on the rack of lamb. And only the best of the game, the plumpest goose and choicest gazelle! Pile it high on the platter. What? Another course, Herodias? And served by your own enchanting daughter? Bring it in!" And so in she danced, lithely serving up the finest cut of all, the head of John the Baptist. Josephus adds the detail that John was beheaded in Antipas' fortress in Machaerus, a walled palace with special quarters for political prisoners on a nearly impregnable rise deep in the hills of Perea.

John's disciples were granted the right to their leader's decapitated body and buried what was left of his remains with all the dignity they could muster in a location not mentioned by either the Gospel writers or Josephus. One tradition—surely spurious—placed John's burial in Sebaste. This was the location of a sumptuous palace of Herod the Great and the site both of Herod's marriage to Mariamne and the execution of his beloved sons Alexander and Aristobulus (Ant. xvi.3.3–4.6, xvi.10.6–11.7). So the three elements present in the story of John's beheading by Antipas (a palace feast, marriage and murder) were

The Hasmonean king Alexander Jannaeus first built a fort at Machaerus; true to form, Herod the Great enlarged the site with another one of his magnificent palaces and constructed a port at the hot springs of Callirrhoe below that facilitated travel across the Dead Sea to Judea. His son, Herod Antipas, inherited the site. Today Machaerus is partially reconstructed, with a large enough collection of recovered building stones and architectural fragments to again prompt the Herodian imagination. Partying in splendor amidst a desert wasteland like only a Herod could do, Antipas threw a birthday bash for himself, inviting the leading men of his kingdom. John, meanwhile, locked up in the mountain's holding tank, no doubt heard the revelry. Eventually he, too, received an invitation to the party, but to be seen, not heard.

The strong hill of Machaerus offers a commanding view of the northern end of the Dead Sea from the east. The King's Highway, Transjordan's historic north-south trunk route, lies ten gnarled miles to the east, close enough to be controlled by the site but far enough away to give Machaerus an aura of rugged invincibility. It was a good place to secure political prisoners—and a tempting target for rebel takeover. During the first centuries B.C. and A.D., Machaerus controlled the eastern frontier of whatever power-may-be that ruled Judea, be it Hasmonean, Herodian, Roman or, with the outbreak of the Great Revolt of A.D. 66, Jewish. (photo: Garo Nalbandian)

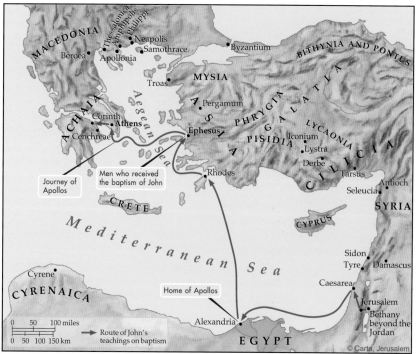

The Influence of John the Baptist in the Mediterranean World.

John was born in a nondescript Judean hill country village, baptized along a stretch of the landlocked Jordan Valley and died in a desert fortress east of the Dead Sea, but his influence reached deep into the Roman world. From the Book of Acts (18:24–19:3) we can track John's teachings on baptism from Judea to Alexandria, then on to the Aegean and, likely, beyond. John's disciples helped to plow the fertile ground around the Mediterranean that was soon sown with the teachings of the Apostle Paul.

The excess waters from the springs of Umm el-'Umdan (Aenon) have carved a deep cut in the marly soil of the region just above their final drop into the twisting bends of the Jordan River. Although they once grew only along the banks, dense reeds now fill the trough, thriving on today's reduced but always muddy flow. The supple reed, flipping in the wind, is useful enough for mats or baskets, but certainly not majestic and long-lived like "a tree planted by the water that extends its roots by a stream" (Jer 17:8). The well-established prophetic image for a life blessed by God fit John; it was Antipas who was the ephemeral reed.

also part of Antipas' father's experience in Sebaste. Apparently the memory of tradition simply blurred people, places and events together. Despondent, John's disciples informed Jesus of the affair (Mt 14:12). To whom else could they go?

When John was in prison, facing the cold stone walls and a diet that probably made him *wish* he had locusts and wild honey—not knowing if he would be executed although the grisly thought must have crossed his mind—he questioned whether or not this Jesus whom he had baptized really was the one who would vindicate the bold turn that his life had taken. Was it all worth it? Was Jesus going to pick up the pieces? Or would the momentum that was building for the Kingdom of Heaven stall out like it had when other messiah figures died (cf. Ant.xiv.9.2; Acts 5:33–39, 21:38)? John sent some of his disciples to Jesus to ask if in fact he was the expected one: "I just need to know." Jesus' reply was the reply of the obvious: the blind see, the lame walk, the lepers are cleansed, the deaf hear, the dead are raised up and the downtrodden are hearing the Good News (Mt 11:2–6; Lk 7:18–23). Don't worry. The Kingdom is in good hands. Then Jesus added, "Blessed is the one who doesn't stumble over me." This last comment wasn't for John's benefit (Jesus was confident John wasn't someone who flipped back and forth like a reed in the wind; cf. Mt 11:7–8; Lk 7:24–25), but for the prophet's disciples. What would *they* do if their master was gone?

And now he was, and John's disciples had to make a choice. Some, such as the disciple Andrew of Bethsaida, brother of Simon Peter, attached themselves to Jesus' growing band (Jn 1:35–42). Others probably scattered or went back home, as Jesus'

own disciples (including Andrew) would do soon after the crucifixion (cf. Mt 26:56; Jn 21:1–3). But some remained loyal to John; baptized by him, they followed and promoted his teachings and manner of baptism, fasting and prayer (cf. Mk 2:18; Lk 11:1). John's movement remained alive and gained ground far outside of the land of Israel, in Egypt and in Asia Minor. Twenty-five years later, in the mid-50s A.D., the Apostle Paul met a group of around twelve people in Ephesus who believed in Jesus, yet had only been baptized according to the baptism of John. Apparently they had learned of John (and perhaps even Jesus) through Apollos of Alexandria, "an eloquent man…mighty in the Scriptures who had been instructed in the way of the Lord and spoke and taught accurately the things concerning Jesus, but was acquainted only with the baptism of John" (Acts 18:24–25, 19:1–3; cf. 1 Cor 1:10–13). Apollos had since moved on to Corinth. How he learned about John in the first place is not known, but the cosmopolitan Jewish community in Alexandria did have ongoing contact with Jerusalem and an eloquent man such as Apollos surely would have been well connected to channels of learning and thought throughout the Jewish world. Paul explained to the twelve that John's baptism of repentance was preliminary to the coming of Jesus, in whom they now should be baptized. Upon doing so, they received the Holy Spirit and entered into the full community of Christians in Ephesus (Acts 19:4–7).

For many of the Jews of Jerusalem and Judea, John the Baptist was a rather pointed reminder that a life worth living was a life characterized by deeds of righteousness. For the emerging Christian movement across the Roman world, John was a bridge to Jesus, "the Lamb of God who takes away the sin of the world" (Jn 1:29). But for Jesus, John was a prophet—yet more than a prophet:

> *Truly, I say to you, among those born of women there has not arisen anyone greater than John the Baptist, yet he who is least in the Kingdom of Heaven is greater than he.* (Mt 11:11)

It's quite an assessment for someone who made quite a scene during his lifetime. And it's also quite an honor, comparatively speaking, for those who followed.

CHAPTER 19
MARY AND JOSEPH
Simple Lives Lived Extraordinarily

For a book that focuses so much on interpersonal relationships, there are not a lot of stories about family life in the Bible. As a result, with relatively few exceptions we know little to nothing about the families of people of Scripture. Who were the wives of Joshua or Jehu, for instance, or of Ezra or Nehemiah? Who were their children? Admittedly the world of the Bible was a man's world, and many of the stories preserved in Scripture are stories of affairs of state or the temple, where family life played an incidental or negligible role. But even those that do speak of domestic affairs tend to omit details we think important, like women's names: it's Jephthah and the-daughter-of-Jephthah, Manoah and the-wife-of-Manoah, Samson and a-woman-of-Timnah, Elijah and the-widow-of-Zarephath, and Peter and the-mother-in-law-of-Peter, for instance. Wives or mothers are mentioned by name in the Bible if they were infertile (Hannah) or fostered palace intrigue (such as David's queens Michal, Ahinoam, Maacah, Haggith and Bathsheba—not a lot of filial love lost among *their* boys), or when their husbands were dead (Naomi and Ruth) or just plain foolish (Abigail and Esther), but only rarely in normal familial roles. The stories of Abraham and his offspring (where perhaps too much of the family dynamic is revealed) are an exception: here the reader is afforded a long peek into the patriarchal tent, but behind the curtain stirred a brood that, on the balance, was rather dysfunctional (or, if the reader prefers, clever, conniving or resourceful). Tranquil families just don't make for good stories. Finally we meet Zechariah and Elizabeth, as stable as the rocky hill country in which they born—then alas, they are just set-up characters for the more important story of John the Baptist. But on their heels come Mary and Joseph (also an opening act, though of the Messiah) who, on the whole, provide one of the best biblical examples of a husband-wife relationship that fostered wholesome family life. Not that the couple didn't have their share of troubles: there was that matter of having to explain Mary's pregnancy to a village where of course it was everyone's business, followed by a quick flight to Egypt as refugees, then Mary's bereavement, apparently, as an all-too-young widow who was left to raise the Savior of the World alone. But in spite of the challenges thrown their way, both Mary and Joseph occupy a place of distinctive honor among all other couples of the Bible and provide a model of dignified speech and

behavior for those who follow.

The story of Mary and Joseph is a Galilee story, with important excursions to Bethlehem, Jerusalem and Egypt. Galilee had a large Jewish population in the first century A.D., and its people maintained a vibrant cultural life centered in towns and villages scattered across the fertile hills and valleys of the region. It wasn't always so—local Israelite settlement had taken quite a hit with the Assyrian invasions of the late eighth century B.C., and a continual influx of Babylonians, Persians, Greeks and Romans, among others along the great international highways of the southern Levant conspired against Jewish efforts to reestablish their own presence in the region. Historians often speak of an attempt on the part of the Hasmonean kings—particularly by Aristobulus in 104–103 B.C.—to "conquer" or "judaize" Galilee, forcibly or otherwise, as part of an ambitious Hasmonean attempt to return lands once controlled by ancient Israel to the Jewish fold. Specific evidence for a premeditated effort such as this is wholly lacking in written sources from the time, however. Josephus, citing the first-century B.C. Greco-Alexandrian historian Timagenes (No. 81), speaks only of Aristobulus' forced circumcision of residents of Iturea in and around Mount Hermon and the Huleh Basin (*Ant.* xiii.11.3), and of an occasion—specific details are not recorded—in which Aristobulus' brother Antigonus returned in glory

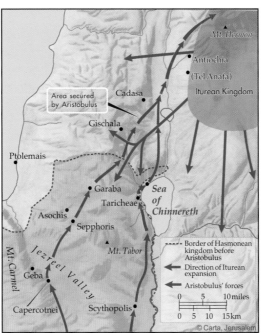

The Campaign of Aristobulus Against the Itureans, 104–103 B.C. *The Itureans were a confederation of Arab tribes that had settled on and around Mt. Hermon by the end of the second century B.C. As the Hasmonean kings began to move northward to fill the vacuum caused by the collapse of Seleucid control in the region, the Itureans moved south in an attempt to do the same. Aristobulus sought to contain the Itureans in their Mt. Hermon home (he never conquered them) and secure Galilee for Jerusalem. Josephus' claim that Aristobulus forcibly converted the Itureans to Judaism is probably an overstatement. What the Hasmonean king seems to have accomplished was to provide an environment in Galilee in which Jews could again prosper.*

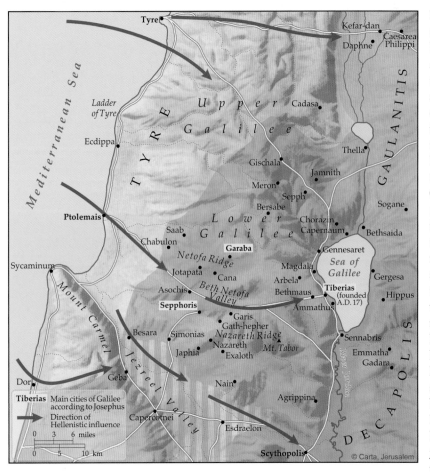

The Galilee of Mary and
Joseph. *Mary and Joseph
were at home in the hills of
Lower Galilee, a region under
the control of Herod the Great
then, after 4 B.C., governed by
his son, Antipas. In the eyes
of a Judean this was a bit of
a frontier land, but for those
stout of spirit who were willing
to work hard, Galilee offered a
comfortable home. At the same
time, corridors of Hellenism
pierced the region, flowing
mainly through the fertile
Jezreel and Beth Netofa valleys.
These offered opportunities
of growth for the intrepid,
but were looked upon with
suspicion by the multitudes who
just tried to get by.*

to Jerusalem having gotten "a very fine suit of ar-
mour, made with fine martial ornaments, in Galilee"
(*Ant.* xiii.11.1; *War* i.3.3). Neither of these references,
both of which Josephus largely makes in pass-
ing, suggest formal campaigns in Lower Galilee or
around the Sea of Galilee, the regions that were
most densely settled by Jews in the north of the land
during the time of Jesus. Nevertheless Galilee seems
to have been an important—although somewhat
peripheral—part of the Hasmonean kingdom, with
a growing effort by zealous Jews—officially or otherwise—bent on reestablishing Jewish religious, political and social life in the region. Certainly we can
also posit some degree of Jewish immigration into
Galilee throughout the decades leading up to the
time of the Gospels, and infer that of those Jews who
moved north, some were attracted by the region's
favorable economic opportunities while others no
doubt were motivated by an ideology shaped by a
"right of return" to the land of the kings of Israel.

The geographical shape of the region made this
both desirable and difficult. Unlike the rugged hills
of Judea where the Jews of Jerusalem could forge
an energetic religious and cultural identity in a region that was largely isolated from the waves of Hellenism washing ashore on the coastal plain below,
Galilee lay open and exposed. Broad valleys bisect
the region, connecting the Mediterranean with the
Rift Valley and beyond and inviting West to meet

East and settle down on its fertile plains. The result was that even though Lower Galilee again
had a large Jewish population in the first century
A.D., distinct and influential corridors of Hellenism
remained in the region, tying Ptolemais and Caesarea to Tiberias and bending the local culture and
economy to Rome. Quite naturally, these corridors
flowed along the valleys themselves as Rome thrust
its tentacles into all of the economically productive
land throughout its Empire. It wasn't for nothing
that Matthew, quoting the prophet Isaiah, labeled
Galilee of the Gospels, "Galilee of the *Gentiles*"
(Mt 4:15; cf. Isa 9:1). Jewish landowners of large estates
in the Jezreel and Beth Netofa valleys (the valleys
that cradle the Nazareth Ridge on the south and
north respectively) generally—and understandably—recognized the personal economic advantages of participating in the system and grew quite
wealthy in the process. But for those who sought to
reestablish a *Torah*-based religious identity in Galilee in the face of the temptations of the world at
hand, such countrymen were simply collaborators.
Many of these Jews would have been more comfortable living high on the hills above the great valleys
below, or in pockets a bit distant from centers of
Hellenism. Or, it could be that Jews who already
lived in more remote areas simply found it easier to
justify their spot in life by turning more directly toward the time-tested demands of Judaism.

In any case, of all of the Jewish villages of Galilee
in the first century A.D. we would be hard pressed
to find one that lay closer to the opportunities afforded such "collaborators," yet stuck in the back-
woods than was Nazareth. This was a small village
of a few hundred people at most, with houses scattered over not more than 40 to 50 acres, largely
inconsequential to the economy of the region and
not mentioned in any documents of the first centuries B.C./A.D. other than the Gospels. (Matthew
and Luke graciously call Nazareth a "city" [Mt 2:23;
Lk 2:4; 4:29] although in the sixth century, even after
the place received attention from pilgrims due to
its associations with Jesus, Jerome still referred to it
as a "hamlet"; *Onomasticon* 141.) Nazareth was nestled
in a small basin of soft, chalky limestone high on
the crest of a rocky ridge rising 1,100 feet straight
out of the Jezreel Valley. The drop to the north, toward Sepphoris and the Beth Netofa Valley, is more
gradual, but steep enough to keep Nazareth off the
main route. Owing to the quality of the soft stone at
the top of the ridge, the residents of Nazareth made
due with relatively poor local building materials, a
weak though adequate spring and soil that was not
terribly productive. It was possible to make a living
in Nazareth, but left to the limits of its own resources the town would never become very prosperous.
On the other hand, the hard limestone ridge down-
slope provided good building materials and a rich

Today the city of Nazareth fills the soft limestone basin on top of the Nazareth Ridge, spilling over the sides into the valleys below. It's a crowded, bustling city, the center of economic life in the mid-Galilee, with a mixed population of Christians, Muslims and, in adjacent Nazareth Illit, Jews. In other words, the Nazareth of today is much like the Sepphoris of the first century, offering its residents opportunities and challenges beyond those typically faced by villagers. Ironically, today's Sepphoris (Zippori) is but a small Jewish village.

terra rosa soil excellent for olives, figs and grapes, and some villagers certainly farmed these areas. Just beyond, the wonderfully fertile valleys at the base of the Nazareth Ridge carried international commerce across the southern Levant. It was the Jezreel Valley to the south (which the Psalmist called "the pasturelands of God"; Ps 83:12) and the smaller yet equally blessed Beth Netofa Valley to the north that served by comparison to punctuate Nazareth's less-favored situation. The residents of Nazareth of course knew their lot in life and realized that for those among them who preferred to stay home, the resources below lay just out of hand. At home in their small basin-bound village, these Nazarenes could physically see only a tight horizon line, and although the vast world over the rim was out of sight, it was never out of mind. Some chose to interact with it, finding work, trade or social opportunities in other villages in the area or even in nearby Sepphoris. Others clung to their chalky basin home and threw up a barrier of religious and political particularism against the Gentiles swirling around their feet, if the in-your-face reaction of the residents of Nazareth at Jesus' favorable mention of Sidonians and Syrians is any indication (cf. Lk 4:24–29). In its many facets, then, the setting of Jesus' home village rightly prompted Nathanael's clipped censure: "Can *anything* good come out of Nazareth?" (Jn 1:46).

For the Jews of Galilee, the choice between participating in the economic opportunities of their demographically mixed region and keeping *Torah* was not clear-cut. Some did both; many likely did neither. It would be difficult to suggest that a working knowledge of *Torah* and the ability or willingness

to keep its provisions—at least as expounded by the Pharisees—was prevalent among the "people of the land" (*am ha-aretz*). As tenants, day laborers and at best small freeholders of bit plots of land, these multitudes were also largely shut out from full participation in the economic affairs of the region. Other Jews found ways to combine the two. The presence of a synagogue in Nazareth (cf. Lk 4:16; remains of the building have not been found) suggests that this was a religiously observant town, at least for those educated in *Torah*. It is to this kosher group that Mary and Joseph belonged, while Joseph's skill as a "carpenter" (*tekton*) likely brought him into contact with Gentiles as well.

Bedrock lies close to the surface on the Nazareth Ridge, a blessing for builders but a bane for farming. From these rocks skilled craftsmen such as Joseph and Jesus wrestled building stone from the ground and carefully shaped it into blocks for homes for the growing families of Nazareth. It was a necessary and helpful trade, and Joseph's family likely prospered as he worked his skills in Nazareth and nearby villages and cities.

Although the village of Nazareth was stuck in a relatively unproductive basin high atop the Nazareth Ridge, rich farmland stretched away in the valleys below. The Beth Netofa Valley, seen here from Cana with a view back toward Nazareth, provided a strong economic base for central Galilee. These flat lands also carried the international highway connecting the Mediterranean port of Ptolemais with the Sea of Galilee and Transjordan, via Sepphoris. With the world at their feet, Mary and Joseph remained loyal to Torah and the call of God on their lives— no small accomplishment in any place or time.

Matthew and Luke provide important information about Mary and Joseph in connection with their stories of the birth and early years of Jesus. Although each offers the reader a different set of episodes, it is possible to weave their narratives into a single, credible and connected storyline and even flesh it out a bit by reasonable suppositions based on other textual evidence and realities of geography, history, social custom and patterns of national and personal behavior. While early and medieval church traditions are useful for examining the development of Christian memory and thought, they also provide additional interesting (and often entertaining) information that highlights the Gospel story.

The circumstances that first placed Mary and Joseph in Nazareth are wholly unknown. According to Luke, each was a resident of the town (Lk 1:26–27, 2:4), but for how many previous generations, if any, their families lived there, and why they chose to do so (Nazareth was a relatively new village in the first century A.D.), it is impossible to say. The apocryphal gospel *Protoevangelium of James*, dated to the mid-second century A.D. and purportedly written by a son of Joseph from an earlier marriage, records the miraculous annunciation and birth of Mary to Joachim, a pious and exceedingly rich man of Jerusalem, and his childless wife Anna; the tradition that localizes Mary's birth in a house under the Church of St. Anne in today's Muslim Quarter of Jerusalem can't be traced back earlier than the fifth century A.D. The *Protoevangelium* continues with the account of how Mary was raised in the Temple from the age of 2 to 12, like a dove receiving food from the hand of an angel, then how she was given to Joseph, an old, widowed carpenter tramping through Judea who heard of her situation from Zechariah and who was specially chosen by the LORD, under his own protests of inadequacy, to be her husband.

Clearly this set of traditions arose from a composite of themes connected with several great men and women of the Bible, including Sarah, Samuel, Elijah, Zechariah the father of John the Baptist and even Mary herself. In reality Joseph was likely older than Mary, although not exceedingly so, and both seem to have had Jerusalem ties only in the sense that Joseph and perhaps also Mary were blood descendants of David (Joseph's genealogy is recorded in Matthew 1:1–16, and Mary's, many argue, in Luke 3:23–38; cf. Lk 1:27, 1:32–34 in which *Mary's* son will be a descendant of David). Joseph also maintained his ties to his family's native city, Bethlehem, the birthplace of David, and likely knew distant relatives there.

The story of Mary and Joseph, however, begins in Nazareth, with the betrothal of the couple already part of the opening scene. Typical of others of the time, Mary's family would have promised her in marriage to Joseph not long after she reached "marriageable age," that is, as soon as she was able to bear children. The marriage itself would take place one or two years later. In the meantime, Mary would continue to live in her father's house, under the umbrella of his authority and honor. The girl—and sometimes even the man—typically had little say in the arrangement, which was orchestrated by the fathers (or eldest brothers) of the two. Marriages were contracted within branches of an extended family to keep the resources and reputation of the family intact. Likely a bride price was paid by the family of the prospective husband; those who adhered to the rabbinic school of Shammai typically offered one *denarius* (about a day's wage), while those following the school of Hillel gave one *prutah*, a mere pittance (*Mishnah, Kiddushin 1.1*). In any case, the amount was largely symbolic—what's money between friends? The betrothal was sealed by witnesses and capped by a village-wide celebration, complete with gift giving (even today, traditional Middle Eastern societies place as much—or more—emphasis on the engagement party as on the wedding; the latter is just the formal "ratification" of the prior intent to forge bonds of unity between two families). Because they were from a small village, almost certainly the families of Mary and Joseph were already related by previous marriages (Mary and Elizabeth, the mother of John the Baptist, were kinsmen; so likely were Mary and Joseph), and the resources, reputation and honor of everyone rode in part on the success of this new union binding the families even tighter together. Anything that ran counter to the purity of the moment placed the honor and reputation of everyone involved—even those not yet born—in jeopardy.

Mary was probably thirteen or fourteen years of age when the attention of Nazareth focused on her upcoming marriage to Joseph. Although most girls were betrothed as soon as they were physically able to extend the family line, the reality of this custom likely didn't lessen the impact of the moment, and mixed parts of excitement, fear, duty and uncertainty as to what it all would feel like came crowding in at once. But on top of that, Mary was confronted with one more element that no one before or since had ever faced: an angel of the LORD appeared to her (that in itself, though highly unusual, was not unprecedented; *cf.* Judg 6:11–12, 13:3; Lk 1:11) and announced the impossible, that she, though still a virgin—would bear a son

> *[who] will be great*
> *and will be called the Son of the Most High;*
> *and the Lord God will give him the throne of his*
> *father David*
> *and he will reign over the house of Jacob forever,*
> *and his kingdom will have no end.* (Lk 1:32–33)

The language was nothing short of messianic. Mary had "found favor with God" (Lk 1:30); her family roots, upbringing, religious and mental constitution, talents, abilities and situation in life all fit exactly with what God Himself considered a worthwhile life to be, and He entrusted the redemption of the world into her hands. And all this without prior experience to the task at hand, no less—as if any amount of formal preparation would have been sufficient. Mary had by birth and by character what couldn't be taught. "Hail, favored one! The LORD is with you!" (Lk 1:28). She responded perhaps a bit boldly for a first-century village girl who had never seen an angel before (who had?), yet who knew good and well what was and wasn't humanly possible: "How can this be? I'm a virgin (and I intend to stay so until I'm properly married!)."

> *The Holy Spirit will come upon you, and the power*
> *of the Most High will overshadow you;*
> *and for that reason the holy offspring will be called*
> *the Son of God…*
> *for nothing will be impossible with God.*
>
> (Lk 1:34–35, 1:37)

And to emphasize that even *this* was not impossible, the angel offered the bit of information that Mary's older cousin Elizabeth, though of course not a virgin, was going to have a special child herself (Lk 1:36). Mary's pregnancy was not only wholly unexpected, it was wholly unprecedented (could the birth of the Messiah be otherwise?). After her initial shock at God's call, Mary passively accepted the inevitable (Lk 1:38), partly from social conditioning, partly from character.

But a quick trip to Elizabeth was also in order. If Mary was going to become pregnant before she was married, things could get rather uncomfortable at home. Elizabeth was family, and Mary needed family now (Elizabeth probably did, too). Surely *she* would understand. The journey from Nazareth to the hill country of Judea, where Elizabeth

and Zechariah lived, took at least six days and was not an easy walk. Mary went quickly, before physical changes to her body would have hindered the journey (Lk 1:39–40). Certainly she took some of the menfolk of her family with her, for protection, support and provision. The roads between Galilee and Judea—through Samaria or, more likely, the route down the length of the Jordan Valley—were fairly well traveled, but certainly no place for a young girl of marriageable age without protection. Women of the street maybe, but not Mary.

Elizabeth sensed that there was something special about the visit (Lk 1:41–45) and when she arrived Mary, in a full dramatic entrance, burst out with praise to God:

During the course of archaeological excavations at Caesarea in 1962, three broken pieces of a dark-grey marble slab were found in the ruins of the 3rd–4th century A.D. *synagogue in the northern part of the ancient city. These three pieces were part of a much longer inscription containing a list of the 24 priestly courses named in 1 Chronicles 24:7–18, with the family name of each course listed alongside the city to which that family moved after the destruction of the Temple in* A.D. *70. The eighteenth line reads: "[the 18th] co[urse, Happizzez], Nazareth" (cf. 1 Chron 24:15). This is the only mention of Nazareth in ancient sources outside of the Gospels and the writings of the Early Church fathers. The Nazareth to which the Happizzez family chose to relocate was already a religiously observant town before* A.D. *70, with an active synagogue life to which Joseph and Jesus belonged.*

This young Bethlehem bride of the late 19th century A.D. *is heavily adorned for her upcoming wedding. She can't be much older than Mary was for hers. Both weddings were carefully arranged by the older men of their families—for Mary's, God himself was also involved— and this poor Bethlehem girl's expression belies her not-so-radiant emotions at what lies ahead. With the weight of the world growing within her, Mary's emotions were likely often similar, in spite of the confidence voiced in* The Magnificat *(Lk 1:46–55).*

The Psalmist didn't know that the shore of the Dead Sea was the lowest place on the face of the earth. He only knew that from Jerusalem the arid wasteland of the Wilderness of Judah dropped away at his feet and ended with a salty splash far below. And he knew that here and there somewhere deep in the folds of the barren hills of the wilderness, it was possible—wondrously so—to find springs, water, and life. These were bits of creation in a mysterious place, metaphors of human birth:

For You formed my inward
        parts,
    you wove me together in
        my mother's womb.…
My frame was not hidden
        from you
    when I was made in secret,
        skillfully wrought in the
        depths of the earth.
(Ps 139:13, 15)

Birth is a miracle itself; for Mary, doubly so.

My soul exalts the LORD,
    and my spirit has rejoiced in God my Savior.
For He has regard for the humble state of His bond
    slave;
for behold, from this time on all generations will
    count me blessed.
For the Mighty One has done great things for me,
    and holy is His name.… *(Lk 1:46–55)*

She couldn't hold it in any longer. Mary's song of praise (*The Magnificat*) is a wonderful composition that draws on themes and phrases from great men and women, psalmists and prophets of the Old Testament (cf. 1 Sam 2:1–10; Job 5:11; Ps 34:2–7, 35:9, 98:1, 103:17, 107:9, 118:15, 132:11; Hab 3:18). The song shows that in spite of her gender and tender years, Mary was steeped in the Hebrew Scriptures and synagogue liturgies. Passive, perhaps, but with a mind like a sponge. Mary stayed with Elizabeth for three months, long enough for the cousins to bind souls but not quite long enough for her to "show." "You have to get back," the older and wiser Elizabeth likely counseled. "Your place is not here. God be with you!" Then it was home.

Back home—and Mary knew something was happening deep within her body. Her soul mate Elizabeth was far away, and apparently no one in Nazareth yet had a clue. And how did this young girl—fast becoming a young woman—think she was going to break the news to Joseph and the families that were *so proud of her?* Matthew spills the beans for the reader of his Gospel story:

Before they came together she was found to be with child—by the Holy Spirit. (Mt 1:18)

And who was going to believe that last part?

"She was found." Baggy clothing and all, Mary couldn't hide it forever. Who noticed first? Probably not Joseph, but someone in her own father's house. Perhaps the men who had accompanied her journey to Elizabeth? "I told you we shouldn't have let her go to Judea! They're a rough lot down there—knocked her up, they did" (which was actually a sophisticated Judean's attitude of the uncouth Galileans, but the sentiment worked both ways). Then, turning to the more obvious villain, "Or maybe it was *you*, Joseph??"

"Mary, how could you?"

Even though Mary and Joseph were not yet married, certain rights of marriage were attached to the state of being betrothed. Infidelity by the woman, for instance (in those days such things were always the woman's fault), constituted adultery, with all the rights of consequence as if the offending party had already been married. Joseph was a righteous man, living in a *Torah*-observant community. The law must be upheld. Mary would be hauled out to the doorway of her father's house and stoned to death by her neighbors, family and friends (Deut 22:13–21; Jn 8:4–5), her last view of home obliterated by men grasping stones, bent on restoring the honor of their fine town. The institution of marriage was too sacred to be treated lightly; the nature of small village life would do the rest. (Thirty years later Jesus refused to condemn a woman caught in the very act of adultery, but the men of Nazareth nearly stoned him for an offense much less bold; Jn 8:1–11; Lk 4:16–30.)

But Joseph was a *righteous* man, and unwilling to put Mary or her family to more shame than was righteously necessary (Mt 1:19). He would divorce her "quietly," without public humiliation, and let her remain in her father's house, protected to the extent that her male kinfolk were willing or able to do, living out her life, forever single, as best that circumstances would allow. This Joseph was resolved to do, even though not knowing who had made her pregnant and shamed to know that, willingly or not, she had turned against him.

But Joseph's aim was interrupted. An angel approached him in a dream and announced that God had a plan, that the son whom his betrothed was carrying and whom he would have the privilege of raising was conceived of the Holy Spirit. Not only that, this Jesus, as he would be called, would save His people—you, Joseph, and your family and the people of Nazareth and Galilee and Judea and beyond—from their sins. Prophecy was being fulfilled. Emmanuel! God is with us, *again* (Mt 1:20–25; cf. Isa 7:14).

Hurrying the time of the marriage, Joseph took Mary as his wife (Mt 1:24). The people of Nazareth must have recognized that Joseph had fulfilled *Torah* in a way that exceeded their understanding of the intent of the law. And now his bride was radiant with relief—and showed.

Just when Mary's life was starting to get back on track, the imperial government of Rome intervened. Caesar Augustus announced that a census would be taken throughout the empire (Lk 2:1). While the practice of holding a census for the purpose of conscription and/or taxation was known in ancient Rome, this particular census, decreed in the closing years of the reign of Herod the Great, is otherwise unattested in historic sources (cf. Acts 5:37 and *Ant.* xviii.2.1, which mention a census for taxation by Quirinius, imperial legate of Syria-Cilicia, in A.D. 6; cf. Lk 2:2). We might speculate that the census was taken during an early term of Quirinius' rule over Syria in anticipation of Herod's death, in an attempt by Rome to ease what could otherwise have the makings of a nasty fight between his ambitious sons (the kingdom divided relatively peacefully in the end). In any case Joseph, of the house and lineage of David, was required in Bethlehem, his ancestral home (Lk 2:3–5).

Legally, it seems, Joseph's ties were still there. By implication, he was still an outsider in Nazareth and the situation of Mary's pregnancy wasn't helping his attempts to blend in. As a woman Mary wasn't legally obliged to make the trip from Nazareth to Bethlehem, but Joseph, not wanting to leave his wife behind to face the "looks" alone, brought her along. The journey wasn't taken lightly; complications related to childbirth were the leading cause of death for women in the ancient world. This time Mary's trip south was undoubtedly more strenuous than the one a few months before. But in a way Joseph might have been relieved, secretly hoping that his wife would be able to give birth in Bethlehem, away from the tensions they were leaving behind. Maybe they could even start a new life together there. The expectant couple arrived in Bethlehem some time before Mary gave birth (Lk 2:6); certainly the laden trip of cards and carols in which Mary gives birth the very night of their arrival compresses events too tightly.

Nor is the image of a crowded inn with an empty stable somewhere in the back forty reasonable. Joseph would have stayed in the home of distant relatives for the duration of his time in Bethlehem, and there is always room at home for more family, however "long lost" they may be. Although specific archaeological data from Bethlehem is lacking, excavations of villages in Galilee and a reasonable comparison with village homes from the ethnographic present (Palestinian houses of the 19th century) suggest that every house of decent size in Bethlehem would have had a guest room (Gk. *kataluma*, incorrectly rendered "inn" in Lk 2:7) for such occasions as this, to greet, feed, lodge and entertain

guests. This room, facing the street or open courtyard of the compound, was the public face of the home. Alas, perhaps because the family was large or due to the commotion of the events of the day, this space was already taken by others. Or, the issue may have been ritual purity: perhaps there was no room (place) for Mary in the guest room *because* she was giving birth and so she was taken to another room for the moment of delivery (the practice continues in traditional Palestinian village homes, although for different reasons). In addition to a more private room in the rear of the home that was occupied by the homeowner and his immediate family, each house also had a room or two that were utilitarian, used for storage or domestic activities and, in inclement weather or at night, as a stable for the family's livestock: a small herd of sheep and goats, and maybe a donkey or two. Germs and sanitation were not an issue. In the mid-second century A.D. Justin Martyr (*Dialogue with Trypho* 78) spoke of Jesus' birth in a cave; in fact for centuries many village homes in the hill country of Judea actually began as walled-in caves, with other rooms added outward as the needs of the family grew. When Mary finally did give birth to Jesus, it was within a tight, welcoming family context. Jesus' first cry would have been heard by everyone in the household compound and, in the stillness of the night, in other homes nearby. The birth was certainly attended by eager and competent midwives.

Some shepherds—by definition of an uncouth reputation and trusted by neither villagers or city folk—paid a visit that night (Lk 2:8–18). The shepherds figure prominently in Luke's account of Jesus' birth, if for no other reason than to highlight Jesus' ministry to social outcasts and the *am ha-aretz*. David had been a Bethlehem shepherd before becoming king (cf. 1 Sam 16:1–23) and Jesus, though destined for another trade, was also born to a kingdom. Not content with another quiet one-on-one conversation, the angels sang full voice that night:

Until the introduction of concrete as a building material, houses of Judea were made wholly of stone. It's relatively easy to find evidence of ancient quarrying in areas of exposed bedrock throughout the hill country, but it is the scarps of hills that have always provided ready-made stone homes made from caves. One simply needs to clear the ground around a suitable cave, wall in the front with nearby stones, leave space for a door and the home is complete: comfortable, snug and quite appropriate for human habitation, at least no less so than a free-standing house made out of the same kind of rock. The information relayed by Justin Martyr that Jesus was born in a Bethlehem cave is wholly reasonable—and not at all a stigma of a poor, rude entrance into the world.

"And in the same region there were shepherds out in the fields keeping watch over their flocks by night" (Lk 2:8). Not likely if it was wintertime! The fields of Bethlehem were far too valuable as grain-producing areas to be used to graze sheep and goats during the wintertime growing season. And, wintertime rains and wind drive all sane people indoors at night anyway. This flock of sheep, with one curious and precocious goat (so they are!), grazes among fig trees in the high hill country in late summer. Soon they will head east, leaving the growing areas behind for the farmer to sow his crop of winter wheat. Christmas will just have to wait for summertime.

For many, the Jesus of the modern church is the Jesus of stained glass, with images to turn the hearts of the faithful to the heavens but seldom representing "how it actually was." The Jesus of the Gospels is a Jesus of history and of faith, and the Christmas story more than any other allows Christians to continue to combine the two in fresh and meaningful ways.

Glory to God in the highest,
*   and on earth peace among men*
*   with whom He is well pleased.*   (Lk 2:14)

This was the climax of special visits paid by God's messengers to expectant mothers and wondering fathers since the time of Abraham (Gen 18:1–15; Judg 13:2–23; 2 Kgs 4:8–17; Lk 1:5–38; Heb 13:2). The climax of "the hopes and fears of all the years" was just beginning.

Luke provides some geographical details about the birth of Jesus that suggest that this first Christmas took place sometime in the summer or early fall, not winter as is celebrated today (the date December 25 was apparently adopted by Western Christians in the fourth century A.D. as a concession to the pagan mid-winter festivals of Saturnalia and Brumalia, celebrated across the Roman Empire on December 17–24 and 25 respectively). When Jesus was born, shepherds from the vicinity of Bethlehem were "out in the fields keeping watch over their flocks" (Lk 2:8). In the growing season of the hill country of Judea, the farmers of Bethlehem sow their fields with wheat and barley in November in anticipation of a spring and early summer harvest (*Pesach*/Passover and *Shavuot*/Weeks are spring harvest festivals). By late December their fields start to sprout with grain. Flocks of sheep and goats would love to feast of the soft green shoots, but only at the risk of incurring the wrath of the hard-working farmer! Rather, in the wintertime Bethlehem shepherds have historically driven their flocks eastward to graze off the scant growth afforded by the winter rains in the Judean wilderness, before the heat of the spring scorches the ground and forces them back up into the hills. Once in the vicinity of Bethlehem, the sheep and goats could forage and fertilize the fields all summer, after the crops had been harvested. Luke continues that the shepherds were in the fields "at night" (Lk 2:8), a pleasant time for shepherds to watch their flocks out-of-doors following the heat of a long summer day, but a miserably cold and wet experience in the winter. If Mary had given birth in December and the family's flocks were nearby, the stable in any case would have been crowded with animals seeking shelter and warmth, leaving no room for the expectant couple. Rabbinic sources (Mishnah, *Shekalim* 7.4) suggest that certain fields in the vicinity of Bethlehem were reserved year round for lambs being raised for Temple (Passover) sacrifice, and it is theologically tempting to suggest that it was these shepherds who paid the first visit to "the Lamb of God who takes away the sin of the world" (cf. Jn 1:29). Perhaps—but even they would have been in the fields at night only in the summertime!

Mary wrapped her baby in swaddling cloths and gently placed him in the manger—and for Jesus, this cozy crib was a fine first home (Lk 2:7). With reversed imagery describing unfaithful Israel, the prophet Ezekiel fills us in on the details of being a midwife:

As for your birth, on the day you were born your navel cord was not cut, nor were you washed with water for cleansing. You were not rubbed with salt or even wrapped in cloths. No eye looked with pity on you to do any of these things for you, to have compassion on you. Instead, you were thrown out into the open field, for you were abhorred on the day you were born.   (Ezek 16:4–5)

Mary's baby wasn't Joseph's. Everyone back home

assumed "illegitimate." Joseph had every right to cast it aside to die in the ditch, then get Mary pregnant the way it was supposed to happen. But like God did with His people, Joseph redeemed his firstborn son:

> When I passed by you and saw you squirming in your blood, I said to you, "Live!" I said to you while you were in your blood, "Live!" (Ezek 16:6)

The proud, redemptive parents were careful to keep *Torah* and so circumcised their baby on the eighth day of his new life (Lk 2:21; cf. Lev 12:1–3; Gen 17:12; Josh 5:2–9). With a yelp of pain and a smear of blood he entered into the Covenant of God's people, receiving the name Jesus ("the LORD is salvation" or "the LORD saves"). It was the right of the father to name his own son. Joseph deferred to the angel (cf. Mt 1:21; Lk 1:59); this was *God's* son, alive in flesh and blood (cf. Rom 8:3; Gal 4:4; Phil 2:7–8; Heb 2:17). He would shed much more of it later.

According to provisions in the *Torah* (Lev 12:1–5), Mary was considered to be ritually unclean from the time of the flow of blood during her delivery to the thirty-third day following the circumcision of her son. When Jesus was forty days old, Mary, with Joseph and her baby, went up from Bethlehem to the Temple in Jerusalem for her to be purified. Like most who visited the Temple, they likely entered the holy precinct through the Hulda Gates in the compound's southern wall, where they had easy access to the public *miqveh* pools for cleansing their bodies from ritual impurities. After the requisite immersion, the young parents, with Jesus, proceeded to the Nicanor Gate on the Temple Mount platform, at the entrance of the Women's Court (Mishnah, *Tamid* 5.6). It was there that Mary offered a sacrifice of two turtledoves—the offering of the poor—as atonement for her post-delivery ritual uncleanness (Lk 2:22–24; cf. Lev 12:6–8). At the same time Mary and Joseph formally presented Jesus to the LORD, fulfilling the *Torah*-command that all firstborn sons were to be given to God as a kind of first-fruit offering (Lk 2:22–23; Num 18:15–16; cf. Ex 13:1–2; Num 3:44–47; 1 Cor 15:23). Then, according to the provisions of the law, they "redeemed" him back to themselves (the verb is quite intentional) for the price of five sanctuary (i.e., Tyrian) shekels, the equivalent of about twenty days' wages paid in a priceless transaction (Num 18:16). This was not an insignificant sum for the newlywed couple. (Jesus would be "purchased" for six times that amount later; Mt 26:14–16, 27:3–6.)

The wonder of the moment was surely overwhelming—redeeming one's firstborn son is always a highlight of the life cycle of a Jewish family, and doing so within the confines of the Temple precinct, though not a required venue, made the act doubly special for this poor couple from Galilee. And there, constantly walking among the colonnaded porti-

coes of the Temple courtyard, now and again climbing the grand staircase leading to the Nicanor Gate and mingling here and there among the faithful pilgrims, were two old and venerable figures, part mystic, part prophet, faithfully and tirelessly waiting for God to bring the Messiah to His people. Simeon was "looking for the consolation of Israel," Anna "for the redemption of Jerusalem" (Lk 2:25, 2:38). Each had a reputation, certainly, in Jerusalem, a city that has always—and still—seems to attract devout, elderly folk, pious and sure that before their lifetimes expire, they will see God act for His people as He has never done before. "Just a little longer; I can hang on"—and in this case, they were right. Both Simeon and Anna recognized the baby Jesus as the one for whom their patient longings represented the anticipation of all Israel (Lk 2:26–38). Jesus was blessed. His parents were amazed. It was a holy moment.

Sometime later—how much later is unknown, but certainly not the night of Jesus' birth or else Mary could have afforded to give a lamb as the offering for her purification—"Magi from the east" made their way to Bethlehem to offer due homage to Jesus (Mt 2:1–12). Herodotus, always content to codify a fantastic rumor, thought the Magi were a class of Persian priests who flaunted awesome powers of magic and astrology; others consider them to have been Nabateans based on imagery found in Isaiah 60:1–7 and the type of gifts they brought to Jesus. More reasonably these Magi were urban scholars from Babylonia (in their day, Parthia), at home among the academies and libraries of Babylon, who fastidiously studied the remnants of a rich and hoary 4,000-year-old Mesopotamian civiliza-

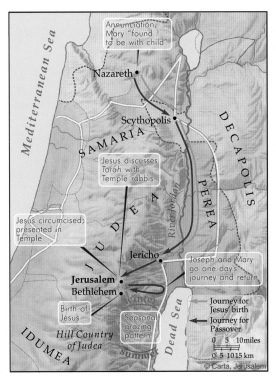

Journeys to Judea. *Mary made the journey south fairly often for a young village woman: first to visit her kinswoman Elizabeth who was also expecting a child, then to Bethlehem where she gave birth to Jesus, then back down to Jerusalem with her family to celebrate Passover when Jesus was twelve. The likely route bypassed Samaria by dropping through the Rift Valley, then climbed back up to Jerusalem via Jericho. This added a day or two to the trip but avoided a land and its people whom the Temple authorities considered unclean.*

During the Great Revolt against Rome of A.D. 66–70, Jews minted their own coins and adorned them with symbols of Jewish life in order to give practical expression to their longing to be free from Rome. This coin shows two baskets overflowing with dates on either side of a date palm, a tree symbolizing righteousness and victory. The inscription, in ancient (Old Testament era) Hebrew script, reads "for the redemption of Zion." It is not possible to separate the religious feelings of Jews who were struggling against Roman occupation from their longing for an independent Jewish political state: in their minds "the redemption of Zion" was a package deal. Seeing the infant Jesus in the Temple, the prophetess Anna "spoke of him to all those who were looking for the redemption of Jerusalem" (Lk 2:38). Her Messiah had come.

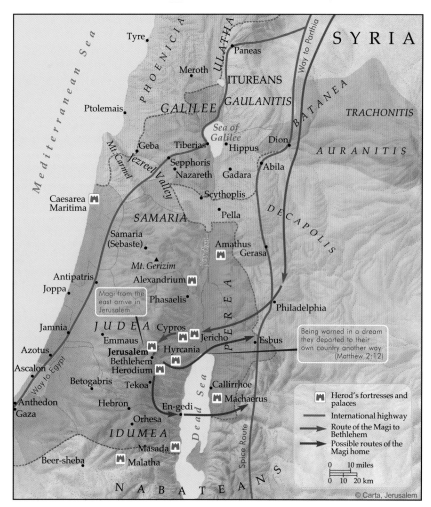

The Journey of the Magi.
Routes for the journey of the Magi follow the path of geographical logic—from the Transjordanian spice route to Jerusalem by way of Jericho, then back east via a more southern route. Any way they went the Magi had to skirt one or more of Herod's palace fortresses. It was a journey of great personal risk, one that took the Magi, like Abraham, far from their comfort zone into a land known only to God. Overcoming every obstacle, the travelers persisted—and rejoiced when at last they gazed at the divine child face-to-face.

tion. By the end of the first century B.C. the use of cuneiform as a literary medium had very nearly expired, but these learned and wise men of Babylon still probed the mysteries of the universe through already ancient cuneiform texts that recorded means of reckoning time and tracking the starry host. In addition, Babylon was home to a large and influential Jewish population that had found it more economically expedient to remain "by the waters of Babylon" (Ps 137:1) than return from exile to Judea, and from them these Magi certainly knew the stories and prophecies of the Old Testament as well (cf. Num 24:17; Isa 60:3).

So the Magi—traditions say three in number and even provide their names: either Bithisarea, Melchior and Gathaspa (Latin) or Balthasar, Melkon and Gaspar (Armenian)—set off on a most remarkable journey, to find a baby who was beginning an even more remarkable journey of his own. They certainly traced one of the great caravan routes of antiquity, north, west and then south along the bend of the Fertile Crescent toward Judea, following roughly the same path that Abraham had trod two millennia before. Geographical logic suggests that once the Magi reached Damascus they probably would have continued to follow the caravan route due south, toward the Arabian Peninsula.

It was perhaps somewhere along this Nabatean spice route that they secured gifts of frankincense and myrrh (aromatic gum resins) and gold. Turning westward at the northern end of the Dead Sea, the Magi would have crossed into Judea at Jericho, passing in the shadow of the large and sumptuous winter palace of Herod the Great. The king was suffering through the last and very paranoid years of his reign. Arriving in Jerusalem, the Magi inquired, perhaps naïvely, for the one "*born king of the Jews*" (Mt 2:1–2). Herod saw only Parthians, bent on grabbing control of his realm and reestablishing a legitimate (though puppet) Jewish ruling line, as they had tried to do at the beginning of his reign thirty-five years before. Although it is unattested in sources outside of the Gospel of Matthew, Herod's response to kill all of the potential candidates who might usurp his throne is true to his character (Mt 2:3–8, 2:16–18).

The Magi presented their lavish gifts to Mary, Joseph and Jesus. Echoes of royal visits such as that of the Queen of Sheba to Solomon abound (e.g., 1 Kgs 10:1–10), as do prophecies that anticipate kings and nations flowing to a rising light in Judea:

> Arise, shine, for your light has come,
>   and the glory of the LORD has risen upon you…
> Nations will come to your light,
>   and kings to the brightness of your rising…
> A multitude of camels will cover you,
>   the young camels of Midian and Ephah;
> All those from Sheba will come.
> They will bring gold and frankincense,
>   and will bear good news of the praises
>   of the LORD….   (Isa 60:1–6)

Warned in a dream not to retrace their steps through Jerusalem, the Magi returned to their eastern homes "by another way" (Mt 2:12). Possibly they left Bethlehem by following the narrow, twisted bottom of the Nahal Kidron, winding their way through the wilderness and past Herod's fortress at Hyrcania to the upper end of the Dead Sea, then around its top to the Transjordanian highway and home. This became the "monk and pilgrim" route connecting Jerusalem and Bethlehem with the Judean Wilderness monasteries during the Byzantine period. Or, they followed the ridge heading southeast out of Bethlehem past the Herodium to En-gedi, then crossed the Dead Sea at the Lisan Peninsula. Either way would have minimized contacts with Herod and his henchmen.

For Joseph and Mary, the practical outcome of the Magi's visit was that they now had adequate funds to live on their own in exile. Mary and Joseph may have been refugees at this point in their lives, but at least they were not destitute. Correctly sensing that Herod wouldn't rest until all threats to his throne were removed, the holy family set off for Egypt (Mt 2:13–15), far from Herod's influence and realm. There was a large Jewish community in Alexandria, and it is perhaps to that city that they headed. For Coptic Christians, the visit by Mary, Joseph and the infant Jesus to Egypt was a great moment in the Gospel story, fulfilling the prophecy of Isaiah "Blessed is Egypt my people" (Isa 19:24–25) and allowing them to become the first Christians. The fourth-century Coptic apocryphal gospel *The History of Joseph the Carpenter,* a purported account by Jesus reminiscing about the faithful deeds of his righteous parents, preserves a memory of many details of the life of the holy family that are not recorded in Scripture, and is a witness to the richness of the Coptic tradition.

In one long episode, events swirling around the baby Jesus flowed from Mesopotamia to Egypt, covering the geographical sweep of the story of Israel from Abraham to Moses to the Exile and Return. It was a momentous swing for a simple, still shamed and nameless couple who hailed from a tiny village lost in the land between.

And now for their Exodus from Egypt. After the death of Herod the Great in 4 B.C., Mary, Joseph and Jesus returned to the land of their birth (Mt 2:19–21; cf. Hos 11:1). There was no pressing reason for them to go all the way back to Nazareth; if home is where the heart is, Bethlehem likely won out as their destination. But Herod's son Archelaus was on the throne in Judea with a reputation even nastier than his father's (Ant. xvii.10.1–10, xvii.13.2). At

(above) Faded paint in a badly damaged semi-dome in the apse of the church at St. Simeon Monastery, Aswan, Egypt, does little to attract the eye or provide visual details of the rich heritage of the saints of the Coptic Church. But it does carry the echoes of a proud memory of Jesus' sojourn in the land of the Nile. This church building and its paintings date to the 10th or 11th century A.D.; Coptic tradition reaches back nearly another millennium beyond, to the very roots of early Christianity.

(right) **Jesus in Egypt According to Coptic Tradition.** Since at least the 4th century A.D., many oral traditions have arisen within the native Egyptian Coptic church to flesh out the visit by the Holy Family to Egypt. Most claim their origin in a divine dream, vision or revelation.

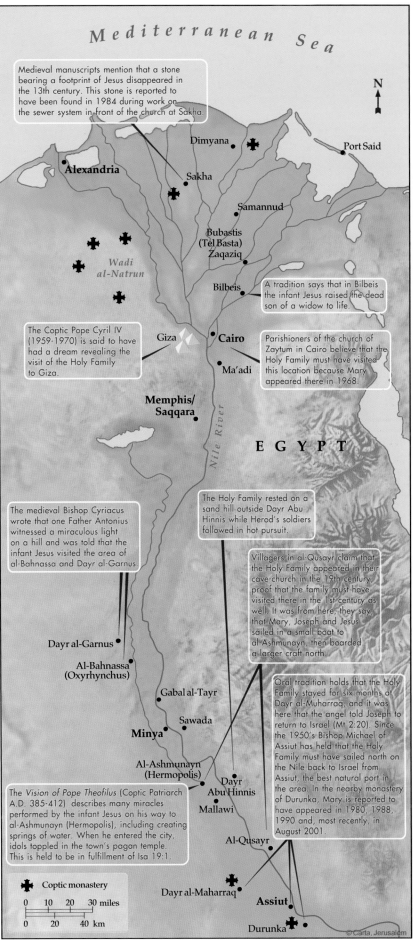

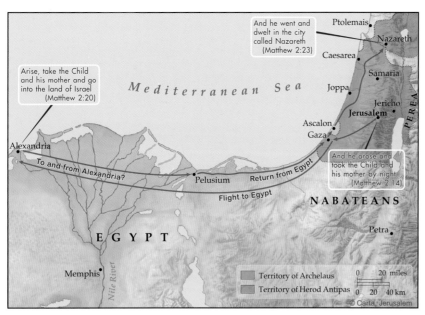

And he went and dwelt in the city called Nazareth (Matthew 2:23)

Arise, take the Child and his mother and go into the land of Israel (Matthew 2:20)

And he arose and took the Child and his mother by night (Matthew 2:14)

Mediterranean Sea

Ptolemais
Nazareth
Caesarea
Samaria
Joppa
Jericho
Jerusalem
Ascalon
Gaza
PEREA

Alexandria
To and from Alexandria?
Pelusium
Return from Egypt
Flight to Egypt

NABATEANS

EGYPT

Petra

Memphis
Nile River

Territory of Archelaus
Territory of Herod Antipas

0   20 miles
0   20   40 km
© Carta, Jerusalem

The Sojourn in Egypt. *Fearing the wrath of Herod, Joseph took Mary and Jesus to Egypt. They would have walked the well-traveled road skirting the Sinai that follows the shore of the Mediterranean Sea, an international route of historic importance, perhaps all the way to the thriving Jewish community in Alexandria. Alexander the Great had marched this way, as did the Assyrian kings Esarhaddon and Ashurbanipal. Coming out of Egypt, this was the military highway for Thutmose III, Amenhotep I, Seti I, Rameses II and Merneptah, the "Pharaohs Triumphant" of Egypt's New Kingdom. But Matthew chose to relate Jesus' exodus from Egypt to the work of Moses: "Out of Egypt I called My Son" (Mt 2:15; cf. Hos 11:1).*

The Hebrew word for "carpenter" is naggar; *Joseph and Jesus would have used the related word* nagar *to refer to the pins projecting from the top and bottom of the door which, when placed into sockets in the lintel above and threshold below, would allow the door to open and close properly. This door and doorway, leading to a storage room off the open courtyard of a home in the Jordanian village of Shawbek, was rather crudely constructed, but it works. Joseph certainly hung many doors in his day, and certainly built walls and doorways as well.*

this point prudence played the better part of valor; with the choice of facing either the wrath of Archelaus or the disparaging looks of people from Nazareth, Joseph, counseled in a dream, chose the latter (Mt 2:22–23).

So it was back to Galilee. With the exception of annual Passover trips to Jerusalem (Lk 2:41), these are silent years during which Jesus "continued to grow and become strong, increasing in wisdom; and the grace of God was upon him" (Lk 2:39–40). Surely Joseph and Mary kept a religiously observant home, were honest and law-abiding citizens and sought to contribute to the welfare of their family and community. The stigma of the "illegitimate" birth lurked in the background, but the urgency of the moment eventually took priority and people surely got on with their lives.

All four Gospel writers speak of Jesus having siblings (Mt 12:46–47; Mk 3:31; Lk 8:20; Jn 2:12). Matthew and Mark identify the boys as James, Joseph/Joses, Judas and Simon, all bearing names common in the world of first-century A.D. Judaism; of the girls, the Gospels are silent (Mt 13:55–56; Mk 6:3). Although a strong interpretative tradition holds that these children must either have been Jesus' half-siblings from an earlier marriage of Joseph or his cousins (so the *Protoevangelium of James,* Jerome, Augustine and a host of other witnesses throughout the ages), the most natural sense of the language of the Gospels indicates that they were Jesus' real brothers and sisters and that Mary's virginity lasted only through the birth of Jesus (cf. Mt 1:25). Altogether there were at least seven children in the family, with Jesus the oldest, an elder brother to be looked up to and admired.

It was a large family to raise, and Joseph was able to provide for them through his trade as a *tekton.* Until quite recently this Greek word has almost universally been translated "carpenter," indicating

a worker in wood (Mt 13:55; Mk 6:3). This understanding has grown in large part from statements by various Church Fathers as early as the second century (Justin Martyr argues that Joseph made plows and yokes) and from the cumulative weight of a host of literary and artistic representations over the last two millennia. The word *tekton,* however, is better rendered "artisan in local building materials," in this case mostly stone, but with some wood and metal. Joseph was, in all likelihood, a master craftsman of buildings and furnishings, certainly not a common day laborer but someone with special skills in construction who could demand a decent wage. Again, drawing on recent ethnographic comparisons, every village (or couple of neighboring villages) in Ottoman Palestine was home to someone who was especially skilled in the more tricky parts of building a home—choosing the best materials, deciding how and where to lay the foundation, fashioning and hanging the door, making a lock and key, and the like. The *tekton* would also be involved in other projects—building or fashioning wine presses, tombs, ossuaries, *mikveh* installations and so forth. The one who did this kind of work well had to be organized, creative and physically strong, possess intuitive on-the-job problem-solving skills, demonstrate competency in applied mathematics and engineering, and have enough initiative and vision to make it all work. The Rabbis recognized the value of this unique mix of skills and considered the "carpenter" (Heb. *naggar*) a specialist who could be consulted on legal matters related to pruning fruit trees (Abodah Zarah 50b). But not only did someone who was a master craftsman in local building materials command a package of highly demanded skills, during the normal course of his work he likely would enter all of the homes in the area and become familiar with the family life and personal needs of everyone around (not unlike a doctor who makes housecalls). And, if work was a little slow at home—as it would be in a small village like Nazareth, where the natural building materials were of a rather inferior quality anyway—he would travel in larger circles in search of adequate work.

It was in this way that Joseph—if this reconstruction is correct, an independent businessman from a conservative and relatively secure small town—likely found work in Sepphoris, a short four-mile walk down ridge to the north. According to Josephus (*Life*, 123), Sepphoris was one of the three chief cities of Galilee in the first century A.D. (the other two were Tiberias—which wasn't founded until A.D. 17—and Garaba), and was the center of political and economic life of the region. The population of the city was decidedly mixed—Jews and Gentiles—with a cosmopolitan flair that no doubt irked people in the poorer villages round about. Sepphoris was destroyed in 4 B.C. as part of the general unrest following the death of Herod the Great, then rebuilt by his son Herod Antipas, tetrarch of Galilee. It was to be a long, drawn-out process and resulted in a city that looked and felt Roman. Much work was available in Sepphoris for specialists who worked in wood and stone, and so it is reasonable to suppose that Joseph—often with Jesus in tow—went there, to the only job site anywhere in the vicinity of Nazareth that offered long-term job security. Perhaps Joseph walked down on Sundays, the first day of the work-week, and returned home each Sabbath. In Sepphoris, both he and Jesus would be exposed to a wide variety of people and ideas that were not part of the normal ebb and flow of life high up in the Nazareth basin.

Joseph and Mary, with their children, made the habit of attending the Passover festival in Jerusalem (Lk 2:41; cf. Ex 23:14–15, 23:17; Deut 16:1–8). The holy city was typically crowded with pilgrims during the eight-day spring freedom festival, among them "relatives and acquaintances" of Jesus' family (Lk 2:44). The year that Jesus was twelve (just old enough to be considered an adult), he spent his Passover in Jerusalem absorbed in detailed and protracted conversations with rabbis in the Temple on Scripture and matters of religious law (Lk 2:42–47). Clearly Joseph had seen to it that Jesus was well taught in the Nazareth synagogue, so much so that David Flusser has termed Jesus "a precocious scholar, one might almost say a young talmudist" (Flusser, *Jesus*, p. 29). Jesus' divine connection to God, combined with the "anything's possible" exuberance of youth, fueled his arguments and surely gained him a reputation among the more staid—and now astonished—Temple authorities. To their amazement, it was indeed possible to get a good rabbinic education in a village in Galilee (cf. Mt 22:15–46; Jn 7:46).

Jesus was so absorbed by his conversations and the wonder of the moment that he missed his family's return trip home. At first Mary and Joseph weren't too worried about their son's safety (even in the Middle East today nobody messes with kids, and Jesus was, after all, already about the age that Mary had been when she was betrothed), but by

the time they got to Jericho (about a day's journey out) and realized he was actually gone they retraced their steps to Jerusalem to find him. Three days of searching produced understandable anxiety (there could have been an accident)—then it was Jesus' turn to be astonished:

> *Why were you looking [all over the city] for me? Didn't you know that I had to be about my Father's business?* (Lk 2:49)

Celebrating Passover with his family took second seat to affairs of the Temple and God's call on Jesus' life. For all Joseph's paternal care, he wasn't Jesus' real father, nor was carpentry Jesus' real calling, or Nazareth his real home. Joseph and Mary simply didn't understand—nor should we necessarily expect them to, yet (Lk 2:50; cf. Lk 2:19). But Jesus had made his point on his bewildered parents. He returned with them to Nazareth, still subject to their authority and continuing "to increase in wisdom and stature, and in favor of God and man" (Lk 2:51–52).

The city of Sepphoris is on the must-see list of archaeological sites in Israel today. Visitors are especially awed by the ancient city's colorful, intricately-designed mosaic floors. These remains and many others, while striking and imaginative, all post-date the time of the Gospels. In the early first century A.D. Sepphoris was a place just being (re)built. Even the theater, shown here early on in its excavation, was only possibly built during the reign of Herod Antipas (3 B.C.–A.D. 39). This makes it unlikely that Joseph or Jesus ever sat in its seats, although it is reasonable to assume that they participated in initial work in the city. A crusader citadel, now the site's museum, sits above.

The "precocious scholar and young Talmudist" at work, holding learned rabbis in the Temple spellbound. This image in stained glass, adorning a window in the chapel of Bethlehem University, Bethlehem, captures the centrality of Jesus in the story. Underneath the haloed aura of the Divine was a sharp and very well-trained mind, clever, witty and practical.

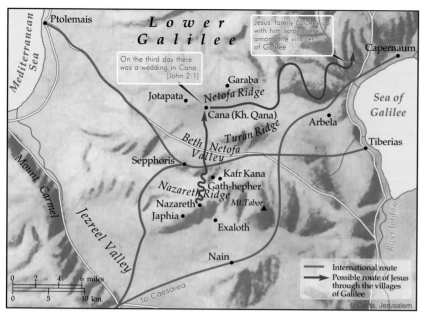

The Wedding at Cana. Jesus' first miracle was at Cana of Galilee, an important Jewish village on the northern end of the Beth Netofa Valley. Like the people of Sepphoris, those who lived in Cana enjoyed the richness of the valley's soil and the economic stability that it brought. Certainly the residents of Cana were better off economically, on the whole, than those of Nazareth, and the elegance of the wedding there would have been a bit out of place in Jesus' home village.

Archaeological excavations in Jerusalem have uncovered an abundance of stone vessels of a variety of types from the first century A.D.: *bowls, plates, cups, trays, lids and, most impressively, large storage jars. These were made of a soft limestone quarried at a site northeast of Jerusalem (Hizma); most were turned on a lathe. They were expensive vessels, and apparently manufactured and used in response to Jewish laws of purity that held that whereas pottery vessels could become ritually unclean, stone vessels remained pure (Mishneh, Kelim 10.1; Parah 3:2). The wedding at Cana was held in a home that had both the means and the reason to possess such stone storage jars (Jn 2:6).*

With the line "I must be about *my Father's* business," Joseph disappears from the Gospel story. Is this a literary device, or does it reflect, as many have concluded, that Joseph died sometime shortly after Jesus' twelfth year? Joseph surely had apprenticed his first-born son in the skills of a *tekton* (cf. Mk 6:3), and likely expected him to inherit the family business. This prompts the question—mostly a theological speculation that cannot be answered: To what extent did Mary and Joseph know where Jesus' calling would take him?

But now Joseph was gone, literarily or in fact, and Jesus was left without a father. As the oldest son he would *de facto* become the head of the family. The Gospel narrative picks up again when Jesus was about thirty years old and ready to begin his public ministry (Lk 3:23). But why so old? In a land where life expectancy hovered around forty years someone who was thirty was already middle-aged. (Alexander had already conquered most of the known world by thirty-two.) Perhaps Jesus, raised as a dutiful son, waited until his siblings had become productive members of society and were in a position to provide for the daily needs of their mother. Once

his ministry began, Jesus showed a tender heart for the fatherless, widows and children, and from this we can safely conclude that his years of preparation were shaped around tangible human needs, including some that his own heart, as a fatherless youth, must have felt (cf. Mt 19:13–15; Lk 7:11–17, 18:1–8, 21:1–4).

Quite early in his public ministry—after he had attracted some disciples but before he was widely known—Jesus went to a wedding. The celebration was in Cana of Galilee, on a Tuesday ("the third day," Heb. *yom shlishi*, still a day for weddings in Israel). While the weight of Early Church tradition locates Cana at Kafr Kana, a large Christian Arab town just down-slope from Nazareth, the more likely location of the site is *Khirbet Qana*, a prominent, bare rise with scattered first-century remains five miles due north, just across the Beth Netofa Valley (the practical travel needs of pilgrims during the early Byzantine period apparently pulled the location of Cana much closer to Nazareth). Mary was invited—certainly she reminisced about her own hurried wedding—and Jesus and his disciples came along as well (Jn 2:1–2). Did Mary ever pause to wonder about her oldest son's marital status?

It is impossible to know who was getting married in Cana, but surely it was either a relative or close acquaintance of Mary and Jesus (a cousin perhaps, or maybe a fellow *tekton* Jesus met at Sepphoris). But the *who* is not as important as the *what*: this was clearly a *kosher* family of some means, who could afford to keep in their home large, expensive jars of stone "for the Jewish ritual of purification" (Jn 2:6). High priests from Jerusalem would be expected to have such articles in their homes, not nameless townsfolk from rural Galilee. Clearly this was a religiously observant home (today we would say it belonged to an Orthodox Jew), who went all-out to celebrate in elegant style (there were many guests and a headwaiter; Jn 2:9–10) in, apparently, a rather large building. Everybody was enjoying themselves, as they should. It was a great moment in life. Then the wine ran out, and Mary (as if it were her business) let Jesus know he should do something about it (Jn 2:3, 2:5). Perhaps Mary was prompting him to tip his Messianic Secret; more likely, she was acting the part of a concerned guest, a bit nosy (it showed she was part of the host's in-group), wanting to receive the public honor that would come her way if the man of her house could solve the problem. (The need to establish and maintain honor cannot be separated from anyone's actions in the Middle East, ancient or modern.) In other words, Mary was playing perfectly the role of a first-century Galilean matron who knew how to entertain and keep a proper house—even if it belonged to someone else. Even though Jesus was the man of her house, the cultural norm prompted Mary to control his social interactions until he either married or moved in to the world of men. Mary still called the shots; Jesus, whose ministry was only just beginning, honored his (dead) father and his mother by obliging (Jn 2:4–8; cf. Ex 20:12). By the time the celebration was over Jesus had performed his first miracle; by serving the best wine last the homeowner had become an extravagantly perfect host; by urging Jesus to act Mary was honored—and a good time was had by all.

Following the wedding at Cana, Jesus started laying the groundwork for what it meant for someone to be his disciple. His mother and brothers caught up with him while he was making his way from village to village in Galilee; something was on their mind. Jesus, occupied with a large crowd, didn't notice while his family, anxious, stood outside, at the edge. If all Mary wanted to do was relay a bit of family news, then a single messenger would have sufficed. But everyone came, clearly prompted by something important, a matter that demanded a family council. While three of the Gospel writers mention the incident, none records the specific reason for the visit, what Mary or the boys said, or Jesus' answer to them (Mt 12:46–50; Mk 3:31–35; Lk 8:19–21). However, from Jesus' response to the crowds upon being told that his family was standing nearby, it is likely that they had some real concerns about what he was doing, or about how he was going about doing it. So Mary and the boys waited, curious to see first-hand how Jesus behaved in public. Were the stories they were hearing about his miracles and following true? And where would it all lead? Galilee had had its share of itinerant, charismatic, crowd-collecting preachers. They usually ended up stirring the crowds against the established power structures, and it never ended happily. "Jesus!" we can hear Mary wanting to say. "Think about what you are doing. Come back home to where you're loved and needed. God can use you there."

Love called, but so did a Greater Love. Home folk tend not to treat their prophets very kindly (maybe they know them too well to let them be prophetic; cf. Mt 13:53–58; Lk 4:16–30), and whether it's through stoning or coaxing, the prophetic voice is often silenced. Not this time.

> My mother and my brothers are the ones who hear
> the word of God and do it.   (Lk 8:21)

Can we hear a tinge of irritation at his family for wanting to hold him back, or a voice of resolve to enlarge God's family whatever the cost (cf. Lk 9:57–62, 11:27–28, 14:26, 18:28–30; Jn 7:5)?

So at least at the beginning of his Galilean ministry, Jesus pulled away from his family ("estranged" would be too hard a word for them, but not for the others of Nazareth; cf. Lk 4:16–30). But it wasn't so for long. Somewhere along the way Jesus' family by blood became part of his family by God. Mary was in Jerusalem with Jesus for the days leading up to his

final Passover. It would be too much to suggest that she knew exactly what was going to happen: even though Jesus repeatedly told his disciples that suffering and death awaited, they seemed not to hear, or to understand (cf. Mt 16:21–23, 17:22–23, 20:17–19). Likely Mary was part of his growing crowd of followers, the ones tracking his wake through Perea that last winter of his life, then across the Jordan River in the vicinity of the place of his baptism and up through the twisted hills of the Judean Wilderness to Bethany on the Mount of Olives where, with another Mary and Martha and Lazarus, he celebrated his last Shabbat Meal. Two days later it was the Triumphal Entry, then days of glory and woe in and around the Temple. Mary must have been there for it all, then finally Jesus' betrayal, trials and the cross. By the time Jesus looked down on her huddled form from the heights of Golgotha, Mary must have been an emotional wreck, without sleep, unable to think or feel or comprehend except to know that her worst fears for her firstborn son had been realized. The stigma of an unwed mother, a birth on the road, the flight to Egypt, the death of her dear husband (may his memory be for a blessing), the rejection she took on herself for her son's denial of a quiet life back home—it was all nothing. *Nothing!* Compared to this.

Jesus looked down—no crowds remained. It was a busy street and people hurried by, pretending not to notice. Rome was very efficient. Only Mary, a couple of other women, and John stood close by. Jesus noticed them; his hour was close:

> Woman—your son.   (Jn 19:26)

Then to John,

> Your mother.   (Jn 19:27)

The beloved disciple became family.

It was the duty of the family to bury one of their own. Jesus' mother, distraught and without means, only watched. The body of Jesus was wrapped for

Perched on top of Khirbet Qana above the Beth Netofa Valley in Lower Galilee, students of the Gospels discuss the words and actions of Jesus when he attended a wedding in Cana somewhere on the same site. The hills of Lower Galilee's Netofa Ridge rise to the north in the distance. Today only intrepid hikers visit the place, approaching either through the wadi behind or via long and fertile fields that stretch southward at its base. There aren't any paved roads for miles. Jesus walked to Cana; so did these students, retracing his steps across the hills and valleys of Lower Galilee. The Cana of pilgrimage and tourist buses—the modern town of Kafr Kana lying much closer to Nazareth—with churches, souvenir shops, restaurants, paved roads and easy vehicle access, offers a very different kind of experience.

In the first century A.D., the Aegean port city of Ephesus was a world center of commerce, trade and Greco-Roman social life. The city's deity was Artemis (Diana), who mythology holds was the Virgin Huntress and twin sister of Apollo. Artemis was the goddess of nature, fertile yet eternally chaste and attractively wild. She was worshipped across the Greco-Roman world and depicted in art as the many-breasted Great Mother. All that's left of her great temple in Ephesus (cf. Acts 19:35) is a massive column and scattered stones. According to an early Christian tradition, the Apostle John brought Mary to Ephesus where she lived out her days, a mother of extraordinary worth in the face of the Great Mother of Rome. It's Mary's legacy that survives.

burial and laid in a borrowed tomb (Lk 23:50–55). The evening came and with it *Shabbat*, a day of rest to remember and celebrate God's creation of life (cf. Ex 20:8–11). For Mary this was the first *Shabbat* of death. Her cosmos had ended.

Early the next morning certain women went to the tomb to properly prepare Jesus' body for burial. The Gospel writers don't mention Jesus' mother among them, but surely her heart was there if not her body and soul. But there was no need. The tomb was empty; Jesus was alive (Mt 28:1–10; Mk 16:1–13; Lk 24:1–12; Jn 20:1–18).

After Jesus' ascension to heaven forty days later, Mary and her sons could be found with Jesus' disciples in Jerusalem, "with one mind, continually devoting themselves to prayer" (Acts 1:14). She had been no quicker or slower than the rest in trying to figure out what the events of the last few weeks—or the last few years—had meant. But now was a time of great transition. Jesus was alive, but in heaven. On earth he would live in the hearts of those who knew him.

The Christian movement began at a cross and a tomb and an upper room in Jerusalem, then spread across the known world and beyond. Jesus' own family, who at first had been skeptical, came around. The Book of Acts indicates that one of the most prominent men in the Jerusalem church was James, without specifying which one among several Jameses mentioned in the New Testament he was (Acts 12:17, 15:12–13; cf. Gal 2:9). Some of the earliest church traditions (e.g. the *Gospel of Thomas* 12, as well as Eusebius and Epiphanius) naturally point to James the brother of Jesus, Mary's next oldest son, as the first bishop of the Jerusalem church. They add that her fourth son, Judas, authored the Epistle of Jude (Jude 1:1) and that Simon, her youngest, also became bishop of the church in Jerusalem. Perhaps so.

Certainly there is precedent in Judaism and the Middle East generally for siblings of the founders of great movements to help continue the cause (e.g. Moses with Aaron and Miriam, and the Maccabees). As for Mary herself, some traditions remember Mary's death (or, her final sleep) to have happened in Jerusalem, on Mount Zion (the location of the Dormition Abbey), and her burial in a cave in the Kidron Valley beneath Gethsemane (first reported in *Transitus Mariae*, much of which dates to the second or third century A.D.). A lesser-held tradition carries Mary with John the Beloved Disciple to Ephesus, the world center of worship of the Great Mother Goddess Artemis, where John became a leader of the most important local church in Asia Minor. Various churches in and around Ephesus mark places where Mary is remembered to have stayed, died and been buried. The Third Ecumenical Council, held at Ephesus in A.D. 431, was called to discuss the nature of the humanity and divinity of Christ, and ended with the adoption of a creed stating that Jesus Christ was "true God and true man" and that his mother Mary, the Holy Virgin, was *Theotokos*, "God-bearer." Given the importance of the debate and the location of its resolution, it was a logical progression: Jesus was born of Mary, Mother of God.

She had come a long way, at least in the minds and hearts of the Early Christian Church. Mary and Joseph sought to live simple, quiet lives, without pretense or fault, according to the commands of *Torah*. Then the hand of God intervened, and their simple lives became quite extraordinary. But it was in their ability to be used of God, even or perhaps especially when the circumstances of their lives became confusing and unclear, that Mary and Joseph showed something even more extraordinary. And in that they became the mother and father of us all.

CHAPTER 20

JESUS
The Anointed One

How do we even begin to define Jesus? Common terms for greatness just don't work. Unique? Certainly, but overused. Heroic? That one sounds terribly out of place. Courageous? Innovative? Legendary? Jesus is so beloved of tradition that for many people his deeds *have* become legendary (unfortunately in every sense of the term), but where then is the immediacy for today? Larger than life? Surely—God himself took on human form, as the Apostle Paul said in Philippians 2:5–8—yet Jesus was also a cultural being who fully participated in the world of first-century A.D. Judaism. Indeed, Jesus' humanity is a window to his divinity (as much as vice versa), a flesh and blood testimony to the fullness of God's desire to speak with, redeem and indwell His people. Jesus was, in the largest sense of the word, *humane*.

But the danger of focusing on his humanity, of course, is that just as people, created in the image of God, promptly turn around and create God in theirs, so we do with Jesus. In fact, the process of re-creating Jesus already began during his lifetime, and in the long centuries since he has become just about anyone for just about any cause, from an Orthodox Jew to a Fine Christian Gentleman, from a backer of the military-industrial complex to a Guevara revolutionary to a Gandhi—or even an initiate of the cult of Isis and Osiris. Everyone wants a piece of Jesus (far too many only if Mary Magdalene is attached), and although he had plenty enough to give, Jesus demanded from everyone that he or she become *his* disciple, not him theirs.

More helpful are common descriptive nouns that arise from the Gospel story: Jesus was a rabbinic scholar, a skilled worker, a friend, a son, a servant, a deliverer, a king, and while these are all certainly aspects of the whole, each by itself is too limiting. So too the biblical titles, some used by Jesus, some by others about him: Son of God (e.g. Mt 4:3, 8:29, 26:63); Son of Man (e.g. Mt 18:11, 25:31, 26:64); Rabbi (Jn 1:38); Teacher (Mt 8:19); Lamb of God (Jn 1:36); Bread of Life (Jn 6:35); Light of the World (Jn 8:12); Good Shepherd (Jn 10:11); Word (Jn 1:1); even Lord (Jn 13:6). These are faces of a multifaceted, highly complex and ultimately very successful individual; but even together they only begin to complete the whole.

Perhaps the best place to start is with the title that most often defines Jesus today, the one that became his name: the Anointed One (Heb. *mashiach*/Messiah; Gk. *christos*/Christ; e.g. Mt 16:16, 27:22; Lk 2:11, 23:2; Jn 7:41–42, 11:27). "Messiah" was a title rooted in the fertile soil of Old Testament expectation, where it was usually attached to a priest (Lev 4:3, 4:5, 4:16, 6:22), a prophet (1 Chron 16:22; Ps 105:15) or a king (most notably Saul and David; 1 Sam 2:10, 16:6, 24:6, 26:9; 2 Sam 22:51, 23:1; Ps 2:2, 132:10) who had been christened (!) with oil and set apart for a special, above-the-norm task of leadership on behalf of the people of Israel. The one who performed the act of anointing had to be someone who already stood in a special relationship with God; a prophet, for instance, such as Samuel who anointed Saul and then David king of Israel (1 Sam 9:22–10:1, 16:1–13). The term

This likeness of David, "the anointed of the God of Jacob, the sweet psalmist of Israel" (2 Sam 23:1), appears on the Scroll of Fire (megillat ha'esh) near Moshav Kesalon in the Judean Hills. Cast in bronze by the renowned sculptor Nathan Rapaport, the monument depicts the Diaspora and return of the Jews to the land of Israel, with glances at Israel's biblical past. Jesus was born "of the house and lineage of David" (Lk 2:4), a direct descendant of Israel's greatest king. He inherited David's messianic role from on high, but spoke of a kingdom in terms more suitable to commoners than royals (e.g. Mt 5:1–7:29, 13:1–52). Jesus was unconventional even in his own day—how much more for we who view him from the distance of time and place!

Tell me the stories of Jesus
   I love to hear,
things I would ask him to
   tell me if he were here:
scenes by the wayside, tales of
   the sea, stories of Jesus,
tell them to me.
    (William H. Parker, 1885)

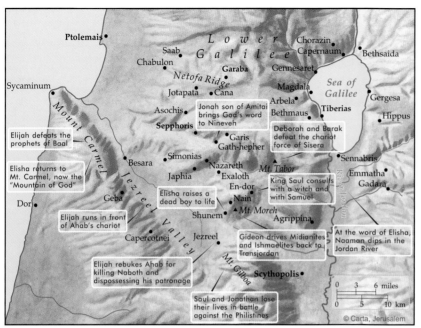

Messianic Associations in Galilee. *As Jesus "grew in wisdom and stature, in favor with God and men"* (Lk 2:52), *he learned how God had redeemed Israel time and again from foreign political and religious oppression in his own homeland, the hills and valleys of Galilee. Elijah, Elisha, Saul, Jonathan, Gideon, Jonah—with neighbors as great as these, Jesus couldn't let his own past go unnoticed.*

"anointed one" took on an increasing significance throughout the biblical period, eventually designating a specific individual whose position and role would not only supersede all anointed ones who had gone before, but usher in God's final Kingdom: this was to be *the* Messiah (Dan 9:24–27).

The coming Messiah figured prominently in Jewish eschatological and apocalyptic literature during the Intertestamental period, giving witness at the turn of the millennium to a heightened expectancy that God would deliver Israel from the cultural and political oppression of Hellenism and Rome (e.g. 1 Enoch 48:10, 52:4; Psalms of Solomon 17–18; 2 Esdras 12:31–33; Testament of Levi 18:2–14; and numerous texts and fragments from Qumran). Indeed, the time was so ripe for deliverance that several self-appointed (self-anointed!) messiah-figures strove to the fore—usually from the religious and social matrix of Jerusalem or freedom-loving Galilee, gathered quick follow-

ings and then just as quickly foundered or were suppressed by the Roman authorities. Among these were Theudas, Judas the Galilean and his sons Jacob and Simon, Athronges, the Egyptian False Prophet and the Prophet in the Desert (Acts 5:36–37, 21:38; Ant. xvii.10.7; xx.5.1–2, 8.6, 8.10). Sometime between A.D. 60 and 62, for example, the procurator Porcius Festus (cf. Acts 24:27)

sent forces, both horsemen and footmen, to fall upon those who had been seduced by a certain impostor who promised salvation and freedom from the miseries they were under if they would but follow him as far as the wilderness. Accordingly those forces that were sent destroyed both the deluder and the deluded who followed. (Ant. xx.8.10)

So too the members of the community of the Dead Sea Scrolls, who died waiting for their messiahs to appear (one "of Israel" to bring political freedom and one "of Aaron" to redeem the Temple; 4Q266 frag.18 iii 12); the Qumran community was destroyed during the Jewish Revolt in A.D. 68. These were trying times for messiahs indeed—and for the hopeful who followed.

Into this matrix (or was it a maelstrom?) came Jesus, who was neither self-anointed nor anointed by someone with established Temple or prophetic authority, but from On High. Having been specially chosen from before birth (from before *conception*; Lk 1:26–38), Jesus "grew and became strong and increased in wisdom; and the grace of God was upon him" (Lk 2:40), then appeared to John to be baptized. Upon rising from the waters of the Jordan River,

the Holy Spirit descended upon him in physical form like a dove, and a voice came out of heaven, "You are My beloved Son; I am well-pleased with you." (Lk 3:22)

Sanctified oil wasn't needed when God did the anointing himself.

Scholars debate the length of time between Jesus' baptism in the waters of the Jordan and his crucifixion in Jerusalem. While many posit a short ministry of one year or less (based on the pattern of the life-expectancy of the other messianic movements of his day), the three Passover festivals recorded in the Gospel of John, if they are sequential rather than simply episodic, suggest a ministry of nearly three years (cf. Jn 2:13, 6:4, 12:1). But it is difficult to mesh the

On the eve of his public ministry Jesus withdrew to the Judean Wilderness for forty days to relive in microcosm Israel's forty-year sojourn through a land of trials and temptation. The test pushed Jesus' physical and spiritual resources nearly to the limit, but he stood firm and Satan, the adversary, withdrew "until a more opportune time" (Lk 4:13). Three years later Jesus retraced his steps through the same wilderness as he made his final ascent from Jericho to Jerusalem, a path made even more difficult by the realization that the Cross lay up ahead.

events of Jesus' life mentioned by John with those recorded in the Synoptic Gospels (Matthew, Mark and Luke) on chronological grounds. Moreover, the geographical clues offered by each Gospel writer are not always straightforward, either (it's a case of both too much information, and too little). Specific data of time and place (where Jesus did what, and when), the foundation of any connected narrative or historical reconstruction, are sufficiently incomplete so as to allow any number of supposed geographical and chronological sequences of the events of Jesus' life. A broad-stroke picture, however, is possible, taking into account that while the focus of Jesus' work was around the Sea of Galilee, certain trips to Jerusalem for the festivals is both historically reasonable and to have been expected.

But first an initial consideration. Jesus was born in Bethlehem of Judea and raised in a conservative home in the out-of-the-way village of Nazareth, nestled in a basin high on a rocky limestone ridge above both the Jezreel and Beth Netofa valleys. Although its specific geographical situation limited Nazareth economically, a short walk from the heart of the village to the rim of the Nazareth Ridge above offered any resident of the town a view of the world: vast stretches of fertile farmland, large cities and busy international thoroughfares. It was in the Jezreel and Beth Netofa valleys that the opportunities and temptations of the Hellenistic and Roman worlds lay, but also here, especially in the view to the south, that a young Jesus could gaze into the arena of his own people's past. One can imagine Jesus as a youth, first learning in the synagogue the stories of the great acts of God that had taken place in his region of Galilee, then replaying those events in his mind as he walked the hills of Nazareth or stood above the great amphitheater of the Jezreel Valley where so many of them had unfolded. There was the victory of Deborah and Barak over Sisera and Jabin (Judg 4:1–5:31), and the story of Gideon's small army defeating the hordes of Midianites and Ishmaelites "like locusts in number" who were bent on devouring the fertile land that God had given to Israel (Judg 6:1–8:21):

Deal with [our enemies now!] as with Midian,
    as with Sisera and Jabin at the torrent of Kishon,
who were destroyed at En-dor,
    who became as dung for the ground.
Make their nobles like Oreb and Zeeb,
    and all their princes like Zebah and Zalmunna,
Who said, "let us possess for ourselves
    the pasturelands of God."   (Ps 83:9–12)

It was on the mountains surrounding the Jezreel Valley, easily seen from the Nazareth Ridge, that Israel's first anointed king, Saul, appealed to the witch at En-dor, then lost his life the next morning in battle against the Philistines (1 Sam 28:1–25, 31:1–13). But it was also here that Elijah and Elisha, God's

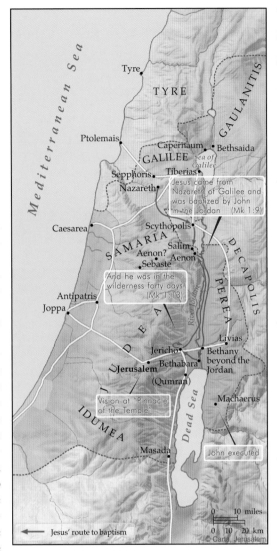

prophets mighty in word and deed, stood strong against the tides of religious paganism, social injustice, misguided political pressure and military invasion that threatened to overwhelm Israel in their day (1 Kgs 18:20–46, 21:1–29; 2 Kgs 4:8-37). To the north was Gath-hepher, hometown of the prophet Jonah,

The Baptism of Jesus and His Sojourn in the Wilderness. *"Jesus arrived from Galilee at the Jordan, to John, to be baptized by him...then was led up by the Spirit into the wilderness to be tempted by the devil"* (Mt 3:13, 4:1). *The setting was most appropriate, full of associations with Moses, Joshua, Elijah and Elisha. Satan tried to derail Jesus' messianic role from the start. Jesus was tried but found worthy; Satan withdrew "until a more opportune time"* (Lk 4:13).

(below) The view from the Nazareth Ridge south into the Jezreel Valley, here framed by the northern slope of Mount Moreh, takes in a portion of one of the greatest battlefields in the ancient world. Today it's all fields, neatly ordered and cultivated and crossed by thoroughfares; in Jesus' day, too, the soil and routes of the Jezreel Valley represented the strength of an economy tied into the world's markets. But it was here that the Israel of Jesus' own past also fought to establish a strong and secure presence in its ancestral homeland. On this particular plot of ground the army of Deborah and Barak defeated the chariot forces of the Canaanite general Sisera, a battle whose significance was not lost on the Jews of Roman Galilee.

187

Several of Jesus' disciples were fishermen, at home on the waters of the Sea of Galilee as in the towns and villages that lined its shore. A life on the sea, even one as confined as this, held adventure and excitement and bred a certain kind of rugged opportunism and confidence that bode well for personal survival. But even this sea had its mean streak, and the fisherman who plied its waters knew that its appetite for wrecked ships would never be satisfied. A dark sky, a blast of wind—and a quick boat ride could quickly turn into a desperate struggle for life.

who spoke a message of forgiveness to all peoples, and beyond, the route the Syrians, Assyrians and Babylonians had used to penetrate, occupy and control the land of Israel. As he grew "in wisdom and stature in favor with God and men" (Lk 2:52), Jesus' messianic awareness must have been forged in part on the realization that his land again lay in the clutches of foreign political and religious domination, and that his Jewish countrymen eagerly anticipated God's mighty hand moving to save, redeem and deliver them from oppression.

And so Jesus grew, but with an understanding that oppression began in the heart. After he was baptized he withdrew immediately to the Judean Wilderness, likely the arid region above Jericho, for forty days, into a landscape and for a period of time that echoed Israel's years of temptation and trial in "the great and terrible wilderness" of Sinai (cf. Deut 1:19). Here, wandering amid rocks, cliffs and endless chalky hills, without adequate food or water, Jesus was tempted by the devil. "You have needs—fill them! You have power—use it! You're the Son of God—prove it! You want to be king?—you *deserve* to be king! *I can help.* Follow me." The devil was enticing and seductive, choosing a moment of weakness to strike deep within (it's his habit), but Jesus stood firm. (Not so his disciples, who would fall from only a gentle push; cf. Heb 2:18, 4:15). The devil left, waiting "for an opportune time" (Mt 4:1–11; Mk 1:12–13; Lk 4:1–13). Jesus, anointed, tried and found worthy, entered a world of need.

He returned to Galilee and began to gather together a band of disciples, as rabbis with something to say tended to do. Eventually great crowds followed, even some who held positions of power and influence, but Jesus was more interested in choosing a special twelve ("those whom he himself wanted… that they might be with him" [Mk 3:13–14]). This was a mixed band, representing in microcosm the hopes and dreams, the socio-economic positions, suspicions and opportunities of Jewish Galilee (Mt 10:2–4; Mk 3:16–19; Lk 6:14–16). Nearly all were from the immediate region, calling the northern shore of the Sea of Galilee home. At least four (Peter, Andrew, James and John) and maybe also Philip were Bethsaida fishermen, which gave this occupation a disproportionately large representation in the band of twelve when compared to the number of fishermen among the residents of Galilee in general. Perhaps this was an "accident of geography" since Jesus' ministry was focused on the northern end of the sea, or, given the reputation of commercial fishermen (tough, independent and shrewd), it was to show that there was room in God's kingdom for anyone. In any case, fishing was a risky business; so would be the task of spreading Jesus' message, and the skills of survival learned in one helped to ensure the success of the other. James and John, whose father Zebedee owned a boat with a sophisticated fishing net and had hired men, stood to inherit a profitable business (Mk 1:19–20). Matthew (Levi), the local tax collector, was on his way to becoming rich at the expense of people like these who toiled night and day on a capricious and unforgiving sea. When Jesus called Matthew (he was one of the last to join the band; Lk 5:27–32), the fishermen disciples who had already cast their lot with Jesus in hope of a better life probably said "Now wait a minute. We know this guy. He and his Rome-loving cronies are the very ones we try to avoid." And Matthew, knowing good and well that he carried the reputation of a collaborator, was perhaps just as surprised at the call, but like the rest, he came. Philip and Andrew had Greek names; Simon was a Zealot (whether he was zealous for *Torah* or for Jewish nationalism is unknown—likely for both—but he certainly wouldn't be caught dead with a name like *Philip* himself). Peter was overly bold (Type-A); Jesus nicknamed James and John "thunderous ones," surely an indication of their personality (Mrs. Zebedee probably had her hands full when they were kids); Thomas doubted (was he a reasoned skeptic, or a bit of a wuss?). At least one, Andrew, was already a disciple of John the Baptist (Jn 1:40), and glad to see that Jesus had made his way to his little corner of the world (Mk 1:16–18). Three (Bartholomew, James the son of Alphaeus and Thaddaeus/Judas son of James) are known only to tradition. And then there was Judas Iscariot, in whom the forces of good and evil wrestled mightily. The surname "Iscariot" may indicate that Judas was "a man (Heb. *Ish*) from Kerioth," a village in

Judea; if so (and there are other possibilities), he was the only southerner in the bunch, a stigma that automatically aroused suspicion above and beyond that which accompanied his role as company treasurer ("You're not from here, and you talk funny"; cf. Mt 26:73). It all made for rather interesting discussions (not to mention personal and professional jealousies) along the way. This was not a rag-tag bunch of down-and-outers who left situations in which they had nothing to gain in order to follow a local charismatic who promised the world. No—each was searching for someone or something (certainly not all knew exactly what at first) who would redeem the times. Andrew got it right from the start: "We have found the Messiah" (Jn 1:41).

Sometime early on, after he heard that his prophetic predecessor John the Baptist had been arrested, Jesus returned to his boyhood home of Nazareth (Mk 6:1–6; Lk 4:14–30; cf. Mt 4:12–13). He was already a man of some renown having done wondrous things in Capernaum and Cana (Lk 4:23; Jn 2:1–12, 4:46–54), a local-boy-done-good. At first Jesus enhanced his reputation as, in the synagogue, he read the words of the prophet Isaiah, no doubt emphasizing the pronouns as he went:

*The Spirit of the LORD is upon **me**,*
    *because he anointed **me** to preach the Gospel*
    to the poor;
*He has sent **me** to proclaim release to the captives,*
    and recovery of sight to the blind;
*[He has sent **me**] to set free those [of you!] who*
    are downtrodden,
to proclaim the favorable year of the LORD.
                    (Lk 4:18–19; cf. Isa 61:1–2)

Gracious words for an audience that, much like Simon the Zealot, was busy trying to wrest a working religious/nationalistic world-view on a rocky island awash in a capricious and unforgiving Gentile sea. Much later, Peter would neatly summarize Jesus' work this way to a Roman centurion stationed at in-your-face Caesarea on the Mediterranean shore:

You know Jesus of Nazareth, how God anointed Him with the Holy Spirit and with power, and how He went about doing good and healing all who were oppressed by the devil, for God was with him.
                    (Acts 10:38)

But it was in the Nazareth synagogue, among

It's a hefty walk from Nazareth to Capernaum, a journey that takes all the sunlight hours of a summer day. After crossing the hills of Lower Galilee, Capernaum first comes into sight at the Arbel Pass, a fissure in the basalt-covered limestone ridge lining the western shore of the Sea of Galilee. The view is one of the most majestic in all of Israel, and it doesn't take too much imagination to think that it may have been one of Jesus' favorites, too. From here Capernaum is still a dot in the haze—it's time to pick up the pace to reach the city by nightfall....

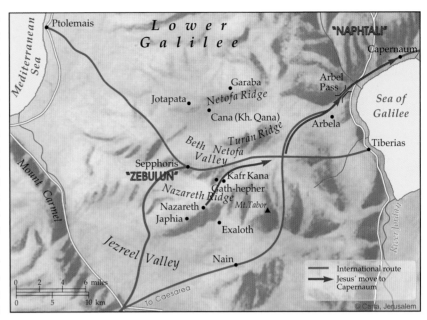

his life-long colleagues, that the Anointed One got into trouble. When Jesus announced that God was also in the business of blessing *Gentiles*—such as the widow of Zarephath (a city between Tyre and Sidon; cf. 1 Kgs 17:8–24), the hated Syrian general Naaman (cf. 2 Kgs 5:1–14) and, by implication, the Hellenists and Romans surrounding and swallowing Nazareth in the first century A.D.—his ultra-nationalistic neighbors cut him short by trying to toss him from the steep rocky mountainside that isolated their village from the imperialistic world of the Jezreel Valley below, into the very arena in which God had worked His mighty deeds on behalf of Israel during the time of the Old Testament (Lk 4:16–30).

Passing from their midst (a local tradition says he jumped off the cliff to escape!), Jesus moved down to Capernaum permanently (Lk 4:31; cf. Mt 9:1), fulfilling the promise of Isaiah, according to Matthew 4:12–16 (cf. Isa 9:1–7) that a great light would arise out of the land of Zebulun (where Nazareth was) and Naphtali (the homeland of Capernaum). Nearly

Jesus' Move from Nazareth to Capernaum. *"Now when Jesus heard that John had been taken into custody, he withdrew into Galilee; and leaving Nazareth, he came and settled in Capernaum which is by the sea, in the region of Zebulun and Naphtali. This was to fulfill what was spoken through Isaiah the prophet: 'The land of Zebulun and the land of Naphtali, by the way of the sea, beyond the Jordan, Galilee of the Gentiles—the people who were sitting in darkness saw a great light, and those who were sitting in the land and a shadow of death, upon them a light has dawned'"* (Mt 4:13–16; cf. Isa 9:1–2).

189

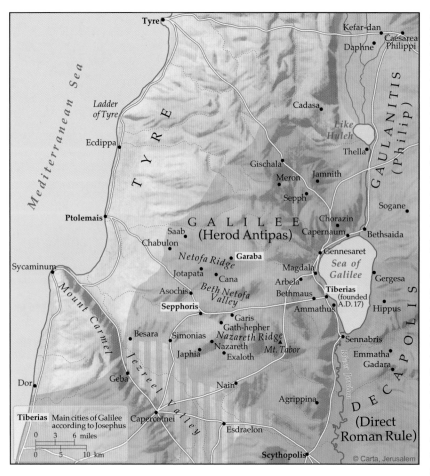

Tiberias | Main cities of Galilee according to Josephus

0 3 6 miles
0 5 10 km

© Carta, Jerusalem

Political Districts Around the Sea of Galilee. *Though really quite small in size, the Sea of Galilee was the meeting place of three distinct regions that represented, in microcosm, the political reality of the much larger first-century Mediterranean world. The local arena of Jesus' ministry was a valuable training ground for his disciples who would one day play a more visible role on a much larger stage. Living in Jerusalem had its advantages, but had Jesus based his ministry there, he likely would not have had the freedom and opportunity to sow seeds as widely as he did.*

eight hundred years earlier, in Isaiah's day, the Assyrians had swallowed up this same "Galilee of the Gentiles" (Isa 9:1) on their march to Egypt. Isaiah's prophetic trajectory, launched in a day of infamy, landed in the fertile ground of first-century Galilee, darkened by the oppression of Rome, lighted by the presence of Jesus.

Leaving Nazareth behind, Jesus "withdrew to the sea with his disciples" (Mk 3:7). "The sea" was of course the Sea of Galilee (Mt 4:18; Mk 1:16), called the Sea of Tiberias in John 6:1 and 21:1 and the Lake of Gennesaret in Luke 5:1. Josephus typically referred to the sea as either "the lake" (it's only eight by twelve miles across; e.g. *Life* 18; *War* ii.21.8), "the lake which the native inhabitants call Gennesar" (after the fertile plain of Gennesaret along its northwestern shore; *War* iii.10.1) or simply "the Gennesar," a name echoed in "the Kinneret," the modern Israeli term for the sea (*War* iii.10.8). Its proper name aside, this was no isolated holiday spot where a soft-handed Jesus wandered about pleasant fields and picturesque villages saying gentle things about life in the bye-and-bye. Rather, in the first century A.D. the narrow shoreline of the Sea of Galilee was a crowded, bustling, rough-and-tumble arena where just about every kind of person that Jesus' disciples would someday meet around the rim of the vast Mediterranean Sea had already congregated, trying to wrest a decent living for themselves and their families in

an unforgiving world. Except for the swampy Lake Huleh lying in the Rift Valley ten miles north (it was largely drained in the late 1950s), the Sea of Galilee is the only natural permanent body of fresh water on the eastern seaboard of the Mediterranean. With its pleasant climate and fertile shoreline soil, the sea was a magnet for settlement and economic ventures whenever a large nation-state dominated the region. In addition, the major international highway carrying traffic through Galilee from the Mediterranean to desert caravan routes beyond Damascus tracked along its northern shore, from Tiberias to Bethsaida-Julias. Capernaum, Jesus' adopted hometown, lay along this route. It was the last town in the political district of Galilee as one headed east.

Governed by Herod Antipas, Galilee was a place where Jews could feel comfortable in their cultural, religious and political identities, in spite of an obvious corridor of Hellenism that carried Rome from Ptolemais to Sepphoris then to Tiberias on the sea. Beyond the Jordan River was Gaulanitis, a region with a decidedly mixed population (Jewish and Gentile) governed by the half-brother of Antipas, Philip. Bordering the Sea of Galilee on the southeast lay a thoroughly Gentile district dominated by ten cities founded with the expressed purpose of disseminating a Greco-Roman world-view throughout the region and thereby holding Rome's eastern frontier against armies beyond. These in-your-face cities were called the Decapolis by the writers of the Gospels (Mt 4:25; Mk 5:20, 7:31; cf. Josephus, *Life* 65, Pliny, *Nat. Hist.* 5.16; Eusebius, *Onomasticon*, 80.16). Whether the Gospel writers understood the term "Decapolis" to indicate a geographical region or a political unity is a matter of debate. It is possible that they used the term rather generically for "eastern gentile regions" of any kind.

In any case, although the three regions that bordered the Sea of Galilee differed demographically and politically in significant ways, the people living in the cities and villages throughout shared a common humanity: everyone worked hard in the fields or on the lake trying to make a decent living; everyone enjoyed the company of family, friends and community; and all wanted security for themselves and their families. The lake was small enough that folks from all sides lived and toiled within sight of each other, and certainly most daily interactions on the street, on the lake or in the marketplace took place without thought of issues of politics or world-view that seemed to preoccupy the professional political and religious leadership of the day. And, the lake was small enough so that news could travel quickly from one shore to another—news of a birth, a death, or a visitor who decided to make a town along the sea his new home, especially if that newcomer had a compelling personality and special powers.

Of the cities and villages around the Sea of Galilee, Capernaum was perhaps the one best suited to become the focal point of Jesus' ministry (cf. Mt 9:1). Josephus provides a welcoming glance:

Along the lake of Gennesar is a region that bears the same name, a place whose natural properties and beauty are quite remarkable. There is not a plant that its fertile soil refuses to produce, and its farmers in fact grow every kind. The quality of the air is so well tempered that even the most opposite varieties of plants thrive there. The walnut tree, which delights in a winter climate, grows luxuriantly right next to palm trees that thrive on the heat, along with figs and olives requiring a milder atmosphere. One might say that nature has taken particular pride in the place…and each of the seasons of the year wish to claim this region for their own.…Besides being favored by its pleasant air, the region is watered by a most fertile spring. The inhabitants of the place call it Capernaum. (War iii.10.8)

Indeed, archaeological evidence supports Josephus' contention that Capernaum was a special place. As many as seven boat docks or fishing piers dating to the first century A.D. have been found along a 2,500-foot stretch of shoreline at Capernaum, some reaching 100 feet into the lake. This was a larger number than were associated with Bethsaida-Julias, Hippus and Tiberias (the main lake cities of Gaulanitis, the Decapolis and Galilee respectively) combined. We can assume that Capernaum was a center not only of fishing but also of attendant industries such as the manufacture and repair of boats and nets, and the curing and preservation of fish (Magdala-Taricheae, downshore to the west, was a similar center; *taricheae* means "salted fish"; cf. Strabo, Geography 16.2.45). The international highway that ran through town fostered the distribution of the daily catch to area markets. Many high-quality basalt millstones were found in the ruins of ancient Capernaum, some for producing olive oil and others for grinding grain—more than a town this size would normally use, suggesting that the economy of Capernaum was bolstered by an industry of heavy agricultural implement manufacture. Like in all villages, many (probably most) of Capernaum's residents were directly involved in agriculture, and so farmed fields and orchards and raised flocks of sheep and goats.

Of course such a place would attract the taxman, someone who had his hands full monitoring revenues derived from both land and sea (Matthew was busy, and into everyone's business). But Matthew's position (and person) were also protected by Rome: apparently one hundred Roman auxiliary troops were garrisoned at Capernaum, stationed to enforce the will of the Empire throughout northeastern Galilee. The residents of the town must have felt their

occupation as acutely as did the people of Jerusalem. These soldiers (comprising a "century") were under the authority of a centurion, in this case an officer who used his position wisely to help (or, to purchase the loyalty of) the residents of Capernaum, for "it was he who built us (i.e., paid for) our synagogue" (Lk 7:1–10). Archaeological foundation remains show that in Jesus' day the synagogue of Capernaum was a large building intended to serve a sizeable congregation. By reason it appears, then, that a good portion of the Jewish residents of the city must have been religious, with not a few scribes and Pharisees, scholars well-educated in matters of *Torah*, at hand (Mt 9:10–13; Mk 2:1–12; Lk 5:21). Jesus' relationship with the scribes and Pharisees was multidimensional,

The rise of Hippus (Sussita) dominates the southeastern shoreline of the Sea of Galilee, today marking the location of the buildings and fields of Kibbutz En Gev at its base. In Jesus' day Hippus, a Decapolis city, was Rome's most intrusive footprint on the sea, a constant and visible reminder to the Jews of Galilee that a new world order was stomping its way through their land. "A city set on a hill cannot be hidden," Jesus said to his Galilean audience on the other side of the sea, perhaps with Hippus in mind (it was certainly in sight). "They're shining their light for all the world to see. Why don't you do the same?" (cf. Mt 5:14–16).

The limestone synagogue of Capernaum dates to either the 2nd and 3rd, or, more likely, the 4th and 5th centuries A.D. Underneath archaeologists found a foundation of black basalt, though not quite on the same line as the building above. Likely this basalt foundation was originally built to support an earlier basalt synagogue in the same location, perhaps dating to the 1st century A.D., conceivably the synagogue paid for by the centurion of Luke 7:5.

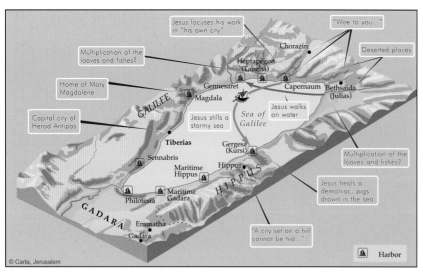

Jesus focuses his work in "his own city"
"Woe to you...."
Chorazin
Multiplication of the loaves and fishes?
Deserted places
Heptapegon (Tabgha)
Gennesaret
Capernaum
Bethsaida (Julias)
Home of Mary Magdalene
Magdala
Jesus walks on water
Sea of Galilee
Jesus stills a stormy sea
Capital city of Herod Antipas
Tiberias
Gergesa (Kursi)
Sennabris
Maritime Hippus
Hippus
Multiplication of the loaves and fishes?
Philoteria
Maritime Gadara
Jesus heals a demoniac; pigs drown in the sea
GADARA
Emmatha
Gadara
"A city set on a hill cannot be hid...."
Harbor
© Carta, Jerusalem

Jesus' Travels Around the Sea of Galilee. *Jesus focused his everyday ministry on the northern shore of the Sea of Galilee, in towns and villages from Magdala over to Bethsaida. It is possible to locate a few events mentioned in the Gospels at other places around the sea, although establishing an overall sequence and itinerary of Jesus' movements is difficult. In the end, much must be handed over to the art of reasonable speculation.*

providing color for the Gospel story and giving indication of his tendency to be both conservative and innovative in matters related to the worldview and personal behavior demanded by *Torah* (e.g. Mt 5:17–48, 23:1–36).

Capernaum also had a doctor. When Josephus injured himself falling from a horse on the Plain of Bethsaida in A.D. 67, he went to Capernaum for medical attention (*Life* 72).

Jesus, too, had practical skills to offer the residents of Capernaum. Trained from his youth as an artisan in wood and stone (Mt 13:55; Mk 6:3; Gk. *tekton* is usually translated rather simply as "carpenter"), Jesus would have had ample opportunity to ply his trade in this bustling city, should he so choose. The rabbis of Jesus' day encouraged every father to teach his son a skilled trade (Mishnah, *Kiddushin* 4.14), and most of the teachers of *Torah* themselves had secondary jobs to supplement their income (e.g., the first-century A.D. sage Hillel the Elder was a manual worker and his disciple Joshua ben Hananiah a charcoal burner; for the period following the destruction of the Temple we know that Rabbi Johanan was a sandal maker, Rabbi Isaac a smith, Rabbi Judah a baker, and so on). Like the tentmaker apostle Paul, we can assume that Jesus continued to partially support

himself (and perhaps even the family he left behind in Nazareth) after he had arrived in Capernaum (cf. Lk 8:2–3; Acts 18:1–4). Jesus' skills as a builder would have been in high demand in an important town like this, allowing him access to homes and families throughout the community. Like a doctor who makes house calls, he would have gained familiarity and credibility in the area by virtue of his ability and willingness to interact on this practical level of everyday human need.

So Jesus' ministry took shape around the Sea of Galilee, centered in his new home of Capernaum. Here, as well as in Chorazin and Bethsaida, Jesus would end up performing most of his miracles and, by implication, their residents would hear most often the good news of God's kingdom (the "gospel"; Gk. *euangelion*; cf. Isa 40:9). Archaeological evidence at Chorazin (*Khirbet Kerraza*) on the slope of the rocky basalt rise two miles above Capernaum suggests that that place was a small village in the first century A.D., while Bethsaida, on the other hand (the remains of which are generally thought to be at the mound of *et-Tell*, now a mile up the Jordan River delta from the sea), had just been elevated to the status of a *polis* by the tetrarch Philip (*Ant.* xviii.2.2). Certainly there were bits and pieces of nondescript settlements in the immediate vicinity (cf. Mk 1:38); it is likely, for instance, that Jesus' fishermen disciples who were "from Bethsaida" actually lived and worked in a cluster of houses dependent on the *polis* nearer the sea (e.g. at *Khirbet el-Araj*; cf. Judg 1:27). Together, these cities and their villages on the northern end of the Sea of Galilee, demarcating a small triangle of land lying mostly within the political district of Galilee, were a good place for Jesus to build his base of operations. We can only imagine most of the specifics, as the Gospel writers fail to mention any of Jesus' visits to Chorazin and record only a very few of his activities in Bethsaida. Ironically, in the end much of what he said and did there was for naught, and Jesus sternly upbraided the residents of all three places for their lack of repentance even though they had witnessed the power of God face to face (Mt 11:20–24; Lk 10:10–15; cf. Mt 3:7–12). But in spite of the cold response to his work Jesus didn't leave this "Evangelical Triangle" behind as he

The ground above Capernaum rises gently but surely to the north. Geologically, this is an uprise (or, plug) of basalt (today labeled the Rosh Pina Sill), blocking free drainage of the Huleh Basin and channeling the flow of the Jordan River to a rapids-filled canyon along its eastern side. The basalt of the sill has eroded into hillsides covered with large boulders, hindering the development of agriculture but providing good grazing land. The largest village up on the sill in the first century A.D. was Chorazin. Just above Capernaum were ample empty places into which Jesus could withdraw when he needed a break from the pressures of ministry along the shore (e.g. Mt 1:35).

had the village of Nazareth. Its geographical setting was too proximate to the spread of the Gospel to do otherwise.

Jesus' ministry in the north carried him throughout Galilee, into the surrounding districts of Gaulanitis and the Decapolis and even to the region of Tyre bordering the Mediterranean coast. However, there is no mention in the Gospel accounts of him ever setting foot in the larger Hellenistic cities of the region: Tiberias, Hippus, Sepphoris, Scythopolis or other cities with similar names or demographics (he once visited "the region of Caesarea Philippi" but apparently not the city itself; cf. Mt 16:13). Some scholars have argued that Jesus' efforts to "keep *kosher*" (as a good rabbi would want to do) prevented him from entering places that were home to so many persons who were ritually unclean according to Jewish law (especially Tiberias, which was built over a cemetery; cf. Ant. xviii.2.3). Perhaps—but by avoiding the Greco-Roman cities of the region Jesus (and the Gospel writers) also sent a message about the hollowness of the ways of the world: "All that stuff related to a Roman world view? It's not necessary for life. We can safely ignore it."

Jesus' first recorded miracle in Capernaum was quick, dramatic and effective, and unwittingly brought him instant publicity. The setting was the synagogue and, like in Nazareth, he was asked to teach on his first *Shabbat* in town (he had been in Capernaum before, and his reputation there remained intact; cf. Lk 4:23). Jesus' words raised the interest of the local scribal establishment, "for he taught as one having authority" (Mk 1:21–22). But before a theological debate could arise that might take him down the same track as the events of Nazareth, Jesus was confronted by a man "with an unclean spirit" (Mk 1:23). In keeping with first-century understandings of medicine, this description of the poor fellow's ailment was rather generic and could have included a variety of emotional or psychological disorders as well as demon-possession. Surely the man was known to the more dignified attendees of the

synagogue, and was feeling the stigma of living a life that was perpetually unclean before them and God. Whatever the exact nature of his ailment, he made quite a stir and Jesus ordered the vigorous-yet-debilitating spirit trapped within to "be quiet and come out!" (Mk 1:23–26). Jesus' command-verbs not only were appropriate to the case at hand, but came to characterize his early Galilean ministry: active, effective work done quietly and in order so that his messianic role would remain in the background until the appropriate time (cf. Mt. 8:4, 9:30; Mk 1:34, 1:44, 5:43, 8:26). No sword-and-glory campaign here. Other Galilee messiahs could walk that road. Jesus' first agenda was to "go about doing good and heal all who were oppressed by the devil" (Acts 10:38), overcoming a force of evil that included Rome but was ever so much larger. The news about him spread quickly throughout the surrounding district of Galilee (Mk 1:28), no doubt carried in part by the easily excited (and justifiably so) multitudes, the ever-present *am ha-aretz* who came to track his every move. In this manner the Gospel came first—at least geographically and chronologically—to the "lost sheep of the house of Israel" (cf. Ezek 34:1–10; Mt 9:35–36, 10:5–6; Lk 15:3–7). The line between quick fame for the sake of a just cause and toiling in relative obscurity until the proper time was a fine one for messiahs to walk,

The heartland of first-century Galilee was the Beth Netofa Valley, a wonderful agricultural plain wedged between the Nazareth Ridge and Cana of Galilee. Jesus must have walked along its pathways and through its fields often. Much recent attention has focused on the valley's main city, Sepphoris, and the role that this largely Hellenistic town may have played in Jesus' early education about the world around him. Fair enough, but it was the country folk living in the smaller villages of the region—places that were tied almost exclusively to the local resources of the land rather than to the opportunities offered by the Ptolemais–Sepphoris–Tiberias highway—to which Jesus' main attention was drawn (cf. Mt 10:5–6). The hearts of such people were full of "good soil," although even some of them resembled rocky places and thorns where the seed of the Gospel didn't easily take hold (Mt 13:1–23).

In the first century A.D. the city of Capernaum was packed with insulae, self-contained blocks of rooms each forming the living space of an extended family. Many of the rooms were approximately 7 by 10 feet in size. The houses grew organically, with rooms added as the family became larger. The first married son, for instance, typically brought his bride to a newly constructed room in the compound. Jesus certainly called a single room in such an insula in Capernaum home (perhaps his was within the confines of Peter's house, now under the Memorial of St. Peter dominating the site). In any case, Jesus used the image of an insula to help his disciples understand what life with their Heavenly Father would be like: "In my Father's house are many rooms....If I go and prepare a place for you, I will come again and receive you to myself, that where I am, there you may be also" (Jn 14:2–3).

The shoreline of Capernaum today is easily identified by the dark basalt and glass Memorial to St. Peter's Church and the partially reconstructed white limestone synagogue behind. The Memorial to St. Peter is built over the remains of an octagon-shaped church of the Byzantine period. Both that church and the synagogue were in use at the same time, reflecting the importance of the site for Christians and Jews during the early centuries A.D., and signaling the practical needs of the congregants of both institutions to develop helpful and friendly relations in town.

and Jesus had his work cut out for him (cf. Mk 1:45).

After the *Shabbat* service in the Capernaum synagogue Jesus went to the home of Peter's mother-in-law, a short walk away. Archaeologists have found that the synagogue of first-century A.D. Capernaum was surrounded by blocks of living quarters (termed *insulae*), each composed of a random aggregate of small rooms and courtyards intended to serve the needs of an extended family and each isolated from its neighbor by a perimeter wall and intervening alley. Four hundred years later a large, octagon-shaped church was built over the ruins of a particular block of houses south of the synagogue, preserving the tradition that that one was the Capernaum home of Peter (his birth home was in Bethsaida; Jn 1:44). One of the rooms in the house, conveniently located below what would become the center of the church, was likely Jesus' own adopted room. It's all a reasonable hypothesis. Peter's mother-in-law was there, sick with a fever, and Jesus healed her, a quiet act of human compassion that restored her to wholeness (Mt 8:14–17; Mk 1:29–31). After sunset, at *motze Shabbat*, the end of the Sabbath (the notice in Mark 1:32 indicates that most of Capernaum's residents kept *Shabbat*), many families brought their sick to Jesus to be healed. Of course he met their needs; what else could he do (Mk 1:32–34)? Early the next morning he pulled away, likely somewhere into the empty grazing land above Capernaum, with the city and its fields, a thoroughfare and the lake stretching away at his feet. There, at the break of dawn, he could see the sweep of his new world come to life, a microcosm of the much larger Mediterranean basin that also lay at hand. Jesus' disciples found him: "Everyone is looking for you," they said (Mk 1:35–37; cf. v. 45). Word was out. The activities of the past twenty-four hours became a template for ministry as Jesus trekked throughout Galilee from

town to town, synagogue to synagogue, heart to heart (Mk 1:38–39). The skilled builder went to work on the kingdom of God.

When he spoke, Jesus often used traveling verbs: "Come" (Mt 11:28; Mk 6:31; Lk 9:23, 18:22; Jn 11:43); "Go" (Mt 5:41, 8:13, 9:6, 17:27; Mk 14:13; Lk 5:14; Jn 7:8); "Follow" (Mt 4:19, 9:9; Lk 9:23, 9:59, 18:22; Jn 10:4–5); "Send" (Mt 9:38, 10:16; Jn 20:21); "Walk" (Mt 9:5, 11:5; Lk 13:33; Jn 11:9–10). He was a man of action and, like the prophets of old, recognized that the everyday act of moving about from one place to the other, usually by foot and over rough or rugged terrain, was a particularly apt image to speak about conditions of the human heart:

> *This is what the LORD says:*
> *"Stand by the roadways and look,*
> * ask about the ancient paths:*
> *Which is the way to what is good?*
> * Then take it and find rest for yourselves."*
>
> (Jer 6:16)

Or,

> *A highway will be there, a roadway,*
> * and it will be called the Highway of Holiness.*
> *The unclean will not travel on it,*
> * but it will be for him who walks that way.*
>
> (Isa 35:8; cf. Acts 19:23)

Jesus' miracles of healing also echoed images of the heart from the Old Testament. He showed special concern for those who couldn't walk (Mt 8:5–13, 9:2–7; Mk 2:1–12; Jn 5:2–17) or see (Mt 9:27–31, 20:29–34; Lk 18:35–43; Jn 9:1–12), whose bodies were marred by leprosy (Mt 8:1–4; Lk 17:11–19) or physical deformities (Mk 3:1–6, 5:25–34), or who were possessed by unclean spirits (Mt 8:16, 8:28–34, 9:32–34, 15:21–28; Mk 1:21–26; Lk 8:2). Certainly many people, with a multitude of other infirmities, also suffered. Most whom Jesus healed, however, had the kind of physical ailments that prophets of the Old Testament used as images to speak about problems of the heart (cf. Isa 6:9–10, 42:7, 42:16, 42:24; Jer 13:10), or that, according to provisions of *Torah*, made a person too unclean to stand before the LORD (e.g. Lev 13:1–14:57; cf. Mishnah, *Bekhoroth* 7.1–7). Jesus' healings met real human needs, but also sent a clear religious signal: if he had the power to heal physical ailments ("Walk! See! Be clean!"), he also had the power to heal the problem of sin ("Walk! See! Be clean!" cf. Lk 5:17–26).

Jesus' travels took him on pathways, through grain fields and along the seashore to places not specified, but likely at first not too far from Capernaum, teaching, healing, helping and touching lives (Mk 1:45, 2:1, 2:13, 2:23, 3:7; Lk 7:1). The entire setting provided great illustrative material for parables (e.g. Mt 13:1–52). It was also time to celebrate life: the Messiah was coming (in his *Chronicles of Narnia*, a modern parable of sorts, C. S. Lewis would write, "Aslan is on the move").

As he went, Jesus seemed almost to go out of his way to be active on the Sabbath (*Shabbat*), the weekly day for spiritual (and physical) refreshment and for rejoicing in creation, in *Torah* and in God's provision for life. "The Sabbath was made for man," Jesus declared, emphasizing its freeing, beneficial aspects, "not man for the Sabbath" (Mk 2:18–28). Most of the scribes and Pharisees would have agreed on the principle, although it was easy to debate details of practice. According to the *Mekhilta de-Rabbi Ishmael* (Shabbata 1.27–28, commenting on Ex 31:14), "The Sabbath is given to you, but you are not surrendered to the Sabbath." Jesus probed further: "Is it lawful to do good on the Sabbath or to do harm, to save a life or to kill?" (Mt 12:9–12; Mk 3:1–4). Again, his question was consistent with early Rabbinic interpretations which held that healing was permitted on the Sabbath if there was otherwise imminent danger to human life: "We should disregard one Sabbath for the sake of saving the life of a person, so that that person may be able to observe many Sabbaths" (*Mekhilta de-Rabbi Ishmael, Shabbata* 1.30). By action and by deed, Jesus sought to live in the freedom of *Torah*, God's word for right living (cf. Mt 5:17). But his attitude toward Sabbath observance was too liberal (or, generous) for many of his more scrupulous colleagues, among them Pharisees who preferred to define *Torah* by drawing tight boundaries around its provisions, and they were generally displeased: of the people whom Jesus healed on the Sabbath, none had an imminent life-threatening condition (Mt 12:2–14; Mk 2:23–3:6; Lk 6:1–11, 13:10–17, 14:1–6; Jn 5:2–17, 7:19–24, 9:13–16).

Throughout, however, Jesus strove to get to the heart of the matter: one's attitude toward God and neighbor is the best indication of the real relevance of *Torah* in one's life (cf. the Sermon on the Mount, Mt 5:1–7:28; Lk 6:20–49). Many of the people of the land responded favorably, and a great multitude from Galilee, Judea, Jerusalem, Idumea and Perea ("beyond the Jordan") followed—all areas with a dominant Jewish majority—but also folks from the vicinity of Tyre and Sidon, Gentile-land (Mk 3:7–8). It was fertile soil, into which good seed fell and produced a hundredfold (Mk 4:1–25).

At one point Jesus' journeys took him to the southern extremity of Galilee, to the city of Nain on the northern slope of Mount Moreh. During the time of the Old Testament the main population center of Mount Moreh was at Shunem (modern Sulam), a city of some size on the southwestern end of the mountain. Shunem lay halfway between Elisha's home in the Jordan Valley (Abel-meholah) and Mount Carmel, a site of ongoing prophetic activity in the ninth century B.C. Walking between the two required an overnight stop, and Elisha typically had rested at the home of a Shunammite farmer and his wife on his journeys. The prophet blessed the childless couple and they soon gave birth to a boy,

the pride of the family and village. Alas!—the child died when he was but a lad and Elisha, in a moment of divine favor, raised the boy to life (2 Kgs 4:8–37). A great prophet had visited God's people, something the townsfolk never forgot; certainly they passed the story of "their" mighty act of God from generation to generation (for the lad, it was the ultimate story to tell his grandchildren). By the time of Jesus Shunem was no more, but people still lived in the area, now clustered in the small city of Nain (the place remains as the Arab village of Nein). When Jesus approached the city he was met by a large funeral procession coming out of the city gate, bearing the body of a young man, the only child of his widowed mother. The poor fellow had just died (burials are still within 24 hours of death in the land) and the grief was intense. Jesus was moved: his own mother Mary was a widow, and now this widow, a stranger, was also bereft of her only child, with no one to provide in her advancing years. But Jesus knew no strangers and, in a tremendous reaffirmation of prophetic authority, brought her son to life (Lk 7:11–15). Everyone glorified God.

> *A great prophet has arisen among us! [Again!].*
> *God has visited His people! [Again!].* (Lk 7:16)

News like this reached even into Judea (Lk 7:17).

It was at this point that the Judea-based disciples of John the Baptist, their master locked up in Herod Antipas' impregnable prison at Machaerus

"Consider the flowers of the field, how they grow. They do not toil or spin, yet I say to you that not even Solomon in all of his glory clothed himself like one of these. But if God so clothes the grass of the field, which is alive today and tomorrow is thrown into the fire, will He not much more clothe you?" (Mt 6:28–30).

Cradling a goat just hours old, this proud shepherd tends his flock on the stark springtime hillside of Machaerus, site of the execution of John the Baptist east of the Dead Sea. In an environment where green pastures are few and far between, a Good Shepherd is more than kind-hearted, he must be adept, resourceful, persistent and committed to placing the needs of his sheep and goats above his own creature comforts. Said Jesus, "the good shepherd lays down his life for his sheep" (Jn 10:11).

deep in Perea, came to Jesus to ask if he was indeed the Expected One come to redeem God's people. Jesus' response?

> Go and report to John what you have seen and heard: the blind receive sight, the lame walk, the lepers are cleansed, the deaf hear, the dead are raised up, and the poor have the Gospel preached to them. Blessed is the one who does not take offense at me.
>
> (Lk 7:22–23)

On another occasion Jesus summed it all up in the prayer that he taught his disciples to pray, just as the Baptist had taught his own disciples: "Thy kingdom come. Thy will be done, on earth as it is in heaven" (Mt 6:10).

Then it was back home to Capernaum. One evening, Jesus declared his intention to "go over to the other side" of the lake (Mk 4:35). The indicator "to the other side" does not require that he traveled to a point exactly opposite the shoreline, but in effect only move from one of the political districts around the lake to another; from Galilee, for instance, to Gaulanitis or back, even though the actual track of sail may have just cut the northeastern corner of the lake (e.g. Mt 14:22; Mk 6:45). This time Jesus was apparently headed from Capernaum to the Plain of Bethsaida or the part of Gaulanitis that edged the plain farther east. But a fierce wind arose, blowing the small boat out to sea (Mk 4:36–37). The season was likely fall or winter, when sudden, unpredictable storms can arise off the Mediterranean, their winds pouring through the east-west ridges and valleys of Lower Galilee then sweeping over the western rim of the sea, quickly churning its surface into the gateway of a watery abyss. Although the largest waves on the Sea of Galilee never exceed five feet, the small boat in which Jesus and his disciples were riding lay deep in the water, nearly swamped by the rolling swell. In Canaanite mythology the god of chaos and death was *Yam*, the Sea Personified, and

the idea that the sea could never be tamed persisted in shaping the fears of even the most experienced Galilee fishermen. It wasn't only Jonah, like Jesus a landlubber by birth, who was almost swallowed alive by the waters (cf. Jonah 1:4–15, 2:5–6):

> [The LORD] spoke and raised up a stormy wind which lifted up the waves of the sea.
> They (the waves? the people on the boat?) rose up to the heavens,
> they went down to the depths;
> their soul melted away in misery.
>
> (Ps 107:25–26)

Jesus, exhausted enough to sleep through all the excitement, was shaken awake by his disciples, then calmly spoke to the wind and the sea as if he would an unruly child ("Hush. Be still"; Mk 4:38–39), or as God first spoke to the cosmic deep at the moment of creation (Gen 1:6, 1:9).

> He caused the storm to be still
> so that the waves of the sea were hushed.
>
> (Ps 107:29)

And now an even greater kind of fear gripped Jesus' disciples. It was sheer awe, the realization of being face to face with something or someone divine. "Who is this, that even the wind and the sea obey him?!" (Mk 4:41).

The ship was blown some distance to a shoreline southeast of Capernaum, just into the land of the Decapolis (Mk 5:1). Variants of the Greek text of the Gospels read that Jesus and his disciples landed in "the country of the Gadarenes" (i.e., the region of Gadara which, though touching the very southern tip of the sea, is an unlikely location for the story) or "the country of the Gerasenes" (the area of Gerasa/Jerash high on the Dome of Gilead, 4,000 feet in elevation and 30 miles inland, clearly an impossible place). Geographic logic prefers the reading "the country of the Gergesenes," the land surrounding the seaside village of Gergesa (Kursi) at the mouth of the Nahal Samakh just beyond the southern border of Gaulanitis. By the sixth century A.D. all three candidates (Gadara, Gerasa and Gergesa) boasted large Byzantine churches dedicated to the memory of the subsequent miracle of the demons and pigs, and local inhabitants of each remain proud of their ties to "the real place" to this day. No matter; the physical setting of Gergesa offers the best fit for

One of the largest Byzantine monastic complexes in Galilee is located at Kursi, ancient Gergesa, at the mouth of the Nahal Samakh marking the border between the Decapolis and Philip's territory (Gaulanitis). Today manicured lawns and well-maintained remains of the past provide a pleasant stop for pilgrims following Jesus around the Sea of Galilee. The larger landscape—the relative location of the hills to fields and sea—provides a nice fit for the details of the story of Jesus' healing the demoniac, prompting an informed historical imagination to reflect on the rest.

the geographical references of the account. A man with an unclean spirit, driven into the wild hills and caves above the town by an unruly gang of demons (and by the powers of social ostracism), someone once wholly part of village life but now cast aside to live in the tombs of the dead and howl uncontrollably with the jackals that haunted the region in the wilds of the night (they still do)—this man, tormenting both himself and the townsfolk, came running to Jesus (Mk 5:2–8). His name was "Legion," his person badly fractured. Jesus commanded that the demons that seized his soul go into a herd of pigs feeding nearby (this was the Decapolis, where people weren't concerned about keeping *kosher*); they promptly drowned themselves in the sea, returning to the watery cosmic abyss from which they had come (Mk 5:9–13). A plausible candidate for "the steep bank on which they were grazing" lies about a mile to the south of the ruins of the ancient village at Kursi, opposite the town's fields, and from there word of Jesus' power began to spread (Mk 5:14–16). Although the man, now healed and in control of his faculties, wanted to accompany the disciples back to Capernaum, Jesus refused him passage and instead gave him back what he needed most: his own family. Besides, his mission field was his own homeland (Mk 5:17–20). The next time Jesus came to the Decapolis he was met by a large crowd of people who were eagerly awaiting his return (Mk 7:31–37). Their comment? "[Jesus] has done all things well" (Mk 7:37). Though Gentiles, they recognized the essence of *shalom* when they saw it.

Jesus returned to Capernaum and, after another period of teaching, healing and ministering to those in need, sent out his special twelve in pairs, two by two, into the towns and villages of Galilee (Mt 10:1–42; Mk 6:7–13; Lk 9:1–6). They went with his encouragement and instruction: don't go to the Gentiles or to the Samaritans but only to "the lost sheep of the house of Israel" (Mt 10:5–6). "Take only what is necessary. Reach as many people as possible. It won't be easy and the time is short, but there is no need to fear." It is impossible to know how long this first mission for the twelve lasted, but the conditions Jesus expected them to face echoed those that these same disciples, as Apostles ("sent ones"), would meet once they left the relative safety and security of Galilee for the "uttermost parts of the earth" (cf. Acts 1:8). Their discipleship would end up being costly; anyone who wanted to join Jesus' growing band might as well know that from the start (cf. Mt 10:24–42).

When the Apostles-in-training returned to Capernaum they gave a good account of their work to Jesus (Mk 6:30; Lk 9:10). It *hadn't* been easy (although it was exciting; before their call they had been just regular folk) and so Jesus took them "to a secluded place" to rest and regroup (Mk 6:31; Lk 9:11).

In the meantime, Jesus had heard that his prophetic predecessor, John the Baptist, had been executed by Herod Antipas (Mk 6:14–29; Lk 9:7–9), and he had reason himself to pause and reflect on the ominous turn that events had taken. His own death surely lay ahead.

The Gospels are unclear as to which side of the lake this secluded place was; according to Luke 9:10 it was near Bethsaida (the sequence of events recorded in Matthew 14:13–34 agrees), and a move from Antipas' territory to the safer quarters of the tetrarchy of Philip certainly made sense for Jesus at this critical point in his ministry. Mark 6:31, 45, however, suggests that Jesus' withdrawal "to a secluded place" must have been somewhere along the shore west of Capernaum since afterward Jesus intended to sail *to* Bethsaida. In the late fourth century A.D. the pious pilgrim Egeria opted for the latter. The record of her travels, now largely lost, inspired a twelfth-century monk of Monte Cassino, Peter the Deacon, to describe the place this way:

> Not far away from [Capernaum, to the west] there are some stone steps where the Lord stood. And in the same place by the sea is a grassy field with plenty of hay and many palm trees. By them are seven springs, each flowing strongly. And this is the field where the Lord fed the people with the five loaves and the two fishes. In fact the stone on which the Lord placed the bread has now been made into an altar.   (Wilkinson, *Egeria's Travels*, 196)

Egeria's choice of Jesus' "secluded spot" was quite near the main route through the region, but who can argue with the pious faithful? At least it was convenient for pilgrims (in the fifth century A.D. a church was built at the site of Egeria's seven springs—Heptapegon, now Tabgha—duly commemorating the place of the multiplication of the loaves and fishes which is remembered to have taken place there). An alternative spot in the vicinity of Bethsaida has never been pinpointed, although secluded places abound in that region both among the rushing channels of the Jordan River delta and on the drier slopes farther east. In any case Jesus' desire to withdraw from the crowds was for naught, as they followed his boat on foot, picking their way

It's one of a pilgrim's favorite views in all of Galilee: a close-up of the boy's lunch that fed a multitude, preserved in a setting of mosaic under the altar of the Church of the Multiplication of the Loaves and Fishes at Heptapegon (Tabgha) on the northwestern shore of the Sea of Galilee. The current church building, erected in 1982, replicates the 5th-century structure and preserves what remains of the original mosaic, including the loaves and fishes, in situ. Apparently the mosaic artist was not a fisherman. The fish he depicted have two dorsal fins, while all those native to the Sea of Galilee have a single dorsal fin. The rest of the mosaic depicts a rich selection of flora and fauna, some local species and others native to the Nile Delta (below). The artist also included a "Nilometer," apparently intended to measure the height of the water of the Sea of Galilee. Josephus (War iii.10.8) reported that "some have thought [the Jordan River above the Sea of Galilee] to be a branch of the Nile."

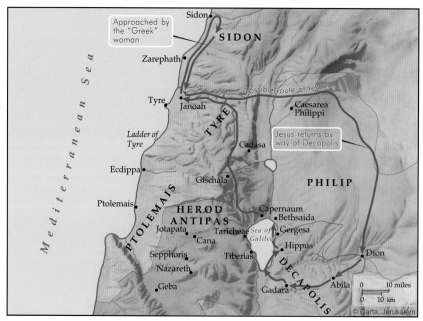

Jesus' Travels in Gentile Lands. *As local opposition to his comments about "keeping kosher" gained steam, Jesus decided to take his disciples to the district of Tyre and Sidon, then over to the Decapolis. His journey likely first crossed the rugged hills of Upper Galilee. Somewhere toward the coast (perhaps near Zarephath between Tyre and Sidon, where Elijah provided for a widow and her boy; cf. 1 Kgs 17:8–24) Jesus was approached by a "Greek" (i.e., Gentile) woman. He returned to the Sea of Galilee through the Decapolis, possibly on an inland route looping through Gaulanitis to the northeast.*

along the rocky shoreline. He must have heard them over the water, clamoring excitedly the entire way. Again, they were "like sheep without a shepherd" (Mk 6:34), now following a familiar voice, satisfied wherever the trip might take them. All met in a place far from towns or provisions. It was springtime, a glorious time to be out and about; Passover was near, and there was much green grass in the place (Mk 6:39; Jn 6:4). Setting aside his own agenda, Jesus spent the entire day with the multitudes, and when it grew late he fed them all, some five thousand people, by miraculous provision from one boy's lunch: five loaves of bread (pita-sized) and two fish (at least one mother had thought ahead!). This is the only miracle, except for the Resurrection, that is recorded in all four Gospels (Mt 14:13–21; Mk 6:33–44; Lk 9:12–17; Jn 6:1–14). Perhaps that says something about the power of the multitudes on the call of the Messiah.

Matthew and Mark record that not long afterward, Jesus again fed a multitude in a desolate place (clues suggest it was also somewhere on the northeastern side of the lake); this time seven loaves and a few fish, multiplied, satisfied four thousand people (Mt 15:32–39; Mk 8:1–9; cf. Mk 7:31). The prophet Elisha had also twice miraculously increased a small amount of food to meet a larger need, once for a widow and her two sons (2 Kgs 4:1–7) and once for a crowd numbering one hundred (2 Kgs 4:42–44). Here, as at Nain, Jesus' actions echoed the prophet, but with a resonance that was much louder than the miracle of old.

After feeding the five thousand, Jesus needed time by himself and so put his disciples in a boat and sent them back across the lake by themselves, late in the evening. The direction that they went depends on the location of the prior episode, although the weight of the evidence suggests they sailed from the region of Bethsaida back toward Galilee

(but cf. Mt 14:34; Mk 6:45). A sudden springtime storm hit the lake, blowing strongly. Mark notes that the disciples, fearing for their lives, strained at the oars to make headway against the wind (Mk 6:48, implying a westward voyage, although it is he who also notes their destination was "to the other side, to Bethsaida," i.e., eastward; cf. Mk 6:45). The geographical clues are as choppy as was the water during the voyage. Map-makers remain adrift; Jesus at least rescued the men in the boat, walking to them on the crashing waves (Mt 14:22–33; Mk 6:47–52; Jn 6:16–21). His disciples were utterly astonished: it was one thing to still the stormy sea; it was quite another to walk out into the liquid jaws of the Cosmic Deep and trample Death under one's feet. All came ashore at Gennesaret on the northwestern shore of the sea (Mt 14:34; Mk 6:53), the waters calm, the disciples likely in the stupor of post-traumatic shock, and another crowd of people, eager, wide-eyed and innocent, waiting to touch their Messiah. Was there no rest for the righteous?

They were back in Galilee again, where Jesus was approached by a contingent of scribes and Pharisees from Jerusalem who took exception with his approach to *Torah*. Either the Capernaum Pharisees had called in reinforcements, or those in Jerusalem had noticed Jesus on one of his trips to the Holy City. The issue was ritual cleansing before meals (Mt 15:1–2; Mk 7:1–5). Jesus responded by bypassing oral tradition with a direct appeal to the written words of Moses (Mk 7:9–13; cf. Ex 20:12, 21:17). Then he turned to the multitudes:

> There is nothing outside a man that can defile him if it goes into him, but the things which proceed out of a person are what defile him.　　(Mk 7:15)

This time he stood squarely against the broad stream of rabbinic tradition. The multitudes offered no argument in reply; the response of the scribes and Pharisees, though not given, was predictable. Later, alone with his disciples, Jesus voiced his opposition to the laws of keeping *kosher* (*kashrut*) and subsumed their effectiveness under the intentions and thoughts of the heart (Mk 7:17–23).

With opposition among his fellow rabbis growing Jesus decided that it was time to make a bold move and so he and his disciples traveled first into the region of Tyre and Sidon, then around and over to the Decapolis. Here it was Gentiles throughout, and Jesus' disciples were clearly out of their comfort zone. When they were approached by a woman whose daughter was demon-possessed Jesus himself was at first reticent to even notice, and his disciples demanded that she be sent away. But the woman persisted, throwing herself on the mercy of the God of Israel ("Lord, Son of David, have mercy on me!"—Jesus' reputation preceded him even here), and he healed her daughter (Mt 15:21–28; Mk 7:24–30;

cf. Mk 3:8). Then it was back to the Decapolis where Jesus healed a deaf man and likely renewed his acquaintance with the fellow he had freed of demons on his previous visit (Mk 7:31–37). One can only imagine other encounters Jesus had in these regions. For his disciples, it was enough to see that the God of Israel had children even among the Gentiles out in the Diaspora (cf. Jesus' comments in the Nazareth synagogue; Lk 4:24–27).

From the Decapolis it was over to Magadan (Mt 15:39) and Dalmanutha (Mk 8:10), two places otherwise unknown in ancient sources (perhaps both are names for the same site). Various suggestions locate them on either the eastern or the western side of the sea. Jesus and his disciples then reentered Bethsaida where he restored sight to a blind man (Mk 8:22–26). As was his pattern up to now, he asked the man who was healed to keep it quiet. But things were about to change dramatically.

From Bethsaida Jesus and his disciples traveled north, likely following the international highway that connected the Sea of Galilee to Damascus (this was a portion of the same "Damascus Road" on which Saul of Tarsus, who became the great Apostle to the Gentiles, would later encounter the risen Christ; cf. Acts 9:1–9). The farther one traveled away from the Sea of Galilee on this route, the more the demographics of Gaulanitis tipped from Jewish to Gentile. Halfway to Damascus, just before the highway left the territory of Philip, travelers necessarily passed through the *polis* of Caesarea Philippi (Panias), nestled against the southern end of Mount Hermon. Here a true Roman city was taking shape, with abundant vegetation fed by a powerful spring (a major source of the Jordan River) issuing out of a large cave at the base of a mammoth limestone cliff. The city was dedicated both to the Greco-Roman god of nature, Pan, and to the divine Caesar Augustus (now dead; Philip's father, Herod the Great, had built a classical Roman temple to Augustus at the mouth of the cave). Philip elevated the place to the capital of his tetrarchy, creating an atmosphere that would make any Rome-oriented traveler from the greater Mediterranean world feel right at home.

It was to the region of Caesarea Philippi, far both in terms of mileage and distance of the heart from Jewish communities in Jerusalem and Galilee, that Jesus brought his disciples to ask, "Who do people say the Son of Man is?" (Mt 16:13). Son of Man was perhaps Jesus' favorite title, and indicated his messianic, eschatological self-awareness (cf. Dan 7:13–14; 1 Enoch 48:2–7, 62:7; cf. 2 Esdras 13:1–58). It was Peter (*Petros*) who answered, "You are the Messiah, the Son of the Living God" (Mt 16:14–16). Jesus followed up with his first and most significant mention of the church, an institution that would be built on "this rock (Gk. *petra*) and the gates of Hades will not prevail against it" (Mt 16:17–19; cf. Mt 18:17, the only

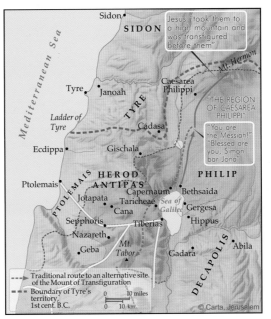

other time the word church occurs in the Gospels). While theologians have long debated the intent of Jesus' use of the term "rock," it remains interesting that his reference was made in the vicinity of the great cliff of Caesarea Philippi, the "toe" of the massive rock of Mount Hermon, a massif made of the kind of hard limestone that provides the best water resources, building materials and soil of all of the rocks of the land of Israel; in other words, a natural resource in which one can find strength, security and everything necessary for life, even in an other-

The Transfiguration. *A critical shift in the flow of the Gospel narrative is marked by a geographical move by Jesus to the northernmost point of the land of Israel. Somewhere in the region of Caesarea Philippi— likely not in the polis itself but certainly in a place under its aura and influence—Jesus prompted a moment of self-realization among his disciples. Who was he? Who were they? Peter spoke up: "You are the Messiah." By these words, Peter also admitted that he was a Messiah-follower. Confessions such as this would build the Church. Afterward Jesus moved to a "high mountain" (Mt 17:1), likely nearby Mount Hermon, where, transfigured with Moses and Elijah, he was confirmed from on high as the beloved Son of God. Now that everyone realized whom everyone was, the action—and the stakes—could intensify.*

The springs at Panias (modern Banias), issuing from the face of a cliff dedicated to the Hellenistic god of nature Pan, are one of the strongest and most refreshing in the entire land of Israel. The imagery of water flowing from the abode of The Divine was popular throughout the Mediterranean world, but it is also a biblical symbol (cf Ezek 47:1–12). Back down in dry and thirsty Jerusalem Jesus brought it all home: "He who believes in me, as the Scripture has said, 'from his inmost being will flow rivers of living water'" (Jn 7:38).

On a clear day the lofty heights of Mount Hermon can be seen from the surface of the Sea of Galilee, from the Nazareth Ridge and even—though rarely—from the higher hills of Samaria. For the Canaanites who called the mountain both Sirion (Ps 29:6) and, more interestingly, Mount Sion (Deut 4:48), the place was akin to the Hellenic Mount Olympus, the abode of the gods. Geographical and theological logic places Jesus' Transfiguration somewhere on its heights, a mountain worthy of an appearance by the prophetic mountaineers Moses and Elijah (Mt 17:3).

A Grand Journey to Jerusalem. *From his Transfiguration on Mount Hermon Jesus "resolutely set his face to go to Jerusalem" (Lk 9:51). For the next nine months the general flow of his journeys was to the south, toward the Holy City. On the way Jesus passed through or touched nearly every region that he had visited before. Although he made two or three quick trips to Jerusalem for specific purposes in the process, the overall sweep of his movements remained fixed on the climax of his journey—the Triumphal Entry, the Cross, the Tomb and the Resurrection.*

wise hostile and pagan environment—just like the church should be.

It was a moment of great expectation. Jesus followed with a jarring dose of reality:

From that time on he began to show his disciples that he must go to Jerusalem, and suffer many things from the elders and chief priests and scribes, and be killed and raised up on the third day. (Mt 16:21)

This was the first of three predictions of his own Passion (cf. Mt 17:22–23, 20:17–19), and if it wasn't enough, Jesus called for a decision from any among his disci-

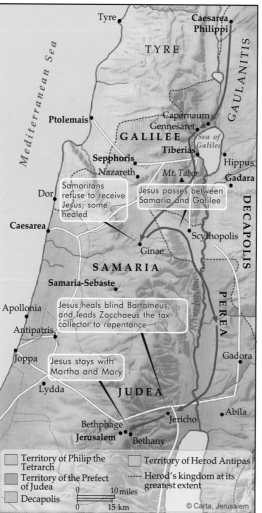

ples who might want to follow:

If anyone wishes to come after me, he must deny himself and take up his cross and follow me. (Mt 16:24)

Was *this* to be the way of the Messiah?

Six days later Jesus took his inner three, Peter, James and John, up to a high mountain where he was transfigured before them. Moses and Elijah, the two greatest prophets of old, also appeared, shining like the sun (Mt 17:1–4; Mk 9:2–4; Lk 9:28–31). While the dominant Byzantine tradition (Origen and Cyril of Jerusalem) places the Transfiguration on Mount Tabor, a prominent peak (elev. 1,929 ft.) on the northeastern corner of the Jezreel Valley conveniently located on the pilgrim route between Nazareth and Capernaum, an alternative voice (Eusebius) suggested that its location may have been on Mount Hermon (elev. 9,233 ft.). Jesus, after all, was already in the vicinity, and Mount Hermon had the advantage of being (north)east of the Rift Valley, the same side of the Jordan River on which Moses and Elijah had spent their final moments on earth before being ushered into the presence of God (Deut 34:1–6; 2 Kgs 2:7–12). High mountains and prophetic revelation go hand-in-hand in the biblical text (cf. Ex 19:10–20:21; 1 Kgs 19:9–18; 2 Pet 1:16–19), and so it was apparently somewhere on the heights of Hermon that Jesus, already in post-resurrection splendor, again heard the anointing-call of God:

This is My beloved Son with whom I am well pleased. Listen to Him! (Mt 17:5; cf. Mk 9:7; Lk 9:35; Mt 3:17; Mk 1:11; Lk 2:14, 3:22)

Jesus was the object of attention, but the intent of the matter was for his disciples. It was a pivotal moment; there was no turning back. Jesus "resolutely set his face to go to Jerusalem" (Lk 9:51).

Mount Hermon was the farthest point from Jerusalem to which Jesus traveled in his years of public ministry. He was there, likely, sometime in the summertime, nine months before the Passover of his crucifixion. And so began the final journey, a nine-month circuitous march touching every area (except for the region of Tyre) which Jesus had visited before, his words and actions building to a climax, his crowd of followers growing like a train of captives ascending on high (cf. Ps 68:18; Eph 4:7–8). It was the beginning of the one Grand Triumphal Entry that climaxed in a procession over the top of the Mount of Olives the Sunday before Passover. Jesus did make a few side-journeys to Jerusalem on the way, for *Succot* and *Hanukkah* (the Festivals of Booths and Dedication; Jn 7:2–10:39) and to raise Lazarus from the dead (Jn 11:1–54), but these don't detract from the force of his main line of march.

Jesus had been in Jerusalem at least twice before as an adult, once when he met Nicodemus, a member of the Sanhedrin who became a secret follower of the Galilean rabbi (Jn 3:1–21, 7:50–52, 19:38–42) and once when he healed a man at the Pool of Bethesda who had been ill for thirty-eight years (Jn 5:1–17). Nicodemus was the kind of fellow who would have been voted "most likely to succeed" by his peers; everything had gone wrong for the man at the pool. Jesus had time (and life-answers) for both.

In between these two visits to Jerusalem Jesus and his disciples had returned to Galilee via Samaria. The typical route taken by Jews between Judea and Galilee followed the eastern side of the Jordan Valley, a path that lay mostly in Perea (friendly Antipas territory) with the added advantage that the best water sources in the valley lay along that side. Although this journey took two or three days longer than did the trek straight up through Samaria, it avoided the distaste of rubbing shoulders with the Samaritans, a people-group with a long and varied history of bad relations with the Jews of Jerusalem (2 Kgs 17:24–26; Neh 4:2; Jn 4:9). A Jew heading north out of Jerusalem would typically spend his or her first overnight either at Anuathu Borcaeus (*Kh. Berqit* at the far end of the Levonah Valley) or Acrabeta (*Aqraba* to the northeast; Mishnah, *Maaser Sheni* 5.2), the last villages in Judea, then make quick work of Samaria in order to reach the Jezreel Valley by sundown, finishing the journey on the third day in Galilee. But on his run through Samaria Jesus stopped halfway, in the village of Sychar beneath Mount Gerizim, as if he had all the time in the world (Jn 4:1–6). He ended up staying two days, and many Samaritans came to believe that he was the Messiah, including the outcast woman at the well, a person as opposite the social spectrum from Nicodemus as Jesus' disciples could imagine (Jn 4:7–43).

These were his earlier journeys to Jerusalem. Now from Mount Hermon Jesus headed south, with the Holy City and a rendezvous at the Cross in sight. When everyone made it as far as the homeland fields of Galilee, Jesus announced his destiny a second time:

> *The Son of Man is going to be delivered into the hands of men and they will kill him, and when he has been killed he will rise three days later.* (Mk 9:31)

Jesus' Early Trips to Jerusalem According to the Gospel of John. *John's Gospel records at least five trips by Jesus to Jerusalem. Most of them coincided with festivals: Passover (Jn 2:13), Succot (Jn 7:3), Hanukkah (Jn 10:22) and possibly Shavuot/Pentecost (Jn 5:1). Each of these trips, plus a fifth in late winter to raise Lazarus from the dead (Jn 11:1–46), anticipated his final journey for Passover and the Passion (Jn 12:1–20:29). At least once he passed from Jerusalem to Galilee through Samaria, stopping in Sychar on the way (Jn 4:7–38). Other times he likely followed the Jordan River route, approaching Jerusalem from the east, the direction from which the Glory of the God of Israel returned to Jerusalem to refill the Temple after the Babylonian Exile (Ezek 43:1–5).*

The disciples had no clue what he was talking about (Mk 9:32; cf. Mt 17:23). A messiah resigned to suffering and death was not on the first-century radar screen. Back up north Jesus had said he was the Messiah and a voice from heaven even confirmed it. But apparently all the disciples wanted to hear was "We're going to Jerusalem," and that implied "to bring in a kingdom." To get themselves ready they promptly exerted no small effort arguing among themselves who would inherit the greater throne (Mk 9:33–34). Jesus let them have it out, then called the twelve together for a lesson in leadership: all pretensions of rank and power had to be set aside; no one was worth following unless they first laid their own life on the line for the others (Mk 9:35).

It is at this point in the narrative flow that we find the best fit for Jesus' "secret trip" to Jerusalem for

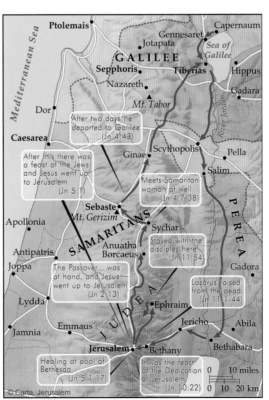

The twin peaks of Mounts Gerizim (left) and Ebal (right), dominating the landscape of Samaria (the hill country of Ephraim and Manasseh), have witnessed millennia of social and political intrigue. Nestled between was Shechem (Roman Neapolis, modern Nablus), the "uncrowned queen of the hills" (so quipped George Adam Smith) from which political aspirations of greatness habitually launched themselves on the surrounding region. In Jesus' day residents of Sychar, a Samaritan village adjacent to Shechem/Neapolis, proudly remembered their temple that had once stood in grandeur on the summit of Gerizim, only to be destroyed by the Jewish king John Hyrcanus in 107 B.C. Against the advice of his wary disciples Jesus rested at Sychar on a journey between Jerusalem and Galilee and found a receptive audience: "Lift up your eyes and look on the fields; they are white for harvest" (Jn 4:35).

The size and depth of the great Pool of Bethesda, now in the compound of the Church of St. Anne in Jerusalem's Muslim Quarter, can be appreciated in spite of the build-up of Byzantine and Crusader-era walls preserving the sanctity of the site. The pool, likely one hundred feet deep, was an important water reservoir for residents of the northern part of Jerusalem in Jesus' day. Nearby stood the massive Antonia Fortress, housing a garrison of Roman troops stationed to keep peace in the city. Their social and religious needs were met in part by use of an Asclepion (a cultic site of healing waters) adjacent to the larger pool. This raises an interesting question: Was the man who had been lying by the water of the Pool of Bethesda for 38 years waiting for the healing powers of the Greco-Roman god Asclepios? "Do you [really] want to get well?" Jesus asked him (Jn 5:6).

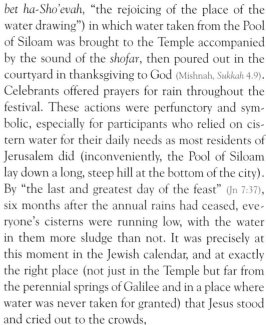

the autumn Festival of *Succot*. Although he knew that his time had not yet come and that a trip to Jerusalem held certain dangers to the proper unfolding of his ministry, Jesus made the journey anyway (Jn 7:1–13). The eight-day pilgrimage festival of *Succot* is a time to rejoice in divine blessings, during which for centuries Jews have celebrated the harvest of summer fruit (grapes, olives, figs and pomegranates), remembered God's provision during Israel's forty-year sojourn in the wilderness, and anticipated the coming of the early rains to break the summer drought (Ex 23:16; Lev 23:39–43; Deut 11:14, 16:13–15)—this even in places in the Diaspora where the seasons and their crops are quite different than in Judea and Galilee. During the Second Temple period the *Succot* celebrations included a water libation (*Simchat*

In May 2004 a municipal utility crew digging to find and repair a sewer line at the southern end of Jerusalem's City of David struck a water system much older than the one they were looking for. Archaeologists Ronny Reich and Eli Shukron, directing the City of David excavations, immediately recognized steps dating to the Second Temple period, subsequently opened to reveal the northern edge of the stepped Pool of Siloam. The pool was fed by an aqueduct channeling water from the southern end of Hezekiah's Tunnel, a water system dating to the 8th century B.C. From this pool water was drawn to pour out as libation in the Temple precincts during Succot. To this pool Jesus sent a man born blind to wash so that he might see (Jn 9:1–12).

bet ha-Sho'evah, "the rejoicing of the place of the water drawing") in which water taken from the Pool of Siloam was brought to the Temple accompanied by the sound of the *shofar*, then poured out in the courtyard in thanksgiving to God (Mishnah, *Sukkah* 4.9). Celebrants offered prayers for rain throughout the festival. These actions were perfunctory and symbolic, especially for participants who relied on cistern water for their daily needs as most residents of Jerusalem did (inconveniently, the Pool of Siloam lay down a long, steep hill at the bottom of the city). By "the last and greatest day of the feast" (Jn 7:37), six months after the annual rains had ceased, everyone's cisterns were running low, with the water in them more sludge than not. It was precisely at this moment in the Jewish calendar, and at exactly the right place (not just in the Temple but far from the perennial springs of Galilee and in a place where water was never taken for granted) that Jesus stood and cried out to the crowds,

> *If anyone is thirsty [and from the look on your faces I can tell that all of you are!], let him come to me and drink. He who believes in me, as the Scripture has said, "From his innermost being will flow rivers of living water."* (Jn 7:37–38)

Jesus didn't quote a specific passage from the Old Testament but cobbled together a number of instances in which the prophets of old had drawn on the image of water flowing from the Temple to speak of the life-giving qualities of the Spirit of God (Ezek 47:1–12; Zech 13:1, 14:8; cf. Isa 44:3, 55:1, 58:11). He was the conduit, channeling life to any one who was willing to drink. And what good was a Messiah-delivered political kingdom if the hearts of its people were dry?

Jesus stayed in Jerusalem for a while, engaging the scribes and Pharisees in dialogue and debate and healing people in need, as he had done throughout Galilee (Jn 7:40–10:21). On the Mount of Olives he refused to condemn an adulterous woman (his own mother had been suspected of the same offense), requiring only that she "go and sin no more" (Jn 8:1–11). On the Sabbath, at the Pool of Siloam, he brought sight to a man born blind (Jn 9:1–12), with the usual consternation following. And, as was the pattern, some people followed; others did not (Jn 10:19–21).

Two months later, in the winter, Jesus was in Jerusalem for the Festival of Dedication (*Hanukkah*; Jn 10:22–39; cf. 2 Macc 10:1–8). Whether he had stayed in the city since *Succot* or returned north between festivals is unknown. But by now his reputation in Jerusalem had grown considerably and some of the city's residents, stirred by the possibilities, pressed for more information:

> *How long will you keep us in suspense? If you are the Messiah, just tell us plainly.* (Jn 10:24)

The climax would come in Jerusalem, but the proper time was not quite ready. In the meantime, Jesus simply asked that everyone judge him by the works that he did "in [his] Father's name" (Jn 10:25, 10:37–38), for, after all, "I and the Father are one" (Jn 10:30). "The Father is in me, and I am in the Father" (Jn 10:38) he said, in the clearest public statement yet that he was the Messiah (cf. Isa 42:1, 43:10, 49:3–6). The crowd picked up stones, clearly upset that by aligning himself so closely to God, Jesus was also claiming to be divine (Jn 10:31–33). He did not dispute the motive for their reaction.

Jesus returned to the lower elevations northeast of Jerusalem and spent the bulk of the winter season there. He probably made it all the way back to Galilee (cf. Lk 9:51–52, 17:11), but in any case his eyes remained steadfastly set on the Passover festival in Jerusalem. At one point he tried to pass through a village in Samaria (he entered the region either from the north or the east) but received a cold reception (Lk 9:51–56). The disciples wanted to call down fire from heaven (cf. 2 Kgs 1:1–16). Jesus, deferring to Torah ("You shall not take vengeance, nor bear any grudge against the sons of your people, but you shall love your neighbor as yourself"; Lev 19:18), replied that he had come to save lives— even Samaritan ones—not destroy them (Lk 9:55–56). Later, in conversation with a Torah scholar, Jesus included Samaritans in the category of "one's neighbor" (he never tired of pushing the envelope; Lk 10:25–37). Given the occasion, Jesus even healed ten Samaritan lepers, requiring only that they show themselves to the (Jewish) priests according to provisions of Torah so they could be formally declared clean before the LORD (Lk 17:11–19; cf. Lev 14:1–32). In this instance, Jesus not only upheld Torah, he sought to bring non-Jews under its umbrella (cf. Mt 5:17).

He apparently spent the bulk of his time that last winter, however, in Perea. Here we can reasonably place the events and teachings of Luke's "Special Section" (9:51–18:30), a narrative flow not included in the other Gospels. Historically Perea, "the other side of the Jordan," was a staging ground for armies or people groups wanting to infiltrate or conquer the land of Israel (e.g. Joshua, Eglon, Jephthah, Tobiah, and the Ammonites, Moabites, Midianites and others generally), and here Jesus went to get ready for his final climb to Jerusalem. He had left Galilee behind to move into position on the Holy City, and because Perea was an area of strong Jewish settlement and, like Galilee, under the political authority of Herod Antipas ("that fox"; Lk 13:32), Jesus was able to continue to build momentum unabated. One senses a real urgency in his movements and teachings, especially here, as the months and weeks grew short:

I say to you, My friends, do not be afraid of those who kill the body and after that have no more that they can do. But I will warn you whom to fear: fear the One who, after He has killed, has authority to cast into hell. Yes, I tell you, fear Him! (Lk 12:4–5)

Be dressed in readiness, and keep your lamps lit… blessed are the servants whom the master will find on alert when he comes. (Lk 12:35–37)

Whoever does not carry his own cross and come after me cannot be my disciple. (Lk 14:27)

Truly I say to you, there is no one who has left house or wife or brothers or parents or children for the sake of the kingdom of God who will not receive many times as much at this time and in the age to come, eternal life. (Lk 18:29–30)

And,

I must journey on today and tomorrow and the next day, for it cannot be that a prophet would perish outside of Jerusalem. (Lk 13:33)

Then, as winter turned to spring and the great Passover freedom festival drew nigh, Jesus announced his coming Passion a third time:

Behold, we are going up to Jerusalem. There all the things that are written through the prophets about the Son of Man will be accomplished. (Lk 18:31)

So far, so good, his disciples thought. Let's go! Then, once more the bombshell:

There He will be handed over to the Gentiles and mocked and mistreated and spit upon, and after they have scourged him they will kill him. But on the third day he will rise again. (Lk 18:32–33; cf. Mt 20:18–19)

And again the inner twelve, who had been privy to Jesus' most personal and intense teachings, didn't understand. No one had been closer to Jesus than James and John, and even they were still thinking, "What's in it for me?" (Mk 10:35–37). But why should

Jesus spent his last winter and early spring in northern Perea, the region "Beyond the Jordan." Living conditions there were similar to those of Galilee: limestone hills, abundant rain, spring water, fertile soil and plenty of vegetation. Moreover, the land was under the authority of Herod Antipas, tetrarch of Galilee. This particular valley is formed by the Wadi es-Sar as it drops into the Plains of Moab opposite Jericho. The rise in the distance carries the Jerusalem–Jericho–Livias–Philadelphia (Amman) highway. Although the Gospel writers do not localize Jesus' travels at any specific spot in Perea, a setting such as this would have been attractive as he continued to build a following for his final march to Jerusalem.

The mountain fortress of Cypros (top right), one of the strongholds of Herod the Great, overlooks the Herodian palace complex at Jericho. Here the remains of an ornate peristyle courtyard, once adorned with frescoes in what is termed the Third Pompeian Style, reflect a grandeur that once was. Zaccheus would have felt at home here, a royal wanna-be though just a lackey in the Roman imperial system; Bartimaeus could only dare hope for a little trickle-down change. Jesus passed by the shadows of Herod's palace on his way to Jerusalem, unimpressed by anything it had to offer.

they understand, really? Everything about the Cross was too dissonant to be believed (Mk 10:38–45).

Now for the final assault. Jesus and his disciples crossed the Jordan River opposite Jericho near the site of his baptism, in the vicinity of the place where, with the command of Moses, Joshua and the children of Israel had entered the Promised Land, and where Elisha, endowed with the double-spirit of Elijah, stepped back into a world of need (Josh 3:1–17; 2 Kgs 2:13–14; Mt 3:13–17; Jn 1:19–34). Then he made his way through the parched nothingness of the Rift Valley to Jericho, an oasis of Roman imperial might awash in an arid sea. Here royal palaces of the Maccabees, Herod the Great and Archelaus still set the tone for the region, shouting the opulent "can-do" of the Empire. Here Rome had placed an agent to collect taxes generated from the Perea-Judea border crossing and the trade in minerals and balsam from the shore of the Dead Sea. Zaccheus, short in stature, salivated at the chance to strike it rich, but in the process collected the special kind of scorn the multitudes reserved for collaborators. Zaccheus did what he could to "get back" at the ungrateful lot through extortion and fraud (it was the way of the Empire; his confession to Jesus "If I have defrauded anyone I will give back four times the amount" was a face-saving way of admitting he *had* taken four times his legal share; Lk 19:1–10). In Zaccheus, Matthew likely recognized a friend—and the need for a Savior (cf. Mt 9:9–13).

Wealth also attracts the very poor, and there sat blind Bartimaeus, a roadside beggar waiting for

crumbs (cf. Mt 15:27). Jesus had time for him, too, and, regaining his sight, a whole Bartimaeus fell into the procession on the way to Jerusalem (Mt 20:29–34; Mk 10:46–52; Lk 18:35–43).

Roads from the east converged at Jericho, funneling most traffic up to Jerusalem along the ridge between the rugged Wadi Mukallik (Nahal Og) and the majestic Wadi Qilt, a rise of 4,000 feet in just thirteen miles. The steepest parts of the road are the initial climb out of the Rift Valley (the "Ascent of Adummim"; Josh 15:7) and the final push up and over the Mount of Olives. Up or down, this leg of the Jerusalem-to-Galilee journey through the Judean Wilderness took a full day by itself, and during his lifetime Jesus walked it several times. It would be a mistake to label this route "the Roman Road to Jericho" in the first century; the road was incorporated into the Roman Road network only in the mid-second century A.D., after the Emperor Hadrian had turned Jerusalem into Aelia Capitolina, a *polis* worthy of Rome's economic attention. Bits and pieces of the remnants of the Roman-Byzantine road (paving, curbing and mile stones) can still be seen by intrepid hikers along the ridge today.

So Jesus climbed one last time, approaching Jerusalem from the east. King David had fled down this route to escape the *coup d'état* of Absalom, then retraced his steps to Jerusalem to receive back his kingdom (2 Sam 15:23, 15:30, 16:1, 16:5, 16:13, 19:15, 19:18, 19:40). When the Babylonians destroyed the first Temple the Glory of the God of Israel had left Jerusalem and stood over the Mount of Olives as the people of Jerusalem were hurled into exile, then returned from the East to fill the rebuilt Temple (Ezek 9:3, 10:18–19, 11:22–23, 43:1–5). Isaiah foresaw the LORD entering Jerusalem from the east, and called for the way to be prepared for His advance on the city:

> Clear the way for the LORD in the wilderness;
>   make smooth in the desert a highway for our
>   God.
> "Let every valley be lifted up,
>   and every mountain and hill be made low;
> let the rough ground become a plain
>   and the rugged terrain a broad valley;
> then the glory of the LORD will be revealed,
>   and all flesh will see it together.   (Isa 40:3–5)

The Gospel writers unanimously connected Isaiah's image to the work of John the Baptist, the great prophetic voice announcing the coming of Jesus (Mt 3:3; Mk 1:2–3; Lk 3:4–6; Jn 1:23), and it is no accident that every time they recorded Jesus' actual approach to Jerusalem, he always came from the east.

Jesus and his disciples climbed to Bethany (el-'Azariyeh), a village on the eastern slope of the Mount of Olives a little less than two miles from Jerusalem (cf. Jn 11:18). This was their Jerusalem-based home, and Jesus apparently stayed there whenever he was in the area (Mt 21:17; Mk 11:11; Lk 10:38–42, 21:37). It was Friday evening, six days before the Passover, and Jesus ate his last *Shabbat* meal with his disciples and some close friends, including Martha, Mary (a Mary other than his mother or Mary Magdalene) and Lazarus, whom he had raised from the dead in Bethany six weeks before (Jn 12:1–2; cf. Jn 11:1–46; *el-ʿAzariyeh* is a corrupted Arabic form of "Lazarus"). Jesus' conversation with Lazarus must have been quite interesting ("What was being in the tomb like…?"). The events of the meal, described by John (12:1–8), closely parallel the accounts of Matthew (26:6–13) and Mark (14:3–9) in which Jesus ate the meal at the home of Simon the Leper, and it is likely that the three Evangelists simply emphasized different aspects of the happenings of a single event. Simon could not have hosted the dinner unless he no longer had leprosy (likely another work of Jesus!), although unfortunately he was stuck with an unclean moniker throughout life. During the meal Mary took an alabaster jar of nard (it was quite expensive; the jar had been imported from Egypt and the nard from northern India; Mk 14:3) and anointed Jesus' head and feet. This was an anointing with a double referent: as Messiah, and for burial.

Jesus spent the entire Sabbath in Bethany. The village lay three times farther from Jerusalem than rabbinic law allowed a person to travel on *Shabbat*, and nearly twice as far as laws of *eruv* (which lengthen the boundaries of *Shabbat* observance in certain instances) would permit (e.g. Mishnah, *Erubin* 3.6, 4.3, 5.9). The next day was Sunday, the first and busiest business day of the week, with crowds of people early on the street making preparations for the upcoming Passover. It was exactly the right time for Jesus to bring his Grand Triumphal Entry to a climax. His choice of transport was a donkey, a humble beast of burden, rather than a warhorse of military conquest (Mt 21:1–9; Mk 11:1–10; Lk 19:28–44; Jn 12:12–19; cf. Zech 9:9). (This is the only time in the Gospel story that Jesus ever rode anything.) He started at Bethphage (of uncertain location but near Bethany; perhaps *et-Tur* or its vicinity on the crest of the southern end of the Mount of Olives), then went over the top of the mount and down. People crowded before and behind holding palm branches, a Jewish symbol of righteousness and freedom during the Second Temple period. From their exuberance alone one would have thought that the Eschaton was coming then and there. "Hosanna" ["Save, now!"]. "Blessed is the kingdom of our father David that is coming!" "Peace in heaven and glory in the highest!" (Mt 21:9; Mk 11:9–10; Lk 19:38). This latter cry echoed that of the angels of nearby Bethlehem at Jesus' birth (Lk 2:14). Everything had come full circle. For his part, Jesus wept over the city and the trials that would surely come its way: "Would that even today you knew the things that make for peace!" (Lk 19:42). The chapel of Dominus Flevit marks the spot where his tears are remembered.

Jesus approached Jerusalem (Mt 21:10–11; Mk 11:11; Lk 19:45). The Gospels don't mention by which gates he entered the city and then the Temple. It is theologically tempting to suggest that he rode straight into the Temple precinct through a gate in the eastern wall of the Herodian complex, although it is more likely that he left his borrowed donkey somewhere outside and climbed the stairs along the southern wall of the Temple enclosure by foot as most who entered typically did. Once inside, he proceeded to the Royal Stoa, the great colonnaded structure of Corinthian order spanning the entire width of the southern end of the Temple Mount, likely the largest building in the Roman world at the time (Ant. xv.11.5). This building, housing the concerns of the Temple's varied financial affairs, was in effect the bank of Jerusalem. It also contained the meeting chambers of the Sanhedrin, Judaism's supreme ruling body. For Jesus, the excesses of the financial end of Temple activities had become an affront to the sanctity of the site and he literally turned the place on its head (Mt 21:12–16; Mk 11:15–18; Lk 19:45–48).

After the Romans destroyed Jerusalem and burned both the city and the Temple in A.D. 70, they minted "Judaea Capta" coins to commemorate their victory. These coins were struck in gold, silver and bronze, and far more exist today than do similar coins commemorating Roman victories over the Egyptians and the tribes of Germany and Spain. The obverse depicts the bust of Emperor Vespasian (his son Titus led the assault on Jerusalem); the reverse shows a Roman soldier standing in triumph behind a humbled Jewish woman representing the captured people of Judea, now in slavery, framed by the words IUDAEA CAPTA. Typically the woman sits beneath a palm tree, the Jewish symbol of righteousness and victory, now spitefully co-opted by Rome. This cold reality was a far cry from the scene of the palm-branch waving crowds welcoming Jesus to Jerusalem the Sunday before Passover.

The largest building on the Temple Mount platform—and possibly in the world at the time—was the Royal Stoa. Built in the Roman basilica style, this structure dominated the southern end of the platform and helped to give Herodian Jerusalem a Western look. The building contained 120 columns set in four long rows each of which, according to Josephus (Ant. xv.11.5), was so massive that it took three men with outstretched arms to cover their circumference. This reconstruction of the Stoa is part of the "Holyland Hotel" Second Temple Model now located at the Israel Museum, Jerusalem. Pieces of columns have been found in excavations in Jerusalem's Jewish Quarter, although of only a "two-man" circumference. They may have come from the Stoa or another building in the vicinity.

Primary access to the Temple Mount in the first century A.D. was through the Hulda Gates located in the massive southern wall that surrounded the Temple enclosure above. A line of Herodian masonry—huge blocks of stone nearly six feet high decorated with a straight-line margin and well-smoothed boss—remains as the bottom course of the southern wall of the Temple Mount. Below were the public miqva'ot *(ritual baths) and a monumental stairway lifting pilgrims to the Temple complex. The margin of the right-hand edge of this particular Herodian stone is ornately carved as a doorjamb, as pointed out by the author's wife, indicating the location of the Hulda Gates. The inner passageway still remains, now sealed by later, rougher, stones. Certainly Jesus crossed this passageway, having first entered the waters of the* mikveh *as he visited the Temple daily the week before of his Passion.*

(below) The remains of this city gate at the southern edge of the Protestant cemetery on Mt. Zion were first uncovered by British archaeologists Bliss and Dickie in 1894–1897. The gate was excavated again by Bargil Pixner and Shlomo Margalit in 1977–1978. Its upper threshold (X) belonged to a gate that was part of the Byzantine city. Both Bliss and Pixner identified the lowest threshold beneath, which dates to the Second Temple period, with the Gate of the Essenes mentioned by Josephus (War v.4.2). The author's daughter graces the street level below. Fr. Pixner used this identification to support his theory of an Essene Quarter on Mt. Zion, supposedly located just inside the gate, and suggested that Jesus' Last Supper meal was taken within that complex. Typical gate nomenclature, however, labels a gate after the place to which travelers go upon exiting. The so-called Gate of the Essenes faces southwest to the watershed ridge route and Bethlehem; the Essene community at Qumran lay to the southeast.

John mentioned this event nearly at the beginning of his Gospel account (Jn 2:13–22), dramatically introducing his readers up front to the far-reaching ramifications of Jesus' divine call. Overturning the Temple money-changers' tables was not something that Jesus could have gotten away with twice!

Jesus spent most of his time the next few days in and around the Temple, returning to Bethany to spend each night with his closest circle of supporters and friends (Mt 21:17; Mk 11:19; Lk 21:37). His time had finally arrived, and he held nothing back. The Temple officials questioned him up front: "By what authority are you doing these things? And who gave you that authority?" (Mt 21:23). Jesus rightly suspected a Catch-22, that he would be condemned whether he said "from God" or "from men," and so he turned the question back on them, asking by whose authority John baptized. Fearing the response of the multitudes if they didn't acknowledge that John's baptism was from God, the chief priests and elders blinked first (Mt 21:24–27).

Jesus then began a long series of teachings—some upbraiding, others more gentle—about the need to get ready for the coming kingdom of God (Mt 21:28–25:46; Mk 12:1–13:37; Lk 20:9–21:36). The climax, sure to win enemies, was his lengthy diatribe against the scribes and Pharisees, said not because of what they taught (Jesus recognized the rightness of Pharisaic authority; Mt 23:2–3), but because of what they did ("they preach, but do not practice"; Mt 23:3). It has been suggested, and probably rightly so, that the scene of this lecture was the public and very crowded grand stairway leading up to the Hulda Gates on the southern end of the Temple precinct, a place where rabbis were known to hold "open court" with their disciples and whomever passed by (Babylonian Talmud, Sanhedrin 11a). From this spot Jesus and his captivated audience (those on the bottom always love to hear criticisms of those on the top) would have been able to see—or to see without much difficulty—most of the objects that he referenced as images of the deeds of the Pharisees: men struggling to carry heavy burdens (v. 4), the "doorway" to the kingdom of heaven (i.e., the Hulda Gates; v. 13), the gold adorning the Temple (v. 16), whitewashed tombs on the Mount of Olives (v. 27) and monumental tombs of the righteous in the Kidron Valley (v. 29). And from these steps Jesus could also see the horizon line: to the east, south and west higher hills crowded the old historic core of Jerusalem (David's city and the Temple Mount), forming the image of a nest in which God had exerted so much effort to hatch and then raise a people to follow Him.

> *O Jerusalem, Jerusalem, killing the prophets and stoning those who are sent to her. How often I wanted to gather your children together like a hen gathers her chicks under her wings, but you were unwilling.* (Mt 23:37)

Sometime toward the end of the week Jesus made preparations to celebrate the Passover meal with his disciples (Mt 26:17–19; Mk 14:12–16; Lk 22:7–13). According to the Gospel of John, however, Jesus and his disciples ate this Last Supper before the start of Passover so that he could die at the same time that the Passover lambs were being sacrificed in the Temple courtyard, as "the Lamb of God who takes away the sin of the world" (Jn 1:29; cf. Jn 19:30–31). Among the many solutions that have been offered for this chronological (and conceptual) difficulty, a recent and creative idea suggests that Jesus ate the last supper meal in Essene facilities on Mount Zion (the southern end of Jerusalem's western hill), where the Passover could be celebrated a couple of days before the official Passover sanctioned by the

Temple authorities (the Essene calendar, based on the sun, differed from the normative Jewish lunar calendar in determining the dates of the festivals). While this suggestion has some merit and many adherents, it allies Jesus too closely to the Essenes for this most critical point in his life, and a chronological solution remains in doubt.

In any case, it is clear that the Last Supper was eaten in the context of a Passover meal (Mt 26:20–29; Mk 14:17–25; Lk 22:14–23; Jn 13:1–17:26) somewhere (confirmed by the cumulative weight of church tradition) on Mount Zion. Partway through the meal Judas Iscariot excused himself (he had previously arranged to sell Jesus to the Temple authorities for thirty pieces of silver, the *Torah* price for a slave accidentally gored by an ox; Mt 26:14–16; Mk 14:10–11; Lk 22:3–6; cf. Ex 21:32). Judas' motives certainly were political; ironically, he was perhaps the first of the disciples to try to come to terms with the reality that Jesus' kingdom was not aimed at driving Rome from Judea and Galilee. While two thousand years of Christian Western civilization have thoroughly vilified Judas as the archetype of sanctimonious hypocrisy (or worse), as a dark, bulbous Shylock driven by avarice and misguided self-zeal, it is likely that he was simply disillusioned, feeling that it was not he but Jesus, so full of promise, who had betrayed the cause. Jesus knew what was going on, but the other disciples were clueless (Mt 26:21–25; Mk 14:17–21; Lk 22:21–23; Jn 18:4). They decided to proceed with more important matters, like finally deciding which of them would be the greatest in the coming kingdom (Lk 22:24–30). "Have they learned *nothing* yet?"—the thought must have crossed Jesus' mind. Becoming a servant for the sake of others is the hardest lesson to learn.

After the meal Jesus and his disciples left the city, crossed the Kidron Valley and started to climb the Mount of Olives. The hour was late (close to or after midnight), the Passover moon was full and high in the sky, and the springtime air cool (cf. Lk 22:55). The eleven disciples probably assumed they were heading back to Bethany for a long and much-deserved sleep, but Jesus stopped on the lower slope of the mount in a familiar place called Gethsemane ("olive press"), nearly crushed by the weight of the events to come (Mt 26:36–46; Mk 14:32–42; Lk 22:39–46; Jn 18:1).

> *Abba, Father, all things are possible for you. Remove this cup from me!* (Mk 14:36)

The disciples all fell asleep. Hush! A quick scramble and Jesus could be over the mountain and gone, to live in the adoration of his fans another day, the awful duty of the Triumphal Entry erased from his mind.

> *Nevertheless, not my will, but Yours be done.* (Mk 14:36)

Suddenly the night was interrupted by a cohort of Roman soldiers and Temple police crashing through the trees. Judas met his old master with a kiss of recognition—and betrayal (Mt 26:47–56; Mk 14:43–52; Lk 22:47–53; Jn 18:1–11). It was a deed fitting the darkness of the night. Jesus was hauled off for a series of hearings and trials before Temple and Roman authorities; Judas, in the horror of a deed that could not be undone, hung himself (Mt 27:3–10; cf. Acts 1:18–20).

Although the weight of the history of interpretation posits that Jesus' several trials all took place within the span of a few hours during the early

These ancient olive trees stand silent watch in the garden of the Church of All Nations at the foot of the Mount of Olives. Their age is measured in centuries, not millennia, though they are often given credit for being the very trees of the Garden of Gethsemane under which Jesus' disciples prayed while he sweat drops of blood. Stately and gracious, the trees themselves see no reason to argue the point.

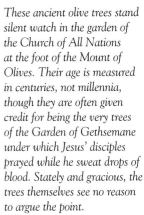

The Russian Orthodox Church of St. Mary Magdalene was erected between 1885 and 1888 by the nationalistic reactionary Czar Alexander III in memory of his mother the Empress Maria Alexandrovna, in a style that reflected the architectural flavor of the Kremlin. The church marks another one of the traditional locations of the Garden of Gethsemane. A midnight service every Easter Saturday calls Jesus anew from the tomb; worshippers leave the darkened church to walk around the building three times, then reenter the just-lighted sanctuary. Mary Magdalene played a very minor role in the Gospel story (in spite of the inventions and machinations of modern novelists), but she was present at Jesus' crucifixion and burial—stricken by the darkness of his crucifixion, enraptured at the light of his resurrection.

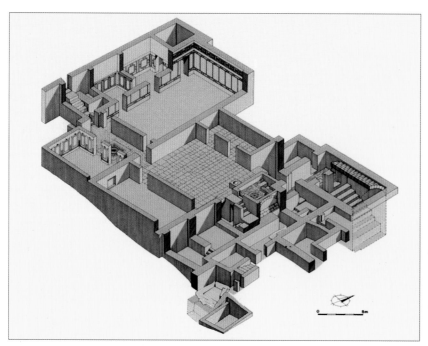

Archaeological excavations in Jerusalem's Jewish Quarter have uncovered large palatial mansions on the crest of the city's western hill (an official/ residential area now termed the Herodian Quarter). This spacious mansion, with large rooms around an open courtyard, was built of well-dressed ashlar stones; some rooms had mosaic floors; the walls of others were adorned with red-colored frescoes and white molded stucco. When fully standing, the view from the mansion's eastern windows took in the Temple, the Royal Stoa and the Mount of Olives. The entire complex is reminiscent of the Gospel's description of the home of the high priest Caiaphas in which Peter, sitting in the open courtyard, was near enough to be seen and heard by Jesus who was being interrogated in an adjacent room (Lk 22:54–62).
(reconstruction: L. Ritmeyer)

morning of the Friday of his crucifixion, there is nothing in the Gospel accounts that demands they all be squeezed into this narrow time-frame. Indeed, such a reconstruction assumes that everyone was so eager to do Jesus harm that laws were broken in the process (e.g. Jewish law forbade capital proceedings at night; Mishnah, *Sanhedrin* 4.1), that none of the members of the Sanhedrin or the host of witnesses called in to testify against Jesus had anything better to do during the wee hours of the night before Passover than hold a kangaroo court, and that both Pontius Pilate (the governor of Judea) and Herod Antipas (tetrarch of Galilee) adjusted their schedules on no notice to hear claims at an hour when royalty should be sleeping, against a man whom they had never met—and whom Pilate most likely never heard of. The Gospel accounts depict Jesus' trials as a hurry-up offense, but this must be read against the backdrop of "haste" in the ancient Mediterranean world which in any instance was several speeds slower than in the modern West. Typical would be the scenario: "Let him sit in prison for awhile like that crazy prophet John the Baptist" (Mt 11:2; cf. Acts 24:24–27). In any case reason would suggest that the trials took place over the course of at least a day, as is consistent with Jewish law that demanded a day's wait in capital cases (Mishnah, *Sanhedrin* 4.1).

First up was Jesus' hearing before Caiaphas, apparently in the high priest's own home, a spacious dwelling with official and private quarters in Jerusalem's wealthy Upper City. (Today the house of Caiaphas is claimed to be both in the Armenian compound on the highest point of Mount Zion and at the Church of St. Peter of Gallicantu downslope to the southeast. Archaeological excavations in Jerusalem's Jewish Quarter have revealed foundations of palatial mansions that must have been

similar in pomp and style to the home of Caiaphas.) In the stress of the moment Peter, always out in front, denied knowing Jesus three times (Mt 26:57–75; Mk 14:53–72; Lk 22:54–71; Jn 18:12–27). Caiaphas accused Jesus of blasphemy, a crime deserving death by stoning according to Jewish law (Mishnah, *Sanhedrin* 7.4; cf. *Sanhedrin* 7.5). The power to execute, however, lay in the hands of Rome (Jn 18:31; Jerusalem Talmud, *Sanhedrin* 1.18a), and so Caiaphas sent Jesus to Pilate, who was staying either "with the troops" in the Antonia Fortress adjacent to the northwestern corner of the Temple Mount or, more likely, in the sumptuous palace of Herod the Great on the western side of the city (in today's Armenian Quarter south of Jaffa Gate). Both buildings would have housed a Praetorium with quarters for soldiers and cells for prisoners (Mt 27:1–14; Mk 15:1–5; Lk 23:1–5). Not sure of the situation and unwilling to risk further exacerbating an already tenuous relationship with his Jewish subjects, Pilate shipped Jesus the Galilean off to Herod Antipas, who was in Jerusalem for Passover. Herod was likely staying in the old Hasmonean palace (remains of this building have not been found) or, if Pilate was at the Antonia, in his father's palace (Lk 23:6–16). Antipas was glad to finally see Jesus face-to-face, hoping that this "magic man of Galilee" would put on quite a show, but Jesus remained silent. Antipas arrayed Jesus in mock tribute, then shipped him back to Pilate where he was tortured by the Roman soldiers before being sentenced to death by crucifixion (Mt 27:15–31; Mk 15:6–20; Lk 23:17–25; Jn 18:28–19:15).

So Jesus, beaten, scourged, mocked and already half-dead, made his last journey, from the judgment hall of Pilate through Jerusalem's crowded streets then outside the city to a place of crucifixion, Golgotha, the Place of the Skull (Mt 27:32; Mk 15:21; Lk 23:26–32; Jn 19:17). His *Via Dolorosa* bore no directional relation to the street of the same name today or to its Stations of the Cross which represent a pious accretion of faithful memories over the centuries. Almost certainly, however, the crucifixion took place within, or very near to, ground occupied by the Church of the Holy Sepulcher. This was a known spot of crucifixion, just outside the city wall and adjacent to an area of tombs dating to the first century. Here Jesus was crucified between two thieves, nailed to a tree with his feet just off the ground and his face nearly eye-level with his accusers and passersby, stark naked, intentionally humiliated and left to the abuses of the hot sun and flies and insects drawn to blood, and of wild animals and birds hungry for a meal:

Punished with limbs outstretched…they are fastened [and] nailed to [the stake] in the most bitter torment, evil food for birds of prey and grim pickings for dogs.
(Pseudo-Manetho, *Apotelesmatica* 4:198–199)

The vulture hurries from dead cattle and dogs and crosses to bring some of the carrion for her offspring.

(Juvenal, *Satires*, 14.77–78)

Laureolus, hanging on no unreal cross, gave up his vitals defenseless to a [wild] bear. His mangled limbs lived, though the parts dripped blood and in all his body was nowhere a body's shape.

(Martial, *Liber Spectaculorum*, 7)

And the people—some mocking, others feigning indifference (according to Quintilian, *Declamationes*, 274, there was no more exemplary deterrent for crime than crucifixion), and yet a few unable to draw themselves from the final horrifying moments of their loved one (Mt 27:33–56; Mk 15:22–41; Lk 23:33–49; Jn 19:18–30). Sometimes it took days to die. Only a few women were faithful to the end, among them Mary Magdalene from whom Jesus had cast a demon, Mary the mother of James and Joses, Salome, and his own mother (Mt 27:55; Jn 19:25–27; cf. Lk 8:2). Mercifully, death came in just a few hours (cf. Mt 27:45).

With the sun angled low in the western sky and the start of Passover at hand, there was haste to get the tortured corpses off of the crosses. Jesus' body was interred in a nearby tomb belonging to Joseph of Arimathea, a member of the Sanhedrin who was sympathetic to his message. There was little time to prepare the body properly for burial, and Nicodemus helped by bringing myrrh and aloes for a kind of hasty mummification (Mt 27:57–61; Mk 15:42–47; Lk 23:50–56; Jn 19:31–42). Both Joseph and Nicodemus risked becoming ritually impure by the venture. Within two or three hours, according to the chronology of the Gospel of John, they would eat the Passover meal, celebrating again redemption from Egypt, looking again for freedom from Rome, wondering....

How the Marys spent the night can only be imagined.

The next day was the Sabbath. No one could possibly come to the tomb (Lk 23:56). The morning after two of the Marys, Mary Magdalene and Mary the mother of James and Joses, and Salome did come—early—with spices to anoint their Messiah for burial. But there was no need. The tomb was empty. Jesus had risen, just like he said (Mt 28:1–10; Mk 16:1–11; Lk 24:1–12; Jn 20:1–18; cf. Mt 16:21, 17:22–23, 20:18–19).

The women told Peter and John, who had to come and see for themselves. Then word began to spread, first to the eleven disciples, then beyond.

Late that afternoon Jesus encountered two men walking to the village of Emmaus and to them he "explained the things concerning himself in all the Scriptures" (Lk 24:13–35; cf. v. 27; Mk 16:12–13). Four places have been suggested as the location of Emmaus: early Byzantine tradition (including the Bordeaux Pilgrim and Jerome) cite the large city of Nicopolis in the Aijalon Valley at the point where the hill country meets the Shephelah (modern 'Imwas);

the Crusaders favored Castellum at modern Abu Ghosh, 7 miles from Jerusalem; a slightly later tradition (apparently also Crusader but strengthened in the Medieval period) preferred el-Qubeibeh in the hills slightly north; and Josephus (War vii.6.6) mentions a village called Emmaus thirty furlongs west of Jerusalem corresponding to Qaloniyeh/Mozah, an Israeli town about four miles west of the Old City today. Three are located along the same natural route, so at least the line of the "Emmaus Road" is not in doubt. The storyline of Jesus' encounter on the road to Emmaus best fits Qaloniyeh/Mozah or possibly either el-Qubeibeh or Castellum, for the two men who ate with the resurrected Jesus (it was his first supper since his Last one) hurried back to Jerusalem that same night. They added their testimony of the risen Lord to that of Simon Peter, and then to others as Jesus made himself known to his disciples in Jerusalem (Mt 28:16–17; Mk 16:14; Lk 24:36–49; Jn 20:19–29; cf. 1 Cor 15:3–8).

Jesus also appeared to some of his disciples on the

The Church of the Holy Sepulcher, described as "the most illustrious edifice in Christendom...grand, reverend, venerable" by a famous American writer who visited the place in 1867 (Mark Twain, The Innocents Abroad), was erected on ground strewn more with tradition than fact. Yet all reasonable evidence points to this building—or at least places in the general vicinity—as enclosing the likely spot of Jesus' crucifixion, burial and resurrection. The church has been enveloped by the Old City of Jerusalem since it was first built by Constantine in the fourth century A.D. Today's building is largely a Crusader "downsizing" of the Byzantine structure.

Approximately 800 rock-cut tombs dating to the Second Temple period have been found in the vicinity of Jerusalem. These represent burials of the more wealthy echelon of Jerusalem's society, only a small percentage of the total population of the city during the time. Of the known tombs, some are quite elaborate with multiple rooms of burial chambers and sophisticated entrances. The use of a rolling stone to seal a tomb's outer doorway was quite rare in the first century, with only two or three known in Jerusalem today. The tomb of Joseph of Arimathea is not known to archaeologists; the incorrectly identified "Herod's Family Tomb" high on the western slope of the Hinnom Valley near to the King David Hotel with rolling stone still in situ, shown here, was discovered in 1892. Perhaps the tomb in which Jesus was laid was of similar construction, although the Hebrew term for "rolling stone," golal, was also used for square, plug stones.

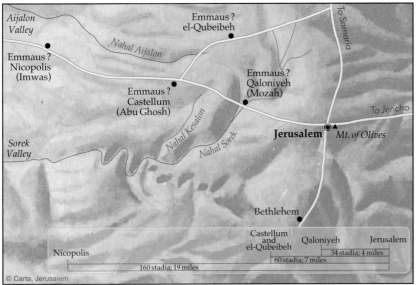

The Road to Emmaus. *The desire to remember and venerate the encounter that two followers of Jesus had with the risen Christ on the Road to Emmaus has led to several competing candidates for the location of the village over the course of Church history (this is an "It-could-have-been-me" story claimed by Everyone). According to most early Greek manuscripts of Luke's Gospel, Emmaus was 60 stadia (about 7 miles) from Jerusalem* (Lk 24:13), *a reading that favors both el-Qubeibeh and Castellum. Some manuscripts (primarily the Codex Sinaiticus) read "160 stadia," supporting the city of Nicopolis. If the distance noted by Luke was "round trip," then a village 30 stadia (3.5 miles) from Jerusalem such as the Emmaus mentioned by Josephus (Qaloniyeh/Mozah;* War vii.6.6) *could also be a candidate for the town.*

(right) Curbstones of the Emmaus Road can be traced for some distance through a short side-branch of the Nahal Soreq (Sorek Valley) connecting Jerusalem's Givat Shaul neighborhood with Motza. These curbstones are part of the Roman road that connected Jerusalem with Nicopolis ('Imwas) 19 miles west and Lydda and Joppa beyond. Although it post-dates the first century, this line of stones provides a helpful reminder of Jesus' walk along the same route during the late afternoon of Resurrection Day. Today the narrow wadi carries Jerusalem's water main (above ground) and high-wire pylons, and is a dump for waste rock aggregate and construction debris for the rapidly expanding city. Though not what it once was, a walk down the Emmaus Road is still pleasant enough, especially as the sun sets and a nearly full moon rises over Jerusalem in the east, as it did for the wide-eyed traveler of Luke 24 hurrying back to the Holy City.

shore of the Sea of Galilee (Jn 21:1–23). Peter had taken them fishing. Interrupting their futile attempts to pull in a large haul, Jesus called them again (cf. Lk 5:1–11). He wasn't about to let his mission die.

Forty days after his resurrection Jesus met the eleven disciples on the Mount of Olives. "The Holy Spirit is coming," he said. "Wait in Jerusalem… And when He comes, you will receive power…" (Acts 1:1–8). "Finally!" the disciples must have thought, still assuming that Jesus was going to restore the kingdom to Israel. But then Jesus continued:

You will be my witnesses both in Jerusalem, and in all Judea and Samaria, and even to the most remote part of the earth. (Acts 1:8)

Witnesses. To make disciples of all nations. To baptize them in the name of the Father, Son and the Holy Spirit. And to teach them everything that he had commanded (Mt 28:19–20).

And now the disciples had a choice: either walk down the backside of the Mount of Olives, retrace their steps through the Judean Wilderness to Jericho, head north and return to what promised to be a secure and profitable future around the shore of the Sea of Galilee, glad for their experiences with Jesus but ready to get back to real life. Or, follow Jesus' footsteps down the western slope of the mount, cross the Kidron Valley and climb back into Jerusalem, carrying their Savior's message to a world waiting for consolation and redemption (cf. Lk 2:25, 2:38). And this they did. Eventually Jesus' followers took the name "Christians" (Acts 11:26)— Christ-ians; Messiah-ians; Anointed Ones; like their Lord filled with His image (cf. Gen 1:26–27) to carry grace and truth (cf. Jn 1:17).

I have come that they may have life, and have it abundantly. (Jn 10:10)

Now there's a life-description worthy of the Messiah on any account.

Multitudes of believers find the fresh beauty of the grounds of the Garden Tomb to be a perfect place to reflect on the death and resurrection of Jesus. Others come as well. Here a group of young Muslim women emerge from the tomb; they had quite a long time of discussion inside. For many in the mix of the population of Jerusalem the resurrection of Jesus is a mystery (cf. 1 Cor 15:51) or a stumbling block (1 Cor 1:23). Yet the witness of the empty tomb, proclaimed by the faithful staff of the Garden Tomb Association, is unwavering. "Why do you seek the living One among the dead? He is not here, but He has risen!" (Lk 24:5–6).

CHAPTER 21
PONTIUS PILATE
The Enforcer

What happens when a person is given unlimited authority in a task related to the common good, then acts with only his own interests in mind? If the assignment is small the potential damage done may not be too great, but woe to everyone in reach if the misfit wields a behemoth's club. So it was with Pontius Pilate, who held the office of prefect of Judea from A.D. 26–36. By most reasonable estimates here was someone who was part butcher, part beholden, part anti-Semite, part man of expediency and part self-made man who worshipped his maker. Pilate burst onto the scene in Judea with a host of veteran actors already following multiple scripts, none of which included lines he was fit to read. It was all a toxic mix. Before the curtain fell he was yanked off stage having made it messier by virtue of his being there and banished to a place of anonymity reserved for actors who fail miserably in their parts. It was not a pretty sight. Justifiably, most modern critics sweep Pilate into a bin labeled "Bad Boys of the Bible," occasionally snatching his mangled reputation to serve as proxy for others throughout history who also have crushed voices of innocence, reason and faith. Attempts to redeem him as a fellow who was well meaning but misunderstood, genuine but somehow misguided, or an honest seeker of truth who just didn't push his curiosity quite far enough largely fall on deaf ears. Let them lie. When ancient sources as diverse in opinion as Philo, Josephus and the Gospels all point in the same direction, it's proper to call a spade a spade.

Rome's decision to appoint Pontius Pilate as prefect of Judea was part of a sequence of events that slowly ratcheted the region from the periphery toward the center of Rome's orbit of control. After Pompey entered Jerusalem in 63 B.C. and brought the Jewish Hasmonean kingdom to an inglorious end, Rome initially tried to maintain control of Judea by backing cooperative members of the disposed Hasmonean royal family, principally Hyrcanus II who as high priest had been a legitimate claimant to the Jewish throne. Hyrcanus proved to be ineffective (most of his subjects despised collaborators) and so in the summer of 40 B.C. the Senate instead appointed a local strongman, Herod the Great, as king. The region placed under Herod's control included Judea, Idumea, Perea, Samaria, Galilee, Gaulanitis, Trachonitis, Auranitis and much of the coast, and remained a client kingdom of Rome throughout the reign of Herod and his sons. Herod

was a man of excess but at least had the presence of mind and sleight of hand to keep a lid on things that would cause Caesar undue concern. His son Archelaus, who inherited Judea, Idumea and Samaria in 4 B.C., was beneficiary of Herod's iron-fisted will but at eighteen appeared too young to know how to add the necessary political and diplomatic finesse to make it all work. Within ten years Archelaus had offended virtually every element of the local population and so in A.D. 6 Caesar Augustus banished him to the northern reaches of Gaul where he could thrash around without hurting anyone (*Ant.* xvii.8.4–9.6, 13.1–4).

When Herod had died ten years earlier, a delegation of influential Jewish leaders, rightly fearing that Archelaus might prove to be even more tyrannical than his father, begged Caesar Augustus not to replace him with a member of the Herodian royal line. In a moment of extreme pragmatism they asked instead that Augustus annex Judea to Syria, the largest and most powerful of Rome's provinces in the east, hoping the governors there would show more grace toward local sensibilities than did Herod (*Ant.* xvii.11.2; *War* ii.6.2). Augustus deferred at the time, but after Archelaus had indeed proven to be a greater despot than his father and sensing an opportunity to capitalize on the desire of the Jewish delegation to place Judea under tighter Roman control (it was a minority though vocal opinion), the emperor belatedly heeded the call. In doing so, however, Augustus bypassed the delegation's specific suggestion and chose instead to create a new province out of the region (*Ant.* xviii.1.1).

He had several options. Provinces within the empire that were stable and generally free from threat were placed under the control of the Roman Senate. Others—and these were the majority in the empire—faced the possibility of ongoing unrest from either external or internal threats and so remained under the direct control of the emperor. Of these "imperial provinces" the more critical, such as Syria, were governed by men of senatorial rank (*legatus Augusti pro praetore*) and supplied with crack legionary troops. Others, including Egypt, Cappadocia, Sardinia and Judea, were placed under the authority of equestrians (*equites*; "knights"), men of proven military ability who were still climbing the ladder of success within the imperial system. Imperial provinces of the equestrian order typically were provided with auxiliary troops (*auxilia*) recruited

One of the rights Caesar granted the prefects and procurators of the Roman Empire was that of minting coins. Each of the governors of Judea (with the exception of Pontius Pilate) struck only coins depicting objects that would not offend Jewish religious sensibilities: sheaves of barley, palm trees and palm branches, bunches of fruit, vines, figs and cornucopia. The coins of Felix showed anchors (a symbol that appeared on Hasmonean coins) and crossed spears. None depicted human faces. Pilate was the only governor of Judea to depict symbols used in Roman pagan worship on his coins: the lituus (augur staff; above, bottom) and simpulum (ladle; above, top). Pilate's choice of symbolism was an unnecessary affront to the people he was assigned to rule, but given his overall patterns of behavior, it was probably to be expected.

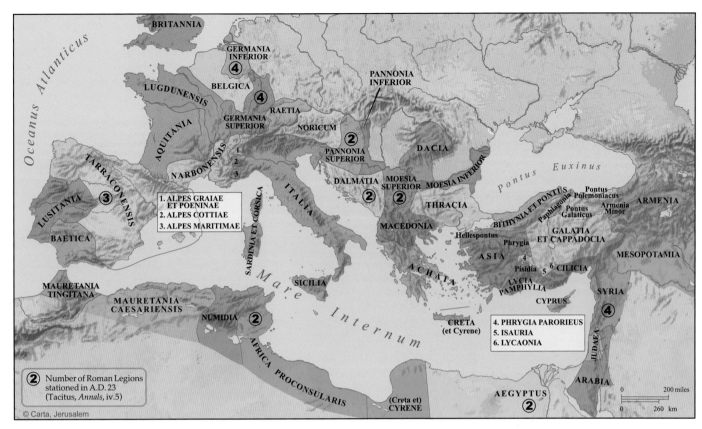

© Carta, Jerusalem

② Number of Roman Legions stationed in A.D. 23 (Tacitus, *Annals*, iv.5)

Provinces of the Roman Empire, A.D. 117. *Slowly, methodically but surely the Roman Empire burst from the mountainous spine of central Italy to swallow the world of the Mediterranean. At its height Rome governed lands from the Atlantic to the Euphrates, from what is now the British Isles to Khartoum. An empire as large as the world had ever known needed to be divided into provinces to be governed effectively. Some, termed "Imperial Provinces," were placed under the direct control of Caesar. Of these, the ones that were the most troublesome or faced an open frontier (such as Syria) were governed by men of Senatorial rank with the help of legionary troops. Egypt was an Imperial Province of a lesser order governed by equestrians, although because of its extreme wealth Roman legions were also stationed there. Little Judea was sandwiched between.*

from within each province. When Archelaus was dismissed in A.D. 6, Judea became a province of this type but with the apparent understanding that the governor of Syria held veto power over internal matters. It was a hook that would come in handy later. With Augustus' decision, then, the people of Judea (including Idumea and Samaria), together with their resources and hopes and dreams for the future, came under the heavy fist of direct Roman rule (*Ant.* xvii.13.5; *War* ii.8.1). For the members of the prior Jewish delegation and their desperate constituency who had asked for relief from the Herods, it proved to be an ominous choice.

Until the reign of Emperor Claudius (A.D. 41–54), the governors of imperial equestrian provinces were called prefects (*praefectus*), a term that was proper for seasoned military officers who commanded five hundred to one thousand troops. (Judah's garrison in the decade leading up to the Great Revolt of A.D. 66–70 was significantly larger, with up to five infantry cohorts of five hundred men each in addition to a squadron of cavalry, and it may have been this large under the early prefects as well; cf. *Ant.* xvii.3.1; xx.6.1; *War* ii.12.5; 111.4.2; Mt 27:54; Acts 10:1, 21:31–36; cf. Lk 7:2.) Only after the reign of Claudius was the title "prefect" replaced by the more familiar term "pro-curator," designating the chief financial officer of a province. Evidence for the use of "prefect" as the proper title for the early governors of Judea comes chiefly in a broken inscription found in archaeological excavations in Caesarea mentioning Pilate as *[praef]ectus Iuda[ea]e.* Josephus' refer-

ences to Pilate as "procurator of Judea" appear to be anachronistic (cf. *Ant.* xviii.3.1; *War* ii.9.2); the writers of the Gospels preferred the more generic title "governor" (*hegemon*) for all higher Roman officials, including the prefect, who served in the region (Mt. 27:2; Mk 13:9; Lk 2:2, 3:1, 20:20).

The prefects of Judea typically were appointed and dismissed by Caesar himself. Until the reign of Claudius, all were natives of Italy, a pattern which probably helped to ensure that the province would be governed by men known by, and particularly loyal to, the emperor. Their duties were directly related to enforcing Rome's will. High on each prefect's job description was control of the auxiliary troops, which for Judea were drawn from the local Hellenistic populations of Caesarea and Sebaste (*Ant.* xx.8.7). If the prefect of Judea needed additional military help he had to appeal to the governor of Syria for access to its legions. (From the time of Tiberius, four of Rome's 25 legions were based in Syria; Tacitus, *Annals* iv.5.) The prefect was also the highest judicial authority in the province, holding the exclusive right to enforce capital punishment (*War* ii.8.1). Additionally, he was responsible for the province's financial affairs, which included levying taxes, implementing the corvée and minting coins. Rome also allowed the prefect to appoint and dispose of high priests, a right necessary for maintaining a firm line of control in the province but something that was a constant show of humiliation for the Jews; over time it further politicized a temple hierarchy already given to power plays and expediency. (The

Herodian kings had been given the same right, but at least they were a local Jewish dynasty.) As a corollary, until the end of the governorship of Pilate the prefect also administered the use of the high-priestly vestments, an act that had practical ramifications as large as its symbolism (Ant. xviii.2.2, 4.3). Any one of these several duties brought the prefect into direct conflict with the powers and people of Judea, and to be effective he had to be a man with refined skills of diplomacy and coercion.

Tiberius (A.D. 14–37) appointed only two prefects over Judea, Valerius Gratus and Pontius Pilate. Each served about ten years. Later procurators typically remained in office for only two years, just long enough for each to gain some experience in the job and enrich themselves for their journey up the power echelon of Rome in the process. Or, engorge themselves on the public good. Emil Schuerer's comments on the matter are sufficient:

> For the good of the provinces concerned, [Tiberius] left [the prefects] as long as possible in their posts because he thought governors behaved like flies on a wounded body; once sated, they then temper their extortions, whereas new men would start with a keen appetite. (History of the Jewish People 1:383)

Tiberius was mistaken with Pilate. And as for the people of Judea—their blood just kept getting sucked out.

This being said, Judea's first three prefects apparently strove for a relatively favorable relationship with their Jewish subjects. These were Coponius (A.D. 6–9?) for whom the gate on the western side of the temple precinct (the Kiponus Gate of Mishnah Middoth 1.3) may have been named, Marcus Ambivulus (A.D. 9?–12) and Annius Rufus (A.D. 12–15). The fourth, Valerius Gratus (A.D. 15–26), had a mixed record. During his long term in office Gratus dismissed and/or appointed no less than five high priests, including Annas, who was fired not long after Gratus took office, and Annas' son-in-law Caiaphas, whom Gratus appointed toward the end of his tenure (cf. Jn 18:13). Caiaphas remained in power throughout the term of Pilate, leading some to suggest, certainly correctly, that at the very least he had gained the trust of the Roman authorities. Likely Rome found Caiaphas a convenient tool to foster Jewish loyalties to the empire, or at least someone who wouldn't rock the boat in the matter. It was a tough spot for a high priest to try to survive, and in a world of politics and strange bedfellows, Caiaphas snuggled up to the prefect.

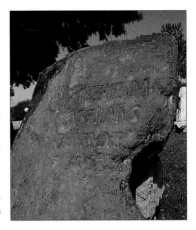

In 1962 an Italian archaeological team uncovered this stone in the theater complex at Caesarea Maritima. The stone was found in secondary use as a common building stone for a stairway built to renovate the theater as a Kolymbethra, a "pool for water games." The inscription reads:
[…] S TIBERIEUM
[…PO]NTIUS PILATUS
[PRAEF]ECTUS IUDA[EA]A
[FECIT]
"…This Tiberium, Pontius Pilate, prefect of Judea, erected."

Originally the stone bore a dedicatory inscription for a Tiberium, or temple, that Pilate built in the city in honor of Tiberius. Pilate is the only known Roman governor who built a temple to a living emperor. Unlike Augustus, Tiberius downplayed efforts to develop a cult to his person, and he likely was not particularly pleased with Pilate's efforts to ingratiate himself in this way.

(photo: Garo Nalbandian)

Governor of Judea	Date of Office (A.D.)	Name of Ruling Caesar	Reference in Josephus	Reference in the New Testament
Coponius	6–9?	Augustus	Ant. xviii.2.2	—
Marcus Ambivulus	9?–12	Augustus	Ant. xviii.2.2	—
Annius Rufus	12–15	Augustus; Tiberius	Ant. xviii.2.2	—
Valerius Gratus	15–26	Tiberius	Ant. xviii.2.2	—
Pontius Pilate	26–36	Tiberius	Ant. xviii.3.1–3, 4.1–2; War ii.9.2–4	Mt 27:2–66; Mk 15:1–15; Lk 3:1, 13:1, 23:1–7, 23:13–25; Jn 18:28–19:15; Acts 3:13, 4:27, 13:28; 1 Tim 6:13
Marcellus	36–?	Gaius/Caligula	Ant. xviii.4.2	—
Interregnum of King Agrippa I	41–44	Claudius	Ant. xviii.3–10; xix.4–8	Acts 12:1, 12:18–23
Cuspius Fadus	44–46	Claudius	Ant. xv.11.4; xix.4.2; xx.1.1; War ii.11.6	—
Tiberius Alexander	46–48	Claudius	Ant. xx.5.2	—
Ventidius Cumanus	48–52	Claudius	Ant. xx.5.2; War ii.12.1	—
Antonius Felix	52–60	Claudius; Nero	Ant. xiv.11.7; xx.7.1, 8.5, 8.7, 8.9; War ii.12.8, 13.7	Acts 23:24–24:27, 25:14
Porcius Festus	60–62	Nero	Ant. xx.8.9, 9.1	Acts 24:27–26:32
Albinus	62–64	Nero	Ant. xx.9.1	—
Gessius Florus	64–66	Nero	Ant. xviii.1.6; xx.9.5, 11.1; War ii.14.3, 14.6, 14.9, 15.1, 16.1	—

The Governors of Judea (Prefects from A.D. 6–41; Procurators from A.D. 44–64)

The second Roman emperor, Tiberius, was born to one of Julius Caesar's military officers and rose through the ranks of the army by waging successful campaigns in Pannonia, Dalmatia, Armenia and Gaul. Tiberius' mother divorced his father and became Augustus' third wife; Tiberius himself married one of Augustus' daughters, Julia. Family life in Caesar's household wasn't smooth, and personal and political rivalries kept Augustus and Tiberius at arm's length. The Emperor eventually adopted Tiberius, helping pave the way for the Senate to appoint him Caesar after Augustus died in A.D. 14. Tiberius' 23-year reign was largely conservative in polity, and unlike his predecessor he played down attempts to be portrayed as divine. Tiberius ruled during the time of the ministry of Jesus (Lk 3:1) and the fledgling years of the early Church. He died on 16 March, A.D. 37, having spent the last eleven years of his life on his several royal estates on the island of Capreae (Capri).

Next after Gratus was Pontius Pilate. Like his immediate predecessors, Pilate appears to have been a native of central Italy. The family name Pontius has been traced, with some likelihood, to the hilly region of Samnium in south-central Italy, 130 miles east of Rome. The specific name Pilate is much more rare; none of its supposed meanings ("armed with a javelin," "bald" and "shaggy") are of any help in shedding light on the origin or character of the man. After what must have been a fairly noticeable career in the equestrian orders of the Roman military, Pilate was appointed prefect of Judea in A.D. 26.

Some scholars (e.g. Menahem Stern) have suggested that Pilate's appointment, which should have been made by Tiberius alone, was influenced by Sejanus, the powerful chief of Caesar's Praetorian Guard. (According to Tacitus, Annals iv.5, Rome was guarded by three city and nine praetorian cohorts.) The suggestion is not without merit—A.D. 26 was the year that Tiberius retired from the daily grind of his job and withdrew to the picturesque Campanian isle of Capreae (Capri) off the coast of Neapolis (Naples), where he owned twelve magnificent villas. He never returned to Rome. It can be expected that in Tiberius' absence someone as well-placed and ambitious as Sejanus would try to buck the Senate and lend a direct hand in helping run the empire ("Who, me? I'm just a loyal servant of Caesar…"). But perhaps more importantly, Sejanus was a known proponent of anti-Semitic policies in Rome (Philo, De legatione ad Gaium [On the Embassy to Gaius] 159–161), and it is likely that he was attracted to Pilate—and vice versa—because the latter fostered the same tendencies. Philo, an Alexandrian Jew, wrote freely and bluntly of the excesses of Pilate, his contemporary, and while it is certain that Philo's own interests as a defender of the faith shaped his opinion of Judea's prefect, his comments do provide a helpful grid to understand Pilate's heavy-handed actions once he assumed control of the province. Pilate was, said Philo, a man "with a very inflexible disposition, merciless and most obstinate," possessed by "most ferocious passions" and someone who was widely feared because of his "corruption, acts of insolence, rapine behavior, habit of insult-

ing people, cruelty, continual murders of people untried and uncondemned, and his never ending, gratuitous and most grievous inhumanity"—a list of seven deadly sins if there ever was one (De legatione ad Gaium, 301–303). If Pilate came to Judea under the sponsorship of Sejanus with anti-Semitic tendencies already in hand, what else could his subjects expect during ten years of free-reign in the province?

Having taken up residency in Caesarea, Pilate wasted no time in offending the Jews under his charge. It almost seems as though he did so deliberately. Josephus cut to the chase in his very first mention of the man:

Now Pilate, the procurator [sic] of Judea, moved the army from Caesarea to Jerusalem to take their winter quarters there in order to abolish Jewish laws.

(Ant. xviii.3.1)

Transferring the army from wintertime Caesarea, where the weather is mild, to cold and wet Jerusalem for the sake of quarters makes no sense, and Josephus quickly—and correctly—smelled an ulterior motive. Indeed, Pilate brazenly showed his hand. The army arrived in Jerusalem with royal ensigns bearing the image of Tiberius, a clear affront to Jewish law and religious sensibilities. All ensigns that had been brought to Jerusalem previously flew without such ornamentation, following Herod's precedent not to depict images in places and palaces that Jews might visit. Pilate's move cannot be excused as a rookie mistake, for the whole operation proceeded under the cover of darkness. The next morning the city was in an uproar. Masses of people marched on Caesarea and for five days demanded that Pilate remove the ensigns that were polluting the Holy City. The protest clearly caught him off-guard and he responded by digging in his heels and passing the blame upward, insisting that Caesar himself would be affronted otherwise (Are we not friends of Caesar?). On the sixth day Pilate had had enough and instructed his army to surround the protesters with orders to draw their swords at his command. But when confronted with death, the Jews "laid their necks bare and said they would rather take their deaths willingly than transgress the wisdom of their laws" (Josephus' retelling of the event comes

Most of what we know about the life and times of the people of Judea during the time of the New Testament has been preserved for us by the Jewish historian Josephus (c. A.D. 37–100). Josephus was trained as a rabbi and a priest and dabbled in various interpretive schools of Torah before eventually joining the Pharisees at age nineteen. During the Great Revolt he commanded the Jewish forces in Galilee. He was a better scholar than soldier, surrendering the fortress of Jotapata (above Cana) to Vespasian in A.D. 67. After becoming Caesar, Vespasian favored Josephus, released him from his status as prisoner-of-war and granted him the emperor's family name, Flavius. Josephus eventually traveled to Rome with Vespasian's son, Titus, the victorious general of the battle for Jerusalem (A.D. 70). There he lived out his years as an author and favorite of the court. Josephus' primary works, Antiquities of the Jews and The Jewish War, are an invaluable, though understandably opinioned, account of the decades of Jewish history that witnessed the destruction of the Temple and the birth of Christianity. This bust is thought to preserve his likeness.

with all his usual flare for the dramatic; *Ant. xviii.3.1;
War ii.9.1–2*). In any case the point was made: Pilate
caved, and the ensigns were removed. It is not clear
if the Jews of Jerusalem were emboldened or just
relieved at the outcome; certainly their suspicions
that Pilate would not shy from confrontation again
were justifiably aroused.

A similar incident is related by Philo of Alexandria *(De legatione ad Gaium, 299–305)*. When Pilate came
to Jerusalem he typically stayed in Herod's palace
in the western part of the city, and at one point he
decorated the palace with golden shields. Although
the shields bore only an inscription mentioning the
name of the donor (certainly Pilate himself) and the
honored recipient (Tiberius), their very presence
represented an imperial affront to the Jews of the
Holy City. It is often suggested that the incident
may have been prompted by the execution of Sejanus in Rome in A.D. 31, and Pilate's subsequent
desire to show a sign of loyalty to Tiberius. In any
case the Jews protested again, and again Pilate resisted, but this time they went above his head and
sent a delegation to carry the matter all the way to
Rome. The circumstances fit a time frame subsequent to the incident of the offending ensigns; Pilate seemed to have learned a lesson about graven
images in the meantime, but for the people of Jerusalem that wasn't enough. Tiberius intervened on
their behalf and forced him to remove the shields;
Pilate installed them instead in the Temple of Augustus in Caesarea. Religious sensibilities and the
common good prevailed; Pilate was called on the
carpet and humiliated in Rome and in Judea. He
didn't wear it well.

Sometime later—Josephus doesn't mention
when—Pilate got into trouble for what probably appeared to him as a simple and necessary improve-
ment in Jerusalem's infrastructure: tapping into a
distant spring and channeling its waters into the city
(Ant. xviii.3.2; War ii.9.4). Although Pilate's aqueduct has
not been positively identified archaeologically, it
was certainly related to the earlier Hasmonean and
Herodian aqueduct system that brought water from
the hills of Hebron into Jerusalem. Pilate probably
increased the length of that system by extending its
upper end to reach additional springs near Hebron.
His offense was that he paid for the project out of
(extorted) temple funds, money that had been designated "Corban" ("devoted"; cf. Mt 7:11) and so was
restricted for sacred use only. The next time Pilate
showed his face in Jerusalem he was beset by another angry mob, this time bold enough "to hurl insults
and abuse the man as crowds of such people usually do" *(Ant. xviii.3.2)*. It had become personal. Pulling a practiced trump card from his pocket, Pilate
again brought armed soldiers onto the scene, this
time dressed as cloaked commoners with armor and
weapons concealed. They mingled with the crowd,

then at a signal attacked, killing many and suppress-
ing the throng by brute force. While Josephus notes
that the severity of the soldiers' reaction against the
crowd exceeded their orders (it was mob against
mob), the Jews of Jerusalem clearly held Pilate responsible for the affair and its bloody aftermath.

Things didn't improve.

*Now there were some…who reported to [Jesus]
about the Galileans whose blood Pilate had mixed
with their sacrifices. Jesus replied, "Do you think that
these Galileans were greater sinners than all other*

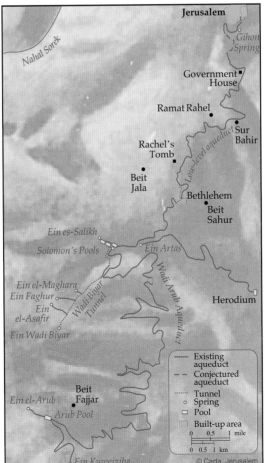

*Pilate's Judean headquarters
were in Caesarea, within the
confines of the sumptuous
palace there, the palace Herod
the Great had built on a
spit of land jutting into the
Mediterranean. Only scattered
building stones remain together
with the outline of the palace's
foundation—rooms centered on
a large rectangular freshwater
pool. Pilate was holed up here
when crowds from Jerusalem
swarmed Caesarea to protest
his pretense in bringing offensive
royal ensigns to their city.*

**The Aqueduct to Jerusalem,
1st Century A.D.** *It was
a massive undertaking:
bringing water from several
springs in the hills of Hebron
to Jerusalem, a twisting
channel, pipe and tunnel route
following hillside contours for
over 40 miles. The aqueduct
was probably begun by the
Hasmoneans, although Herod
the Great properly gets credit
for overseeing the construction
of most of its length. Pilate's
addition was likely somewhere
in the aqueduct's upper,
southern extremities, although
it is impossible to identify any
specific section as his from the
extant remains.*

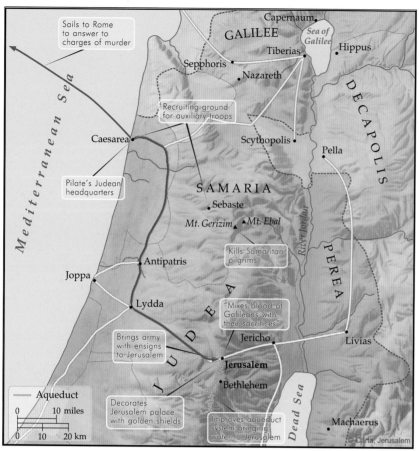

Sails to Rome to answer to charges of murder

GALILEE

Capernaum

Sea of Galilee

Tiberias

Hippus

Sepphoris

Nazareth

DECAPOLIS

Recruiting ground for auxiliary troops

Scythopolis

Pella

Caesarea

Pilate's Judean headquarters

SAMARIA

Sebaste

Mt. Gerizim   Mt. Ebal

Kills Samaritan pilgrims

River Jordan

PEREA

Antipatris

Joppa

Lydda

"Mixes blood of Galileans with their sacrifices"

Jericho

Livias

Brings army with ensigns to Jerusalem

JUDEA

Jerusalem

Bethlehem

Dead Sea

Aqueduct

0   10 miles

0   10   20 km

Decorates Jerusalem palace with golden shields

Improves aqueduct system bringing water to Jerusalem

Machaerus

© Carta, Jerusalem

Mediterranean Sea

Pontius Pilate, Prefect of Judea, A.D. 26–36. *Pilate held the office of prefect of Judea longer than any other man except for Valerius Gratus. The record of his activities is also lengthier than that of his colleagues, due in no small measure to his antagonistic attitude toward the Jews and that his term in office coincided with the adult ministry of Jesus. Most of Pilate's offenses were inflicted in Jerusalem, home to a Jewish way of life worth fighting for. Pilate never learned the ideological language of the people under his charge, and his reign imploded in the end.*

Galileans because they suffered this fate? I tell you no—but unless you repent, you will all likewise perish."   (Lk 13:1–3)

Some scholars have suggested that this massacre mentioned in the Gospel of Luke was a spillover of the "crowd-control" following the riot over the aqueduct, but the details are sufficiently different—and Pilate's character sufficiently obstinate—to see them as two separate events. Pilate had no authority in Galilee (that province was part of the tetrarchy of Herod Antipas), but when a number of Galileans ran afoul of his will while on a holy pilgrimage to Jerusalem, his response was true to form. The particulars are unstated but easily imagined—if asked, Pilate probably would have called it insurrection. Luke's comments on the matter may be taken to mean that the pious travelers were killed in the very act of offering sacrifices in the Temple—an outrage of unprecedented proportions that Josephus surely would have mentioned if they had—or, more likely, that they were involved in some sort of violent demonstration (or caught in its backlash) during their pilgrimage to the city. Whatever the circumstances, it was likely part of the cause of the antagonism between Antipas and Pilate—this, and the fact that Pilate, a rank foreigner, had taken over the inheritance of Antipas' half-brother Archelaus (cf. Lk 23:12). When the subject of the massacre was brought up to Jesus, he refused to get into politics (Jesus con-

sistently avoided entanglements of that kind) and simply noted that the wrath of God toward unrepentant sinners far exceeded anything that Pilate could muster. God and people were the focus; Pilate was just a detail of time and place. Few others could dismiss the prefect that easily.

But in the end could Jesus? Somewhere in the middle of Pilate's lengthy term of office Jesus of Nazareth, Son of David and Son of God by birth but a resident of insurrection-prone Galilee by upbringing, made his final pilgrimage to Jerusalem. His entrance down the Mount of Olives the Sunday morning before Passover was dramatic—triumphant, even—as crowds of people waved palm branches, giving fervent expression to their longing for redemption and freedom from political overlords. Shouts of "Hosanna (Save, now!)" and "Blessed is the king who comes in the name of the LORD!" echoed into the city (Mt 21:9; Lk 19:38). Jerusalem was already crowded with pilgrims getting ready for the Passover, the Jewish freedom festival *par excellence*, when it was easy for thoughts of redemption from bondage in long-ago Egypt to blur with hopes for freedom from Rome. Modern estimates suggest that the population of the city may have doubled in size whenever the Jewish pilgrimage festivals rolled around; the city not only pulsed with the excitement of the moment but with the anticipation that each new year might be the year of the Messiah at last. Rome had a long history of dealing with such matters, and Pilate probably sent extra troops to Jerusalem to offset any populist tendencies that might give rise to expressions of freedom that threatened Rome (cf. *War* i.4.3, ii.1.3, ii.12.1, v.5.8). He himself would also typically come to the city for the festival to keep a personal watch on things. But this year the week before Passover started badly for Pilate—a report no doubt reached his desk that the crowds couldn't even wait for the holiday to begin before clamoring for some rabbi from Galilee to overthrow the government. Extra care had to be taken. Pilate didn't need another incident, but he also couldn't hope that the crowds that had so welcomed Jesus to Jerusalem would just go away. He couldn't afford any unnecessary confrontations that would rouse Tiberius' ire again. With Sejanus dead Pilate no longer had a buffer to help absorb Caesar's blows should trouble arise out in the provinces.

Certain members of the temple hierarchy also wanted Jesus gone. The Gospels say "from envy" (Mt 27:18; Mk 15:10)—apparently that Jesus was attracting too large a following—but many members of Jerusalem's priesthood, especially Sadducees comfortable with the *status quo*, had no patience for movements clamoring for revolutionary change. Thanks to Judas Iscariot's "inside job" Jesus was taken off the streets quickly and quietly. His disciples scattered under cover of darkness; only Peter and John followed, furtively hugging the shadows, hardly daring to draw close (Mt 26:47–56; Mk 14:43–52; Lk 22:47–62; Jn 18:1–16).

As high priest, Caiaphas was responsible for a complex weave of political and religious interests in Judea and Galilee and throughout the Diaspora, with multiple constituencies clamoring for leadership and attention. His feet were firmly planted on both sides of the fence that divided Jerusalem from Rome; it was a rather delicate place to stand, and above all he needed no one to kick one of his feet out from under him or to give the barbed wire a "twang." Get rid of Jesus, and things would quiet down. Representing the temple hierarchy, Caiaphas accused Jesus of blasphemy, then, after consultation, delivered him to Pilate for the sentence of death (Mt 26:57–27:2; Mk 14:53–15:1; Lk 22:63–23:1; Jn 18:12–27). Rome alone held the authority to execute (Jn 18:31; Jerusalem Talmud, *Sanhedrin* 1.18a).

Pilate had no interest in internal Jewish religious matters unless they touched on issues of security and control—he probably resented being drawn into what he considered the quirky controversies of the Jews—and so the charge against Jesus was given with the appropriate nuance:

> We found this man misleading our nation, forbidding us to give tribute to Caesar and saying that he himself is the Messiah, a king. (Lk 23:2)

Pilate preferred the direct approach and immediately set the tone for the direction of the inquiry: "Are you the king of the Jews?" Absent an ideology of the Messiah, the question was quite impossible for any normal person living in Judea or Galilee to answer. At most someone could have dared to reply "I am the rightful king of *Judea*," of a bounded territorial unit currently under the control of Pilate himself. But to respond "Yes, I am king of the Jews" would have meant either that Judea should be divided into Jewish and Gentile sub-provinces, or worse, it would have made the accused king over a minority population scattered throughout the many districts of the empire, clearly a conceptual and practical impossibility for Rome. The threat of

a Messiah was the threat of carving up the empire. Pilate had to take the case seriously and so he asked the Messianic question in a way that mocked the validity of its claims.

Jesus' reply was also direct, but provocative: "You have said so" (Ellis Rivkin has called it "Delphic"; *What Crucified Jesus*, 104)—as if Pilate's pronouncement had any objective relevance in the matter of God's Messiah. Then Jesus fell silent (Mt 27:11–14; Mk 15:2–5; Lk 23:2–5).

Only the Gospel of John records further conversation between the two. Interrogation was standard procedure in an investigation by a Roman magistrate when the accused refused to plead his case (Pliny the Younger, *Epistulae* x.96.2–3; Eusebius, *Historia ecclesiastica* v.1.20–22). Here it started with Pilate distancing himself from the maddening people under his control. "I am not a Jew," he hissed. "How should I know what you have done?" (Jn 18:35). Jesus' response was reasoned and calm:

> My kingdom is not of this world. If it were, my servants would be fighting by now for my release.
> (Jn 18:36)

(*Your* kingdom is not *what?!*)

Pilate had to regain the edge: "So you admit that you *are* a king?" To the matter-of-fact prefect, Jesus' reply was incomprehensible:

> You have said [correctly] that I am a king. For this I have been born, and for this I have come into this world, to testify to the truth. Everyone who is of the truth hears my voice. (Jn 18:37)

(*Your* voice? Mine is the one that counts!") Then the snarl: "*What is truth?!*" (Jn 18:38). In the cold world of political expediency, truth is whatever it has to be.

Pilate had had enough. If he passed sentence of execution, he risked another riot by the crowds who last he heard were still looking for the Messiah. But if he turned Jesus loose, he risked further alienating the local religious authorities who wanted him dead. And Caiaphas, who was supposed to be sensitive to Rome's interests, was pressing the affair! Hearing that Jesus was a Galilean, Pilate shipped him across town to Herod Antipas, who had also come to Jerusalem for the Passover. This time Antipas could deal with his own mess!

The tetrarch of Galilee was not opposed to

Josephus' description of Jerusalem's Royal Stoa includes the following line: "The number of columns was 162, each of which had a capital ornamented in the Corinthian style of carving, which caused amazement by the magnificence of its whole effect" (Ant. xv.11.5). This Corinthian capital, carved of hard limestone (of the local mizzi hilu variety) and still nearly perfect after being buried in the rubble of Second Temple Jerusalem for nineteen centuries, attests to the grandeur of Herod's city. The acanthus leaves across the bottom are not quite as elaborate as those of classic Corinthian capitals; the center panel contains lilies, a common Jewish symbol of the time. In all, the capital is witness to the persuasive power of Rome in the face of persistent Jewish forms in the Holy City. (NEAEHL)

The tomb of the high priestly Caiaphas family was found in archaeological excavations directed by Zvi Greenhut in 1990 within the grounds of the Jerusalem Peace Forest, just over a mile southeast of the Old City of Jerusalem. Although the tomb had been robbed in antiquity, the bones of over 60 persons remained, together with an ossuary inscribed "Joseph son of Caiaphas" (above). According to Josephus (Ant. xviii.2.2; 4.3) this was the full name of the high priest who presided at the trial of Jesus. The ossuary's rich and detailed ornamentation (left), the most exquisite of any ossuary found in Jerusalem, attests to the importance of the man whose bones were laid within. The ossuary actually contained the bones of six people, including a 60-year-old man who was probably Caiaphas himself. (NEAEHL)

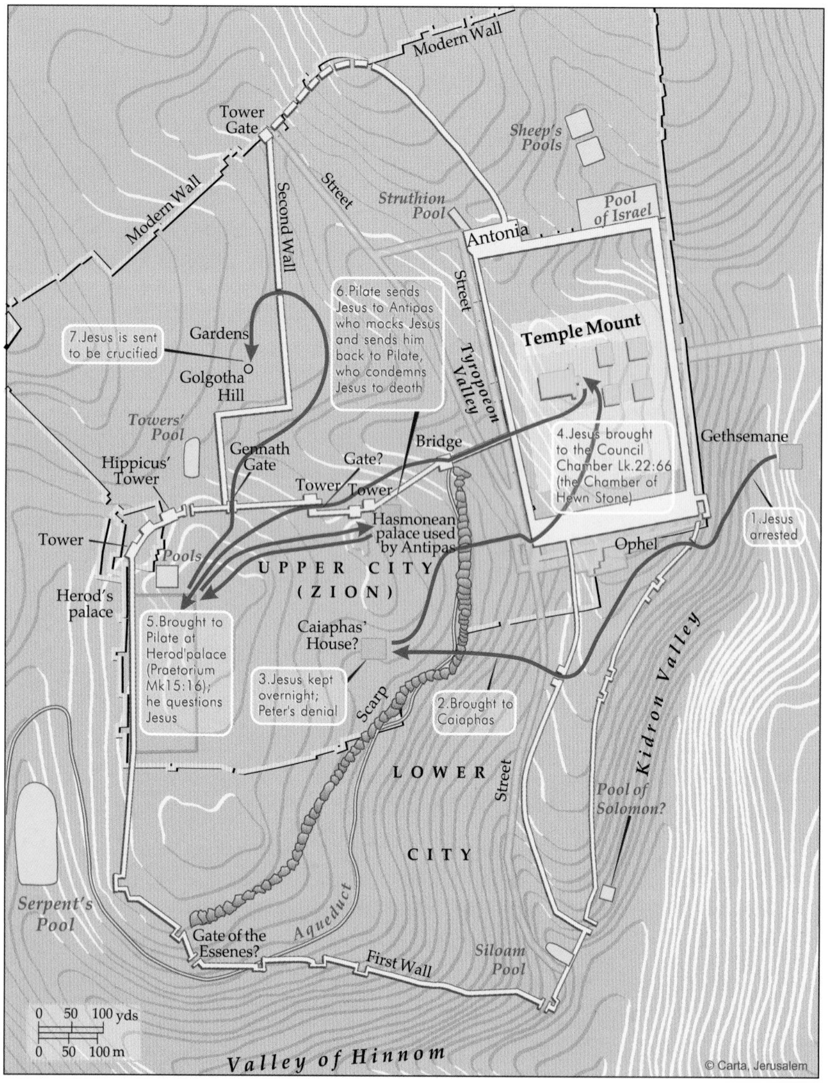
Modern Wall
Tower Gate
Sheep's Pools
Modern Wall
Second Wall
Street
Struthion Pool
Pool of Israel
Antonia
Street
6.Pilate sends Jesus to Antipas who mocks Jesus and sends him back to Pilate, who condemns Jesus to death
Temple Mount
7.Jesus is sent to be crucified
Gardens
Golgotha Hill
Tyropoeon Valley
Towers' Pool
4.Jesus brought to the Council Chamber Lk.22:66 (the Chamber of Hewn Stone)
Gethsemane
Bridge
Gennath Gate
Gate?
Hippicus' Tower
Tower
Tower
Hasmonean palace used by Antipas
1.Jesus arrested
Tower
Pools
Ophel
UPPER CITY (ZION)
Herod's palace
5.Brought to Pilate at Herod'palace (Praetorium Mk15:16); he questions Jesus
Caiaphas' House?
3.Jesus kept overnight; Peter's denial
Scarp
2.Brought to Caiaphas
Kidron Valley
LOWER
Street
Pool of Solomon?
CITY
Serpent's Pool
Gate of the Essenes?
Aqueduct
First Wall
Siloam Pool
0 50 100 yds
0 50 100 m
Valley of Hinnom
© Carta, Jerusalem

The Arrest, Trials and Crucifixion of Jesus—A Possible Sequence. *The Gospel accounts agree that Jesus was arrested, brought before Jewish and Roman authorities for interrogation and sentencing, and led outside the walls of Jerusalem to be crucified. What is not clear is the sequence of the events of Jesus' trial(s) or their location within Jerusalem. About all that is sure is that the* Via Dolorosa, *a modern series of narrow, arched and stepped streets leading from the Sisters of Zion Convent (the location of the Antonia Fortress) to the Church of the Holy Sepulcher (Golgotha), is a route more of faith than fact. The uncertainty of the known route aside, the events surrounding Jesus' crucifixion and Resurrection remain the founding fact of Christianity.*

seeing Jesus; he had already executed John the Baptist (Mt 14:1–12) and now wanted a good look at the prophet's cousin, the miracle worker from Nazareth. Antipas grilled Jesus well, but the prisoner maintained his silence. Without extradition to Galilee there was little Antipas could do other than taunt Jesus and send him back to Pilate (Lk 23:6–12).

Thanks for nothing. It was time to finish the case. But perhaps Pilate could have a little fun in the process, undercutting the claim of Jesus' accusers and picking away at the absurdity of the perpetual political-religious mix of Judaism that had given him such trouble in the past. And so Pilate announced his decision, wholly unexpected by everyone: "I find no fault in him" (Lk 23:13–16; Jn 18:38).

No fault? Who was Pilate trying to kid? He had just heard Jesus as much as admitting to be the King of the Jews! Pilate was ready to throw Jesus back to the multitudes from which he came, a near-martyr returned to his partisan following to live and lead a revolt another day. (He had no clue who Jesus really was.) The religious authorities were incensed—they knew that another attempt at insurrection would prompt an even harsher response from their I'll-never-forget-you-humiliated-me-before-Caesar prefect. Pilate was setting the crowds up against their own leaders, relishing the thought of creating an opportunity to crush once and for all their seething and arrogant hope for an independent Jewish state. (Although he had been in the province for half a decade, Pilate still had no real clue who the Jews were, either.) Let the crowds force the hand of their own leaders this time!

A convenient tool lay at hand. According to recent custom, Pilate could offer to release one prisoner from custody at Passover time. He gave the crowds a choice: Barabbas or Jesus (Mt 27:15–20; Mk 15:6–9; Jn 18:39–40). Barabbas was a local insurrectionist and murderer, but as far as we know not someone who claimed to be the Messiah. There was no particular reason why anyone (except for his own family) would want him back on the street, and we can assume that many wanted him to remain locked up. Jesus was the crowd's hero and savior. Pilate figured that the choice would be obvious, and that a mass call to release Jesus would force the Jewish authorities to cave before popular will. *They* could be humiliated this time. And if it gave him justifiable reason to turn his troops loose again, so much the better.

But once again, Pilate had misunderstood his foes. By now the Jewish authorities had swayed the emotional crowds to *their* side—Jesus was a messianic *fraud* who would only lead them all astray. Better to get rid of him now than to incur the wrath of Rome one more time (Mt 27:20; Mk 15:11). Everyone quickly closed ranks and demanded Jesus' execution. Pilate was obstinate—he knew how to dig in his heels, too, and tried again and again to swing the momentum back (Mt 27:21–23; Mk 15:12–14; Lk 23:18–23). But in the end the growing mob pulled the ultimate trump card: "If you release Jesus, you're no friend of Caesar" (Jn 19:12). *That* was the one thing Pilate couldn't have. So he caved, but not before literally washing his hands of the matter (Mt 27:24): "You'll get what you deserve someday. And don't blame me when you do." Then he nailed down a final warning, a sign of mock tribute fastened to Jesus' cross, pointing in shame to The King of the Jews—"*this* is what happens to messiahs. Don't even think about being one."

In the end, as the trials and tribulations of a prefect go, Pilate's day could have been worse. His own agenda had been thwarted, it is true, but he had avoided a riot, solved a difficult case to the satisfaction of the accusers (much to his own chagrin, but he would have to live with that), kept Rome out of the matter, saved his own neck in the process (*that* was more important), and been able to throw some barbs at the people who had dared buck his authority in the past. And only one person had to be sacrificed—and he wasn't even a Judean.

From the ground it looked as though Jesus had been caught in a riptide of competing egos and pulled under by cross-currents of conflicting agendas, paying the highest price in the process. In reality, the Creator of the World had orchestrated events so that the Savior of the World could pay the highest price for human sin. But Pilate cared nothing for that.

By such mixed doses of in-your-face and dodge-and-feint, Pilate rode herd over the Jews under his watch and care. But things couldn't go on indefinitely. Ironically, the sequence of events that led to Pilate's downfall didn't happen in Judea but in Samaria, the portion of his territory that had a sizeable Gentile base (centered in the cities of Caesarea and Sebaste). Samaria was also home to the Samaritans, a schismatic people group once close to Judaism who clung to the tradition that Moses had intended Mount Gerizim to be the holy mountain of Israel. An unnamed Samaritan mystic (Josephus, who had no reason to protect Samaritan sensibilities, called him "one who thought lying was a thing of little consequence and who contrived things to please the multitudes"; Ant. xviii.4.1) inspired a crowd to converge on Mount Gerizim and look for sacred vessels that Moses had buried somewhere on the mountain. But they came armed; this was no effort at objective archaeology. Sensing a messianic-type revolt, Pilate sent the army to meet them on the road near the village of Tirathaba (an unknown location but likely in one of the valleys touching Mt. Gerizim on the north or east) to prevent their ascent up the mountain; some were killed, others fled; many were taken prisoner. Their recondite leader was executed straightaway. It was quick, easy and decisive—ignore public opinion, and life can go on as it should (Ant. xviii.4.1).

But this time Pilate couldn't outrun the crowds. Even though the official Samaritan leadership likely saw their unfortunate mystic as a bit of a kook, they

Pilgrims from Italy pray and sing their way through the streets of Jerusalem following the Stations of the Cross. Centuries of tradition have etched in stone holy moments of Jesus' final journey along the Via Dolorosa: where he fell, where he met his mother, where Simon of Cyrene took the cross, where Veronica wiped his face, where he fell again, and again. By now Pilate had gotten on with his day, the matter put aside, more important things to attend to. He did order soldiers to guard Jesus' tomb lest anything unexpected should happen. A martyr's body could be as dangerous to a crazed following as the martyr himself....

couldn't let Pilate's attack on their community go unanswered. A delegation reported the matter to Vitellius, governor of the province Syria, claiming that Pilate had murdered members of a harmless crowd. Vitellius, tired of Pilate's excesses, pulled rank and sent him to Rome to finally answer to the emperor directly for his heavy-handed ways (Ant. xviii.4.2). A friend of Vitellius named Marcellus, who had been given the privilege of delivering the news to Pilate, stayed on as temporary prefect of Judea. At the next Passover festival Vitellius, who understood that pro-Jewish policies were in Rome's best interest, went up to Jerusalem to a hero's welcome. Knowing change was in order, he ordered tax relief, removed cozy Caiaphas from the high priesthood and returned the control of the priestly vestments to the temple authorities (Ant. xviii.4.3). Judea breathed a collective sigh of relief.

In the meantime, while Pilate was en route to Rome, Tiberius died—and with this, the contemporary sources for the prefect's life fall silent. Pilate's involvement in the trial and execution of Jesus, however, guaranteed that he would not be forgotten. In the early fourth century A.D. Eusebius, bishop of Caesarea, wrote that during the reign of Tiberius' successor Gaius (Caligula; A.D. 37–44), "calamities forced [Pilate] to an unavoidable suicide, for the penalty of God, it seems, followed hard after him" (Historica ecclesiastica ii.7). A likely scenario is that Pilate

This ancient pavement, made of large, smooth flagstones, is located in the basement of the Sisters of Zion Convent on today's Via Dolorosa in the Muslim Quarter of Jerusalem's Old City. The pavement is inscribed with markings thought to be a "gameboard" of the type used by Roman soldiers to idle away their time while on duty far from home (close-up photo, above). Perhaps they played "the Game of the King," in which an unfortunate prisoner was taunted and abused while being forced to pretend to be king for the day. The Antonia Fortress almost certainly stood here in the first century A.D., with a Praetorium housing Jerusalem's contingent of Roman soldiers assigned to enforce the Empire's will in this independent-minded city. All of this prompted the suggestion long ago that these very stones are part of the Pavement (lithostrothon) mentioned in John 19:13 where Pilate condemned Jesus to death. It's a popular stopping point for pilgrims tracing Jesus' final journey to the Cross, even though archaeologists have now shown the pavement to be dated to the 2nd century A.D. A reasoned historical supposition locates Pilate's activities in Herod's royal palace in the western part of the city instead.

Pontius Pilate in History and Tradition. *It is natural that a man as closely tied to the death of Christ as was Pilate would become easy prey for weavers of tradition and legend. The details of Pilate's life that are supplied by Josephus are largely limited to events that took place in Judea. Early Church traditions differ on what happened to the man after Jesus' crucifixion; for some he was a saint, for others a demon. In the two millennia since, Pilate's character and career have become a favorite template for works of art, literature and song, most casting him in a justifiably negative light.*

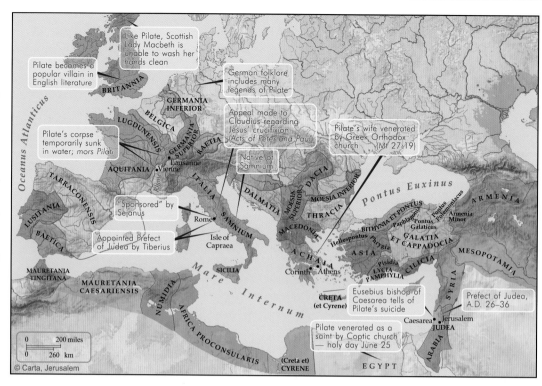

was found guilty of crimes against Rome's interests and chose to die honorably rather than at the hand of his employer. The spurious but influential *Mors Pilati* ("Death of Pilate"), a Latin document dated no earlier than the fifth century A.D., relates that Pilate's corpse was sunk in Rome's Tiber River but that "malignant and filthy spirits" clinging to his body so agitated the waters that he was drawn out and sunk again in the Rhone near Vienne (in southeastern Gaul). But those waters also churned and so his body was moved again, to the territory of Lausanne where the evil spirits plagued that land. Pilate's unfortunate remains were finally buried in a pit surrounded by mountains somewhere high in the western Alps "where to this day," reports *Mors Pilati*, "certain diabolical machinations are said to bubble up." Tradition accomplished what history didn't.

Certain early Church traditions sought to exonerate Pilate for his role in the death of Jesus, preferring instead to place full blame for the act on the Jews (e.g. Tertullian, *Apologia* 21.24, and *The Acts of Peter and Paul* in which Pilate sends a letter to the Emperor Claudius blaming the crucifixion of Jesus, a

benevolent miracle-worker, on "the wickedness of the Jews"). Anti-Semitism never rests, but fortunately the earliest Church creed proclaimed a more accurate understanding:

I believe in God, the Father Almighty,
the Creator of heaven and earth,
and in Jesus Christ, His only Son, our Lord:
Who was conceived of the Holy Spirit,
born of the Virgin Mary,
suffered under Pontius Pilate,
was crucified, died and was buried.
He descended into hell.
The third day He arose again from the dead.
He ascended into heaven
and sits at the right hand of God the Father Almighty,
whence He shall come to judge the living and the dead.
I believe in the Holy Spirit, the holy catholic church,
the communion of saints,
the forgiveness of sins,
the resurrection of the body,
and life everlasting.
Amen. (The Apostle's Creed)

And here Pilate's legacy should lie. God needed a human instrument so that His grace could flow through Jesus into all the world. Like Pharaoh, Nebuchadnezzar and Cyrus before, Pilate was called into the divine plan. His unfortunate personality served God's purposes even though it seemed like nothing but grief and chaos at the time. The Empty Tomb demanded first a crucifixion. In *this* instance at least, the will that Pilate enforced was God's.

The XIIth Station of the Cross, where Jesus died, was first identified by Constantine in the early 4th century. Here Constantine erected a wooden cross in memory of his Savior and built a massive church surrounding both it and the tomb in which Jesus was thought to have been laid. In A.D. 417 the Emperor Theodosius II replaced Constantine's cross with a cross of gold and precious stones, more fitting with a Rome that was becoming Byzantium, and the push to beautify and beatify the site was on. Today the Church of the Holy Sepulcher bears little resemblance to the Roman killing fields that lay outside the walls of first-century Jerusalem. The church pulsates with the prayers of the faithful, mixed with equal doses of tourists' gawks and power politics. These pious nuns genuflect daily at the altar that stands over the very spot that tradition has fixed as the place of the cross, a constant reminder that while Pontius Pilate is dead and gone, the faith of the Jesus whom he tried to exterminate lives on.

CHAPTER 22

PETER
Out in Front

Simon Peter was quite a character. Bold, energetic, a real go-getter, always out in front, asking questions, wanting answers, engaging the moment. This was Mr. Type-A: competitive; driven to succeed, wanting to be a part of things; taking on—and being given—multiple tasks; someone whose bold exterior made it hard to admit mistakes; who, when frustrated, tended to withdraw. If Jesus needed something done, Peter was there. If the disciples needed someone to stand up, there he was. If the Master was threatened, he was there. But when things really turned sour, there *went* Peter, distancing himself from failure. He was perhaps the most fully human of Jesus' followers, wholly believable in word and deed, perhaps a little too much so for comfort. Peter's life has been tracked by what he did, by the ebb and flow of his personality, and by how the church's collective memory of him has resonated down the centuries. The events of Peter's life can also be traced "on the ground," from the tight arena of the Sea of Galilee to the vastness of the Mediterranean. A geographical view such as this scans the horizon of a life that was first rooted to a tight shoreline, then gradually but inexorably opened to a world very much bigger that the one he called home.

Peter (or, more properly, Simon, his name by birth; cf. Jn 1:42) was a fisherman by trade, who wrestled a living for himself and his family from the sea. He grew up on the water, learning life skills from his father John, likely also a Galilee fisherman (cf. Jn 1:42). The Plain of Bethsaida, Peter's home (Jn 1:44), encompassed the outlet of the Jordan River and other, smaller tributaries that fed the northeastern corner of the Sea of Galilee. The waters lacing the region carried ample deposits of organic material on which fish could feed, and offered a fertile breeding ground where they could spawn, live and be caught by eager eyes peering from above. Peter often walked the shore near his Bethsaida home looking for schools of fish feeding among the rocks and reeds close to the water's edge, trapping them in a circular cast net thrown at just the right moment and with just the right twist of his wrist (Mk 1:16). This was a safe way to harvest the lake, relatively inexpensive and risk-free. Peter also plied the waters of the sea by boat, toiling long nighttime hours on end, trying to read the mood of sea and sky (cf. Mt 16:1–3; Lk 12:54–56), hoping that the fish, invisible in the depths below, might have congregated just where he had decided to drop his net (Lk 5:1–7).

But sometimes it was the sea, turned wild at a moment's notice, that would catch the fishermen, pulling their bodies down into a watery grave. The old Canaanite god of chaos and death, *Yam* (lit. "sea"), still swallowed predators into the world of the prey. This practical aspect of the ancient pagan worldview never quite let go of the first-century "moderns" who called the liquid abyss home. Fishermen needed a backbone stronger than those who spent their lives on shore, and it was this toughness in the face of uncontrolled risk that engendered personalities who would someday risk their lives spreading the Gospel across other seas.

Fishermen also used the sea to their advantage, quickly going where foot traffic was unable, chasing opportunities, for instance, or running from the taxman (e.g. Matthew; Mt 9:9). If contemporary documents from Roman Egypt are any indication, Caesar's local representative took a hefty percentage of every haul from the Sea of Galilee, perhaps 30–40% (*Tebtunis Papyri*, 701). Peter by instinct would have dodged Matthew the revenuer whenever he thought he could get away with it.

The Big Fisherman. Shepherd of the Church. Holder of the Keys of the Kingdom. In a lifetime buoyed by self-confidence, swamped by blunder and denial, and rescued by the Holy Spirit, the Apostle Peter strode from the shores of Galilee to distant coastlands across the Mediterranean. This one-ton bronze statue of Peter in full stride welcomes visitors to the Meditation Garden at Capernaum. The form is solid though full of motion, the face determined yet caring. The artist, Philadelphia sculptor Charles Madden, read well the passions of the man whose energy and devotion gave living shape to the earliest days of the church.

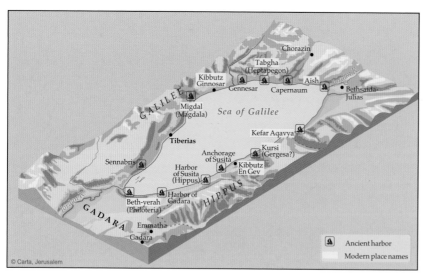

⚓	Ancient harbor
	Modern place names

Ancient Harbors on the Sea of Galilee. *When the water level in the Sea of Galilee is low, it is possible to make out piles of boulders jutting from shore. These are traces of harbors and anchorage points that served villages and cities around the lake in the first century. Ancient Capernaum boasted as many as seven piers, the most of any town around the lake. Some of the sea's best fishing was found just east of Capernaum, in the area of the Jordan delta, and to the west at the warm springs of Heptapegon (Tabgha). Curiously, no ancient harbor has yet been found at Tiberias, the capital of Galilee during the time of Jesus' ministry.*

Rabbinic tradition had mixed feelings about people who sailed the seas:

> A man should not teach his son to be a donkey-driver or a camel-driver, or a barber or a sailor or a herdsman or a shopkeeper, for their craft is the craft of robbers…[yet] most of the sailors are saintly,
>
> (Mishnah, *Kiddushin* 4.14)

meaning of course that some were not. For those who lived by the sea, the opportunity to act like a scoundrel always lay close at hand. Like everyone else in the lower echelons of Galilee's economy (and this was the vast majority of the people), Peter had to learn to "make his own way." He was a rough-and-tumble sort of guy who fought continually to get life to work for him.

Simon Peter's brother, Andrew, was also a fisherman. The blood of their brotherhood ran deep. As boys, they seem to have been raised in a *kosher* home (cf. Acts 10:14), where *Torah* was kept to the extent that it could be in Galilee. This was not always easy, and later rabbinic tradition records several ways that *Torah* impacted how one fished. The rabbis determined, for instance, which kinds of fish were *kosher* and hence were com-

mercially viable for Jewish homes (those that had fins and scales; Mishnah, *Hullim* 3.7); whether or not one could empty a net on the Sabbath that had been laid the day before (Mishnah, *Shabbat* 1.6); and how closely a net could be thrown to a school of fish that had already been spotted by someone else (Babylonian Talmud, *Baba Bathra* 21b). To what extent such scruples actually held to the day-to-day activities of Galilean Jewish fishermen in the first century is unknown, but likely the intent was similar.

In any case, Andrew likely was more spiritually sensitive than his brother, for something prompted him to journey down the Jordan Valley to Bethany where John the Baptist was offering a baptism of repentance for the forgiveness of sins (Mk 1:4; cf. Acts 2:38). Andrew came under the influence of the Baptist and was counted as one of his disciples. But when John baptized Jesus, Andrew was so taken by "the Lamb of God who takes away the sin of the world" that he became Jesus' disciple instead (Jn 1:29, 1:35–40). Correctly sensing that here at last was the One sent from God, Andrew quickly told his brother: "We have found the Messiah!" Seeing solid potential in the fisherman, Jesus didn't ask Simon if he, too, wanted to follow. Leaving no room for application forms or interviews, Jesus simply said straight away, "You are Simon the son of John. You shall be called Cephas" (Aramaic for "rock"; the Greek form *Petros*, "Peter," was more appropriate for the larger Greek-speaking world of the time; Jn 1:42). With that, Peter was caught, though it was a long time reeling him in.

Simon returned to Galilee and resumed life right where he had left it. Sometime later Jesus came back north and, leaving Nazareth, brought his fledgling ministry to the shoreline Peter knew so well. It was the morning following an unsuccessful night of fishing, and Peter and his fellow fishermen (James and John the sons of Zebedee, who would also soon follow the Master; Mt 4:21–22; Mk 1:19–20; Lk 5:9–11) were cleaning and preparing their nets for what they hoped would be a better catch next time out. Jesus, with eager listeners in tow, got into Peter's boat and used it as a pulpit to teach the multitudes. There was no necessary reason for him to have done so—there were plenty of places to speak from the shore—except that he apparently wanted to engage Peter in the conversation. Peter certainly overheard

The view of the Sea of Galilee from the rise above Capernaum to its eastern shore takes in the sweep of waters around which the Gospel story was born. The sea is nicely confined by a rim of hills that nearly fill its perimeter and offer an arena for life that can be seen and seized by anyone with the confidence and competence to do so. Peter was a big fish in a small pond here. But when he was thrown into the Mediterranean, a sea with a landless horizon line, he not only survived but thrived, and carried the message of Jesus all the way to Rome.

everything Jesus said—especially the last part: "Put down your nets into the deep water for a catch" (Lk 5:1–4). He protested—what could landlubber Jesus, eloquent as he was, teach *him* about fishing? Yet Peter did as Jesus commanded, perhaps half out of prior conviction, half to prove his own point—and to his surprise pulled in a huge catch. His response betrayed both amazement and an exposed sense of unworthiness: "Go away from me Lord, for I am a sinful man (my trying to keep *kosher* notwithstanding)." But Jesus pulled on the line. "From now on you will be catching men" (Lk 5:5–11).

Matthew (4:18–22) and Mark (1:16–20) record a shorter version of Peter's call, or perhaps a second call somewhat later since the details of the fishing expedition in their account differ from those of Luke. Peter was the kind of fellow who needed to feel the tug of the hook more than once, though once he did decide to follow, he did so wholeheartedly, "leaving everything to follow Him" (Lk 5:11). Yet there is no reason to think that Peter left fishing entirely. The focus of his life certainly changed, but he brought his talents along. After all, Peter still had easy access to boats—they seemed to always be at hand for Jesus' travels from shore to shore; he fished for tax money at Jesus' behest (Mt 17:24–27) and stepped right back into fishing after Jesus' crucifixion (Jn 21:3). When his travels eventually took him far out onto the coastal plain, Peter ended up settling for awhile in a house in Joppa by the sea (Acts 10:6). Fishing was in his blood—and besides, it was still way too early in church history to think in terms of professional ministry.

Peter quickly became the leader of Jesus' twelve disciples, and of the inner circle of three. In every list of names his appears first (Mt 10:2–4, 17:1, 26:37; Mk 3:16–19, 5:37; Lk 6:14–16, 8:51). Peter was a born leader, but a detail of geography might also help explain why he was able to stay out front. Peter was from Bethsaida in Gaulanitis, the territory of Philip, yet he married a Capernaum gal (Mt 8:5, 8:14; Mk 1:21, 1:29–30; Jn 1:44) and seemed to be at home as much in her father's household as in his. Certainly he used Capernaum as a base for fishing the northwestern shore of the sea. Of all Jesus' disciples it was perhaps Peter then who had the greatest number of contacts along the northern shore, who was best known in both Bethsaida and Capernaum, and so who already commanded a broad base of attention.

Not long after his call, Peter's mother-in-law became ill with a debilitating fever. Because her husband plays no role in the episode (Mt 8:14–17; Mk 1:29–31; Lk 4:38–39) it is likely that he was dead and that Peter had stepped in to assume responsibility for the home. Neither Peter's wife nor any of their children appear in the Gospel narrative, although 1 Corinthians 9:5 indicates that she eventually accompanied him on his travels. Rather, the focus of

Peter's work in the Gospels was on ways "that [Peter] might be with Him, i.e., Jesus," instead (Mk 3:13; cf. Mt 19:28–29).

For the first few months of Jesus' ministry Peter, like the rest of the disciples, listened, learned and absorbed all that he could. These were days of awe and anticipation as Jesus moved from one village to the next, from Galilee to Gaulanitis and the Decapolis and back, healing, teaching and meeting needs.

Sometimes Peter's understanding of what it meant to live right—to "keep *kosher*"—was challenged, such as when a woman who had had a flow of blood for twelve years touched Jesus and became well. According to Levitical and rabbinic law the woman was in a state of perpetual uncleanness, since her blood flow never stopped (Lev 15:19–30). She knew that before God and the religious authorities she was unclean, and had learned to hide

This first-century A.D. *mosaic from Migdal (Taricheae, which means "the place where fish were salted") on the northwestern shore of the Sea of Galilee depicts a boat typical of the craft that plied the waters of the sea during the time of the New Testament. The boat was propelled by a single mast fitted with a square-rigged sail and two oars on either side. A fifth crewman steered with a long rudder. Fully loaded, a boat of this kind could transport twelve people or carry nets, equipment and crew for a night of open-water fishing.*

An early-morning mist clouds the Sea of Galilee as fishermen from Kibbutz En Gev winch in their nets, hopeful of the kind of catch that Peter hauled up after Jesus commanded, "Put down your nets into the deep water!" (Lk 5:4–7; cf. Jn 21:6, 11). With modern equipment the details of fishing have changed, yet the essentials remain: the importance of teamwork, the bonds of camaraderie, the necessity of hard work, the risk of the unknown—and the pleasant satisfaction of a day's work well done.

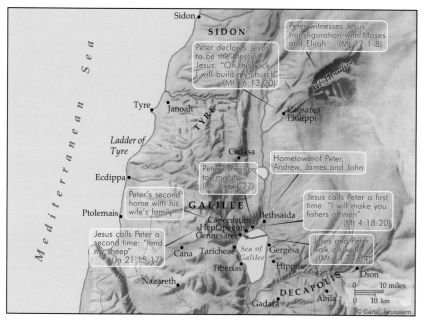

Peter with Jesus in Galilee.
The Gospels include more stories involving Peter than any other of Jesus' disciples. Of these, only some can be located in a specific place, but they are enough to see that wherever Jesus went, there was Peter, following his every footstep across land and sea. Capernaum was an "adopted" home for both, and became a convenient anchorage point for their ministry around the lake.

her condition well. Peter was at Jesus' side as she approached, furtive yet bold, the crowd close and everyone jostling everyone else. Rabbinic tradition held that once the hemorrhaging woman touched Jesus her uncleanness should have passed to him, then on to everyone who happened to be touching him at the moment, including likely Peter himself. But this time cleansing power flowed the other way, purifying and healing *her*, making her whole. "Go in peace," Jesus said. *Shalom.* For the woman, for the first time in more than a decade, life could be the way it was supposed to be (Mk 5:25–34; Lk 8:43–48).

Jesus was on his way to the home of a synagogue official named Jairus when the bleeding woman touched him. Though he was steeped in the laws of purity, Jairus was more concerned at the moment with his own daughter who was on the point of death and needed Jesus' healing touch. Just when Jesus healed the woman with the flow of blood, some of

Jairus' servants ran to tell him that his daughter had died—there was no need to bother the rabbi. Jesus disagreed. Taking Peter, James and John, he entered Jairus' house. According to rabbinic law, a corpse exuded the highest level of uncleanliness and the house and everything that overshadowed the body within, including people, became ritually unclean by virtue of being there (Mishnah, *Kelim* 1.4; *Oholoth* 1.2–4, 3.4). Jesus strode right in anyway, seized the dead girl by the hand and spoke "Child, arise!" (Mk 5:21–24, 5:35–43; Lk 8:40–42, 8:49–56). His touch and spoken word were personal, (re)creating and giving life to the dead (cf. Gen 1:26–27, 2:7). Of Jesus' disciples only his inner three witnessed the event. Peter, the spokesman, surely told the other nine what he saw. Jesus knew that a student *knows* something only when he has to find the right words to teach it to others.

Sometime later, in the spring of the year when storms could blow up quite suddenly, the disciples were heading across the lake in a boat. It was night; everyone was tired after a long day with the multitudes; Jesus had just fed 5,000 people with only five loaves of bread and two fish (Mt 14:13–21). The boat was full, riding quite low in the water, some distance from land, when suddenly the wind picked up. The waves were "contrary"—against them—crashing into the boat (Mt 14:22–24). Tired and worn, the disciples quickly realized the seriousness of their situation. A later rabbinic tradition preserves a legend of how some sailors might have responded:

Rabbah said: Seafarers told me: The wave that sinks a ship appears with a white fringe of fire at its crest, and when stricken with clubs on which is engraven "I am that I am, Yah, the Lord of Hosts, Amen, Amen, Selah," it subsides.

(Babylonian Talmud, *Baba Bathra* 73a)

Ever more practical, Peter simply strained at the oars (Mk 6:47–48). Then, out of the storm came a fig-

Partially reconstructed walls trace the dimensions of small rooms lying within blocks of houses (insulae) in ancient Capernaum. These living spaces date to the first century A.D. and are typical of village homes in the Galilee during the time of Jesus. Archaeologists have suggested that one particular room among the many was used as a meeting place for Christians as early as the late first century A.D.; above it a large octagon-shaped church was built in the second half of the fifth century formally commemorating the space below as the room in Peter's house that Jesus called home. Today, the ruins of the Byzantine structure are preserved by a new church, "St. Peter's Memorial," erected by the Franciscan Custody of the Holy Land exactly above. This building, with a glass floor to allow the faithful to peer down into time, is slung on exterior pillars so that no support columns penetrate the sacred space below. The church is sometimes maligned as a "spaceship," although its Italian architect, Ildo Avetta, intended the image to reflect a boat sailing the waters of the sea.

ure walking on the water. It was Jesus to the rescue. Peter, probably half crazed with the excitement of the moment, had to be a part of it all and asked Jesus to "command me to come to you on the water" (Mt 14:25–28). What he surely meant was "tell me I really do have the courage, and command the waves to hold me up." And so they did—until he realized what he was doing and started to sink. Now it was *his* hand that Jesus seized, drawing him back from the brink of death, giving him a second chance at life. It was personal—no second-hand sailor's legends here—and for the first time Peter realized that this one, *this One*, was *himself* the Son of God (Mt 14:29–33; cf. Mt 8:27, 9:8). Seeing, listening and taking part, Peter was starting to learn.

Eventually some scribes and Pharisees came up from Jerusalem to confront Jesus on matters of religious purity. Jairus' daughter aside, things had to be done properly, even up in Galilee. Jesus stated his case, reversing the polarity of ritual uncleanness: "It is not what enters into the mouth that defiles the man, but what proceeds out of the mouth that defiles him" (Mt 15:11). Peter, who had kept *kosher* all his life and would continue to do so for a long time yet (cf. Acts 10:14), asked Jesus what he meant. Jesus' reply spoke of matters of the heart:

> The things that proceed out of the mouth come from the heart….It is these that defile the man, not eating with unwashed hands. (Mt 15:18–20)

With that, Jesus took his disciples directly into Gentile territory, toward Tyre and Sidon and the Hellenized coast (Mt 15:21). Someday, sooner than Peter could yet imagine, he would make a similar trip and come face-to-face with God's call to the Gentiles (Acts 10:1–48). In the meantime, Jesus took him by the hand and led him through the motions, teaching him "how to observe all that [he] commanded" (cf. Mt 28:20). Peter was a good study. By-and-by, here and there, many who followed Jesus turned back and no longer walked with him. Jesus asked his lead disciple, "Do you, too, want to go away?" But by now Peter knew that not only was he caught, he was caught willingly.

> Lord, to whom shall we go? [It is] you [who] have the words of eternal life. We have believed and have come to know that you are the Holy One of God. (Jn 6:68–69)

Their journey together was about to reach a new level. Jesus took his disciples up to the district of Caesarea Philippi, a Gentile region north of the Sea of Galilee. There, far from the meld of multitudes that was always at his feet and within the geographical and world-view context that reflected, in microcosm, the basin of the Rome-gripped Mediterranean Sea, Jesus asked his disciples "Who do you say that I am?" Peter spoke right up; others might say that Jesus was John the Baptist, Elijah, Jeremiah

or one of the prophets, but Peter was sure that *he* knew: "You are the Messiah, the Son of the living God" (Mt 16:13–16). The answer was correct, concise and complete. Cognitively, Peter knew; but in terms of the ramifications of the revelation, he still had a long way to go. After informing Peter that he would play a foundational (rock-like) role in establishing the church (the extension of God's people worldwide), Jesus announced that he himself would soon go to Jerusalem to be abused and killed. Peter would have none of it—such things weren't supposed to happen to the Messiah (Mt 16:17–21). His response was strong, decisive and big-brother protective:

> God forbid, Lord! This shall never happen to you!" (Mt 16:22)

Jesus' reply was equally forceful, calling *that* attitude the camp of Satan (Mt 16:23).

Peter was rebuked, but not demoted. Discipleship, he had to learn, would be costly (Mt 16:24–26). Even his ego would be at risk. Six days later, with James and John, he saw Jesus, Moses and Elijah transfigured "on a high mountain apart." The location was most likely somewhere on the upper slopes of Mount Hermon east of the Jordan Valley, above Caesarea Philippi (Mt 17:1–3). Eager again to prove his worth, Peter volunteered to quickly make huts for each of them: "It is good we are here to help…" (Mt 17:4). What *that* was, was gibberish—the nervous response of someone who knew he should be doing something but had no idea what. It had been an emotional week, and Peter's roller coaster dipped and turned. Fortunately God himself interrupted the moment:

> This [Jesus] is my beloved Son. Listen to him! (Mt 17:5)

Returning to Capernaum, Peter was eager to ask questions. He knew that something quite special

The massive cliff at Caesarea Philippi (Banias) is decorated with niches that once held sacred statues dedicated to Pan, the Greco-Roman god of nature and fertility. Ruined foundations of temples and ceremonial courtyards still line the site. Here, on pagan holy ground, Herod the Great built a temple to Augustus, the divine Caesar, to bolster cultural and political connections between his kingdom and Rome. "You are Peter, the rock," Jesus told his lead disciple in the vicinity of the place. "And upon this rock (the image was striking) I will build my church, and the gates of Hell—(even Rome itself!)—will not overpower it" (Mt 16:18).

The Hasmonean kings established the principle that the annual temple tax, one-half shekel according to the sanctuary weight paid by every Jewish male over twenty years of age (cf. Ex 30:13), was to be paid with the Tyrian shekel. The choice appears odd, as the coin's obverse shows the Phoenician god Melqart and the reverse the Greco-Roman eagle. Although this half-shekel depicts graven images, it was apparently judged to be less offensive than coins minted by the Romans themselves. The silver content of the coin was tightly regulated (14.5 grams of silver; Jewish coins, minted without graven images, were generally struck with inferior metals). Perhaps Jerusalem's high priests conceded the coin's images in favor of its dependability. There was apparently a Tyrian shekel in the mouth of the fish that Peter hooked to pay the annual temple tax for himself and Jesus (Mt 17:24–27). (photo: L. Ritmeyer)

Stretching heavenward, the upper branches of a fig tree unfold their new spring leaves at the same time that its first fruit—early, inedible green figs called paggâ—pokes from the tree's light gray branches, otherwise bulbous and bare. These figs will ripen somewhat by early summer, but passersby prefer to wait for the better-quality figs that the tree will produce later in the season. Jesus passed by a fig tree at Passover time and found only leaves—not only was it not time for ripe figs, the pre-season paggâ weren't there either—and cursed the tree because it held no promise for fruitfulness. Peter was impressed: "Look! It withered!" (Mk 11:12–14, 11:20–25). Jesus used the moment to impress upon his lead disciple the power of faith and, by implication, the need to remain faithful—and fruitful.

was swirling around Jesus and that both by force of personality and divine choice he was going to play a leader's role in it all. The anticipation, the possibilities, were boundless. Jesus had started talking about going to Jerusalem to die (Mt 16:21, 17:22–23, 20:17–19), but surely, Peter thought, he could help straighten that sort of thing out if and when it would actually come. One more tangled net to wash and clean!

In the meantime, Peter started to work on some practical issues. The taxman came calling to ask for payment of the annual dues owed the Temple, wondering why Jesus was in arrears. Peter covered for his Master: "Of course we pay," then went to Jesus and fished around for why they hadn't. Jesus' reply was that as the Son of God he was exempt, but that no offense should be given and of course both of them would make good on the amount (Mt 17:24–27; cf. Mt 22:15–22). Or, after Jesus spoke of forgiveness, it was Peter out of a need to organize and control who asked for clarification. "How often shall I forgive? I'm big enough to do it up to seven times!" Jesus countered that there was to be no end to forgiveness: Do it "seventy times seven," he said, giving a number that surpassed practicality of purpose for sincerity of the heart (Mt 18:21–22). Or, when Jesus spoke in parables, it was Peter who looked for a specific point of application: "Is this for us, or for everyone?" (Lk 12:41). Peter was a tell-me-exactly-what-I-should-do kind of guy. Jesus refused to quantify: a good servant should just know what his Master wants and strive to do it continually (Lk 12:35–48).

Peter was also a bottom-line kind of guy: "Look. We've left everything and followed you. What do we get out of it?" (Mt 19:27). That question, coming as Jesus was about to begin his final climb to Jerusalem and the Cross, must have hurt, although the Gospel writers don't betray Jesus' inner thoughts. All Peter and the others saw coming was a Triumphal Entry into Jerusalem. So Jesus' reply:

Truly I say to you, in the new world, when the Son of man shall sit on his glorious throne, you who have followed me will also sit on twelve thrones judging the twelve tribes of Israel. And every one who has left houses or brothers or sisters or father or mother or children of lands for my name's sake, will receive a hundredfold and inherit eternal life. (Mt 19:28–29)

Jesus' words were of the world-to-come, a rabbinic concept (ha-olam ha-ba) that included reward for the righteous, especially for the righteous sufferer (cf. Exodus Rabbah 52.3; Babylonian Talmud, Sanhedrin 101a; Ta'anith 25a; Avodah Zarah 65a). Wholly consistent with Jewish expressions of future reward, Jesus couched his terms with reference to realities of the present. Surely Peter seems to have qualified; like Job, whatever loss he absorbed would be restored, if not here and now, then and there (cf. Job 42:10–16). But with Jesus, there was always a tag line:

But many that are first will be last, and the last first. (Mt 19:30)

And which of these would Peter be?

Then the climb to Jerusalem, up and over the Mount of Olives to the cheering throngs. Peter and the others followed Jesus into the Temple and witnessed their coming king in action—overturning the moneychangers' tables, challenging insincerity and corruption, energizing the crowds, leading the charge, speaking of the days to come (Mt 21:1–24:3; Mk 11:1–13:3; Lk 19:28–21:4). There was some local opposition, but that was to be expected. Everything was proceeding right on schedule for a coronation. Peter was anxious and, with Andrew, James and John, pulled Jesus aside at the end of a busy day. They were on the Mount of Olives, overlooking a city pressed with the cares of the day.

Tell us, when will these things be, and what will be the sign when all these things are going to be fulfilled? (Mk 13:4)

Jesus' reply was ominous. Hard days were coming, days of persecution and turmoil. And he didn't say exactly when, only "watch therefore, for you know neither that day nor the hour" (Mt 24:4–25:46; Mk 13:5–37; Lk 21:8–36). It all seemed so immediate, yet so far away.

For Peter and John, things more pleasant lay at hand. It was the morning of the eve of Passover (*erev Pesach*) and Jesus asked them to prepare the meal (Lk 22:7–13). This was a real privilege, and they wouldn't let him down. Everything had to be exactly right, a fitting climax to a week of anticipation, the right beginning to the real freedom and redemption that surely lay just ahead.

The meal was intimate, the setting secure. But for Peter, something wasn't quite right. By all appearances he was Jesus' right-hand man, the second in command, yet Jesus had given the seats of honor at the table (those at his right and left hand; cf. Mt 20:21, 22:44) to John and Judas—Judas!—instead (Jn 13:23–26). Peter had to sit somewhere "down table," in a seat of lesser importance. Then, during the order of service (*seder*), Jesus himself stood up to wash the feet of everyone in the room. The Master—a common servant? Peter would have none of it, until Jesus reminded him:

If I do not wash you, you have no part with Me.

(Jn 13:8)

Never one to go only part way, Peter, in nervous and confused energy, quickly conceded:

Lord, then wash not only my feet but my hands and head also.

(Jn 13:9)

But dark clouds formed; a chill swept the room. Jesus announced he was going to be betrayed by someone within the circle of twelve. Unbelievable! Peter was dumbfounded. (Mt 26:20–25; Mk 14:17–21; Lk 22:21–23; Jn 13:21–30). Then the climax: after the meal, as they were making their way through the still city to the garden of Gethsemane, Jesus announced he would be going away and Peter himself would deny even knowing him. Impossible! "I'm ready to go with you to prison and even to death!" (Lk 22:31–34; cf. Mt 26:30–35; Mk 14:26–31; Jn 13:36–38). Faithful Peter had brought a sword (cf. Jn 18:10).

Later that night, in the Garden of Gethsemane, the world fell in. A cohort of soldiers surrounded Jesus and his groggy disciples. The sudden realization of the moment slapped Peter awake, and he whopped off the ear of the emissary of the high priest Caiaphas (Mt 26:47–55; Mk 14:43–49; Lk 22:47–53; Jn 18:10–11). It was a gutsy move in the shadow of the Temple Mount. If he were as good with a sword as he was with a net, Peter probably would have been hauled off with Jesus. As it was, after Jesus was taken away he followed—he *had* to follow, though at a distance, as an unknown. He made it as far as the inner courtyard of the house of the high priest. Sev-

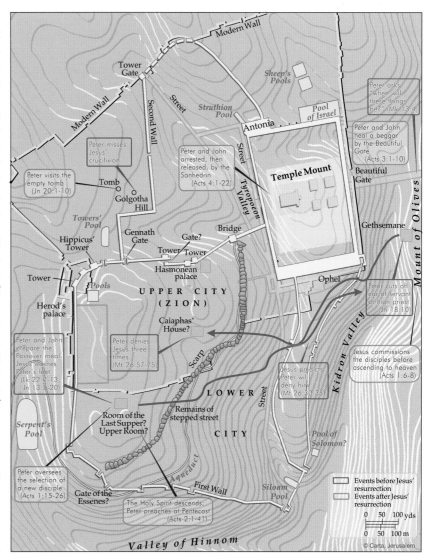

eral people approached, sure that he was part of the Jesus-conspiracy. Peter couldn't take any chances—there were probably spies everywhere. Cornered, he succumbed to the fatal power of self-preservation and denied his Master three times. Jesus, just inside, heard it all. Morning broke. It was a new day—and Peter, realizing what he had done and crushed by the irreversibility of the events, ran for his life (Mt 26:56–75; Mk 14:50–72; Lk 22:54–62; Jn 18:25–27).

He missed seeing Jesus die. He was probably wandering the streets in a daze when it happened.

It must have been a tortuous *Shabbat*.

Early the morning after, Mary Magdalene, Mary the mother of James, and Salome came to Peter, running:

They have taken away the Lord out of the tomb and we do not know where they have laid him!

(Jn 20:2)

What a panic! The tomb was already violated. Responsible Peter would know what to do. But he didn't—he and John examined the tomb and found it to indeed be empty, then spent the rest of the day

Peter in Jerusalem. *Before Jesus' resurrection Peter was brash and defensive; afterward, bold and confident. Jerusalem became the center of his activity as he played the pivotal role in the founding and earliest days of the church. The small band of Jews who believed that Jesus was the Messiah took their charge seriously so that "repentance for forgiveness of sins would be proclaimed in Jesus' name to all the nations, beginning from Jerusalem"* (Lk 24:47).

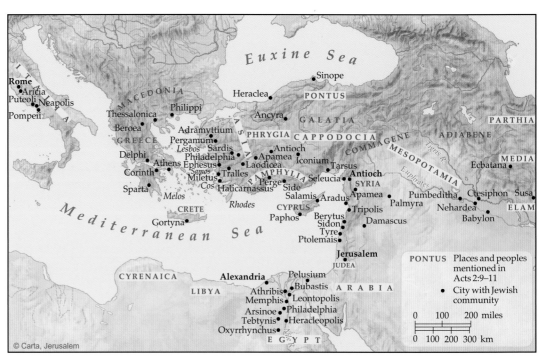

The Jewish Diaspora in the Time of Jesus. By the time Christianity was first established, Jewish communities could be found throughout the lands of the eastern Mediterranean and ancient Near East. Each centered on a local synagogue where Jewish teachings and traditions fostered an active social and spiritual life. Scattered throughout were God-fearers: Gentiles who were interested in, and sympathetic to, Jews and Jewishness. Jews from across the known world were present in Jerusalem when the Holy Spirit descended at Pentecost; those who responded helped to prepare the groundwork for the Gospel to spread "from Jerusalem and all Judea and Samaria to the uttermost parts of the earth" (Acts 1:8).

"Me? With Jesus?! I've never heard of the guy!!" Peter's denial, both incredulous and believable, has echoed down the halls of time. This image is found in the courtyard of the Assumptionist Church of Saint Peter in Gallicantu ("of the cock crowing") in Jerusalem. Cast by Robert Shiloh, it captures the moment of the self-preservation of denial, the most human of all of Peter's emotions.

not comprehending what might have happened (Lk 24:12; Jn 20:1–10). Reports filtered back to the disciples: the women said they saw an angel who told them Jesus had risen from the dead and would meet everyone back in Galilee, and Mary Magdalene said she saw the resurrected Lord himself. But Peter scarcely knew whether—or how—to believe (Mt 28:1–8; Mk 16:1–11; Lk 24:1–11; Jn 20:11–18). That evening, as the disciples (*sans* Thomas) were gathered together in a closed room (they were hiding from who knew what, scared, suspicious of everything, hoping yet not daring to hope), the resurrected Jesus appeared to them all. Then two who had been on the road to Emmaus confirmed that they, too, had seen Jesus (Lk 24:13–35; Jn 20:19–25). He was alive.

Sometime later, Peter and six other disciples went back to the Sea of Galilee and started fishing again. It seems to have been a first, small attempt to get on with their lives. What the resurrection actually meant hadn't sunk in, and Peter apparently had grown edgy just waiting around Jerusalem. But there, out on the water, in the early morning, it all came back. Not their luck in fishing—they toiled all night and still caught nothing—but Jesus' call. "Cast your net on the right side," a voice from the shore commanded. And when they did, the haul was immense (Jn 21:1–6, 11; cf. Lk 5:1–4). Peter immediately recognized Jesus and couldn't wait to get to shore. They shared a common meal—simple fare of loaves and fishes, but it was with Jesus. An early church tradition codified by the pious pilgrim Egeria in the fourth century A.D. places the breakfast in the same location as Jesus' earlier multiplication of the loaves and fishes (at Heptapegon, modern Tabgha). It's a convenient collapsing of events onto a single spot of holy ground. For Peter, the multitudes were gone but that didn't matter. Jesus had returned (Jn 21:7–11).

After breakfast, Jesus asked Peter three times if he loved him. Peter had denied Jesus three times and had a lot of making-up to do. Now each time Peter replied that yes, he did, but his choice of words (in Gk. *phileo* rather than *agape*) was somewhat noncommittal. For the moment, Jesus would have to take what he could get. With each assertion Jesus commissioned his lead disciple: "Tend my sheep" (Jn 21:15–17). Peter had started out as a fisherman but ended up a shepherd (cf. Lk 5:10). This change of vocation was apt: not only were shepherds the image of choice of Old Testament writers who wanted to illustrate effective, redemptive leadership in ancient Israel (e.g. Ps 23:1, 80:1; Isa 40:11; Jer 31:10; cf. Ezek 34:1–10;

Zech 11:4–17; 1 Pet 2:25, 5:1–4), but in common terms a shepherd's goal was to keep sheep healthy and whole; fishermen killed fish. Years later, Peter wrote about Jesus' sufferings to Christians living out in the Roman world. He spoke of their experiences as his own:

> And [Jesus] himself bore our sins in his body on the cross so that we might die to sin and live to righteousness; for by his wounds you were healed. For you were continually straying like sheep, but now you have returned to the Shepherd and Guardian of your souls. (1 Pet 2:24–25)

Peter's encounter with Jesus had become a template for everyone.

Forty days after his resurrection Jesus gathered his disciples to the top of the Mount of Olives where he commissioned them to speak on his behalf "in Jerusalem, in all Judea and Samaria, and even to the uttermost parts of the earth" (Acts 1:6–8). From where they stood they could see all of Jerusalem and some of the hills of Judea; Samaria lay only a few miles north; the "uttermost parts of the earth" began twenty miles west, on the Hellenized coastal plain. Lifetimes of work were at hand, and Peter took the lead to not disappoint his Master and Lord.

After Jesus ascended to heaven the disciples (now apostles, envoys, "sent ones") entered the fray. They walked down the mount, and then up into the city where memories of Jesus' crucifixion were still raw on the ground. All returned to the upper room in which they had been staying, perhaps the same place they had eaten the Passover meal six weeks before (once again tradition doesn't fail) and, along with a small crowd of faithful (including Jesus' mother and brothers), awaited the Holy Spirit whom Jesus had promised to send (Acts 1:9–14). Peter, anxious, couldn't wait to begin. With Judas dead there was a hole in the band of disciples and Peter proposed that it be filled with someone who had been with Jesus from the beginning. Lots were cast (the Spirit moved even though He had not yet formally filled the room) and Matthias was enrolled with the eleven (Acts 1:15–26).

The festival of *Shavuot* ("Weeks"; Gk. *pentekoste*, lit. "fifty") was at hand. Like Passover fifty days before this was a pilgrimage festival when Jews from across the Diaspora, from Parthia to Rome, filled Jerusalem (cf. Acts 2:8–11). The celebrations of *Shavuot* marked the end of the annual grain harvest in Judea. By the end of the third century A.D. at least, if not earlier, the festival also began to commemorate the giving of *Torah* on Mount Sinai, God's gracious provision of life-instruction for his people (Babylonian Talmud, *Pesachim* 68b). On the first day of this *Shavuot* Jesus' followers were all together "in one place" when the Holy Spirit descended onto—into—them like flames of fire, with the sound of a rushing

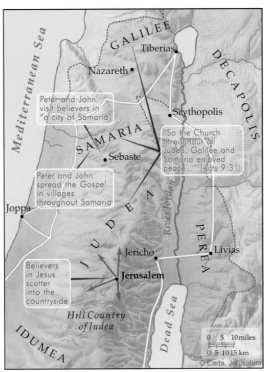

wind. It was God's creative spirit/wind (Heb. *ruah*; cf. Gen 1:2) and his empowering presence all wrapped up into one, a gracious provision of life-power for his people (Acts 2:1–3). Early church tradition (Cyril of Jerusalem, early fourth century A.D.) remembers the place as the same upper room in which the Last Supper was eaten (and why not?). Recent suggestions place the gathering on or near the stairway leading to the southern (Hulda) gates of the Temple Mount (also why not?) near the public *mikva'ot* (ritual immersion pools) where people from across the Jewish world would have been able to hear Peter's words, and where the many who embraced Jesus as Messiah that day could have been be baptized (cf. Acts 2:41). The coming of the Holy Spirit caused quite a stir, as many who were filled began to speak

"From Jerusalem to Judea and Samaria…" *Under opposition by Saul of Tarsus (soon to become Paul the Apostle), believers in Jesus headed for the hills, scattering throughout Judea, Samaria and eventually Galilee. When the Jerusalem church heard that people in Samaria were coming to faith in Christ, Peter and John went to "a city in Samaria," perhaps Sebaste, to check out the situation personally. They found the Samaritan's belief to be genuine, and the church, by the power of the Holy Spirit, took a giant step forward.*

Linford Stutzman and students of the Gospel reflect on Peter's second call from a life of fishing, at a spot on the northern shore of the Sea of Galilee that tradition remembers as the place of his breakfast with the resurrected Jesus (Jn 21:1–17). *A hymn with a flowing melody line, composed by the Spanish priest Cesareo Gabarain, carries the moment:*

Lord, you have come to the lakeshore…
  with your eyes you have searched me,
  kindly smiling, have spoken my name.
Now my boat's left on the shoreline behind me,
  by your side I will seek other seas.

"…to the Uttermost Parts of the Earth." *Joppa had been Judah's port, on and off, for centuries. Although way out on the coast, it was certainly known to the Jews of first-century Jerusalem, and a place where many of them could feel comfortable along with an otherwise Hellenized shore. Caesarea, on the other hand, was a new city, thoroughly Roman, that offered both opportunities and threats for Jews. From its synagogue the revolt began that led to the destruction of Jerusalem in A.D. 70, and from its port the Gospel was launched into the Mediterranean world. For Peter, the jump from Joppa to Caesarea was the push that altered his life—and that of the church—forever.*

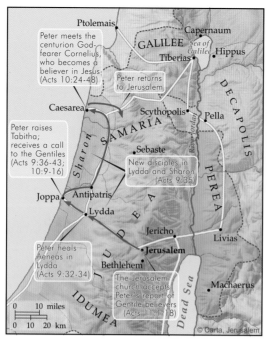

A double dose of the presence of God—descending as a dove, then radiating like tongues of fire—fills the apse behind the chancel of St. Peter's Church in Joppa (Yafo). Peter missed seeing Jesus' baptism in the Jordan River (his brother Andrew likely was present), but he certainly felt the onrush of the Holy Spirit at Pentecost when he received power from on high. With its presence, he was finally able to live the words of Jesus.

in other known languages (Acts 2:4–13). Seizing the moment, Peter addressed the crowd and explained that God had just fulfilled words of the prophet Joel:

"And it shall be in the latter days," said God,
  "that I will pour forth of my Spirit on all mankind…
and it shall be that everyone who calls on the name of the Lord will be saved."

(Acts 2:17–21; cf. Joel 2:28–32)

This was Peter's first public sermon, and with it and the power of the Spirit of God the church was born. Three thousand people repented and were "baptized in the name of Jesus Christ for the forgiveness of sins" (Acts 2:37–42; cf. Mk 1:4). Certainly many were pilgrims who returned to their homes across the Roman world carrying news about Rabbi Jesus the Messiah as they went.

The church was born, but Peter and all the rest considered themselves fully Jewish—nothing had changed, yet everything had. Peter continued to observe *Shabbat* and the holidays (Acts 2:1), eat *kosher* food (Acts 10:14) and go to the Temple to pray (Acts 2:46, 3:1). But filled with the power of the Holy Spirit, his energy found full release in the direction of the words and teachings of Jesus.

On one visit to the Temple he and John met a man who had been lame from birth, a beggar at the eastern gate called Beautiful. The man asked for alms; "in the name of Jesus Christ the Nazarene" Peter and John gave him back his health. Jesus' power to heal still stirred the city (Acts 3:2–10). Crowds gathered in the Portico of Solomon, likely the eastern colonnade of the Temple's public courtyard, where Peter preached his second sermon, focusing on Christ crucified and risen again (Acts 3:11–26). He was quick to point out the role that the people of Jeru-

salem played in delivering Jesus to the sentence of death, and their need to repent before God ("…I know that you acted in ignorance, just as your rulers also did"; Acts 3:17). Many responded favorably.

The temple authorities, though—especially the aristocratic Sadducees who had a *status quo* to protect (cf. Acts 5:17)—were not pleased that this Jesus movement was resurrected from the dead (it should have been taken care of back at Passover…). They arrested Peter and John and hauled them before the high priest (Acts 4:1–7). Peter had avoided facing Caiaphas during Jesus' trial by choosing to deny his involvement in that affair, but now he was in the hot seat himself and responded boldly and at length. Jesus, who had spoken only one sentence to Caiaphas during his hearing (Mt 26:64), would have been proud. Unable to dispute the miracle that had taken place and unwilling to risk unrest among the crowds who were taken in by it all, the temple authorities turned Peter and John loose with a warning to stop speaking in the name of Jesus. Encouraged by the body of believers and by their own confidence in the resurrected Christ, Peter and John only spoke out more boldly (Acts 4:8–31).

The fledgling body of believers grew by leaps and bounds (at this early stage the movement was not yet a "church," just a community of Jews who believed that Jesus was the Messiah and sought to shape their lives accordingly; the term "Christian" wasn't coined until a decade later, up in Syrian Antioch; Acts 11:26). The movement was characterized by a willingness of each of its members to help the other, as in a family in which the financial and personal needs of one are met by the abilities of others (Acts 2:43–47, 4:32–37). When two new followers of Jesus, Ananias and his wife Sapphira, secretly put their own needs over those of the new community to which they now belonged, Peter confronted them for lying to God and the Holy Spirit (Acts 5:1–11). For centuries the two foundational values of Jewish (and Israelite) village life had been family and land, and all decisions that affected the individual were made with the continuity of one's family on one's ancestral land in mind. By the time of the New Testament these values were starting to break down as complex economic structures (some of which were related to the influx of Hellenism and Roman political control, others to urbanization) began to alienate people from their families and/or their family land. The earliest community of Jesus' followers in Jerusalem sought to fill the need to belong by encouraging its members to pool their resources for the benefit of their new "family" in Jesus (cf. Mt 12:46–50). When Ananias and Sapphira sold a plot of (ancestral?) land and gave only a portion of its proceeds to the common pot, withholding the rest for their own use, they disinherited not only their own blood descendants but cheated their new family as well (cf. Moses' curses against those among the people of Israel who acted against their covenant with God in secret; Deut 27:15, 17–18, 24). Shocked that they should be found out, both fell dead at Peter's feet.

Peter continued to speak and heal in the name of Jesus, and the movement continued to grow (Acts 5:12–16). Clearly the prior warning by the temple authorities had gone unheeded and several of the apostles, including Peter, were rounded up again in an attempt to squash the movement (Acts 5:17–18). Between the excesses of Rome, the crazy ideas of fanatics and the fickle mood of the masses, the local leaders of Jerusalem already had their hands full keeping a lid on their city; further divisions among the people wouldn't serve anyone's interests (especially theirs). But an angel of the Lord opened the prison doors that night and commanded Peter and the apostles to

Go, stand and speak to the people in the temple the whole message of this [new] life. (Acts 5:20)

Of course they listened to the angel rather than the high priest. When brought in again the next morning for another hearing, Peter simply replied "We must obey God rather than men" (Acts 5:21–32). The Sanhedrin was fit to be tied. If God were to speak, surely he would do so through proper temple channels! One of their members, Gamaliel (as a Pharisee, he was more in tune with the needs of the masses and their susceptibility to following charismatic holy men than were the aristocratic Sadducees) cautioned prudence. If Peter's crowd followed the pattern of other messianic movements whose leaders had been killed, it would surely soon spin itself out. But if it really *were* of God, opposition would be fruitless. Again the Sanhedrin turned the apostles loose with a stern warning; emboldened, Peter spoke even more forcefully in the name of Jesus (Acts 5:33–42).

With this kind of start it wasn't long before the body of believers spread from "Jerusalem to all Judea and Samaria" (cf. Acts 1:8). Opposition in Jerusalem was spearheaded by a zealous Pharisee, Saul of Tarsus, who inadvertently helped the cause when believers in Jesus scattered before his blows into the countryside, carrying the apostles' message with them (Acts 8:1–4). Philip the Evangelist (cf. Acts 6:3–6) proclaimed Christ in "the city of Samaria," likely Sebaste, a city with a large Gentile population from which both Herod the Great and the prefects had drawn soldiers to man Rome's occupying army (Acts 8:5–8). When word reached Jerusalem that there were now believers there, in a community that clearly stood on the edge of mainstream Judaism (if not outside the rabbinic boundaries altogether), Peter and John went down (the verb in Acts 8:5 is used in terms of elevation, not compass direction) to assess the situation. Finding the response genuine

Neither Josephus or the Mishnah mentions the "Beautiful Gate" by which Peter and John healed the lame beggar in Acts 3, although Josephus does refer to a gate "of Corinthian bronze" (War v.5.3) outside of the sanctuary that may be another name of the same. Likely both are the gold-colored gate at the entrance to the Women's Court of the Temple at the bottom of the photo. An alternative suggestion is to equate the "Beautiful Gate" with the Nicanor Gate at the top of the curved steps leading into the inner Court of Israel and the Temple itself (cf. Acts 3:2). Both would have been prime locations for beggars.

(Simon the magician, who offered to purchase the Spirit with money was a notable exception), they prayed for the Holy Spirit to reveal Himself to the Samaritan believers (Acts 8:9–24). Empowered, Peter preached the gospel in many Samaritan villages on the way back to Jerusalem (Acts 8:25). In terms of locus of ministry and world-view, he had come a long way from home.

Now that he had broken out of the geographical and cultural barriers that enclosed Jerusalem, Peter traveled throughout Judea, Samaria and, likely, even Galilee with the good news (Gospel) of Jesus. His journeys eventually took him toward the coast (Acts 9:31–32). The year was around A.D. 37, and everyone in Judea and Samaria was breathing a sigh of relief because Pontius Pilate, the overbearing Roman prefect, had been removed from office and his replacement, Marcellus, voiced a conciliatory stance toward the Jews. Saul of Tarsus, in the meantime, had seen the risen Christ in a vision as he was traveling to Damascus to oppose the growing body of believers there, and ended up joining them instead (cf. Acts 9:1–30). Eventually Saul would come to Peter in Jerusalem and be accepted by its body of Jewish believers in Jesus (Gal 1:18). Meanwhile,

the church throughout all Judea and Galilee and Samaria enjoyed peace, being built up. Continuing in the fear of the Lord and in the comfort of the Holy Spirit, it continued to increase. (Acts 9:31)

Traveling west, Peter made his way to Lydda, just out of the hill country of Judea, then all the way to Joppa on the sea, healing the sick and raising the dead as he went (Acts 9:32–42). News about Jesus spread up and down the coast, a Hellenized land that was the gateway of "the uttermost parts of the earth" (Acts 1:8). Here Peter was far out of his comfort zone (understandably so), and so vis-

Boats, cars and people converge at the port of Joppa (Yafo) on a sunny Shabbat afternoon in late winter. Not many keeping kosher here! The spirit of internationalism still reigns on Judea's coast. The spires of the old city tell the tale of the ancient coastline: the lighthouse to bring commerce safely home; the minaret and church bell tower guiding the ways of the faithful. Under the courtyard next to the bell tower (of St. Peter's Church) remains were found of the Roman city. Tradition holds that the mosque (under the minaret) marks the site of the home of Simon the Tanner, where Peter stayed when he was in town. The building is a private home today.

ited (quite naturally) cities with sizeable Jewish populations. His base of operations was the home of another man named Simon, a tanner who lived at the edge of Joppa by the sea (cf. Mishnah, *Baba Bathra* 2.9) and who was also a Jewish believer in Jesus (Acts 9:43). Leatherworking, though a necessary trade, was a nasty, smelly business, and its practitioners, considered unclean by Jewish law, were generally despised by those who were religiously observant (Lev 11:39–40; Mishnah, *Shabbat* 1.2; *Megillah* 3.2; *Ketuboth* 7:10). By staying with Simon the tanner, Peter was pushing his security envelope just about as far as it could go.

One bright day Peter was on the rooftop for a meal and noontime prayers when out of the blue he had a vision of a great white sheet sailing down from heaven, filled with every kind of animal that Levitical and rabbinic law considered unclean. The Greek word used here for sheet, *othone*, is also the technical term for the sail of a ship, and to Peter the sheet descending from the sky certainly represented the cultural pollution of the Hellenistic world that kept popping up over his western horizon (cf. Ps 57:20). Three times a command, clearly from God, ordered Peter to eat from the squirming, squiggly mess. Peter, who had kept the Jewish dietary laws all his life, of course refused. Surely, he must have thought, it was a divine test (or maybe a trick?), that if he ate, he would be giving his heart and soul to the Hellenists who had sailed to Judea to spit on the ways of *Torah*. Peter had denied Jesus three times before—he wouldn't do it again (Acts 10:9–16)! As soon as the vision passed there was a knock at the gate: it was soldiers, wanting to take him to the centurion at Caesarea for questioning. In his gut he must have assumed that he was being arrested again, and this time, out in exposed Gentile land, it was serious. But reassured by the Holy Spirit Peter went willingly, though he took along some of his

colleagues for support (Acts 10:17–23). The next day in Caesarea he had a frank discussion with Cornelius, a centurion of the Italian cohort (Peter couldn't have found someone who better represented "the uttermost parts of the earth" if he had tried). But Cornelius was also a God-fearer who was attracted to the tenets of Judaism (Acts 10:24–43). Upon hearing the Gospel, Cornelius and those whom he had gathered to hear Peter believed, and though all were Gentiles, the Holy Spirit fell on them, too. Seizing the moment, Peter baptized everyone into the body of believers in Jesus (Acts 10:44–48).

When Peter returned to Jerusalem he had some explaining to do. The Jewish believers who had heard of his exploits down in Caesarea were not pleased. "You went to uncircumcised men and ate with them!" they scolded (Acts 11:1–3). Peter was firm and compelling in his reply: "What God has cleansed, no longer consider unholy" (Acts 11:8; cf. Acts 10:15)—or in other words, everything that God created, is good (Gen 1:31). His Jerusalem colleagues acquiesced (Acts 11:16–18).

About a decade had passed between the coming of the Holy Spirit in Jerusalem and His descent on Cornelius' family in Caesarea. During that time the church had grown consistently, sometimes rapidly, under favorable conditions and amid controversy, both within and without. Peter had grown, too—he had found other seas.

In A.D. 41 Herod Agrippa I took the throne of Judea, Samaria and Caesarea (it was a reward of friendship by Claudius, the new emperor in Rome). The Jews in his realm were genuinely happy that one of their own, rather than another Latin prefect, was again the local ruler of the land. Agrippa favored his Jewish subjects and came down hard on the growing band of Christians. He executed James the brother of John with the sword (Acts 12:1–2).

Seeing that his actions pleased the Jews, Agrippa arrested Peter as well, at Passover, likely in either A.D. 43 or 44 (Agrippa would die in the summer of A.D. 44 after a short reign in the fast lane; *Ant.* xix.8.2). As he sat in prison Peter must have remembered the tragic events of the Passover a decade earlier when Jesus had also been arrested, then executed. But the same was not to be Peter's fate: the night before Agrippa planned to parade Peter before the people, an angel of the Lord escorted him out of prison. After quickly reporting to a desperate and despondent gathering of Christians who were praying for his release, Peter disappeared (Acts 12:3–19).

And with this, except for a few quick references that pop up here and there in the rest of Acts and the Epistles, Peter largely fades from the literary scene of the New Testament. Of course he played an important role at the first Apostolic (Jerusalem) Council, speaking up in favor of bringing Gentiles into the larger community of (Jewish) believers without requiring them to become circumcised or keep Jewish ceremonial laws (Acts 15:6–12). In a note that is somehow related—though how is highly debated—the Apostle Paul told the church in Galatia that while in Antioch he had confronted Peter for appearing to backtrack on his commitment to the Gentiles after being confronted by Jews zealous for *Torah* (Gal 2:7–16). From Antioch Peter's travels took him generally westward, although a single connected journey cannot be posited. His first epistle was addressed to "pilgrims of the dispersion scattered throughout Pontus, Galatia, Cappadocia, Asia and Bithynia" (1 Pet 1:1), all regions of the high country of northern and western Anatolia, and it is likely that he had actually visited the people to whom he wrote. Notes by Paul in 1 Corinthians 1:12 and perhaps 9:5 suggest that Peter also taught and baptized in Corinth.

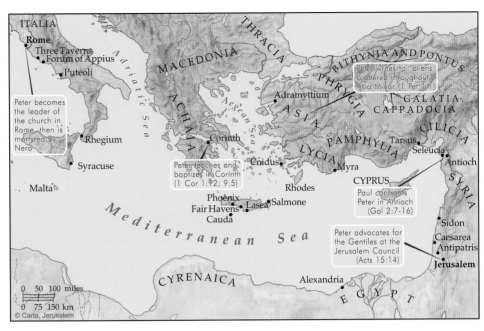

Finally he came to Rome, the "Babylon" from which he wrote his first epistle (1 Pet 5:13) and where, according to the early church fathers, he and Paul established the church in the city. The accounts vary (cf. Irenaeus, *Adversus omnes haereses* iii.1.1 and Eusebius, *Historia ecclesiastica* ii.25.8), but all point to Peter as the first bishop (later called pope) of the church in Rome. Somewhere along the way, according to Eusebius (*Historia ecclesiastica* iii.39), Peter transmitted an eyewitness account of his experiences with Jesus to Mark, who committed them to writing as the second Gospel.

It was in Rome that both Paul (first) and then Peter were eventually martyred for their faith (cf. the testimony of 1 Clement 5–6). The executions took place in the reign of the noxious emperor Nero (A.D. 54–68), likely during his first grand and gory persecution of Christians in A.D. 64 (cf. Jn 21:18–19). Later tradition (e.g. the sixth-century *The Acts of Peter and Paul*) holds that Nero had Paul beheaded and Peter crucified, both for causing the death of Simon Magus (the Samaritan magician of Acts 8:9–24 who just happened to pop up in Rome and accuse Peter and Paul of all sorts of nefarious deeds). Peter took his cross unflinchingly (cf. Mt 16:24):

"Since my Lord Jesus Christ, who came down from the heaven upon the earth, was raised upon the cross upright, and He has deigned to call to heaven me, who am of the earth, my cross ought to be fixed head down most, so as to direct my feet toward heaven; for I am not worthy to be crucified like my Lord." Then, having reversed the cross, they nailed his feet up. (The Acts of Peter and Paul)

Numerous literary works appeared in the early centuries of Christianity purporting to describe further (previously hidden) teachings and exploits of the apostle. These include the Gnostic writings *Acts of Peter and the Twelve Apostles*, the *Epistle of Peter to Philip* and the *Apocalypse of Peter*. All are certainly more a witness of responses to various heresies within the church than a reflection of the man himself. More to the point is Peter's own testimonial, portraying himself not as a fisherman but as a shepherd's shepherd whose first care was for sheep:

I exhort the elders among you, as your fellow elder and witness of the sufferings of Christ and a partaker also of the glory that is to be revealed, shepherd the flock of God among you, exercising oversight not under compulsion but voluntarily. (1 Pet 5:1–2)

So in the end Peter was still out in front, though not for self-assertion (he had done plenty of that in his younger years), but simply guiding and protecting the people under his charge as Jesus had him, keeping them healthy and whole.

*He waited after no pompe and reverence
Ne maked him a spiced conscience,
But Cristes lore and his apostles twelve
He taughte, but first he folwed it hymselve.*
(Chaucer, *Canterbury Tales*, 525–528)

Peter's Journey to Rome.
Although it is not possible to draw a single continuous route following Peter from Jerusalem to Rome, clues in the New Testament and in writings of the early church fathers suggest that his steps generally tracked the direction of the travels of the Apostle Paul. It is reasonably clear that the two great apostles to the Gentiles met a similar fate, martyrdom at the bloody hands of Nero sometime before the outbreak of the Jewish revolt of A.D. 66–70. That was a decade that would change the world.

Jesus' call on Peter's life carried him from sea to shining sea, from the security of Galilee to the unbounded opportunities of the Mediterranean. By the time his own sun had set, Peter had carried Jesus' message of good news to faraway Rome, the capital of a cultural and political order that had washed across most of the known world. The roll of the Roman sea was unrelenting; the Gospel tide would prove to be more so.

233

CHAPTER 23
PAUL
Living Under Grace

Alexander the Great's battle against the Persian king Darius at Issus was portrayed in a masterful full-color mosaic at Pompeii (2nd–1st century B.C.). One can almost hear the noise of battle and smell the stench of smoke and death amid the crush of titans on the scene. This early clash of east-meets-west didn't bode well for the kingdoms of the Levant and Mesopotamia. The Issus battlefield was in the neighborhood of Tarsus, home of the great Apostle Paul. His effort at carrying the Gospel of Jesus into the world of Alexander was also a struggle and sometimes ended in shed blood (his own, for instance). But his fight was on a different level. Paul described it this way: "Our struggle is not against flesh and blood, but against the rulers, against the powers, against the world forces of darkness, against the spiritual forces of wickedness in the heavenly places. Therefore take up the full armor of God" (Eph 6:12–13).

It was perhaps as dramatic a shift in outlook and career as anyone could make—a man wholly driven in one direction, then totally committed to another. Rabbi Saul of Tarsus turned Paul the Apostle to the Gentiles. Saul was, in his own words, fully immersed in the world of Pharisaic Judaism:

Circumcised the eighth day, of the nation of Israel, of the tribe of Benjamin, a Hebrew of Hebrews; as to Torah, a Pharisee; as to zeal, a persecutor of the church; as to the righteousness that is in Torah, found blameless. (Phil 3:5–6)

Yet when the risen Jesus met him face to face (or, light to face; Acts 9:3–4), his inner being was transformed:

[Whichever of these] things were gain to me, those I have counted as loss for the sake of Christ…[that I might have] the righteousness which comes from God on the basis of faith, that I may know Him and the power of His resurrection and the fellowship of His sufferings, being conformed to His death, in order that I may attain to the resurrection from the dead. (Phil 3:7, 9–11)

Armed with a new name (Acts 13:9) and a (re)newed identity, Paul became the greatest Christian evangelist of the first century. Yet he was also totally taken (obsessed?) with his own unworthiness to be called an apostle:

For I am the least of the apostles, and not fit to be called an apostle, because I persecuted the church of God. (1 Cor 15:9; cf. Eph 3:8; 1 Tim 1:15)

Self-deprecating? There is no reason to doubt his sincerity—or his understanding of God's grace:

By the grace of God I am what I am, and His grace toward me did not prove vain; but I labored even more than all of them, yet not I, but the grace of God with me. (1 Cor 15:10)

What might seem arrogant from the mouth of anyone else was simply Paul, living under grace. And by doing so, he was the great bridge that carried Christianity out of Judaism (cf. Rom 11:17–24), a humble though powerful servant of God who more than anyone was responsible for taking the message of the life, death and resurrection of Jesus the Jewish Galilean to Gentiles living in "the uttermost parts of the earth" (Acts 1:8). And the world has never been the same for his efforts.

Saul of Tarsus was as well suited as anyone to be that bridge. He was born probably about a decade after the birth of Jesus, though a world away, in Tarsus, the largest city in the Roman province of Cilicia on the northeastern corner of the Mediterranean Sea (Acts 9:11, 22:3). The eastern end of the province, dominated by a large, fertile plain, was home to a thriving Greek and Jewish population in the first century A.D. Near the easternmost city on this plain, Issus, Alexander the Great had won his decisive battle against Darius the Persian in 333 B.C., opening the east to Hellenism. At the opposite, western end, ten miles inland, lay Tarsus, a center of Hellenistic education and culture that rivaled Alexandria and Athens (Strabo, *Geography* xiv.5.13). Behind Tarsus towered the great Taurus Mountains, a rugged 10,000-foot wall separating continental Asia from Asia Minor. These mountains are pierced by the Cilician Gates, a formidable pass due north of Tarsus that carried most of the traffic between East and West in ancient times. Tarsus was a major trade center and gateway in the Roman world, as Istanbul is the gateway between Europe and Asia today.

As a result, Saul's Tarsus contemporaries and forerunners were, by definition, "of the world," cosmopolitan and connected. In 41 B.C. Antony had commanded Cleopatra to meet him in Tarsus (she arrived lounging on a decorated barge, dressed like Venus; Plutarch, *Antony*). The philosopher Athenodo-rus of Tarsus was one of the tutors and confidants of the future Caesar Augustus (Strabo, *Geography* xiv.5.14; cf. Dio Cassius, *History* lvi.43.2). Antipater, a native product of a school of Stoicism in Tarsus, became head of a similar school in Athens. Many of the residents of Tarsus, includ-

ing some Jews, were granted Roman citizenship by Pompey and Antony in the last half of the first century B.C.; perhaps Saul's father or grandfather were among that number. (In a tradition that cannot be verified, Jerome relates that Paul's ancestors had migrated to Tarsus from Gischala in Upper Galilee when Pompey conquered Judea in 63 B.C.; *De viris illustribus* 5.) In the late first century B.C. Athenodorus reorganized the political leadership of Tarsus by placing an inner aristocracy of Roman citizens on top (just under himself), to which Saul's family may have been connected (Strabo, *Geography* xiv.5.14). Certainly Paul's ties to the place were on his mind when he was being manhandled by a mob in Jerusalem toward the end of his life: the first words out of his mouth were "I am a Jew of Tarsus in Cilicia, a citizen of no insignificant city!" (Acts 21:39). His roots were deeply intertwined with the penetrating reality of the Hellenistic world.

But they were thrust just as deeply into traditional Judaism. Paul's abbreviated autobiography "[I am] a Hebrew of Hebrews..." (Phil 3:5) suggests that in spite of his father's likely connections to the politics and economy of Tarsus, members of his family maintained strict control of their Jewishness and were careful not to assimilate (or not to assimilate too much) to the glories of Hellenism that so defined their home town. Both Saul and his father were, after all, Pharisees (Acts 23:6). It is a tribute to their devotion to the "traditions of the elders" that, though living far out in the Diaspora and in a city that flaunted all the world had to offer, Paul would still remember and value his ancient tribal ties ("...of the nation of Israel, of the tribe of Benjamin..."; Phil 3:5). Geographically, Israelite tribal boundaries had broken down with the fall of Israel and Judah over half a millennium before. Prior to that, in the ninth century B.C., the small territory of Benjamin in particular had been sliced in two with the larger portion being incorporated into the southern Kingdom (Judah) and a thin northern slice absorbed by the northern Kingdom (Israel; 1 Kgs 15:16–22). Yet the Benjaminite tribal identity persisted. Great men had hailed from the tribe of Benjamin: Ehud the judge and deliverer (Judg 3:15–30), Samuel the prophet (1 Sam 1:19–20) and Saul the first king of Israel (and perhaps the rabbi's namesake; 1 Sam 9:1–2, 9:15–16), men who had forged strong personal and corporate identities in their tiny tribal land between. Saul of Tarsus was proud of his Benjaminite roots (and justifiably so), and of his Jewish identity ("...as to the righteousness which is in *Torah*, blameless"; Phil 3:6). It was an awareness forged on the anvil of confidence and made strong in the face of confrontation, then tempered into a shield of survival skills that the Jews of Tarsus (and other cities!) wielded to withstand the worst of the Diaspora's seductions in their own land between.

Sometime early in life Saul (and his family) moved to Jerusalem where he received a traditional rabbinic education (Acts 22:3, 26:4; cf. Acts 23:16). He was joined to the aged rabbi Gamaliel (the Elder), one of the leading Pharisaic scholars of the day (Acts 22:3). Gamaliel was the grandson (or possibly the son) of Hillel, the founder of the more liberal of the two schools of the Pharisees in the late first century B.C. (the other was the school of Shammai). Although his credentials as a teacher of Bible and preserver of rabbinic tradition were impeccable (at one point he had served as president of the Sanhedrin), Gamaliel was also a student of Greek literature and advocated tolerance toward Gentiles. He wrote numerous legal directives (*takkanot*), many of which ended with the distinctive tagline "as a precaution for the common good" (Mishnah, *Gittin* 4:2–3). (This tolerant attitude certainly lay behind his counsel to the Sanhedrin to spare Peter's life when the apostle was arrested for teaching and healing in the name of Jesus; Acts 5:33–40.) Saul, certainly fluent in Greek, Hebrew (Acts 21:37–40) and Aramaic and arguably conversant in Latin, was one of Gamaliel's prize students:

I was advancing in Judaism beyond many of my contemporaries among my countrymen, being more extremely zealous for my ancestral traditions.

(Gal 1:14)

Unlike the Sadducees who were well positioned in the aristocratic circles of Jerusalem, individual Pharisees often needed income-producing jobs in order to make ends meet (cf. Mishnah, *Kiddushin* 4.14; and *Pirke Avot* 2.2 which finds value in combining the study of *Torah* with "worldly business" to avoid the pull of sin). For Saul of Tarsus and, certainly, his father, this trade was tent-making (possibly of the more fashionable leather rather than goat-hair "Bedouin-type" variety; Acts 18:3). This was a practical skill that had usefulness throughout the Roman Empire wherever there were travelers and soldiers far from home, that is to say wherever Saul happened to be. Certainly he didn't let his upbringing,

The Babylonian Talmud (Sanhedrin 11a) relates an instance when Rabbi Gamaliel the Elder, teacher of Saul of Tarsus, dictated three short letters (epistles?) concerning fine points of Torah while seated on the broad processional staircase leading to the southern, Hulda Gate entrance of the Temple Mount. The letters were addressed to "our brethren in Upper and Lower Galilee," to "our brethren of the Upper South and of the Lower South," and to "our brethren of the exile of Babylon, the exile of Media, and the other exiles of Israel." It is tempting to place Saul of Tarsus on these stairs as well (the worn ones are original) as he sat in Gamaliel's "seminary classroom." After Gamaliel died, the sages remembered the esteemed rabbi for his saintliness: "When Rabban Gamaliel the Elder died, the glory of Torah ceased and purity and abstinence perished" (Mishnah, Sotah 9.15).

Saul's Early Years. *Saul's early journeys carried him across the biblical landscape, from the doorway of Mesopotamia to the edge of Egypt, from Jerusalem into the wilderness then back to the Promised Land. Every place he went was full of historic associations, of stories, teachings and traditions that entered his mind and soul and forged his Jewish identity. Jerusalem was the center, but in the end the periphery became the core as Saul set his sights on bringing the Gospel to the Gentiles.*

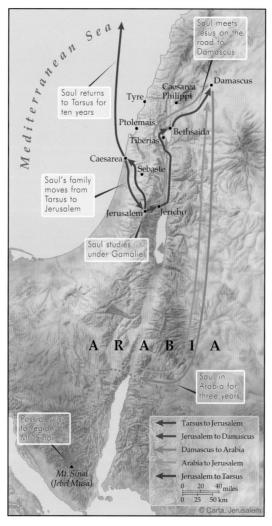

a promising career as a respected Jerusalem-based Pharisee (cf. Acts 26:5). Perhaps someday he could even become a member of the Sanhedrin. He decided to build his reputation by publicly opposing the new and fast-growing group of Jews (centered in Jerusalem and led by Peter, James and John) who preached that Jesus of Nazareth, *crucified*, had not only risen from the dead but was the long-awaited Messiah whom God had sent "to bless you by turning every one of you from your wicked ways" (Acts 3:26; cf. Acts 2:14-36, 3:11–26). Their message was a clear affront to Saul, who had been trained in all righteousness by the best teacher of righteousness of his day. For Saul, the catalyst was the work and words of Stephen, a leader in the Jesus movement and apparently a member of Jerusalem's Synagogue of the Freedmen, who took the case for Jesus to his congregation. Among the members of the synagogue were men from Cilicia (perhaps some of Saul's family) who, with Saul, took offense at the new message (Acts 6:5–15). Stephen was stoned for his testimony (he was the first martyr of the early church); Saul witnessed and gave full assent to the act (Acts 7:54–8:1), then led the charge against the believers in Jerusalem:

> [He] began ravaging the church [and], entering house after house and dragging off men and women, he would put them into prison.
>
> (Acts 8:3; cf. Acts 22:4, 26:9–11)

The community scattered; Saul followed in quick pursuit. Armed with letters of extradition signed by the high priest against any believers in Jesus whom he might find in Damascus, Saul journeyed north (Acts 9:1–2). His route necessarily passed through Jesus-territory (eastern Galilee), then took him up onto the flats of Gaulanitis (the Golan), through or near the vicinity of the district of Caesarea Philippi where Jesus had first announced the coming phenomenon of the church (Mt 16:13–20). As Saul was approaching Damascus he swung by Mount Hermon, the mount of Jesus' Transfiguration, a place of Word and Light (cf. Mt 17:1–8). Somewhere in the vicinity—although the significance of place surely evaded him—Saul met the resurrected Jesus as

privileged in terms of Roman citizenry and top-notch rabbinic education, get in the way of the fair and honored practice of earning one's own living. And even when everyone else respected him as chief of the apostles, Paul remained dependent on the work of his own hands (Acts 18:3, 20:34–35; 1 Cor 4:12; 1 Thess 2:9; cf. Acts 28:30).

Having finished his formal education at the feet of Gamaliel, Saul of Tarsus looked forward to

This Israeli army post on Mount Bental (now decommissioned), built into the shell of an extinct volcano, is one of several that command the flats of the Golan Heights (Gaulanitis). Mount Hermon rises to the north. The "road to Damascus" lies on the plain below (a specific track cannot be determined). Throughout recorded history the Golan has been a field of parry and thrust, advance and retreat: Syria (Aram-Damascus) v. Israel, or Syria v. the states and peoples of southern Transjordan. The overriding issues are strategic: open and exposed, here boundaries easily shift and new realities take hold. When Saul of Tarsus encountered God somewhere on this expanse, his own sense of territory, space, ownership and loyalty were altered dramatically.

PAUL'S FIRST MISSIONARY JOURNEY: AD 48

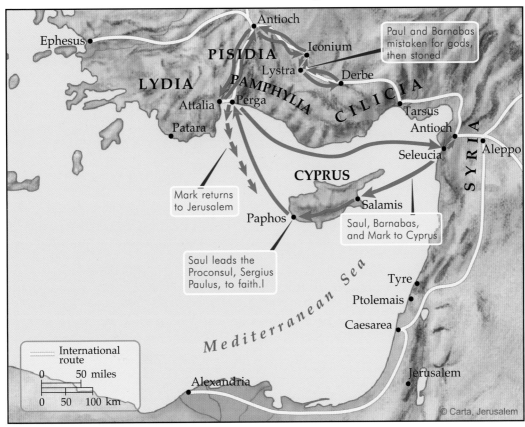

PAUL'S SECOND MISSIONARY JOURNEY: AD 50–52

The wastelands that cradle the land of Israel on the east and south have been a place of divine revelation from the beginning of time. In the biblical story God met Moses face-to-face deep in the Sinai, first at the burning bush, then at Horeb, the Mountain of God. Led by God, armed with Torah and wrapped in the command of destiny, Israel entered their promised land from the deserts of the east, a theophany melded to the human soul:

> The LORD came from Sinai,
>   and dawned on them from Seir.
> He shone forth from Mount Paran.... *(Deut 33:2)*

The "Arabia" of the Roman Empire encompassed this same sweep of awe-filled geography, and somewhere in its full emptiness the three-year wilderness wandering of Saul of Tarsus brought the converted rabbi face-to-face with "the bare immensities of God" (to borrow a poetic line from Amy Blank, "Moses Speaks").

light and a voice of clear command (Acts 9:3–6). On the road to oppose "the Way" (Acts 9:2), Saul fell in stride behind his new Rabbi. He was led, blind, to the home of a man called Judas who lived on Straight Street in Damascus where, after three days of blindness and fasting, a disciple named Ananias prayed for him to regain his sight. The transformation was instant: Saul immediately recognized Jesus as the Son of God, was baptized and began to declare such in the synagogues of the city (Acts 9:7–22; cf. Acts 22:16). His Damascus-road experience was so powerful that Saul mentioned it at least twice in his own defense later in life (Acts 22:1–16, 26:9–20).

Saul's boldness completely turned the tables and now it was he, traitor to the cause, who was the object of persecution and threat. He escaped Damascus by being let down over the wall in a basket at night (Acts 9:23–25)—his opponents had enlisted the help of the governor of Damascus in their efforts (2 Cor 11:32–33)—then fled into Arabia for three years (Gal 1:17–18). In the second century A.D. the Roman province of Arabia encompassed both Nabatean Transjordan and central and southern Sinai. Paul's use of "Arabia" in Galatians 1:17 is probably generic enough to include the same, and it is tempting to see him retracing the steps of both Elijah and Moses to Mount Sinai in order to sort out the ramifications

of his new faith in Jesus face-to-face, as it were, with God himself (cf. Ex 19:1–25; 1 Kgs 19:1–18; Gal 4:25).

Eventually Saul returned to Damascus (Gal 1:15–17; some would place his flight from the city via the basket here), then made his way back to Jerusalem as he of course had to do. There he found himself the subject of rumors and innuendos—all understandable given his career the last time he was in town (Acts 9:26). It was sometime in the middle 30's A.D.; Saul was about 30 years old (cf. Lk 3:23) and ready to embark publicly on a new kind of ministry—for Jesus, rather than against him. Peter, with Barnabas, took the lead in welcoming Saul into the community of believers in Jerusalem; it took a personality as strong as Peter to convince the fledgling Christian community that Saul was now one of them (Acts 9:27–28; Gal 1:18–19). Saul's old comrades—the Hellenistic (Greek-speaking) Jews of Jerusalem and likely most of his earlier supporters in the Sanhedrin—were less forgiving and so Peter and the others hustled him off to Caesarea (it would become a familiar port-of-call), then back home via the string of ports along the northern Levantine (Syrian) shore to Tarsus (Acts 9:29–30; Gal 1:21).

There followed ten quiet years in the historical record, largely silent but certainly not unproductive. We can easily assume that Saul was quite active for the sake of the Gospel throughout Cilicia during this time, perfecting his skills in teaching, preaching and persuading both Jews and Gentiles to follow Jesus Christ the risen Lord. His efforts were not without persecution (cf. 2 Cor 11:24–25), and perhaps the emotional and spiritual torment that lay behind his admission of inner-conflict in Romans 7:14–25 (cf. Gal 5:17–18) found free-rein in his soul during these early years. Throughout, the leaders of the church in Jerusalem heard of Saul's work and were pleased (Gal 1:22–24).

The first city to see large numbers of Gentiles come to faith in Jesus as the Messiah was Antioch

Damascus in the Time of Saul. *Lying on a pleasant plain east of Mt. Hermon, watered by the Amana and Parphar rivers and commanding the main north-south trade route of the southern Levant, Damascus enjoys the reputation as the oldest continuously inhabited city on earth. During the time of the Old Testament Damascus was home to a local Aramean city-state that constantly absorbed the cultural and military blows of larger powers to the north and south (the Hittites, Egyptians, Assyrians, Babylonians, and Persians). Under the Seleucids of the Hellenistic period the city was completely replanned and laid out as a rectangle bisected by two parallel streets. The longest of these streets, a colonnaded "cardo" fronted by the city's theater and palace, was "the street called Straight" (Acts 9:11).*

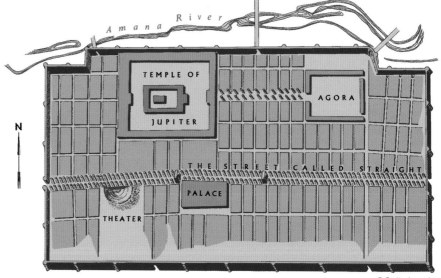

in Syria, the third largest city in the Roman Empire and one well positioned on the trade routes of the eastern Mediterranean. The process was one of cross-fertilization: Jewish believers who had fled Jerusalem scattered to Phoenicia, Cyprus and Antioch where they spoke to Jews, while others (Hellenistic Jewish believers?) from Cyprus and Cyrene came to Antioch and brought the message about Jesus to the Gentiles. The church in Jerusalem sent Barnabas up to Antioch in order to assess the situation (Acts 11:19–24). As a Levite of Cypriot birth (cf. Acts 4:36–37), Barnabas would have had the proper sensitivities to understand the challenges that a large influx of Gentiles would bring to a phenomenon that so far had been primarily Jewish. Barnabas in turn brought Saul down from Tarsus, who readily spent a full year in Antioch bearing fruitful ministry (the soil of Antioch was likely fertile in part because of spill-over of Saul's work in neighboring Cilicia). It was here that the believers were first called "Christians," followers of "Christos," the Messiah (Acts 11:25–26).

The decade of the 40's A.D. was in general a time of poor harvests and economic scarcity across the Roman world (Dio Cassius, *Roman History* lx.11; Suetonius, *Claudius* 18; Tacitus, *Annals* xi.4, xiii.43), and a particularly severe famine struck the region of Judea and Syria around the year A.D. 46. The church in Antioch rode out these hard times due to the overall prosperity of their city and commissioned Barnabas and Saul, with Titus (a believer in Jesus though an uncircumcised Gentile; cf. Gal 2:1, 2:3), to carry relief funds to their poorer brethren down in Jerusalem. Such offerings were gladly received, as Judea's perpetually marginal resource base ensured that the Jerusalem church would never become economically self-sufficient even though its members supported each other generously (Acts 11:27–30; cf. Acts 2:44–45, 4:36–5:1-2, 6:1, 24:17; Rom 15:26–27; 1 Cor 16:1–4). Indeed, the eagerness of the members of the Jerusalem community to share their goods with one another may have been a practical necessity for this very reason.

This was Saul's first visit to Jerusalem in fourteen years (although the chronological note in Gal 2:1 may indicate that it was 14 years since he had first left Jerusalem for Damascus), and he took advantage of his time in the city to argue forcefully with James, Peter and John for full acceptance of the Gentiles—even those who remained uncircumcised—in the community of the church. (It is noteworthy that James, not Peter, appears at the head of the list as the leader of the Jerusalem church, and that at this point in his ministry Saul recognized the need for Jerusalem's support—if not outright approval—of his work.) In the end it was agreed that Saul would continue to concentrate his efforts on bringing the good news of Jesus to the Gentiles (with the blessing of the church in Jerusalem),

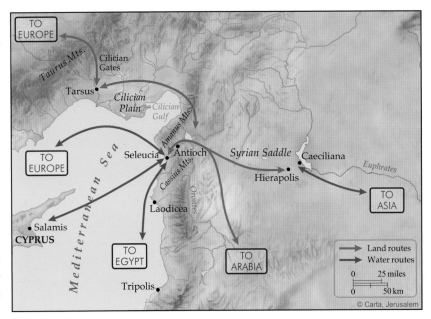

while the Jerusalem leadership would remain focused on spreading the Gospel to the Jews (Gal 2:1–10; cf. Acts 22:21; Rom 1:14, 16:18). It was a formative, though informal, council. With it, the stage was now set for Saul to become the Apostle Paul (Acts 13:9). The curtain rose on a new act in the Gospel story. The scenery had changed: the contained arc of the Fertile Crescent had given way to the vast amphitheater of the Mediterranean Basin.

Barnabas and Paul (now using his Greek name *Paulos* rather than the Greek form of his Hebrew name, *Saulos*; cf. Acts 13:9) returned to Antioch. They were commissioned by the leaders of Antioch's international church to follow the call of the Holy Spirit:

"Set apart for Me Barnabas and Saul for the work to which I have called them." (Acts 13:2)

The Holy Spirit didn't give details; like Abraham, they were just to go (Acts 13:1–3; cf. Gen 12:1, 12:4) and, like the patriarch who had started in Ur, their general direction of travel was to the west, into a land that for them was yet unknown. Paul and his various traveling companions would be constantly on the move, sometimes settling down for a while (Abraham's Beer-sheba would become Paul's Ephesus; his Hebron, Paul's Rome) but then journeying on; approaching new places, forging new relationships; no longer at home anywhere but gradually becoming so everywhere in the new land of his divine call—with an unwavering faith in a new Covenant and a harvest as vast as the stars of the open Mediterranean sky and the grains of sand along its endless shore (cf. Gen 15:5, 22:17).

And if you belong to Christ, then you are Abraham's descendants, heirs according to promise. (Gal 3:29)

Taking a young John Mark, Barnabas's cousin, as their assistant (Acts 13:5; cf. Acts 12:12; Col 4:10), Paul and Barnabas sailed from Seleucia (Antioch's bustling

International Gateways of the Northeastern Mediterranean. *The lands lying along the northeastern shore of the Mediterranean Sea are the most important hinge linking together the continents of the Eastern Hemisphere. Antioch, the third largest city in the Roman Empire, together with its port, Seleucia, lay on the most critical joint of this hinge—a pass between mountain ranges funneling sea traffic inland and land routes toward the sea. The church that arose here in the first century A.D. was necessarily, and by definition, international. Of course "it was in Antioch that the disciples were first called Christians" (Acts 11:26). Tarsus, controlling the southern end of the Cilician Gates, was a funnel-city in its own right. As a new Christian Paul spent ten years spreading the Gospel in this strategic region, a world with a geographical and historical setting as different from the tightness of Jerusalem as one might imagine.*

Paul's First Missionary Journey, c. A.D. 48. *Paul carried the message of the Gospel first into relatively familiar territory, fairly close to home. He started in Cyprus, the land of Barnabas' and John Mark's birth (and where that duo would eventually focus their work), then headed north to the Anatolian mainland. Paul's trek through southern Galatia connected the main cities on its international thoroughfare, a familiar route that also passed through his home city, Tarsus. Having evangelized southern Galatia, the stage was set for greater trips ahead.*

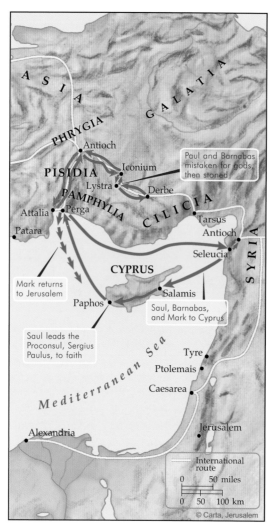

"I have been on frequent journeys, in dangers from rivers, dangers from robbers, dangers from the Gentiles, dangers in the city, dangers in the wilderness, dangers on the sea, dangers among false brethren. I have been in labor and hardship, through many sleepless nights, in hunger and thirst, often without food, in cold and exposure" (2 Cor 11:26–27). *It was anything but easy being the greatest apostle to the Gentiles, but the paths Paul blazed across the Roman world, from the highlands of Anatolia (here) to Rome, lit a fire for the Gospel that has never been extinguished.*

port) to Cyprus. It was a natural starting point for their journey: not only was Cyprus the island bridge between Phoenicia and the Aegean but Barnabas (and probably also John Mark) were Cypriot nationals. Rich in natural resources and historic associations, Cyprus offered a brilliant mosaic of cultures and people groups hailing from across the eastern Mediterranean, including a large, vibrant and, apparently, relatively tolerant Jewish community. Paul and his small team landed at Salamis on Cyprus' eastern shore, then worked their way westward the

length of the island to Paphos, the provincial capital, teaching in synagogues along the way. This became their *modus operandi*: even though Paul's ministry focused on Gentiles, he typically made contacts first in a city's synagogue (he was still a skilled and personally observant rabbi, after all, and continued to love his people to his dying day; cf. Acts 18:18, 20:16, 21:23–26; Rom 1:16, 9:1–5, 10:1–4, 11:1–24). Diaspora synagogues were lively centers of interaction between Jews and interested Gentiles (God-fearers), and so provided natural forums for anyone who wanted to discuss matters related to religious and cultural identity. The island's proconsul, Sergius Paulus, was well-acquainted with his Jewish subjects, and as a result of Paul's preaching and miracle-working he heard about, then believed, in the work and power of Jesus. In the process Cyprus became the first Roman province to be governed by a Christian (Acts 13:4–12); for Paul it couldn't have been a more promising start.

From Paphos Paul and his companions sailed northwest to Perga, a large port city in Pamphylia where for reasons unknown John Mark left them to return to Jerusalem (Acts 13:13). This would prove to be a point of contention between Paul and Barnabas later on (cf. Acts 15:36–39). From there they crossed the rugged Taurus Mountains to Pisidian Antioch, a moderately-sized city in southern Galatia lying a hard two weeks' walk from the coast (Acts 13:13–14). Perhaps the "dangers from rivers" and "dangers from robbers" mentioned in 2 Corinthians 11:26 refers to this part of Paul's travels—or certainly something similar. Arriving in town they naturally headed first to the synagogue where Paul preached a message of Jesus "through whom everyone who believes is freed from all things from which you could not be freed through the *Torah* of Moses" (Acts 13:39). Most of the Jews in attendance were understandably opposed to the message, although Paul's words were generally well received by God-fearing Gentiles (Acts 13:15–49). Facing opposition, Paul and Barnabas fled southeast along the main trade route that connected Galatia with Syria, to Iconium, where his strategy—and the results—were the same (Acts 13:50–14:5).

From Iconium Paul and Barnabas continued to Lystra (on a future journey Paul would meet Timothy there, who was destined to become his most-beloved disciple; Acts 14:6–7; cf. Acts 16:1–2). Upon healing a man who had been born lame, the apostles were promptly hailed as the Greek gods Hermes and Zeus by the priest of the local Zeus temple, their own protests notwithstanding (Acts 14:8–18). Paul's opponents from Pisidian Antioch and Iconium, however, arrived and quickly set things straight, stoning them on the edge of town and driving them farther east to Derbe. From there it was a fairly short walk back to Tarsus and Paul likely would have returned home were it not for the positive response to the Gospel he found in Derbe and the surrounding region (Acts 14:19–21). Encouraged, he decided instead to retrace his steps back through Lystra, Iconium and Pisidian Antioch,

> strengthening the souls of the disciples, encouraging them to continue in the faith and saying, "Through many tribulations we must enter the kingdom of God." (Acts 14:22)

This was full in the face of an opposition that thought it had gotten rid of him the first time (the stones still lay by the side of the road). Tracking back through the Taurus Mountains, Paul and Barnabas sailed from Attalia (the modern resort city Antalya) to Syrian Antioch where they were well received by their sending church (Acts 14:21–28).

The realistic prospect of a Gentile-majority in the young church didn't sit well with most of the leadership in Jerusalem and a delegation arrived in Antioch intent on making the point that Gentiles could become part of the church only if, as Jewish proselytes, they were first circumcised (Acts 15:1; Gal 2:11–21). Clearly the Jerusalem church was thinking in terms of belief in Jesus as a movement *within* Judaism rather than something that could—or should—exist on the outside. The term "Christian" had originated in a Gentile context—in Paul's dear Antioch—and it was high time the folks up there acknowledged their connection to Jerusalem. It is likely that these "Judaizers" (as they are often called in the secondary literature) made follow-up visits to the churches that Paul and Barnabas had planted in Galatia, anxious to correct any misinformation that might have been spread in the Apostle's zeal to bring the message of Jesus to both Jew and Greek (cf. Gal 1:6–9, 3:1, 4:12–5:15, 6:12–13). A credible case can be made that Paul wrote his letter to the Galatians—a primer on justification by faith—as his first epistle, quickly, from Antioch, in response to these in-house challenges to his work. Paul even went toe-to-toe with Peter on the issue (Gal 2:11–14).

The matter was serious enough to prompt a formal discussion in Jerusalem. To what extent should Gentiles conform to Jewish religious practices in order to be considered part of the church? Put in more far-reaching terms, to what extent did the movement of believers in Jesus see themselves as Jewish, or as something else? And who called the shots? Jerusalem? Paul and Barnabas of course attended this Jerusalem Council, in A.D. 49 or 50, and argued convincingly for full Gentile inclusion, without circumcision, into the otherwise predominantly Jewish church. At the same time they willingly conceded that no one should practice idolatry or immorality, or participate in feasts in pagan temples (Acts 15:2–21). Such actions, Paul concurred, were enough to separate believers in Jesus from their Roman neighbors, but he hoped that they would also be sufficient to continue to mark Jewish believers

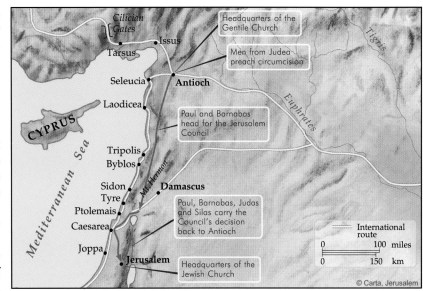

as being good Jews. He miscalculated the response. While the decision of the Jerusalem Council paved the way for a truly universal church, it also cast the die for an eventual split between church and synagogue. The divergence was slow but inexorable; the actions of Paul and the Jerusalem leadership were a mere beginning of the process.

Paul and Barnabas, together with Judas Barsabbas and Silas, two leaders of the Jerusalem church, carried a formal letter from the council back to Antioch (Acts 15:22–35). Yet the extent to which Paul actively supported these actions *as a decision of the council* is a matter of debate. Operating in the Diaspora, he apparently never really recognized the need for the council in the first place as he failed to appeal to its decision in any of his letters that discussed the specific issues it addressed (cf. Rom 2:25–29, 3:29–30, 14:1–23; 1 Cor 8:1–13 and Galatians if it were written subsequent to the council's decision). Paul was well aware that some in the Jerusalem church considered him a bit of a loose cannon. Never mind: "We who are strong ought to bear the weaknesses of those without strength" (Rom 15:1), whomever they be! His mission lay out in the real world, where the call of the Gospel had to advance hand-in-hand with practicality (but not expediency; cf. Rom 6:1–7; 1 Cor 9:19–23; 2 Cor 3:17; Gal 3:28).

After a short stay in Antioch, likely still in A.D. 50, Paul asked Barnabas to accompany him on a return trip to the churches they had established in Galatia. Barnabas wanted to bring his cousin John Mark along; Paul point-blank refused, remembering too clearly John Mark's bail-out back in Perga (Acts 15:36–38; cf. Acts 13:13). After a sharp disagreement (Paul never lacked for saying exactly what was on his mind), Barnabas and John Mark returned to Cyprus to focus on spreading the Gospel in their homeland. Paul tapped Silas instead, and the two set

The Jerusalem Council, A.D. 49 or 50. Within two decades of its birth the church began to polarize between Jewish and Gentile factions, with bases of operation at opposite ends of the Levant. The Jerusalem Council aimed at forging a working agreement between the two on the issue "who is a Christian." Paul and Barnabas attended; their route "through both Phoenicia and Samaria" (Acts 15:3) could have taken them either by land or by sea. If by land, their likely route would have been through the great Beq'a Valley separating the Lebanon and Anti-Lebanon mountain ranges, a walk of a couple of weeks. The sea journey would take less than half the time (against the current but with the winds); the ship would have put in each night at one or another of the Syrian or Phoenician harbors strung along the coast.

241

Sweeping through the highlands of Phrygia and Galatia, Paul, Silas and Timothy first tried to push north, into Bithynia, but were prevented from continuing "by the Spirit of Jesus" (Acts 16:6). Eventually churches were established in Bithynia and neighboring Pontus (cf. 1 Pet 1:1), but Paul's footsteps had already taken him elsewhere. The hills here, between modern Ismit and Iznik, lively Turkish cities east of the Marmara Sea, are typical of the landscape that Paul traversed as he headed west, through Mysia and toward the doorway of Europe.

off overland to Galatia (Acts 15:39–41). The result: two teams in the field rather than one, a net gain for the early church. Silas (a short-form of the Latin name *Sylvanius*) was a leader in the Jerusalem church (Acts 15:22, 15:32) but also a Roman citizen (Acts 16:37). Like Paul, he was culturally bilingual and so an excellent fit for the task at hand.

Paul and Silas crossed Cilicia to Tarsus, threaded their way through the Cilician Gates and leveled out on the edge of the high interior plateau behind the Taurus Mountains at Derbe. Passing through Lystra where Paul had been stoned, he and Silas picked up Timothy, a young disciple with mixed parentage (his mother was a Jewish believer in Jesus; his father Greek) on the way. Timothy represented the nuances and challenges of the geographical and spiritual world into which Paul was journeying, a reality

that the nascent church was learning how to face. Assimilate? Confront? When in Rome do as the Romans? And in Jerusalem…? Timothy came along, but only after Paul circumcised him "because of the Jews who were in those parts" (Acts 16:1–3). Why this was necessary after Paul had just insisted that Gentile believers did not need to be circumcised to join the church—rebuking Peter for kowtowing to the religious scruples of the Jerusalem leadership in the meantime (Gal 2:11–14)—must have been clear in Paul's mind; it has not always been so to others. Paul had made his point back in Jerusalem; as a soldier in the trenches (2 Tim 4:7; cf. 1 Tim 1:18–19, 6:12) he reserved the right to fight proactively as front-line situations arose.

The three journeyed on, through Galatia to Pisidian Antioch then north into the bracing Phrygian highlands. Skirting Bithynia, they descended to the west through the fresh, wooded hills of Mysia south of the Marmara Sea. Although these regions were well populated and could have offered a lifetime of worthy and profitable service, the Spirit of Jesus pulled Paul, Silas and Timothy on to Troas, a lively port on the Aegean just south of the Hellespont (Acts 16:4–8). There they picked up Luke "the beloved physician" (Col 4:14), who would travel with Paul intermittently and chronicle not only their journeys together but the earliest history of the church (the Book of Acts). For those parts of the journey on which he accompanied Paul, Luke was able to enrich the narrative detail of Acts through his keen observations of time, people and place.

At Troas, just south of the spot that Alexander the Great (of Macedon) had entered Asia to spread the glories of Hellenism (and himself) across the East, Paul had a vision compelling him to travel to Macedonia and preach the Gospel on European soil (Acts 16:9–10). Gladly heeding his "Macedonian call," Paul and his companions sailed across the northern Aegean, skirting the small but rugged island of Samothrace (its majestic peak, at 5,328 feet, is the highest point in the Aegean), to Neapolis, Macedonia's easternmost port. Thirteen miles inland, over a low rise, lay the grand plain of Philippi, dominated by the city of the same name, the first European objective of the Apostle and his three protégés. Philippi had been founded as a Greek city

Paul's Second Missionary Journey, A.D. 50–52.
Paul's second journey broke new ground for the growing church. Not only did he cross the great geographical divide from Asia to Europe but he brought the Gospel to Gentiles of ill repute—Corinthians—many of whom weren't even good pagans let alone likely candidates for a life wrapped in Torah. "But God has chosen the foolish things of the world to shame the wise, and the weak things of the world to shame the strong" (1 Cor 1:27). It took some doing, but by the grace of God even the Corinthian church came around.

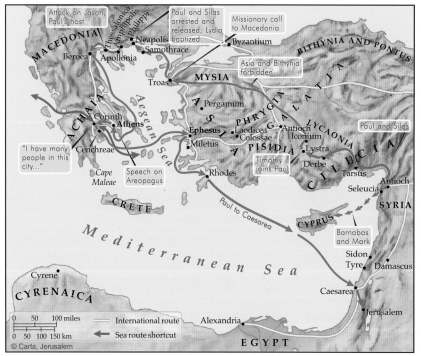

by Alexander's father Philip of Macedon in 360 B.C. (Diodoros Siculus, *History* xvi.8); the world view of Moses that the golden-haired conqueror had tried to overwhelm with the seductive beauties of Hellenism was about to invade his father's namesake city.

The Jewish community in Philippi was quite small and there was no proper synagogue in town, so on the Sabbath Paul went to the place where Jews tended to meet in good weather, alongside a river (probably the Gangites) outside the city gate. Here he met a group of women that included Lydia of Thyatira, an agent for distributing expensive purple cloth in the region (Thyatira, in western Asia Minor, was a prominent center of dyting). Lydia became the first convert in Europe and was baptized along with her household (Acts 16:13–15). This was the foothold that Paul needed, and his work gained strength.

As usual, opposition was close at hand but this time trouble came from an unexpected source. A local holy woman, a slave girl with a "spirit of divination" (Gk. *pythona*, one who gave oracles by the power of Apollo), pestered Paul with incessant prattle. He drove her chattering spirit out, much to the chagrin of her owner who made a tidy profit on its oracles (Acts 16:16–20). Paul had tampered with private property rights in a Roman colony (cf. Acts 16:12), but the formal charges against him rang of age-old anti-Semitism:

> As Jews, these men are throwing our [fine] city into confusion, proclaiming customs that it is not lawful for us, [good] Romans, to accept or observe.
>
> (Acts 16:21)

And Paul and Silas were beaten and thrown into prison. That night, an earthquake jarred open the doors; the jailer, shocked, believed in the power and grace of Jesus, and he and his household were baptized. The next morning Paul and Silas insisted on their rights as Roman citizens (they spoke out officially, certainly in Latin) and were released with all proper attention and protocol. Paul, Silas and Timothy journeyed on, leaving a new local church and, apparently, Luke, behind (Acts 16:22–40; 1 Thess 2:2). The church in Philippi would become one of Paul's favorites, and supported him generously along his way (cf. Phil 1:3–11, 4:15–16).

The trio traveled the *Via Egnatia* (the great Roman military road connecting Illyricum with Thrace) through Amphipolis and Apollonia to Thessalonica, the capital of Macedonia. Thessalonica was a thriving city, a large-ship port on the largest bay of the Balkans, with a majestic view of Mount Olympus, the "throne" of Zeus, across the bay to the southwest. Here, surrounded by a cosmopolitan flair that was much to Paul's liking (as were Athens, Corinth and Ephesus), the apostles quickly established another church, this one primarily among the God-fearers in town. "God-fearers"—Gentiles with sensitivities for things Jewish—generally were a buffer between Romans and Diaspora Jews; when they threw their loyalty to Jesus in any particular place, the local Jews sometimes felt a bit vulnerable before the foreignness of Rome. This time the Jews staged a mass demonstration against Paul (Acts 17:1–6), accusing him of treason against the Emperor (and hopefully securing their own place in the process):

Ten miles south of the Hellespont and the fabled city of Troy, the Mysian port of Troas received the shipping lanes binding Asia to Macedonia in the first century A.D. Paul found an open door for the Gospel here but didn't stay long, preferring to cross into Europe instead (2 Cor 2:12–13). Today the site is called Eskistanbul (Old Stambul), a small town and pier nestled in expansive though largely overgrown ruins of the ancient site. Persistent visitors can wander for hours and find bits and pieces of the past scattered here and there amidst the sand and grassy fields along the shore. Here pilings from the Roman harbor splash from the sea, beckoning a sail west. It was from here that Paul heeded his Macedonian call.

Alexander the Great (of Macedon) crossed the Dardanelles into Asia at the Hellespont; the Apostle Paul, sailing from Troas, reversed the favor. Shrouded in the myths of time, Agamemnon, Achilles and a host of other Greek heroes fought to restore the honor of Helen at Troy, not far away. The Dardanelles' narrowest sea connection between Asia and Europe is here, at Çanakkale, the region's popular tourist center. Today, Çanakkale is most crowded on March 18, Turkish Victory Day, and April 25, Anzac Day, commemorating the bloody Gallipoli campaign of the First World War. In an area saturated with historical associations of past, present and future, Paul carried the Gospel of peace to a world that has never seemed to tire of war.

Judaism, and then Christianity, spread into the greater Roman world where the culture was raw and rich, the gods diverse, the buildings ornate and the people dressed and spoke funny. But not all was unfamiliar. Much of the northeastern Mediterranean, from Judea to Achaia, shared a common landscape: the sea giving way to broad level plains backed by a rise of limestone hills. And the climate, at least at the lower elevations, is generally uniform: hot, dry summers; cool, wet winters. Hillsides and soil suitable for grapevines and olive and fig trees abound, with grazing land on the arid slopes above. The view here, in the northeastern Peloponnesus at Mycenae, is typical of the whole. In spite of the difficulties of travel, Paul was comfortable getting around in the Mediterranean basin. At least the land itself had a familiar look many places he went.

They act contrary to the decrees of Caesar, saying that there is another king, Jesus. (Acts 17:7)

The circumstances were desperate and remind the reader of the mob at Jesus' crucifixion (cf. Jn 19:1–15). The Roman magistrates defused the problem by extracting a pledge from Jason, Paul's host in the city; the money paid evidently guaranteed that the offending party would leave town and not return (Acts 17:8–9). Paul, Silas and Timothy moved on to neighboring Berea, mindful of the bind into which they had gotten the new church and for which they were largely responsible. In his first letter to the Thessalonian believers, probably written at Corinth later in his journey, Paul defended his work there ("you yourselves know that our coming to you was not in vain..."; 1 Thess 2:1–16), then bared his desire to return:

But we, brethren, having been taken away from you for a short while—in person, not in spirit—were all the more eager with great desire to see your face [again]. For we wanted to come to you—I, Paul, more than once—yet Satan hindered us.

(1 Thess 2:17–18)

And in a sincere pledge of his favor: "You are our glory and joy" (1 Thess 2:20).

Their reception at Berea, on the western edge of the swampy Thessaly plain, was more favorable than in Thessalonica, and many Jews and Gentiles there accepted Paul's teachings. Here were eager students, "examining the Scriptures daily to see whether these things were so" (Acts 17:11). Eventu-

ally the ones who had driven Paul out of Thessalonica heard of his success in Berea and forced him to move on again, this time completely out of their territory (Acts 17:10–14). Paul left Silas and Timothy behind and headed for the Aegean coast where he caught a ship to Athens. He immediately sent for his companions—they likely had remained in Berea either to try to smooth things over or to monitor the situation and let Paul know when it might be safe for him to return. From Athens Paul sent Timothy back to Thessalonica (1 Thess 3:1–3) and Silas to somewhere in Macedonia—probably Philippi (Acts 18:5). All this going back and forth shows the ease of travel in the mid-first century A.D. Roman world, but also hints at the behind-the-scenes logistical hustle and bustle, from one unfamiliar city to another, of trying to make the whole thing work. Everyone needed healthy doses of the Spirit, improvisation and sweat.

Paul's stay in Athens was relatively brief (only a few days?) and he failed to make significant inroads among its sophisticated population. Perhaps he planted a church there, although the New Testament fails to mention one. Paul preached in the synagogue to Jews and God-fearers and in the marketplace (*agora*) to whatever Greeks happened to stop and listen. In between he wandered around looking at the sights, like any first-time visitor to a city of awe (Acts 17:16–17, 17:23). Though no longer the political capital of Achaia, Athens nevertheless was aesthetically beautiful and retained its reputation for culture and learning that it had forged five centuries before, during the Golden Age of classical Greece. Writing later, Luke caught the essence of the place:

Now all the Athenians and the strangers visiting there used to spend their time in nothing other than telling or hearing something new. (Acts 17:21)

Ivory tower, meet the local trendy bar.

Athens boasted a number of philosophical schools and Paul, filled with both wonder and indignation, warmed to the task of challenging both the reason-loving Stoics and the pleasure-seeking Epicureans. (They had called him an "idle babbler," after all, literally a "seed-picker," *spermologos*, after birds that flitter and jerk from furrow to furrow across a freshly sown field.) The setting was the Areopagus (the "hill of Ares" or "Mars Hill"), a large rise of limestone northwest of the acropolis where the city's Council of the Areopagus often met to hear and decide civic issues. There, before the council, Paul defended the Gospel by referencing an Athenian altar he had seen that was dedicated "to an unknown god." It was a convenient springboard to speak of the God of the Jews and the resurrected Jesus. Paul gained a mixed reaction: some sneered (as usual, because he mentioned Jesus' resurrection) while others asked for another hearing (Acts 17:18–34).

PAUL'S THIRD MISSIONARY JOURNEY: AD 53–57

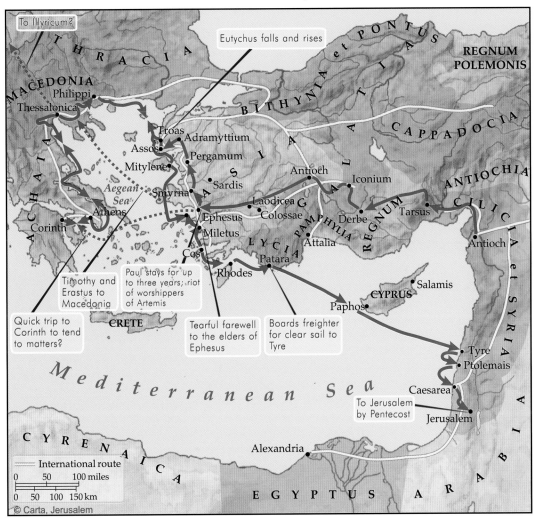

PAUL'S JOURNEY TO ROME: AD 60–61

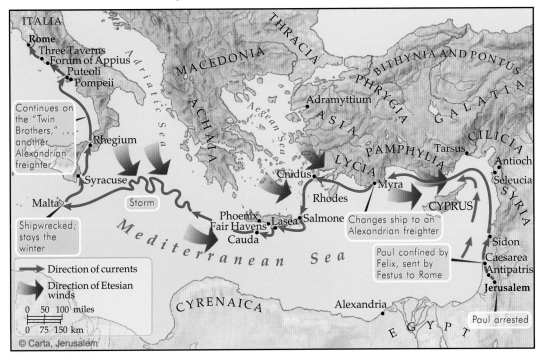

And just as in early times the Strait of Sicily was not easy to navigate, so the high seas, and particularly the sea beyond Maleae [the southeastern point of the Peloponnesus] also were not, on account of the contrary winds. Hence the proverb, "But when you double Maleae, forget your home." At any rate, it was a welcome alternative for the merchants both from Italy and from Asia to avoid the voyage to Maleae and land their cargoes [at Corinth]. And also the duty on what by land was exported from the Peloponnesus and what was imported to it fell to those who held the [city's] keys. (Strabo, Geography viii.6.20)

All of this made Corinth a bustling boomtown in the first century A.D., a place of unbounded energy and bawdy gusto with a population of about half a million people, many of whom were rough, opportunistic and self-made men—or, a place exactly opposite erudite Athens. Athens read poetry; Corinth heave-hoed—and caroused. Paul was fascinated and stayed eighteen months (Acts 18:1, 18:11).

He put in initially with Aquila and Priscilla, Jewish believers who had themselves just arrived in Corinth having fallen victim to the Emperor Claudius' expulsion of the Jews from Rome (likely in A.D. 49 or 50; Seutonius, Claudius 25.4. No mention is made as to how Rome got a church in the first place.) For Paul it was a fortuitous arrangement: not only did they share the same tent-making trade, but Aquila and Priscilla were no doubt full of current information about opportunities to spread the Gospel in Rome (this was Paul's ultimate goal). So he settled in, part-time tent-making, part-time "reasoning in the synagogue every Sabbath" (Acts 18:1–4). Nearby, at Isthmia (on the portage route that crossed the isthmus), the Isthmian Games were held every other spring, including in the spring of A.D. 51, when Paul was in town. These were the second most important of the pan-Hellenic festivals, and provided a ready market for travelers who needed temporary (tent)

"Now while Paul was waiting for [Silas and Timothy] in Athens, his spirit was being provoked within him as he was observing the city full of idols" (Acts 17:16). The Temple in Jerusalem contained no images; those in Athens were very nearly nothing but. While in Athens Paul certainly climbed the Acropolis and wandered among its monuments and shrines. Among the most striking is the Erechtheion, built according to the Ionic order in the late 5th century B.C. in honor of the mythic god-king Erechtheus. The roof of the porch projecting from the southern side is supported by six Caryatids, columns in the shape of full female figures. Impressed by the grandeur but not the world-view it represented, Paul called the whole thing "idols," then told the Athenians of "the LORD of heaven and earth [who] does not dwell in temples made with hands" (Acts 17:24).

In the end Paul didn't stay in Athens long. Perhaps he sensed that too much time would have to be spent untangling the webs of words churned out by the academy and he preferred the plain-spoken folk of a thoroughfare city like Corinth instead. And so Paul traveled west, across the narrow isthmus joining the Achaean mainland to the Peloponnesus, the tumbled, mulberry leaf-shaped peninsula dangling into the Mediterranean. The highly irregular coastline of Achaia brought the sea close to the province's dissected interior, creating a land wholly oriented toward the Mediterranean. Because the sea journey around the Peloponnesus was lengthy and dangerous, many ship captains preferred instead to download their cargo and drag it across the three-mile isthmus beneath Corinth. That city, then, became perhaps the greatest seaport of the east-central Mediterranean, as the geographer Strabo explained:

Corinth is called "wealthy" because of its commerce, since it is situated on the Isthmus and is master of two harbors, of which the one leads straight to Asia and the other to Italy, and it makes easy the exchange of merchandise from both countries that are so far distant from each other.

The Areopagus is a large hill of rough limestone, mostly bare today, rising just west of—and overshadowed by—the city's famed Acropolis. The name indicates "the hill of Ares [Mars]," the god of War, but also was given to the ruling civic council that once held session on its summit. Paul's defense of "the unknown God" took place "in the midst of the Areopagus" (Acts 17:22), likely here, on Mars Hill, but perhaps in council chambers elsewhere. Today it's a scramble to the top: the sixteen badly worn steps leading to the summit belay a slippery climb and descent.

housing, as well as athletic imagery for the apostle's spiritual exhortations (e.g. "run in such a way that you may win"; 1 Cor 9:24–27).

When Silas and Timothy joined Paul in Corinth (cf. 2 Cor 1:19; 1 Thess 3:6), he began to devote more of his time to speaking publicly about Jesus. This drew the customary response, and to signal his intent to focus on bringing the Gospel to the Gentiles Paul began to use the house of Titius Justus, a proselyte who lived next to the synagogue, as a meeting place instead of the synagogue. In a timely vision God himself assured Paul of success in Corinth:

> ...do not be silent, for I am with you...and have many people in this city.　　(Acts 18:5–11)

Crispus, a leader of the synagogue, became a believer in Jesus, as did others with special skills for ministry, including those whom Paul mentioned by name in his letters to the Corinthians (e.g. 1 Cor 1:11–15, 16:15–18). Many, however, came from the lower classes of society, folks who were not very wise, mighty or noble, or who had been out-and-out scoundrels (1 Cor 1:26, 6:9–11). The church in Corinth grew mightily, but had special needs (bad habits were hard to break) and Paul eventually wrote as many as four letters to them urging unity and clean living (cf. 1 Cor 5:9; 2 Cor 7:8):

> Do you not know that you are a temple of God and that the Spirit of God dwells in you?　　(1 Cor 3:16)

Having laid the foundation for the Corinthian church and each "temple" within (1 Cor 3:10), and being absolutely convinced that the power of the Gospel could change lives even there (1 Cor 1:18, 2:4–5; 2 Cor 4:7–11), Paul eventually moved on. Aquila, Priscilla (Acts 18:18) and certainly Timothy joined him on his homeward journey; Silas apparently stayed behind (in any case his name drops from the written sources from this point in Paul's travels). Paul caught a ship at Cenchrea, a small port on the Aegean side of the isthmus that sported a striking bronze statue of Poseidon thrust toward the sea. Before sailing he "had his hair cut, for he was keeping a vow" (Acts 18:18). This act was certainly to mark the end of a vow that was consistent with *Torah* provisions for a Nazarite (although the particulars are unstated; Num 6:13, 6:19–20; cf. Acts 21:23–26), rather than a concession to the pagan practice of cutting one's hair to ensure safe sea voyage as some have maintained (cf. Juvenal, *Satires* xii.81). There is no other mention of Paul passing through Cenchrea, yet a church arose in the city led by Phoebe, a deaconess(!) (Rom 16:1–2). Paul's ship put into the port of Ephesus and he stayed there just long enough to be missed. Leaving Aquila and Priscilla behind and promising to return "if God wills" (He certainly did), Paul sailed on (Acts 18:19–21).

Given the rudimentary nature of ancient navigation, the best time of the year for open-water sailing

on the Mediterranean was from late May to early September, when the prevailing Etesian winds blew most favorably from the northwest. The fall and spring winds were risky; winter was downright dangerous. A ship heading into the Mediterranean from Judea typically hopscotched the Phoenician and Syrian coastline north, then ran west above Cyprus under the winds sweeping off Asia Minor, remaining within site of land all the while. The return voyage, in the summertime, was direct: a run across the open sea from Greece to Caesarea would take from three to five days, full-sail. By this means Paul soon reached Caesarea, Judea's main (and growing) Mediterranean port. Welcomed ashore by an architectural footprint that looked as though it could have been stamped anywhere around the Mediterranean (the Roman soul of its founding father, Herod the Great, had seen to that), Paul cleared customs and then went up to Jerusalem. After reporting to the leaders of the church there, he returned to Antioch sometime in late A.D. 52, his second missionary journey completed (Acts 18:22).

The church in Antioch was no doubt pleased with what they heard, and Paul could scarcely wait to head out again. The Roman world was large; many centers of Christianity had yet to be founded, and established ones needed strengthening. Paul's focus would continue to be on the Empire's imperial routes and its major cities where strategically-placed churches could grow and eventually carry the Gospel into the surrounding countryside. And so he set off again, sometime in A.D. 53, overland through Galatia and Phrygia, likely retracing earlier steps and renewing old and dear acquaintances in Derbe, Lystra, Iconium and Pisidian Antioch (Acts 18:23). If Timothy had not stayed behind in Ephesus, he certainly accompanied Paul now (Lystra, his home, remained a magnet). From Phrygia Paul made his way "through the upper country" toward Ephesus (Acts 19:1). His route probably dropped off the Anatolian plateau into the broad Maeander river valley,

The Temple of Apollo in Corinth, built in the Doric order like Athens' Parthenon, sat on a cliffy rise at the center of the city's crowded agora. Constructed in the 6th century B.C., the temple already reflected hoary antiquity when Paul first visited the site. Today's ruins, though sparse, still carry the grandeur and good looks for which its dedicated deity, Apollo (the god of medicine, music, reason, light and truth), was known. The city's mighty acropolis, the Acrocorinth, rises behind. On its height once stood a temple of Aphrodite, the lovely seductress whose servants helped foster Corinth's reputation for immorality. Church members were not immune, and Paul had his hands full in the place (1 Cor 6:9–20; 2 Cor 12:20–21).

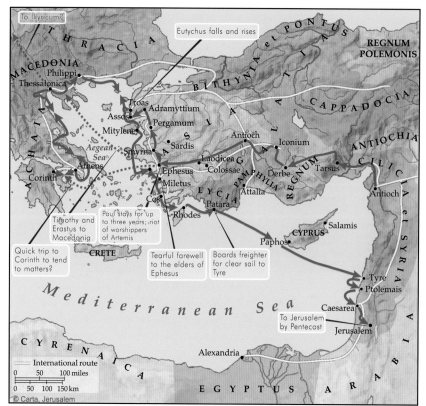

To Illyricum?

Eutychus falls and rises

REGNUM
POLEMONIS

THRACIA
MACEDONIA
Philippi
Thessalonica
Troas Adramyttium
Assos Pergamum
Mitylene
Aegean Sea Smyrna Sardis
Athens Ephesus Laodicea Antioch Iconium
Corinth Miletus Colossae
Derbe Tarsus
Cos Attalia Antioch
Patara
Rhodes
CYPRUS Salamis
Paphos
Tyre
Ptolemais
Caesarea
CRETE
Jerusalem

Timothy and Erastus to Macedonia

Paul stays for up to three years; riot of worshippers of Artemis

Quick trip to Corinth to tend to matters?

Tearful farewell to the elders of Ephesus

Boards freighter for clear sail to Tyre

To Jerusalem by Pentecost

Mediterranean Sea

CYRENAICA
Alexandria
EGYPTUS ARABIA

International route
0 50 100 miles
0 50 100 150 km
© Carta, Jerusalem

Therefore be imitators of God, as beloved children, and walk in love, just as Christ also loved you and gave himself up for us, an offering and a sacrifice to God as a fragrant aroma. (Eph 5:1–2)

One gets the feeling that Paul gained great satisfaction from his work in Ephesus.

Not so with those troublesome Corinthians. From Ephesus Paul spent much of his time tending to matters back in freewheeling Corinth, where the temptations of the world remained fresh and old patterns died hard. His first three letters to the Corinthians (the book known as First Corinthians, a prior letter, and a stern one written subsequently; 1 Cor 5:9, 16:8; 2 Cor 2:1–4, 7:5–16) were perhaps all sent from Ephesus, and a frustrated Paul may also have made a quick trip to Corinth to attend to things personally (2 Cor 2:1, 12:14, 13:1). For sure from Ephesus he dispatched Timothy and the disciple Erastus to minister to churches in Macedonia (Philippi and Thessalonica?; Acts 19:22; cf. Rom 16:23; 2 Tim 4:20).

Paul's work in Ephesus was quite fruitful, and he gained fame (or, notoriety) by preaching and driving out evil spirits there ("God was performing extraordinary miracles by the hands of Paul"; Acts 19:11). Eventually so many Ephesians turned to Jesus that the local merchants who sold idols and trinkets of the city's patron goddess, Artemis (Diana), began to suffer economically and brought the matter to the attention of the entire town. Everyone gathered in the theater where those most loyal to Artemis pressed their claim on the religious sensibilities—and economic loyalty—of the others ("Great is Artemis of the Ephesians!"). The assembly quickly dissolved into mass confusion and a near riot. The town clerk eventually restored order, and shortly afterward Paul decided to leave town, partly for his own safety, partly to forestall a backlash against the church (Acts 19:23–20:1).

Sometime in A.D. 55 or 56 Paul made his way via Troas to Macedonia (Acts 20:1; 2 Cor 2:12–13). At this point the data are scattered and it is not possible to trace his subsequent travels through Macedonia and Achaia with any degree of certainty. One can justifiably assume that Paul visited churches he had previously founded throughout the region and planted more to the west, perhaps as far as Illyricum (today's east Adriatic coast from Albania to Croatia; Rom 15:19). Paul stayed in Achaia—almost certainly Corinth—for three months (Acts 20:2–3), and it is likely that he wrote his fourth letter to the Corinthians (the Book of Second Corinthians) from Philippi just before arriving, out of joy that the Corinthian church was finally coming around (cf. 2 Cor 2:1–2). Perhaps it was while he was in Corinth that Paul penned his greatest epistle of all, to the Romans, a well-reasoned argument of how the

Paul's Third Missionary Journey, A.D. 53–57. *Paul's third missionary journey was a combination of new work and follow-up as he founded churches and strengthened ones visited previously. His base of operations was Ephesus where he "fought with wild beasts" (1 Cor 15:32; cf. 2 Cor 1:8)—perhaps a veiled reference to human foes, perhaps just matter-of-fact. He also declared "the whole purpose of God" (Acts 20:27) so effectively that the church in Ephesus grew mightily (cf. Rev 2:2–3). Paul could return to Jerusalem pleased with his efforts and with the outpouring of God's Spirit among the Gentiles.*

on the way passing through the cities of Colossae and Laodicea (at the upper end of the Lycus River, one of the Maeander's tributaries). Toward the end of his life when he was imprisoned in Rome, Paul would write letters to churches in these two cities (Col 1:2, 4:10, 4:15–16; cf. Col 2:1).

Making good on his promise to return to Ephesus, Paul remained in the city for up to three years (Acts 19:8, 19:10, 20:31; cf. Acts 18:20–21). There he found "a wide door for effective service" (1 Cor 16:8–9) and used Ephesus as a base of operations to reach people from all areas of the province of Asia (Acts 19:10, 19:26). The city of Ephesus was well-positioned for this effort as it lay at the juncture of two important overland routes through Asia (one ran north-south along the coast; another stretched east back to Colossae) and boasted the province's main Aegean harbor. For three months Paul focused his work in the synagogue of Ephesus, then found more useful facilities in the "hall (Gk. scholé) of Tyrannus" where he "reasoned daily" for two years (Acts 19:8–10). Tyrannus' hall may have been a place of public gathering where open philosophical discussions were held in the morning (cf. Juvenal, *Satires* vii.222–226), allowing Paul to rent the place in the afternoon (or, if Tyrannus was a disciple, perhaps use it *gratis*). In any case he settled in, remaining in Ephesus longer than at any other city of his journeys (with the possible exception of Rome). Years later, when he was a prisoner in Rome, Paul wrote his letter to the Ephesians, a mature treatise on the blessings and responsibilities of living the Christian life:

Paul likely passed through the region of Colossae on his third missionary journey, perhaps founding and certainly encouraging the church in the city. Not much in the way of ruins can be seen at the site today, but the view from the summit of the tel takes in the sweep of the geographical seam where the eastern heights of Phrygia drop into the fertile Lycus Valley. The residents of Colossae enjoyed just the right combination of seclusion and connectedness. The mountains above and countryside round about offer wonderful grazing land for sheep, which in ancient times were known for their especially soft wool. Prior to the first century, when the Phrygians controlled their own kingdom, Colossae had been an important center for dying and distributing this wool (termed colossinus), but by the time of the New Testament the city's fortunes had declined. Yet from the tone of inscriptions found in the region it is apparent that the Colossians were enthusiastic about life and enjoyed the opportunities that still came their way.

death and resurrection of Jesus provides justification and righteousness to all who have faith in him.

Paul longed to visit Rome on his way to even more distant places such as Spain, but first wanted to make a trip back to Jerusalem (Rom 15:22–25; cf. Acts 19:21). He retraced his steps through Achaia and Macedonia, collecting on the way a large monetary contribution for the relief of the poorer members of Jerusalem's churches (Rom 15:26–27; Strabo [Geography vii.34] knew of many gold mines in the vicinity of Philippi). The contribution strengthened the ties between these Jewish and Gentile congregations, and reminded the churches in Macedonia of their spiritual indebtedness to Jerusalem. After celebrating Passover in Philippi (in A.D. 57, the likely year, Passover was April 5–12 according to the Gregorian calendar) Paul, with Luke, sailed to Troas where he stayed for a week (Acts 20:1–6). Final farewells were hard to make, and Paul preached one of his lengthier sermons late into the night before he was to leave (those who fell asleep as he droned on, such as Eutychus, can be forgiven! Acts 20:7–12).

Luke and several other disciples sailed for Assos while Paul, by choice, made his way overland, apparently walking alone. The journey by land from Troas to Assos is neither long (about 25 miles) nor unduly difficult, yet one would think that a day's sail with his companions would have been more comfortable for the apostle (he wasn't getting any younger!). Paul clearly needed some time alone, knowing an emotional meeting with the elders of Ephesus lay ahead. From Assos it was a glorious springtime journey threading his way among the islands off the coast of Asia (Luke, ever with an eye for detail, kept careful track of the time and route throughout; Acts 20:13–16).

Paul knew that if he stopped at Ephesus he would never get away and so he sailed past the harbor and around a spit of land to Miletus at the mouth of the

Maeander River, about thirty miles south. (Perhaps the ship was a private hire, or else it would surely have stopped at Ephesus on its journey around the coast of Asia.) His heart was clearly torn: half ached to remain in Ephesus, the other longed to be in Jerusalem by Pentecost four weeks hence. Premonitions in hand, he met the leaders of the church of Ephesus in Miletus for a heart-wrenching farewell:

You yourselves know, from the first day I set foot in Asia, how I was with you the whole time, serving the Lord with all humility and tears and trials...and now, bound by the Spirit, I am on my way to Jerusalem, not knowing what will happen to me there,

One ancient city on everyone's must-see list in Turkey is Ephesus, the great harbor town where Paul the Apostle spent three years establishing a base of operations for Christian ministry in Asia. An impressive amount of the city's grandeur is still left for easy public viewing, although most of the extant remains post-date Paul's sojourn there. Ephesus boasts one of the largest theaters of the Roman world: nearly 500 feet in diameter, it held upwards of 25,000 people, an estimated one-tenth to one-twentieth of the city's population. The pro-Artemis riot that cut short Paul's ministry in Asia rocked the theater's cavernous hold; he wisely viewed the proceedings from outside, then quickly left town.

249

Ruins of the picturesque city of Assos, where Paul rejoined ship for his springtime journey to Caesarea, climb a steep volcanic hill rising out of the Gulf of Adramyttium on Mysia's western shore. The Greek-style theater, built in the late 4th century B.C., faced the island of Lesbos beyond a strait in the Aegean Sea, while the Temple of Athena, the city's goddess and favorite daughter of Zeus, graced the summit of the rocky acropolis behind. The harbor from which Paul sailed has silted in completely, and a modern breakwater curves into the sea at its side. Nowadays the entire place is typical of Aegean tourist havens: choked roadways and crowded dockside cafes. Paul preferred to walk into town—it's still not bad advice!

except that the Holy Spirit solemnly testifies to me in every city that bonds and afflictions await me.… And now, behold, I know that all of you will no longer see my face…and [so] I commend you to God.…
(Acts 20:18–35)

Leaving Miletus in tears, Paul's ship skipped along the southwestern coast of Asia Minor, making port every night (in Cos, then Rhodes, then Patara). In Patara he, Timothy and Luke transferred to a larger freighter bound for Tyre and made straight sail by means of the favorable Etesian winds, passing the southern tip of Cyprus on the way. Paul visited churches in Tyre and Ptolemais before ending his sea journey at Caesarea. Again he cleared customs, this time bringing a large amount of hard currency into the country. He had made good time: Pentecost was still about ten days off (Acts 20:36–21:8).

Paul's premonitions that something awaited him in Jerusalem were not unfounded (cf. Rom 15:31). A prophet from Judea, Agabus, came down to Caesarea to warn him personally that he would be arrested there. Paul ascended to the Holy City anyway; it would be his last visit to Jerusalem and he arrived—and left—in style. Early in his journeys Paul had traveled with one or two companions, entered unknown cities and put in where he could at night. But now it was close to the end and he had an entourage who even pre-arranged his housing (e.g. Acts 20:4–5, 21:5, 21:15–16). Meeting with James and the elders of the church in Jerusalem, Paul gave a glowing report of the spread of the Gospel among the Gentiles (Acts 21:18–19). A quarter century had passed since the Pentecost when the Holy Spirit had first empowered the earliest believers in Jesus, and over the years the church had grown with remarkable success.

On each of his missionary journeys Paul faced the issue of how closely Jews living in the Diaspora who had come to faith in Jesus should keep normative Jewish religious practices. The issue was raised

again as soon as he arrived in Jerusalem. So as not to cause undue offense to both the temple authorities and his fellow believers who adhered to strict *Torah* observance, Paul willingly visited the *miqveh* for ritual purification, then sponsored temple sacrifices for four Jewish believers who were finishing a period of vows (Acts 21:20–26; cf. 1 Cor 6:12, 9:22; "…and when in Jerusalem, do as the Jerusalemites"). In the process, toward the end of the festivities of Pentecost (*Shavuot*), some pilgrims with whom he had bumped heads somewhere back in Asia and who were in town for the holiday accused him (mistakenly? intentionally? conveniently?) of bringing a Gentile into the Temple. If the charges were true, it would be a clear and blatant violation of the compound's sacred space. A great commotion ensued, out of which Paul was plucked by a squadron of Roman soldiers who were permanently garrisoned in the Antonia, the fortress overlooking the Temple Mount. As he was being led away, Paul faced the crowds and gave an impassioned defense of his ministry—it was a simple though powerful testimony of how God had personally chosen him to bring the message of Jesus to the Gentiles. The next morning, since he was accused of breaking Jewish, not Roman, law, Paul was handed over to the Sanhedrin for a formal hearing (Acts 21:27–22:30).

Paul's appearance before the Sanhedrin was rocky, with the Pharisees lending a sympathetic ear and the Sadducees upset that his very *raison d'être* for ministry and life involved the reality of the resurrection from the dead (Acts 23:6–10; cf. *Ant.* xviii.1.4; 1 Cor 15:1–58). Things got so raucous that Paul was again taken into Roman custody and a plot was hatched to take his life. Warned of the conspiracy by his own nephew (like Mordecai for Esther, it was fortuitous that Paul had a close relative on the street; cf. Esth 2:21–22, 4:4–14), Paul alerted Claudius Lysias, the commander of the garrison, who promptly ordered his immediate evacuation to Caesarea, the provincial seat of government. The initial leg of this journey, through the rough hills from Jerusalem to Antipatris, was made with a heavy armed guard under the cover of darkness, apparently to lessen the threat of ambush. Paul rode a horse, the only time we hear of him riding on anything other than a boat in his travels. The case was brought directly to the procurator, Antonius (or, Claudius) Felix (A.D. 52–60?), who sequestered Paul in Herod's Praetorium (Acts 23:12–35).

Felix enjoyed one of the longer terms as procurator of Judea, perhaps because he was well connected to Rome's imperial aristocracy (he married one of the granddaughters of Antony and Cleopatra; Tacitus, *Historiae* 5.9). It may be for this reason that he was able to get away with strong-arming his subjects for as long as he did (cf. *Ant.* xx.8.9; Tacitus, *Historiae* 5.10; *Annales* 12.54). Felix was rather efficient in rounding up

members of militant groups that festered within the borders of his province (bandits, partisans, messiah-wanna-be's and the like; *Ant.* xx.8.5–6; *War* ii.13.2, 13.4; cf. Acts 21:38), actions that must be seen in light of the surge in popular unrest that would lead to open revolt against Rome less than a decade later (ignited in A.D. 66, in Caesarea; *War* ii.18.1). Certain elements in the religious leadership of Jerusalem were sympathetic with Felix's response to these groups, for their own positions, too, were jeopardized by mass civil unrest. It was this opening that the high priest Ananias seized to charge Paul before Felix, throwing him in with the rabble ("we have found this man to be a real pest…"; Acts 24:1–9). Felix deferred to the prisoner, partly because he sensed a difference in intent in the actions of the accused, partly to give Paul time to come to the realization that a well-placed bribe would win his freedom (pocketfuls of money didn't pass through Caesarea unnoticed; Acts 24:10–26). Paul preferred to bide his time in prison—it was a loose confinement, with rights of open visitation—and met Felix often for talks at the highest levels.

The case bogged down in the system. Two years later, in A.D. 60 (possibly 59), Felix was cycled out of office and his replacement, Porcius Festus, brought in. The new procurator wisely began his term by offering certain informal concessions to the Jews of Jerusalem and so placed Paul's unresolved case high on his agenda. Festus convened a formal hearing in Caesarea but Paul cut the proceedings short by playing the ultimate trump card of any Roman citizen who ran afoul of provincial authorities: he appealed directly to Caesar (Acts 25:1–12). This right, in its current form, had been modified early in the reign of Augustus when the emperor forbade a local magistrate from killing, scourging, chaining or torturing Roman citizens who had appealed to Caesar, or preventing them from going to Rome to personally present their cases. Paul apparently thought that his fortunes in Judea would not improve under Festus and sensed an opportunity to move on, in effect arranging free and direct passage to the city of his dreams (cf. Acts 19:21, 23:11). As the new kid on the block Festus drew on the wisdom of Agrippa II, who was in town paying due respects to the new procurator, on how to formally present the case to Nero (Acts 25:13–27). Agrippa II was an interested party: not only was he the great-grandson of Herod the Great and king of Chalcis, Gaulanitis and parts of Galilee and Perea, he held the right to appoint high priests in Jerusalem and control temple finances (*Ant.* xix.5.2, 7.1; xx.1.1–3).

Paul was equally interested in the chance to declare the power of the Gospel to a king, and did so with great eloquence. This was clearly the first time Festus heard such claims of religious truth, and he was stunned: "Paul, are you out of your mind? Your nose has been in the books so long you've gone crazy!" (Acts 26:24). Agrippa, of course familiar with the thought patterns of Jews (and becoming so with Christians), was incredulous for other reasons: "In such a short time you think you will persuade me to become a Christian?!" (Acts 26:28). He rightly saw, however, that Paul's actions were an intra-Jewish affair that did not warrant charges against Roman law, and advised Festus accordingly (cf. the similar decision of Gallio, proconsul of Achaia, when Paul was in Corinth; Acts 18:12–17). But things had gone too far for Festus to ignore Paul's legal right of appeal and the desire of the temple leadership to get rid of the guy, and so he arranged for the prisoner's transfer to Rome (Acts 26:1–32). For Paul it was the crowning opportunity of a lifetime of service to the Gospel: not only had he booked free passage to Rome, he had a chance to meet the Emperor face-to-face. Even more optimistically—it would be a totally unrealistic hope—if Nero would judge the case favorably, Paul could win legal recognition of Christianity as a viable sect (in Paul's eyes, as the fulfillment) of Judaism.

It was already getting late in the shipping season when Paul, together with other prisoners bound for Rome (all under the custody of a centurion named Julius), were put on board a ship heading north along the Phoenician coast. Paul did not travel alone—Luke, at least, accompanied him, as likely did others who had been with him on previous journeys. Julius allowed Paul to disembark at Sidon (and probably at other ports as well) to greet friends on the way (Acts 27:1–3). Their ship was a small trading vessel typical of those that plied the waters and ports of the eastern Mediterranean, now on its homeward voyage to Adramyttium on the Aegean coast of Asia, across the bay from Assos. The voyage was not without difficulty as "the winds were contrary." The captain had some trouble making decent headway as his ship made its way between Cyprus and the

Arrested in Jerusalem under the charge of bringing a Gentile into the Temple, Paul was hauled off to Caesarea where the procurator Felix sequestered him in Herod's Praetorium. A reasonable interpretation of the historical and archaeological evidence places the Praetorium in this complex of rooms surrounding a large square courtyard, adjacent to Herod's grand "Promontory Palace" jutting into the Mediterranean Sea. If the identification is correct, it's easy to imagine Paul hearing the waves break on the shore every day of his two-year imprisonment in Caesarea, or seeing countless ships come and go from the busy harbor just upshore. Captive in the land that still best defined his own identity, Paul longed for the day when he could sail for Rome.

Paul's Journey to Rome, A.D. 60 (Fall) to 61 (Spring)

Luke tells the story of Paul's shipwreck journey to Rome (Acts 27–28) with all the skill of a good Roman historian, giving details of sailing the high seas that only an eyewitness could know. Homer's sailing stories have the clear ring of myth; Strabo's Geography is meticulous but so massive in scope that he could not possibly have seen everything he described (certainly not the fanciful things). Luke, trained as a physician, had an eye for observation and put his skills to good use, holding his readers at rapt attention: "…they observed a bay with a beach and resolved to drive the ship onto it if they could. So casting off the anchors and leaving them in the sea while at the same time loosening the ropes of the rudders and hoisting the foresail to the wind, they headed right for the beach. But they struck a reef…" (Acts 27:39–40).

Cilician coast, hugging the inlets of the rough Asian shore as it went. The steady westward current in this tight corner of the Mediterranean helped overcome the strong headwinds.

At the port of Myra on the Lycian coast the centurion Julius, his prisoners and Paul's companions transferred to a large Alexandrian freighter bound for Italy (Acts 27:4–6). This ship was heavily loaded with 276 people (it could also hold up to 70 tons of Egyptian wheat; cf. Acts 27:37–38), trying to make its final run before the unpredictable fall winds might shut down the shipping lanes. It is estimated that Rome reaped (or, raped) 150,000 tons of wheat from Egypt's Nile Delta and Faiyum each year, enough to feed its population for four months (Rome's annexation of Egypt in 30 B.C. was blatant economic imperialism). All of this moved annually between May and October (Myra was a regular port-of-call for ships from Egypt), with the first and last runs taxing the seamanship of every worthy captain. This final voyage was a roll of the dice—sitting in port for six months somewhere en route was needlessly expensive, and the thought of shipwreck due to the sudden onset of an early winter storm always lay at hand. It was well after "the fast" (*Yom Kippur*, the Jewish Day of Atonement, fell on September 22 in A.D. 60, the likely year of Paul's voyage) and strong prevailing winds slowed the trip considerably. The freighter found shelter from the northwesterly gale by sailing along the southern side of Crete, though it now faced the open sea. The captain tried to wait out the winds at Fair Havens, by Lasea, a small bay protected by a bit of a cape on the west. A momentary break in the weather prompted the centurion (who by force of might was the supreme authority on board) to try to find better winter anchorage at Phoenix, a decent port farther along the Cretan shore. This was against the pointed advice of the ship's captain and Paul. The Apostle was not unfamiliar with the secrets of the sea—he had been

shipwrecked twice before, even spending a day and night adrift on the open water (2 Cor 11:25)—but also never shied from sharing his opinion on a matter (Acts 27:7–13).

It was all for naught. A fierce northwesterly wind bore down from the Aegean, driving the ship below the tiny, last-gasp island of Clauda then out to open sea.

> *Those who go down to the sea in ships,*
> *who do business on the great waters;*
> *they have seen the works of the LORD,*
> *and his wonders in the deep.*
> *For he spoke and raised up a stormy wind,*
> *which lifted up the waves of the sea.*
> *They rose up to the heavens, they sent down to the depths;*
> *their soul melted away in their misery.*
> *They reeled and staggered like drunken men….*
>
> (Ps 107:23–27)

Tired, hungry, cold and thoroughly wet to the bone, the crew and passengers could only trust in the encouragement of Paul and wait for the end. After fourteen battered days the ship ran aground off the small island of Malta, beneath Sicily (Acts 27:14–44). Ship and cargo were lost; the passengers all made it safely to shore where they spent the winter under the hospitality of the islanders (Acts 28:1–10).

In the spring of A.D. 61 Julius and the prisoners in his charge, including Paul, caught passage for Rome on an Alexandrian ship that had found safe winter anchorage at Malta. The relatively quick voyage touched Syracuse on Sicily, then Rhegium at the tip of the Italian "boot" before landing at the marvelous port of Puteoli, just beyond Pompeii and the Isle of Capreae (Capri). The church in and around Rome was already strong, and many believers in towns from there to Puteoli came down to meet the famed evangelist. They gladly escorted the centurion and his prisoners up the *Via Dormitiana* then the *Via Appia* (the Appian Way) into Rome (Acts 28:11–15). There Paul was placed under loose house arrest where for two years, living at his own expense, he openly preached the Gospel of Jesus to all who would hear (Acts 28:16–31).

The Book of Acts—the best and only connected source on the life of the Apostle Paul—ends here. In one sense it is enough—the Gospel had reached the center of "the uttermost part of the earth" (cf. Acts 1:8) and its greatest advocate and ambassador was speaking freely in his new home and, likely, (though with escort permission) in its streets. But history easily melds with tradition, and although the early post-Acts sources are scant, reasonable lines can be drawn to finish Paul's story.

The most pressing question is what happened to Paul in Rome. All evidence agrees that he was eventually executed by Nero—his Roman citizenship granted him rights of status, protection and appeal in life, but also dictated that if execution should come, it be by beheading with the sword (1 Clement 5:5–7; Eusebius, *Historia ecclesiastica* ii.25.6; cf. 2 Tim 4:6–18). The late (sixth century A.D.) *Acts of Peter and Paul* (80) provides the requisite details as the Church remembered them at the time: Paul was led in chains to a point three miles south of Rome on the *Via Ostia* called *Aquae Salviae*, near a pine tree, where some soldiers did the bloody deed. His eyes were veiled with a handkerchief graciously lent to him by a one-eyed woman; the splattered cloth absorbed Paul's healing power and when it was returned to the woman by God himself, her sight was restored (cf. Acts 19:11–12). And why not? Paul deserves the memory. Of course the spot was consecrated by a memorial chapel in the fifth century A.D. Eusebius (*Historia ecclesiastica* ii.25.7) citing Gaius, a church historian of the late second century, notes that the "trophies of the Apostles"—the tombs of Paul and others—could be pointed out in his day in the Vatican and on the Ostian Way. Other traditions abound. As in Jerusalem, holy places in Rome multiplied and Paul was able to do in death what for all of his talents he could not accomplish in life—be in more than one place at the same time.

But *when* Paul was martyred, and what he may have accomplished in the meantime, remains a matter of speculation. He (and Peter) certainly succumbed either during Nero's first great persecution of the church in A.D. 64, or sometime within the next two or at most three years. Scraps of evidence suggest that Paul may have been released from Rome after his initial imprisonment and traveled again in the Mediterranean (to Crete—Tit 1:5; Macedonia again—1 Tim 1:3; and Nicopolis in Epirus, on the Adriatic side of Achaia—Tit 3:12). And of course there is the matter of the trip to Spain (cf. Rom 15:22–25). The testimony of Clement of Rome (c. A.D. 96) assures us that Paul "went to the extreme limits of the West" (1 Clement 5:7); this has often been understood as indicating the realization of Paul's greatest geographical goal. Sufficient time is

also needed for Paul to have composed most or all of his epistles to the churches in Ephesus, Philippi, Colossae and Laodicea, and letters to Philemon, Timothy (twice) and Titus. The earlier date of his death compresses events while the latter allows for more options; nothing is certain. Like with all great men, some dreams must have been left on the table. At least he reconciled with John Mark before the end (2 Tim 4:11).

In his penetrating discourse on justification by faith—much of which grew out of the ministry of the Spirit during painful personal experiences—Paul wrote confidently that "where sin increased, grace abounded even more" (Rom 5:20; cf. Rom 7:7–20). Paul's life was overly full, with opportunity but also challenge. Dangers of every kind lay always at hand—if it wasn't the road, it was the people on it, or at its end (2 Cor 11:23–29). Being "all things to all people" yet unwaveringly faithful to the call of Jesus was humanly nearly impossible. Yet the extent to which Paul succeeded can be measured by the grace that filled his life.

The grace of the Lord Jesus Christ and the love of God and the fellowship of the Holy Spirit be with you all. (2 Cor 13:14)

Amen.

Geologically, the coastlines of the Aegean, southern Italy and to some extent the extreme northwestern corner of the Levant are "discordant," that is, the inland mountain ranges run at right angles to, rather than parallel to, the sea. As a result the shore is quite rugged, with deep bays, estuaries and inlets that have provided ample opportunity for the development of seaborne communication and trade. Chains of offshore islands, especially in the Aegean, beckon ships safely abroad. Westward shipping lanes in the Roman world hugged the mainland shores as ships fought to make headway against the prevailing winds; if a boat was blown out to open water, it could easily be lost at sea.

This relief of Nike, the winged goddess of Victory, once graced one of the upper corners of the Heracles Gate at Ephesus. Though likely dating to the second century A.D., this Nike in full flight attests to the control (victory? or stranglehold?) that Rome exerted across the Mediterranean in the days of the Apostle Paul. "Every person is to be in subjection to the governing authorities, for there is no authority except from God," Paul wrote to the Romans (13:1), sound advice for a church struggling for recognition and rights. But the point of interaction of the individual with the Roman system was to be quite different: "Do not be conformed to this world but be transformed by the renewing of your mind, so that you may prove what the will of God is, that which is good and acceptable and perfect" (Rom 12:2).

CHAPTER 24
JOHN
Someone Who Deserved the Last Word

And then there was John. By all estimations he was the youngest of the twelve disciples, and the one of whom Jesus seemed to have been the most fond. The favorite, perhaps, like Joseph among his ten older brothers (cf. Gen 37:3), although it's difficult to think in terms of Jesus "playing favorites." With Peter and James he was part of Jesus' inner three, eager, quick, attentive—and impressionable, as youth always are. Perhaps Jesus saw him as his own son, the one he would never have. "Train up a child in the way he should go," says the proverb, "and when he is old he will not depart from it" (Prov 22:6). And as John grew, from "the [younger] brother of James" (Mk 5:37) to "the disciple Jesus loved" (Jn 19:26, 21:20) and then to "the Elder" (2 Jn 1:1; 3 Jn 1:1) and became, likely, the last of the Apostles to breathe the air of this fine world, he gained not only an insider's view of the heart and mind of Jesus but a glimpse of the Divine. John wrote the last Gospel and (nearly) the last of the New Testament epistles. Then, reaching back through the vivid thickness of Scripture and dragging his hand across the rich literature of the Intertestamental period, he drew out just the right language and imagery for the last of all biblical books, the Revelation, a magnificent work summarizing the essence and anticipating the fullness of God's touch on Time and Place. John was beloved, and the survivor. When one considers all of the affirmations of the founding generation of the Church, it was he, as its first Great Elder Statesman, who most deserved the last word.

When Gospel readers first meet John he is the junior partner of a profitable fishing enterprise plying the shallows and open waters along the northeastern shore of the Sea of Galilee. Peter the seasoned fisherman was perhaps already the boss, in team with his brother Andrew and Zebedee and Zebedee's two sons, James and John (Lk 5:3, 10; cf. Mt 4:18–22; Mk 1:16–20). They owned their own boats and some nice fishing equipment, and could afford the services of hired hands. All were likely from the region of Bethsaida, where dark basaltic soil and an abundance of fresh water join in a bounded plain that reflects the exuberance of nature. Southward toward the sea the Bethsaida Plain gives way to marshes, estuaries and inlets, a tangled mass of green-meets-blue teeming with wildlife, a fisherman's paradise. And into this pleasant corner of the sea walked Jesus, from Galilee to Gaulanitis, fishing for men. Andrew, who was a disciple of John the Baptist, already knew him (Jn 1:35–40). Peter came along quickly, as did James and John (Mt 4:21–22; Mk 1:19–20; Lk 5:1–11). John was probably in his late teens, part of a band of brothers that remained inseparable even when others joined the call (it was "Peter, Andrew, James and John," then the rest in a list of eight that doesn't roll off the tongue quite as easily; Mt 10:2–4; Mk 3:16–19; Lk 6:12–16).

When he wrote his own account of the life of Jesus sometime after the other three Gospels were already becoming part of the fabric of Christian Scripture (cf. Jerome, *De viris illustribus,* ix) John not only didn't provide a list of Jesus' twelve disciples, he deferred from even mentioning his own name in the narrative, using instead the personal circumlocutions "the other disciple" (Jn 18:15–16, 20:2–4) or "the disciple Jesus loved" (Jn 13:23, 19:26–27, 21:7, 21:20). The other Gospel writers could provide blow-by-blow accounts of their Master's words and deeds; John preferred to distill Jesus' life to its essence:

> In the beginning was the Word [Gk. *logos,* yes, but also Heb. *davar,* the intimate expression of God's creative existence], *and the Word was with God, and the Word was God....And the Word became flesh and dwelt among us, and we saw His glory, glory of the only begotten from the Father, full of grace and truth.* (Jn 1:1, 1:14)

John's home was on the water's edge of the Plain

This modern Zebedee and his two sons enjoy the sun and water on a quiet afternoon along the northern shore of the Sea of Galilee. Their perch is part of the first-century harbor at Heptapegon (Tabgha), which juts into the water a little west of Capernaum. Warm springs at Heptapegon attracted both people and fish in Jesus' day, as well as the tradition that it was here that Jesus ate a post-resurrection breakfast with his disciples. John, familiar with the anchorage, joined Peter, James, Thomas and Nathanael for the meal (Jn 21:1–11).

of Bethsaida, but the geography of his Gospel centers on Jerusalem. In language both soaring and simple, John the Gospel writer focused on Jesus' work in the Holy City and especially events of that last Passover (the account fills nearly half his book). For Jesus' life John gives an alternate geography and an alternate chronology. (When an author is intimately familiar with his subject, the full touch of reality can override rigidity of normal historiographic form.) Adopting the terminology of the great linguist Kenneth Pike (*Language in Relation to a Unified Theory of the Structure of Human Behavior*, ch. 2), social scientists strive to reach a view of others that is "emic," an insider's view, one "gone native." For Jesus this emic view was achieved, as much as anyone, by John.

Letting "no one despise his youth" (cf. 1 Tim 4:12), John stayed close to Jesus—foot in footprint, as it were—for the three years they were together. He doesn't appear very often in the Gospel accounts, but when he does it is in connection with memorable events. John was there at the beginning, when Jesus healed Simon Peter's mother-in-law following services one *Shabbat* morning in Capernaum; that evening "the whole city gathered at the door" (Mk 1:29–34). One can imagine John taking mental notes: "For this is the message which you have heard from the beginning," he would write years later, "that we should love one another" (1 Jn 3:11). One of the synagogue officials, Jairus, certainly noticed as well, and when his own young daughter fell deathly ill sometime later he called Jesus to touch her "so that she will get well and live" (Mk 5:21–23). But by the time Jesus had reached Jairus' home the girl had died. Taking only Peter, James and John inside, the Word touched flesh, restoring her to life. John was an eyewitness, an intimate, and kept well the first-hand testimony that Jesus was entrusting to him:

> *What was from the beginning, what we have heard, what we have seen with our eyes, what we have looked at and touched with our hands, concerning the Word of Life….What we have seen and heard we proclaim to you also, so that you too may have*

(right) It's springtime on the lakeside end of the Plain of Bethsaida, where water meets green and wildlife abounds. There are no towns out here today, and campers stick to the high ground at the water's edge. A little beyond and the paths quickly become overgrown and submerged by high lakewater. Josephus' horse stumbled in these marshes during the battle for Galilee in A.D. 67, spilling and badly injuring the wrist of rider; he reports that he was carried to Capernaum for medical care (Life 72). Hikers need to take caution for other reasons—it's easy to disturb wild boars (the author speaks from experience) or critters that lurk in the depths. Khirbet el-Araj, the lakeside ruins of a small village in the immediate vicinity, is identified by some (e.g. Mendel Nun) as the Bethsaida of Peter, Andrew, James and John. For the disciples, it would be difficult to grow up here and not be adventurous….

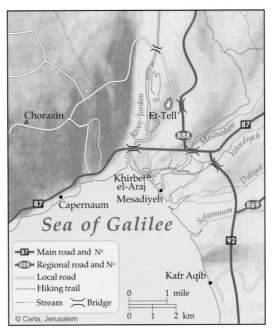

fellowship with us; and indeed our fellowship is with the Father, and with His Son Jesus Christ.

(1 Jn 1:1–3)

So too at Jesus' Transfiguration on Mount Hermon where, in the presence of Moses and Elijah, the inner three saw Jesus' face "shine like the sun, and his garments as white as light…and [heard] a voice out of the cloud announcing, 'This is My beloved Son with whom I am well-pleased. Listen to him!'" (Mt 17:2–5; cf. Mk 9:2–8; Lk 9:28–36). The solid height of Mount Hermon is visible in the wintertime to anyone in a boat in the middle of the Sea of Galilee, its snowy crown (cf. Jer 18:14) thirty-five miles to the north rising 10,000 feet above the green Bethsaida Plain—though often its top is shrouded in clouds. For the young, robust fisherman John, this must

The Plain of Bethsaida.
While the Gospel accounts are silent as to the home of Zebedee and his family, the association of James and John with Peter and Andrew, who were from Bethsaida (Jn 1:44), suggests that all hailed from the same town or its close vicinity. The prominent mound of et-Tell ("the ruin") bears the imprimatur of the Survey of Israel map office, the Israel Antiquities Authority and the Vatican as the location of the Bethsaida of the Gospels, and it is easily visited by vehicle and foot traffic. Khirbet el-Araj, tucked in an isolated spot among the marshes at water's edge, offers an alternative location much closer to the fishing opportunities of the sea, although the archaeological record of first-century remains there is inconclusive. The excavators of et-Tell suggest that the shoreline of the plain in the first century was located somewhat farther north than it is today, bringing open water much nearer the mound of et-Tell. They argue further that Khirbet el-Araj was a Byzantine village and the ground on which it was located was formed as a result of a major earthquake and landslide in the centuries after the close of the Gospels.

John with Jesus in Galilee, Samaria and Judea. *"What we have heard, what we have seen with our eyes, what we have looked at and touched…"* (1 Jn 1:1). *John was an active witness and a devoted follower of Jesus, taking everything in, soaking it up, defending his Master and Lord. Certainly he was close to the action throughout Jesus' ministry although he is fronted in the Gospel storyline only occasionally. But those occasions come at critical points in the narrative flow, and show John to be a disciple worthy of one who had the last word.*

(below) This fishing boat finds its home anchorage at Kibbutz En Gev on the eastern side of the Sea of Galilee. It's a hard-working craft for hard-working men who ply the waters of the sea. Nowadays they look mostly for sardines. The boat's seine net is folded, covered and ready for the next sail. Once out to water, the net is let down in a large circle, then drawn together ("pursed") and hauled up with the catch. The Gospels call sardines "small fish"; a few, with bread, were a dietary staple for the local population. Contemplating how to feed 4,000 people, Jesus asked his disciples, "How many loaves do you have?" They answered, "Seven, and a few small fish" (Mt 15:34).

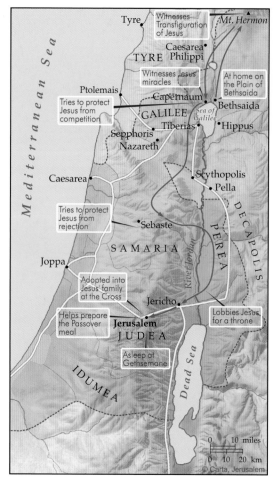

have been a favorite view of home, and now he was *up there*, wrapped in light and voice and cloud and in the presence of God Himself. He and the others were stunned, unsure of what to make of it all (Mt 17:6–10). Again, much later, with the perspective of time and a lifetime of reflection on the character of God behind him, John could pinpoint the essence of a double theophany of Father and Son:

This is the message we have heard from Him and announce to you, that God is Light, and in Him there is no darkness at all…[and] the darkness is passing away and the true Light is already shining.

(1 Jn 1:5; 2:8)

But in the meantime John was still young and rough around the edges (a true Son of Thunder; cf. Mk 3:17), eager but not yet very wise, sure that something that would involve him was happening and convinced that that alone made him special. So back in Capernaum he proudly told Jesus that he had tried to stop someone outside their group of twelve who was doing miracles in Jesus' name. "Don't hinder him," Jesus replied. "Whoever is not against us, is for us" (Mk 9:38–40; Lk 9:49–50). Then, as they began to move toward Jerusalem and he to the cross, Jesus and his disciples were refused hospitality in a Samaritan village. John was ready to call down fire (and thunder!) from heaven: "Whoever is not for us must be against us!" Again Jesus told John to leave well enough alone. "The Son of Man did not come to destroy men's lives, but to save them" (Lk 9:51–56).

Then the climax. Approaching Jericho, John sensed the excitement. They would soon climb to Jerusalem where Jesus the Messiah would bring in the kingdom and he, Jesus' favorite, would not only see it happen but be a part! So John and his brother James (at the urging of their mother, who, like Jesus' own mother, was part of the popular movement massing on the Holy City) asked that they might be able to share thrones with Jesus, one on the right, the other on the left. It was only to be expected. And Mrs. Zebedee was only trying to find public honor for herself and her family through the deeds of her sons, as any mother in the ancient Mediterranean world would do. The other disciples were quite put out by it all—Peter, probably, the most—and Jesus had to sort it all out. God alone, he said, would decide who sits where; in the meantime it's about serving others (Mt 20:20–28; Mk 10:35–45; cf. Lk 22:24–27)—and in this business there are no hired hands! This was—and remains—as counter-culture a pronouncement as Jesus would make. Again, John summed it up nicely:

Do not love the world nor the things in the world. For all that is in the world…the boastful pride of life, is not from the Father, but is of the world.

(1 Jn 2:15–16)

But the journey from "what's in it for me" to "how can I help you" was a long one. It was first up and over the Mount of Olives for the Triumphal Entry, then a few days listening to Jesus in and around the Temple precinct speaking freely of the evils of self-serving leadership, of troubled times ahead and of God's coming kingdom (Mt 21:1–25:46; Mk 11:1–13:37; Lk 19:28–21:38). When it was time, Jesus did publicly

With strong voices and lively steps, sisters from the Missionaries of Charity (Order of Mother Teresa) attached to a work on the Mount of Olives sing their way in a joyful Palm Sunday processional into Jerusalem. From the Gospel accounts, the crowds at Jesus' Triumphal Entry must have been just as excited. Perhaps John was one of the two disciples who arranged for a donkey to be Jesus' mount (cf. Mt 21:1–6); certainly he was fully part of the moment. A mosaic panel (below) of the famed "Dionysus Mosaic" from Sepphoris (3rd–4th century A.D.) depicts a reminiscent scene, although the purpose of celebration was clearly different. Here men, women and children carry wreaths, fruit and other objects in preparation for the Dionysus festival, a Greco-Roman celebration of feasting and theater-going aimed at pleasing the senses. Most wear garlands. One well-dressed young fellow rides a donkey sidesaddle, with legs crossed and upper body turned toward the procession. With his right hand he guides the animal; his left is raised and open. Crowds love a parade; who wouldn't want to join along? Jesus offered a different reason to celebrate.

honor John, first by granting him and Peter the privilege of preparing the Passover (Lk 22:7–13), then by inviting John to sit at his right hand during the meal (Jn 13:23–25; cf. Jn 21:20). The conversation here would be most intimate, a kind of "pillow-talk," and John listened carefully. He was the only Gospel writer to record at length Jesus' comments around the table, and noted well that Jesus chose his words so as to speak of their relationship as if they were family (Jn 14:1–17:26). "I will not leave you as orphans," Jesus promised (Jn 14:18), and repeatedly spoke of God as Father—as kin, not king (Jn 14:2, 14:6–10, etc.). One wonders if Zebedee, like Joseph, was dead. Then Jesus spoke of coming together, becoming "one" (Jn 17:20–26):

> In my Father's house are many rooms…I go to prepare a place for you and will come again and receive you to Myself, that where I am, there you may be also. (Jn 14:2)

This was exactly the practice for marriages in first-century Judea and Galilee: the prospective groom would build a new room within the confines of his father's house, then escort his bride there (the public processional was moment of marriage) where they would begin their new life together. John filled out the image as he wrote the vision that climaxes the Book of Revelation, with the Church as the bride of Christ (Rev 21:2, 21:9).

After the meal Jesus and his disciples walked out of the city by moonlight and crossed the narrow floor of the Kidron Valley. The massive Herodian masonry of the Temple Mount rose like a canyon wall behind; darkened orchards clung to the steep slope of the Mount of Olives ahead. Eight men lagged; one was already lost. Jesus took Peter, James and John a little beyond (Mk 14:32–33). The moment was melodramatic to the point of being heavy, too thick for quick movement, like wading through neck-deep water.

> My soul is deeply grieved to the point of death; remain here and keep watch. (Mk 14:34)

A slow, squeezing crush, the weight of the universe pressed onto a single fulcrum—blood, sweat and tears. "NOT ME!…Yes, for them" (Mk 14:36). Then rapid movement as Jesus was arrested, swallowed by darkness and hauled off to trial. Peter and John followed at a shadowy distance, making it as far as the inner courtyard of the high priest's compound. Both witnessed the scurrying-about of initial proceedings; John heard Peter deny any involvement in the affair (Jn 18:15–27). The beloved disciple alone, with the Marys, stayed with Jesus all the way to the cross. There, with a death rattle in his throat, Jesus gave Mary and John to each other. "Your son." "Your mother" (Jn 19:25–27). John was no longer just a disciple; he was *family*.

He was also the first disciple to make it to the empty tomb, his young legs outracing Peter for the honor of being the first eyewitness to *something*, though he didn't understand what (Jn 20:1–10). In the next few days Jesus appeared to all of his disciples at least twice in Jerusalem, where Great Acts of God were supposed to happen (Jn 20:19–29). But it wasn't

John, the Post-Resurrection Apostle. *With Peter and James, John became a leader in the early church in Jerusalem. It is important to note that while he was in Jerusalem, John never acted alone, only in the company of other Apostles, most notably Peter. This may indicate that he held a somewhat junior role in the Jerusalem "triumvirate," or that church leadership there was somewhat of a cooperative effort. It is impossible to know when John moved his own work and ministry to western Asia. That he went to Ephesus at all can also not be proven, although there is no compelling reason to doubt the traditions that report that he did. In Ephesus John's authority seems to have been unquestioned, and his work in establishing and maintaining churches throughout the region was vital to the success of Christianity in the Roman world.*

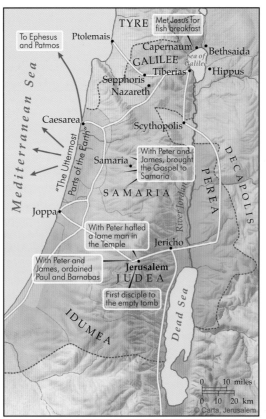

cf. 2 Jn 1:1; 3 Jn 1:1; Rev 1:4) of the church that the Apostle Paul loved so much. During the time of the Book of Acts John is always found in silent company with Peter: healing a lame man in the Temple (Acts 3:1–4:31), verifying the work of Philip in bringing the Gospel to the people of Samaria (Acts 8:4–15), and commissioning Paul and Barnabas to carry Jesus' message to the Gentiles (Gal 2:7–9). Later, after he moved to Ephesus (this is according to Jerome, *De viris illustribus* xvii–xviii), John ordained one of his own disciples, Polycarp, as bishop of Smyrna, and Papias, another worthy student, bishop of Hierapolis. The church in Smyrna seems to have been one of John's favorites, and he spared it criticism when addressing the Seven Churches of Revelation late in life (Rev 2:8–11). It was likely in Ephesus, as echoed by the testimony of Jerome (*De viris illustribus* ix), that John wrote the four New Testament books that bear his name. What *is* clear is that John had witnessed the spread of the Gospel from Jerusalem to Samaria to the uttermost parts of the earth (cf. Mt 28:16–20; Acts 1:8).

But John also suffered for the sake of the Gospel. His brother James was the first of the Apostles to be martyred for the faith, cut down by the sword of Herod Agrippa I around A.D. 42 or 43 in a move to strengthen mainline Temple authority (Acts 12:1–2). John's soul was weighed heavily by the failings of Christians throughout the province of Asia who didn't share the same intensity for the things of Jesus that he had grown to love (Rev 2:1–4:22). And at least part of his latter years were spent in exile on Patmos, a small, rocky (volcanic) and very irregularly-shaped Aegean island lying about sixty miles off the Ephesus port. Rome banished political prisoners and dissidents to Patmos (and neighboring islands; Pliny the Elder, *Naturalis historia* 4:69–70; Tacitus, *Annals* 4:30), and a number of early Church historians report that John was exiled there in the 14th year of the emperor Domitian (A.D. 95; Irenaeus, *Adversus omnes haereses* v.30.3; Eusebius, *Historia ecclesiastica* iii.18; Jerome, *De viris illustribus* ix; cf. Rev 1:9). John would have been about eighty years old at the time. It was no place for an octogenarian. Eusebius gives the cause as "his witness to the divine word"; by John's own account it was "because of the word of God and the testimony of Jesus" (Rev 1:9). The implication is that John must have transgressed Roman law by refusing to worship the emperor. It is, in any case, consistent with what is known of the divine personality cult that swirled around Domitian. The emperor brutally persecuted both Jews and Christians (he was an equal-opportunity despot) starting in or around A.D. 90; the purge was lifted only after he was assassinated on 16 September A.D. 96.

Banishment to Patmos usually carried a life sentence, but John was released under the benevolent hand of Nerva, Domitian's successor, who allowed him to return to Ephesus, likely in late A.D. 96 or

until he met them in the middle of the mundane back home, calling for a catch of fish along the north Galilean shore, that it all started to sink in. John was the first to recognize Jesus *there*, back in real life: "It is the Lord!" (Jn 21:1–7).

John was of course present with the other disciples when Jesus ascended to heaven on the Mount of Olives, when Matthias was chosen to replace Judas among the twelve, and when the Holy Spirit descended at Pentecost (Acts 1:6–2:42). And it is was quite natural that he, Peter and James were recognized as leaders of the growing Jesus movement, both by those within the sect and those who stood opposed. Yet we know very little about John's specific activities during the earliest years of the church—this whether he was in Jerusalem or in Ephesus, where the cumulative weight of church tradition holds that he lived out his days as the leader (*presbuteros*, "Elder";

With eyes drawn upward to Jesus' downward glance, John was adopted into his Messiah's family, on earth and as it was in heaven. The moment was depicted by the Italian artist Dragoni in 1990 on a relief adorning the sanctuary wall of the Peter Memorial church at Capernaum, on the shore of the Sea of Galilee.

THE ROMAN EMPIRE (100's A.D.) AND THE EXPANSION OF CHRISTIANITY (300's A.D.)

BOSPHORUS

Black Sea

SARMATIA

Sinope

BITHYNIA
AND
PONTUS

CAPPADOCIA
Samosata

Caesarea

GALATIA

LYCAONIA CILICIA

Ancyra

Aleppo SYRIA Hamath

Nicomedia

Antioch

Tarsus

Damascus

Bostra

Tripolis

Tyre

Jerusalem

Petra

ARABIA
(PETRAEA)

Heraclea

Byzantium

ASIA

Pergamum

LYDIA PAMPHYLIA

Sardis Lystra

Smyrna Ephesus

Patara

Rhodes

EGYPT

Pelusium

Alexandria Memphis

Durostorum

THRACE

Philippi

Crete

Aegean
Sea

Gortyna

DACIA

Viminacium Novae

MOESIA

MACEDONIA

Thessalonica

EPIRUS

Delphi

ACHAIA

Athens Corinth

Sparta

Cyrene

CYRENAICA

Aquincum

Brigetio

Mediterranean Sea

PANNONIA

ILLYRICUM
(DALMATIA)

NORICUM

Aquileia

RAETIA

Pola

Adriatic
Sea

Ancona

Cannae

Rhegium

Syracuse

Lugdunum

Mogontiacum

GERMANIA

Vienna

Massalia

NARBONENSIS

Arelate

Narbo

ITALY

Rome Neapolis

Tyrrhenian
Sea

Sicily

Hadrumentum

BELGICA

Lutetia

LUGDUNENSIS

AQUITANIA

Corsica

Sardinia

Carthage

AFRICA

TRIPOLITANIA

North
Sea

Vetera

Eburacum

Deva

BRITANNIA

Londinium

Burdigala

Caralis

Hippo

Cirta

Lambaesis

NUMIDIA

Tarraco

TARRACONENSIS

Carthago Nova

Caesarea
Mauretania

MAURETANIA

Atlantic Ocean

Merida

Corduba

BAETICA

Tingis

Seville

Cadiz

LUSITANIA

Ancient cities that
exist today are
underlined in red on
the modern overlays

▢ Extension of the Roman Empire in the 100's A.D.

▢ Expansion of Christianity through the 300's A.D.

AridOcean/shutterstock.com

259

The Seven Churches of Revelation. *The seven churches addressed by John in Revelation 2–3 are all located along an important circle route encompassing the most populated and profitable region of the Roman province of Asia. The distance between each on the Roman road network varies from between 25 and 100 English miles; the total circuit covers 350 miles. (Nowadays some bus pilgrims, in a mad dash, try to visit all seven churches in a single day.) During its founding centuries Christianity took deep root in the fertile valleys of west-central Asia. By spreading beyond, its legacy remains.*

Zeus was the head of the Greek pantheon; his counterpart Jupiter reigned over the mass of Roman deities. Mature yet ageless, Zeus carried the cares of the cosmos, first and foremost those wrapped up in the affairs of his own indulgent family. With gods and goddesses like Apollo, Ares, Poseidon, Athene, Artemis and Aphrodite milling about his feet, the great father-god Zeus had his hands full. Here he looks concerned. He should be—with the spread of the Gospel throughout the Mediterranean, the myths of the Greeks and his own supposed existence were about to be overwhelmed by the message of the Cross.

early 97 (Eusebius, *Historia ecclesiastica* iii.20). According to Irenaeus, whose teacher was John's disciple Polycarp (*Adversus omnes haereses* iii.3.4), John lived into the reign of Trajan (A.D. 98–117). Jerome (*De viris illustribus* ix) tells us that John died "worn out by old age …in the sixty-eighth year after our Lord's passion and was buried near the same city" (i.e., in A.D. 98 in Ephesus). Eusebius (*Historia ecclesiastica* iii.39) noted that already by his own day (the early fourth century) there were two tombs in Ephesus "both still called John's," and allowed for the possibility (he called it a "probability") that one belonged to the Apostle and the other to a man of the same name who wrote the Book of Revelation. Eusebius' was one of a growing host of voices trying to sort out various claims about the beloved disciple in the earliest generations of the Church. In any case, John's death coincided with the passing of Herod Agrippa II, the last of the Herodians; the Temple had gone up in flames almost a generation before (A.D. 70). It was becoming more and more clear that Judaism and Christianity would be moving along divergent paths. A new era had begun.

While in exile John might have had permission to roam Patmos freely, interacting with the local inhabitants as he wished. The island is about 20 square miles in size, or about the same size as land the width of the northern shore of the Sea of Galilee reaching two miles inland. But without the familiar greenery of Galilee it was a small cage in which to pace. Or, a prisoner in exile was sometimes sentenced to forced labor—or worse: a life with fetters, scant food and clothing and compelled to sleep on bare ground in a dark prison (cf. Acts 16:22–24). While on Patmos John spoke of himself as a "bondservant" and "fellow par-

taker in the tribulation and kingdom and perseverance which are in Jesus" (Rev 1:1, 1:9). This suggests that his situation on the island was less than pleasant, although specific details are lacking. Certainly this was the place where John received the awesome and awful visions of the climax of God's great work in the world that he wrote—either on Patmos or after he returned to Ephesus—as the Apocalpyse, Revelation (cf. Rev 1:11, 21:10). Of course a grotto in the hills above the ancient town of Patmos, midway along the island's rugged western coast and with a view in the direction of Rome, is remembered to be the cave in which John received these visions. And who could prove otherwise? Nearby stands the influential Greek Orthodox monastery of St. John the Divine, once the most important spiritual center in all the Aegean, founded by St. Cristodoulus of Nicaea in the eleventh century.

To draw a map of God's Revelation to John would be to plot events of heaven and earth—then, now and forever (cf. Rev 1:8, 1:17–19). The language the apostle used to express what he saw "on the Lord's day" while in exile on the island (Rev 1:9–10) is cryptic, symbolic and highly graphic, intended to conceal as well as to reveal. Images fixed on a page, viewed or read in only two dimensions, don't seem to suffice; adding a third (i.e., projecting each episode of Revelation "in the round" of John's time and place) helps, but many readers prefer to grasp for a "fourth dimension," special insight, for instance, or an angle that fits events of their own day. Options for understanding the book abound (it has been a hermeneutical happy hunting ground for ages).

Seven places mentioned in the opening chapters of Revelation, at least, are known—cities in the Roman province of Asia in which important, though also clearly representative, churches could be found in the late first century A.D. These are Ephesus, Smyrna, Pergamum, Thyatira, Sardis, Philadelphia and Laodicea. Each was well situated on the network of imperial routes that tied Asia to lands of the eastern Mediterranean; three, Ephesus, Smyrna and Pergamum, each claimed the privileged title "First of Asia." John mentioned the cities in a clockwise order that follows the great circle route of the province. Surely he had visited them, likely more than once, during his years in Ephesus, and knew firsthand the heart-condition of each. And to each church (and reader) John gave a personal challenge to remain faithful and to overcome (Rev 2:1–3:22).

Then came an extended vision of "what must take place after these things" (Rev 4:1). The opening scene was in heaven (Rev 4:1–4); the last (a never-ending end) was "a new heaven and a new earth, for the first heaven and the first earth passed away and there is no longer any sea" (Rev 21:1). It was an altered geography to be sure—but for the people of highland Judea, whose formative experiences were

Apostles and Evangelists	Final Destination	Fate	Patristic (or Later) Sources
Peter	Rome	Crucified head downward by Nero	1 Clement 5–6; Eusebius, *Historia ecclesiastica* ii.25, iii.1; *The Acts of Peter and Paul*
Andrew	Scythia	Manner of death unstated	Eusebius, *Historia ecclesiastica* iii.1
	Scythia	Stoned and crucified	*Martyrdom of Andrew*
	Patrae in Achaia	Crucified by the proconsul Aegeates for converting and estranging his wife	*Acts of Andrew*
	Lydia in Asia	Hung from a tree and stoned	Ethiopian *Synaxarium*
James "the Great"	Jerusalem	Executed by the sword by Herod Agrippa I	Acts 12:1–2
John	Patmos and Ephesus	Died of natural causes	Eusebius, *Historia ecclesiastica* iii.20; Jerome, *De viris illustribus* ix
Philip (often confused with Philip the Evangelist)	Hierapolis in Asia	Manner of death unstated	Eusebius, *Historia ecclesiastica* iii.31, 39
	Hierapolis in Asia	Crucified head downward	*Acts of Philip*
Bartholomew	India	Manner of death unstated	Eusebius, *Historia ecclesiastica* v.10
	Parthia/Armenia	Flayed alive and beheaded	*Preaching of St. Andrew and St. Bartholomew*
	"Cities on the Mediterranean coast"	Placed in a sack full of sand and thrown into the sea by King Agrippa	*Martyrdom of St. Bartholomew*
Matthew/Levi	Unstated	Died of natural causes	Clement, *Stromata* iv.9
Thomas	Parthia	Manner of death unstated	Eusebius, *Historia ecclesiastica* iii.1
	India	Pierced by four spears	*Acts of Thomas*
James son of Alphaeus "the Less"	Ostrakine in the Sinai	Crucified	Nicephorus ii.40
	Persia	Crucified	*Martyrologium Hieronymi*
	Jerusalem	Stoned	Ethiopian *Synaxarium*
Thaddaeus/Judas son of James	Edessa	Manner of death unstated	Eusebius, *Historia ecclesiastica* i.13, ii.1; *Acts of Thaddaeus*
Paul	Rome	Beheaded by Nero	1 Clement 5–6; Eusebius, *Historia ecclesiastica* ii.25; *The Acts of Peter and Paul*
John Mark	Alexandria	Manner of death unstated	Eusebius, *Historia ecclesiastica* ii.16, 24
	Alexandria	Dragged through the streets of the city	*Paschal Chronicle*; *Acts of Mark*
Luke	Bithynia	Died of natural causes at age 74	*Prefatio vel Argumentum Lucae*

the stuff of mountains and wilderness, rocks and wadis, a re-created, sea-less landscape was to be expected. Viewed through an ancient Semitic lens, the sea remained untamed and untamable, a symbol of the instability and uncertainty of life, the abyss-home of "a beast rising up" (Rev 13:1–10), the epitome of evil both anti-Christ and anti-God. And so in the fulfillment of John's vision, just as at Creation and the Exodus, the sea was again pushed aside for dry land to appear, birthing a special place both proper and fit for God's people to live (Gen 1:6–13; Ex 14:13–29; cf. Gen 8:1–19; Josh 3:14–17; 2 Kgs 2:7–8, 2:13–14; Isa 57:20). The center of this re-creation was a new Jerusalem, "coming down out of heaven from God, made ready as a bride adorned for her husband" (Rev 21:2).

In between these glimpses of a heavenly geography John portrayed a maddening whirl of divinely-orchestrated chaos on earth—judgment, trial and tribulation—focusing on that other city, "Babylon the great, the mother of harlots and of the abominations of the earth" (Rev 17:5; cf. Rev 14:8, 16:19). Babylon and all that it represented up and down the timeline, from what was done by Nebuchadnezzar to the deeds of Domitian and countless others of the same stripe throughout history, was the great enemy of God's people and their Jerusalem home. But then, in the great climax to not only Revelation and the story of the Bible but all human history, John saw Babylon fall, and it and everything that pulls people away from God were cast into a body of water even more horrifying than the sea-home of evil, the Lake of Fire (Rev 18:1–24, 20:11–15). It was totally unlike any lake John had ever fished around! Our inability to place this lake on a map does nothing to detract from the force of its reality. In its stead John saw "a river of the water of life, clear as crystal, coming from the throne of God and of the Lamb" (Rev 22:1; cf. Ezek 47:1–12), a pastoral scene reminiscent of Eden

"So Great a Cloud of Witnesses." *Traditions regarding the founders of the Church abound. The chart on the previous page presents a select and representative sample, indicating the extent to which the Christian community spread by the end of the first century* A.D. *and the dangers to life and limb that its leaders faced in the process. Tradition holds that only a few died a natural death. Several were remembered as having taken up their own cross; most succumbed to the kinds of deaths that the writer of Hebrews noted were part and parcel of a life of faith* (Heb 11:32–40)*: "For consider Him who has endured such hostility by sinners against Himself, so that you will not grow weary and lose heart"* (Heb 12:4)*.*

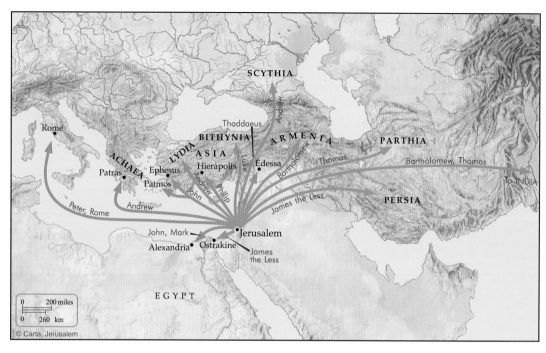

"It is finished. I am the Alpha and the Omega, the Beginning and the End. To the one who thirsts I will give [life] as a gift from the spring of living water" (Rev 21:6)*. This mosaic is from the Byzantine chapel at Khirbet Harmeshith on the grounds of the biblical landscape reserve Ne'ot Kedumim, southeast of Israel's Ben-Gurion Airport.*

now created for all. And with it, maps are no longer relevant.

The twelfth-century English abbot Aelred of Rievaulx reflected well on the character of John, comparing him to Peter, the apostle who always wanted the first word:

To Peter [Jesus] gave the keys of his kingdom; to John he revealed the secrets of his heart. Peter, therefore, was the more exalted; John, the more secure....Peter...was exposed to action, John was reserved to love. (De Amicitia Spirituali 3.117)

And so John lived from beginning to end, secure and hopeful though not without trial. With his eyes set steadfastly on the power of the love of God, the resurrection of Jesus and the fellowship of the Holy Spirit, he endured. And by the example of his love and the love shown to him, we can do no less.

With the inscription okeanos, *"ocean," this experienced fisherman stands as conqueror of the seas. The mosaic is part of an extended depiction of man's appreciation for, and dominance of, nature, which adorns the southern aisle of a sixth-century church in Petra, Jordan. Its mood is part and parcel of the headiness of the Byzantine period at full flower, when Christianity had penetrated both sea and desert. The Roman world had become Christian, in name if not in conviction. "Whoever is born of God overcomes the world," wrote John toward the end of the first century* A.D. *Then he added, "this is the victory that has overcome the world—our faith"* (1 Jn 5:4)*. One wonders to what extent the beloved apostle would have recognized the building that arose on the foundation that he and his fellow eyewitnesses of Jesus had laid.*

262

AFTERWORD

In the eastern, rural, patriarchal and essentially unchanging world of the Bible, people were dedicated to fostering and preserving two basic resources: family and land. Everyone defined his or her own identity by where they stood in an unbroken chain of forefathers long dead and descendants not yet born, a family line that was bound to a particular plot of real estate. One's sense of belonging was circumscribed by the limits of one's ancestry and ancestral land. This was as true for the residents of towns and villages of the ancient Near East as it was for persons scattered around the rim of the Mediterranean. Even peoples whose lifestyle was relatively mobile, such as the ancient equivalent of nineteenth century A.D. Bedouin, developed patterns of social interaction based on rights to specific grazing lands and water sources that were protected and passed down from generation to generation. One's heirs were one's sons, who inherited family lands. In an equally real sense one's heir was also the land, which inherited sons as caretakers for the next generation.

But in the biblical world land and children were more than just resources. Practically speaking, they were also markers of wealth, of security and of peace, values common to the human endeavor everywhere. And, given the geographical and historical realities of the ancient Near Eastern and Mediterranean worlds, these values and their underlying resources were honored, maintained and protected at all costs. Simply put, they were worth fighting for.

In this part of the world one's roots always run deep, where they easily become entangled with the roots of some other family or clan, tribe or people trying to stay put in the same region. This clearly complicates life, and fosters a fluid mix of relationships that at one moment threaten efforts at *shalom* (life the way it's supposed to be), the next protect it. For the ancients, one's family-land chain *had* to survive (this was more true for persons of the time of the Old Testament than the New, but remained a major definition of social behavior in the time of the Gospels). The greatest tragedy that could befall a family was not that someone would die but that the person do so before providing an heir. Equally tragic was the individual or family who was displaced from their ancestral land, whether by invasion, exile or oppressive economic systems. And so, for instance, the story of the patriarchs and matriarchs, a not-quite-yet-a-family to whom God promised both children and land and who then promptly spent the next four generations acting in such a way so as to put both in jeopardy. Or Naomi, who returned from a Moabite exile childless and landless before everything was put right by the actions of her kinsman-redeemer. Or Rizpah, who restored honor and life to the line of her dead husband by bringing his body back to rest in the land of his forefathers. But then the apostles—Peter, Paul, John and the others—who died far from home in order to give birth to a much larger family of God, choosing in the end people over land to fill out Jesus' command to make disciples, not kingdoms, in his name (Mt 28:18–20; Acts 1:7–8).

Whatever else the lands of the Middle East might be, they are (and always have been) "God's testing ground of faith" (Jim Monson, *Regions on the Run*, 5). Perhaps this has something to do with geographical characteristics of the region itself—that it stands in the middle of three continents and so is pushed and pulled by political and economic interests from all sides. Maybe it has something to do with the persistent practice of defining one's identity and reason for being as the sum of "place" + "God's will for me in that place." Or perhaps it just seems so because we are privileged to have received such a long and detailed written record of human and divine activity *here*, where so much of the world traces its intellectual and spiritual roots, rather than somewhere else. Never mind—the land of the Bible remains a place typically suitable for human life, and grasping its stories allows us readers to not only participate in them but to better face any future, in partnership with God, in which our resources—whatever they might happen to be—are stretched desert-thin.

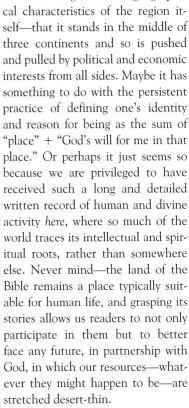

The track record of human activity in the Middle East has not been a particularly good one (we all have a little Judas in us). Yet its future rests in the hands of its children, we who reach back for direction, up for strength and forward to give shape to tomorrow. God wills that we don't reach alone, but hand-in-hand with Him. He shapes and molds opinion, cleans hearts, changes lives and redeems the times. And He reserves the right to step into human history whenever and however He wants. We live as Esther, for such a time as this; as Mary and Joseph, extraordinarily; and as Paul, under grace. But we also live together, in community with God and each other, and for this reason and cause our divine-human efforts will not be in vain.

P. H. W.
Mt. Zion, Jerusalem
October, 2008

BIBLIOGRAPHY

The works listed below are a small sample of books and articles that provide insights into the history, geography, personality and cultural background of each of the great people of the Bible whose stories have been related here. The actual number of relevant works is vast, and the choice used for any study will vary.

Aharoni, Yohanan, Avi-Yonah, Michael, Rainey, Anson F., and Safrai, Ze'ev. *The Carta Bible Atlas*. 4th ed. Jerusalem: Carta. 2002

Avi-Yonah, Michael, ed. *The World History of the Jewish People: The Herodian Period*. New Brunswick, NJ: Rutgers, 1975

Baly, Denis. *The Geography of the Bible*. Rev. ed. New York: Harper & Row, 1974

Bright, John. *A History of Israel*. 4th ed. Louisville: Westminster John Knox, 2000

Brichto, Herbert Chanan. *Toward a Grammar of Biblical Poetics: Tales of the Prophets*. New York: Oxford, 1992

Edersheim, Alfred. *The Life and Times of Jesus the Messiah*. Grand Rapids: Eerdmans, 1956

Ferguson, Everett. *Backgrounds of Early Christianity*. 2nd ed. Grand Rapids: Eerdmans, 1993

Flusser, David. *Jesus*. Jerusalem: Magnes Press, 1997

Freyne, Sean. *Galilee: From Alexander the Great to Hadrian, 323 BCE to 135 CE*. Edinburgh: T & T Clark, 1998

_____. *Jesus a Jewish Galilean: A New Reading of the Jesus Story*. Edinburgh: T & T Clark, 2004

Hallo, William W. and Simpson, William Kelly. *The Ancient Near East: A History*. New York: Harcourt, Brace, Jovanovich, 1971

Har-el, Menashe and Wright, Paul H. *Understanding the Geography of the Bible: An Introductory Atlas*. Jerusalem: Carta, 2005

Hengel, Martin. *Crucifixion*. London: SCM Press, 1977

Heschel, Abraham J. *The Prophets*. New York: Harper & Row, 1962

Horsley, Richard A. *Bandits, Prophets and Messiahs: Popular Movements at the Time of Jesus*. San Francisco: Harper & Row, 1985

Jeffrey, David Lyle, gen. ed. *A Dictionary of Biblical Tradition in English Literature*. Grand Rapids: Eerdmans, 1992

King, Philip J. and Stager, Lawrence E. *Life in Biblical Israel*. Louisville: Westminster John Knox, 2001

Malina, Bruce. *Windows on the World of Jesus: Time Travel to Ancient Judea*. Louisville: Westminster/John Knox, 1993

Matthews, Victor H. and Benjamin, Don C. *The Social World of Ancient Israel, 1250–587 BCE*. Peabody, MA: Hendrickson, 1993

Mazar, Amihai. *Archaeology of the Land of the Bible*. New York: Doubleday, 1990

Monson, James M. *Regions on the Run: Introductory Map Studies in the Land of the Bible*. Rockford, IL: Biblical Backgrounds, 1998

Murphy-O'Connor, Jerome. *The Holy Land: An Oxford Archaeological Guide from Earliest Times to 1700*. 4th ed. Oxford: Oxford University, 1998

Notley, R. Steven and Safrai, Ze'ev. *Eusebius, Onomasticon: The Place Names of Divine Scripture*. Leiden: Brill, 2005

Nun, Mendel. *The Sea of Galilee and Its Fishermen in the New Testament*. Ein Gev: Kibbbutz Ein Gev, 1989

Olmstead, Albert T. "The Calculated Frightfulness of Ashur-nasir-pal." JAOS 38 (1918): 219–263

Pritchard, James B., ed. *Ancient Near Eastern Texts Relating to the Old Testament (ANET)*. Princeton, NJ: Princeton, 1955

Rainey, Anson F. and Notley, R. Steven. *The Sacred Bridge*. Jerusalem: Carta, 2006

Ramsay, William M. *St. Paul: The Traveler and Roman Citizen*. Rev. ed. Ed. by Mark Wilson. London: Angus Hudson, 2001

Rasmussen, Carl G. *NIV Atlas of the Bible*. Grand Rapids: Zondervan, 1989

Richardson, Peter. *Building Jewish in the Roman East*. Waco: Baylor University, 2004

Rivkin, Ellis. *What Crucified Jesus: The Political Execution of a Charismatic*. Nashville: Abingdon Press, 1984

Roitman, Adolfo. *Envisioning the Temple: Scrolls, Stones, and Symbols*. Jerusalem: The Israel Museum, 2003

Samuel, Maurice. *Certain People of the Book*. New York: Union of American Hebrew Congregations, 1955

Stern, Ephraim, ed. *The New Encyclopedia of Archaeological Excavations in the Holy Land (NEAEHL)*. 4 vols. Jerusalem: Israel Exploration Society and Carta, 1993

Whiston, William, transl. *Josephus: Complete Works*. Grand Rapids: Kregel, 1960

Wilkinson, John, transl. *Egeria's Travels*. London: SPCK, 1971

Witherington, Ben, III. *New Testament History: A Narrative Account*. Grand Rapids: Baker, 2001

Wright, Paul H. *Understanding the New Testament: An Introductory Atlas*. Jerusalem: Carta, 2004

INDEX

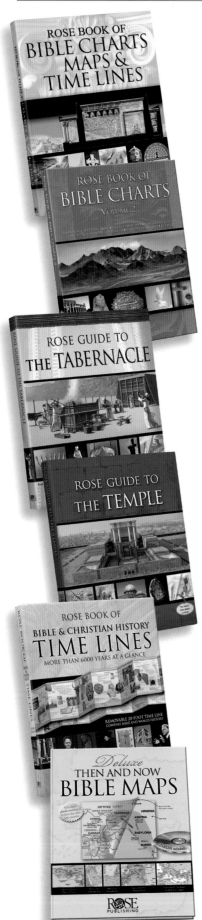

Rose Book of Bible Charts, Maps & Time Lines

Dozens of popular Rose Publishing Bible charts, maps, and time lines in one spiral-bound book. Reproduce up to 300 copies of any chart free of charge.

- Christianity, Cults & Religions
- Denominations Comparison
- Christian History Time Line
- How We Got the Bible
- Tabernacle
- Jesus' Genealogy
- Bible Time Line
- Bible Bookcase
- Bible Overview
- Ark of the Covenant
- Islam and Christianity
- Bible maps
- Trinity
- Temple and High Priest

Hardcover. 192 pages. ISBN: 9781596360228

Rose Book of Bible Charts Volume 2

Here are dozens of popular Rose charts in one book! Topics include • Bible Translations comparison chart • Why Trust the Bible • Heroes of the Old Testament • Women of the Bible • Life of Paul • Christ in the Old Testament • Christ in the Passover • Names of Jesus • Beatitudes • Lord's Prayer • Where to Find Favorite Bible Verses • Christianity and Eastern Religions • Worldviews Comparison • 10 Q & A on Mormonism/Jehovah's Witnesses/Magic/Atheism and many others!
Hardcover with a spine covering a spiral binding. 240 pages ISBN: 9781596362758

Rose Guide to the Tabernacle

Full color with clear overlays and reproducible pages. The Tabernacle was the place where the Israelites worshiped God after the Exodus. Learn how the sacrifices, utensils, and even the structure of the tabernacle were designed to show us something about God. See the parallels between the Old Testament sacrifices and priests' duties, and Jesus' service as the perfect sacrifice and perfect high priest. See how:
• The Tabernacle was built • The sacrifices pointed Jesus Christ • The design of the tent revealed God's holiness and humanity's need for God • The Ark of the Covenant was at the center of worship. Clear plastic overlays show inside/outside of the tabernacle. Hardcover. 128 pages. ISBN: 9781596362765

Rose Guide to the Temple

Simply the best book on the Temple in Jerusalem. It is the only full-color book from a Christian viewpoint that has clear plastic overlays showing the interior and exterior of Solomon's Temple, Herod's Temple, and the Tabernacle. Contains more than 100 color diagrams, photos, illustrations, maps, and time lines of more than 100 key events from the time of King David to modern day. It also includes two full-color posters: the Temple of Jesus' time and the stunning National Geographic poster on the Temple Mount through time. You will understand how the Temple looked, its history, and its biblical importance.
Hardcover. 144 pages. ISBN: 9781596364684

Rose Book of Bible & Christian History Time Lines

Six thousand years and 20 feet of time lines in one hard-bound cover! This unique resource allows you to easily store and reference two time lines in book form. These gorgeous time lines printed on heavy chart paper, can also be slipped out of their binding and posted in a hallway or large room for full effect.
• The 10-foot Bible Time Line compares Scriptural events with world history and Middle East history. Shows hundreds of facts; includes dates of kings, prophets, battles, and key events.
• The 10-foot Christian History Time Line begins with the life of Jesus and continues to the present day. Includes key people and events that all Christians should know.
Hardcover. ISBN: 9781596360846

Deluxe Then and Now® Bible Maps Book with CD-ROM!

See where Bible places are today with Then and Now® Bible maps with clear plastic overlays of modern cities and countries. This deluxe edition comes with a CD-ROM that gives you a JPG of each map to use in your own Bible material as well as PDFs of each map and overlay to create your own handouts or overhead transparencies. PowerPoint® fans can create their own presentations with these digitized maps.
Hardcover. ISBN: 9781596361638